THE WORKS

OF

MR. RICHARD HOOKER

The Works of That Judicious and Learned Divine Mr. Richard Hooker
Seventh Edition
Originally published by Oxford at the Clarendon Press, 1888

This edition published 2009 by
Regent College Publishing
5800 University Boulevard
Vancouver, British Columbia V6T 2E4 Canada
Web: www.regentpublishing.com
E-mail: info@regentpublishing.com

Views expressed in works published by Regent College Publishing are those of the author and do not necessarily represent the official position of Regent College (www.regent-college.edu).

ISBN 978-1-57383-359-2 (Volume 1)

THE WORKS

OF THAT LEARNED AND JUDICIOUS DIVINE

MR. RICHARD HOOKER

WITH AN ACCOUNT OF HIS LIFE AND DEATH

BY ISAAC WALTON

ARRANGED BY

THE REV. JOHN KEBLE, M.A.
LATE FELLOW OF ORIEL COLLEGE, OXFORD

SEVENTH EDITION

REVISED BY

THE VERY REV. R. W. CHURCH, M.A., D.C.L.
Honorary Fellow of Oriel College, and Dean of St. Paul's

AND

THE REV. F. PAGET, D.D.
Canon of Christ Church, and Regius Professor of Pastoral Theology
in the University of Oxford

VOL. I

REGENT COLLEGE PUBLISHING
Vancouver, British Columbia

"*All things written in this booke I humbly and meekly submit to the censure of the grave and reverend Prelates within this land, to the judgment of learned men, and the sober consideration of all others. Wherein I may happely erre as others before me have done, but an heretike by the help of Almighty God I will never be.*"

HOOKER, MS. Note on the title leaf of the "Christian Letter."

THE WORKS

OF THAT LEARNED AND JUDICIOUS DIVINE

MR. RICHARD HOOKER

WITH AN ACCOUNT OF HIS LIFE AND DEATH

BY ISAAC WALTON

ARRANGED BY

THE REV. JOHN KEBLE, M.A.
LATE FELLOW OF ORIEL COLLEGE, OXFORD

SEVENTH EDITION

REVISED BY

THE VERY REV. R. W. CHURCH, M.A., D.C.L.
Honorary Fellow of Oriel College, and Dean of St. Paul's

AND

THE REV. F. PAGET, D.D.
Canon of Christ Church, and Regius Professor of Pastoral Theology in the University of Oxford

VOL. I

REGENT COLLEGE PUBLISHING
Vancouver, British Columbia

"All things written in this booke I humbly and meekly submit to the censure of the grave and reverend Prelates within this land, to the judgment of learned men, and the sober consideration of all others. Wherein I may happely erre as others before me have done, but an heretike by the help of Almighty God I will never be."

HOOKER, MS. Note on the title leaf of the "Christian Letter."

NOTE TO THE SIXTH EDITION.

IN this Edition the General Index has been somewhat altered and enlarged. A separate Index of all Texts of Holy Scripture quoted in Hooker's Works, and a Glossary of Words strange either in themselves or in Hooker's use of them, have been added. In the preparation of the Glossary valuable help has been most kindly given by F. J. Furnivall, Esq., one of the Honorary Secretaries of the Philological Society.

November 1862.

NOTE TO THE SEVENTH EDITION.

THIS Edition is a reprint of Mr. Keble's Edition, with some slight corrections and additions.

The Text has been again revised by comparison with the various original Editions, whether published in Hooker's lifetime, or after his death. A few oversights in Mr. Keble's careful collation of these Texts have been corrected. Further, the printer's copy from which Book V. was printed, with Whitgift's signature and corrections in Hooker's handwriting, procured for the Bodleian by Mr. Coxe, has been collated by Dr. Paget, Professor of Pastoral Theology, with the first edition. An account of this MS. will be found prefixed to Book V.

Mr. Keble's orthography and punctuation have been preserved, except in a few older forms, which are more than mere matters of spelling, and in the forms of Old Testament names, which Hooker, like most writers of the time, took from the Septuagint or Vulgate.

The Glossary, added to in the Sixth Edition by Mr. Furnivall, has been further enlarged; and an Index is given of the writers cited by Hooker, showing the range and character of his reading. Some additions to the Notes have been furnished by the Rev. Edward Marshall, late Fellow of C. C. C., Oxford, and Vicar of Sandford St. Martin. They are marked M. or E. M.

R. W. CHURCH.

1887.

GENERAL CONTENTS.

VOL. I.

	PAGE
EDITOR'S PREFACE	ix—cxxi
WALTON'S DEDICATION TO BISHOP MORLEY	cxxiii
PREFACE TO THE FIRST EDITION OF THE LIFE OF HOOKER	1
LIFE OF HOOKER	3
APPENDIX TO THE LIFE OF HOOKER	88
FURTHER APPENDIX TO THE LIFE OF HOOKER	100
SPENSER'S PREFACE TO THE READER	121
PREFACE TO THE BOOKS OF THE LAWS OF ECCLESIASTICAL POLITY	125
OF THE LAWS OF ECCLESIASTICAL POLITY—	
THE FIRST BOOK	197
THE SECOND BOOK	286
THE THIRD BOOK	337
THE FOURTH BOOK	416

VOL. II.

OF THE LAWS OF ECCLESIASTICAL POLITY—	
THE BODLEIAN MS. OF BOOK V [1887]	v
THE FIFTH BOOK	1
HOOKER'S DEDICATION TO ARCHBISHOP WHITGIFT	ibid.
APPENDIX TO BOOK V	537

VOL. III.

	PAGE
OF THE LAWS OF ECCLESIASTICAL POLITY:—	
THE SIXTH BOOK	1
APPENDIX TO BOOK VI	108
OF THE LAWS OF ECCLESIASTICAL POLITY—	
THE SEVENTH BOOK	140
THE EIGHTH BOOK	326
APPENDICES TO BOOK VIII	456
A SERMON ON THE CERTAINTY AND PERPETUITY OF FAITH IN THE ELECT	469
A LEARNED DISCOURSE ON JUSTIFICATION, WORKS, AND HOW THE FOUNDATION OF FAITH IS OVERTHROWN	483
TRAVERS'S SUPPLICATION TO THE COUNCIL	548
HOOKER'S ANSWER TO TRAVERS'S SUPPLICATION	570
A LEARNED SERMON ON THE NATURE OF PRIDE	597
A REMEDY AGAINST SORROW AND FEAR: DELIVERED IN A FUNERAL SERMON	643
JACKSON'S DEDICATION TO THE FIRST OF TWO SERMONS ON PART OF ST. JUDE	654
THE FIRST SERMON	659
THE SECOND SERMON	681
A SERMON FOUND AMONG THE PAPERS OF BISHOP ANDREWS	700
INDICES	711
TEXTS	713
AUTHORS	730
SUBJECTS	737
GLOSSARY	793

ADDITIONS AND CORRECTIONS TO THE SEVENTH EDITION.

Vol. I. p. liii, l. 22, *for* Mus. Bodl. 55. 20 *read* Bodl. MS. e Mus. 55. Art. 20.
Vol. III. p. 526, note ³, l. 10, *for* e *read* a : l. 16, *for* tenui *read* tenue.
„ „ p. 599, note ², *for* Sc. 4 *read* Sc. 1.

The Editors are indebted for the following to the Rev. E. MARSHALL :—

Vol. I. p. 227, note ². The earliest known occurrence of this saying is in Alcuin. Admon. ad Carol. M. § ix. 'Nec audiendi sunt qui solent dicere, Vox populi, Vox Dei, cum tumultuositas vulgi semper insaniæ proxima est.' Ep. cxxvii. Alcuin. Opp. t. i. p. 191 ed. Froben. 1777.

„ „ p. 251, note ². See Cic. de Nat. Deor. lib. i. cc. 15, 41, with a further reference to Gaisf. Paroem. Gr. p. 252 (for the Greek proverb), and to Pliny and Juvenal, in the note of A. Schott, ibid.

„ „ p. 314, note ¹, l. 18, 'Greece of Greece.' Mr. Evelyn Abbott points out that Athenaeus refers this title of Athens to Thucydides: Θουκυδίδης δὲ ἐν τῷ εἰς Εὐριπίδην ἐπιγράμματι Ἑλλάδος Ἑλλάδα (ἔφη), v. p. 187 E. The epigram is preserved among the Ἐπιτύμβια of the Anthologia Palatina (vii. 45, Anth. Graec. t. 1, p. 235. Tauchn.), where there occurs at v. 3 : Πατρὶς δ' Ἑλλάδος Ἑλλάς, Ἀθῆναι.

„ „ p. 315, note ⁷. For original Greek see p. 317, note ².

„ „ p. 393, note of 1886. Cf. Cic. de Rep. lib. iii. ap. S. Aug. Contr. Jul. iv. 12.

Vol. II. p. 44, note ². There is a copy of the edition of 1707 in the Bodleian Library.

„ „ p. 53, note ². See the De Ebrietate, c. xxxvi (tom. i. p. 377 ed. 1742), τὰ δόρατα καὶ τὰ νοητὰ θεωρήματα ὧν αἰσθηταὶ ταῦτα εἰκόνες.

„ „ p. 260, note ¹, last line, *for* 1354 *read* 1654.

„ „ p. 302, note ¹. These words are condensed from Boet. de Consol. Lib. IV, Pros. iv. *ad fin.*

„ „ p. 406, note ², l. 15, *for* 'the Levant' *read* 'those of the Levant.'

„ „ pp. 407, note ¹, l. 12, 417, note ². The passage referred to as from Ignatius is in Pseudo-Ignatius, 'the long recension' of Bishop Lightfoot, Vol. II. sect. ii. p. 786.

„ „ p. 515, note ¹. The words occur in Regulæ juris utriusque, tom. i. p. 269, col. 1, Lugd. 1587.

Vol. III. p. 441, note ¹. Add to quotation from Bishop Cooper, S. Ambr. Serm. contr. Auxent. § 5. Ep. xxi., Tom. II. p. 865, ed. Bened.

„ „ p. 523, note ⁴. The passage is translated from the 'Epistola M. Buceri in Evangelistarum enarrationes nuncupatoria ad præclaram Acad. Marpurg., MDXXX,' of which Epistle the running title is ' De Servanda Ecclesiæ Unitate M. Buceri Epistola Nuncupat.' There is a copy in the Bodleian Library.

„ „ p. 622, l. 4 from foot. The quotation is from Digesta, Lib. L. Tit. xvii. 109, where edd. 1553, 1575 read 'prohibere (non) potest': ed. Berol. 1870 (Mommsen) 'prohibere potest.'

„ „ p. 666, ll. 2 *sqq*. The reference is to St. Hilary de Trinitate, lib. IX, c. x. p. 990, ed. Bened.

„ „ p. 703, l. 2 *sq*. These words occur almost *verbatim* in S. Greg. M. Hom. in Evang. xxxvii. § 1. Tom. I. p. 1627, ed. Bened.

EDITOR'S PREFACE.

THE first object of the present publication is, to exhibit the remains of the great and venerable writer (all, unfortunately, more or less imperfect) in as correct a form as could be attained, by reference, throughout, to the original editions; and in some few cases, to MS. copies.

1. In respect of the Life of Hooker, by Walton—which has a sort of customary right to appear first in all collections of his remains, and a right, surely, which no one would wish to disturb, who can enter into the spirit either of the biographer, or of his subject—the reader will find some considerable variations from the copy which appears in most former editions: of which the following is the account. The life was first written at Archbishop Sheldon's suggestion to correct the errors of that by Bishop Gauden, which had come out in 1662. The first edition bears date 1665; the date of the Introduction is fixed to the year before, by the expression, "I must look "back to his death, *now sixty-four years past:*" for Hooker died Nov. 2, 1600. In 1670, it was reprinted, together with the lives of Donne, Wotton, and Herbert, and the collection was dedicated, as the separate life had been, to Walton's intimate friend (if he might not be called his patron) Bishop Morley. It was so popular as to reach a fourth edition in 1675: and from that, which was the last that had the author's corrections, the present reprint has been made. To the best of the Editor's knowledge, the copy of the Life prefixed to the editions of Hooker since 1666, was taken from Walton's first edition. For although there were at least two reprints of Hooker before Walton's death, one in 1676 and one in 1682, (he died Dec. 15, 1683,) the Life remained uncorrected: and this circumstance not being observed by Dr. Zouch led him to select for his edition a text which undoubtedly Walton

Editor's Preface.

himself had discarded. Dr. Wordsworth in his Ecclesiastical Biography saw and corrected the mistake. It is remarkable that it should have escaped Strype's notice when he inserted his corrections and additions in the reprint of 1705. Some of the principal variations are set down in the notes to the present edition: but without exact collation of the two texts.

The general result, in the Editor's opinion, is favourable to Walton's veracity, industry, and judgment. The advantage he possessed was great in his connexion[1] with the Cranmer family, Hooker's near neighbours and most intimate friends. Of this connexion Walton's biographers do not appear to have thought much, if it was at all observed by them; though it was this in all probability which gave the colouring to his whole future life, introducing him into societies and pursuits from which otherwise he seemed far removed. At the same time the Editor has no wish to deny, that which is apparent of itself to every reader—the peculiar fascination, if one may call it so, by which Walton was led unconsciously to communicate more or less of his own tone and character to all whom he undertook to represent. But this is like his custom of putting long speeches into their mouths: we see at once that it is his way, and it deceives no one. Perhaps the case of Hooker is that in which the biographer has on the whole produced the most incorrect impression of his subject. He seems to have judged rather from anecdotes which had come to his knowledge, than from the indications of temperament which Hooker's own writings afford. Otherwise he might perhaps have seen reason to add to his commendation of him for meekness and patience, that those qualities were by no means constitutional in him. Like Moses, to whom Walton compares him, he was by nature extremely sensitive, quick in feeling any sort of unfairness, and thoroughly aware of his own power to chastise it: so that his

---

[1] This marriage of the Archbishop's great-niece with a simple London shopkeeper would seem to shew that Hooker's own marriage, however ill-assorted in other respects, would not be considered as disparaging to his station in society. The woman might be, as Antony Wood describes her, "clownish and silly;" but in point of rank and education, according to the fashion of that time, there was no reason why she might not become the wife of a country clergyman, though of an old family, and nephew of a member of parliament. Churchman, her father, had been wealthy, and the family bore arms, as appears by the Hookers' pedigree.

forbearance (which those only can judge of, who have acquainted themselves with the writings of his opponents) must have been the result of strong principle, and unwearied self-control. Again, Walton or his informants appear to have considered him as almost childishly ignorant of human nature and of the ordinary business of life: whereas his writings throughout betray uncommon shrewdness and quickness of observation, and a vein of the keenest humour runs through them; the last quality we should look for, if we judged only by reading the Life. In these respects it may seem probable that if the biographer had been personally acquainted with his subject, the picture would have been somewhat modified: in no others is there any reason, either from his writings or from contemporary evidence, to doubt the accuracy of his report.

[2] It will be observed that in the Notes and Appendix to the Life, some use has been made of the collections of Mr. Fulman, which are preserved in C. C. C. Library, to the number of twenty-two volumes; of which an account may be seen in Dr. Bliss's edition of the Athenæ Oxonienses, iv. 242: as also an account of the collector, who had been the *alumnus* and amanuensis of Hammond, and was the friend and literary adviser of Antony Wood. He was also acquainted with Walton, as appears from his Appendix to the Life of Hooker, p. 89 *n.*²; and from an indorsement in Fulman's hand, on some papers which will be found, vol. iii. p. 108 of this edition. All therefore that he knew about Hooker he had communicated to Walton, no doubt, before 1675: and therefore little or no direct additional information was to be expected, or occurs, in his papers.

The chief use now made of them has been to extract a few passages relating to Reynolds, Hooker's tutor, and undoubtedly the leader of the Moderate Puritanical party in the University at that time. A specimen of his tone and principles may be seen in the Further Appendix to the Life, Nº. ii: which letter, with all that we read of Reynolds, tends to put in a strong light his pupil Hooker's entire independence of thought, and the manner in which he worked his way towards other views than those in which he had been trained. For it may be observed that his uncle, John Hooker or Vowel, was rather a keen partisan, as he had been at one time an associate, of Peter Martyr and others of the more uncompromising foreign Reformers: as his historical fragments, inserted in Holinshed, may shew. Hooker's connexion again with Bishop Jewel; with Dr. Cole, President of C. C. C., who had been forced on the society by the Queen's government[1]; and with Cole's party in the College; were all things calculated, as far as they went, to give him a bias towards the extreme which was accounted most contrary to Romanism. And indeed the deep and sincere dread with which he regarded the errors and aggressions of Rome, is apparent in every part of his writings: and so much the more instructive will it prove, should we find him of his own accord embracing those catholic opinions and practices, which some in their zeal against popery may have too lightly parted with, but which Rome alone could not give, neither should we allow her indirectly to take them away.

The other short pieces, subjoined to the Life in this edition, are accounted for by notes as they severally occur.

[3] 2. If Hooker's works were arranged in the order of their composition, (a course which is so far preferable to any other, as it gives the completest view of the progress of the writer's own mind, and any modifications which his opinions may have undergone,) the Sermons relating to the controversy with Travers, 1585–6, would naturally come first in order. For that controversy not only preceded the Laws of Ecclesiastical Polity in order of time, but actually led to the first idea and undertaking of the great work [2]. However, in the present publication, the precedent of all former ones has been respected; but it will be for future editors to consider whether they may not advantageously invert this order.

The statement of Walton, that the dispute in the Temple led immediately to the design of Hooker's Treatise, is incidentally confirmed by a passage in the Sermon on pride, which appears from internal evidence to have been a subsequent part of the same course, to which the discourses censured by Travers belonged. The passage occurs in a portion of the Sermon now for the first time printed [3]. He is speaking of the difference between moral or natural, and positive or mutable law: "which "difference," he says, "being undiscerned, hath not a little "obscured justice. It is no small perplexity which this one

[1] Strype, Parker, i. 528.   [2] See Life, p. 65, 66.   [3] See vol. iii. p. 618.

Occasion and Progress of the Ecclesiastical Polity. xiii

"thing hath bred in the minds of many, who beholding the
"laws which God himself hath given abrogated and disan-
"nulled by human authority, imagine that justice is hereby
"conculcated; that men take upon them to be wiser than God
"himself; that unto their devices His ordinances are con-
"strained to give place; which popular discourses, when they
"are polished with such art and cunning as some men's wits
"are well acquainted with, it is no hard matter with such tunes
"to enchant most religiously affected souls. The root of which
"error is a misconceit that all laws are positive which men
"establish, and all laws which God delivereth immutable. No,
"it is not the author which maketh, but the matter whereon
"they are made, that causeth laws to be thus distinguished."
Such as are acquainted with the argument of the first three
books of Ecclesiastical Polity, will perceive at once in the
paragraph just cited the very rudiment and germ of that
argument: which, occurring as it does in a sermon which
must have been preached within a few months of the discourse
on Justification, shews how his mind was then employed, how
ripe and forward his plans were, and how accurate Walton's
information concerning them.

Accordingly, the summer of 1586 may be fixed on as the
time of his commencing the work: and after six years and
more, i.e. on the 9th of March, 1592–3[1], the four first books
were licensed to "John Windet[2], dwelling at the signe of the
"Crosse Keyes near Powle's Wharffe." Most of the work
was therefore composed in London, amidst the annoyance of
controversy, and the interruption of constant preaching to
such an audience as the Temple then furnished. For it was
only in July 1591, that he obtained what he had so long
wished for, a quiet home in the country, viz. at Boscomb near
Salisbury.

Four days after the entry at [3] Stationers' Hall, the MS. was

[1 So stated by Walton. But in the Stationers' Registers published by Mr. Arber (II. 295), the entry is "John "Windet, 29 Januarie, [159$\frac{2}{3}$] entred "for his copie, *The lawes of ecclesi-* "*asticall policie*, eight bookes, by Rich- "ard Hooker. Auctorized by the lord "archbishop of Canterburie his grace "under his hand."] 1886.

[2 Windet was one of the publishers commonly employed by persons of Hooker's way of thinking: we find him about this time publishing a work of Dr. Bridges, and the tract called "Querimonia Ecclesiæ."

[3 Supposing the entry was March 9th. But it was really January 29th.] 1886.

Editor's Preface.

Editor's Preface.

sent to Lord Burghley: and it is not unlikely that the delay which ensued in the printing was occasioned by him. For the first edition bears date 1594[1]. There is a MS. note of Hooker's on a pamphlet called "the Christian Letter," &c. (hereafter to be spoken of) which would lead to the supposition that Burghley as well as Whitgift had seen and approved the unpublished work. The writers or writer of the Letter, having brought sundry doctrinal exceptions to the books of the Laws of Ecclesiastical Polity, had appealed to the author[2], as to what he thought in his conscience would be the sentence of bishops and divines, were his work, and two others just then published[3], to be authoritatively examined by such and such persons, and compared with the formularies of the Church. To this challenge part of Hooker's reply is, "The books you "mention have been perused. They were seen and judged "of before they came abroad to the open view of the world. "They were not published as yours is. As learned as any "this nation hath saw them and red them before they came "to your hands. And for any thing that I could ever yet "learn, the learneder they are that have given sentence con- "cerning the same, the farder they have differed from this "your virulent, uncharitable, and unconscionable sentence."

Besides Whitgift and Burghley, we know that Hooker availed himself of the judgment of his two friends, Cranmer and Sandys[4], (if they were within reach;) and there is much reason to suppose that Dr. Reynolds also was consulted[5]. With Saravia he was unacquainted, until he went into the neighbourhood of Canterbury[6].

[4] As for assistance in the way of books, there is every mark of his having been abundantly supplied during the preparation of his work. In several cases he quotes foreign productions, which from the dates of their publication could have been only just out of the press in time to be so cited. Every thing probably was sent to Whitgift: and his stores, it may be supposed, were placed at Hooker's command.

[1 The title-page is without any date in the Bodleian and other copies. Walton says 1594 (p. 69 infra), and this date is sometimes inserted in contemporary handwriting.] 1886.

[2] Page 44.

[3] "Querimonia Ecclesiæ;" and "Bancroft's Dangerous Positions."

[4] See Life, App. p. 104; and vol. iii. notes on B. vi.

[5] B. vi. App. in vol. iii. 109, 112.

[6] Life, p. 74.

He observes a remarkable accuracy in citation, especially of the passages which he means to refute. Sometimes indeed he abridges, where Cartwright is unnecessarily verbose (a fault against which that writer was not much on his guard): but there is not (as the Editor believes after minute examination) a single instance of unfair citation. That the reader may judge of this for himself, the rule of the present edition has been, scrupulously to point out all particulars in which the passages produced to be refuted, or otherwise in the way of argument, at all vary from their originals. We learn from a note of Sandys[1], on the sixth Book, that Hooker's " discourse " had credit of sincerity in the former books especially by " means of setting down Mr. Cartwright's and W. T[ravers]'s " words in the margent wheresoever they were impugned." As an instance of his care we may observe, that the copy of the Christian Letter, on which his notes are made, has nearly all the errata, which are marked at the end, corrected in the body of the pamphlet by his own hand.

Editor's Preface.

[5]   The *Editio Princeps*[2] itself is a small folio, very closely, but clearly, and in general most accurately, printed. The present edition professes to be a reprint of it, except in some matters of punctuation, and in many of orthography. As to the former: amidst great general exactness (to which also the little remaining MS. bears witness) there occur sometimes whole pages in which almost all the smaller stops are omitted in a manner which could scarcely be intentional: and there the liberty has been taken of arranging them in the way which seems most agreeable to the author's general

[1] Vol. iii. 136.

[2] The Editor takes this opportunity of acknowledging his obligations to the Rev. Dr. Bliss, Registrar of the University of Oxford, for the use of a copy of this rare volume, including also the fifth Book, first edition, in correcting the press: and also for the following note regarding the two. "The four " first books were, according to Maun-"sel, printed in 1592-3. Walton how-"ever (and he is probably right) says " that they did not appear till the year " 1594. The fifth was published by " itself in 1597, the printer being the "person who executed the first part in " 1594. It is singular that neither " Ames nor Herbert" (who notice the first part, Typograph. Antiq. vol. ii. p. 1230,) "knew any thing of the fifth " book. What they say of the four " first, is quoted from Maunsel" (Catalogue, part i. p. 59) "and the Sta-"tioners' Register."

[In this edition, the editions published in Hooker's lifetime (Books I-IV. 1594 (?), Book V. 1597) are denoted by the sign A.; Dr. Spenser's reprint of I-IV. 1604, called by him the second edition, by the sign B.] 1886.

Editor's Preface. system of punctuation. Care however has been taken not unwarrantably to determine by this process the meaning of clauses, which might fairly be left ambiguous. However, both in this question and still more in that of spelling, the Editor acknowledges that he should himself prefer an exact reprint of the original, excepting of course palpable errors of the press. In one respect especially, i.e. as a specimen and monument of language, ancient books lose very much of their value by the neglect of ancient orthography. But this, it was feared, could not be remedied without making the work less fit for general use. All that remained was to take care that no word should be lost, added, or mistaken: and this it has been endeavoured to ensure by more than one exact collation.

In verifying the quotations, there has been occasional difficulty; first, from their being very often no otherwise appropriated to a particular spot in the text, than as standing opposite to it in the margin, without any letter or mark of reference: a circumstance which has caused them to be misplaced in subsequent editions, not unfrequently by whole pages. The author seems to have become aware of the inconvenience before he published the fifth book; for in that, with few exceptions, letters of reference are inserted. It is remarkable amidst so much accuracy that the titles of books quoted should have been given in many cases so very erroneously and imperfectly, as to lead to the supposition that the press was not corrected by the author, nor by any scholar on his behalf. This has added considerably to the labour inseparable from the task of verifying quotations of that date, when "Chrysostom saith," "Augustine saith," or the like, was the received method of alleging the Fathers and Schoolmen. And in more cases than the present Editor could have wished, his endeavours to trace the quotation have as yet proved fruitless: a thing particularly to be regretted in such a writer as Hooker, much of whose argument depends on authority, and on the exact wording and context of passages produced. Where tracing the reference was not beyond his skill, the Editor has with few exceptions thought it right to insert the whole passage referred to in the notes: and in doing so, has been almost invariably impressed with admiration, not only at the depth and fulness of the writer's knowledge, but also at his fairness as well as skill in the conduct of his argument. It will be found of course, that in disputing with Romanists, he generally alleges by preference Roman Catholic authorities; and with Puritans, the writings of the reformers of Zurich and Geneva. And in some cases, where his authorities at first sight might be accounted but a gratuitous ostentation of learning, it may appear that they were severally representatives of so many classes or schools whose agreement in some common point it was of consequence to exhibit. An example may be seen in b. vii. c. xi. 8 (iii. 209 $n.^1$): and another in b. i. c. viii. 3 (i. 227 $n.^3$); where an array of quotations is produced in support of what appears at first sight a truism, but it will perhaps be found that the writers quoted are in fact, as has just been said, representatives of those systems in philosophy and theology which are most opposed to each other, and that it might be of use to shew them expressly assenting in common to that one principle of natural reason at least.

[6] The greatest liberty taken with the text by the present Editor has been the breaking it up into numbered paragraphs and sections, and inserting, by way of running title, the chief topics of as many paragraphs as the space would conveniently receive. In doing this he is well aware that he has to a certain extent taken on himself the duties of a commentator. As such he has endeavoured to execute his task faithfully: but he cannot flatter himself that in so long a work (the arrangement of which, in many places, is rather fine and subtle, than easy and prominent) he has always succeeded in drawing his partition-lines exactly, or in hitting and describing precisely the characteristic topic of each paragraph. However, it was but a choice of two evils: and it seemed better that critical students should occasionally have to correct such errors for themselves, than that popular readers should be altogether deterred by the wearisome uninviting form of the text.

3. These remarks apply as well to the second portion of the work as to the first. That second portion, containing the fifth book alone, came out, as is well known, in 1597, altogether in the same form as its predecessors. It seems to have excited great and immediate attention; one result of which was the appearance of a pamphlet often to be mentioned in the notes to the present edition, of which therefore

xviii *Christian Letter: Occasion of it:*

Editor's Preface. in this place it is necessary to give some account. It is entitled, "A Christian Letter of certaine English Protestants, "unfained favourers of the present state of Religion, author-"ised and professed in England: unto that Reverend and "learned man, Mr. R. Hoo. requiring resolution in certain "matters of doctrine (which seeme to overthrow the founda-"tion of Christian Religion, and of the Church among us) "expreslie contained in his five books of *Ecclesiastical Policie.* "1599." It is a small 4to. of 49 pages, and bears no printer's name. Some account of it may be seen appended to the Life of Hooker in Dr. Wordsworth's Ecclesiastical Biography; and the whole has been annexed, in the form of notes, to Hanbury's edition of Hooker, London, 1831. Its general drift may be gathered from the opening sentences [1].

"[2] When men dreame they are asleepe, and while men "sleepe the enemie soweth tares, and tares take roote and "hinder the good corne of the Church before it be espied. "Therefore *wisemen through silence permitt nothing looselie to* "*passe away as in a dreame.* Your offer then, Maist. *Hoo.* is "godly and laudable, to *enforme men of the estate of the church* "*of God established among us.* For the teachers of righteous "things are highlie to be commended. And he that leadeth "men rightlie to judge of the church of God is to be beloved "of all men. Howbeit sometimes goodlie promises are meere "formal, and great offers serve onely to hoodwinke such as "meane well. And as by a faire shew of *wishing well,* our first "parents were fowlie deceaved; so is there a cunning framed

---

[1] Here and elsewhere the copy of the "Christian Letter" referred to is one in the Library of C. C. C. Oxon; with the use of which the Editor has been most kindly favoured by the President: a copy enriched with a good many notes in Hooker's own handwriting. Nearly all these notes will be found in this edition, subjoined (with so much of the pamphlet itself as seemed necessary to make them intelligible) to those portions of the work respectively to which the pamphlet in each case referred.

[2] Hooker, marg. note. "That it "was not my purpose though it were "my profession to write for men's in-"formation concerning the state of the "Church of England. That they "which are sincere minded men indeed "were almost deceyved by the fair "speeches wherewith I cloke and coulor "mine intent. That calling at the "length their wittes unto them they saw "very great presumptions whereby I "might be taken for a close enimy to "the faith and doctrine of this Church, "in shew a mainteiner of the govern-"ment of God's house, indeed an in-"cendiarie, one set to fier the house of "God for other men's better opportu-"nitie to rifle it."

"method, by excellencie of wordes, and intising speeches of
"man's wisdome, to beguile and bewitch the verie Church of
"God. And such as are used for this purpose come in sheepes
"clothing. For he translateth himself into an angel of light,
"who blindeth all men with utter darkness.

"When we, therefore, your loving countrymen, (unfaynedlie
"favouring the present state, and embracing from our heartes
"the gospel of Christ, as it is preached and professed in
"England, being readie every hower to give up our lives for
"God's glorie and the honour of our Queene[1],) having so
"goodlie a champion to offer combat in our defence, were made
"verie secure, and by the sweete sounde of your melodious
"stile, almost cast into a dreaming sleepe: wee happelie
"remembring your preface that there might bee some *other*
"*cause*, opened at the length our heavie eyes, and casting
"some more earnest and intentive sight into your manner
"of fight, it seemed to us that covertlie and underhand you
"did bende all your skill and force against the present state
"of our English church, and by colour of defending the
"discipline and governement thereof, to make questionable
"and bring in contempt the doctrine and faith itselfe. For
"we saw the theme and the cause you have in hand to be
"notable simples, whereof a skilful popishe apoticarie can
"readilie make some fine potion or sweete smelling oint-
"ment, to bring heedlesse men into the pleasant dreame of
"*well-weening*, while they closelie set on fire the house of
"God. And may wee not trulie say that under the shewe
"of inveighing against Puritanes, the chiefest pointes of popish
"blasphemie are many times and in many places by divers
"men not obscurelie broached, both in sermons and in writing:
"to the great griefe of many faithful subjectes, who pray
"for the blessed and peaceable continuance of her most
"gracious Majestie, and of the estate of the Church of Jesus
"Christ as it is now established among us? And verelie
"such a thing offered itselfe unto our eyes in reading your
"bookes, and we had not skill howe to judge otherwise of the
"handling of your penne and of the scope of your matter."
Then, challenging him to reconcile his positions with the
Thirty-nine Articles, and the Apologies and other writings

---

[1] Hooker, marginal note. "Who driveth you to this profession?"

of the defenders of the Anglican Church, they produce their charges against him, to the number of twenty-one; of which the following are the heads. 1. The Deity of the Son. 2. The Coeternity of the Son, and proceeding of the Holy Ghost. 3. The Holy Scriptures contain all things necessary to Salvation. 4. Holy Scripture above the Church. 5. Of Free-Will. 6. Of Faith and Works. 7. The virtue of Works. 8. Works of supererogation. 9. None free from all Sin. 10. Predestination. 11. The visible Church, and the Church of Rome. 12. Of Preaching. 13. Of the Minister's Office. 14. Of the Sacraments. 15. Of Christ's Institution. 16. Necessity of Baptism. 17. Of Transubstantiation. 18. Of speculative Doctrine. 19. Of Calvin and the reformed Churches. 20. Schoolmen, Philosophy, and Popery. 21. The Stile and Manner of writing. Specimens of the method of attack adopted on most of these heads will be found in the notes to this edition, appended to those passages in the Ecclesiastical Polity, which drew forth the several criticisms. It was considered unnecessary to reprint the whole pamphlet; enough appearing in this way to inform the reader's judgment concerning it, and to enable him to decide whether there be much probability in a notion which some entertained at the time, that the appearance of so formidable an antagonist actually hastened the death of Hooker.

[7] On this point, over and above the presumption arising from the pamphlet itself, we possess the unquestionable evidence, curious on many other accounts, of Hooker's own MS. memoranda towards a vindication of himself, entered, as above stated, on the margins and fly-leaves of a copy of the "Christian "Letter," now preserved in the library of C. C. C. Oxford. These memoranda are in a very rough state, having been evidently set down at various times, some of them quite on the spur of the moment, and all clearly without the smallest intention of their ever meeting any eye but his own. So that the Editor for some time had serious doubts of the propriety of making them public. Some of them however are intrinsically so valuable; others so curious, as affording specimens of the way in which important discussions begin as it were to germinate in such a mind as that which planned and executed the Books of the Laws of Ecclesiastical Polity; a third sort again such perfect samples (so to speak) of his man-

ner and sentiments, that inserting them seemed on the whole more just to the truth, and to the Author's memory. Accordingly almost all of them will be found *in locis* among the notes to this edition: and amongst other things, it is apprehended they will clearly shew, whether any annoyance which he may have felt was at all mixed up with the notion, that he had a dangerous adversary to encounter, or whether it arose simply from disgust at what he considered to be malicious and unfair treatment: although in general his tone is rather playful than angry. It is clear that he knew, or strongly suspected, who the writer of the pamphlet was. For in p. 44, making answer to a passage which challenged him to submit his books to revision by authority, and which designated them as "notable "bellows to blow up the coals of sedition and fiery civil war "between all Christian churches, and to make all people who "read them to fall either flatly to atheism or backward to "popery;"—in answer to this, which he calls a "virulent "unconscionable and uncharitable sentence," having stated, as before, p. xiv of this Preface, that his work had already undergone such a revision as was demanded, he proceeds as follows: "But the best is, they are not many that sate on the bench "from which this sentence hath proceeded. It is your owne. "As for them against whom you give it, I think they take "you for no competent judg." In the same page, they call on him to "tell them roundly and soothly, If the reverend "Fathers of our Church, *assisted by* some of the approved "divines of both universities, did reade, peruse and examine "your bookes and those two other bookes[1], whether they "would not judge in their conscience and give sentence with "their mouthes, that by those three writinges the Church of "England, and all other Christian churches are undermined." His note is, "Why *assisted?* Are your reverend Fathers in- "sufficient to judg of such a matter without assistants from "the universities. Besides, what a wise question this! I must "tell you what other men will speake and think in their con- "sciences touching bookes which you condemne." "Again I "must tell you whether I have not as bad an opinion of myself "and mine own writings, as you have of both. Did ever man "heere such questions proposed by one that were (*sic*) in his

[1] "Querimonia Ecclesiæ," and Bancroft's "Dangerous Positions."

"right witts? But see how coler and rage doth make you
"forget your self. You plainly avouch that all the ministers
"which be godly and all the churches which be Christian are in
"those three books traduced openly and notoriously detected:
"and all the articles of our religion checked.

"You have asked my judgment of three books. Let me
"ask yours touching three other, and as I find your answere
"reasonable so I will accordingly frame mine own. I pray sir
"what sentence will you give concerning M. Calv. Lectures
"upon Amos[1], touching the booke called Vindiciæ contra
"Tyrannos[2], and of the Ecclesiastical History[3] almost fully
"printed out in the Blackfriers[4]?"

[8] From this and other portions of the memoranda which will be found here and there in the present edition, it is manifest that the author considered himself as dealing with a single opponent in the name of many: and that he did not rate that opponent very highly in any respect: in short, that there is no reason to question the statement of Dr. Covel, in his reply to the Christian Letter, dedicated to Archbishop Whitgift, and published by authority, A.D. 1603. Covel was patronised by Whitgift, and seems to have undertaken the Defence at his suggestion. In his address to the reader, he says, "Our Church hath had some enemies, more openly dis-
"content in the case of discipline, than they now appeare;
"whom to satisfie with reason, Maister Hooker indevoured
"with much paines: that which might have contented all,
"was in divers a spurre to a more violent coler: for medicines
"how profitable soever worke not equally in all humours.
"From hence proceeded a desire in some to make a question

---

[1] Specified no doubt on account of the famous passage on c. vii. 13; in which the royal supremacy was attacked by Calvin: see E. P. viii. iv. 8.

[2] For some account of this book see E. P. viii. ii. 8 (iii. 347 *n*.[1]). It may seem by the manner in which the mention of it is here introduced, that Hooker was inclined, with Bancroft, to ascribe it to Beza. The argument however depends not on who was the writer, but on the acceptation which the book obtained among the reformers both here and abroad: which seems to have been at any rate very considerable.

[3] On this work the editor has not been able to obtain any information. If it were a translation, abridgment, or reprint of the Magdeburgh Centuries, it would come under the same description as the two former; see b. viii. *ubi supra*.

[4] This instance may shew how well informed Hooker was about works *in the press*, &c.; no doubt by Whitgift's means. See p. xiv of this.

"of things whereof there was no doubt, and a request for
"resolution of some points wherein there was no danger:
"to this end a Letter (which heere is answered) was pub-
"lished by certaine Protestants (as they tearme themselves)
"which I heare (how true I know not) is translated into
"other tongues: *this they presume hath given that wound
"to that reverend and learned man, that it was not the
"least cause to procure his death.* But it is farre otherwise;
"for *he contemned it in his wisdome* (as it was fit) and yet
"in his humility would have answered it, if he had lived."
He adds, "I staid the time, and a long time, until some
"elder and of riper judgment might have acquitted me
"from all opinion of presumption in this cause; which
"being not done by them whom many reasons might have
"induced to this defence, I could not for that part which
"I beare in that church, whose government was defended by
"Maister Hooker, with patience endure so weake a letter
"anie longer to remaine unanswered. And herein I have
"dealt as with men (although to me unknown) of some
"learning and gravitie, to whom peradventure in manie re-
"spects I am farre inferiour; and yet for anie thing I know,
"or appeareth in this letter, they may be clothed with the
"same infirmities that I am. But if this had beene by him-
"self performed (*which I heare he hath done, and I desire
"thee to expect it*) thy satisfaction (gentle reader) would
"have beene much more; yet vouchsafe in thy kindnesse to
"accept this." In p. 9, Covel begs the writers of the letter
to receive from him what they had required from Hooker:
"a charitable, direct, plain, and sincere answer: which, no
"doubt of it, from himselfe had bin far more learned and more
"speedy, if he could either have resolved to have done it, or
"after he had resolved could have lived to have seen it finished.
"But first of all, he was loath to entermeddle with so weake
"adversaries, thinking it unfit (as himselfe said) that a man
"that hath a long journey should turne backe to beate everie
"barking curre; and having taken it in hand, his urgent and
"greater affaires, together with the want of strength, weak-
"ened with much labour, would not give him time to see it
"finished. Yet his minde was stronger than his yeares, and
"knew not well how to yeeld to infirmitie. Wherein if he

"had somewhat favoured himselfe, he might peradventure "have lived to have answered you; to the benefite of the "Church, and the comfort of a great number."

Evidently the writer of these sentences had no access to Hooker's papers, and his general reasonings shew as much: for he is commonly content to clear up the points objected to by production of his author's context, and collections from other parts of his writings. However, the same impression seems to have been made on him as on Hooker, by the perusal of the Christian Letter: viz. that it was the production not of many, but of one; and that one, a person before versed in the Puritan controversy, and now desirous, under cover of anxiety for evangelical doctrine, to insinuate the principles of the Genevan discipline in all their disturbing force. Thus in p. 3, Covel says, "It is much easier to answer those shadows "of reason, wherein these *admonishers* do please themselves, "than by their silence to make them confess that they are "fully answered:" where the word "admonishers" printed in Italics evidently points at the compilers of the famous Admonition to the Parliament. Again, p. 5; "Those whom we "must make adversaries in this cause are men not known "either by name, religion, or learning. . . .It may be peradven- "ture the zeal of some one, who desirous to gain an opinion "among his followers undertaketh to speak as from the minds "of many . . . .Whosoever they are, as I cannot easily conjec- "ture, so I am not curious to know." In p. 46, he speaks to the unknown compilers of "the rest of their writings in "that kind:" and in p. 136, tells them, "themselves were "able to witness that Hooker had not shunned to encounter "the best of the Disciplinarian faction in our land."

Covel, therefore, as well as Hooker himself, countenances the idea that the pamphlet proceeded from some veteran or veterans in the cause of Puritanism, afraid to speak out, for what reason is not hinted, but probably because of late the government had been acting decisively against that party: and also on account of the great effect on men's minds, which had been produced by the publications as well of Hooker himself, as of others hereafter to be specified. On the whole, it seems very clear that the Christian Letter may be regarded as a kind of document, expressing the views and feelings of the Puritans of that generation: which being understood, the question as to the author's name, however curious, is comparatively of little moment. Cartwright and Travers were both living at the time, the one in Warwick, master of the hospital, the other in Dublin, Provost of Trinity College; but both of them apparently had finally retired from the controversy; and the style of the letter will be found on examination very unlike either of theirs. John Field, another leading admonitioner, had been dead since 1588[1].

[9] Hooker's notes on this pamphlet are here printed from the original, preserved (as above mentioned) in the library of C.C.C.; and collated with two transcripts, in interleaved copies of the tract, the one also in C. C. C.[2], the other in Trinity College, Dublin (A. 5. 22): for which latter collation, as for all that comes from the Dublin library, the reader will understand that he is indebted to Dr. Cotton, the present Dean of Lismore. These transcripts have been eminently useful in supplying portions where the original had worn out, and in confirming readings which might have been otherwise doubtful. On comparing the two, they appear to have been made independently of each other: that in C. C. C. seems the earlier and more accurate. In one instance, the Dublin copy inserts a note, of which no vestige occurs in the original. A few of the memoranda, which the Editor conceived might be worth preserving, but for the insertion of which in the notes no convenient place had occurred, will be found at the end of this Preface.

4. But Hooker's preparations in his own defence had proceeded further than these brief and scattered hints. In the library of Trinity College, Dublin, (MS. B. 1. 13) is what is described in the catalogue as "a Treatise by Hooker, on "Grace, the Sacraments, Predestination, &c.:" which in three passages[3] clearly indicates itself to have formed part of the

---

[1] Dr. Wordsworth in his Christian Institutes, i. 90, states the writer of the Pamphlet to have been Dr. Andrew Willett, Author of the *Synopsis Papismi*.

[2] Thus described in the Catalogue of MSS. C. C. C. 1682. "215." (now E. i. 15.) "A Letter against Mr. "Hooker's Polity, printed in the year "1599, interleaved, with some part of "an Answer to it of Mr. Hooker's. "Sed hic videtur esse exemplar recen-"tius, ipsum vero autographum est "penes me Tho. Norgrove."

[3] Compare in this edition, vol. ii. 538, with i. 222, *n.*[2]; and ii. 556 with p. 216, *n.*[1], and Chr. Letter 15-17; and see ii. 542, *n.*[3].

Editor's Preface.

intended reply to the Christian Letter. It contains much valuable matter, although in a very undigested and imperfect form: with the exception perhaps of the portion concerning Predestination, which is much the largest of the three, containing in the MS. twenty closely written folio pages, whereas the other two, on Grace and on the Sacraments, contain but six and four respectively. We may conjecture that this more finished part was not now for the first time written, but rather that the revival of the dispute on Predestination led the author to revise papers which he had prepared more than ten years before, when Travers first attacked him on the subject. For in the Answer to Travers's Supplication, § 23, he states himself to have "promised at some convenient time to "make the points then agitated clear as light both to him "and to all others." Now the points were the very same which the Christian Letter had now called in question. If this conjecture be warrantable, it will follow, that we cannot certainly reckon upon these fragments as exhibiting Hooker's latest and most matured judgment on all the mysterious topics introduced in them: although the distinct reference to the Lambeth Articles at the end must undoubtedly be regarded as a deliberate summary of the general conclusions at which he had then arrived. Of the second fragment, that on Sacraments, it may seem questionable whether it is rightly placed as part of this controversy. As far as it goes, it is wholly defensive, against Romanists; but it might be intended as introductory to a view of the question from the other side. The whole of these fragments will be found in the Appendix to the fifth book. Their genuineness is morally demonstrable. The writer uses the first person in speaking of the books of Ecclesiastical Polity, and refers to the Christian Letter in a way which coincides remarkably with Hooker's own MS. memoranda. Compare (e.g.) the mention of *aptness* and *ableness* in the Fragment, p. 538, with a note in p. 11, of the pamphlet, which will be found in this edition, E. P. i. vii. 6. But indeed it is hardly necessary to dwell on minute marks of this kind, so strong and clear is the internal evidence throughout. To say nothing of favourite idioms, and turns of language; the views themselves, philosophical and theological; the mode of developing those views; the allegations from the Fathers and Schoolmen, and the way of translating them; the introduction and management of rapid historical sketches; the quiet and sustained majesty of style; and more perhaps than all, the deep awe with which sacred things are approached: are so many tokens of ownership, impossible to be counterfeited. One quality indeed is wanting: there are few if any traces of that instinctive playfulness of humour, which breaks out so often in his former controversial writings. It would seem as if he had determined to be more than usually guarded in his manner of speaking of his adversaries on this occasion: a circumstance not a little remarkable, when compared with the notes on the Christian Letter, many of them so keenly expressive of his first sharp sense of their unfair usage of him.

[10] 5. The Appendix to the fifth Book contains moreover the letter of George Cranmer to Hooker, which in all editions since 1666 immediately follows the life by Walton. Being in a great measure historical, it was judged more convenient to place it in the order of time; and so placed, it bears a striking testimony to the effect of Hooker's labours even at that early period, and to the apparently declining condition of the Puritan interest[1]; and we may judge a little of the support and encouragement which it must have afforded to his wearied and anxious mind, when he found his old friend and pupil, now rapidly rising, in the expectation of all their contemporaries, to the highest places of the state[2], yet unchanged in affection for him, and bringing his varied experience and

---

[1] The conclusion is particularly calculated to excite serious reflections on the possible cause of the revival of that interest, in so fearful a way, within the very next generation. "The clergy," says Cranmer, "especially those of both universities, "are to be exhorted to preach Christ "crucified, the mortification of the "flesh, the renewing of the spirit: "not those things which in time of "strife seem precious, but passions "being allayed, are vain and child-"ish." There is a remarkable coincidence between this and the language of King Charles I. about thirty years after, when being at Woodstock he commended to the faculty of divinity at Oxford, as the best subject whereof to treat, "Jesus Christ and "Him crucified." See Jackson's Works, ii. 565.

[2] "Queen Elizabeth, confiding in "her own princely judgment and "opinion, had formed so favourable "an opinion of Cranmer's worth and "conduct, that she would have him "and none other, to finish and bring "the Irish war to a propitious end: "which not deceiving her good conceit of him, he nobly achieved, though "with much pains and carefulness." Lloyd's State Worthies, p. 665, as quoted by Dr. Bliss, in his edition of the Ath. Oxon. i. 701.

Editor's Preface. independent judgment to the zealous support of the views to which he was himself devoted.

This letter is reprinted from the original, first published in 1642: the year in which, as may be gathered from Wood, Ath. Oxon. iii. 577, the parliamentarians plundered the library of Henry Jackson, rector of Meysey Hampton, Gloucestershire, who had had the care of Hooker's remains committed to him by Dr. Spenser[1]. In that way possibly some loyal person might get hold of the letter, and publish it as a seasonable warning. That Jackson himself was not the publisher is evident from the mistakes in the prefixed advertisement[2], which he could not well have passed over: that Walton was not, may be gathered from his silence on the subject, where he introduces the letter at the end of the Life of Hooker. At the same time, connected as he was with the Cranmers, such introduction on his part undoubtedly proves the document genuine. Some remarkable differences appear on collating the letter as printed by him (1675) with the edition of 1642, which would lead to a suspicion that he was not aware of that publication. The result of the collation the Editor proposes to give at the end of this preface; where whoever will take the trouble of examining it will see, it is hoped, sufficient reason for the preference given to the text of 1642 above that of Walton's copy.

[11] 6. So far, the task of verification has proved easy: but on proceeding to the sixth book, the ground, as is well known, entirely changes. The clearest way perhaps of exhibiting the whole case, will be first to recapitulate all that is known of the fate of the three last books in common, and then to

---

[1] See Life of Hooker, Further Appendix, No. i. p. 103.

[2] Life, p. 17. It may be as well to specify the corrections there made by Walton in the extract from the version of Camden. The Advertisement says, "In C. C. C. he proceeded and continued M.A. *of six years standing* before he removed:" Walton, "he continued M.A. *for some time* before," &c. The Advertisement, "He then betook himself *to secretary Davison*:" Walton, "He then betook himself to *travel, accompanying* "*that worthy gentleman sir E. Sandys,*" &c. The Advertisement, "After sir H. Killigrew's death, he accompanied sir E. Sandys, &c. and after his return was sought after by the most noble lord Mountjoy:" Walton, "After sir H. Killigrew's death he was sought after by the most noble lord Mountjoy." These corrections, which Walton must have obtained from the Cranmers, seem to shew that they were not, any more than Jackson, concerned in the original publication of the letter.

explain the course taken in the present edition severally with each of the three: for it so happens that they stand respectively upon distinct and very unequal grounds of evidence.

First, there can be no reasonable doubt that the author left them completed for publication. Of this fact, we have two, if not three, contemporary statements, independent of each other: first, that of Dr. Spenser in his preface to the first edition of the collected five books; "[1] He lived till he saw "them perfected:" secondly, that of Covel, (Just and Temp. Defence, p. 149;) "Those three books of his, which from his "own mouth, I am informed that they were finished." To which in all probability might be added the testimony of the Cranmer family, of whom, it may be supposed, Walton received the anecdote related in the Life, p. 84.

Next, his papers with the rest of his chattels were given by his last will to his wife, whom he left sole executrix under the supervision of a person of the name of Churchman, probably her father, (see Bishop Andrewes' Letter, p. 91 *n.* [7]) in conjunction with his own friend and pupil, Sandys. The will is dated Oct. 26, and Hooker died Nov. 2. Only five days afterwards Dr. Andrewes, being then at the court, wrote to Dr. Parry, who was, as it may seem, intimate with the Churchman family, and near at hand, requesting him to provide without delay for the security of the papers. He writes in a tone of the greatest anxiety, and regrets that he should be so late in giving this hint, having but just been informed of Hooker's death. Inquiry, it may be presumed, was made accordingly, and nothing satisfactory elicited from the widow. For the next thing we are told is, that at the end of a month, the archbishop sent one of his chaplains to inquire after the three remaining books, "of which she would not, or could not, "give any account:" but that after an interval of three months more, suspicions having arisen, she was summoned before the privy council, and in a preliminary examination confessed to the archbishop, that many of her husband's writings had been burned and torn by a Mr. Charke, (probably the same who married her daughter,) and another minister who dwelt near Canterbury. Here her statement closes; for she died suddenly before the examination could be resumed.

[1] See hereafter, p. 97.

Editor's Preface.

Such is the narration of Walton, communicated to him about the year 1624, "by one that well knew Mr. Hooker and the "affairs of his family:" i. e. apparently, by William the brother of George Cranmer, or by one of his sisters: the father and aunts of Walton's first wife. To which must be added the statement of Bishop King, also a contemporary of Hooker's, communicated through the Bishop's son to Walton, with the express intention of its being made public in his name. See hereafter, p. 103. This evidence is surely distinct enough, and has as much claim to be attended to as contemporary evidence has in general. Of course it does not prove that the widow's account was true, but it does prove that the papers were not forthcoming, that she was called on to undergo official examination regarding them, and that such and such was the result of the examination, according to the belief of those who were most concerned to know. It is true, no record of the transaction remains in the council books; but it does not appear from Walton's account that it ever came officially before the council. On the whole, the conclusion is irresistible: that the completed books were irrecoverably gone; and all that remained was to secure and arrange what was left of the rough draughts. These, it may be supposed, Mrs. Hooker gave up to the archbishop, on occasion of the aforesaid inquiry, i.e. about March, 160$\frac{8}{9}$. And he committed them to the care of Dr. Spenser, not only, doubtless, as an intimate college friend of the author, but also as one of the nearest surviving representatives of George Cranmer, who of all others would have been fittest for the trust, had he been alive. But he unfortunately had fallen at the battle of Carlingford, Nov. 13, 1600, only eleven days after his friend and tutor, and in all probability before he could be aware of his death.

[12] To Spenser then, who had married Cranmer's sister, and who afterwards became President of the college, the task of editorship was by preference intrusted: the rather, as it may seem, because he was one of those with whom Hooker had most freely communicated on his great work, during its progress. And the single remaining composition of Spenser himself (single, if we except his preface to his edition of the Polity) is quite sufficient to evince his entire sympathy with Hooker's views; at least, his thorough aptness as a learner in that

school. It is a posthumous publication, a sermon at St. Paul's Cross on Isaiah v. 2, 3 : full of eloquence and striking thoughts ; the theological matter almost entirely, and sometimes the very words, being taken from those parts of Hooker, in which he treats of the visible Church. It may be added, that Spenser from the beginning appears to have belonged to that party in his college, which feared Puritanism as well as Romanism, and that his appointment to the office of Greek Lecturer, in 1577, had been vehemently opposed by Reynolds [1]. Both he and Bishop King were at the time of their common friend Hooker's death resident in London, and neighbours, Spenser vicar of St. Sepulchre's, and King rector of St. Andrew's, Holborn. The first step the former took in fulfilment of the archbishop's charge regarding Hooker's remains, was the re-publication of the five Books of Polity, with a preface (reprinted in this edition): in which he distinctly announces the purpose of giving to the world the three remaining books, dismembered and defaced as they were. This took place, according to Wood, in 1604. The edition contained the five books, "without any addition or diminution what-"soever." But the editor's labours that year began to be interrupted by the new Translation of the Bible, in which he was engaged as one of the Westminster committee : and no progress appears to have been made with Hooker until his return to Oxford again. But in 1607, on the death of Reynolds, he was elected President of C.C.C., his and Hooker's friend King having been made Dean of Ch. Ch. in 1605.

[13] He found in the college a young scholar of the name of Henry Jackson, of the city of Oxford, skilful and industrious in translating, arranging, and compiling: him Spenser employed, as Walton says, "to transcribe for him all Mr. "Hooker's remaining written papers;" and he evidently entered on the work with an editor's partiality, and was disposed to take to himself the editor's credit, which indeed Spenser, as far as appears, was in no wise inclined to deny him. He began with what may be called the Opuscula : publishing in the years 1612, 13, 14, several of the Sermons, to be noticed hereafter in their places : among which that on Justification had so rapid a sale, that a new edition was

---

[1] See Further Appendix to the Life of Hooker, No. iv. p. 114.

xxxii *Death of Spenser. Fate of Hooker's Remains:*

Editor's Preface. required in a few weeks. It seems to have been intended that the eighth book of the Polity, for whatever reason, should appear first, by itself: and Fulman has preserved three fragments of letters by Jackson, all dated 1612; the first, as it seems, early in the year, stating that the President had put the eighth book into his hands, and that he was entirely taken up with the task of "polishing" and arranging it. The second letter, dated in September, represents him as just putting the last hand to the same book: and the third, of Dec. 21, complains "that the President, as he, Jackson, had "reason to think, meant to edit it in his own name, although "its revival (for he could call it no less) was the work of him, "Jackson, alone: a plain case of one man bearing off another "man's honours."

Thus far the business of publication had advanced when Dr. Spenser died, 3 April, 1614. At his death, he bequeathed Hooker's papers "as a precious legacy" to Dr. King, who in 1611 had been made Bishop of London. Thus they were taken out of Jackson's custody, at a time when he was not very kindly affected towards any one who might interfere with the interest in them which he considered himself to have acquired. The rest of their history, as a collection, is soon told. Bishop King's son informs Walton, that his father preserved them until his death, which happened March 30, 1621[1]. Afterwards they continued in his, Henry King's hand, till Archbishop Abbot claimed them for Lambeth Library. They were conveyed to him by Dr. Barkham his chaplain, who, being dean of Bocking, was probably a neighbour of King, then archdeacon of Colchester. This must have taken place before September 1633. It is remarkable, that while they were under Laud's custody, no thought of completing the edition seems to have been entertained. The reports on the state of the MSS. were probably discouraging, and a false notion might prevail, of undue countenance likely to be afforded to the innovators by certain portions. However, the papers remained undisturbed, except by occasional copyists, (with whom the eighth book seems to have been most in favour,) until Dec. 28, 1640, when the Archbishop was committed for high treason, and his library was made over to the

---
[1] Ath. Oxon. ii. 296.

First Publication of the Sixth and Eighth Books. xxxiii

custody of Prynne[1]. From him it passed to Hugh Peters, by a vote of the Commons, June 27, 1644. Nothing more is known of the fate of the original papers : and certainly it is no great wonder, if whilst they remained in such hands, the friends of the Church looked suspiciously at the publication of any thing which professed to have formed part of them.

Editor's Preface.

14]   7. To record those publications in their order: The first occurs as early as 1641, from the Oxford press, under the sanction of no less a person than Archbishop Ussher. Of this an account will be given in speaking of the Appendix to Book Eight in this edition.

The second of the Hooker Fragments which appeared was the letter of George Cranmer already mentioned, in 1642. Reasons have been given above, against ascribing the editorship of this either to Jackson or to Walton : but it may have passed through the hands of Ussher ; who appears to have spent the whole of that year, either in Oxford or in London : and ground may perhaps appear by and by for a reasonable conjecture as to the channel by which he became possessed of this and some other pieces.

The third was a far more important relic. In 1648, according to Wood, (Ath. Oxon. i. 695,) but according to the copy[2] which has been used in correcting the press of this edition, in 1651[3], came out " Of the Lawes of Ecclesiasticall " Politie, the Sixth and Eighth Books. By Richard Hooker. " A work long expected, and now published, according to the " most authentique copies. London, printed by R. B. [Richard " Bishop,] and are to be sold by [John Crook, 1648] George " Badger in St. Dunstan's Churchyard in Fleet-street." small 4to. pp. 226[4]. An account of the authorities from which this publication was professedly made may be seen in the Life, p. 95 *n.*[1]. Six MSS. are there mentioned : but it may be suspected that the statement relates to the eighth book only. At least, the Catalogus MSS. Anglic. mentions but one copy of the sixth book, nor have the researches made with a view to the

---

[1] See H. Wharton's Preface to the Troubles, &c. of Archbishop Laud.
[2] From the Library of C. C. C. with a few marginal notices and corrections by Fulman.
[3] Wood however was right : as appears by a copy with which the Editor has been favoured, since the first publication of this Preface, by the Rev. J. S. Brewer, of Queen's College, Oxford.
[4 Designated in Mr. Keble's notes by the sign E. vol. iii. p. 1. *n.* b.]

VOL. I.   C

present edition succeeded in producing any more: whereas of the eighth no fewer than four have been examined. The text, therefore, of the two books, though accidentally published together at first, must be severally accounted for.

To speak at present of the Sixth only: Dr. Cotton has collated for this edition a MS. (B. 1. 13) in the library of Trinity College, Dublin: which has proved of very great service, not only in correcting the many and often palpable errors of the first printed copy, but also in arranging the whole with a view to the argument. "The MS.," Dr. Cotton says, "is evidently "written by an amanuensis; but there are every where marks "that Archbishop Ussher had read it over most carefully, as " he has corrected with his own hand the errors of the copier, "even in the most minute particulars. You will perceive, be- "sides the verbal discrepancies, considerable difference in the "punctuation, many sentences being materially altered in "sense by it. Also, that the book is divided into sections, as " are the first five: which adds to the lucidity of the work, as " does likewise the breaking of it into several paragraphs." Dr. Elrington, to whom the Editor is obliged for the first notice of these important fragments at Dublin, adds, that " in " the catalogue is the following note," relating to the marginal remarks of Ussher; " The editor of the printed copy has seen "these notes, but has made some small omissions." Dr. Elrington further remarks, that the MS. had the appearance of being written out for the press. It may be proper to add, that in this edition the arrangement thus sanctioned by Ussher is generally adopted as to the leading divisions, though not always as to chapters or sections: and that in all cases of departure from the reading of the first edition, (except matters of mere punctuation and obvious errors of the press,) the change is made on authority of the Dublin MS.

[15] 8. But concerning this Sixth Book, a very material inquiry remains. At first sight, of all the three questionable books, this is in one respect by far the most perplexing. As it stands at present, it is an entire deviation from its subject. For whereas the plan of the whole treatise required in this part a full discussion of the claim of lay elders to a part in church jurisdiction; and whereas the title distinctly propounds that subject; it is clear and certain, that of the whole book as it

stands the two first chapters only and the first section of the third chapter have any relation to that subject. The remainder, being nineteen twentieths of the whole, is a series of dissertations on Primitive and Romish Penance, in their several parts, confession, satisfaction, absolution. This anomaly, which every reader must have observed, and which in any writer carried so far would be extraordinary, but in Hooker of all writers is quite unaccountable, is explained at once by a document, which the present Editor has had permission to copy from the original in C. C. C. library: and which he has subjoined as an appendix to the sixth book. It appears that Hooker, having finished the treatise on lay elders, forwarded it, as had been his custom with former portions of his work, to his friends and confidential advisers, Cranmer and Sandys: and the paper alluded to gives the result of their criticism. It is in their own handwriting; Cranmer's part (which was afterwards reviewed by Sandys) filling twenty-four folio pages, and Sandys' part, which is more closely written, occupying six pages more. Its genuineness is ensured, not only by internal evidence, (for who would ever have thought such a paper worth forging?) but also by the attestations of Walton and Fulman, which the reader will find, vol. iii. p. 108 *n.*[1]. This document would have been worthy of preservation, were it only for the good sense and accurate reasoning, by which, even in such disjointed fragments, the writers have contrived to throw light on many parts of a curious and important subject: or again as a pleasing monument of the entire, affectionate confidence, which subsisted between Hooker and his two pupils: occupied as they were in lines of life very far removed from his, Cranmer as a diplomatist, Sandys as a member of parliament: but as a document in the question of the genuineness of the (so called) sixth book, these notes are in truth quite decisive. First, it will be found that among them all there are not so many as four instances, in which the *catchwords* at the beginning of the note occur in the text as it stands. Next, the whole subject-matter of their remarks, the scriptural and other quotations referred to, indicate an entirely different work. There is not a word about penitency, auricular confession, absolving power: but (in the third place) the frame of the whole, and each particular as far as it can be understood, implies the annotators to have had before them a work really addressing itself to the question of lay Elders, and meeting all the arguments, which, as we know from contemporary writers, the upholders of the Puritan platform were used to allege.

[16] As far as can be gathered from the very scanty notices remaining, it may seem that Hooker, entering as Sandys thought rather too abruptly on his subject, treated of these following heads. 1. Of the natural connection between the two powers, of Order and of Jurisdiction. 2. Of the best way of drawing the line between Ecclesiastical and Civil Causes. 3. Of the principle of Courts Ecclesiastical, and the meaning of, "Tell the Church." 4. Of the Church's Anathema: in which he seems to have made three degrees, and to have considered St. Paul's expression, Rom. ix. 3, as referring to excommunication. Cranmer's remark on this is very striking, and very much in unison with the little that remains of him besides. 5. What offences are excommunicable; under which head the question recurred of the limits of church and state power, and Sandys lays down that it is an error to make the sovereign a mere lay person. 6. Effects of excommunication (probably against Erastus). Distinction between the Church's anathema and that of a mere ecclesiastical judge. Whether temporal judgment on the excommunicated person might ever be expected to ensue. The case of Victor cited; probably to moot the question of the effect of a wrong excommunication. The Epicurean tendency of slighting excommunication was pointed out in the next place; and frivolous proceedings in ecclesiastical courts deprecated as leading to such contempt. 7. The interference of presbyterial jurisdiction with sovereign authority was next urged against Beza. 8. The precedents of Jewish Polity were considered; (on which head down to the time of Jehoshaphat a valuable abstract of the discourse is given in one of Cranmer's notes.) 9. The pleas were examined, which the defenders of the eldership were accustomed to urge from the New Testament: especially Rom. xii. 8; 1 Cor. xii. 28; Acts xiv. 23; 1 Tim. v. 17. 10. He proceeded to the precedents usually alleged on this subject from the Fathers: having both in this and the part next before an eye particularly to T. C. part iii. tract 8. The book appears to have concluded as it

began; rather too abruptly for the taste of the friendly revisers. Each of them recommends an appropriate conclusion: Cranmer suggesting that it might be well to add some remarks on the indirect political inconveniences of the lay eldership; Sandys, on the other incongruities of the Geneva platform; the essential distinction of pastor from teacher; the arrangements of their consistories, their synods, and the like.

Somewhat after this sort, judging by the fragments which remain, did the argument of the sixth book proceed: and every one who has read Whitgift, Bancroft or Bilson on the one hand, Beza or Cartwright on the other, will be aware that these are the topics which Hooker must have introduced in order to perform the service which he had undertaken. It now appears, in point of fact, that he did so. But the treatise which embodied his views on the subject, and which one may collect from these indistinct notices to have been more valuable by far in its constructive than in its destructive part, has disappeared, even in its rough outline, with the exception perhaps of a few sentences near the beginning.

[17] The question has been asked[1], "If it be true, as is "alleged, that different MSS. of the last books did not agree, "if even these disagreements were the result of fraud, why "should we conclude that they were corrupted by the Puri- "tans rather than by the Church?" It is presumed that the fact now demonstrated, namely the suppression of the entire book on lay elders, supplies of itself an answer to this question. For if there was one point in their system, on which the Puritans of the sixteenth century were more sensitive, and piqued themselves more[2] than on the rest, this of lay elders was that point. Suppose a party of them in Hooker's study, according to the report made to Walton; the sixth book was that which they would first lay violent hands on. A churchman would be under no temptation of the sort: if he wanted to tamper with any part, he would sooner select parts of books vii. and viii., in which he might think unguarded concessions

---

[1] Hallam's Constitutional Hist. of Engl. c. iv. vol. i. p. 236. 4to. 1827. note.

[2] See E. P. Pref. iv. 5, and note; and Querimonia Ecclesiæ, p. 219. "Non "tam bonis displicet novum hoc senio- "rum genus, quam placet Puritanis. "Nam cum omnia quæ nobis propo- "nunt plurimum semper dilaudant, ... "præclarum tamen hunc seniorum con- "sessum tanti faciunt, ut eo uno totius "Ecclesiæ salutem niti existiment."

xxxviii *Conjecture as to the present Sixth Book.*

Editor's Preface. made to the prejudice of regal or episcopal authority. As it is, there can be no question that far "other than verbal "changes have been made in the loose draught which the "author left;" and surely there are also very considerable appearances of the MS. having been once in the hands of Puritans. Bishop Andrewes's letter proves how much he apprehended such a thing at the time; we know from a statement of Travers, and by the pedigree subjoined to this preface, that his kindred, in all likelihood Puritans, were connected with the Hookers by marriage: there is also reason to believe that Hooker's own daughter married into a Puritan house: add to this only so much of the Cranmer family's statement to Walton, as it was impossible for them to be mistaken in: and whether we believe the widow Hooker's account of the Puritan ministers' interference or no, it cannot be said that the case is clear of all suspicion of the kind.

But to return to the Sixth Book. As has been said, with regard to nineteen twentieths of it the case is made so clear by these notes, that it might perhaps have been more consistent with the duty of an editor, had the whole of it after c. iii. § 1, been separated entirely from the Books of Ecclesiastical Polity, of which, undoubtedly, the author never meant it for part. The reasons or impressions which told against such an arrangement will be found in the second note on this sixth book. But the change may perhaps be made with advantage in a future edition, i.e. by far the greater portion of the book may be separated, not from Hooker's remains altogether, but from forming part of the Ecclesiastical Polity. For although it be found in the wrong place, yet is there no cause whatever to account it ascribed to a wrong author. It is full of instruction, piety, and eloquence; it has every internal proof of being Hooker's. Its appearing where it does may be reasonably accounted for, without supposing any further liberties taken by the Puritans, if we only imagine it in a heap of papers, accidentally coming next to a sketch of the preamble of the Sixth Book. Any one eager to publish might seize on it, and with no deliberate purpose of deceiving, or as is most likely for mere purposes of trade, might send it abroad with the misnomer now detected. The wonder is that such a critic as Ussher should have corrected it, as it seems he had done, for the press, without being aware of its total deviation from the question: and that Walton, and perhaps still more that Fulman, should have had the notes of Cranmer and Sandys in his possession, without discovering the interpolation in the sixth book.

[18] 9. On the Seventh Book, and the evidence for its genuineness, a very few words may suffice. The first publishers of the sixth and eighth in 1648 and 1651, state those two books to have been preserved in the hands of Andrewes and Ussher, "with great hopes the seventh would have been recovered, "that they might have been published to the world's view at "once: but," they add, "endeavours used to that purpose have "hitherto proved fruitless." In fact, no trace of the book appears until 1662, when Gauden, just then promoted to the see of Worcester, (the person whose name appears in so questionable a light in the affair of the Εἰκὼν Βασιλικὴ,) set forth a new edition of Hooker, augmenting it by this seventh book and some paragraphs at the end of the eighth. In his title-page and preface he uses very sounding language, and even gives his readers to understand, that the work was now entirely recovered [1] to the state in which Hooker left it. He distinctly

---

[1] Titlepage: "The works of Mr. "Richard Hooker, (that Learned, "Godly, Judicious, and Eloquent "Divine,) vindicating the Church of "England, as truly Christian, and duly "Reformed: in Eight Books of Ecclesiastical Polity. Now compleated, "as with the Sixth and Eighth, so "with the Seventh, (touching Episcopacy, as the Primitive, Catholic, and "Apostolic government of the Church,) "out of his own MSS. never before "published. With an account of his "Holy Life, and Happy Death, written "by Dr. John Gauden, now Bishop "of Exeter. The entire Edition dedicated to the King's most excellent "Majesty, Charles II: by whose Royal "Father (near his Martyrdom) the "former Five Books, (then only extant) "were commended to his dear children, "as an excellent mean to satisfy private "scruples, and settle the public Peace "of this Church and Kingdom." Dedication to the King: "I know not "what to present more worthy of your "Majesty's acceptance, and my duty, "than these elaborate and seasonable "works of the famous and prudent "Mr. Richard Hooker, now augmented, "and I hope compleated with the three "last books, so much desired, and so "long concealed. The publication of "which volume so *entire*," &c. And below: "To this *compleated edition*, "I have added such particular accounts "as I could get, of the author's person," &c. Preface: "By the care of some "learned men, especially of the Right "Reverend Father in God, Gilbert, "now Lord Bishop of London, those "genuine additions are now made of "the three last books, promised and "performed by him, but long concealed "from public view, not without great "injury to the public good." And, p. 23, "Himself expired amidst his "great undertakings to the impotent "joy of his antagonists: who finding "themselves worsted and sorely wounded

says, "The seventh book, by comparing the writing of it with "other indisputable papers, or known MSS. of Mr. Hooker's, "is undoubtedly his own hand throughout. The eighth is "written by another hand, as a copy, but interlined in many "places with Mr. Hooker's own characters, as owned by him. "The best and surest test of the genuineness or legitimacy of "these three now added books, will be the weight, or learned "solidity of the matter, also the grave, but eloquent and "potent manner of handling each subject; ... This only "may be suspected (as is said) that in some places he had "not put to his last polishing or consummating hand." And, p. 40: "When these excellent books shall obtain their "deserved place in men's heads and hearts, ... I shall have "no cause to repent of the pains, yea pleasure, I have taken "in giving the world this renewed view of Mr. Richard "Hooker, and his now completed works."

On examining the sixth and eighth books in Gauden's impression, no material improvement occurs. What MSS. he had appear to have agreed on the whole with the printed text: excepting the aforementioned addition to the eighth book, of which something will be said in its place. It is extraordinary that in speaking of the seventh he should, as will have been seen, omit altogether to say where he found the MS., how he came by it, and what he did with it: nor does

"... by this great archer, in his five "first books, yet received some comfort "in this, that they escaped the shot of "his last three, which he never pub-"lished, and which they hoped he had "never finished; or if he did complete "them, they found (as is by some "imagined) some artifice so long to "smother and conceal them from the "public, till they had played such an "after-game, as they thought was only "able to confute Mr. Hooker, and to "blot out by the sword the impres-"sions of his pen. But Providence "in time hath not only confuted those "men's projects and confidences, but "also brought forth those esteemed "abortions, the three last books, with "such lineaments of their father's vir-"tue and vigour on them, that they "may be easily and justly owned for "genuine, although (perhaps) they had "not the last politure of their parent's "hands. Their strength shews them "to be a legitimate progeny, however "they may seem to want something "of that beauty and lustre which always "attended Mr. Hooker's consumma-"tion." He next goes on to give what seems by its form intended as a sort of analysis of the three last books, but from its matter one might almost conjecture, that he had hardly read more of them than their titles. He then proceeds, p. 26: "Such as they are, "it is thought meet to present them to "the reader; each of them is by learned "critics judged to be genuine or authentic, "though possibly not so complete or ex-"act as the curious author intended."

he leave any clue whatever for the guidance of future inquirers. For the genuineness, then, of this portion of the work, our only direct testimony is the affirmation of Dr. Gauden. In other words, we are left to make up our minds by internal evidence only. Not that Gauden had, as far as is known, any political or theological views, which would lead him to take liberties with the MSS., nor that there is any appearance of their having been tampered with on any such ground: the suspicion which occurs is rather, that forgery or at least interpolation may have been practised, in order to promote the sale of the work.

19] Under such circumstances it is satisfactory to find, that the internal evidence of this seventh book is on comparison even more decisive than either that of the sixth or of the eighth. The course of argument and flow of style are more sustained, and more decidedly characteristical. The translations from the Fathers are of the same stamp: and this is a point of extreme delicacy, a point in which Hooker perhaps is unequalled amongst English writers. It is true that in certain portions, especially towards the end, there is some verbosity, and a considerable degree of repetition [1]. But this may be thought to arise in part from the editor's uniting, as members of a continuous treatise, what were in fact independent sketches of matters to be somewhere introduced. Such sketches, if not checked by comparison, would incidentally run into each other.

From the manner in which the pages of Gauden's edition are numbered, it would seem that this seventh book must have come into the editor's hands after the sixth and eighth books, and subsequent parts of the volume, had gone to the press [2]. For the paging goes regularly on to the end of the fifth book, p. 345: the sixth commences, in a way not easily accounted for, at p. 137, and goes on to p. 183; the seventh is interposed, paged from 1 to 75; and then the former reckoning is resumed, the eighth commencing at p. 184, and so on to the end of the volume. The printing is full of errors: but that is common to the whole edition.

Now all these marks of unskilful editorship, however un-

---

[1] Compare e. g. the corresponding part of the fifth book.

Printers, as in his Hieraspistes: see that work, p. 320. ed. 1653.

[2] Or he may have employed two

Editor's Preface. pleasant to the reader, supply in reality no mean argument in favour of the genuineness of the composition. For who would think it worth while to forge blunders? who for example, employed in setting off a spurious copy to the best advantage, would ever have left such an error as that [1], so well known to all unfriendly critics on Hooker, where in discussing the opinion of St. Jerome on the divine right of Bishops, he or some one else had made a private note on the MS. and the printers have inserted it, incoherent as it is, in the body of the text? Such carelessness in the mode of publication, although it may render particular expressions more doubtful, certainly goes far to negative all idea of deliberate forgery on a large scale. Added to the mass of internal evidence, it may warrant us in accepting this seventh book, hastily written as it is in many parts, for a real though mutilated and otherwise imperfect relic.

It may further appear to have the implied sanction of Walton himself, and of Archbishop Sheldon, inasmuch as the one having by the other's direction undertaken to correct some of Gauden's principal mistakes, no charge is insinuated of want of fidelity in this, the most material part of his task: on the contrary the whole is reprinted without hesitation in the next edition, 1666; the Life by Walton being for the first time prefixed.

[20] 10. We come now to the Eighth Book: on the subject of which (no doubt from its immediate bearing on the political questions of the time) most curiosity seems to have been felt, and to have led to a greater multiplication of copies or extracts. As stated above, it was first published, but avowedly in a mutilated form, A.D. [1648] 1651. It broke off at the words "to give judgment," vol. iii. p. 438, of this edition. But as far as it went, it concurred in the sequence of its parts with the text which Gauden afterwards gave, and with three out of the four now existing MSS.

Dr. Bernard in his Clavi Trabales[2], 1661, published some additional fragments out of the papers of Archbishop Ussher, occupying that work from p. 64 to 94. These fragments relate, the first, p. 64—71, to the Jewish polity, as affording a precedent for something like the Anglican supremacy; which notion is maintained against the objections of Stapleton; the

---

[1] Vol. iii. p. 164. [2] See App. by Walton, p. 95.

The Eighth Book, in Gauden's Edition.   xliii

second, p. 71, 72, to the King's claim of a share in church jurisdiction; the third, p. 73—76, to his prerogative in church legislation; the fourth, p. 77—86, to the appointment of Bishops by the king; the fifth, p. 86—92, to the same subject as the second, jurisdiction; the sixth, p. 92—94, is the opening of a treatise on the King's exemption from church censure. With these were printed short marginal notes, and what Dr. Bernard calls "confirmations and enlargements," under the archbishop's own hand. In one or two of these entries, he says in the margin, "This is," or "This is not, in the common "books or copies of Mr. Hooker's MS.:" meaning by the "common" books or copies, not those in print, 1651, (as is evident from his affirming in one instance the "common "books" to have a passage which the printed copies then had not,) but his meaning was to refer to the ordinary *Manuscripts* of b. viii : and the passage is mentioned here simply for the purpose of remarking, that copies must have been rather frequent at that time, in order to justify such an expression.

Gauden next year confirmed the publication of Bernard by adding the passage which begins, "As therefore the person of "the King," &c. (p. 438,) and ends in p. 444, at the words "the truth therein:" and also that on the power of Legislation, which begins in Clavi Trabales at "The cause (case) is "not like;" and ends, p. 76, abruptly in the middle of a sentence at the words "hath simply." Gauden's edition, adopting this paragraph, completes it : and thereby shews that itself was not in these portions borrowed from the Clavi Trabales, but had other copies to rely on; which also is evident from the omission of much important matter found in the pamphlet. The comparison strengthens the idea of Gauden's good faith, while it lessens that of his industry and skill in such work. He subjoined also another fragment, on the limits of obedience to sovereigns; which the present edition transfers to an appendix, for reasons to be assigned in their place. All succeeding editors have followed him. The text now given will be found, in very many material points, widely at variance with either of these: many portions added, some few omitted, and the parts which remain transposed in such a manner, as to form on the whole an entirely new

Editor's Preface.

Editor's Preface. arrangement. It is the Editor's duty now to account for these changes. And as in so doing he will have to mention the names of more than one friend, to whose assistance he is deeply indebted, and of more than one public body, who have liberally granted him the most unreserved use of their stores of information; he is desirous here of expressing, once for all, his gratitude for such kind permission and invaluable assistance.

[21] The MSS. of the eighth book, which have been collated for this edition, are four in number: and the Editor is not aware of any others now existing. The first (Q), in the library of Queen's College, Oxford (R. 29. i.), was the property of Dr. Thomas Barlow, Provost of that College, and Bishop of Lincoln from 1675 to 1691; in whose handwriting appear a few corrections and insertions, chiefly in the way of collation with the printed text. He was an intimate friend of Bishop Sanderson; so that possibly this may be the very MS. mentioned as having been seen by Sanderson, in the Appendix to Hooker's Life by Walton, p. 97. It coincides indeed, except *in minutis*, with the received text; and this at first sight may appear not to have been the case with the MS. of which Walton is there speaking; or rather Fabian Philips as quoted by Walton. But Sanderson's expression is on the whole not inapplicable to the received text; although Walton seems to have judged otherwise. It is simply this: that "he had seen "a copy, in which no mention" (i.e. of course, no approving mention) "was made of the supreme governor's being ac-"countable to the people." Is any such doctrine taught in the received text? It speaks indeed positively of the people's implied consent being in theory the origin of government, but it expressly denies in one place[1] the practical accountability which some would infer from this; nor is that denial withdrawn or qualified in any other part of the book. All things considered, it seems a fair conjecture, that Mr. Philips may have mistaken what he heard Bishop Sanderson say, which as reported by him comes to very little: and that the Bishop may rather have remarked on the *positive* inconsistency of Hooker's doctrine with the conclusion on behalf of which it was alleged. If he did, his remark would be amply borne out by the place referred to, which occurs in Barlow's MS. as well

[1] E. P. viii. ii. 10.

as in the rest; and therefore Barlow's MS. may be that which Sanderson professed to have seen: though it certainly never could have had much pretension to the honour of being an autograph.

The second copy (L) is in the library of the Archbishop of Canterbury, at Lambeth, (MS. 711. N°. 2) and was, by permission of his Grace, most carefully collated for this edition by the Rev. C. A. Ogilvie, of Balliol College, Oxford, his Grace's chaplain. Nothing is known of the history of this copy. Of its date thus much is ascertained, that it must have been later than 1624. Like the Queen's MS. it differs from the old printed text only in minute verbal points.

The third MS. (C) is in the library of Caius College, Cambridge; and for the collation of it the Editor is indebted to the Rev. Thomas Thorp, fellow and tutor of Trinity College; a favour of which those only can judge who know how irksome the task of collating is, and to what a load of pressing avocations it was in this instance voluntarily superadded. This Caius MS. appears to be in some respects a less careful transcript than either of the two before mentioned; and there are a few variations in critical passages, which a fanciful person might imagine to have been made intentionally: but on the whole it belongs to the same class as the others. All three are in fact different copies of the received text.

22] But the same repository to which every part almost of the present edition is so largely indebted, the library of Trinity College, Dublin, has supplied a fourth MS. of this eighth book, far more nearly approaching to completeness than the printed copies as they stand at present, or as they might be amended from the other three MSS. It is designated in the Dublin Catalogue, MS. C. 3. 11, and in the notes to this edition by the letter (D). The important service of collating it has been performed by Archdeacon (now Dean) Cotton. The result is (to use his own words) "a great number of variations "from the printed text of most important character; even so "far as to assert for denial, and to deny for assertion, and to "make sense where was none, and better sense where was in- "different. Besides these, and considerable improvement in "punctuation, division into sections and paragraphs, &c. (such "as was noticed in the sixth book,) you have a considerable

Editor's Preface.

"accession of new matter, together with a totally different "arrangement of the several portions of the book. Doubt- "less, we are still far from having the book as Hooker himself "would have published it; yet by the aid of this our MS. "the *disjecta membra* are somewhat more decently arranged "than before." On this opinion of a most competent judge, as well as on his own conviction, (in which he feels morally certain that every person on inquiry will concur,) the Editor has felt himself justified in acting so far as to adopt the Dublin MS. for the basis of this edition: noting carefully at the foot of the page every variation from the original edition and other MSS. which at all affects the sense, and inserting in the Appendix a Table, which will bring into one view the difference of arrangement between this and former editions, and will shew what quantity of additional matter has been supplied.

The concluding portion of this eighth book, as it stood in Gauden's edition, which has been followed in all subsequent reprints, was a fragment on the Divine sanction under which human laws are to be obeyed, beginning at "Yea, that which "is more," and ending at "if so be we can find it out." The Editor has now taken the liberty of separating this portion from the body of the book, and throwing it into the Appendix, No. 1: for although it occurs in all the MSS. he is convinced that it is no part of the treatise, but belonged most probably to a sermon or sketch of a sermon on obedience to authority, which Jackson, or some other arranger of the papers, erroneously annexed to the chapter on Ecclesiastical Legislation, which it immediately follows in the Dublin MS., as well as in the received text, although from the altered arrangement of the former it occurs in the fifth chapter instead of the conclusion of the book. It commences with two or three sentences which are found *verbatim* in the third book, c. ix. § 3; a circumstance decisive, as it may seem, against its being a part of the eighth book. For although a writer may silently transfer a passage from one work of his own to another, or from a printed work to a mere sermon, it is hardly conceivable that he should repeat a whole paragraph, without notice, in a subsequent part of the same work. This fact, then, and the little coherence of the whole with the course of

The MS. (D) not that used in Clavi Trabales. xlvii

discussion in the book where it has appeared, determined the Editor to remove that portion into the Appendix: its case being the same with that which bears the name of the sixth book: no reason to doubt that it is the production of Hooker, only wrongly assigned to a place in the Ecclesiastical Polity.

23] The *Clavi Trabales* may also be considered as an independent authority for those portions of the text which occur in it: i.e. it clearly was not printed from any of the existing MSS. Not from either of the three English ones, because two thirds of its contents are absent in them all: not from the Dublin MS., for the following reasons, which are given in the words of Dr. Cotton, the collator. "It is certain that "besides the copy now collated, Archbishop Ussher once "possessed another, and almost equally certain that that other "(*as likewise the seventh book*) was also in Trinity College "library. 1. The Dublin MS. has not the marginal notes, "'Copied from Ussher's own hand,' which Bernard gives, "marked with an asterisk. 2. At p. 76, Bernard says, 'Here "this breaks off abruptly;' whereas our MS. does not break "off here, but pursues the argument farther. 3. Again, at "p. 94, our MS. adds one more sentence to the part with "which Bernard finishes:" (which is, "On earth they are "not accountable to any.") 4. It moreover contains many "pages not formerly printed, nor yet printed by Bernard: "who, we must therefore suppose, did not find these in *his* "MS. But there once was another copy, even in Trinity "College library. In the Catalogus MSS. Angliæ, &c. fol. "1696, is a list of the Dublin MSS. sent in by Provost "Brown. This mentions, marked I. 50, "Books 6, 7, 8. of "Mr. Hooker's Eccl. Polity.' On looking to an old cata-"logue preserved in the library, I find the same entry. Now "at present, book vi. is bound with several other pieces, by "Hooker and others, and on one of the blank covers is "marked I. 50. This is *in folio*. But book viii. is *a small* "*quarto*, bound by itself; lettered 'Church Government;' "and entered in the catalogue not under Hooker, but as 'a "Discourse against Cartwright and others;' and never could "have formed part of 50; nor is it written in the same kind "of hand. The books appear to have been rebound about "100 or 120 years ago."

Editor's Preface.

xlviii   *Account of " A Discovery of the Causes," &c.*

Editor's Preface.   However, the hope thus occasioned of recovering, not only an additional copy of the eighth book, but also a MS. of the seventh, has unfortunately proved vain. After the most exact inquiry, none such appear to exist in the Dublin library. Whether therefore the copy of the eighth used by Bernard was the same with that indicated in the above paragraph, must remain doubtful: it may however be added, that the facts to a certain extent tally with the statement, made on the appearance of the first edition, that "*two* copies in the "hands of the Lord Archbishop of Armagh had been com- "pared before publication."

[24]   11. There is one short paper more, which may by possibility have relation to this eighth book, as the conclusion of the whole work: and which the reader will therefore find inserted in the Appendix, Nº. ii. It was put out at Oxford, 1641, by Leonard Lichfield, printer to the University; with the title: " A Discovery of the Causes of these Contentions "touching Church Government, out of the Fragments of "Richard Hooker." It stood as preamble to a Collection of Tracts or Extracts, by Andrewes, Ussher, Reynolds, and others; the general drift of the publication being to recommend a sort of compromise in Church government, of the kind to which Ussher is believed to have been favourable. The immediate occasion in all likelihood was the discussions which led to the University Remonstrance for the Church, presented to parliament[1], Apr. 27, 1641. Ussher was at that time in Oxford or in London, having come to England for refuge from the troubles in Ireland: and it seems nearly certain that he sanctioned this publication; although his biographer[2] do not directly assert it. But in Trinity college library (D. 3. 3) is a MS. copy of this paper, which Dr. Cotton has collated with the printed text; adding to his collation the following statement. "The above is in "the handwriting of some person unknown. The marginal "references to Scripture are in Ussher's hand, as likewise

---

[1] Wood, Hist. and Antiq. Univ. Oxon. i. 350. ed. 1674.

[2] Parr, Life of Ussher, p. 44, " 1641. "This year there was published at "Oxford (among divers other treatises "of Bishop Andrewes, Mr. Hooker, "and other learned men, concerning "Church government) the Lord Pri- "mate's 'Original of Bishops and Me- "tropolitans.'"

Reasons for doubting the Genuineness of that Paper. xlix

"are several slight corrections in the text. It is highly *Editor's*
"probable that this is the very MS. from which the printed *Preface.*
"copy was taken: more especially as at p. 5. line 22. (of the
"printed copy) Ussher has added a sidenote to the printer;
"'*A larger space betwixn these;*' which has been followed:
"the space left there being wider than between any other
"two paragraphs of the tract." This seems decisive as to
the fact, that Ussher originally edited the collection in question. Of course he must have believed this fragment to be really Hooker's. If such were the case, it may have been a sketch for a conclusion to the whole eight books: in accordance perhaps with the plan which Cranmer in the last paragraph of his letter recommended. The use of the second person ("*ye* are not ignorant," p. 4; "*you* do hear and read," p. 6) would seem to indicate that the conclusion was meant to be addressed, as the Preface had been, by way of expostulation, to the seekers of reform. But in truth the internal evidence is not strongly in favour of the genuineness of this piece. In substance it has nothing to recall so great a name, and there is a kind of point in its turns and transitions, ingenious enough, but in nowise characteristic of Hooker. The remark on Alexander Bishop of Alexandria, and his proceedings against Arius, is little in harmony with Hooker's known approbation of the policy of Archbishop Whitgift, and with his tone and manner, where in the fifth book he has to speak of the very same part of history. No doubt the paper was found in Hooker's study, but if it was not found in his own handwriting, its authorship may well be doubted of. Still, in deference to Archbishop Ussher, it was judged right to insert it in this edition.

25] 12. The reader has now before him an account of the materials, by the aid whereof it has been endeavoured to present this immortal but yet imperfect work, in a form somewhat more accurate, and more inviting to common readers, than it has hitherto worn. On the history of the MSS. since nothing distinct is told us, it is in vain to speculate much: but there are one or two obvious conjectures, which it may be right just to mention, if only for the chance of giving hints, which (it is barely possible) may lead to more successful researches in the same or in other quarters.

1 Eighth Book: Conjectural History of the received Text.

Editor's Preface.

It will be remembered that the first person who appeared as taking interest, at least as feeling alarm, concerning the Hooker papers, was Bishop Andrewes in his letter to Parry. It seems not unlikely, that in course of transmission from Hooker's study through Lambeth to Dr. Spenser, some of them, or transcripts from them, may have lingered in Andrewes's hands. One sermon we know was found in his study, and published for the first time by Walton long after; and it seems on the whole not to be doubted, that if any one was allowed to take copies of the rough draught of the missing books at that time, Andrewes would have been anxious to do so. Accordingly we find that among the copies stated to have been compared before the first publication, one had been in his possession: and we are afterwards given to understand that either the sixth or the eighth book, or both, were actually printed from a copy preserved in his hands, of which copy afterwards Ussher had obtained the custody. For that Ussher had in some way access to Andrewes's papers, the publication by him of the Summary View of Church Government out of Andrewes's rude draughts, 1641, may evince beyond all question. Not that Ussher was then the actual editor; for he would not of course call himself, as he is called in the Address to the Reader, "a Mirror of Learning;" but that he permitted the books to be printed from his MSS. And thus we seem to have arrived at a tolerable ground for considering the received text as so far guaranteed to us by Andrewes and by Ussher.

This publication took place in 1651 [1648]: when of course the Primate as yet knew nothing of the far more correct and enlarged copy now existing in Dublin: of which however there can be no doubt that it was at some time in his possession. He died in 1656: therefore this MS. must have fallen into his hands within those five [seven] years: a time during which, as he found by unpleasant experience, the treasures of retired students were not unfrequently wandering about for sale, having formed part of the spoil of the civil war in various quarters. Now in the course of the war, as before mentioned, one of the libraries which had suffered in this way was that of Henry Jackson, the rector of Meysey-Hampton, and original editor, under Spenser, of Hooker's remains. It is possible, therefore, that a MS. from Jackson's library might fall into Ussher's hands. But is there any ground for imagining that such a MS. as the amended copy of the eighth book existed there? There is just ground enough, the Editor apprehends, for a plausible conjecture, and no more. The conjecture is this: that when Jackson delivered up the papers after Spenser's death into the custody of Bishop King, he may have retained the completer copy of the last book, (which he represents in a fragment preserved by Fulman as being absolutely "restored "to life" by him,) and that he may have handed over to the executors only the rough draught, from which, in course of time, so many transcripts have been made. His own expressions shew that he was precisely in the frame of mind which would make a person likely to take such a step: and perhaps it must be owned that the temptation was not inconsiderable. He writes in December, 1612, "Puto Præsidem nostrum "emissurum sub suo nomine D. Hookeri librum octavum, "a me plane vitæ restitutum. Tulit alter honores." And in April, 1614, Spenser dies, and the MSS. are reclaimed. Is it doing Jackson any great injustice to suppose that in his pique he retained his more finished copy: being, as Antony Wood says, "of a cynical" as well as "of a studious temper?" And if he did, the mode has already been pointed out, how that copy or a transcript of it might fall into Ussher's hands; and consequently might come to be deposited in the library of Trinity College, when the remains of the Primate's books and MSS. were lodged there after the restoration. This, it is repeated, is no more than conjecture: but such as it is, it may give a possible explanation of the great superiority of that single copy; leading us to suppose, that it is either Jackson's own, or one taken from his.

As to the seventh book, if it ever existed (as it certainly appears to have done) among Ussher's MSS., he must clearly have acquired it within the last five years of his life: but where it could have been preserved, we have no means of ascertaining. This only is evident; that it formed no part of the collection of Bishop Andrewes. It might have been in Lambeth, where at that time Ussher would hardly have found access: or it might have formed part of Jackson's store, as was just now conjectured with regard to the eighth book. In

lii *Account of the Sermons on Assurance and Justification:*

Editor's Preface.

any case, to prove it genuine, we must come back to internal evidence.

[26] 13. The few remaining Opuscula of Hooker may be arranged in two classes: the first comprising the Sermons on Habakkuk, and the controversy with Travers which arose out of some of them; the other, what may be called Miscellaneous Sermons. In the present edition, the order in which they stand has been a little changed, with a view to this arrangement. First in the first class is placed the Sermon on the Certainty and Perpetuity of Faith in the Elect: which appears, both from the mention of it by Travers and Hooker in their dispute, and from the order of the texts, to have preceded the famous discourse on Justification; itself being preceded by one on Predestination, which has not come down to us. This sermon on Assurance was originally published by Jackson, under Spenser's guidance, [at Oxford] in 1612. The Editor regrets that he has not been able to procure a copy of that date: but the inconvenience is the less, as this and other of the sermons, regarding which he labours under the same disadvantage, viz. those on St. Jude and that on Pride, were reprinted with the whole of Hooker's works then extant, in 1622[1], by William Stansby, a London bookseller, apparently under the superintendence of Jackson himself. So Wood expressly affirms; and the preface with Stansby's initials subscribed is not unlike Jackson's manner of writing. To the edition of 1622, therefore, in default of an earlier one, recourse has been had for correcting the present impression.

Next comes the famous discourse on Justification, the curiosity excited by which at the time of its delivery is so vividly described by Walton and Fuller: and when it was published, so many years afterwards, we learn by a fragment of a letter of Jackson's, that the first impression was exhausted in a few days[2]. "Edidi ante paucos dies tractatus quosdam "D. Richardi Hookeri, qui omnium applausu (excipio Puri- "tanos ut vocant) ita excepti sunt, ut necesse jam sit typo- "grapho nostro novam editionem parare, quæ prima illa "emendatior, mea cura, Deo volente, proditura est." Accord-

[1 First in 1618, with Books i-iv. (*fourth* ed.) 1617.]

[2] Ap. Fulm. x. 86 The letter is dated Sept. 1612. The Tracts were at first published with Wickliffe's Wicket.

ingly the Sermon on Justification was reprinted in the course of the following year, 1613; from a copy of which reprint, in C. C. C. library, the press has now been corrected. On comparison with a copy of the former year, preserved in St. John's College, it seems that Jackson had kept his word, and that considerable emendations were made. Moreover, Dr. Cotton has discovered and collated for this edition a good and old MS. of this sermon, among the relics of Ussher in Trinity College Dublin, A. 5, 6, 4°. It was entered in the catalogue under the word "Sermon," not being known to be Hooker's. Dr. Cotton describes it as "contemporary, seemingly written "in the same hand as is the Answer to Travers' Supplica-"tion," presently to be mentioned. It contains several good readings, and some notes in an unknown handwriting: but what is remarkable, it omits all the notes which are printed with the sermon, although many of them seem to carry strong internal evidence of their being Hooker's.

Editor's Preface.

This sermon gave immediate occasion for "Walter Travers' "Supplication to the Council," which therefore comes next in the volume. It is a reprint of the first edition, by Joseph Barnes, Oxford, 1612, 4°: corrected from a MS. in the Bodleian (Mus. Bodl. 55. 20) evidently the work of a copyist, with some careless omissions. Much the same may be said of Hooker's Answer, which was published by Jackson along with Travers' attack. But the text of the Answer has now the additional benefit of a MS. (A. 5, 22. fol. 37) apparently contemporary, in Trinity College, Dublin; collated also by Archdeacon Cotton. It is said in the catalogue to be Hooker's own handwriting: but this point surely is more than doubtful. However, there are readings in the MS. which it is hoped will be found real improvements.

The sermon "of the Nature of Pride," the last remaining of the supposed series on Habakkuk, will also be found in this edition corrected from a MS. (B. 1. 13. folio) preserved in the same library, and supposed, like the last, but on no good ground, to be in Hooker's own handwriting. In this copy, at the end of the sermon as it was published by Jackson, appears the following note: "Huc usque excusum "exemplar: sequentia in eo non habentur." What follows, is a continuation of the sermon, described in the Dublin catalogue as being "five times so much in quantity as that which is "already printed." Of the genuineness of this portion, never till now published, there can be no doubt. The internal evidence alone would be almost decisive: and in addition, there is the express testimony of Archbishop Ussher. For it appears that "he procured this unprinted portion to be copied "in a very fair hand as if for publication, or at least better "preservation." Such is the statement of Dr. Cotton, who transcribed the whole from the copy so made, taking care afterwards carefully to collate every part with the original, which is in a most cramped and difficult hand. In the course of transcribing he found that "several words had not been read at "all by the original copier; others he had read wrong, and "some few short clauses he had omitted." On the whole, although the Editor has failed to procure a copy of the *editio princeps*, as well of this sermon as of those on St. Jude, and on the Certainty and Perpetuity of Faith, yet by the aid of Dr. Cotton and this Dublin MS. he hopes that it will be presented to the reader in a tolerably correct form. It is much to be regretted that the fragment proceeds no further, breaking off as it does, at a most interesting and critical point of one of the chiefest controversies between this church and Rome. But the loss, it should seem, is irrecoverable: and perhaps under all the circumstances, we ought, instead of repining, to congratulate ourselves that so much yet remains.

[27] 14. This additional portion of the Sermon on Pride is the last unprinted fragment of Hooker which the Editor has been able to recover. The remaining contents of the volume are the Funeral Sermon, called a Remedy against Sorrow and Fear; printed from the original edition of 1612: the Sermon on St. Matthew vii. 7, printed also from the original edition, viz. as it was published by Walton at the end of his Life of Bishop Sanderson, 1678; in the titlepage to which he describes it as "found in the study of the late learned Bishop Andrewes[1]:"

---

[1] Walton, Preface to Sanderson's Life. "As in my queries for writing "Dr. Sanderson's Life, I met with "these little Tracts annexed; so in my "former queries for my information "to write the Life of venerable Mr. "Hooker, I met with a sermon, which "I believe was really his, and [it is] "here presented as his to the reader. "It is affirmed, (and I have met with "reason to believe it,) that there be "some artists that do certainly know an "original picture from a copy, and in "what age of the world, and by whom

Sermons on St. Jude; their Genuineness questionable. lv

and the two Sermons on part of St. Jude, printed, not from the original edition, which the Editor after much inquiry has failed in procuring a sight of, but from the reprint of 1622. This failure he the more regrets, as there may appear on minute examination more internal reason for questioning the genuineness of these two sermons than of any thing besides which bears the name of Hooker. For, first, the style of writing and tone of argument are in many places marked by a kind of sharpness and quickness, and here and there by a vagueness of phraseology, far removed from the sedate majesty which reigns in all Hooker's known compositions[1]: secondly, there runs through the whole a vein of heightened rhetorical expression[2], quite opposite to his usual guarded way of dealing with all delicate points of doctrine: and thirdly, the appeal made here[3] to men's consciousness on their own spiritual condition, cannot easily be reconciled with the doctrine of the Sermon on the Certainty of Faith, or with the jealousy expressed in the fifth book of Ecclesiastical Polity regarding the rule of men's private spirits. On the whole, if

Editor's Preface.

"drawn. And if so, then I hope it may "be as safely affirmed, that what is here "presented for theirs is so like their "temper of mind, their other writings, "the times when, and the occasions "upon which they were writ, that all "readers may safely conclude, they "could be writ by none but venerable "Mr. Hooker, and the humble and "learned Dr. Sanderson."

[1] E. g. 1 Ser. § 1. "a *sweet* lesson." § 4. "The prophets were not like harps "or lutes: *they felt, they felt,* the power "and strength of their own words." (Compare Spenser's "God's love to His "Vineyard," p. 7. "As for that old "vineyard, *it is burnt, it is burnt* with "fire.") § 6. "If any man doth love "the Lord Jesus (and woe worth him "that loveth not the Lord Jesus) here- "by we may know that he loveth him "indeed." § 7. "A *mingle-mangle* of "religion and superstition, ministers "and massing priests, light and dark- "ness, truth and error, traditions and "scriptures." § 9. "The *maddest people*

"*under the sun.*" Serm. ii. § 10. "How suddenly they *pop down* into "the pit." "*O then* to fly unto God." § 11. "Is there not *a taste, a taste* "of Christ Jesus in the heart of him "that eateth?" § 22. "He was able "*to safe conduct* a thief from the cross "to Paradise."

[2] E. g. § 12. "If these men had "been of us indeed (*O the blessedness* "*of a Christian man's estate*) they had "stood surer than the angels that had "never departed from their place." § 14. "It is as easy a matter for the "spirit within you to tell whose you "are, as for the eyes of your body to "judge where you sit, or in what place "you stand." ii. § 18. "If I break my "very heart with calling upon God, "and wear out my tongue with preach- "ing; if I sacrifice my body and soul "unto Him, and have no faith, all this "availeth nothing."

[3] Serm. i. § 13, 14. Compare Serm. on Certainty, &c. p. 474; and E. P. v. 9.

Editor's Preface. the sermons be Hooker's, which the Editor is far from positively denying, they must be referred to a date in his life earlier than any other of his remains; to a time when he may have hardly ceased to affect the tone of others, both in composition and in doctrine, instead of writing and thinking for himself. There is a date given in one of them, which would harmonize well enough with such a conjecture. "I must," says the preacher, "advertise all men that have the testimony "of God's holy fear within their breasts to consider, how in-"juriously our own countrymen and brethren have dealt with "us by the space of *twenty-four years* from time to time, . . . "never ceasing to charge us, some with heresy, some with "schism, some with plain and manifest apostasy." There are, it would seem, but two dates, from which these twenty-four years can be reckoned; viz. 1558, when Queen Elizabeth came to the throne; and 1569 or 1570, when the bull of Pius V. declaring her excommunicate and deposed, was issued and sent into England. This latter would bring down the date of the sermon in question to 1593–4: a time, at which, for the reasons above assigned, it seems most improbable that Hooker could have written them. It remains that if they be indeed his, they were preached in the 24th or 25th of Elizabeth, 1582–3: when he was not quite thirty years old, having commenced preacher at St. Paul's Cross, as Walton informs us, in 1581. If the other supposition be preferred, viz. that the two sermons are not Hooker's, it is not necessary to charge Jackson, their original editor, with intentional fraud. They might be found among Hooker's papers[1], might even be corrected with his own hand, (of which there are considerable indications,) without being his own compositions. But a critic like Jackson, more zealous than refined, himself evidently of the Reynolds school in theology, might excusably overlook or undervalue objections of that nature. In sum, thus much appears unquestionable: that we should not be safe in referring to these two sermons, for the matured and deliberate judgment of the Author of the Laws of Ecclesiastical Polity, concerning any great point.

The several contents of these volumes being thus accounted

---

[1] If a conjecture might be ventured, in his early days, was not unlikely to Reynolds, or Spenser perhaps himself have written such discourses.

for in their order, it remains for the Editor, first, to record his respectful gratitude to the many friends and helpers, who either out of their private stores, or as having custody of public or collegiate repositories, have aided him one and all with the most unreserved kindness[1], many of them with no small labour to themselves; and next, to express an unaffected wish, that the task of arranging materials so provided had fallen into the hands of some person of more editorial skill, more leisure from unavoidable interruption, and far more historical and theological reading. Such as the volumes are, they exhibit, he believes, in some form or other, all that remains of the venerable and judicious Hooker: and it is pleasant and reasonable to hope that their many defects will be hereafter supplied by some one more amply qualified for the task.

[28] It may be useful in this place, and also just and fair to preceding labourers in the same field, if some notice be inserted of the former editions of Hooker: although the Editor has reason to fear that his list, even as a list, is imperfect, and he certainly has no intention of pronouncing any judgment on their comparative merits.

Of the books which came out in the Author's lifetime an account has already been given. The first reprint was that of the four first Books, by Dr. Spenser, in 1604[2]. Wood, in his account of Spenser[3], says, "He did about four years after "Hooker's death publish the five books of Ecclesiastical Polity "together in one volume, with an Epistle before them, sub-"scribed I. S." The truth seems to be that Spenser only reprinted the four first books, to bind up with the remaining copies of the fifth. It is remarkable that the titlepage[4] of this

---

[1] Several names have been mentioned; that of one to whom the publication is more deeply indebted than to any except Dr. Cotton, is omitted from scruples of private feeling: but one, the Editor must here take the liberty of adding, that of the President of Hooker's college, Dr. Bridges, whose friendliness in intrusting the Editor with the valuable relics of Hooker there preserved has been felt all along as an additional call for every effort to do justice to his sacred memory.

[2] The Editor has never met with a copy, but has been favoured with an account of one by the Rev. T. Lathbury, of Bath.

[3] Ath. Oxon. ii. 146. [Signed T. S. ed. 1604. J. S. ed. 1617.]

[4] But so on titlepage of the first ed. 1594.]

edition promises the whole eight books: the remains of the three last being then in Spenser's custody, waiting to be arranged and published in a second volume. The five books were reprinted, as above stated, in 1617[1]; the Preface to which calls it the *fourth* edition; reckoning probably the two publications in Hooker's lifetime as the first and second. To these in [1618 and] 1622 Henry Jackson added the second volume, comprising Travers's Supplication with Hooker's Answer, the Sermons on Habakkuk, the Funeral Sermon, and those on part of St. Jude. All these he had before edited separately. There was a reprint in 1632, which speaks of itself as the *sixth* edition: that in 1622 having been the fifth. These are all which the Editor has met with of what may be called Dr. Spenser's editions[2]: and they appear on the whole more free from gross blunders than most of those which came after. Nothing more need be said here of Gauden's edition of 1662, which added the seventh book, besides a life of Hooker and a Dedication to King Charles II. (the latter prefixed to most of the following editions.) Gauden's too was the first collection which contained the other two imperfect books. It is unfortunate, considering the little pains taken to correct it, that this edition should have been acquiesced in as a basis, by subsequent publishers, to the end of the 17th century: only with the substitution of Walton's Life, which at once superseded Gauden's on its first appearance. Editions of this description came out, all in folio, in 1666, 1676, 1682. In 1705, Strype revised the Life for the publishers, and made some improvements; but there is no appearance of his having done much to Hooker's works. However, there were several corrections made, and the series of editions which may be called Strype's, of which in the last century there were many, are on the whole greatly superior to Gauden's: i.e. the copies of 1705, 1719[3], 1723, (which is generally pointed out as the best edition of all,) 1739, &c. In 1793, the first 8vo. edition issued from the Clarendon Press, under the superintendence of Bishop

---

[1] The fifth book has a separate title, 1616, but paging continuous.]

[2] He has since been informed of a seventh reprint in 4to, by Bishop, of London, 1639.

[3] There was also an edition in large folio printed at Dublin, by subscription, 1721. It does not appear that the publisher was at all aware of the remains of Hooker in Trinity College library. The only addition to Strype's of 1705 is the Preface by Dr. Spenser.

Randolph. The only material variation made in it was the insertion of Andrewes's letter to Parry, which the Bishop had found in the Bodleian. Other editions in the same form have appeared since, but there are only two which require particular notice. The one in two volumes, (London 1825,) by the Rev. W. S. Dobson, of St. Peter's College, Cambridge: a great improvement on all that had been done since Gauden, especially in the laborious task of verifying quotations. The present Editor is particularly bound to acknowledge his obligations to this useful but unpretending publication, having taken it as the groundwork on which to introduce the readings from the MSS. or original editions. The only remaining edition which requires to be mentioned was executed in 1831, by Mr. B. Hanbury, with considerable spirit and industry, but in some parts with a degree of haste, and in many with an expression of party feeling, tending to lessen its usefulness greatly. It is corrected from the *Editiones Principes*, where the Editor had access to them; and, besides many notes, contains an enlarged Index, Hooker's Letter sent to Burghley with a copy of his work, as given by Strype, a Life of Cartwright by the Editor, the whole of the "Christian Letter," distributed in the notes, and the "Just and Temperate Defence" by Covel, annexed to the fifth book.

Here, it may be, strictly speaking, the task of the present Editor ought to terminate. But there are two large subjects intimately connected with it, to which it appears desirable to invite particular attention. One, the state of the Puritan controversy just at the time when it was taken up by Hooker, and the mode in which it was conducted by him and his contemporaries: the other, his views on certain questions in theology, collateral indeed to that controversy, but at least equally momentous with any thing in it, questions apparently beyond his original anticipation, at which in course of discussion he successively arrived, and kept them in sight afterwards with a religious anxiety proportioned to his deep sense of their vital importance.

29] In the annals of the Church, with more certainty perhaps than in those of the world, we may from time to time mark out what may be called *turning points;* points in which every

Editor's Preface.

thing seems to depend on some one critical event or coincidence, at the time, possibly, quite unobserved. It is awful, yet encouraging, to look back on such times, after the lapse of ages and generations, and to observe the whole course of things tending some one evil way, up to the very instant when it pleased God in His mercy to interfere, and by methods of which we now can see more than contemporaries could, to rescue, it may be, not only that generation, but succeeding times also, and among the rest, ourselves and our children, from some form of apostasy or deadly heresy.

One of these critical periods in our own church history, if the Editor mistake not, is the latter portion of the sixteenth century: and the character and views of Hooker mark him (if we may venture to judge of such a thing without irreverence) as one especially raised up to be the chief human instrument in the salutary interference which Divine Providence was then preparing. In order to have a clearer notion of the peril in which he found the truth, and of the process by which he was trained to be its defender, it may be well if we first consider the previous position of the governors of this church, relatively to the Genevan or Puritan party.

Now the *nucleus* of the whole controversy was undoubtedly the question of church authority: not so much the question as to the reach and limits of that authority, (which subject he fully discusses in the early part of his great work,) as that which takes up the latter part of the treatise, and which he himself denominates the " last and weightiest remains of this " cause [1]: " the question, namely, with whom church authority resides. On this point, in Hooker's time, as now, the Christian world in Europe (speaking largely) was divided into three great parties. The first, that of the ultramontane Roman Catholics, who judging that consent of Christian antiquity in any rule was equivalent to an universal sanction of authority, only second (if it were second) to express enactment of holy Scripture ; and wrongly imagining that they could establish such consent for the paramount authority of their popes and councils; refused the civil government any further prerogative in church matters, (i. e. as they interpreted, in all matters of conscience,) than merely

[1] Book vi. near the beginning.

that of executing what the said popes and councils should decree.

The second party was that of the Ghibellines in the empire, of the prerogative lawyers in the kingdom of France, of Henry the Eighth in England, and generally of all in every country who maintained more or less expressly the claims of the local governments against the papacy: their common principle (with innumerable shades of difference, and some of them very deeply marked) being this; that church laws and constitutions are on the whole left by Providence to the discretion of the civil power. To this latter party, whether on principle or on account of the exigency of their position, most of the early reformers attached themselves. Its theory was implied in the general course of proceeding, both of the Lutherans in Germany, of the Zuinglians in Switzerland, and of Archbishop Cranmer and other chief leaders of the separation between England and Rome: in their *general* course of conduct, not in all their measures; for in such extensive and complicated movements thorough consistency is out of the question, without some visible authority more entire and permanent than any which existed for the reformers, as a body, to acknowledge.

30] To these two parties, which had subsisted in much the same form, at least down from the age of Gregory VII, the events of the Genevan Reformation and the character and views of Calvin had added a third, about thirty years after the rise of Luther; a party which agreed with the Roman Catholics in acknowledging a church authority independent of the state, but differed from them as to the persons with whom such authority was intrusted; assigning it, not to the successors of the Apostles as such, but to a mixed council of Presbyters, lay and spiritual, holding their commission, not as an inward grace derived from our Lord by laying on of hands, but as an external prerogative, granted (so they thought) by positive enactment of holy Scripture. The rapid progress of this system, wherever it was introduced at all under favourable circumstances, proves that it touched some chord in human nature which answered to it very readily: while the remarkable fact, that not one of the reformers besides ever elicited the same theory for himself, but that it is in all instances traceable to Calvin and Geneva, would seem to be very nearly decisive against its claim to scriptural authority. Its success is in fact neither more nor less than a signal example of the effect producible in a short time over the face of the whole church, by the deep, combined, systematic efforts of a few able and resolute men. For that their efforts were combined and systematic, not in Geneva and France only, but as far as ever they could extend the arms of their discipline, no one can doubt, who is at all acquainted with the published correspondence of Calvin first, and in the next generation, of Beza. Two such men following each other, and reigning each his time without a rival in their own section of Christendom, went far towards securing to their party that unity of proceeding, in which, as was just now remarked, Protestants generally were in that age very deficient. This has been remarked by Hooker himself, in the course of his unpublished memoranda above mentioned, where he proposes a comparison between Calvin and Beza[1]. "Hereby," says he, "we see what it is for any one church or place of "government to have two, one succeeding another, and both "in their ways excellent, although unlike. For Beza was "one whom no man *would* displease, Calvin one whom no "man *durst*." He goes on to specify some particulars of Calvin's influence: "His dependants both abroad and at "home; his intelligence from foreign churches; his corre-"spondence every where with the chiefest; his industry "in pursuing them which did at any time openly either "withstand his proceedings or gainsay his opinions; his "writing but of three lines in disgrace of any man as forci-"ble as any proscription throughout all reformed churches; "his rescripts and answers of as great authority as decretal "epistles." Thus far Hooker, speaking of Calvin. And any one who will consult Strype's Annals will find incidentally very sufficient proof of the same kind of authoritative interference in English affairs on the part of Beza, throughout Queen Elizabeth's reign.

[31] There were predisposing circumstances, which made England at that time a promising field for the efforts of the foreign presbyterians. Some of these are touched on by

---

[1] See vol. i. p. 134, of this edition.

Hooker himself in his Preface, and by G. Cranmer in his Letter on the Discipline. It may be useful here to mention a few others, which could not be so clearly discerned, at least not discussed so freely, by contemporaries. First and most obviously, the unpopularity of the Romish party, through the cruelty of Queen Mary and her advisers, and their total disregard of English feelings and opinions. One very striking proof of the extent to which this prevailed is the publication of the well-known pamphlets by Knox[1] and Goodman[2], in which, with a view to the case of England even rather than of Scotland, it was maintained that royal authority could not be vested in a female, and that, wherever vested, it might be forfeited, by maladministration, into the hands of the people. A person of the acuteness and vigilance of the Scottish reformer, (for with all his vehemence no one knew better how to take the tide of popular opinion,) a dexterous politician like Knox would never have ventured on such a step, without good grounds for supposing that the old feeling of hereditary loyalty was fast giving way before the gathering discontent. The same remark in some measure applies to Whittingham, who seems to have been as much as any one responsible for Goodman's book, to which he wrote a Preface. He was of a temper sufficiently cool and calculating, and not likely to commit himself in such a cause without good grounds for expecting it to be popular. And it is not perhaps easy to say how far their efforts might have succeeded, had not the failure of issue from Queen Mary, and her early demise, given a new turn to the opinions and movements of men. It would almost seem as if providentially the leaders of the Puritans had been led on to suffer these indications of their real views to escape them in good time, and so to give Elizabeth a warning, which all her life long cooperated with her natural disposition and theological opinions, in keeping her on her guard against them. But however the publications might be counteracted, the mere fact of their appearing shews to what an extent, in the judgment of competent observers, the English protestants of that

Editor's Preface.

---

[1] "The first Blast of the Trumpet "against the monstrous Regiment of "Women." 1556 or 1557.

[2] "How Superior Powers ought to "be obeyed." 1558.

Editor's Preface.

[32] day were disposed to acquiesce in whatever movement appeared to take them farthest from Rome.

Another feeling, which to the end of the century continued acting in the same direction, was sympathy with the foreign protestants; not the foreign protestants generally, for the Lutheran and Zuinglian sections of Germany and Switzerland were then in comparative peace, and presented little to excite much interest on the part of those who watched them at a distance. The struggle, the excitement, the suffering, and the ardour, were all in those countries where the reformation had taken its line in obedience to Geneva: in France, namely, and in the Netherlands. It is well known what sympathy was kindled in Elizabeth's court by the first news of the massacre of St. Bartholomew; which, it may be remarked, took place the very year when the English Puritans began to be more open and combined in their efforts, first in parliament for legalizing the discipline, and afterwards in their several districts, for establishing it without law. And Hooker's own works have many incidental marks of the great and increasing interest, which was naturally felt here in the varying fortunes of the Hugonots. Of course it will be seen that such interest, as far as it had any bearing on the differences among protestants themselves, would strengthen most effectually the hands of that party, which had the perfectest agreement with the persecuted abroad, and seemed at first view most irreconcilable with the persecutors.

And as the fortunes of Genevan protestantism in France would secure for it that fellow-feeling here, which attaches itself to a band of confessors and sufferers for the truth, so its fortunes in Scotland would attract such as love to be on the winning side. We have it on very high authority, the authority of Dr. Thomas Jackson[1], that the first impulse towards puritanism in his neighbourhood, Newcastle, was given by Knox himself, acting in King Edward's time as a kind of missionary under the direction of the council. Afterwards, when the door had been opened to change in his own country, neither he nor his successors in the management of the Kirk ever lost sight of their kindred party in England. In Bancroft's Dangerous Positions may be found repeated assertions,

[1] Works, iii. 273 [fol. 1673].

and several instances, of the support which the Puritan agita- *Editor's*
tors constantly received from that quarter: such as their pro- *Preface.*
curing one Waldegrave, a printer devoted to their cause, to
be king's printer in Edinburgh, in the minority of James VI.
And it is known that Penry, the author of the Marprelate
libels, when he was most active in that line, resorted to Scotland for refuge and cooperation. The course of the new
reformation in short was notoriously such as Bancroft has
expressed, quaintly but not unaptly, in the titles of his sections: first comes " Scottish Genevating," and then " English
" Scottizing, for Discipline."

In aid of all these feelings, after a while, came the resentment occasioned by the dethroning bull of pope Pius, which
made it seem a matter of plain loyalty and patriotism, to
secede from the Romish Church in every thing as completely
as possible.

Accordingly, we find that not only in the parliaments of
Elizabeth, but also in her cabinet, at least for the first thirty
years of her reign, there existed a very strong bias in behalf
of the Puritan party. Not only such persons as Knolles and
Mildmay, and others who were Calvinists and Low Churchmen on principle; nor again only such as Leicester, who may
be suspected of looking chiefly to the spoils which any great
church movement might place at his disposal: but even
Burghley and Walsingham, it is well known, were continually
finding themselves at issue with the Archbishop of the day
concerning the degree of discouragement due to the reformers.
So that as far as the government was concerned, nothing but
the firmness of the Queen herself, supporting first Parker and
afterwards Whitgift, prevented the adoption of the new model,
at least in those parts of it which did not apparently and
palpably intrude on royal authority. To our argument it does
not much matter, whether this tendency in such men as
Burghley and Walsingham, were occasioned by any supposed
necessity for conceding to popular opinion, or whether it were
really the conscientious bias of their minds: but one symptom
of the latter we may here observe, viz. that in their appointments, when left to themselves, they evidently gave a preference to the Puritan side. Thus Walsingham having provided a divinity lecture at Oxford, with the sole declared view

of resisting and discrediting Romanism, nominated Reynolds the first reader of his lecture: indeed it seems to have been endowed expressly for him. And Burghley employed as domestic chaplain and tutor to his children, Walter Travers, the well-known antagonist of Hooker, and author of the book *de Ecclesiastica Disciplina*, not the least able and influential of the treatises which Geneva was continually pouring into this country.

Without investigating more deeply laid grounds of error, principles which must make the struggle with Puritanism at all times painful and arduous, even such a superficial view as has now been attempted may serve to give some idea of the amount of disadvantage under which they laboured, who had to conduct that controversy on the side of the existing Church down to the middle of Elizabeth's reign. There is hardly need to add express mention of the certainty, under such circumstances, that whatever they said and did would be tainted with the name and suspicion of papistry; so easily affixed, and so hard to shake off, wherever men demur to the extreme of what are denominated protestant opinions.

[33] Our argument now requires a brief account of the mode in which those who preceded Hooker had considered it best to meet the invasion from Geneva: confining attention still to the question, in whom church authority is properly vested: which question, as was remarked in the outset, forms a kind of centre around which the other points of the controversy gradually came to arrange themselves. It is evident, (speaking largely,) that there were but two ways of meeting the claim of the New Discipline: the one, the way of the early Church, of which the doctrine of papal supremacy is a perversion and excess: the other, the way which in modern times has been very generally denominated Erastian; though far indeed from being an invention of Erastus, since in every kingdom of Europe the Roman claims had been resisted on the like principles for centuries before he was born. The peculiarity of Erastus' teaching lay rather in his refusing all right of *excommunication* to the Christian Church. However, it has become usual to designate from him the theory in question, which would rest the government of the Church, spiritual as well as civil, altogether in the Christian magis-

trate: thus entirely denying the principle, on which the Genevan innovation proceeded; whereas the High Churchmen (as they were called) of a later age, would grant the principle, but deny the application: they would allow that a succession of governors exists in the Church, of apostolical authority, not to be superseded by man; but they would deny the claim of Geneva to that succession; maintaining, what undoubtedly *prima facie* church history would seem to teach, that the Bishops are the true heirs of the apostles in their governing powers as well as in their power of order.

Now, since the episcopal succession had been so carefully retained in the Church of England, and so much anxiety evinced to render both her liturgy and ordination services strictly conformable to the rules and doctrines of antiquity, it might have been expected that the defenders of the English hierarchy against the first Puritans should take the highest ground, and challenge for the Bishops the same unreserved submission, on the same plea of exclusive apostolical prerogative, which their adversaries feared not to insist on for their elders and deacons. It is notorious, however, that such was not in general the line preferred by Jewel, Whitgift, Bishop Cooper, and others, to whom the management of that controversy was intrusted, during the early part of Elizabeth's reign. They do not expressly disavow, but they carefully shun, that unreserved appeal to Christian antiquity, in which one would have thought they must have discerned the very strength of their cause to lie. It is enough, with them, to shew that the government by archbishops and bishops is ancient and allowable; they never venture to urge its *exclusive* claim, or to connect the succession with the validity of the holy Sacraments: and yet it is obvious that such a course of argument alone (supposing it borne out by facts) could fully meet all the exigencies of the case. It must have occurred to the learned writers above-mentioned, since it was the received doctrine of the Church down to their days; and if they had disapproved it, as some theologians of no small renown have since done, it seems unlikely that they should have passed it over without some express avowal of dissent; considering that they always wrote with an eye to the pretensions of Rome also, which popular opinion had in a great degree mixed up with this doctrine of apostolical succession.

lxviii *The Reformers, why slow to admit Apostolical Succession.*

Editor's Preface. One obvious reason, and probably the chief one, of their silence, was the relation in which they stood to the foreign protestant congregations. The question had been mixed up with considerations of personal friendship, first by Cranmer's connection with the Lutherans, and after King Edward's death, by the residence of Jewel, Grindal, and others at Zurich, Strasburgh, and elsewhere, in congregations which had given up the apostolical succession. Thus feelings arose, which came, insensibly no doubt, but really and strongly, in aid of the prevailing notion that every thing was to be sacrificed to the paramount object of union among protestants.

[34] To these theological sympathies with the German reformers must be added the effect of political sympathies with the imperialist party, and generally speaking with the advocates of civil interference in the Church in the several nations of Europe. Some who cared little for religion at all, and others who had no objection to the doctrines of Rome, had united nevertheless with the zealots of the new opinions in promoting changes which they considered necessary for the deliverance of their respective countries from priestly usurpation. In England, as in other countries, the leading protestant divines had availed themselves largely of the cooperation of these numerous and powerful parties: and had occasionally committed themselves to statements and principles, which would stand greatly in their way, if ever they found it requisite to assert the claims of apostolical episcopacy.

Add to this, what the papacy itself had done, and was daily doing, to weaken all notions of independent authority in Bishops: of which policy the full development may be seen in the proceedings of the Italian party at Trent, and their efforts to obtain an express declaration from the council, that no prelate had any power in the Church, except what he received through the successors of St. Peter. So that on the one hand a large section of the reformers had a direct interest in making light of apostolical claims, and on the other, no inconsiderable portion of the opponents of innovation were prepared beforehand to concede this point. Indeed, when we consider the joint effect of all these interests, so various in themselves, yet concurring to disparage primitive episcopacy, the wonder will be, not that apostolical claims were not advanced to the full extent by the opponents of the Puritans in England, but rather that any thing like apostolical succession is left amongst us. It is indeed, throughout modern English history, a continually recurring theme of admiration and of thankfulness.

Editor's Preface.

Should it be asked, how such accomplished divines, as Jewel and others of his class undoubtedly were, could permit themselves, for any present benefit to the Church, so to waver in so capital a point, with the full evidence of antiquity before their eyes; it may be replied, first of all, that in some sort they wanted that full evidence with which later generations have been favoured. The works of the Fathers had not yet been critically sifted, so that in regard of almost every one of them men were more or less embarrassed, during the whole of that age, with vague suspicions of interpolation. The effect of this is apparent in various degrees throughout the controversies of the time; but on no question would it be more felt than on this, of the apostolical succession and the frame of the visible Church: because that was a subject on which, more continually perhaps than on any other, temptations to forgery had arisen: and also because the remains of St. Ignatius in particular, for a single writer the most decisive of all who have borne witness to apostolical principles, were all that time under a cloud of doubt, which was providentially dispelled in the next age by the discovery of a copy unquestionably genuine. This consideration, as it accounts (among other things) for the little stress which Hooker seems to lay on quotations from St. Ignatius, to us most important and decisive: so it must in the nature of things have placed his predecessors, of whom we are now speaking, under a considerable disadvantage, as compared with the writers of the following century: and in all candour should be taken into account, on the one hand by those who would take advantage of the silence of the reformers to disparage the apostolical succession; on the other hand by the advocates of that doctrine, to prevent their judging too hardly of the reformers themselves for their comparative omission of it.

Further; it is obvious that those divines in particular, who had been instrumental but a little before in the second change of the liturgy in King Edward's time, must have felt themselves in some measure restrained from pressing with its entire force the ecclesiastical tradition on church government and orders, inasmuch as in the aforesaid revision they had given up altogether the same tradition, regarding certain very material points in the celebration, if not in the doctrine, of the holy Eucharist. It is but fair to add, that the consideration last suggested, viz. indefinite fear of interpolation in the early liturgies, may have told with equal or more force in justifying to their minds the omissions in question. This subject also since their time has been happily and satisfactorily cleared up [1]. But whether it were this, or extreme jealousy of practices which had been made occasions of abuse, or whatever the cause might be, the fact is unquestionable, that certain services had been abandoned, which according to the constant witness of the remains of antiquity had constituted an important portion of the Christian ritual: e.g. the solemn offering of the elements before consecration for the living and the dead, with commemoration of the latter, in certain cases, by name. It should seem that those who were responsible for these omissions must have felt themselves precluded, ever after, from urging the necessity of Episcopacy, or of any thing else, on the ground of uniform Church Tradition. Succeeding generations obviously need not experience the same embarrassment to the same extent: since they have only to answer for bearing with the innovation, not for introducing it.

To all these causes of hesitation we must add the direct influence of the Court, which of course on this as on all similar occasions would come strongly in aid of the Erastian principle. It is well known to what an extent prudential regards of this kind were carried by the several generations of the Anglican Reformers.

On the whole, (and the remark is made without any disrespectful thought towards them,) it was very natural for them to waive, as far as they did, the claim of exclusive divine authority in their defences of episcopal rights; nor ought their having done so to create any prejudice, in such as deservedly hold them in respect, against that claim itself.

[35] Lest it should be imagined that we are here conceding more than we really mean to concede regarding the views of

---

[1] See Palmer's Origines Liturgicæ.

the writers in question, two propositions are subjoined, as comprising the substance of the argument by which they resisted the demands of the Puritans.

1. The whole Church, being naturally the subject in which all ecclesiastical power resides, may have had originally the right of determining how it would be governed.

2. Inasmuch as the Church did determine from very early times to be governed by Bishops, it cannot be right to swerve from that government, in any country where the same may be maintained, consistently with soundness of doctrine, and the rights of the chief magistrate, being Christian.

This statement, of Whitgift's opinions in particular, it were easy to verify by extracts from his Defence against Cartwright. His object was, evidently, to maintain the episcopal system, i.e. the government of the Church by three orders, without at all entering on the matter of apostolical succession. Natural reason, and Church history, spoke, he thought, plainly enough. There was no occasion to settle the question, whether the charter granted by our Lord to the Twelve, was granted to them and the whole Church, or to them and the heirs for ever of their spiritual power, set apart by laying on of their hands.

Practically, perhaps, and in reason, even such a mode of arguing ought to have prevailed against the arrogant innovations which it was intended to meet. But being as it was far from the whole truth, (was it ever stated as such by those who advanced it?) it could not either correspond to the standard, which those would naturally form to themselves who looked much to Christian antiquity; or satisfy those feelings and expectations in mankind generally, which the true church system was graciously intended to supply. Cartwright therefore, inconclusive as his reasoning was, and unsubstantial his learning, appeared to maintain his ground against Whitgift. About the same time the death of Archbishop Parker made room for Grindal in the metropolitical see; whose connivance at the conduct of the Puritans is well known, and generally alleged as not the least of the causes which contributed to the increase of their influence. When the Queen interfered to repress them, and chastise him, it was in such a manner as to give the whole an air chiefly of political precaution, and to encourage the idea

Editor's Preface. that the defenders of the Church were in fact identifying her almost entirely with the state. About this juncture came out Travers's famous Book of Discipline; very much superior to Cartwright's publications in eloquence and the skill of composition, though not at all more satisfactory in argument. Altogether the current was setting strongly in favour of the innovators, up to the time when Whitgift became Archbishop. Acute and indefatigable as he was in his efforts to produce a reaction, not only by his official edicts and remonstrances, but by his disposal of preferment also, and the literary labours which he encouraged, there was no one step of his to be compared in wisdom and effect with his patronage of Hooker, and the help which he provided towards the completion of his undertaking. It is true that in the course of the ten years which preceded that publication many things happened which had the same tendency. Abundant experiment was made elsewhere of the mischief occasioned by extreme protestant principles: and at home, the Marprelate libels and Hacket's conspiracy had disgusted all reflecting and conscientious men. A new generation had arisen both in Oxford and Cambridge, which by the comparative tranquillity of the times enjoyed more leisure from pressing disputes, and had a better chance of considering all points thoroughly, than any one could have during the hurry of the Reformation. And (what was most important of all) the feverish and exclusive dread of Romanism, which had for a long time so occupied all men's thoughts as to leave hardly any room for precautions in any other direction, was greatly abated by several intervening events. First, the execution of Queen Mary, though at the cost of a great national crime, had removed the chief hope of the Romanist party in England; and had made it necessary for those, who were pledged at all events to the violent proceedings of that side, to disgust all British feeling by transferring their allegiance to the king of Spain. And when, two years afterwards, his grand effort had been made, and had failed so entirely as to extinguish all present hope of the restoration of Popery in England; it is remarkable how immediately the effect of that failure is discernible in the conduct of the church controversy with the Puritans. The Armada was destroyed in July. In the February following was preached and published the famous

Saravia's Judgment on the Divine Right of Bishops.

Sermon of Bancroft at St. Paul's Cross, on the duty of trying the spirits; which sermon has often been complained of by Puritans and Erastians as the first express development of high church principles here. It may have been the first published: but there is internal evidence of the same views having existed long before, in some of the Treatises which appeared successively on that side of the question during the four or five subsequent years.

[36] For example, Saravia in his three Tractates gives proof that the sentiments complained of in Bancroft's sermon had been long familiar to him, and that their being unacceptable to his countrymen abroad was one chief reason of his finally establishing himself in England [1]. Now Saravia's judgment of

---

[1] In his first Treatise, (1590,) Preface to the Reader, he says, "Sæpius "his 26 annis, quid sentirem de epi-"scoporum ordine, in familiari collo-"quio amicis exposui." In his Dedication, (to Whitgift, Hatton, and Burghley,) "Ego ab ecclesiis Belgicis hinc "evocatus, illic vixi diversis in locis "totos decem annos, quo tempore duo "quædam maximi momenti illis eccle-"siis deesse judicavi, quæ a me pie dis-"simulari non possunt: nempe honorem "et convenientem dignitatis gradum "ministerio, evangelio jam authoritate "publica recepto, non dari; deinde opes "in societate civili æstimationi reti-"nendæ necessarias negari." Afterwards, "De his malis non raro conquestus sum "apud eos quibuscum familiaris eram "... Tandem mei officii esse judicavi, "quæ exactius consideranda tum ipsis "ecclesiarum ministris, tum imprimis or-"dinibus Belgicis proponere aliquando "cogitaveram, nunc his tribus libris "Latino sermone vulgare." In his address to the Ministers of Lower Germany he begins thus: "Non raro cum "plerisque vestrum, cum Leidæ agerem, "deploravi ecclesiarum quæ istic sunt "statum," &c. And below, "Constitu-"eram, si apud vos mansissem, super "hac re Dominos Status convenire ... "Sed meum consilium primo mors "Dom. Principis Aurantiæ remorata "est, deinde Dom. Comitis Leicestriæ "gratia, ne id facere viderer aut alieno "tempore, in summa consternatione "reip. aut fretus favore et consilio Dom. "Comitis." And again, "Apud meos "fratres et collegas, et nonnullos ex "magistratu urbis Gandavi, meam sen-"tentiam dissimulare non potui. Sed "fateor me non ita libere fuisse locu-"tum, ut in hac disputatione facturus "sum; verebar enim ne nuper ad Christi "fidem conversos offenderem."

From all which it appears that Saravia held in substance the opinions of these treatises, (and among the rest the doctrine of Apostolical Succession exclusively in Bishops,) since the year 1564, when he lived at Ghent; retained those opinions in Jersey, where he went before 1566; and was confirmed in them in England both before and after his residence for ten years in Holland, which ten years must have ended before 1587, when Leicester finally returned from the Low Countries. The substance therefore of his work was long anterior to Bancroft's Sermon, although it did not appear till more than a twelvemonth after. Its publication at that particular time in England may be regarded as another symptom of the alteration in tone concerning such matters occasioned by the destruction of the Armada.

lxxiv *Progress of Apostolical Views; Saravia; Sutcliffe;*

Editor's Preface.

the divine right of Bishops was such as is expressed in the following passages; a few out of many which occur in his first treatise. The title of that treatise is, "Concerning "the various degrees of Ministers of the Gospel, *as they* "*were instituted by the Lord, and delivered on by the* "*Apostles*, and confirmed by *constant* use of *all* Churches." In his dedication, after exposing the error of those who would make church goods public property, he mentions as one thing which tended to encourage that error, the notion that the superiority of Bishops over presbyters was not of any divine institution: and adds, "Our fathers and all the old "theologians believed that the controuling prudence of one "man was *divinely* appointed in the church of each city or "province, for avoiding schism and repressing the rashness "of the many." Thirdly, and especially, in his Address to the Reader he speaks thus fully to the point: "There are "some" (the Erastians) "who think that all controul of man-"ners is to be left entirely to the civil magistrate, and con-"fine the ministry of the Gospel to bare preaching of the "word of God and administering the Sacraments; which being "impossible to be made out by the word of God, or by any "example of the Fathers, I wonder that such a thought could "ever enter into the mind of a theologian. Others there are "who assign the power of church censures to Bishops, and "to Presbyters who are both called and really are such, with "that authority which God gave to the Apostles and to those "who after them should be Bishops of the Church. The third "sort are those who rejecting the order of Bishops, join to "the pastors elders chosen for a time, to whom they commit "the whole government of the churches, and discipline eccle-"siastical." Then he proceeds to enumerate the forms of civil polity, and adds, "To no nation did God ever appoint "any certain and perpetual form of government, which it "should be unlawful to alter according to place and times. "*But of this government whereof we are now discoursing* "*the case is different, for since it came immediately from* "*God, men cannot alter it at their own free will.* Nor is "there any occasion to do so. For God's wisdom hath so "tempered this polity, that it opposes itself to no form of "civil government... Bishops I consider to be necessary to

"the Church, and that discipline and government of the
"Church to be the best, and *divine*, which religious Bishops,
"with Presbyters truely so called, administer by the rule of
"God's word and ancient councils."

Saravia, then, is a distinct and independent testimony to the doctrine of exclusive divine right in Bishops. He had worked it out, as appears, for himself; he had made material sacrifices for its sake ; and he seized the first opportunity of making it public allowed him by the caution of the English government, hitherto so scrupulously sensitive in behalf of the foreign reformers. And since Saravia was afterwards in familiar intercourse with Hooker, and his confidential adviser when writing on nearly the same subjects, we may with reason use the recorded opinions of the one for interpreting what might seem otherwise ambiguous in the other.

[7] The same year and the year following (1591), Matthew Sutcliffe, afterwards Dean of Exeter, an acute and amusing but not always very scrupulous controversialist, published several treatises against the Puritan discipline ; the tone of which may be judged of by the following complaint of Penry; (Petition to the Queen, 1590 or 1591.) "Mat. Sutcliffe hath "openly in Latin defaced foreign churches, of whom D. Whit-"gift and others have always written honourably. Whereby "it is likely there will arise as dangerous troubles to the "churches about discipline as hath grown by the question of "consubstantiation." He probably alludes to the Tract "De "Presbyterio," in which Sutcliffe had handled the subject of lay elders with small veneration for the French and Genevan arrangements.

Next to Sutcliffe in order of time comes an anonymous Latin treatise, entitled "Querimonia Ecclesiæ ;" a work more particularly to be noticed here, because it should seem from a passage in the Christian Letter, that Hooker himself was at that time suspected of having some concern in it. The passage in the Letter occurs in p. 44. "We beseech you "therefore in the name of Jesus Christ, and as you will "answer for the use of those great gifts which God hath "bestowed upon you, that you would return and peruse "advisedly all your five books, compare them with the articles "of our profession set out by public authority, and with the lxxvi *Querimonia Ecclesiæ, a Witness to Apostolical Views.*

Editor's Preface.

"works apologetical and other authorized sermons and homi-
"lies of our Church, and of the reverend Fathers of our land,
"and with the holy Book of God, and all other the Queen's
"Majesty's proceedings, and then read and examine with an
"indifferent and equall mind a book set out in Latin, called
"*Querimonia Ecclesiæ*, and another in English late come
"abroad, speaking of Scotizing and Genevating, and Allo-
"brogical discipline:... and tell us... whether the reverend
"Fathers of our Church would not give sentence... that by
"those three writings the Church of England and all other
"Christian churches are undermined." Hooker's reply to
this challenge (which has been given above, p. xxii) consists in
a similar challenge to his adversary to give his opinion of
three Calvinistic works, in two of which the royal supremacy
in religion, and in the third the very principle of irresponsible
authority in Kings, had been expressly controverted. He
does not, it will be observed, at all disavow the connection, or
at least the strong sympathy, which had been hinted at as
subsisting between him and the author of the "Querimonia
"Ecclesiæ." That tract, it may be worth remarking, was
printed by Windet, the person whom Hooker himself employed for both portions of the Ecclesiastical Polity, and
Saravia for the first edition of his three treatises ; which
Windet in all probability was the same who appears in the
pedigree of the Hooker family as the eldest son of an aunt of
Hooker's. Be that as it may, the coincidence between the
views of Hooker and those of the anonymous pamphlet is
very striking on many topics, while on others there is quite
variation enough to prove the two testimonies independent
of each other.

[38] Now on the point of church government, the "Querimonia"
is, if any difference, even more express than Hooker in
insisting on the divine origin and indispensable necessity of
the episcopal order. The writer (speaking, as throughout, in
the person of "Ecclesia") enumerates the want of discipline as
the second of four grave defects, by which, he says, our western
reformation has been generally blemished ; the first being,
disparagement of the fasts of the Church. His language
concerning episcopacy, and those who had so irreverently
dispensed with it, is such as the following (speaking of Aërius

and his followers ancient and modern): "Optimæ illi disciplinæ "reciderunt nervos, qui... eam, quæ sæpe mihi salutem attulit, "episcopalem auctoritatem improbe violarunt." Again, referring as it seems to an expression of Beza, which had obtained great currency; "Aërius... presbyterum episcopo dignitate "adæquandum censuit: episcopatum nostri *a Diabolo insti-* "*tutum* contendunt." In the sketch which he draws of the fallen state of the Church in all parts of Christendom, when he comes to the protestants, he says, " Ita episcoporum am- "bitionem reprehendunt, ut episcopalem interdum ordinem "repugnent: ita superstitionem condemnant, ut permulta "simul religionis tollant ornamenta." When he comes to particular countries it is remarkable that he says not a word of Scotland. In p. 81, he affirms, "Princeps ille noster "Christus, etiamsi non omnes disciplinæ partes præscripsit, "communes tamen proposuit regulas, quas in regenda Ecclesia "semper intueri oportet." In p. 83, he gives specimens of things, "quæ tota observat Dei Ecclesia, et instituta sunt ab "Apostolis vel apostolicis viris, et perpetuo prosunt Chris- "tianæ societati:" which therefore "religiose ubique reti- "nenda judico;" and his examples are, Lent; the holidays of our Saviour; different offices in the Church, and degrees in the ministry, including not only diocesan Bishops, but Archbishops, Primates or Metropolitans, and Patriarchs. Here then is another strong instance of the alteration in tone on which we are remarking: and the writer, whoever he might be, was no common person; as will further appear when reference is made to him, for illustration of Hooker's opinions on other matters, some of them even more important than this of episcopacy.

The last writer now to be mentioned is one whose work came out in the very same year with the first part of Hooker's, 1593-4: Bilson, then Warden, afterwards Bishop of Winchester, author of "the Perpetual Government of Christ's "Church:" a more elaborate and complete work than either of the former, full of good learning and sound argument, regularly arranged and clearly expressed. He, it may be observed, makes in his Preface an acknowledgment similar to that which will be presently quoted from Hooker himself; "the credit of "the first devisers" of the new discipline "did somewhat

Editor's Preface.

Editor's Preface. "deceive me." His principles of church government are such as follows: "The power of the keys was first settled in the Apos- "tles before it was delivered unto the Church ; *and the Church* "*received it from the Apostles, not the Apostles from the Church:*" p. 104. And, p. 106. "The authority of their first calling "liveth yet in their succession, and time and travel joined with "God's graces bring pastors at this present to perfection; yet "the Apostles' charge to teach, baptize, and administer the "Lord's Supper, to bind and loose sins in heaven and in "earth, to impose hands for the ordaining of pastors and "elders: these parts of the apostolic function are not decayed, "and cannot be wanted in the Church of God. *There must* "*either be no Church, or else these must remain; for without* "*these no Church can continue.*" And, p. 107. "As the "things be needful in the Church, so the persons to whom "they were first committed cannot be doubted... The service "must endure as long as the promise; to the end of the "world... Christ is present with those who succeed his "Apostles in the same function and ministry for ever." And, p. 244. "Things proper to Bishops, that might not be com- "mon to them with presbyters, were singularity in succeeding, "and superiority in ordaining." 247. "The singularity of one "pastor in each place descended from the Apostles and their "scholars in all famous churches in the world by a perpetual "chair of succession, and doth to this day continue, but where "abomination or desolation, I mean knavery or violence, in- "terrupt it." From p. 108 to 112 is a course of direct reasoning to the same purpose.

[39] It were easy to multiply quotations: but enough perhaps has been advanced to justify the assertion, that while Hooker was engaged on his great work, a new school of writers on church subjects had begun to shew itself in England: men had been gradually unlearning some of those opinions, which intimacy with foreign Protestants had tended to foster, and had adopted a tone and way of thinking more like that of the early Church. The change in the political situation of the country gave them opportunity and encouragement to develope and inculcate their amended views. At such a time, the appearance in the field of a champion like Hooker on their side must have been worth every thing to the defenders of

Apostolical order: and that he was then considered as taking the field on their side is clear from the manner in which, as we have seen, he was attacked, and from the names with which his was associated, by the Puritans. In later times, a different construction has very generally been put on his writings, and he has commonly been cited by that class of writers who concede least to church authority, as expressly sanctioning their loose and irreverent notions. And yet he has distinctly laid down, and adopted as his own, both the principles and the conclusion of the stricter system of antiquity. The principles, where he asks so emphatically, "What angel "in heaven could have said to man, as our Lord did unto "Peter, 'Feed my sheep; preach; baptize; do this in re- "membrance of me; whose sins ye retain, they are retained, "and their offences in heaven pardoned whose faults you shall "on earth forgive?' What think we? Are these terrestrial "sounds, or else are they voices uttered out of the clouds "above? The power of the ministry of God translateth out "of darkness into glory; it raiseth men from the earth, and "bringeth God himself down from heaven; by blessing visible "elements it maketh them invisible grace; it giveth daily "the Holy Ghost; it hath to dispose of that flesh which was "given for the life of the world, and that blood which was poured "out to redeem souls; when it poureth malediction upon the "heads of the wicked, they perish, when it revoketh the same "they revive. O wretched blindness, if we admire not so "great power; more wretched if we consider it aright, and "notwithstanding imagine that any but God can bestow "it[1]!" Can we help wondering, that the author of these sentiments should be generally reckoned among those, who account the ministry a mere human ordinance? Again, it is certain from Hooker's own express statement, that the ministry of which he entertained these exalted ideas was from the beginning an episcopal ministry. "Let us not," he says, "fear to be herein bold and peremptory, that if any "thing in the Church's government, surely the first institution "of bishops was from heaven, was even of God; the Holy "Ghost was the author of it." Nay, he has marked his opinion yet more forcibly, by stating elsewhere, that he had

[1] E. P. V. lxxvii. 1.

not thought thus always[1]. "I myself did sometimes judge "it a great deal more probable than now I do, merely that "after the Apostles were deceased, churches did agree "amongst themselves for preservation of peace and order, to "make one presbyter in each city chief over the rest, and to "translate into him that power by force and virtue whereof "the Apostles ... did preserve and uphold order in the "Church." This he calls "that other conjecture which so "many have thought good to follow," whereas "the general "received persuasion held from the first beginning" was, "that "the Apostles themselves left bishops invested with power "above other pastors."

There is something very significant in the list of authorities, from whose opinion or conjecture of the equality of bishops and presbyters he here specifies his own dissent. They are first the Waldenses; then Marsilius the jurist of Padua, an extreme partizan of the imperial cause against Rome; then Wicliffe, Calvin, Bullinger, (as representing the Zuinglians,) Jewel, who had tolerated, and Fulke who had maintained, the presbyterian principle in their controversies with the Romanists. By Hooker's distinctly specifying all these authorities, every one of whom stands, as it were, for a class or school, and putting on record his dissent from them, all and each, it should seem as if he were anxious to disengage himself openly from servile adherence to any school or section of Protestants, and to claim a right of conforming his judgment to that of the primitive or catholic Church, with whomsoever amongst moderns he might be brought into agreement or disagreement.

[40] The passages above cited are such as cannot well be explained away: and if (as many will be ready to assert) they are expressly or virtually contradicted by other passages of the same author, the utmost effect of such contradiction must be to neutralize him in this controversy, and make him unfit to be quoted on either side. But is it so certain, that his reasonings and assertions elsewhere are at variance with these unequivocal declarations? Appeal would probably be made, first of all, to the line which he has adopted in his second and third books: whereof the second is taken up with sifting that main principle of the Puritans, that nothing should be done

[1] E. P. VII. xi. 8.

without command of Scripture; the third, in refuting the expectation, grounded on that principle, that in Scripture there must of necessity be found some certain form of ecclesiastical polity, the laws whereof admit not any kind of alteration. But it may be replied, that all his reasonings in that part of the treatise relate to the *a priori* question, whether, antecedently to our knowledge of the fact, it were necessary that Scripture (as a perfect rule of faith) should of purpose prescribe any one particular form of church government. The other question, of history and interpretation, how far such a form *is* virtually prescribed in the New Testament, he touches there only in passing, not however without very significant hints which way his opinion leaned [1]. "Those things," says he, "which are of principal weight in the very particular form of "church polity (although not that form which they imagine, "but that which we against them uphold) are in the Scrip- "tures contained." And again, "If we did seek to maintain "that which most advantageth our own cause, the very best "way for us, and the strongest against them, were to hold "even as they do, that there must needs be found in Scrip- "ture some particular form of church polity which God hath "instituted, and which for that very cause belongeth to all "churches, to all times. But with any such partial eye to "respect ourselves, and by cunning to make those things "seem the truest which are the fittest to serve our purpose, is "a thing which we neither like nor mean to follow. Where- "fore that which we take to be generally true concerning "the mutability of laws, the same we have plainly delivered." This passage is perhaps one of the strongest which the adversaries of ancient church order could adduce in support of their interpretation of Hooker. But what does it amount to? Surely to this, and no more: that he waives in behalf of the episcopal succession the mode of reasoning from antecedent necessity, on which the Puritans relied so confidently in behalf of their pastors, elders and deacons. Here, as in all other cases, he recommends the safe and reverential course of inquiring what the New Testament, as interpreted by natural reason and church history, contains, rather than determining beforehand what in reason it ought to contain.

[1] E. P. III. x. 8.

lxxxii *Hooker's Concessions related to Points of Detail:*

Editor's Preface. But even in this place he not obscurely implies, and in other parts of the same dissertation he expressly affirms, that the result of such reverential inquiry into the meaning of God's later revelation would be in favour of the episcopal claims[1]. "Forasmuch as where the clergy are any great multitude, "order doth necessarily require that by degrees they be dis-"tinguished; we hold there have ever been and ever ought "to be in such case at leastwise two sorts of ecclesiastical "persons, the one subordinate unto the other; as to the "Apostles in the beginning, and to the Bishops always since, "we find plainly, both in Scripture and in all ecclesiastical "records, other ministers of the word and sacraments have "been... So as the form of polity by them set down for per-"petuity is... faulty in omitting some things which in Scrip-"ture are of that nature; as namely the difference that ought "to be of pastors, when they grow to any great multitude." His manner of speaking of the foreign protestants tallies exactly with this view[2]. "For mine own part, although I see "that certain reformed churches, the Scottish especially and "the French, have not that which best agreeth with the sacred "Scripture, I mean the government that is by bishops,... "this their defect and imperfection I had rather lament in "such case than exagitate, considering that men oftentimes, "without any fault of their own, may be driven to want that "kind of polity or regiment which is best." There is nothing here to indicate indifference in Hooker with regard to the apostolical succession; there is much to shew how unwilling he was harshly to condemn irregularities committed under the supposed pressure of extreme necessity.

[41] On the whole, it should seem that where he speaks so largely of the mutability of church laws, government, and discipline, he was not so much thinking of what may be called the constitution and platform of the Church herself, as of the detail of her legislation and ceremonies: although it has become somewhat hard for a modern reader to enter into this construction of his argument, because the notion which he had to combat, of every the minutest part of discipline being of necessity contained in Scripture, has now comparatively become obsolete; whereas the episcopalian controversy

[1] E. P. III. xi. 18.   [2] E. P. III. xi. 14.

is as rife as ever. We are therefore unavoidably apt to survey with an eye to that controversy portions of his argument, in which, if we were better acquainted with the notions of the first Puritans, we might perceive that he was not thinking at all about it. If we take this observation along with us, and weigh well the amount of the statements above quoted on the episcopal side, we shall not perhaps hesitate to set down Hooker as belonging to the same school in ecclesiastical opinions with Bilson and the author of the "Querimonia:" and for those times undoubtedly the weightiest, although not perhaps the most open and uncompromising advocate of their views: the substance of those views being, that episcopacy grounded on apostolical succession was of supernatural origin and divine authority, whatever else was right or wrong.

If moreover we would fully estimate the value of Hooker's testimony in particular to the divine right of Bishops, we must add the following considerations. First, that such opinions were contrary to those in which he had been brought up. For his uncle, who had the entire superintendance of his education, was an intimate friend of Peter Martyr, and as his remains shew, likely in all questions to take that side which appeared most opposite to Romish tradition. And of his tutor Reynolds we have already spoken; he was a leader in the Puritan cause, and no doubt did his very best to leaven such a mind as Hooker's, a mind naturally full of affectionate docility, with Genevan notions in preference to those of antiquity. On this particular point, the exclusive divine right of episcopacy, there are extant letters and remonstrances from Reynolds, occasioned by the preaching of Bancroft's sermon above mentioned, sufficient by themselves to shew how deeply he was imbued with doctrines most abhorrent from those of his great pupil.

Secondly, that may be remarked here, which must be remembered throughout in reading Hooker by those who would weigh and measure his expressions truly; viz. that whatever he wrote was more or less modified, in the wording of it if not in the substance, by his resolution to make the best of things as they were, and in any case to censure as rarely and as tenderly as possible what he found established by authority.

These two feelings will account in some good measure for

the admission in the seventh book[1], an admission, which, after all we have seen, may appear somewhat anomalous; that "there may be sometimes very just and sufficient reason to "allow ordination without a bishop." The excepted cases, according to Hooker, are two: first that of a supernatural call, on which little needs now to be said, although some of the leading foreign reformers, Beza for one, were content to have it urged on their behalf; thereby, as it may seem, silently owning an instinctive mistrust about the reality of their commission. The other "extraordinary kind of vocation is, when "the exigence of necessity doth constrain to leave the usual "ways of the Church, which otherwise we would willingly "keep: where the Church must needs have some ordained, "and neither hath nor can have possibly a bishop to ordain: "in case of such necessity the ordinary institution of God "hath given oftentimes and may give place." Here, that we may not overstrain the author's meaning, we must observe first with what exact conditions of *extreme* necessity, *unwilling* deviation, *impossibility* of procuring a bishop to ordain, he has limited his concession. In the next place, it is very manifest that the concession itself was inserted to meet the case of the foreign Protestants, not gathered by exercise of independent judgment from the nature of the case or the witness of antiquity. Thirdly, this was one of the instances in which unquestionably Hooker might feel himself biassed by his respect for existing authority. For nearly up to the time when he wrote, numbers had been admitted to the ministry of the Church in England, with no better than Presbyterian ordination: and it appears by Travers's Supplication to the Council, that such was the construction not uncommonly put upon the statute of the 13th of Elizabeth, permitting those who had received orders in any other form than that of the English Service Book, on giving certain securities, to exercise their calling in England. If it were really the intention of that act to authorize other than episcopal ordination, it is but one proof more of the low accommodating notions concerning the Church which then prevailed; and may serve to heighten our sense of the imminent risk which we were in of losing the Succession. But however, the apparent decision

---

[1] Ch. xiv. 11.

of the case by high authority in church and state may account for Hooker's going rather out of his way, to signify that he did not mean to dispute that authority.

At the same time it is undeniable, that here and in many other passages we may discern a marked distinction between that which now perhaps we may venture to call the school of Hooker, and that of Laud, Hammond, and Leslie, in the two next generations. He, as well as they, regarded the order of Bishops as being immediately and properly of Divine right; he as well as they laid down principles, which strictly followed up would make this claim exclusive. But he, in common with most of his contemporaries, shrunk from the legitimate result of his own premises, the rather, as the fulness of apostolical authority on this point had never come within his cognizance; whereas the next generation of divines entered on the subject, as was before observed, fresh from the discovery of the genuine remains of St. Ignatius. He did not feel at liberty to press unreservedly, and develope in all its consequences, that part of the argument, which they, taught by the primitive Church, regarded as the most vital and decisive: the necessity, namely, of the apostolical commission to the derivation of sacramental grace, and to our mystical communion with Christ. Yet on the whole, considering his education and circumstances, the testimony which he bears to the bolder and completer view of the divines of the seventeenth century is most satisfactory. Their principles, as we have seen, he lays down very emphatically; and if he does not exactly come up to their conclusion, the difference may be accounted for, without supposing any fundamental variance of judgment. It seems to have been ordered that in this, as in some other instances, his part should be "serere arbores, quæ alteri sæculo prosint." His language was to be φωνᾶντα συνέτοισιν, more than met the ear of the mere ordinary listener, yet clear enough to attract the attention of the considerate; and this, it will be perceived, was just what the age required.

42] As to the relation of the ecclesiastical to the civil power: the proposition, that the whole body of the Church is properly the subject in which power resides, is repeatedly

Editor's Preface. acknowledged, *in terminis*, by Hooker himself[1]: as indeed it was the received doctrine of all protestants in his time, and also of that numerous section of Romanists, which maintained the prerogative of councils as against the Pope. It seems to have been borrowed by analogy from the Roman Law, of which the fundamental proposition is[2], "Quod principi "placuit, legis habet vigorem: utpote cum lege regia, quæ "de imperio ejus lata est, populus ei et in eum omne suum "imperium et potestatem conferat." Those who are familiar with the reasoning of Hooker on the origin of civil government, in the first and eighth books, will at once recognise the elements of that reasoning in those few words of Justinian. A remarkable fact, that the liberal politics of modern days should delight to base themselves on the very same tenet, which was the corner stone of the Cæsarean despotism of old. By Hooker, however, it was so completely assumed as an axiomatic principle of all government, that he transferred it without scruple to ecclesiastical legislation, and as long as he could have the benefit of it in support of the system which he wished to uphold, was little anxious to dwell even on the apostolical charter, which he has himself elsewhere asserted, in behalf of that system. As therefore in respect of kingly power he sufficiently secured existing authority by calling it, once conferred, irrevocable, although it were at first a trust from the body of the people, so in respect of episcopal power it ought, by his rule, to make practically little difference, whether it were appointed by Christ Himself to certain persons, or whether[3] "they from the Church do receive the power which "Christ did institute in the Church, according to such laws "and canons as Christ hath prescribed, and the light of "nature or scripture taught men to institute." In either case, whatever other portions of the Church system might continue voluntary, this part of it, the hereditary monarchy of the Apostles' successors, ought on Hooker's principles to be accounted indefeasible, where it could be had. As far as regards their power of order, he allows, nay strongly enforces this; but when he comes to their power of dominion, feeling himself

---

[1] E. P. VIII. vi. 1.
[2] Dig. i. iv. 1 [Inst. i. ii. 6] quoted by Hooker, E. P. VIII. vi. 11.
[3] E. P. VIII. vi. 3.

embarrassed by the received notion of the supremacy, he *Editor's Preface.* changes his ground, and recurs to the prime theory of government; according to which, the Christian state being one with the Church, and the sovereign by irrevocable cession the representative of the whole state, the same sovereign must necessarily, in the last resort, represent the whole Church also, and overrule even the Apostles' successors as well in legislation and jurisdiction as in nomination to offices.

It is true, that in these large concessions to the civil power, Hooker always implies, not only that those who exercise it are Christians, but also that they are sound and orthodox churchmen, in complete communion with the Church which they claim to govern. Where that condition fails, on his own principles the identity or union of Church and state is at an end; and the Church, as a distinct body, is free without breach of loyalty to elect officers, make laws, and decide causes for herself, no reference at all being had to the civil power.

[43] It were beyond the scope of this Preface to inquire, whether this limitation amount, even in theory, to a real safeguard; since all questions relating to the churchmanship of the sovereign are by the supposition in every case to be ultimately decided by the same sovereign himself: or again, practically, whether it have not terminated in rendering the Church throughout protestant Europe too much a slave of the civil power: neither is this the place to dwell on the grave reflection which naturally arises, how dangerous it is trusting in human theories, where God has so plainly spoken out by the voice of His ancient Church; nor to expatiate on the peril in which the very power of order in bishops is involved, as soon as their inherent powers of ecclesiastical jurisdiction and dominion are surrendered: both resting, to so great an extent, on the same Scriptures and the same precedents. But it may be allowable just to point out one fallacious proposition, which seems to have had a great share in making such a reasoner as Hooker thus inconsistent with himself and with antiquity. It is simply this, the notion which his reasoning, and all Erastian reasoning, implies, that *coordinate authorities are incompatible;* that the sovereign is not a sovereign, if the Church is independent. Surely this is as untenable, as if one denied the sovereignty of the king under the old constitution

of England, because the houses of lords and commons had certain indefeasible privileges, independent of him. If *their* veto, for example, on acts of *civil* legislation, did not impeach the king's temporal sovereignty, why should *the Church's* veto impeach the same sovereignty, in case a way could be found of giving her a power over any proposed act of *ecclesiastical* legislation? Hooker himself supplies, obviously enough, this correction of his own argument, where he reasons concerning civil power, that it must be limited before it be given; and concerning ecclesiastical, that though it reside in the sovereign as the delegate of the whole Church, yet it must always be exercised "according to such laws and canons as Christ "hath prescribed, and the light of Nature or Scripture taught "men to institute."

[44] Thus much on the point of church government, the immediate matter of controversy between Hooker and the Puritans. But there is cause to regard his appearance in the Church as most timely on other grounds, some of them yet higher and more sacred. Beginning as he did, from a point not far short of what may be truly called extreme protestantism, he seems to have been gradually impressed with the necessity of recurring in some instances to more definite, in others to higher views, to modes of thinking altogether more primitive, than were generally entertained by the Protestants of that age. Circumstances (fully related in his life) having determined him to undertake his large treatise, and the character of his mind and studies having determined him to lay the foundation deep, and begin far back, he found there, as he went on, opportunities of inculcating his gradually improving views, (the more effectually perhaps because not obtrusively) concerning one after another of almost all the great controversies. This may be the true account of many dissertations, or parts of dissertations, which might otherwise appear to be introduced on insufficient grounds. From time to time he lays hold of occasions for establishing rules, and pointing to considerations, by which the mind of the reformed church might be steadied against certain dangerous errors, which the opinions of some early reformers, too hastily adopted or carried too far, were sure to produce or encourage. At the same time he desired

to shew Roman catholics (for whose case especially we may constantly discern him providing with charitable and anxious care) that there might be something definite and primitive in a system of church polity, though it disavowed the kind of unity on which they are taught exclusively to depend.

Of these collateral subjects, the first to be mentioned on all accounts is the Catholic doctrine concerning the Most Holy Trinity. Hooker saw with grief and horror what had taken place in Geneva, Poland, and elsewhere: how crude notions of the right of private judgment, and of the sufficiency, to each man, of his own interpretations of Scripture, had ended in the revival of the worst and wildest blasphemies. He saw in the writings of that reformer especially, whose influence was greatest in this and the neighbouring countries, he saw in Calvin a disposition to treat irreverently, not only the Creeds, the sacred guards provided by the Church for Christian truth, but also that holiest truth itself, in some of its articles[1]. He knew who had called the Nicene Creed "frigida cantilena;" had treated the doctrine expressed in the words, "GOD OF "GOD, LIGHT OF LIGHT," as a mere dream of Platonizing Greeks; and had pressed, in opposition to that formula, for the use of the word αὐτόθεος, in relation to the Son. These, it may be presumed, were some of the reasons why Hooker so anxiously availed himself of the opportunity which the question of the sacraments afforded him for entering at large on the sacred theology of the Church, and exhibiting it in its primitive fulness. The controversy in which he was directly engaged required no such discussion. But when these alarming symptoms are recollected, we cease to wonder at his pausing so long upon it.

It is observable that the author of the Christian Letter, a person evidently most jealous of Calvin's honour, has selected for the very first point of his attack on Hooker a passage in which the subordination of the SON is affirmed. "We crave "of you, Maister Hoo. to explain your owne meaninge where "you saye, (b. v. p. 113[2],) 'The Father alone is originallie "that Deitie which Christ originallie is not.' Howe the

---

[1] See Bishop Bull, Def. Fid. Nic. iv. i. 8.   [2] Of the original edition; in this, ch. liv. 2.

Editor's Preface.

"Godhead of the Father and of the Sonne be all one, and yet "originallie not the same Deitie: and then teach us how "farre this differeth from the heresie of Arius, who sayeth of "God the Sonne, 'There was when he was not,' who yet "graunteth that He was *before all creatures,* 'of thinges "which were not.' Whether such wordes weaken not the "eternitie of the Sonne in the opinion of the simple, or at the "least make the Sonne inferior to the Father in respect of "the Godhead; or els teach the ignorant, there be many "Gods." On which Hooker's note is, "The Godhead of the "Father and of the Sonne is no way denied but graunted to "be the same. The only thing denied is that the Person of "the Sonne hath Deitie or Godhead in such sort as the "Father hath it." Again, Christian Letter, p. 7. "We pray "your full meaning where you say, 'The coeternitie of the "Sonne of God with His Father, and the proceeding of the "Spirit from the Father and the Sonne, are in Scripture "nowhere to be found by express literal mention'... Whether "such maner of speeches may not worke a scruple in the "weak Christian, to doubt of these articles; or at the least to "underproppe the popish traditions, that menne may the "rather favour their allegations, when they see us fain to "borrow of them." This complaint they support by citing various texts of Scripture, which as they supposed express the doctrines in question. Hooker remarks in the margin, "These places prove that there is undoubted *ground* for "them in Scripture, whence they may be deduced, as is "confessed in the place cited (lib. i. n. 13[1]): but that "they are literally and *verbatim* set down you have not "yet proved[2]."

The attack, the reply, and the principle on which the reply turns, are all worthy of the gravest consideration on the part of those who are at all tempted to disparage the authority of primitive interpretation through excessive dread of Romish inventions.

[45] The like reverential care and watchful forethought is most apparent in all that has fallen from Hooker's pen on the

---

[1] Chap. xiv. 2.
[2] This note is preserved only in the Dublin Transcript of the notes on the Christian Letter.

Incarnation of the Most Holy Son of God. While the apprehensions of other theologians, contemplating the growth of Puritanism, were confined to points of external order and the peace of the visible Church, Hooker considered the very life and substance of saving truth to be in jeopardy, as on the side of the Romanists, so on that of the Lutherans also, by reasonings likely to be grounded, whether logically or no, on the tenet which they taught in common of the proper ubiquity of our Saviour's glorified body in the Eucharist[1]. Evidently it was a feeling of this kind, rather than any fear of exaggerating the honour due to that blessed Sacrament, which reigns in those portions of the fifth Book, where he lays down certain limitations, under which the doctrine of the Real Presence must be received. The one drift and purpose of all those limitations is, to prevent any heretical surmise, of our Lord's manhood now being, or having been at any time since His Incarnation, other than most true and substantial. Whatever notion of the real presence does not in effect interfere with this foundation of the faith, that, the genuine philosophy of Hooker, no less than his sound theology, taught him to embrace with all his heart. No writer, since the primitive times, has shewn himself in this and all parts of his writings more thoroughly afraid of those tendencies, which in our age are called Utilitarian and Rationalist. If at any time he seem over scrupulous in the use of ideas or phrases, from which the early Fathers saw no reason to shrink, it is always the apprehension of irreverence, not of the contrary, which is present to

Editor's Preface.

---

[1] There is a remarkable passage in the eighth book, in which he betrays the same jealousy, not without reason, of some incautious positions of Cartwright. That diligent copyist of the foreign reformers had borrowed, probably from Beza, the strange notion, that our Lord in the government of His Church has a superior, viz. His Father; but in the government of kingdoms is merely alone and independent; a notion which, carried out as far as it will go, has an evident tendency towards Nestorian error. So Hooker appears to have felt: and accordingly, without saying as much, he disposes of it by simply repeating the catholic doctrine, and challenging the authors of the questionable position to produce their authority for it, either in Scripture or in the nature of the case. Nor was this any new feeling, but it was an apprehension which he had conceived or adopted from the very beginning of his theological career. See a very significant note (if it be his) on the Sermon of Justification: where he charges both Papists and Lutherans with "denying "the foundation by consequence" on this point.

xcii *Relation of the Eucharist to the Resurrection of the Dead.*

Editor's Preface.

his mind. For example, let the three following passages only be well considered and compared: i. e. as they stand with their context; for in these critical parts more especially, no separate citation can ever do Hooker justice.

1. "[1]Christ's body being a part of that nature, which "whole nature is presently joined unto Deity wheresoever "Deity is, it followeth that His bodily substance hath every "where a presence of true conjunction with Deity. And foras- "much as it is by virtue of that conjunction made the body of "the Son of God, by whom also it was made a sacrifice for the "sins of the whole world, this giveth it *a presence of force* "*and efficacy* throughout all generations of men." 2. "[2]Doth "any man doubt, but that even from the flesh of Christ our "very bodies do receive that life which shall make them glorious "at the latter day, and for which they are already accounted "parts of his blessed body? Our corruptible bodies could "never live the life they shall live, were it not that here they "are joined with His body which is incorruptible, and that His "is in ours as a cause of immortality; a cause by removing "through the death and merit of His own flesh that which "hindered the life of ours. Christ is therefore, both as God "and as man, that true vine whereof we both spiritually and "corporally are branches. The mixture of His bodily sub- "stance with ours is a thing which the ancient Fathers dis- "claim. Yet the mixture of His flesh with ours, they speak "of, to signify what our very bodies, through mystical con- "junction, receive from that vital efficacy which we know to "be in His; and from bodily mixtures they borrow divers "similitudes, rather to declare the truth than the manner of "coherence between His sacred and the sanctified bodies of "saints." 3. "[3]As for any mixture of the substance of His "flesh with ours, the participation which we have of Christ "includeth no such kind of gross surmise."

A striking exemplification of the difference of doctrine between Hooker and those who preceded him occurs on comparing the second of the above-cited passages with the language of Bishop Jewel on the same subject[4]. "Ye" (Harding) "say, 'The raising of our flesh is also assigned

[1] E. P. V. lv. 9.
[2] Ibid. V. lvi. 9.
[3] E. P. V. lvi. 13.
[4] Def. of Apol. part 2. c. 21. div. 1.

"in the holy Scripture to the real and substantial eating "of Christ's flesh.' But whence had ye these words, M. "Harding? Where found ye these Scriptures? Dissemble "no longer: deal plainly and simply: it is God's cause. "For a show ye allege these words of Christ written by "St. John: 'He that eateth my flesh and drinketh my blood "hath life everlasting; and I will raise him up again at "the last day.' These words we know, and the eating of "Christ's flesh we know, but where is your 'real' and "'substantial,' and 'carnal[1]' eating?...... Neither these "words nor the former ('except ye eat the flesh of the Son "of Man, and drink his blood, ye have no life in you') "pertain directly to the Sacrament."

46]   In treating on this subject of the Incarnation, that which comes next in order has been in some respects unavoidably anticipated; i.e. Hooker's doctrine concerning the holy Sacraments. Here he saw reason to practise the same circumspection, in regard of the Sacramentarians, as before, on the question of ubiquity, in regard of the Romanists and Lutherans. The erroneous theory to be obviated was one most seducing to the pride of human reason; the construction, namely, which would explain away, *first*, the Communion of Saints itself, and *secondly*, the instrumentality of sacramental signs in that Communion, so as to dispense with every thing supernatural in either.

The germ of the first error is probed[2] (as it were) in the following remarkable passage. "It is too cold an interpreta-"tion, whereby some men expound our being in Christ to "import nothing else, but only that the selfsame nature which "maketh us to be men is in Him, and maketh Him man as "we are. For what man in the world is there, which hath "not so far forth communion with Jesus Christ? It is not "this that can sustain the weight of such sentences as "speak of the mystery of our coherence with Jesus Christ." Whether the particular misinterpretation here specified were common in those days, or no[3], certainly it is in unison with

---

[1] The word "carnal," it will be observed, is added by Jewel to the quotation from his opponent.

[2] E. P. V. lvi.

[3] The following appear to be instances of it. Cranmer, Doctrine of the Sacrament, Works, vol. ii. p. 406. "Hilary...... although he saith that

that mode of thinking, which inclines men to be uneasy, until they have rid their creed as they think, as nearly as possible, of all mysterious meaning. Such persons, having been even constrained by inevitable force of Scripture to adopt one great mystery, the proper Incarnation of our Lord Jesus Christ, endeavour at least to obviate the necessity of the other, the real, substantial Participation of Christ by His saints.

[47] It is only a part of the same general view, that the Sacrament should be regarded simply as expressive actions; or tokens, morally at most, but in no wise mystically, conducive to the complete union of the renewed soul with God: a heresy, the disavowal of which by Hooker[1] is, as might be supposed, express, reiterated, and fervent, in proportion to his deep sense of its fatal consequence, and to the probability which he saw of its one day generally prevailing. Whatever such anticipations he might form, have been fully and fatally confirmed by subsequent experience.

"Christ is naturally in us, yet he saith also that we be naturally in Him . . . He meant that Christ in His incarnation received of us a mortal nature, and united the same unto His divinity, and so we be naturally in Him." And again, Answer to Gardiner, b. iii. in vol. iii. 263. "As the vine and branches be both of one nature, so the Son of God taking unto Him our human nature, and making us partakers of His divine nature, giving unto us immortality and everlasting life, doth *so* dwell naturally and corporally in us, and maketh us to dwell naturally and corporally in Him." And p. 265. "Where you say that Christ uniteth Himself to us as man, when He giveth His body in the Sacrament to such as worthily receive it; if you will speak as Cyril and other old authors used to do, Christ did unite Himself to us as man at His incarnation." So determined was Cranmer in this interpretation, that even in such passages as the following he expounds the μυστικὴ εὐλογία, not of the blessing in the Eucharist, but of Christ's taking our flesh. "The Son is united unto us," says St. Cyril, "corporally by the mystical benediction, spiritually as God." "In that place," says Cranmer, "the mystical benediction may well be understood of His incarnation." vol. iii. 264.

[1] E. P. V. lvii. 1. "It greatly offendeth, that some, when they labour to shew the use of the holy Sacraments, assign unto them no end but only *to teach* the mind, by other senses, that which the word doth teach by hearing," ibid. 5. "We take not Baptism nor the Eucharist for bare *resemblances* or memorials of things absent, neither for *naked signs* and testimonies assuring us of grace received before, but (as they are indeed and in verity) for means effectual whereby God, when we take the Sacraments, delivereth into our hands that grace available unto eternal life, which grace the Sacraments represent or signify."

But not only does this great writer with religious horror disavow the Zuinglian notion, that the sacraments are only valid as moral aids to piety; he is also very full and precise in guarding against another theory, less malignant, but hardly less erroneous and unscriptural, (though unhappily too much countenanced in later days;) the theory which denies, not indeed the *reality*, but the *exclusive* virtue, of the Sacraments, as ordinary means to their respective graces. He hesitates not to teach, with the old Christian writers, that Baptism is the *only* ordinary mean of regeneration, the Eucharist the *only* ordinary mean whereby Christ's body and blood can be taken and received. He is far from sanctioning the too prevalent idea, that every holy prayer and devout meditation renders the faithful soul a partaker of Christ, in the same sense that His own divine Sacrament does. His words concerning Baptism are: "[1]As we are not naturally men without birth, so "neither are we Christian men in the eye of the Church of "God but by new birth; nor according to the manifest ordi- "nary course of Divine dispensation new born, but by that "Baptism which both declareth and maketh us Christians." Concerning the Eucharist and Baptism both; "It is not ordi- "narily His will to bestow the grace of sacraments on any, "but by the sacraments[2]." He expounds the awful declarations in the sixth chapter of St. John, without all controversy,

Editor's Preface.

---

[1] E. P. V. lx.

[2] Compare (inter alia) the following passages: Cranmer, Defence, &c. b. iii. c. 2. vol. i. p. 357. "They say, that good "men eat the body of Christ, and drink "His blood, only at that time when "they receive the Sacrament; we say, "that they eat, drink, and feed, of "Christ continually, so long as they be "members of his body." And Jewel, Reply to Harding, art. 5. div. 2. p. 238, 9. "Our doctrine, grounded upon God's "holy word, is this: that as certainly "as Christ gave His body upon the "cross, so certainly He giveth now the "selfsame body unto the faithful; and "that not only in the ministration of "the Sacrament, . . . but also at all times, "whensoever we be able to say with "St. Paul, 'I think I know nothing "but Jesus Christ, and the same "Christ crucified upon the Cross.'" Should it occur to any one that the doctrine blamed in the text, is but in accordance with that of the church of England, in her rubric concerning spiritual communion, annexed to the Office for Communion of the Sick: he may consider whether that rubric, explained (as if possible it must be) in consistency with the definition of a sacrament in the Catechism, can be meant for any but rare and extraordinary cases; cases as strong in regard of the Eucharist, as that of martyrdom, or the premature death of a well-disposed catechumen, in regard of Baptism.

Editor's Preface. of that heavenly feast[1]; considering our Saviour to have spoken by anticipation of what He meant ere long to ordain. A mode of interpretation the more remarkable on Hooker's part, as in embracing it he was contradicting an authority which he held in most especial reverence; that of his own early patron, Bishop Jewel, whom he designates as "the "worthiest divine which Christendom hath bred by the space "of some hundreds of years[2]." This is therefore as strong an example as could be given of the freedom and courage of Hooker's theological judgment: nor will it be unprofitable to compare his tones of unaffected reverence with the peremptory language, almost amounting to scornfulness, of Jewel on the same subject. One instance, from the Defence of the Apology, has already been quoted. Others may be found in the following places: Part ii. c. 12. div. 3. "The "Sacrament is one thing, and Christ is another. We eat "Christ only by faith; we eat the Sacrament only with the "mouth of our body. When Christ spake these words, 'He "that eateth me, shall live by me;' he spake only of himself "to be eaten spiritually by faith: but he spake not one word "there of the Sacrament. He that knoweth not this, knoweth "nothing." And Reply to Harding, art. viii. div. 16. p. 292. "Christ in these words, as is witnessed by all the holy "Fathers, speaketh not of the Sacrament, but of the spiritual "eating with our faith; and in this behalf utterly excludeth "the corporal office of our body."

[48] The opinions we form on the Sacraments are sure to mingle, insensibly perhaps to ourselves, with our views of every part of practical religion. Hooker's judgment on the reality and exclusiveness of the spiritual grace of Baptism and the Lord's Supper being thus distinct and unquestionable, we are prepared to find him speaking of church ceremonies in general, and of every part and instrument of communion with the visible Church, in a very different manner from that which now commonly prevails. More especially in regard of those observances, which, though not strictly sacraments, according

---

[1] As did St. Augustine, (among other places,) in his sermon on the 54th verse. "Corpus dixit escam, san-"guinem potum; Sacramentum fide-"lium agnoscunt fideles; Audientes "autem quid aliud quam audiunt." t. v. 640.

[2] E. P. II. vi. 4.

to the more precise definition of the word, have yet in them somewhat of a sacramental nature, and were ever accounted, in the early Church, means toward several graces. Take, for example, the sign of the cross in Baptism[1]. He dwells indeed much on its use by way of instruction; whether "to put us "in mind of our own duty, or to be a memorial, sign or monu- "ment of God's miraculous goodness towards us:" which is much the same definition as a rationalist would give of Baptism or the Eucharist itself. But Hooker has other expressions, which imply that for aught we know it may be more than this. He calls the cross, "in some sense a mean "to work our preservation from reproach." He likens it to God's mark set on the forehead of His chosen in the vision of the Prophet Ezekiel. He approves of the custom adopted by the primitive Christians, of referring to it, as they did by constant crossing, whenever their baptismal integrity was in danger, and refreshing it as it were and burnishing it up in those foreheads, in which it had been impressed as God's own signature at Baptism. In other words, he makes it one among many things, which may be, if God so please, supernaturally as well as morally means of grace; and what more would Zuinglius or Hoadly have allowed concerning the blessed Eucharist itself?

Again, to imposition of hands in confirmation, in receiving penitents, or in other solemn acts of blessing, he scruples not to attribute the same virtue which the Fathers every where acknowledge. "[2] Our warrant," he says, "for the great good "effect thereof is the same which Patriarchs, Prophets, Priests, "Apostles, Fathers, and men of God have had for such their "particular invocations and benedictions, as no man, I sup- "pose, professing truth of religion, will easily think to have "been without fruit."

In respect therefore of these things, which (to use Hooker's own expression) though not sacraments, are *as* sacraments, and which perhaps it might not be amiss to denominate *sacramentals*, it will be seen that Hooker, liberal as he is sometimes accounted, was at least as far from proud and faithless indifference as he was from irrational superstition.

[1] E. P. V. lxv.   [2] E. P. V. lxvi. 7.

Editor's Preface. Even of those parts of the ancient ritual, which he dared not wish to restore, he makes mention in such a tone, as to shew that he deeply lamented the necessity of parting with them. He compares them to the rank growth of over fertile grounds: he acknowledges that although "now superstitious in the " greater part of the Christian world," yet in their first original they sprang from "the strength of virtuous, devout, or " charitable affection," and " could not by any man be justly " condemned as evil." In a word, his language regarding them comes to this: that the Church is fallen and become unworthy of them, instead of their being in themselves unmeet for the Church.

Nor can such sentiments on his part be summarily disposed of by calling them " errors of that day," " relics of Romanism, " not yet throughly purged out." For, as we have had occasion more than once to remark, Hooker's bias by education and society, the bias " of the day" as it was likely to influence him, lay quite on the other side. Every sentiment like that just quoted was a return to something which had grown out of fashion, an attempt, if the expression may be allowed, to " lock the wheel" of extreme innovation. It is certain that the divines most approved in Hooker's time go far beyond him in a seeming willingness to explain away every thing of deeper meaning in Church services. The common topics of Jewel for example, and Cranmer, when they treat of ceremonies, are the supposed origination of some of them from heathen or Jewish customs, or from mere childish fancy; the absolute indifferency of those even which are more properly Christian; and the arbitrary power of national churches over them, which they press, not in the guarded tone of our thirty-fourth article, but without any kind of scruple or remorse. We nowhere find in the Ecclesiastical Polity such contemptuous mention of the old usages of the Church, as in that writer, who being asked by a Romanist, how he could prove from St. Augustine, that altars might be pulled down, and vows of poverty disallowed, as also the keeping of Lent and the use of consecrated oil, made this short reply, " His " altars, his vows, his Lents, and his oils, be answered suffi- " ciently otherwheres." How different from Hooker, who earnestly bespeaks our reverence for primitive ordinances, not only "as betokening God's greatness and beseeming the "dignity of religion," but also "as concurring with celestial "impressions in the minds of men:" a phrase which implies that such ordinances may be real means of sundry graces, though not of those vital graces which are appropriate to the two blessed Sacraments; nor of any graces, *certainly*, or by virtue of express promise.

[49] The truth is, Hooker's notion of ceremonies appears to have been the legitimate result of a certain high and rare course of thought, into which deep study of Christian antiquity would naturally guide a devout and reflective mind. The moral and devotional writings of the Fathers shew that they were deeply imbued with the evangelical sentiment, that Christians as such are living in a new heaven and a new earth; that to them "old things are passed away," and "all "things are become new;" that the very inanimate creation itself also is "delivered from the bondage of corruption into "the glorious liberty of the children of God." Thus in a manner they seem to have realized, though in an infinitely higher sense, the system of Plato: every thing to them existed in two worlds: in the world of sense, according to its outward nature and relations; in the world intellectual, according to its spiritual associations. And thus did the whole scheme of material things, and especially those objects in it which are consecrated by scriptural allusion, assume in their eyes a sacramental or symbolical character.

This idea, as it may serve to explain, if not to justify, many things, which to modern ears sound strange and forced in the imagery of the Fathers and in their interpretations of Scripture; so it may be of no small use in enabling us to estimate rightly the ceremonials of the Church. The primitive apostolical men, being daily and hourly accustomed to sacrifice and dedicate to God even ordinary things, by mixing them up with Christian and heavenly associations, might well consider every thing whatever as capable of becoming, so far, a mean of grace, a pledge and token of Almighty presence and favour: and in that point of view might without scruple give the name of μυστηρία or sacraments to all those material objects which were any how taken unto the service of religion: whether by Scripture, in the way of type or figure; or by the Church, introducing them into her solemn ritual. In the writings of St. Cyprian[1], for example, to go no further at present; we have the homer full of manna, gathered by each of the Israelites, denominated "the sacrament of Christ's equal and im-"partial grace;" the words of the *Pater noster*, considered as meaning far more than at first meets the ear, are "the "sacraments of the Lord's Prayer;" the Church's rule for keeping Easter, with many other like points, are so many "sacraments of Divine service;" the cross is "a sacrament "of salvation;" St. Cyprian, having collected a number of what would now be called fanciful allusions, to console and encourage certain martyrs in their sufferings, is thanked by those martyrs for "his constant care to make known by his "treatises hidden and obscure sacraments." In these and innumerable similar applications of the term, it will perhaps be found that such words as "figure," "symbol," "emblem," do by no means come fully up to the force annexed to it by the Church and ecclesiastical writers. God omnipresent was so much in all their thoughts, that what to others would have been mere symbols, were to them designed expressions of His truth, providential intimations of His will. In this sense, the whole world, to them, was full of sacraments.

No doubt such a view as this harmonizes to a considerable degree with Platonism; no doubt, again, it has much in common with the natural workings and aspirations of poetical minds under any system of belief. Still, should it appear, on fair inquiry, to have been very early and very generally diffused; should we find unconscious disclosures of it among Christian interpreters and moralists quite down from St. Clement and St. Ignatius; these things would seem to indicate that it may have been a real part of the very apostolical system; grounded as it plainly might be on such scriptures as were just now mentioned.

[50] Thus then we seem to discern a kind of theory, silently pervading the whole language and system of the Church, much to this effect: that whereas all sensible things may have other meanings and uses than we know of; spiritual and heavenly relations, associations, resemblances, apt to assist men in realizing Divine contemplations; the Church (no one

[1] Ed. Baluz. p. 157; 206; 144; 159; 161.

Ceremonies, a Part of the Church's Spiritual Sacrifice. ci

of course can say how far by celestial guidance at first) selected a certain number and order of sensible things ; certain actions of the body, such as bowing at the name of Jesus, and turning towards the east in prayer ; certain forms of matter, such as the cross and ring ; generally or always significant in themselves, and very instructive, one might almost say needful, to children and men of childlike understanding and knowledge ; such things as these the Church of God instinctively selected for her ceremonies, and combined them by degrees into an orderly system, varying as circumstances might require in different dioceses, but every where constituting a kind of perpetual sacrifice ; offering to the Most Holy Trinity so many samples (if we may so call them) or specimens of our common hourly actions, and of the material objects in which we are most conversant, as tithes are a sample and specimen of our whole property, and holy-days, of our whole time : likely, therefore, as tithes and holy-days are, by devout using to bring down a blessing on the whole.

Hence it would follow, that those fragments of the primitive ritual, which are still, by God's providence, allowed to remain amongst us, are to be cherished as something more than merely decent and venerable usages. They are authorized, perchance divinely authorized, portions of the Church's perpetual spiritual sacrifice ; and the omission of *such* ceremonies, how imperative soever on individuals, acting by authority of their own particular church, must needs bring a grave responsibility on the churches themselves which may at any time direct such omission. Unquestionably circumstances might arise to justify them, such as are mentioned in the short discourse on ceremonies, prefixed to our Common Prayer : but the burden of proof in every case would lie on those omitting, not on those retaining the usage.

It is not affirmed that this view of Church ceremonies is any where expressly set down, either by Hooker or by his guides, the early Fathers. But surely something like it lies at the root of their mystical interpretations of Scripture, and of their no less mystical expositions of many portions of their ritual. Nay, it may have given many hints towards the framing that ritual itself, as far as we can judge of it after so many transformations. Surely also, on this point as on many others,

Editor's Preface.

Editor's Preface.

Hooker's sympathy with the fourth century rather than the sixteenth is perpetually breaking out, however chastened by his too reasonable dread of superstition.

Fasting, which may in some respects very well stand for one of the sacramentals just mentioned, affords a very prominent and decisive instance. For although the Church of England, by God's favouring providence, has retained the primitive system of fasting in greater perfection than any other among those bodies which have come to be separated from the Roman communion; yet even here also, at a very early period of the reformation, that evil tendency began to be disclosed, which in our days, we see, has led too generally to the undisguised abandonment of this part of Christian discipline. Now the Querimonia Ecclesiæ, which for reasons above stated may be regarded as a kind of exponent of the views of Hooker and his school in theology, expatiates, as one of its leading topics, on the prevalent neglect of Church fasts, and the revival of Aërius' error in the reformed churches. It should seem that the Utilitarians of those days could only imagine one *moral* use of fasting: they could not approve of it as a periodical expression of penitence, or as helping to withdraw the mind from earth, and supply it with heavenly contemplations. Consequently, prescribed universal fasts were to them unmeaning superstitions. And the result was, as Hooker not obscurely hints[1], and the writer of the Querimonia more openly affirms, that among protestants religious abstinence was becoming rather discreditable than otherwise. Here we seem to perceive the reason why Hooker thought it needful in his fifth book to go so far back in vindication of fasting itself. And we know that his course of life bore continual witness to his deep sense of the importance of that duty.

He differs indeed from the writer of the Querimonia, as to the apostolical institution of Lent. The pamphlet is very full for the affirmative; but the Ecclesiastical Polity says, "It doth not appear that the Apostles ordained any set and "certain days to be generally kept of all." This is noted

---

[1] E. P. V. 2. lxxii. "The world "being bold to surfeit doth now blush "to fast, supposing that men when they "fast, do rather bewray a disease, than "exercise a virtue."

here by the way, as decisive against making Hooker responsible for the Querimonia, as the authors of the Christian Letter tried to do; unless we suppose him to have changed his opinion about Lent between 1592, the date of the Querimonia, and 1597, when the fifth book was published. This however is no difference in principle, since both agree in adopting St. Augustin's rule, that what is universally observed in the Church, yet not commanded in Scripture nor in any general council, cannot well be of less than apostolical origin. The variance therefore about Lent amounts only to this; that the Querimonia considers the historical evidence sufficient to prove reception by the whole Church, Hooker not so.

[51] There is another branch of the same subject, on which their agreement is more complete; though here also the anonymous author speaks out more clearly sentiments, of which Hooker, coming after, is content to imply rather than express his approbation. In each we find a parallel between the heresy of Aërius on fasting, and the low disparaging notions of that duty, becoming at that time prevalent among many Protestants. This comparison is distinctly made in the Querimonia, as indeed there was ample reason: Beza having gone so far, in one of his tracts against Saravia, as to take part avowedly with Aërius, and endeavour to exculpate him from the charge of heresy. The controversy having proceeded so far, it is obvious that Hooker, writing as he does of Aërius, must have had an eye to Beza as well as to Cartwright. Evidently his wish was to hold up Aërius, as a warning *in terrorem* to Protestants generally, so far as they were tempted to fall into errors like his: only to make the warning more impartial and instructive, he subjoins tacitly, and by implication, another and an opposite parallel, viz. between the error of Tertullian in his Montanizing days, and some errors of the church of Rome in her rules on the subject of Fasting.

The last thing now to be observed in this very important portion of Hooker's Treatise, is the thorough practical good sense which the conclusion of it evinces. Among other benefits of fasting he enumerates the following; "That "children, as it were in the wool of their infancy dyed with "hardness, may never afterwards change colour; that the "poor, whose perpetual fasts are necessity, may with better "contentment endure the hunger, which virtue causeth others "so often to choose," &c. This is a specimen of the way in which Hooker, in the midst of his lofty and sometimes subtle speculations, observed and entered into men's daily pursuits and feelings; how he contrived (if one may so speak) to know what all sorts of persons are really about: a merit the more needful to be remarked in him, as it is one for which his readers and the readers of his Life have generally been apt to give him but little credit; but, certainly one of the highest merits which can be attributed to a practical divine, and not one of the least rare. In the eyes of plain unlearned persons, who read merely for practical improvement, this is what will ever give Hooker a peculiar value, as compared with many of no small name in theology; with Hall for instance, with Barrow, or with Warburton. He enters into the real feelings of men, and balances the true relative importance of things, in a manner which no depth of learning, or power of language, no logical or rhetorical skill could insure; and without which, to persons of the description now mentioned, no talent or energy can make theology interesting.

On festival days the opinion of Hooker is well known. He urges the perpetual observance of the Lord's day (carefully separating from it the name of Sabbath) on a mixed ground of ritual and of moral obligation; considering the general requisition of natural piety to be determined to a seventh part of time by the Decalogue. For saints' days again he regards the same obligation as being in like manner determined, only not by God's own voice, but by the authorized legislation of His Church. Praise, Bounty, and Rest, according to the law of nature, and the analogy of holy Scripture, constitute the proper elements of each kind of festival. Thus diametrically are the views of Hooker opposed, on the one hand, to the profane and insolent indifference of some following generations towards all festivals but Sunday; on the other, to the affectation of respect, almost more insolent and profane, which some persons are in the habit of bestowing on the Sunday itself. The rest of that blessed day is now too commonly enforced on reasons of mere economy and expediency, far indeed removed from Hooker's representation of it as a sacrifice of one-seventh part of our time to God; just as in those days to such a degree had popular opinion swerved from the primitive rules, that many, and among them even a writer in our own Homilies, were fain to plead, in behalf of fasting, the supposed preservation of pasturage, and encouragement of fisheries[1], instead of simply referring the duty to its own high and spiritual grounds. Admirable as these two chapters are throughout, in no respect do they call for more attentive consideration, than as a melancholy testimony to the total decay of religion properly so called, i.e. of the service of God, in an age so boastful of its own religion as the present.

Another development of the same principle occurs, in passing from the consideration of festivals and fasting days to that of churches, church lands, and tithes. Hooker evidently delights in resting the claim of both on one and the same ground of natural piety, warranted rather than expressly ordained by the Gospel of Jesus Christ. "Sith we know[2] "that religion requireth at our hands the taking away of so "great a part of the time of our lives quite and clean from "our own business, and the bestowing of the same in His; "suppose we that nothing of our wealth and substance is "immediately due to God, but all our own to bestow and "spend as ourselves think meet? Are not our riches as well "His, as the days of our life are His?" A tenth of our substance, no less than a seventh of our time, is, in Hooker's judgment, part of the grand sacrifice which we all owe to God continually, and the payment whereof is the great business of our lives.

52] Again; whatever has been once so dedicated, be it land, or house, or treasure, or church furniture, that Hooker regards as absolutely devoted and inalienable. The diverting it wilfully away from sacred purposes he deems no less than plain sacrilegious impiety: the same kind of sin as profaning holy days; or as if a clergyman should abandon God's special service, and try to become a mere layman again, after his solemn vow of dedication to the altar. It is very observable

---

[1] Compare E. P. V. lxxii. 1.   [2] V. lxxix. 1.

Editor's Preface. on what principle Hooker defends the English reformation from this charge of sacrilege, to which it would seem at first sight liable, on account of the unsparing plunder of monastic property. He is far from acquiescing in the ordinary political plea of "changed circumstances," "comparative uselessness," and the like. His sentence (right or wrong) is, that the property in question was never, strictly speaking, clerical. He professes it not to be his meaning "to make the state of " bishopric and of those dissolved companies" (the monasteries) " alike; the one no less unlawful to be removed than the " other. For those religious persons were men which followed " only a special kind of contemplative life in the common- " wealth, they were not properly a portion of God's clergy, " (only such amongst them excepted as were also priests,) " their goods (that excepted which they unjustly held through " the Pope's usurped power of appropriating ecclesiastical " livings unto them) may in part seem to be of the nature " of civil possessions, held by other kinds of corporations, " such as the city of London hath divers. Wherefore, as " their institution was human, and their end for the most part " superstitious, they had not therein merely that holy and " Divine interest which belongeth unto Bishops, who being " employed by Christ in the principal service of His Church, " are receivers and disposers of His patrimony, . . . which " whosoever shall withhold or withdraw at any time from " them, he undoubtedly robbeth God Himself[1]." According to this statement, the goods of the religious houses under Henry VIII. were lay corporate property, forfeited (as was judged) by abuse. To resume it, therefore, and apply it to other lay purposes, might be dishonest or arbitrary, but could not well be sacrilegious. Should this view appear paradoxical, it will but the more amply illustrate Hooker's deep conviction of the impiety of alienating things once hallowed. That being granted, the following dilemma ensued. He must either expressly condemn a principal part of the settlement at the reformation in England, confirmed and carried on as it had

[1] E. P. VII. xxiv. 23. Contrast with this, Cranmer's Answer to the Devonshire Rebels, art. xiv. vol. ii. p. 242. And vol. i. p. 319, where he silently sanctions Henry the Eighth's usurpations, not only of monastic but of cathedral property.

been by subsequent monarchs; or else (which he chose to do) must deny the sacredness of the confiscated property. So evident to Hooker's mind was the proposition, that whatever has been once dedicated to Almighty God can never cease to be His, but by His own cession.

53] It is but a continuation of the same process of thought, where Hooker expresses his sense of the real sanctity of consecrated places, and his horror at the hard and profane notions of the Brownists or Independents on that subject, which were just then beginning to prevail among some of the reformed, though far from the alarming acceptance which they find at present. And again, where he dwells so long and so earnestly on the great mistake which the Puritans committed in their estimate of the relative importance of the parts of public service; where he shews himself so full of regret at their presumption in undervaluing scriptures and written prayers, and their fond superstition in reckoning sermons only "the quick "and forcible Word of God[1]:" wherever, in short, he inculcates more or less directly the momentous truth, that a church is a place of solemn homage and sacrifice, not only nor chiefly a place of religious instruction; a place of supernatural even more than of moral blessings. For although he disclaim the existence of any sacrifice, properly so called, in the ritual of the Church, it is clear enough that this expression must be restrained to expiatory sacrifices. Take the word *sacrifice* in its other senses, for eucharistical or penitential homage, and it is very plain that by Hooker's own account, prayers, tithes, festival days, church ceremonies, are so many sacrifices, truly and properly so called. Nay, the very establishment of a national church, instead of being merely, as modern theorists hold, a national expedient for securing instruction to the people, ought also on Hooker's principle to be regarded as a grand public sacrifice: a continued act of religious worship and homage, offered to God on the part of kings and states.

So far, the Catholic Church has been considered as a channel of supernatural grace; in which light chiefly Hooker regards it all through the fifth book. Again, his doctrine

[1] E. P. V. xxii. 10.

Editor's Preface.

concerning the Church, considered as a witness to the truth, that is to say, in her relation to the rule of faith, may be found at large in the three first books. His principle is that of the sixth article of our Church, so admirably developed by Laud in his conference with Fisher: viz. that in doctrines supernatural, holy Scripture is paramount and sole: reason and Church authority coming in as subsidiary only, to interpret Scripture or infer from it; but in no *such* point ever claiming to dictate positively where Scripture is silent[1]. Nevertheless they teach, that in regard of rites and customs, which are a sort of practical deductions from truths supernatural, apostolical tradition, derived through Church records, if any can be proved really such, must be of force no less binding, than if the same were set down in the very writings of the Apostles. "For both," says Hooker, "being known "to be apostolical, it is not the manner of delivering them "unto the Church, but the author from whom they proceed, "which doth give them their force and credit."

[54] On Hooker's doctrine concerning the covenant of grace, a very few words must here suffice. His compositions on that subject are mostly of an early date, when, as has been exemplified, he hardly seems to have acquired the independence of thought, which appears in the Polity. And the writer to whose interpretations he had been taught to defer most constantly, and with deepest reverence, undoubtedly was St. Austin. In treating of justification, his great care was, of course, to exclude all notion of merit: of merit, i. e. as a ground of dependence, not as a qualification for supernatural blessings, divinely given to the baptized as members of Christ, for in that sense he himself allows the name, and hints no ambiguous censure on the affectation of shrinking from it, sanctioned as it is by the constant use of antiquity[2]. This exclusion of our own desert he represents, as many writers before and since have done, by the things which

---

[1] See especially i. 14.

[2] E. P. V. 72. 9. "I will not dispute . . . whether truly it may not be said that penitent both weeping and fasting are means to blot out sin, means whereby through God's unspeakable and undeserved mercy we obtain or procure to ourselves pardon, which attainment unto any gracious benefit by him bestowed the phrase of antiquity useth to express by the name of merit." Comp. Disc. of Justification, § 21.

Christ did and suffered being imputed to us for righteousness: and in this sense earnestly presses against the schoolmen and the council of Trent, that justifying righteousness is not inherent. But whilst he thus separates justification from sanctification *in re*, he is careful (plainly with an eye to Antinomian abuse) to maintain that the two are always united *in tempore*. "The Spirit, the virtues of the Spirit, the habitual "justice which is engrafted, the external justice of Jesus "Christ which is imputed, these we receive all at one and "the same time; whensoever we have any of these, we have "all; they go together[1]." He allows that the word *justification* is sometimes used (e.g. by St. James) so as to imply sanctification also; that in this sense we are justified by works and not by faith only; and that this is essential, and inseparable, as a result and evidence of the former; so that however "[2] by the one we are interested in the right of in-"heriting," yet without the other we must not look to be "brought to the actual possession of eternal bliss." On the whole, the differences, which at first sight would appear considerable, between Hooker's teaching, and that of Bishop Bull on this subject, will be found on examination rather verbal than doctrinal: turning upon their use of certain modes of expression, and upon their interpretation of particular texts, rather than on their conceptions of the process itself and order of Divine mercy in the salvation of sinners. Hooker, for instance, adopts without scruple the phrase of Christ's imputed righteousness: which Bull disavows and argues against as unscriptural. Hooker again reconciles St. James with St. Paul by making the one speak of the righteousness of justification, the other of that of sanctification: a distinction which seems to correspond nearly with the first and second justification of some other protestant commentators, and is disapproved by Bull, whose mode of harmonizing the two Apostles is to shew, that the works rejected by St. Paul are not Christian works, not those required by St. James, but that these on the contrary are included in St. Paul's faith; as all right principles include and imply corresponding practice, when occasion arises. But since Hooker on the one hand makes the two justifications

Editor's Preface.

[1] Disc. of Justif. § 21.   [2] Ibid. § 6.

which he insists on inseparable and contemporaneous; and Bull, on the other, disclaims with all possible earnestness all notion of condignity, in faith alike and in works, and in every thing else that is ours; it should seem that, really and practically, there is no such great difference between them.

[55] With regard to the points usually called Calvinistic; Hooker undoubtedly found the tone and language, which has since come to be characteristic of that school, commonly adopted by those theologians, to whom his education led him as guides and models; and therefore uses it himself, as a matter of course, on occasions, where no part of Calvinism comes expressly into debate. It is possible that this may cause him to appear, to less profound readers, a more decided partisan of Calvin than he really was. At least it is certain that on the following subjects he has avowed himself decidedly in favour of very considerable modifications of the Genevan theology. First, of election; the very ground of his original controversy with Travers was his earnestly protesting, in a sermon at the Temple, against irrespective predestination to death: a protest which he repeated in the Ecclesiastical Polity[1]; and afterwards drew out at large in the fragment of an answer to the Christian Letter. The sum of it is this: "The nature of God's good-"ness, the nature of justice, and the nature of death itself, "are all opposite to their opinion, if any will be of opinion, "that God hath eternally decreed condemnation without the "foresight of sin as a cause. The place of Judas was *locus* "*suus*, a place of his own proper procurement. Devils were "not ordained of God for hell-fire, but hell-fire for them; "and for men so far as it was foreseen that men would be "like them."

But the extent to which, on this and some other topics, Hooker was willing to admit modifications of Calvinism, may be judged of accurately by the conclusion of the fragment just quoted, which consists of eight propositions, so worded, as to shew clearly that they are altered from the famous articles of Lambeth; so that on comparing the two, the degrees by which Hooker stopped short of extreme Calvinism will

---

[1] V. xlix. 3.

become apparent even to the very eye. Now the first article of Lambeth affirms eternal predestination and reprobation both: Hooker's, predestination only, omitting all mention of reprobation. The second Lambeth article is not only negative, denying the foresight of any good in man to have been the ground of predestination to life; but also affirmative, that its only ground is the will of the good pleasure of God: Hooker omits the affirmative part, and sets down the negative only. The third Lambeth article states the number of the elect to be definite and certain, so that it can be neither increased nor diminished: Hooker, far less hard and peremptory in tone, says, "To him the number of his elect is definitely known." The fifth pair of articles relates to perseverance in grace, and presents so remarkable a difference, that it may be right to insert both here, for avoiding of apparent or inadvertent misrepresentation.

LAMBETH Art. 5.	HOOKER.
Vera, viva, justificans fides, et Spiritus Dei sanctificans non extinguitur, non excidit, non evanescit in electis aut finaliter aut totaliter.	That to God's foreknown elect, final continuance of grace is given.

It could hardly be without meaning, that he omitted those expressions of the article, which seemed to imply that justifying faith and sanctification, where real, must of course be indefectible. Yet this of all the tenets, commonly designated as Calvinistic, was that which in his earlier productions he seems to maintain with least hesitation. For example; in the sermon on the Certainty and Perpetuity of Faith; "In this "we know we are not deceived, neither can we deceive you, "when we teach that the faith *whereby ye are sanctified* "cannot fail; it did not in the prophet, it shall not in you." Also (*inter alia*) in the Discourse of Justification[1]: "If he

---

[1] § 26. In these, (by the way,) as in all Hooker's earlier works, it is observable that he employs undoubtingly the phraseology appropriate to the Christian covenant to express the spiritual condition of Jews and Patriarchs: just as Bishop Jewel and others continually affirm the spiritual graces of the Sacraments to have been the portion of such as Abel, Abraham, or David, as truly

"which once hath the Son, may cease to have the Son, though it be for a moment, he ceaseth for that moment to have life. But the life of them which have the Son of God is everlasting in the world to come. Because as Christ being raised from the dead dieth no more, death hath no more power over Him; so justified man, being allied to God in Jesus Christ our Lord, doth as necessarily from that time forward always live, as Christ, by whom he hath life, liveth always[1]." And even in the Ecclesiastical Polity[2] he uses the following strong expressions concerning a believer's first participation of Christ's grace. "The first thing of his so infused into our hearts is the Spirit of Christ: whereupon ... the rest of what kind soever do both necessarily depend and *infallibly also ensue.*" It is not quite clear why a person holding such an opinion as this should scruple to receive the fifth Lambeth Article: yet Hooker it seems had such a scruple[3]. It may be, that when he came to weigh more exactly his own doctrine of the Sacraments, he felt that it could not well stand with the supposed indefectibility of grace. For how could or can any person, beholding what numbers fall away after Baptism, hold consistently, on the one hand, that real sanctifying grace can never be finally forfeited; on the other, that it is given at Baptism? which latter, Hooker unquestionably holds: for these are his words[4]: "Baptism is a sacrament which God hath instituted in his Church, to the end that they which receive the same might thereby be incorporated into Christ, and so through his most precious merit obtain as well that

as of the saints of the new covenant. This was one dogma of the school of extreme protestantism, from which Hooker began afterwards gradually to withdraw himself: and as a symptom of his doing so may be remarked, that in no part of his dissertation on Sacraments in the fifth book of the Ecclesiastical Polity does he argue at all from this supposed identity of the Jewish with the Christian Sacraments; rather his whole train of thought is such as strictly to confine the sacramental grace of Christ to the heavenly kingdom which He set up after his incarnation.

[1] Comp. St. Aug. De Peccat. Merit. &c. i. 26, 27. t. x. p. 15.
[2] V. lvi. 11.
[3] In which he would be confirmed by that writer of whom among human authorities he speaks most highly, St. Augustin: who undoubtedly held baptismal justifying grace, and as undoubtedly considered it as capable of forfeiture; ascribing perseverance to a supervening special gift. See De Corrept. et Grat. c. 18—21. t. x. 759.
[4] E. P. V. lx. 2.

"saving grace of imputation which taketh away all former
"guiltiness, as also that infused Divine virtue of the Holy
"Ghost which giveth to the powers of the soul their first dis-
"position towards future newness of life." This is one passage
among many attributing to baptism when not unworthily
received, and therefore in all cases to infant baptism, no less
than justifying or pardoning grace, together with the first in-
5] fusion of that which sanctifies. It is for those who suppose
the writer an uncompromising Calvinist, to explain how these
representations can be reconciled with Calvin's doctrine, of the
absolute perpetuity of justifying and of the first sanctifying
grace. It is not here meant to deny that such reconciliation
may be possible: but the Editor has never yet met with it.
And until some way be discovered of clearing up this difficulty, it will be at least as fair in the advocates as they are
called of free-will, to quote Hooker's doctrine of the sacraments,
as in predestinarians to insist on his doctrine of final perseverance. The rather, as the next, the sixth Lambeth article, which
lays it down that all truly justified souls have full assurance
of faith concerning their own pardon and salvation; this
article is totally omitted by Hooker: no doubt for the same
kind of reasons as induced him, writing on the Certainty and
Perpetuity of Faith, to make so large allowance for the little
understanding men have of their own spiritual condition.
The modifications of the three remaining articles are much
less considerable; they are, first, "that inward grace whereby
"to be saved is deservedly not given to all men:" where the
word "deservedly" is an insertion of Hooker's, anxious to
counteract all notions of arbitrary punishment. Secondly,
that "no man can come to Christ, whom God by the inward
"grace of his Spirit draweth not." Hooker contents himself
with this anti-Pelagian proposition: whereas the Lambeth
divines added, "Not all men are drawn by the Father to
"come to his Son." Next, whereas they nakedly affirm, "It
"lies not in the will or power of each individual to be saved
"or lost:" Hooker, charitably and cautiously, guards the
assertion; "It is not in every, no not in any man's own mere
"ability, freedom or power, to be saved; no man's salvation
"being possible without grace." And lastly, he adds a
distinct reserve in behalf of the claim of practical obedience on

Editor's Preface.

Hooker's note on "A Christ. Letter" etc. p. 20. | *Ibid. p. 22.* | *Ibid. p. 24.*

Note by G. Cranmer on B. 6. of Eccl. Polity.

p. 20. Marriage feast in Cana? Although yt be no necessary consequence, yet some presumption yt is that if any such thing had beene vsed in ye Church before Victor, yt would at some tyme or other haue beene mentioned. And therefore if any testimony may could heere be alleaged of ye devvses of excommunicated before Victor, it would be very fitt. Fr. B. i. and y. like if you cannot call to remembrance any cleare testimony, it may be D. Raynoldes were able to furnish you, &c a word in his owne eare, when you send your booke.

Note by E. Sandys on B. 6. of Eccl. Polity.

83
84

The above are all from MSS. preserved in C.C.C. Library Oxford.

every soul of man. "God is no favourer of sloth: and there-
"fore there can be no such absolute decree touching man's
"salvation as on our part includeth no necessity of care and
"travail." On this there is a deep silence in the Lambeth
propositions.

[57] So much for the points which it was considered material to
enumerate, as best exemplifying the gradual but decisive change
which English Theology underwent in the hands of Hooker.
The results of his publications were great and presently per-
ceptible: a school of writers immediately sprung up, who by
express reference, or style, or tone of thought, betray their admiration of Hooker; Covel, Edwin Sandys, Field, Raleigh [1],
and others; and what was infinitely more important, Hooker
had his full share in training up for the next generation, Laud,

---

[1] The following sentences from the History of the World, which must have been finished before 1615, may serve to illustrate this observation: "This was "the order of the army of Israel, and "of their encamping and marching; "the tabernacle being always set in the "middle and centre thereof. The re-"verend care, which Moses the Pro-"phet and chosen servant of God had, "in all that belonged even to the out-"ward and least parts of the tabernacle, "ark and sanctuary, witnessed well the "inward and most humble zeal borne "towards God himself. The industry "used in the framing thereof and every "and the least part thereof; the cu-"rious workmanship thereon bestowed; "the exceeding charge and expense "in the provisions; the dutiful ob-"servance in the laying up and pre-"serving the holy vessels; the solemn "removing thereof, the vigilant at-"tendance thereon, and the provident "defence of the same, which all ages "have in some degree imitated, is now "so forgotten and cast away in this "superfine age, by those of the *Fa-*"*mily*, by the Anabaptists, Brownists, "and other sectaries, as all cost and "care bestowed and had of the Church, "wherein God is to be served and "worshipped, is accounted a kind of "popery, and as proceeding from an "idolatrous disposition; insomuch as "time would soon bring to pass (if it "were not resisted) that God would be "turned out of churches into barns, "and from thence again into the "fields and mountains, and under the "hedges; and the offices of the min-"istry (robbed of all dignity and re-"spect) be as contemptible as those "places; all order, discipline, and "church government, left to newness "of opinion and men's fancies; yea, "and soon after, as many kinds of re-"ligions would spring up, as there are "parish churches within England; "every contentious and ignorant per-"son clothing his fancy with the spirit "of God, and his imagination with "the gift of revelation; insomuch as "when the truth, which is but one, "shall appear to the simple multitude "no less variable than contrary to "itself, the faith of men will soon "after die away by degrees, and all "religion be held in scorn and con-"tempt." b. ii. c. 5. § 1. Elsewhere (c. 4. § 4.) Sir Walter Raleigh quotes Hooker by name for his definition of law: one among the many incidental proofs of the great authority which Hooker's work had acquired in so very few years.

Hammond, Sanderson[1], and a multitude more such divines: to which succession and series, humanly speaking, we owe it, that the Anglican church continues at such a distance from that of Geneva, and so near to primitive truth and apostolical order. There have been and are those, who resort, or would be thought to resort, to the books of Ecclesiastical Polity, for conclusions and maxims very different from these. King James II, it is well known, ascribed to Hooker, more than to any other writer, his own ill-starred conversion to Romanism: against which, nevertheless, if he had thought a little more impartially, he might have perceived that Hooker's works every where inculcate that which is the only sufficient antidote, respect for the true Church of the Fathers, as subsidiary to Scripture and a witness of its true meaning. And the rationalists on the contrary side, and the liberals of the school of Locke and Hoadly, are never weary of claiming Hooker as the first distinct enunciator of their principles. Whereas, even in respect of civil government, though he might allow their theory of its origin, he pointedly deprecates their conclusion in favour of resistance. And in respect of sacramental grace, and the consequent nature and importance of Church communion, themselves have never dared to claim sanction from him.

[58] It is hoped that this republication of his remains, by making them in certain respects more accessible, will cause them to become more generally read and known: and surely the better they are known, the more entirely will they be rescued from the unpleasant association, and discreditable praise, just now mentioned; the more will they appear in their true light, as a kind of warning voice from antiquity, a treasure of primitive, catholic maxims and sentiments, seasonably provided for this Church, at a time when she was, humanly speaking, in a fair way to fall as low towards rationalism, as the lowest of the protestant congregations are now fallen, Bold must be he who should affirm, that great as was then her need of such a defender, it at all exceeded her peril from the same quarter at the present moment. Should these volumes prove at all instrumental in awakening any of her children to

---

[1] See especially Hammond, Works, vol. i. p. 669; and Pierce's Letter at the end of Walton's Life of Sanderson.

a sense of that danger, and in directing their attention to the primitive, apostolical Church, as the ark of refuge divinely provided for the faithful, such an effect will amply repay the Editor, not only for the labour of his task, which to one more skilful would have been comparatively nothing, but for that which must otherwise be always a source of some regret to him—the consciousness, namely, of having undertaken an office, for which in many respects he knew himself to be so very imperfectly prepared.

The chief circumstance important to be stated on this reprint of the edition of 1836, is, that the whole of the Dublin MSS. of Hooker have been carefully collated for it a second time by Dr. Todd and Mr. Gibbings; and all the resulting variations of any importance will be found inserted in their proper places. They have ascertained what it is on many accounts satisfactory to know; that the notes on the Sermon on Justification, supposed to be Archbishop Ussher's, and given as his in the former edition, are unquestionably by another hand. Mr. Young, of the College of Arms, has kindly revised the Pedigree of the Hooker family, and corrected it from documents in the library of that institution: towards which object valuable information has been furnished by Mr. Dalton, of Dunkirk House in Gloucestershire. The Editor gladly avails himself of this mode of acknowledging the obligation he feels to all these gentlemen for their valuable and friendly aid.

March, 1841.

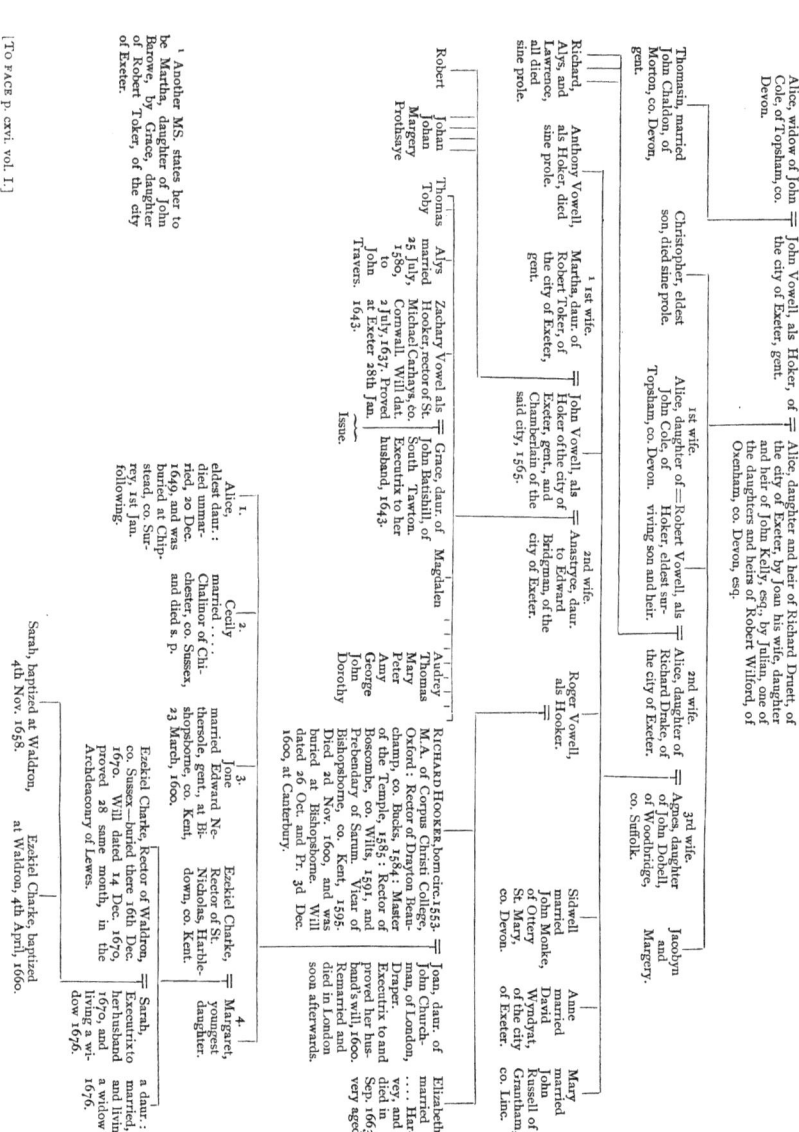

APPENDIX TO PREFACE.—No. II.

Collation of the first edition of G. Cranmer's Letter on the New Church Discipline with Walton's edition, 1675. See in this edition, vol. ii. p. 598—609.

Readings of first Edition.	Readings of Walton.
P. 598, l. 21. diffidence	defiance
599, l. 1. emprese	impress
— l. 11. is mightily	did mightily
— l. 12. to possess	possess
— l. 13. to lose	if lost
— l. 20. workmen	workman
— l. 21. they find	and they find
— l. 31. cap and surplice	the cap and surplice
— l. 32. government then established	government established
— l. 36. in Latin	and in Latin
600, l. 13. desired of the common people	desired by all the common people
— l. 17. acknowledging	by acknowledging
— l. 24. further to proceed	to proceed further
— l. 26. was in fact	was also in fact
— l. 27. that undone	that to be undone
601, l. 6. out of a pease cart	out of a pease cart in Cheapside
— l. 20. their entering	they entered
602, l. 4. prayers	prayer
— l. 7. were they rather	were they not rather
— l. 8. aloof	aloof off
— l. 8. and loath	as being loath
— l. 8. the Spirit	that Spirit
603, l. 4. hath taken	have taken
604, l. 4. both lawful	is both lawful
605, l. 8. might so be salved	might be salved
— l. 16. erection	erections
— l. 23. τὸ ἴδιον	distraction
606, l. 9. they are not able	that they are not able
— l. 10. with dislike	with a dislike
608, l. 1. open to advantage	open an advantage
— l. 6. somewhat overflow	so often overflow
— l. 13. erection	and erection
— l. 23. their sovereign	or their sovereign
— l. 37. or of innovation	or innovation
— l. 42. common people, judges	common people who are judges
609, l. 2. for want	and for want
— l. 30. of infinite	of the infinite
— l. 38. shod, girt	should be girt
610, l. 6. what men	that what men
— l. 10. but things	but even things

APPENDIX TO PREFACE.—No. III.

Memoranda for an Answer to the "Christian Letter," omitted in the notes to this Edition[1].

Titlepage.] The title of my answere this. To the Penman of a Letter intitled Christian[2], [and published with his name against whom it is writ,] in the name of certain English Protestants.

Ibid.] "Credo Apostolos nostros, nec cum suspicerentur ab ho-"minibus inflatos fuisse, nec cum despicerentur elisos. Neutra "quippe tentatio defuit illis viris; nam et credentium celebrabantur "præconio, et persequentium maledictis infamabantur." Aug. Doct. Christ. iii. c. 20. [t. iii. 54.]

"Prorsus si quid veri me tenere vel scio vel credo vel puto, in "quo aliter sentis; quantum dat Dominus, sine tua injuria conabor "asserere." Aug. ad Hieron. Ep. 15. [t. ii. 167.]

As hitherto I have alwaies framed my selfe to respect truth with reverence, and error with compassion, soe I would be loath to begin in you a chaunge of that course, wherein I could never yet find any inconvenience.

It appeareth cleare throughout the course of his whole booke that this fellow did in no one point of doctrine understand either what he pretendeth the Church of England to establish, or what he allegeth as said by the adversarie; or what he would beare men in hand to be contradicted by the one and craftily upheld by the other; but sheweth such pittiful and palpable ignorance even in every article, as for mine own part I am ashamed that the common enemy of us both should see, being forward enough thereby to imagine that great blindnes must needs reign there where such a champion as this fighteth without eyes.

P. 2.] "Pericles convitiis certare recusat, quod qui vincat victo "deterior sit." Phil. Jud. p. 138. De Agricult. p. 133.

"Veritas est lux quam Sophistæ, consuetudo, conjectura, et falsus "testis corrumpunt.

"Deus rerum omnium certissimus, et similis incerto." Tertul. p. 635.

"Sapiens in eo quod est sapiens, intentio ejus est perquirere veri- "tatem, non facere dubitationes, et ponere involutiones in opinio- "nibus." Aver. Disp. Metaph. fol. 148. p. 1.

---

[1] The references are to the pages of the printed Letter, on which the original memoranda occur.

[2] The portion in brackets has a line drawn across in the original, and consequently omitted in the Dublin and C. C. C. Transcripts.

"Qui falsum aliquid in principio sumunt, verisimilitudine inducti, "necesse est eos in ea quæ consequuntur incurrere." Lactant. p. 178. (l. 3. c. 24.)¹.

"Necesse est falsa esse quæ rebus falsis congruunt." p. 178.

"Cum primis habuerint fidem, qualia sunt ea quæ sequuntur non "circumspiciunt, sed defendunt omni modo, cum debeant prima "utrumne vera sint an falsa ex consequentibus judicare." p. 178.

"Sermo de scientia quam Deus gloriosus de se et de aliis habet "est prohibitus. Quanto magis ponere eum in scriptis. Nam non "pervenit intelligentia vulgi ad tales profunditates; et cum disputa- "tur ab eis, in hoc destruitur divinitas apud eos. Quare disputatio "eis de hac scientia prohibita est, cum sufficiat in fælicitatem eorum "ut intelligant id quod potest percipere intelligentia eorum. Quare "lex cujus intentio prima fuit docere vulgus non defecit circa intelli- "gentiam harum rerum ex iis quæ sunt in homine, sed ad faciendum "intelligere aliqua de Deo indiguit assimilatione ejus, instrumentis "humanis. Ut dixit, 'Manus ejus fundavit terram, et dextra ejus "mensuravit cœlum.' Et hæc quidem quæstio est propria sapientibus, "quos dedicavit Deus veritati." Aver. fol. 208.

"Aliquando est opinio, quæ erit venenum in aliquibus hominibus, "et nutrimentum in aliis." fol. 209.

"Cum impossibile sit quin loquamur in hac quæstione, dicimus "de ea secundum quod requirit vis loquelæ de ea, et apud eum "qui non est assuefactus in rebus in quibus se debet exercere ante "considerationem in hac quæstione." fol. 209.

Γνῶμαι αἱ μὲν τῶν ἄρτι μανθάνειν ἀρχομένων ἄστατοι καὶ ἀνίδρυτοι.

P. 36. "Where is it revealed . . . . that angels' perpetuity is the "hand that draweth out celestial motion! . . . Do you not mean the "angels which kept not their first estate," &c.] What a misery is it to be troubled with an adversary into whom a man must put both truth and wit.

Ibid. On "warrant of present grace in the very work wrought of "baptism."] See Mornæus, Misc. p. 773.

P. 40. "When those officers" (of Geneva, who had expelled Calvin) "like unto filthy froth, were cast out, the one accused of "sedition going about to escape through a window, falling down "headlong, by the pease" (weight) " of his body, was so hurt that "within few days he died: another for murder was put to death, "and the two other being accused for ill government in a certain "embassage, forsook the country, and were condemned being "absent," &c.] Not unlikely but men, when they fail of their hope,

---

¹ The reference in (¹) seems to be entered in the original in Fulman's hand.

Editor's Preface. Appendix 3. and are at a stop in their purposes, may grow desperate; as Achitophel, Hacquet, Coppinger, and such like melancholiques.

P. 45. "In all your bookes ... the *ingenuous schoolemen* almost "in all points have some finger."] As if you should say, the brave and courtly husbandmen, the high spirited shepperds, the victorious friars, the brave and prudent scullers on Thamesis, or any other the like unfit and mischosen titles. A term as fit as is a saddle for a cow's back. Were it fit for me to say of reformers, they are hir majestie's fair and well favoured [subjects]?

P. 46. "As a man afar off beholding a briar tree all blown over "with his flowers, with great desire approacheth near unto it, and "findeth himself deceived; so the delight of reading your book," &c.] What a goodly show there is in the blossoms of a briar tree. No tree in all the field or forest fit to serve your turn in this comparison, but the briar tree only? Indeed the briar is noted for a proud aspiring tree, carrying a more ambitious mind than either the olive tree or vine, although it bring forth nothing worthy to be accounted of. But, good sir, the heart of the tree you see not; it may be the kind you also mistake; and as for the fruit, you are not ignorant how distasteful all fruits are when the tongue is scorched and blistered with heat.

Ibid. "Sometime it seemeth to us that we perceive great flourish-"ing of warlike and glistering weapons, and to hear the loud outcries "and noise of them which pursue their enemies in battle, thundering, "gunshot, tossing of spears, and rattling of harness," &c.] O brave gallant! This martial spirit of yours doth surely deserve a knighthood, but that you are a man more willing to be heard than known in the field; neither do you, like a Pyrgopolimius, swell, and so break, but from big words you proceed, as a valiant champion should do, to deadly blows.

P. 47.] I doubt not but if you once attain to understand the rudiments and principles of Christian religion, which with good helps may be done in reasonable time; those other gifts of speech and writing, wherewith it hath pleased God to indue you in very good handsome measure, may do good for the edifying of poor country people, in case you apply your talent that way, and leave the controversies of religion to other men that have bestowed their time on them.

Ibid. "That you would be careful not to corrupt the English "Creed," &c.] Be you careful to understand the English Creed, which as yet you do not. Read some good Catechism, and take the help of divines allowed by authority, that they may a little better make it sink into your head, before you meddle again with matters of religion.

Add here such sentiments as the Fathers use for admonition to shallow witted men, and consolation, although they be not able to argue and dispute in matters of doctrine: which thing belongeth not to them, but to others, whom God hath more enabled for that purpose.

P. 48.] "Now in all these things, good Maister Hoo. though "we thus write, we do not take upon us to censure your books, "neither rashly to judge of you for them; but because .... he "that toucheth our faith toucheth the apple of our eye; we could "not but utter our inward grief, and yet in as charitable manner, "as the cause in hand would suffer."] As if Cassius and Brutus, having slain Cæsar, they should have solemnly protested to his friends, they meant him nothing but mere good-will and friendship. Only they feared lest the commonwealth should take harm by his means. Was there any friend he had so ill-minded, as not to believe such honest protestations?

An imitation of this conclusion in the person of Cassius and Brutus. You have given me as many stabs as my body could receive at your hands: although in effect, I praise God for it, none of them deadly, whatsoever your intent were. But for this once I will take your word without further reply; and am content to let the world think, if it will, that as you have done me, so likewise you have meant me no evil in any thing hitherto written; not in traducing me as an underminer, not in, &c.

Forget not here to use that of Solomon, Prov. xxvi. 18, "As a "madman who casteth firebrands, arrows, and death, so is the man "that deceiveth his neighbour, and saith, Am not I in sport?"

P. 49. At the foot of their conclusion.] "Hæc pro animi nostri "pura conscientia et Domini ac Dei nostri fiducia rescripsi. Habes "tu literas meas et ego tuas. In die judicii ante tribunal Christi "utraque recitabuntur." Cyprian. ad Papin. [Pupian.] Ep. 66. in fine.

Hooker's note on "A Christ. Letter" etc. p. 20.   *Ibid. p. 22.*   *Ibid. p. 24.*

If sermons be the word of God in the same sense that scripture are his word, if there be no difference between preaching and prophetic shapeings of Christ and the unjust preaching ministers saying, the only between... [manuscript largely illegible]

Note by G. Cranmer on B.6. of Eccl. Polity.

p. 20. Marriage feast in Cana? Although yt be no necessary consequence, yet some presumption yt is that if any such thing had beene vsed in ye Church before Victor, yt would at some tyme or other haue beene mentioned. And therefore if any testimonye could heere be alleaged of ye devise of excommunication before Victor, it would be very fitt. For this and ye like if you cannot call to remembrance any cleere testimony, it may be D. Raynolds were able to furnish you, wth a word writing vnto him, when you send your booke.

Note by E. Sandys on B.6. of Eccl. Polity.

83
84

Ambrose Bishop] Ambrose Archbishop.
wch may be thought odd by men that way allreadie affected.
Ambrose last mentioned] odd but more then they have any sound peece of proofe for] After so I would avoid ye reasons vsing
"graunt any thing to them ex professo, seriò ōr eagerly to signifie that ye cannot it not for truth, rather but admitt it by way of disputation to shew your owne weakenes.

The above are all from MSS. preserved in C.C.C. Library Oxford.

TO THE

RIGHT HON. AND RIGHT REV. FATHER IN GOD,

GEORGE[1], LORD BISHOP OF WINCHESTER,

DEAN OF HIS MAJESTY'S CHAPEL ROYAL,
AND PRELATE OF THE MOST NOBLE ORDER OF THE GARTER.

MY LORD,

I HERE present you with a relation of the life of that humble man, to whom, at the mention of his name, princes, and the most learned of this nation, have paid a reverence. It was written by me under your roof: for which, and more weighty reasons, you might, if it were worthy, justly claim a title to it: but indeed, my Lord, though this be a well-meant sacrifice to the memory of that venerable man; yet I have so little confidence in my performance, that I beg your pardon for subscribing[2] your name to it; and desire all that know your Lordship to receive it, not as a dedication, by which you receive any access of honour, but rather as a more humble and a more public acknowledgment of your long continued, and your now daily, favours to

your most affectionate,

and most humble servant,

IZAAK WALTON.

Nov. 28, 1664.

[1] [Morley.]
[2] [Corrected to "superscribing" in the dedication to the collected lives, 1675, which is the same with this, *mutatis mutandis*.]

PREFACE

TO THE

FIRST EDITION OF THE LIFE OF HOOKER,

PUBLISHED IN 1665.

TO THE READER.

I THINK it necessary to inform my reader, that Dr. Gauden (the late[1] Bishop of Worcester) hath also lately wrote and published the life of Master Hooker[2]. And though this be not writ by design to oppose what he hath truly written, yet I am put upon a necessity to say, that in it there be many material mistakes[3], and more omissions. I conceive some of his mistakes did proceed from a belief in Master Thomas Fuller, who had too hastily published what he hath since most ingenuously retracted[4]. And for the bishop's omissions, I suppose his more weighty business, and want of time, made

---

[1] [Dr. Gauden died in 1662. His edition of Hooker, dated that year, bears marks of great haste.]

[2] [By Archbishop Sheldon's desire, as Gauden states himself in p. 1, which perhaps made the Archbishop the more anxious to obtain a more correct life by Walton: see note on p. 3. of this volume.]

[3] [E. g. "A little living called "Buscomb in the West, to which "*the college of C. C.* presented "him: and *afterward,* that other, "not much better, in *Lincolnshire,* "called Drayton Beauchamp." p. 12. "He ever lived a single life." (Fuller C. H. IX. 235, "living and "dying a single man.") ibid. "He was prebendary of Canter- "bury." p. 25. "He made no "will." ibid.]

[4] [Fuller, Worthies of England; p. 276, ed. 1662. "Here I must "retract two passages in my "Church History. For whereas "I reported him to die a bache- "lor, he had wife and children," [marg. "From the mouth of his "sister lately living at Hogsden" (qu. Hoxton?) "near London."] "though indeed such as were nei- "ther to his comfort when living, "nor credit when dead. Secondly, "his monument was not erected by "Sir E. Sandys, (a person as pro- "bable as any man alive for such "a performance,) but by Sir W. "Cooper, now living in the castle "of Hartford."]

him pass over many things without that due examination, which my better leisure, my diligence, and my accidental advantages, have made known unto me.

And now for myself, I can say, I hope, or rather know, there are no material mistakes in what I here present to you that shall become my reader. Little things that I have received by tradition (to which there may be too much and too little faith given) I will not at this distance of time undertake to justify; for though I have used great diligence, and compared relations and circumstances, and probable results and expressions, yet I shall not impose my belief upon my reader; I shall rather leave him at liberty: but if there shall appear any material omission, I desire every lover of truth and the memory of Master Hooker, that it may be made known unto me. And, to incline him to it, I here promise to acknowledge and rectify any such mistake in a second impression[1], which the printer says he hopes for; and by this means my weak (but faithful) endeavours may become a better monument, and in some degree more worthy the memory of this venerable man.

I confess, that when I consider the great learning and virtue of Master Hooker, and what satisfaction and advantages many eminent scholars and admirers of him have had by his labours, I do not a little wonder, that in sixty years[2] no man did undertake to tell posterity of the excellences of his life and learning, and the accidents of both; and sometimes wonder more at myself, that I have been persuaded to it; and, indeed, I do not easily pronounce my own pardon, nor expect that my reader shall, unless my introduction shall prove my apology, to which I refer him.

---

[1] [Of Walton's care to fulfil this engagement, some instances will be pointed out in the notes on the ensuing Life.]

[2] [In round numbers: from his death in 1600, to the publication of his Life by Bishop Gauden in 1662.]

THE LIFE

OF

MR. RICHARD HOOKER.

THE INTRODUCTION.

I HAVE been persuaded by a friend[1], whom I reverence, and ought to obey, to write *The Life of* RICHARD HOOKER, the happy author of five (if not more) of the eight learned books of *The Laws of Ecclesiastical Polity*. And though I have undertaken it, yet it hath been with some unwillingness, because I foresee that it must prove to me, and especially at this time of my age, a work of much labour to inquire, consider, research, and determine, what is needful to be known concerning him. For I knew him not in his life, and must therefore

---

[1] [Thus explained in the Epistle to the Reader, prefixed to the Lives of Donne, Wotton, Hooker, and Herbert, when first collected (in 1670) into one volume. "Having "writ these two lives," (of Dr. Donne and sir H. Wotton,) "I "lay quiet twenty years, without "a thought of either troubling "myself or others, by any new "engagement in this kind, for I "thought I knew my unfitness. "But, about that time, Dr. Gauden "(then Lord Bishop of Exeter) "publisht *the Life of Mr. Richard* "*Hooker*, (so he called it,) with so "many dangerous mistakes, both "of him and his books, that dis- "coursing of them with his Grace, "Gilbert" [Sheldon] "that now is "Lord Archbishop of Canterbury, "he enjoined me to examine some "circumstances, and then rectify "the bishop's mistakes, by giving "the world a fuller and a truer "account of Mr. Hooker and his "books, than that bishop had done; "and, I know I have done so. And, "let me tell the reader, that till "his Grace had laid this injunction "upon me, I could not admit a "thought of any fitness in me to "undertake it: but, when he had "twice enjoined me to it, I then "declined my own, and trusted his "judgment, and submitted to his "commands: concluding, that if I "did not, I could not forbear ac- "cusing myself of disobedience; "and, indeed, of ingratitude for "his many favours. Thus I be- "came engaged into the third life." N. B. This is quoted from the edition of 1675.]

not only look back to his death, (now sixty-four years past,) but almost fifty years beyond that, even to his childhood and youth, and gather thence such observations and prognostics, as may at least adorn, if not prove necessary for the completing of what I have undertaken.

This trouble I foresee, and foresee also, that it is impossible to escape censures; against which I will not hope my well-meaning and diligence can protect me, (for I consider the age in which I live,) and shall therefore but entreat of my reader a suspension of his censures, till I have made known unto him some reasons, which I myself would now gladly believe do make me in some measure fit for this undertaking: and if these reasons shall not acquit me from all censures, they may at least abate of their severity; and this is all I can probably hope for.

My reasons follow.

About forty years past[1] (for I am now past the seventy of my age[2]) I began a happy affinity with William Cranmer, (now with God,) grand nephew unto the great archbishop of that name; a family of noted prudence and resolution; with him and two of his sisters I had an entire and free friendship: one of them was the wife of Dr. Spencer, a bosom friend, and sometime com-pupil with Mr. Hooker in Corpus Christi college in Oxford, and after, President of the same. I name

---

[1] [Is. Walton was born Aug. 9, 1593. The marriage referred to by the word "affinity" must be dated therefore about 1623. "From one "or two entries in the parish regis- "ter of St. Dunstan, Fleet-street, "there is reason to believe that "Walton was twice married:" (the second marriage connecting him, as is well known, with Bishop Ken:) "of his first wife nothing is "now known, but that her Christian "name was Rachel.

"'Aug. 25, 1640, Rachell wife "of Isaak Walton was buried.'"

"By her he had two sons. "Henry baptized October 12, 1632, "and buried October 17, following. "Another Henry baptized March "21, 1634, buried Dec. 4. follow- "ing." Dr. Bliss's note in Athen. Oxon. I. 690. In the Appendix, Walton says that George Cranmer's sister was his (Walton's) aunt. This passage shews that he means his aunt *by marriage:* and we may conclude that his first wife was Rachel, daughter of William Cranmer, one of the younger sons of Thomas, son of Edmund, who was brother to the Archbishop, and archdeacon of Canterbury. Dr. Zouch, apparently on the strength of the passage in the Appendix alone, states (vol. II. p. 314.) that "Isaac Walton's *mo- "ther* was the daughter of Ed- "mund Cranmer:" which is evidently inconsistent with the manner of speaking in the text.]

[2] ["I have almost attained the "declining year of fifty of mine "age." Robert Beal ap. Strype, A. IV. 116.]

them here, for that I shall have occasion to mention them in this following discourse; as also George Cranmer their brother, of whose useful abilities my reader may have a more authentic testimony than my pen can purchase for him, by that of our learned Camden and others.

This William Cranmer, and his two forenamed sisters, had some affinity, and a most familiar friendship with Mr. Hooker, and had had some part of their education with him in his house, when he was parson of Bishop's-Borne near Canterbury; in which city their good father then lived. They had (I say) a part of their education with him, as myself, since that time, a happy cohabitation with them; and having some years before read part of Mr. Hooker's works with great liking and satisfaction, my affection to them made me a diligent inquisitor into many things that concerned him: as namely, of his person, his nature, the management of his time, his wife, his family, and the fortune of him and his. Which inquiry hath given me much advantage in the knowledge of what is now under my consideration, and intended for the satisfaction of my reader.

I had also a friendship with the reverend Doctor Usher, the late learned Archbishop of Armagh; and with Doctor Morton, the late learned and charitable Bishop of Durham; as also with the learned John Hales, of Eton College[1]; and with them also (who loved the very name of Mr. Hooker) I have had many discourses concerning him; and from them, and many others that have now put off mortality, I might have had more informations, if I could then have admitted a thought of any fitness for what by persuasion I have now undertaken. But, though that full harvest be irrecoverably lost, yet my memory hath preserved some gleanings, and my diligence made such additions to them, as I hope will prove useful to the completing of what I intend. In the discovery of which I shall be faithful, and with this assurance put a period to my introduction.

[1] [Archbishop Usher died 1655, aged 75; Bishop Morton 1660, aged 96; Mr. Hales 1656, aged 72.]

THE LIFE.

IT is not to be doubted, but that Richard Hooker was born at Heavy-tree[1], near, or within the precincts, or in the city of Exeter; a city which may justly boast, that it was the birthplace of him, and Sir Thomas Bodley; as indeed the county may, in which it stands, that it hath furnished this nation with Bishop Jewel, Sir Francis Drake, Sir Walter Raleigh, and many others, memorable for their valour and learning. He was born about the year of our redemption 1553[2]; and of parents that were not so remarkable for their extraction or riches, as for their virtue and industry, and God's blessing upon both[3]; by which they were enabled to educate their children in some degree of learning, of which our Richard Hooker may appear to be one fair testimony; and that nature is not so partial, as always to give the great blessings of wisdom and learning, and with them the greater blessings of virtue and government, to those only that are of a more high and honourable birth.

His complexion (if we may guess by him at the age of

---

[1] [Fuller, Worthies of England, p. 264. "Richard Hooker was "born at Heavy-tree." (marg. "MS. of baronet Northcott.") Gauden, Life, p. 7. "This only "is certain on all hands, that he "was born in the west, either in, "or not far from, the city of Ex- "eter; only Dr. Vilvain, an ancient "and learned physician in Exeter, "informs me, that he was born in "Southgate-street in Exeter, anno "1550." Fulman, MSS. tom. x. fol. 26. "Richardus Hooker ap. "Heavy-tree juxta civitatem Ex- "oniam natus est circa finem Martii "mensis, anno 1554 ineunte." No trace of him remains in either of the register books of the cathedral, St. Mary Major, or Heavitree. In the register of burials of St. Mary Major are the following entries: Agnes Hoker, (possibly his sister,) 18 Oct. 1590: William, and Richard, both 16 Nov. following: another William, 25 March, 1592: Anstice, the wife of Mr. John Hoker, (and therefore Hooker's aunt by mar- riage,) 25 March, 1599: John Hoker the younger, (his first cousin,) 8 Nov. 1601: Robert, 23 Oct. 1602.]

[2] [There is authority for this in the register of the President of C. C. C. Oxford. "1573. Dec. 24. ".... quendam Ricdum Hooker "*viginti annorum* ætatis circiter "festum Paschæ proxime futur."]

[3] ["His great grandfather John "Hooker was mayor of Exeter "1490. Robert Hooker, esquire, "his grandfather, was mayor 1529." Dr. Bliss's note to Ath. Oxon. I. 693. "The family of Hoker was "highly respectable. John Hoker," mentioned above, "was of a wor- "shipful house and parentage, and "represented this city in parliament "during the several reigns of Edw. "IV., Rich. III., and Hen. VII. "As a magistrate he was distin- "guished for probity, learning, and "diligence: as a Christian and ci- "tizen, he was exemplary for good "conduct and abundant charities. "He was elected into the civic chair "in 1490, and died three years after,

forty[1]) was sanguine, with a mixture of choler; and yet, his motion was slow even in his youth, and so was his speech, never expressing an earnestness in either of them, but an humble gravity suitable to the aged. And it is observed (so far as inquiry is able to look back at this distance of time) that at his being a schoolboy he was an early questionist, quietly inquisitive, why this was, and that was not, to be remembered? why this was granted, and that denied? This being mixed with a remarkable modesty, and a sweet serene quietness of nature; and with them a quick apprehension of many perplext parts of learning imposed then upon him as a scholar, made his master and others to believe him to have an inward blessed divine light, and therefore to consider him to a little wonder. For in that, children were less pregnant, less confident, and more malleable, than in this wiser, but not better, age.

This meekness, and conjuncture of knowledge with modesty in his conversation, being observed by his schoolmaster, caused him to persuade his parents (who intended him for an apprentice) to continue him at school, till he could find out some means, by persuading his rich uncle, or some other charitable person, to ease them of a part of their care and charge; assuring them, that their son was so enriched with the blessings of nature and grace, that God seemed to single him out as a special instrument of His glory. And the good man told them also, that he would double his diligence in instructing

"Robert his son was the youngest of twenty, but lived to witness the successive deaths of all his brothers and sisters, and to inherit the whole of the family property. He was registrar of the archdeaconry of Barnstable, and 'became chief and principal of St. Mary the More's parish;' was a great peacemaker, and eminently zealous and attentive to the duties of first magistrate of his native city, in 1529. The pestilence which made such havoc in Exeter in 1537, numbered this Robert among its victims. His will is preserved in the corporation archives, and bears date 7 Aug. 1534, in which he makes provision for his wife Agnes, and seven children, Roger, Sydwell, Anne, Alice, Mary, Juliana, and John." (From the tenor of the will, it may be conjectured that all but the last were the issue of previous marriages. The details of the will evince much public spirit, and considerate benevolence.)

For the whole of this information, as well as the account of John Hooker, *alias* Vowell, in a subsequent note, the editor is indebted to the Rev. Mr. Oliver, of Exeter.]

[1] [About 1594, when he moved into Kent, and the Cranmer family, Walton's informants, became acquainted with him.]

him, and would neither expect nor receive any other reward than the content of so hopeful and happy an employment.

This was not unwelcome news, and especially to his mother, to whom he was a dutiful and dear child; and all parties were so pleased with this proposal, that it was resolved, so it should be. And in the mean time, his parents and master laid a foundation for his future happiness, by instilling into his soul the seeds of piety, those conscientious principles of loving and fearing God; of an early belief that he knows the very secrets of our souls; that he punisheth our vices, and rewards our innocence; that we should be free from hypocrisy, and appear to man what we are to God, because first or last the crafty man is catcht in his own snare. These seeds of piety were so seasonably planted, and so continually watered with the daily dew of God's blessed Spirit, that his infant-virtues grew into such holy habits, as did make him grow daily into more and more favour both with God and man; which, with the great learning that he did after attain to, hath made Richard Hooker honoured in this, and will continue him to be so to succeeding generations.

This good schoolmaster, whose name I am not able to recover, (and am sorry, for that I would have given him a better memorial in this humble monument, dedicated to the memory of his scholar[1],) was very solicitous with John Hooker[2], then chamberlain of Exeter, and uncle to our Richard, to take his nephew into his care, and to maintain him for one year in the university, and in the mean time to use his endeavours to procure an admission for him into some college, though it

---

[1] ["In 1561, the school is said to "have been new built, ceiled, and "seated, by a common contribu-"tion, at the request of *Mr. Wil-*"*liams*, the then master." Carlisle's Account of Endowed Grammar Schools, I. 271. tit. Exeter High School.]

[2] ["John Hoker, younger son of "Robert Hoker, by his wife Agnes "Doble, was born in Exeter about "1524. He was sent early to Oxford," either to Exeter college or C.C.C., "but whether he took a "degree, Wood was unable to as-"certain. Leaving the university, "he went to Strasburgh, and be-"came a pupil of Peter Martyr. "In 1555, after he had been some "years returned home, he was "elected first chamberlain of Exe-"ter: an office for which his MSS. "shew that he was admirably qua-"lified. Sir Peter Carew sent him "to Ireland to negotiate his private "affairs, and procured his election "as burgess for Athenry, in the "Irish parliament, 1568. He represented Exeter in the English "parliament of 1571. He married, "first Martha, daughter of Robert "Tucker, of Exeter, gentleman: "2dly, Anstice, daughter of Edward Bridgman. Prince says that

were but in a mean degree; still urging and assuring him, that his charge would not continue long; for the lad's learning and manners were both so remarkable, that they must of necessity be taken notice of; and that doubtless God would provide him some second patron, that would free him and his parents from their future care and charge.

These reasons, with the affectionate rhetorick of his good master, and God's blessing upon both, procured from his uncle a faithful promise, that he would take him into his care and charge before the expiration of the year following, which was performed by him, and with the assistance of the learned Mr. John Jewel; of whom this may be noted, that he left, or was, about the first of Queen Mary's reign, expelled out of, Corpus Christi college in Oxford, (of which he was a fellow,) for adhering to the truth of those principles of religion, to which he had assented and given testimony in the days of her brother and predecessor Edward the Sixth; and this John Jewel having within a short time after a just cause to fear a more heavy punishment than expulsion, was forced, by forsaking this, to seek safety in another nation; and, with that safety, the enjoyment of that doctrine and worship, for which he suffered.

But the cloud of that persecution and fear ending with the life of Queen Mary, the affairs of the church and state did then look more clear and comfortable; so that he, and with him many others of the same judgment, made a happy return into England about the first of Queen Elizabeth; in which year this John Jewel was sent a commissioner or visitor of the churches of the western parts of this kingdom, and especially

"he died in November 1601 : but "the entry of his successor's ap- "pointment, 15 Sept., states the "vacancy to have been made by "his death." But it is certain that he outlived his nephew Richard, for "his portrait in the council cham- "ber was taken in 1601, æt. 76. "In early life he used to sign him- "self John Vowell, *alias* Hoker : "but in late years, John Hoker, "*alias* Vowell."

The following portions of Holinshed's Chronicles were furnished by him : 1. An addition to the Chronicles of Ireland, from 1546 to 1586. 2. A Catalogue of the Bishops of Exeter. 3. A Translation of the Irish History of Giraldus, with notes : which he dedicated to Sir W. Raleigh. 4. A description of the city of Exeter, and of sundry assaults given to the same. "He also "took pains," says Wood, "in "augmenting and continuing to "the year 1586, the said first and "second volumes of Chronicles, "which were printed at London, "1587 :" Holinshed having died about 1580. Of his other writings, see an account in Prince's Worthies of Devon, 387, 8.]

of those in Devonshire, in which county he was born; and then and there he contracted a friendship with John Hooker, the uncle of our Richard[1].

About the second or third year of her reign, this John Jewel was made Bishop of Salisbury[2]; and there being always observed in him a willingness to do good, and to oblige his friends, and now a power added to this willingness: this John Hooker gave him a visit in Salisbury, and besought him for charity's sake to look favourably upon a poor nephew of his, whom nature had fitted for a scholar, but the estate of his parents was so narrow, that they were unable to give him the advantage of learning; and that the bishop would therefore become his patron, and prevent him from being a tradesman: for he was a boy of remarkable hopes. And though the bishop knew, men do not usually look with an indifferent eye upon their own children and relations, yet he assented so far to John Hooker, that he appointed the boy and his schoolmaster should attend him about Easter next following at that place; which was done accordingly; and then, after some questions and observations of the boy's learning, and gravity, and behaviour, the bishop gave his schoolmaster a reward, and took order for an annual pension for the boy's parents, promising also to take him into his care for a future preferment; which he performed; for, about the fifteenth[3] year of his age, which was *anno* 1567, he was by the bishop appointed to remove to Oxford, and there to attend Dr. Cole[4], then president of Corpus Christi college; which he

---

[1] [Their common intimacy with Peter Martyr would naturally make them friends when they met. The Commission is mentioned in Strype, Ann. I. i. 248; bearing date July 19, 1559.]

[2] [Consecrated January 21, 15$\frac{58}{59}$. Strype, An. I. i. 230. Park I. 127. Queen Elizabeth came to the throne Nov. 17, 1558. In the first edition it was "in the third year, &c."]

[3] [In the first edition it was "fourteenth."]

[4] ["1545, July 28, William Cole "made Scholar of C. C. C. 1568, "July 19, President." The latter date convicts Walton of a slight mistake in this passage. The following is Strype's account of Dr. Cole's election: "A notable visita-"tion of C. C. C. in Oxford hap-"pened this year. The occasion was "this: upon the avoidance of the "presidentship of that house, the "Queen sent letters to the fellows, "recommending Wm. Cole to their "choice to supply that place; a "sober and religious man, who had "been an exile under Queen Mary. "But notwithstanding, being well "affected towards popery, they re-"jected the Queen's letter, and "chose for their president one Ro-"bert Harrison, formerly of that "house, but gone from thence for "his favour to the Romish religion.

did; and Doctor Cole had (according to a promise made to the bishop) provided for him both a tutor (which was said to be the learned Doctor John Reynolds[1]) and a clerk's place[2] in that college: which place, though it were not a full maintenance, yet with the contribution of his uncle, and the continued pension of his patron, the good bishop, gave him a comfortable subsistence. And in this condition he continued unto the eighteenth year of his age, still increasing in learning and

"The Queen, hearing this, pronounced their election void, and again commanded them to elect Cole. But they still refused, urging that their former election was according to their consciences and their oaths. Soon after, Horn, Bishop of Winchester, their visitor, was sent down to place Cole, which he did; but first was fain to force the college gates, being shut against him." (In the next paragraph, by an oversight, a letter of this year's date on the state of the college is ascribed to George Cranmer, then only three years old.) Strype then proceeds; "Corpus Christi was procured by the Archbishop to be this year visited by commission from the Queen to the said Bishop of Winton, Secretary Cecil, Cooper, and Humfrey, doctors of divinity, and Geo. Ackworth, LL.D., an officer of the Archbishop's. Where lighter punishments were inflicted upon lesser crimes, and three notorious papists expelled, whose names were Reynolds, Windsor, and Napier." Strype, Parker, I. 528, 9.]

[1] ["John Reinolds was born in Devonshire 1549, made scholar of C. C. C. 1563. Ap. 29," (so that he was just B.A. when Hooker entered,) "President, by exchange of the deanery of Lincoln with Dr. Cole, December 14, 1598; died May 21, 1607." Fulman, from the President's Register. In t. ix. 168, he gives the following extract of a letter from Reynolds on the study of divinity, which is inserted here, as throwing light upon the principles on which Hooker's college education was conducted.

——"You shall doe well if in harder places you use the judgment of some godly writer, as Calvin and Peter Martyr, who have written best on the greatest part of the Old Testament.

"And because it is expedient to joyne the reading of some compend of scriptures, and summe of all divinity, together with the scriptures, I would wish you to travaile painfully in Calvin's Institution of Christian Religion, whereby you shall be greatly profited, not onely to the understanding of the scripture, whereof it is a brief and learned commentary, but also to the perceiving of poynts of doctrine, whither all things doe appertaine, and may of us be applied.

"* * * * touching noting, you know I doe not like the common custome of common places. The best in my judgment is, to note in the margent, or in some paper book for that purpose, the summe and method of that which you read. As for example sake, Mr. Bunny hath done very well in Calvin's Institutions, shewing all his method, and summe of every section in his Compendio etc. which book you may well joyne with the reading of Calvin, to understand his order and method the better."

See also the Appendix to the Life of Hooker, No. II. Of Bunney, see A. O. II. 219.]

[2 His name appears in lists of poor scholars (among them E. Spenser and L. Andrewes) helped by a London citizen, Thos. Nowell (1571-75). Cf. *Spending of T. Nowell*, ed. by Dr. Grosart, p. xxii, and pp. 220-226.]

prudence, and so much in humility and piety, that he seemed to be filled with the Holy Ghost, and even like St. John Baptist, to be sanctified from his mother's womb, who did often bless the day in which she bare him.

About this time of his age he fell into a dangerous sickness, which lasted two months: all which time his mother, having notice of it, did in her hourly prayers as earnestly beg his life of God, as the mother of St. Augustin did[1] that he might become a true Christian; and their prayers were both so heard, as to be granted. Which Mr. Hooker would often mention with much joy, "and as often pray that he might "never live to occasion any sorrow to so good a mother; of "whom, he would often say, he loved her so dearly, that he "would endeavour to be good, even as much for her's, as for "his own sake."

As soon as he was perfectly recovered from this sickness, he took a journey from Oxford to Exeter, to satisfy and see his good mother, being accompanied with a countryman and companion of his own college, and both on foot; which was then either more in fashion, or want of money, or their humility made it so: but on foot they went, and took Salisbury in their way, purposely to see the good bishop, who made Mr. Hooker and his companion dine with him at his own table; which Mr. Hooker boasted of with much joy and gratitude when he saw his mother and friends: and at the bishop's parting with him, the bishop gave him good counsel, and his benediction, but forgot to give him money; which when the bishop had considered, he sent a servant in all haste to call Richard back to him; and at Richard's return, the bishop said to him, "Richard, I sent for you back "to lend you a horse which hath carried me many a mile, "and, I thank God, with much ease;" and presently delivered into his hand a walking staff, with which he professed he had travelled through many parts of Germany[2]. And he said, "Richard, I do not give, but lend you my horse; be sure you "be honest, and bring my horse back to me at your return "this way to Oxford. And I do now give you ten groats[3] to

---

[1] [Confess. lib. III. 11, 12.]

[2] [He was lame, and had suffered much by long journeys on foot. See Dr. Wordsworth's Eccl. Biog. IV. 21, 25, 30.]

[3] ["It is well known that pieces "of ten groats, or 3s. 4d. were cur-"rent at this time." Dr. Zouch.]

"bear your charges to Exeter; and here is ten groats more,
"which I charge you to deliver to your mother, and tell her,
"I send her a bishop's benediction with it, and beg the con-
"tinuance of her prayers for me. And if you bring my horse
"back to me, I will give you ten groats more, to carry you
"on foot to the college: and so God bless you, good Richard."

And this, you may believe, was performed by both parties. But, alas! the next news that followed Mr. Hooker to Oxford was, that his learned and charitable patron had changed this for a better life[1]. Which may be believed, for that as he lived, so he died, in devout meditation and prayer; and in both so zealously, that it became a religious question, Whether his last ejaculations, or his soul, did first enter into heaven[2]?

And now Mr. Hooker became a man of sorrow and fear: of sorrow, for the loss of so dear and comfortable a patron; and of fear, for his future subsistence. But Mr. Cole raised his spirits from this dejection, by bidding him go cheerfully to his studies, and assuring him he should neither want food nor raiment, (which was the utmost of his hopes,) for he would become his patron.

And so he was for about nine months, and not longer; for about that time, this following accident did befall Mr Hooker.

Edwin Sandys (sometime bishop of London, and after Archbishop of York[3]) had also been in the days of Queen Mary forced, by forsaking this, to seek safety in another nation; where for some[4] years Bishop Jewel and he were companions at bed and board in Germany; and where, in this their exile, they did often eat the bread of sorrow, and by that means they there began such a friendship as lasted till the death of Bishop Jewel, which was in September 1571.

---

[1] [Bishop Jewel died 23 Sept. 1571. See his monument in Salisbury cathedral.]

[2] ["It is hard to say, whether "his soul, or his ejaculations ar-"rived first in heaven, seeing he "prayed dying, and died praying." Quoted by Doctor Zouch from Fuller, Ch. Hist. ix. 102.]

[3] [Installed bishop of London, July 20, 1570. (Strype, Grind. 242.) archbishop of York, March 13, 157$\frac{6}{7}$. (Str. An. II. 2, 42.)]

[4] [Originally, "many years." Now Jewel came to Frankfort in the summer of 1554, and found Sandys there, (E. B. IV. 30,) and continued with him, there and at Strasburgh, till July 1556, when Jewel went with P. Martyr to Zurich, (ibid. 34,) but Sandys returned to Frankfort. See Troubles at Frankfort, in Phœnix, II. 170, 119, 121.]

A little before which time the two bishops meeting, Jewel began a story of his Richard Hooker, and in it gave such a character of his learning and manners, that though Bishop Sandys was educated in Cambridge, where he had obliged and had many friends; yet his resolution was, that his son Edwin, should be sent to Corpus Christi college, in Oxford, and by all means be pupil to Mr. Hooker, though his son Edwin was not much younger than Mr. Hooker then was: for, the bishop said, "I will have a tutor for my son, that "shall teach him learning by instruction, and virtue by ex-"ample; and my greatest care shall be of the last; and (God "willing) this Richard Hooker shall be the man into whose "hands I will commit my Edwin." And the bishop did so about twelve months, or not much longer[1], after this resolution.

And doubtless as to these two a better choice could not be made; for Mr. Hooker was now in the nineteenth year of his age; had spent five in the university; and had by a constant unwearied diligence attained unto a perfection in all the learned languages; by the help of which, an excellent tutor[2], and his unintermitted studies, he had made the subtilty of all the arts easy and familiar to him, and useful for the discovery of such learning as lay hid from common searchers; so that by these added to his great reason, and his industry added to both, he did not only know more of causes and effects; but what he knew, he knew better than other men. And with this knowledge he had a most blessed and clear method of demonstrating what he knew, to the great advantage of all his pupils, (which in time were many,) but especially to his two first, his dear Edwin Sandys, and his as dear George Cranmer[3]; of which there will be a fair testimony in the ensuing relation.

---

[1] [The words "or not much "longer" were added by Walton on revisal.]

[2] [Bishop Hall to Bishop Bedel, at Venice: "Since your departure "from us, Reynolds is departed "from the world . . . . . He alone "was a well furnisht library, full "of all faculties, of all studies, of "all learning. The memory, the "reading, of that man were near to "a miracle." Quoted by Dr. Zouch, from Hall's Epist. Dec. I. Ep. 7.]

[3] [Edwin Sandys born Dec. 1560. or 1561; made scholar of C. C. C. 1577, Sept. 16. President's Register. George Cranmer born Oct. 14, 1565; scholar of C. C. C. Jan. 10, 157⅞, but not then sworn by reason of extreme youth. Ibid. Sandys

This for Mr. Hooker's learning. And for his behaviour, amongst other testimonies this still remains of him, that in four years he was but twice absent from the chapel-prayers; and that his behaviour there was such as shewed an awful reverence of that God which he then worshipped and prayed to; giving all outward testimonies that his affections were set on heavenly things. This was his behaviour towards God; and for that to man, it is observable that he was never known to be angry, or passionate, or extreme in any of his desires; never heard to repine or dispute with Providence, but, by a quiet gentle submission and resignation of his will to the wisdom of his Creator, bore the burthen of the day with patience; never heard to utter an uncomely word; and by this, and a grave behaviour, which is a divine charm, he begot an early reverence unto his person, even from those that at other times, and in other companies, took a liberty to cast off that strictness of behaviour and discourse that is required in a collegiate life. And when he took any liberty to be pleasant, his wit was never blemished with scoffing, or the utterance of any conceit that bordered upon, or might beget a thought of looseness in his hearers. Thus mild, thus innocent and exemplary was his behaviour in his college; and thus this good man continued till his death, still increasing in learning, in patience, and piety.

In this nineteenth year of his age, he was, December 24, 1573, admitted to be one of the twenty scholars of the foundation[1]; being elected and so admitted as born in Devon or Hantshire, out of which counties a certain number are to be elected in vacancies by the founder's statutes[2]. And now, as he was much encouraged, so now he was perfectly incorporated into this beloved college, which was then noted for an eminent library, strict students, and remarkable scholars. And indeed it may glory, that it had Cardinal Poole,

then was but 11 or 12, Cranmer but 7 or 8, when they were first put under Hooker's care: Cranmer being akin to him.]

[[1] B.A. Jan. 14, 157¾. Note in Clarendon Press Series, Hooker, p. xxvii.]

[2] ["Natum in comitat. Devo-"niensi, elect. pro comitat. South." Regist. C. C. C. In the same register, ten leaves further on, at the bottom of the page is the following marginal note: "Hooker migrat in "dioc. Exon. per electionem Bod-"ley in *scholarem*." Milo Bodley was a Devonshire scholar, (in the style of the statutes, *discipulus*,) admitted Aug. 6, 1562, who being now made probationer fellow, (*scholaris*,) made room for Hooker, who was still only a *discipulus*, to be reckoned on his own county.]

but more, that it had Bishop Jewel, Dr. John Reynolds, and Dr. Thomas Jackson, of that foundation[1]. The first famous for his learned Apology for the Church of England, and his Defence of it against Harding. The second, for the learned and wise menage of a public dispute with John Hart (of the Romish persuasion) about the head and faith of the church, then printed by consent of both parties. And the third, for his most excellent Exposition of the Creed, and other treatises: all, such as have given greatest satisfaction to men of the greatest learning. Nor was Doctor Jackson more noteworthy for his learning, than for his strict and pious life, testified by his abundant love and meekness and charity to all men.

And in the year 1576, Febr. 23, Mr. Hooker's grace was given him for Inceptor of Arts; Dr. Herbert Westphaling, a man of note for learning, being then vice-chancellor; and the act following he was completed Master[2]; which was anno 1577, his patron Doctor Cole being vice-chancellor that year, and his dear friend Henry Savill of Merton College being then one of the proctors. It was that Henry Savill that was after Sir Henry Savill, Warden of Merton college, and Provost of Eton: he which founded in Oxford two famous lectures, and endowed them with liberal maintenance. It was that Sir Henry Savill, that translated and enlightened the History of Cornelius Tacitus with a most excellent comment; and enriched the world by his laborious and chargeable collecting the scattered pieces of S. Chrysostome, and the publication of them in one entire body in Greek; in which language he was a most judicious critick. It was this Sir Henry Savill, that had the happiness to be a contemporary, and familiar friend to Mr. Hooker, and let posterity know it.

---

[1] ["1523, Feb. 14, Reginald Poole "made fellow of C. C. C.; 1539, Aug. "19, John Jewel, made scholar; "1596, March 24, Thomas Jack"son, scholar." From the President's Register.]

[2] [Fulman, MSS. t. VIII. p. 1, inserts from the Convocation book, "1577, Comitiis, Julii 8ᵛᵒ, Magistri "in Facultate Artium 100, (Dudley "Cancellario, Westfaling Vice-can"cellario) inter quos Rich. Hooker, "Corp. Chr. ... Gulielm. Cole, post"rid. Comit. Vice-cancell." In IX. 85, he says, "Gul. Cole, Vice-can"cellarius, e collegio nostro primus, "et usque hodie solus, 1572, 3."

Dr. Westphaling was then canon of Ch. Ch. His name appears (1582) in the list of divines especially commissioned to confer with recusants. Strype, Whitg. I. 198. His consecration as Bishop of Hereford, 158¾, ib. 467.]

And in this year of 1577, he was so happy as to be admitted fellow of the college[1]: happy also in being the contemporary and friend of that Dr. John Reynolds, of whom I have lately spoken, and of Dr. Spencer; both which were after, and successively, made Presidents of Corpus Christi college[2]: men of great learning and merit, and famous in their generations.

Nor was Mr. Hooker more happy in his contemporaries of his time and college, than in the pupilage and friendship of his Edwin Sandys and George Cranmer, of whom my reader may note, that this Edwin Sandys was after Sir Edwin Sandys, and as famous for his *Speculum Europæ*[3], as his brother George for making posterity beholden to his pen by a learned Relation and Comment on his dangerous and remarkable travels; and for his harmonious Translation of the Psalms of David, the Book of Job, and other poetical parts of Holy Writ, into most high and elegant verse. And for Cranmer, his other pupil, I shall refer my reader to the printed testimonies of our learned Mr. Camden, of Fines Morison, and others[4].

" This Cranmer, (says Mr. Camden, in his Annals of Queen
" Elizabeth[5],) whose Christian name was George, was a gen-
" tleman of singular hopes, the eldest son of Thomas Cranmer,
" son of Edmund Cranmer, the archbishop's brother: he spent
" much of his youth in Corpus Christi college in Oxford,
" where he continued master of arts for some time before he
" removed, and then betook himself to travel, accompanying
" that worthy gentleman Sir Edwin Sandys into France,
" Germany, and Italy, for the space of three years; and after
" their happy return he betook himself to an employment

---

[1] [" 1577, Sept. 16. Mr. Bar-"foote, Vice-præs. admisit Ric. Hooker in Artib. Magistrum æt. annor. 23, circiter fest. Pasch. ultimo præterit. nat. in dioc. Exon. elect. pro com. *Surriensi*." Regist. C. C. C.]

[2] [1598, Dec. 14, John Reinolds made President of C. C. C.; 1607, Jun. 9. John Spenser, ditto. Ibid.]

[3] [" Europæ Speculum: or, a View or Survey of the State of Religion in the Western Parts of the World; wherein the Roman religion, and the frequent policies of the church of Rome to support the same, are notably displayed; with some other memorable discoveries and memorations. Hagæ Comitis, 1629."]

[4] [The first edition added the name of the Lord Totness. The passage in Morison's Itinerary is in part ii. p. 83, 84.]

[5] [As translated by R. N. Lond. 1635, with additions by the author. See Major's edition of Walton's Lives, p. 443.]

"under Secretary Davison[1], a privy counsellor of note, who
"for an unhappy undertaking, became clouded and pitied;
"after whose fall, he went in place of secretary with Sir Henry
"Killegrew in his embassage into France; and after his death
"he was sought after by the most noble Lord Mountjoy, with
"whom he went into Ireland, where he remained until in a
"battle against the rebels near Carlingford, an unfortunate
"wound put an end both to his life and the great hopes that
"were conceived of him[2]: he being then but in the thirty-
"sixth year of his age[3]."

Betwixt Mr. Hooker, and these his two pupils, there was a sacred friendship; a friendship made up of religious principles, which increased daily by a similitude of inclinations to the same recreations and studies; a friendship elemented in youth, and in an university, free from self-ends, which the friendships of age usually are not: and in this sweet, this blessed, this spiritual amity they went on for many years: and, as the holy Prophet saith, so "they took sweet counsel "together, and walked in the house of God as friends." By which means they improved this friendship to such a degree of holy amity as bordered upon heaven: a friendship so sacred, that when it ended in this world, it began in that next, where it shall have no end.

And, though this world cannot give any degree of pleasure equal to such a friendship, yet, obedience to parents, and a desire to know the affairs, manners, laws, and learning of other nations, that they might thereby become the more serviceable unto their own, made them put off their gowns, and leave the college and Mr. Hooker to his studies; in which he was daily more assiduous: still enriching his quiet and capacious soul with the precious learning of the philosophers, casuists, and schoolmen; and with them, the foundation and reason of all laws, both sacred and civil; and indeed, with such other learning as lay most remote from the track of

---

[1] ["He proceeded M.A. 1589, "two years after Davison's fall." Fulman.]

[2] ["Our author Cranmer hath "written other things, as I have "heard Mr. Walton say, but [they] "are kept private to the great pre-"judice of the public." Wood, Ath. Oxon. I. 700.]

[3] [This is taken, with certain corrections, from an advertisement prefixed to Cranmer's Letter on the Discipline, when it first appeared, 1642.]

common studies. And as he was diligent in these, so he seemed restless in searching the scope and intention of God's Spirit revealed to mankind in the sacred scripture: for the understanding of which, he seemed to be assisted by the same Spirit with which they were written; He *that regardeth truth in the inward parts,* making him to *understand wisdom secretly.* And the good man would often say, that "God abhors con-"fusion as contrary to his nature;" and as often say, that "the scripture was not writ to beget disputations and pride, "and opposition to government; but moderation, charity, and "humility, obedience to authority, and peace to mankind: "of which virtues," he would as often say, "no man did ever "repent himself upon his death-bed." And, that this was really his judgment, did appear in his future writings, and in all the actions of his life. Nor was this excellent man a stranger to the more light and airy parts of learning, as musick and poetry; all which he had digested, and made useful; and of all which the reader will have a fair testimony, in what will follow.

In the year 1579, the chancellor of the university[1] was given to understand, that the public Hebrew lecture was not read according to the statutes; nor could be, by reason of a distemper that had then seized the brain of Mr. Kingsmill[2], who was to read it; so that it lay long unread, to the great detriment of those that were studious of that language: therefore, the chancellor writ to his vice-chancellor, and the university, that he had heard such commendations of the excellent knowledge of Mr. Richard Hooker in that tongue, that he desired he might be procured to read it: and he did, and continued to do so, till he left Oxford.

Within three months after his undertaking this lecture (namely, in October 1579[3]) he was, with Dr. Reynolds and others, expelled his college; and this letter, transcribed from Dr. Reynolds his own hand, may give some account of it.

[1] [The Earl of Leicester's letter to this effect is extracted by Fulman from the convocation register, July 14, 1579. MSS. VIII. 183.]

[2] [Thomas Kingsmill, fellow of Magd. Coll. was Regius Professor of Hebrew from 1569 to 1591.]

[3] [Probably 1580. See note 1, p. 20.]

To Sir Francis Knolles[1].

"I am sorry, right honourable, that I am enforced to make
"unto you such a suit, the which, I cannot move it, but I
"must complain of the unrighteous dealing of one of our
"college; who hath taken upon him, against all law and
"reason, to expel out of our house both me and Mr. Hooker,
"and three other of our fellows, for doing that which by oath
"we were bound to do. Our matter must be heard before

---

[1] [This letter has been collated with a copy in Fulman's MSS. IX. 180. He probably furnished Walton with it. In p. 182 he says, "It should seem that in October "1580, J. B. took occasion to ex-"pel J. R. and others: though I "once thought it to be in 1579, "and so told Mr. Walton, who "thereupon added the year, which "was not in the copy, but in the "margin:" probably he means the margin of the above letter. The same day, Reynolds wrote as follows to Walsingham:
(Fulman, IX. 174.) "Non pu-"taram futurum unquam, illus-"trissime Walsinghame, ut cujus "benevolentiam in meis commodis "procurandis expertus essem, ejus "auxilium ad injurias depellendas "implorare cogerer. Verum unius "hominis impotens ambitio, dum "omnia perrumpit jura, quo velifi-"cetur cupiditati suæ, si me solum, "esset levius, sed una quinque "nostrum e collegio ejecit: quam "injuste non dico; relinquo judici "decidendum Episcopo Wintoni-"ensi; quem et leges nostræ nobis "in controversiis judicem esse "volunt, et æquum fore judicem, "ipsius religio, fides, probitas per-"suadent. Veruntamen, quia nobis "insultant adversarii præoccupatum "esse animum episcopi, et obvalla-"tum ita, ut nullum vel locum vel "aditum relicturus sit querelis nos-"tris: a tua dignitate suppliciter "rogamus ut eum per literas sol-"licitare digneris, ne sinat legitimæ "defensionis locum nobis inter-"cludi. Non petimus ut locis "restituamur pristinis, quibus su-"mus ejecti. Nam ea, si jure "judicabimur amisisse, neque de-"sideramus, neque possumus acci-"pere, licet offerantur ultro, quia "vetamur jurejurando. Justitiam, "justitiam petimus et æquitatem; "petimus ut audiatur, ut expenda-"tur causa nostra: ne veritas calum-"niis, potentia jus opprimatur. Si, "quæ sunt facta, jure sunt facta: "causam non dicimus quin maneant "immota. Sin et per injuriam est "in nos grassatus, et quod per "scelus ausus est id per vim obti-"nebit: nos quidem feremus ut "poterimus, neque dubitamus quin "Deus patientiæ et consolationis, "cum æquos nobis animos, tum "mali solatia sit daturus. Sed "collegium nostrum in sordibus "erit et mœrore. Sed Academia "nostra lugebit casum suorum ci-"vium. Sed illi quibus pietas, "quibus conscientia, quibus virtus "est curæ, causam justissimam ab "iniquissima de gradu dejici lamen-"tabuntur. Verum ista ne eve-"niant in tua, Vir illustrissime, "multum est manu. Quem in "finem duo sunt quæ abs te peti-"mus: unum, ut Episcopum Win-"toniensem per literas interpelles, "ne patiatur injuria nos opprimi; "examinetur res in judicio, agamus "causam utrique suam, ferat pal-"mam justitia, cedat victoria veritati. "Alterum, ut nobilissimum comi-"tem Varvicensem placatum mihi "reddas: quo nesciente, sine dubio, "rei iniquitatem, hæc injuria nobis "facta est; ut Chrysogonus libertus "Syllæ Sextum Roscium oppressit

"the Bishop of Winchester[1], with whom I do not doubt but
"we shall find equity. Howbeit, forasmuch as some of our
"adversaries have said, that the bishop is already forestalled,
"and will not give us such audience as we do look for;
"therefore I am humbly to beseech your honour, that you
"will desire the bishop by your letters to let us have justice;
"though it be with rigour, so it be justice: our cause is so
"good, that I am sure we shall prevail by it. Thus much
"I am bold to request of your honour for Corpus Christi
"college sake, or rather for Christ's sake; whom I beseech to
"bless you with daily increase of His manifold gifts, and the
"blessèd graces of His Holy Spirit.

"Your Honour's,
"in Christ to command,
"JOHN RAINOLDES."

"London, October 9, 1579."

This expulsion was by Dr. John Barfoote[2], then vice-president of the college, and chaplain to Ambrose earl of Warwick. I cannot learn the pretended cause; but, that they were restored the same month is most certain.

"imprudente L. Sylla. Atque uti-
"nam ex te cognoscat quam sim
"integer ab eo scelere, quod inimici
"mei apud illum impingunt falso,
"quo generosum viri nobilis ani-
"mum in me inflamment: me
"facere quæ facio, non æquitatis
"studio, non legum tuendarum,
"non collegii nostri: sed ut ejus
"voluntati ac studio resistam, et
"quasi triumphum de eo reportem.
"Deus, qui revelabit arcana cordi-
"um, mihi testis est, has voces
"sceleratas esse calumnias; et veniet
"tempus, veniet, quum hoc venenum
"aspidum sub labiis iniquorum da-
"bit justus Judex ipsis ebibendum.
"Meas itaque petitiones æquitate
"causæ nostræ subnixas, tuæ am-
"plitudini: tuam amplitudinem et
"universæ causæ nostræ successum
"Dei gratiæ commendo. Londini,
"9 Octobr."
In the same volume, fol. 85,

Fulman has the following entry:
"Great expectation of Dr. Cole re-
"signing, first in favour of J. Bar-
"foote, afterwards of J. Reynolds,
"1580:" (the date of Hooker's expulsion.)]
[1] [If Oct. 1579 be the right date of this letter, the bishop here meant is Horn: if 1580, his successor, Watson. Strype, Grindal, 380.]
[2] [Fulm. X. 68. says of him, "Natus in agro Hantoniensi, circa "Festum Purificationis $154\frac{7}{8}$; æt. "16, admiss. in Discip. Feb. 5, "$156\frac{8}{9}$; Scholaris 1566. Dec. 13; "Ambrosio Comiti Warwicensi a "sacris; cujus auctoritate Archi-"diaconus Lincolniensis, Apr. 1, "1581. Ob. 1595." Bishop Cooper made him archdeacon. See a report from him to Archbishop Whitgift, of his peremptory dealings with some puritan ministers, in Strype, Ann. III. 1, 349.]

I return to Mr. Hooker in his college, where he continued his studies in all quietness for the space of three years[1]; about which time, he entered into sacred orders, being then made Deacon and Priest; and, not long after, was appointed to preach at St. Paul's Cross[2].

In order to which sermon, to London he came, and immediately to the Shunammite's house; (which is a house so called, for that, besides the stipend paid the preacher, there is provision made also for his lodging and diet for two days before, and one day after his sermon.) This house was then kept by John Churchman, sometime a draper of good note in Watling-street, upon whom poverty had at last come like an armed man, and brought him into a necessitous condition: which, though it be a punishment, is not always an argument of God's disfavour, for he was a virtuous man: I shall not yet give the like testimony of his wife, but leave the reader to judge by what follows. But to this house Mr. Hooker came so wet, so weary, and weatherbeaten, that he was never known to express more passion, than against a friend that dissuaded him from footing it to London, and for finding him no easier an horse; supposing the horse trotted, when he did not: and at this time also, such a faintness and fear possest him, that he would not be persuaded two days' rest and quietness, or any other means could be used to make him able to preach his Sunday's sermon; but a warm bed, and rest, and drink, proper for a cold, given him by Mrs. Churchman, and her diligent attendance added unto it, enabled him to perform the office of the day, which was in or about the year 1581.

And in this first public appearance to the world, he was not so happy as to be free from exceptions against a point of doctrine delivered in his sermon, which was "That in "God there were two wills; an antecedent, and a consequent "will: his first will, that all mankind should be saved; but "his second will was, that those only should be saved, that "did live answerable to that degree of grace which he had

---

[1] [Corrected, by Walton, from "three *or more* years."]
[2] [Altered from, "in obedience "to the college statutes he was to "preach either at St. Peter's, Oxford, or at St. Paul's Cross, "London; and the last fell to his "allotment."]

"offered, or afforded them[1]." This seemed to cross a late opinion of Mr. Calvin's, and then taken for granted by many that had not a capacity to examine it, as it had been by him before, and hath been since by Master Henry Mason[2], Dr. Jackson[3], Dr. Hammond[4], and others of great learning, who believed that a contrary opinion entrenches upon the honour and justice of our merciful God. How he justified this, I will not undertake to declare: but it was not excepted against (as Mr. Hooker declares in his rational answer to Mr. Travers) by John Elmer[5], then Bishop of London, at this time one of his auditors, and at last one of his advocates too, when Mr. Hooker was accused for it[6].

But the justifying of this doctrine did not prove of so bad consequence, as the kindness of Mrs. Churchman's curing him of his late distemper and cold; for that was so gratefully[7] apprehended by Mr. Hooker, that he thought himself bound in conscience to believe all that she said: so that the good man came to be persuaded by her, "that he was a man of

---

[1] [See E. P. v. 49, and Fragment III. of the Answer to "A Christian "Letter," &c. In 1595, Dr. Baro, Margaret Professor of Divinity at Cambridge, was attacked for preaching the same doctrine almost in the same words. Strype, Whitgift, II. 298. and III. 347.]

[2] [First of Brasennose college, Oxford, afterwards chaplain of C.C.C. and by Bishop King, of London, made rector of St. Andrew's Undershaft; from which being expelled in 1641, he retired to Wigan, his native place, and died there in August 1647, aged about 74. The treatise of his referred to by Walton is "Certain passages in "Mr. Sam. Hoard's book, entitled, "God's Love to mankind mani-"fested by disproving His absolute "decree for their damnation." It was answered by Dr. Twiss in 1653. See Wood's Ath. Oxon. III. 220, 172.]

[3] [Works, II. 173, 202. III. 793. ed. 1673.]

[4] [In his Letters to Dr. Sanderson, on God's Grace and Decrees, Works I. 663, &c. and especially Letter I. §. 28 .... 51, 70 .. 72. and Third Letter of Prescience, §. 58. ed. 1684.]

[5] [By whose nomination probably Hooker preached: "it having been "of long time customary for the "Bishops of London to summon "up from the universities, or else-"where, persons of the best abilities "to preach those public sermons, "whither the Prince and court, and "the magistrates of the city, besides "a vast conflux of people, used to "resort." Strype, Life of Aylmer, 201.]

[6] [This may refer to the year 1584/5, when Hooker was made Master of the Temple, partly by the recommendation of Bishop Aylmer. Strype, Ann. III. I, 352: although in Whitg. I. 344. he says, "Sandys, Bishop of Lon-"don."]

[7] [In the register of C. C. C. is the following; an instance, probably, of Hooker's gratitude: "1581, 21 "Jun. Ego Gulielmus *Churchman* "vicesimo primo Junii admissus "sum et juratus in subsacristam "hujus collegii."]

"a tender constitution;" and "that it was best for him "to have a wife, that might prove a nurse to him; such "an one as might both prolong his life, and make it more "comfortable; and such an one she could and would pro- "vide for him, if he thought fit to marry." And he not considering that "the children of this world are wiser in "their generation than the children of light;" but, like a true Nathanael, fearing no guile, because he meant none, did give her such a power as Eleazar was trusted with, (you may read it in the book of Genesis,) when he was sent to choose a wife for Isaac; for, even so he trusted her to choose for him, promising upon a fair summons to return to London, and accept of her choice; and he did so in that or about the year following. Now the wife provided for him, was her daughter Joan, who brought him neither beauty nor portion; and for her conditions, they were too like that wife's, which is by Solomon compared to "a dripping house[1]:" so that the good man had no reason to "rejoice in the wife of his "youth," but too just cause to say with the holy Prophet, "Wo is me, that I am constrained to have my habitation in "the tents of Kedar!"

This choice of Mr. Hooker's (if it were his choice) may be wondered at; but let us consider that the prophet Ezekiel says, "There is a wheel within a wheel;" a secret sacred wheel of Providence (most visible in marriages), guided by his hand, that "allows not the race to the swift," nor "bread "to the wise," nor good wives to good men: and he that can bring good out of evil (for mortals are blind to this reason) only knows why this blessing was denied to patient Job, to meek Moses[2], and to our as meek and patient Mr. Hooker. But so it was; and let the reader cease to wonder, for "afflic- "tion is a divine diet;" which, though it be not pleasing to mankind, yet Almighty God hath often, very often imposed it as good, though bitter physick to those children whose souls are dearest to him.

---

[1] [Proverbs xix. 13. "The con-"tentions of a wife are a continual "dropping."]

[2] [Originally "*as some think*, to "meek Moses." Why the altera-tion was made is not clear, especially considering Hooker's own interpretation of the place in scripture here referred to. See E. P. v. c. 62. par. 24.]

And by this marriage the good man was drawn from the tranquillity of his college[1]; from that garden of piety, of pleasure, of peace, and a sweet conversation, into the thorny wilderness of a busy world; into those corroding cares that attend a married priest, and a country parsonage; which was Draiton Beauchamp in Buckinghamshire (not far from Ailesbury, and in the diocese of Lincoln); to which he was presented by John Cheny, esq. then patron of it, the 9th of December 1584, where he behaved himself so as to give no occasion of evil, but (as St. Paul adviseth a minister of God) "in much patience, in afflictions, in anguishes, in necessities; "in poverty, and no doubt in long-suffering;" yet troubling no man with his discontents and wants.

And in this condition he continued about a year, in which time his two pupils, Edwin Sandys and George Cranmer[2], took a journey to see their tutor; where they found him with a book in his hand (it was the Odes of Horace), he being then, like humble and innocent Abel, tending his small allotment of sheep in a common field, which he told his pupils he was forced to do then, for that his servant was gone home to dine, and assist his wife to do some necessary household business. When his servant returned and released him, then his two pupils attended him unto his house, where their best entertainment was his quiet company, which was presently denied them; for "Richard was called to rock the cradle[3];" and the rest of their welcome was so like this, that they stayed but till the next morning, which was time enough to discover and pity their tutor's condition; and they having in that time rejoiced in the remembrance, and then paraphrased on many

---

[1] [The college at that time was less tranquil than usual: as might be expected after the strong measures taken in 1568. Mr. Fulman's papers contain many instances, besides those which have been adduced, of the turbulence and faction by which it was long infested.]

[2] [Originally, "were returned from "travel, and took a journey," &c. Now it appears from Fulman's papers, vol. VIII. that Sandys was made regent M. A. July 8, 1583; Cranmer, not till July 13, 1589. This seems to shew that they went abroad together *after* their visit to Hooker, and of course confirms Walton's correction.]

[3] ["This narrative reminds me "of a domestic picture in the Life "of Melancthon, who was seen by "one of his friends with one hand "rocking the cradle of his child, "with the other holding a book." Zouch, Life of Walton, subjoined to Walton's Lives, II. p. 370, note.]

of the innocent recreations of their younger days, and other like diversions, and thereby given him as much present comfort as they were able, they were forced to leave him to the company of his wife Joan, and seek themselves a quieter lodging for next night. But at their parting from him, Mr. Cranmer said, "Good tutor, I am sorry your lot is fallen in "no better ground as to your parsonage: and more sorry "that your wife proves not a more comfortable companion "after you have wearied yourself in your restless studies." To whom the good man replied, " My dear George, if saints "have usually a double share in the miseries of this life, I "that am none, ought not to repine at what my wise Creator "hath appointed for me, but labour (as indeed I do daily) to "submit mine to his will, and possess my soul in patience and " peace."

At their return to London, Edwin Sandys acquaints his father[1], who was then Archbishop of York, with his tutor's sad condition, and solicits for his removal to some benefice that might give him a more quiet and a more comfortable subsistence; which his father did most willingly grant him, when it should next fall into his power. And not long after this time, which was in the year 1585[2], Mr. Alvie (Master of the Temple) died, who was a man of a strict life, of great learning, and of so venerable behaviour, as to gain so high a degree of love and reverence from all men, that he was generally known by the name of Father Alvie. And at the Temple reading, next after the death of this Father Alvie, he the said Archbishop of York being then at dinner with the judges, the reader and benchers of that society, met with a general condolement for the death of Father Alvie, and with a high commendation of his saint-like life, and of his great merit both towards God and man; and as they bewailed his death, so they wished for a like pattern of virtue and learning to succeed him. And here came in a fair occasion for the bishop to commend Mr. Hooker to Father Alvie's place, which he did with so effectual an earnestness, and that seconded with so many other testimonies of his worth, that Mr. Hooker

---

[1] [Corrected from "then bishop "of London, and after archbi-"shop."]

[2] He was dead, and the place void in the month of August, anno 1584. J. S. [John Strype.]

was sent for from Draiton Beauchamp to London, and there the mastership of the Temple proposed unto him by the bishop, as a greater freedom from his country cares, the advantage of a better society, and a more liberal pension than his country parsonage did afford him. But these reasons were not powerful enough to incline him to a willing acceptance of it: his wish was rather to gain a better country living, where he might "see God's blessing spring out of the earth, and be "free from noise" (so he exprest the desire of his heart), "and eat that bread which he might more properly call his "own in privacy and quietness." But, notwithstanding this averseness, he was at last persuaded to accept of the bishop's proposal; and was by patent for life made Master of the Temple the 17th of March, 1585[1], he being then in the thirty-fourth year of his age.

[2][But before any mention was made of Mr. Hooker for this place, two other divines were nominated to succeed Alvey; whereof Mr. Walter Travers, a disciplinarian in his judgment and practice, and preacher here in the afternoons, was chief, and recommended by Alvey himself on his deathbed, to be master after him: and no marvel, for Alvey's and Travers's principles did somewhat correspond. And many gentlemen of the house desired him; which desire the lord treasurer Burghley was privy to, and by their request, and his own inclination towards him, being a good preacher, he moved the queen to allow of him; for the disposal of the place was in her. But Archbishop Whitgift knew the man, and his hot temper and principles, from the time he was fellow in Trinity college, and had observed his steps ever after: he knew how turbulently he had carried himself at the college, how he had disowned the English established church and episcopacy, and went to Geneva, and afterwards to Antwerp,

Endeavours for Travers to be Master of the Temple.

---

[1] This you may find in the Temple records. William Ermstead was Master of the Temple at the dissolution of the priory, and died 2 Eliz.
Richard Alvey, Bat. Divinity, Pat. 13 Feb. 2 Eliz. *Magister sive Custos Domus et Ecclesiæ novi Templi;* died 27 Eliz.
Richard Hooker succeeded that year by patent, *in terminis,* as Alvey had it, and he left it 33 Eliz.
That year Dr. Balgey succeeded Richard Hooker. [The year meant by Walton is no doubt 158$\frac{4}{5}$.]

[2] [The portions between brackets are the additions of Mr. Strype, who revised the Life of Hooker for the edition of his works printed 1705.]

to be ordained minister, as he was by Villers[1] and Cartwright and others, the heads of a congregation there; and so came back again more confirmed for the discipline. And knowing how much the doctrine and converse of the master to be placed here would influence the gentlemen, and their influence and authority prevail in all parts of the realm, where their habitations and estates were, that careful prelate made it his endeavour to stop Travers' coming in; and had a learned man in his view, and of principles more conformable and agreeable to the church, namely one Dr. Bond, the queen's chaplain, and one well known to her. She well understanding the importance of this place, and knowing by the archbishop what Travers was, by a letter he timely writ to her majesty upon the vacancy, gave particular order to the treasurer to discourse with the archbishop about it.

<small>Opposed by the archbishop.</small>

The lord treasurer, hereupon, in a letter, consulted with the said archbishop, and mentioned Travers to him as one desired by many of the house. But the archbishop in his answer, plainly signified to his lordship that he judged him altogether unfit, for the reasons mentioned before; and that he had recommended to the queen Dr. Bond as a very fit person. But however she declined him, fearing his bodily strength to perform the duty of the place, as she did Travers for other causes. And by laying both aside, she avoided giving disgust to either of those great men. This Dr. Bond seems to be that Dr. Nicholas Bond that afterwards was President of Magdalen college, Oxon, and was much abused by Martin Mar-prelate.

These particulars I have collected from a letter of the archbishop to the queen, and other letters that passed between the archbishop and the lord treasurer about this affair, while the mastership was vacant. The passages whereof, taken verbatim out of their said letters, may deserve here to be specified for the satisfaction of the readers.

And first, in the month of August, upon the death of the former master, the archbishop wrote this letter unto the queen:

<small>The archbishop to the queen</small>

"It may please your majesty to be advertised, that the "mastership of the Temple is vacant by the death of Mr.

---

[1] [Of whom see some account in Strype, Whitg. I. 477.]

"Alvey. The living is not great, yet doth it require a learned, concerning
"discreet, and wise man, in respect of the company there: the vacancy of the
"who being well directed and taught may do much good Temple.
"elsewhere in the commonwealth, as otherwise also they may
"do much harm. And because I hear there is a suit made
"unto your highness for one Mr. Travers, I thought it my
"duty to signify unto your majesty, that the said Travers
"hath been and is one of the chief and principal authors of
"dissension in this church, a contemner of the book of
"Prayers, and of other orders by authority established; an
"earnest seeker of innovation; and either in no degree of the
"ministry at all, or else ordered beyond the seas; not accord-
"ing to the form in this church of England used. Whose
"placing in that room, especially by your majesty, would
"greatly animate the rest of that faction, and do very much
"harm in sundry respects.

"Your majesty hath a chaplain of your own, Dr. Bond,
"a man in my opinion very fit for that office, and willing
"also to take pains therein, if it shall please your highness
"to bestow it upon him. Which I refer to your most gra-
"cious disposition; beseeching Almighty God long to bless,
"prosper, and preserve your majesty to his glory, and all our
"comforts.

"Your majesty's most faithful servant and chaplain,
"JO. CANTUAR."

"From Croyden,
"the   day of August, 1584."

Next, in a letter of the archbishop to the lord treasurer, dated from Lambeth, Sept. 14, 1584, he hath these words:

"I beseech your lordship to help such an one to the master- The arch-
"ship of the Temple, as is known to be conformable to the bishop to the lord
"laws and orders established; and a defender not a depraver treasurer.
"of the present state and government. He that now readeth
"there is nothing less, as I of mine own knowledge and ex-
"perience can testify. Dr. Bond is desirous of it, and I know
"not a fitter man."

The lord treasurer in a letter to the archbishop, dated from Oatlands (where the queen now was), Sept. 17, 1584, thus wrote:—

"The queen hath asked me what I thought of Travers The lord treasurer to the archbishop.

"to be master of the Temple. Whereunto I answered, that "at the request of Dr. Alvey in his sickness, and a number "of honest gentlemen of the Temple, I had yielded my allow-"ance of him to the place, so as he would shew himself con-"formable to the orders of the church. Whereunto I was "informed, that he would so be. But her majesty told me, "that your grace did not so allow of him. Which I said "might be for some things supposed to be written by him in "a book intituled, *De Disciplina Ecclesiastica.* Whereupon "her majesty commanded me to write to your grace to know "your opinion, which I pray your grace to signify unto her, "as God shall move you. Surely it were great pity that any "impediment should be occasion to the contrary; for he is "well learned, very honest, and well allowed and loved of "the generality of that house. Mr. Bond told me, that your "grace liked well of him; and so do I also, as one well "learned and honest; but, as I told him, if he came not to "the place with some applause of the company, he shall be "weary thereof. And yet I commended him unto her ma-"jesty, if Travers should not have it. But her majesty thinks "him not fit for that place, because of his infirmities. Thus "wishing your grace assistance of God's Spirit to govern your "charge unblameably,

"Your grace's to command,
"WILL. BURGHLEY."

" From the court at Oatlands,
"the 17th Sept. 1584."

Part of the archbishop's letter in answer to this was to this tenor:

The archbishop in answer to the letter of the lord treasurer.

"Mr. Travers, whom your lordship names in your letter, "is to no man better known, I think, than to myself. I did "elect him fellow of Trinity college, being before rejected "by Dr. Beaumont for his intolerable stomach: whereof I "had also afterwards such experience, that I was forced by "due punishment so to weary him, till he was fain to travel, "and depart from the college to Geneva, otherwise he should "have been expelled for want of conformity towards the "orders of the house, and for his pertinacy. Neither was "there ever any under our government, in whom I found "less submission and humility than in him. Nevertheless if

"time and years have now altered that disposition (which I
" cannot believe, seeing yet no token thereof, but rather
" the contrary), I will be as ready to do him good as any
" friend he hath. Otherwise I cannot in duty but do my
" endeavour to keep him from that place, where he may
" do so much harm, and do little or no good at all. For
" howsoever some commend him to your lordship and others,
" yet I think that the greater and better number of both
" the Temples have not so good an opinion of him. Sure
" I am that divers grave, and of the best affected of them,
" have shewed their misliking of him to me; not only out
" of respect of his disorderliness, in the manner of the com-
" munion, and contempt of the prayers, but also of his neg-
" ligence in reading. Whose lectures, by their report, are
" so barren of matter, that his hearers take no commodity
" thereby.

" The book *De Disciplina Ecclesiastica*, by common opi-
" nion, hath been reputed of his penning, since the first
" publishing of it. And by divers arguments I am moved
" to make no doubt thereof. The drift of which book is
" wholly against the state and government. Wherein also,
" among other things, he condemneth the taking and paying
" of first fruits, tenths, &c.[1] And therefore, unless he will
" testify his conformity by subscription, as all others do,
" which now enter into ecclesiastical livings, and make proof
" unto me that he is a minister ordered according to the
" laws of this church of England, as I verily believe he is
" not, because he forsook his place in the college upon that
" account; I can by no means yield my consent to the
" placing him there, or elsewhere, in any function of this
" church."]

And here I shall make a stop; and, that the reader may
the better judge of what follows, give him a character of the
times, and temper of the people of this nation, when Mr.

---

[1] [Fol. 88. "Quum omnis hic
" locus de ecclesia nostra indignis-
" sime spoliata a doctissimo viro
" Martino Bucero perpurgatus sit
" eo libro quem ante memini, quum-
" que eodem libro non solum Im-
" propriationum, sed et Annalium
" (quæ ejusdem species quædam
" esse videntur) Collationum, Re-
" signationum, et aliarum nundina-
" tionum et spoliationum direp-
" tiones prosecutus sit: malo hæc
" ex eruditissimis illius scriptis
" peti, quo majorem autoritatem
" oratio hæc habere possit."]

Hooker had his admission into this place: a place which he accepted, rather than desired: and yet here he promised himself a virtuous quietness, that blessed tranquillity which he always prayed and laboured for; that so he might in peace bring forth the fruits of peace, and glorify God by uninterrupted prayers and praises: for this he always thirsted and prayed: but Almighty God did not grant it: for his admission into this place was the very beginning of those oppositions and anxieties, which till then this good man was a stranger to; and of which the reader may guess by what follows.

In this character of the times, I shall, by the reader's favour, and for his information, look so far back as to the beginning of the reign of Queen Elizabeth; a time, in which the many pretended titles to the crown, the frequent treasons, the doubts of her successor, the late civil war, and the sharp persecution for religion that raged to the effusion of so much blood in the reign of Queen Mary, were fresh in the memory of all men; and begot fears in the most pious and wisest of this nation, lest the like days should return again to them, or their present posterity. And the apprehension of these dangers begot a hearty desire of a settlement in the church and state; believing, there was no other probable way left to make them sit quietly under their own vines and fig-trees, and enjoy the desired fruit of their labours. But time, and peace, and plenty, begot self-ends; and these begot animosities, envy, opposition, and unthankfulness for those very blessings for which they lately thirsted, being then the very utmost of their desires, and even beyond their hopes.

This was the temper of the times in the beginning of her reign[1]: and thus it continued too long: for those very people that had enjoyed the desires of their hearts in a reformation from the church of Rome, became at last so like the grave, as never to be satisfied, but were still thirsting for more and more: neglecting to pay that obedience, and perform those vows which they made in their days of adversities and fear: so that in short time there appeared three several interests,

[1] [See a note on these words in Dr. Wordsworth's Eccl. Biog. IV. 217.]

each of them fearless and restless in the prosecution of their designs; they may for distinction be called, the active Romanists, the restless Nonconformists (of which there were many sorts), and, the passive peaceable Protestant. The counsels of the first considered and resolved on in Rome: the second in Scotland, in Geneva, and in divers selected, secret, dangerous conventicles, both there, and within the bosom of our own nation: the third pleaded and defended their cause by establisht laws, both ecclesiastical and civil; and, if they were active, it was to prevent the other two from destroying what was by those known laws happily establisht to them and their posterity.

I shall forbear to mention the very many and dangerous plots of the Romanists against the church and state; because what is principally intended in this digression, is an account of the opinions and activity of the Nonconformists; against whose judgment and practice, Mr. Hooker became at last, but most unwillingly, to be engaged in a book-war; a war which he maintained not as against an enemy, but with the spirit of meekness and reason.

In which number of Nonconformists, though some might be sincere, well meaning men, whose indiscreet zeal might be so like charity, as thereby to cover a multitude of their errors; yet, of this party, there were many that were possest with a high degree of "spiritual wickedness;" I mean, with an innate restless pride and malice. I do not mean the visible carnal sins of gluttony and drunkenness, and the like, (from which good Lord deliver us,) but sins of a higher nature, because they are more unlike God, who is the God of love and mercy, and order, and peace; and more like the Devil, who is not a glutton, nor can be drunk, and yet is a devil; but I mean those spiritual wickednesses of malice and revenge, and an opposition to government: men that joyed to be the authors of misery, which is properly his work, that is the enemy and disturber of mankind; and thereby greater sinners than the glutton or drunkard, though some will not believe it. And of this party, there were also many, whom prejudice and a furious zeal had so blinded, as to make them neither to hear reason, nor adhere to the ways of peace: men, that were the very dregs and pest of mankind: men whom pride and self-conceit had made to overvalue their own pitiful, crooked wisdom so much, as not to be ashamed to hold foolish and unmannerly disputes against those men whom they ought to reverence, and those laws which they ought to obey; men that laboured and joyed first to find out the faults, and then to "speak evil of government," and to be the authors of confusion: men, whom company, and conversation, and custom had at last so blinded, and made so insensible that these were sins, that, like those that "perisht "in the gainsaying of Core," so these died without repenting of these "spiritual wickednesses," of which the practices of Coppinger and Hacket[1] in their lives, and the death of them and their adherents, are God knows too sad examples; and ought to be cautions to those men that are inclined to the like "spiritual wickednesses."

And in these times which tended thus to confusion, there were also many of these scruplemongers that pretended a tenderness of conscience, refusing to take an oath before a lawful magistrate[2]: and yet these very men, in their secret conventicles, did covenant[3] and swear to each other, to be assiduous and faithful in using their best endeavours to set up the presbyterian doctrine and discipline; and both in such a manner as they themselves had not yet agreed on[4], but, up that government must. To which end there were many that wandered up and down, and were active in sowing discontents and sedition, by venomous and secret murmurings, and a dispersion of scurrilous pamphlets and libels against the church and state; but especially against the bishops; by which means, together with venomous and indiscreet sermons, the common people became so fanatic, as to believe *the bishops to be Antichrist,* and the only obstructors of God's Discipline; and at last some of them were given over to so bloody a zeal, and such other desperate delusions, as to find

---

[1] [See Camden. Ann. pars ii. pag. 34. ed. 1627. Strype, Ann. IV. 95.]
[2] [Strype, Whitg. I. 502. II. 25. 28. III. 120. I. 351, 357. Hooker, Pref. to E. P. viii. 13.]
[3] [By subscription. Strype, Whitg. III. 239. II. 13.

Dr. Wordsworth thinks Walton inaccurate in the mention of their *swearing.* But see Strype, Parker, II. 285. Collier, E. H. II. 544.]
[4] [Dr. Bancroft proves their disagreement at large; Survey of the pretended holy Discipline, c. 9-19, 24, 34.]

out a text in the Revelation of St. John, that "Antichrist "was to be overcome by the sword." So that those very men [1], who began with tender and meek petitions [2], proceeded to admonitions [3], then to satirical remonstrances [4], and at last having like Absalom [5] numbered who was not, and who was, for their cause, they got a supposed certainty of so great a party, that they durst threaten first the bishops, and then the Queen and parliament [6]; to all which they were secretly encouraged by the earl of Leicester, then in great favour with her majesty, and the reputed cherisher and patron-general of these pretenders to tenderness of conscience; his design being, by their means, to bring such an odium upon the bishops, as to procure an alienation of their lands, and a large proportion of them for himself; which avaricious desire had at last so blinded his reason, that his ambitious and greedy hopes seemed to put him into a present possession of Lambeth-house [7].

And to these undertakings the Nonconformists of this nation were much encouraged and heightened by a correspondence and confederacy with that brotherhood in Scotland [8]; so that here they became so bold, that one [9] told the Queen

---

[1] [That is, the very same class or party: Sampson, Humphrey, &c. being the leaders of the Petitioners; Cartwright, Travers, Field, &c. of the Admonitioners; Penry, Udall, and others, of the Remonstrants.]

[2] [E. g. In the Convocation 1562. Strype, Ann. I. 1, 500.
Foster, alias Colman, his petition to Secretary Cecil, 1569. Ann. I. 2, 350.]

[3] [The two Admonitions to the Parliament, 1572.]

[4] [The tracts under the name of Martin Marprelate, and the like, 1588.]

[5] [2 Sam. xv.]

[6] [Hooker, Pref. to E. P. viii. 13.]

[7] [Fuller, C. H. book ix. 130. "Leicester cast a covetous eye on "Lambeth house, alleging as good "arguments for his obtaining there-"of, as ever were urged by Ahab "for Naboth's vineyard."]

[8] [See the Letter of the general Assembly to the Bishops of England, Strype, Parker, III. 150.
"Since the liberty of prophesying "was taken up, which came but "lately into the northern parts, "(unless it were in the towns of "Newcastle and Barwick, where "Knox, Mackbray, and Udall had "sown their tares,) all things have "gone so cross and backward in "our church, that I cannot call the "history for these forty years or "more to mind, or express my ob-"servations upon it, but with a "bleeding heart." Dr. T. Jackson, Works, vol. III. p. 273.
"It was in the year 1550, or very "near it, that the famous Scotch "divine, John Knox, was appointed "preacher to Berwick, and after "that to Newcastle." Strype, Memorials, II. 1. 369.]

[9] Mr Dering. ["If you have "said sometime of yourself, *tan-*

openly in a sermon, "She was like an untamed heifer, that
"would not be ruled by God's people, but obstructed his
"discipline." And in Scotland they were more confident,
for there they declared her an Atheist[1], and grew to such a
height as not to be accountable for any thing spoken against
her; *nor for treason against their own king, if it were but
spoken in the pulpit*[2]; shewing at last such a disobedience to
him, that his mother being in England, and then in distress,
and in prison, and in danger of death, the church denied the
King their prayers for her[3]; and at another time, when he had
appointed a day of feasting, their church declared for a general
fast in opposition to his authority[4].

To this height they were grown in both nations; and by
these means there was distilled into the minds of the common
people such other venomous and turbulent principles, as were
inconsistent with the safety of the church and state: and
these opinions vented so daringly, that, beside the loss of life
and limbs[5], the governors of the church and state were forced
to use such other severities, as will not admit of an excuse,
if it had not been to prevent the gangrene of confusion, and
the perilous consequences of it; which, without such prevention, would have been first confusion, and then ruin and
misery to this numerous nation.

These errors and animosities were so remarkable, that they
begot wonder in an ingenious Italian, who being about this
time come newly into this nation, writ scoffingly to a friend
in his own country, to this purpose, "That the common
"people of England were wiser than the wisest of his nation;
"for here the very women and shopkeepers were able to
"judge of predestination, and determine what laws were fit

"*quam ovis*, 'as a sheep appointed
"to be slaine,' take heed you heare
"not now of the Prophet, *tanquam*
"*indomita juvenca*, 'as an untamed
"and unrulie heifer.'" (from Jerem.
xxxi. 18.) Wordsworth, Eccl. Biogr.
IV. 226. Walton probably took
the anecdote from Fuller, Church
Hist. b. ix. p. 109. See more of
Deering, Strype, Ann. II. 1. 398,
&c.]
[1] Vide Bishop Spotswood's History of the Church of Scotland.
[B. VI. Ann. 1596. p. 419. edit.
1655.]
[2] [Ibid. p. 330. (1584.) p. 421.
(1596.)]
[3] [Spotswood, p. 354. (1586.)]
[4] [Ibid. 324. (1582.)]
[5] [Penry was executed May 1593.
Barrow and Greenwood the month
before. Strype, Whitg. II. 175, &c.
Stubbs and Page lost their right
hands, for the book against the
Queen's marriage, 1580.]

"to be made concerning church-government; and then, what were fit to be obeyed or abolisht: That they were more able (or at least thought so) to raise and determine perplext cases of conscience, than the wisest of the most learned colleges in Italy: That men of the slightest learning, and the most ignorant of the common people, were mad for a new, or super, or re-reformation of religion; and that in this *they appeared like that man, who would never cease to whet and whet his knife, till there was no steel left to make it useful.*" And he concluded his letter with this observation, "That those very men that were most busy in oppositions, and disputations, and controversies, and finding out the faults of their governors, had usually the least of Humility and Mortification, or of the power of Godliness."

And to heighten all these discontents and dangers, there was also sprung up a generation of godless men; men that had so long given way to their own lusts and delusions, and so highly opposed the blessed motions of his Spirit, and the inward light of their own consciences, that they became the very slaves of vice, and had thereby sinned themselves into a belief of that which they would, but could not believe; into a belief which is repugnant even to human nature (for the heathens believe that there are many gods), but these had sinned themselves into a belief, that there was no God; and so, finding nothing in themselves but what was worse than nothing, began to wish what they were not able to hope for, namely, "that they might be like the beasts that perish;" and in wicked company (which is the atheist's sanctuary) were so bold as to say so, though the worst of mankind, when he is left alone at midnight, may wish, but is not then able to think it; even into a belief that there is no God. Into this wretched, this reprobate condition, many had then sinned themselves [1].

And now when the church was pestered with them, and with all those other forenamed irregularities; when her lands were in danger of alienation, her power at least neglected, and her peace torn to pieces by several schisms, and such

---

[1] [See Cranmer's Letter to Hooker.]

heresies as do usually attend that sin, for heresies do usually outlive their first authors; when the common people seemed ambitious of doing those very things that were forbidden and attended with most dangers, that thereby they might be punished, and then applauded and pitied; when they called the spirit of opposition a tender conscience, and complained of persecution, because they wanted power to persecute others; when the giddy multitude raged, and became restless to find out misery for themselves and others; and the rabble would herd themselves together, and endeavour to govern and act in spite of authority: in this extremity of fear, and danger of the church and state, when, to suppress the growing evils of both, they needed a man of prudence and piety, and of an high and fearless fortitude; they were blest in all by John Whitgift his being made Archbishop of Canterbury; of whom Sir Henry Wotton that knew him well in his youth, and had studied him in his age, gives this true character: "that he was a man of reverend and "sacred memory; and of the primitive temper; a man of "such a temper, as when the Church by lowliness of spirit "did flourish in highest examples of virtue[1]." And indeed this man proved so.

And though I dare not undertake to add to this excellent and true character of Sir Henry Wotton; yet, I shall neither do right to this discourse, nor to my reader, if I forbear to give him a further and short account of the life and manners of this excellent man; and it shall be short, for I long to end this digression, that I may lead my reader back to Mr. Hooker, where we left him at the Temple.

John Whitgift was born in the county of Lincoln, of a family that was ancient, and noted to be both prudent and affable, and gentle by nature; he was educated in Cambridge; much of his learning was acquired in Pembroke-hall, (where Mr. Bradford the martyr was his tutor); from thence he was removed to Peter-house; from thence to be Master of Pembroke-hall; and from thence to the Mastership of Trinity college: about which time the Queen made him her chaplain; and not long after, Prebend of Ely[2], and then Dean of

---

[1] [Reliquiæ Wottonianæ, p. 19, ed. 1651.]

[2] [This he had not from the Queen, but from Bishop Cox.

Lincoln; and having for many years past looked upon him with much reverence and favour, gave him a fair testimony of both, by giving him the bishopric of Worcester, and (which was not with her a usual favour [1]) forgiving him his first-fruits; then by constituting him Vice-president of the principality of Wales. And having experimented his wisdom, his justice, and moderation in the menage of her affairs, in both these places; she in the twenty-sixth of her reign made him Archbishop of Canterbury, and not long after of her privy council; and trusted him to manage all her ecclesiastical affairs and preferments. In all which removes, he was like the ark, which left a blessing upon the place where it rested [2]; and in all his employments was like Jehoiada, that did good unto Israel [3].

These were the steps of this bishop's ascension to this place of dignity and cares; in which place (to speak Mr. Camden's very words in his Annals of Queen Elizabeth [4]) " he devoutly " consecrated both his whole life to God, and his painful " labours to the good of his church." And yet, in this place he met with many oppositions in the regulation of church-affairs, which were much disordered at his entrance, by reason of the age and remissness of Bishop Grindal [5], his immediate predecessor, the activity of the Nonconformists, and their chief assistant the Earl of Leicester; and indeed, by too many others of the like sacrilegious principles. With these he was to encounter; and though he wanted neither courage nor a good cause, yet he foresaw, that without a great measure of the Queen's favour, it was impossible to stand in the breach that had been lately made into the lands and immunities of the Church, or indeed to maintain the remaining lands and rights of it. And therefore by justifiable sacred insinuations, such as St. Paul to Agrippa, ("Agrippa, believest

---

Strype, Whitg. I. 26, and Paule's Life of Whitg. in Wordsworth, E. B. IV. 321, from which latter Walton took most of the particulars here related.]

[1] ["A rare gift for her, who was "so good an huswife of her re-"venues." Fuller, C. H. b. x. p. 25.]

[2] [2 Sam. vi. 11.]

[3] [2 Chron. xxiv. 16.]

[4] [Camden's *Britannia*, translated by Holland, p. 338, ed. 1610.]

[5] Or rather by reason of his suspension and sequestration, which he lay under (together with the Queen's displeasure) for some years, when the ecclesiastical affairs were managed by certain civilians. J. S.

"thou? I know thou believest,") he wrought himself into so great a degree of favour with her, as, by his pious use of it, hath got both of them a great degree of fame in this world, and of glory in that into which they are now both entered.

His merits to the Queen, and her favours to him, were such, that she called him *her little black husband*, and called his servants *her servants*[1]: and she saw so visible and blessed a sincerity shine in all his cares and endeavours for the Church's and for her good, that she was supposed to trust him with the very secrets of her soul, and to make him her confessor: of which she gave many fair testimonies; and of which one was, that "she would never eat flesh in Lent "without obtaining a license from her little black husband;" and would often say, "she pitied him because she trusted him, "and had thereby eased herself, by laying the burden of all "her clergy-cares upon his shoulders, which he managed with "prudence and piety."

I shall not keep myself within the promised rules of brevity in this account of his interest with her majesty, and his care of the Church's rights, if in this digression I should enlarge to particulars; and therefore my desire is, that one example may serve for a testimony of both. And, that the reader may the better understand it, he may take notice, that not many years before his being made archbishop, there passed an act or acts of parliament[2], intending the better preservation of the church-lands, by recalling a power which was vested in others to sell or lease them, by lodging and trusting the future care and protection of them only in the crown: and amongst many that made a bad use of this power or trust of the Queen's, the Earl of Leicester was one[3]; and the bishop having, by his interest with her majesty, put a

---

[1] [Paule's Life of Whitgift in Wordsworth's Eccl. Biog. IV. 387.]

[2] [1 Eliz. c. 19; 13 Eliz. c. 20, &c. See Blackstone's Commentaries, II. 319, 320, 321, Coleridge's edition; and Collier's Eccl. Hist. II. 430, 422.]

[3] [E. g. "The Earl of Leicester, "in a suit to her Majesty, upon the "decease of Barnes, Bishop of "Durham, moved her to take to "herself divers bishops' lands, the "bishopricks being then void, to "the value of 1,200*l.* yearly rent; "and to settle upon them impropri- "ations in the room thereof." The fee-simple of a large portion of such lands to be afterwards granted to him, the earl. Strype, Ann. III. i. 689.]

stop to the earl's sacrilegious designs, they two fell to an open opposition before her; after which, they both quitted the room, not friends in appearance: but the bishop made a sudden and a seasonable return to her majesty, (for he found her alone,) and spake to her with great humility and reverence, to this purpose:

"I beseech your majesty to hear me with patience, and "to believe that your's and the Church's safety are dearer "to me than my life, but my conscience dearer than both: "and therefore give me leave to do my duty, and tell you, "that *princes are deputed nursing fathers of the Church, and* "*owe it a protection;* and therefore God forbid that you "should be so much as passive in her ruins, when you may "prevent it; or that I should behold it without horror and "detestation; or should forbear to tell your majesty of the "sin and danger of sacrilege. And though you and myself "were born in an age of frailties, when the primitive piety "and care of the Church's lands and immunities are much "decayed; yet, madam, let me beg that you would first "consider that there are such sins as profaneness and sacri-"lege; and that, if there were not, they could not have "names in Holy Writ, and particularly in the New Testa-"ment. And I beseech you to consider, that though our "Saviour said, 'He judged no man;' and to testify it, "would not judge nor divide the inheritance betwixt the two "brethren, nor would judge the woman taken in adultery; "yet in this point of the Church's rights he was so zealous, "that he made himself both the accuser and the judge, and "the executioner too, to punish these sins; witnessed, in "that he himself made the whip to drive the profaners out "of the temple, overthrew the tables of the moneychangers, "and drove them out of it. And I beseech you to consider, "that it was St. Paul that said to those Christians of his "time that were offended with idolatry, yet committed sacri-"lege, 'Thou that abhorrest idols, dost thou commit sacri-"lege?' supposing, (I think,) sacrilege the greater sin. This "may occasion your majesty to consider that there is such "a sin as sacrilege; and to incline you to prevent the curse "that will follow it, I beseech you also to consider, that "Constantine the first Christian emperor, and Helena his

"mother [1], that King Edgar [2], and Edward the Confessor [3],
"and indeed many others of your predecessors, and many
"private Christians, have also given to God, and to his
"Church, much land, and many immunities, which they
"might have given to those of their own families, and did
"not; but gave them for ever as *an absolute right and sacri-*
"*fice to God:* and with these immunities and lands, *they*
"*have entailed a curse upon the alienators of them* [4]; God
"prevent your majesty from being liable to that curse,
"which will cleave unto church-lands, as the leprosy to the
"Jews.

"And, to make you that are trusted with their preservation,
"the better to understand the danger of it, I beseech you
"forget not, that to prevent these curses, the Church's land
"and power have been also endeavoured to be preserved (as
"far as human reason, and the law of this nation, have been
"able to preserve them) by an immediate and most sacred
"obligation on the consciences of the princes of this realm.
"For they that consult Magna Charta [5] shall find, that as
"all your predecessors were at their coronation, so you also
"were sworn before all the nobility and bishops then pre-
"sent, and in the presence of God, and in his stead to him
"that anointed you, 'to maintain the church-lands, and the
"rights belonging to it;' and this you yourself have testified
"openly to God at the holy altar, by laying your hands on
"the Bible then lying upon it. And not only Magna Charta,
"but many modern statutes have denounced a curse upon
"those that break Magna Charta: a curse like the leprosy,
"that was entailed on the Jews [6]; for as that, so these
"curses have and will cleave to the very stones of those
"buildings that have been consecrated to God; and the
"father's sin of sacrilege hath and will prove to be entailed
"on his son and family. And now, madam, what account
"can be given for the breach of this oath at the last great

---

[1] [Fuller, Ch. Hist. B. I. p. 23.]
[2] [Ibid. B. II. p. 131, 132.]
[3] [Ibid. B. II. p. 143.]
[4] [Hooker, E. P. V. 79, 14.]
[5] ["The first article of Magna "Charta is, 'Que les Eglises de "Engleterre seront franches, et aient "les dreitures franches, et enterinés, "et plenieres.'" Dr. Zouch. See Hooker, ubi sup.]
[6] [Deut. xxviii. 27, 35.]

"day, either by your majesty, or by me, if it be wilfully, or
"but negligently violated, I know not.

"And therefore, good madam, let not the late lord's ex-
"ceptions against the failings of some few clergymen prevail
"with you to punish posterity for the errors of this present
"age; let particular men suffer for their particular errors,
"but let God and his Church have their inheritance: and
"though I pretend not to prophecy, yet I beg posterity to
"take notice of what is already become visible in many fami-
"lies; *that church-land added to an ancient and just inherit-*
"*ance, hath proved like a moth fretting a garment, and secretly*
"*consumed both;* or *like the eagle that stole a coal from the*
"*altar, and thereby set her nest on fire, which consumed both her*
"*young eagles and herself that stole it*[1].

"And, though I shall forbear to speak reproachfully of
"your father; yet I beg you to take notice, that a part of
"the Church's rights, added to the vast treasure left him by
"his father, hath been conceived to bring an unavoidable
"consumption upon both, notwithstanding all his diligence
"to preserve them. And consider that after the violation
"of those laws, to which he had sworn in Magna Charta,
"God did so far deny him his restraining grace, that as king
"Saul after he was forsaken of God fell from one sin to
"another; so he, till at last he fell into greater sins than
"I am willing to mention. Madam, *religion is the foundation*
"*and cement of human societies:* and when they that serve
"at God's altar shall be exposed to poverty, then religion
"itself will be exposed to scorn, and become contemptible;
"as you may already observe it to be in too many poor vicar-
"ages in this nation. And therefore, as you are by a late
"act or acts of parliament entrusted with a great power to
"preserve or waste the Church's lands; yet dispose of them
"*for Jesus' sake, as you have promised to men, and vowed to*
"*God; that is, as the donors intended;* let neither falsehood
"nor flattery beguile you to do otherwise: but put a stop to
"God's and the Levite's portion, I beseech you, and to the
"approaching ruins of His Church, as you expect comfort
"at the last great day; for, *Kings must be judged*. Pardon

---

[1] [Æsop's Fables, by L'Estrange, fable 72.]

"this affectionate plainness, my most dear sovereign, and let me beg to be still continued in your favour, and the Lord still continue you in his."

The Queen's patient hearing this affectionate speech, and her future care to preserve the Church's rights, which till then had been neglected, may appear a fair testimony, that he made her's and the Church's good the chiefest of his cares, and that she also thought so. And of this there were such daily testimonies given, as begat betwixt them so mutual a joy and confidence, that they seemed born to believe and do good to each other: she not doubting his piety to be more than all his opposers, which were many; nor doubting his prudence to be equal to the chiefest of her council, who were then as remarkable for active wisdom, as those dangerous times did require, or this nation did ever enjoy. And in this condition he continued twenty years[1], in which time he saw some flowings, but many more ebbings of her favour towards all men that had opposed him, especially the Earl of Leicester: so that God seemed still to keep him in her favour, that he might preserve the remaining church-lands and immunities from sacrilegious alienations. And this good man deserved all the honour and power with which she gratified and trusted him; for he was a pious man, and naturally of noble and grateful principles: he eased her of all her church cares by his wise menage of them; he gave her faithful and prudent counsels in all the extremities and dangers of her temporal affairs, which were very many; he lived to be the chief comfort of her life in her declining age, and to be then most frequently with her, and her assistant at her private devotions; he lived to be the greatest comfort of her soul upon her death-bed, to be present at the expiration of her last breath, and to behold the closing of those eyes that had long looked upon him with reverence and affection. And let this also be added, that he was the chief mourner at her sad funeral; nor let this be forgotten, that within a few hours after her death, he was the happy proclaimer, that King James (her peaceful successor) was heir to the crown.

---

[1] [He was confirmed Archbishop, Sept. 23, 1583, and died Feb. 29, $160\frac{3}{4}$.]

Let me beg of my reader, that he allow me to say a little, and but a little, more of this good bishop, and I shall then presently lead him back to Mr. Hooker; and, because I would hasten, I will mention but one part of the bishop's charity and humility; but this of both[1]: he built a large almshouse near to his own palace at Croyden in Surrey, and endowed it with maintenance for a master and twenty-eight poor men and women; which he visited so often, that he knew their names and dispositions; and was so truly humble, that he called them Brothers and Sisters: and whensoever the Queen descended to that lowliness to dine with him at his palace in Lambeth, (which was very often,) he would usually the next day shew the like lowliness to his poor brothers and sisters at Croyden, and dine with them at his hospital; at which time, you may believe, there was joy at the table. And at this place he built also a fair free-school, with a good accommodation and maintenance for the master and scholars; which gave just occasion for Boyse Sisi[2], then ambassador for the French king, and resident here, at the bishop's death, to say, "The bishop had published "many learned books; but a free-school to train up youth, "and an hospital to lodge and maintain aged and poor people, "were the best evidences of Christian learning that a bishop "could leave to posterity." This good bishop lived to see King James settled in peace, and then fell into an extreme sickness at his palace in Lambeth[3]; of which when the King had notice, he went presently to visit him, and found him in his bed in a declining condition, and very weak; and after some short discourse betwixt them, the King at his departure assured him, "He had a great affection for him, and a very "high value for his prudence and virtues, and would endeavour "to beg his life of God for the good of his Church." To which the good bishop replied, *Pro ecclesia Dei, Pro ecclesia Dei:* which were the last words he ever spake; therein testify-

---

[1] [Paule, in Dr. Wordsworth's Eccl. Biog. IV. 391, 392.]

[2] [Jean de Thumery de Boissise, counsellor to King Henry IV: who signed the commercial treaty with England, 1606, (Rymer, xvi. 645,) and was afterwards ambassador of France in the duchy of Cleves, (Sully, Mem. VII. 245, ed. Liege 1788,) and in Denmark (ibid. 285.)]

[3] [He was seized with palsy at Whitehall, just after an audience of the King. Paule's Life, 397.]

ing, that as in his life, so at his death, his chiefest care was of God's Church.

This John Whitgift was made archbishop in the year 1583. In which busy place he continued twenty years and some months; and in which time, you may believe, he had many trials of his courage and patience; but his motto was, *Vincit qui patitur:* and he made it good.

Many of his many trials were occasioned by the then powerful Earl of Leicester, who did still (but secretly) raise and cherish a faction of Nonconformists to oppose him; especially one Thomas Cartwright, a man of noted learning; some time contemporary with the bishop in Cambridge, and of the same college, of which the bishop had been master: in which place there began some emulations, (the particulars I forbear[1],) and at last, open and high oppositions betwixt them; and in which you may believe Mr. Cartwright was most faulty, if his expulsion out of the university can incline you to it.

And in this discontent[2] after the earl's death (which was 1588,) Mr. Cartwright appeared a chief cherisher of a party that were for the Geneva church-government; and, to effect it, he ran himself into many dangers both of liberty and life; appearing at the last to justify himself and his party in many remonstrances, which he caused to be printed, and

---

[1] [Strype, Whitg. b. I. c. 4, 8. Ann. I. ii. 372. . . 382. II. i. 1—5. Bp. Cooper, Admon. 146. "Many "know that a repulse of a dignity "desired was the cause that our "schism brake forth, and hath so "eagerly continued."]

[2] [In the edition of 1723, and I believe in all following editions, this passage stands as follows, the errors having been rectified, and several additions made, as it seems, by Strype:

"Long before the earl's death " . . . . . Mr. Cartwright appeared " . . . . . in many remonstrances, "especially that called the Admo- "nition to the Parliament. Which "last he caused to be printed; to "which the Doctor made an Answer, "and Cartwright replied upon him: "and then the Doctor having re- "joined to his reply, (however Mr. "Cartwright would not be satisfied,) "he wrote no more, but left &c. "[And to posterity he left such "a learned and useful book, as "does abundantly establish the re- "formation and constitution of our "Church, and vindicate it against "all the cavils of the innovators.] "After some time, the Doctor being "preferred to the See, first of Wor- "cester, and then of Canterbury, "Mr. Cartwright, after his share of "trouble and imprisonment, (for "setting up new presbyteries in "divers places against the esta- "blished order,) having received "from the archbishop many per- "sonal favours, retired himself to a "more private living."]

to which the bishop made a first answer, and Cartwright replied upon him: and then the bishop having rejoined to his first reply, Mr. Cartwright either was, or was persuaded to be, satisfied: for he wrote no more[1], but left the reader to be judge which had maintained their cause with most charity and reason. After some silence, Mr. Cartwright received from the bishop many personal favours, and betook himself to a more private living, which was at Warwick, where he was made master of an hospital, and lived quietly, and grew rich[2]; and where the bishop gave him a license to preach, upon promise not to meddle with controversies, but incline his hearers to piety and moderation: and this promise he kept during his life, which ended 1602, the bishop surviving him but some few months, each ending his days in perfect charity with the other.

[It is true, the archbishop treated Cartwright with such J. S. civility as gained much upon him, and made him declare unto his patron, the Earl of Leicester, how much the archbishop's humane carriage had endeared him to him; and withal shewed his desire that he might have liberty sometimes to have access to him; professing that he would seek to persuade all with whom he had concern and converse, to keep up an union with the church of England. This, I say, is certain; but it is not so certain, that the archbishop gave Cartwright a license to preach. It appears, that in the year 1585 he refused to grant it him, however solicited by Leices-

---

[1] [There is an error here, which may be traced to Fuller, C. H. b. ix. p. 102. "It will not be amiss to "set down what writings, pro and "con, passed on the occasion of "this book," (the Admonitions to the Parliament, 1572,) "between "two eminent authors of opposite "parties. 1. The Admonition, "first and second, made by Mr. "Cartwright. 2. The Answer to "the Admonition by Dr. John "Whitgift. 3. The Reply to the "Answer to the Admonition by "Mr. Tho. Cartwright. 4. The "Defence of the Answer by Dr. "John Whitgift. This last kept "the field, and (for ought I can find) "received no solemn refutation." To which he adds many conjectures on the possible causes of Cartwright's silence: not being at all aware of the Second Reply, a much larger work than the first; which Second Reply came out in two parts, 1575 and 1577.]

[2] ["We find him at this time "growing rich in the town of War- "wick (there master of an hospital) "by the benevolence and bounty of "his followers: where he preached "very temperately, according to his "promise made to the Archbishop." Fuller, C. H. b. x. p. 2, almost verbatim from Paule's Life of Whitgift: see Wordsworth's Eccl. Biog. IV. 366.]

ter's own letter to do it; and notwithstanding Cartwright's promises, he required more space of time to be satisfied of his conformity. For the elucidation whereof, and some further light into this matter, let both these letters be read and considered; the former of the earl to the archbishop; the latter of the archbishop to the earl.

"My good Lord,

The Earl of Leicester to the Archbishop concerning Mr. Cartwright.

"I most heartily thank you for your favourable and "courteous usage of Mr. Cartwright, who hath so exceed-"ing kindly taken it also, as, I assure your Grace, he cannot "speak enough of it. I trust it shall do a great deal of "good. And he protesteth and professeth to me, to take "no other course, but to the drawing of all men to the "unity of the Church: and that your Grace hath so dealt "with him, as no man shall so command him, and dispose "of him, as you shall: and doth mean to let this opinion "publicly be known, even in the pulpit, (if your Grace "so permit him,) what he himself will, and would all others "should do, for obedience to the laws established. And if "any little scruple be, it is not great, and easy to be re-"formed by your Grace; whom I do most heartily entreat "to continue your favour and countenance towards him, "with such access sometimes as your leisure may permit. "For I perceive he doth much desire and crave it, &c. "Thus, my good lord, praying to God to bless his Church, "and to make his servants constant and faithful, I bid your "Grace farewell.

"Your Grace's very assured friend,

"ROB. LEICESTER."

"At the court, this 14th of July."

To which letter the archbishop returned this answer:

"My singular good Lord,

The Archbishop to the Earl.

"Mr. Cartwright shall be welcome to me at all times, and "using himself quietly, as becomes him, and as I hope he "will, he shall find me willing to do him any good: but to "grant unto him, as yet, my license to preach, without "longer trial, I cannot; especially seeing he protesteth

"himself to be of the same mind he was at the writing of
"his book, for the matter thereof, though not for the manner;
"myself also, I thank God, not altered in any point by me
"set down to the contrary; and knowing many things [in his
"book] to be very dangerous. Wherefore, notwithstanding I
"am content and ready to be at peace with him, so long as
"he liveth peaceably; yet doth my conscience and duty
"forbid me to give unto him any further public approbation,
"until I be better persuaded of his conformity. And so
"being bold to use my accustomed plainness with your good
"lordship, I commit you to the tuition of Almighty God;
"this 17th of July, 1585."]

And now after this long digression made for the information of my reader concerning what follows, I bring him back to venerable Mr. Hooker, where we left him in the Temple; and where we shall find him as deeply engaged in a controversy with Walter Travers[1], a friend and favourite of Mr. Cartwright's, as the bishop had ever been with Mr. Cartwright himself; and of which I shall proceed to give this following account.

And first this; that though the pens of Mr. Cartwright and the bishop were now at rest[2], yet there was sprung up a new generation of restless men, that by company and clamours became possest of a faith which they ought to have kept to themselves, but could not: men that were become positive in asserting, "that a Papist cannot be saved:" insomuch, that about this time, at the execution of the Queen of Scots[3], the bishop that preached her funeral sermon (which was Dr. Howland[4], then Bishop of Peterborough) was reviled for not being positive for her damnation. And besides this boldness

---

[1] ["Mr. Walter Travers, whom I "may term the neck (allowing Mr. "Cartwright for the head) of the "Presbyterian party." Fuller, C. H. b. ix. 136.]

[2] [Here the editions since Strype nsert "and had been a great while." The latter portion of Cartwright's Second Reply was published 1577.]

[3] [Feb. 8, 158⅞.]

[4] [By a note in Dr. Zouch's edition, given also by Dr. Wordsworth, it appears that Dr. Wickham, Bishop of Lincoln, not Bishop Howland, preached the sermon on this occasion. Fuller, ix. 181, says, "she was buried in the quire of "Peterborough, and Dr. Wickham, "bishop of Lincoln, preached her "funeral sermon; causelessly carped "at by the Martin Mar-Prelate, as "too favourable concerning her "final condition."]

of their becoming gods, so far as to set limits to His mercies; there was not only one *Martin Mar-prelate*[1], but other venomous books daily printed and dispersed; books that were so absurd and scurrilous, that the graver divines disdained them an answer. And yet these were grown into high esteem with the common people, till Tom Nash appeared against them all; who was a man of a sharp wit, and the master of a scoffing satirical merry pen, which he employed to discover the absurdities of those blind, malicious, senseless pamphlets, and sermons as senseless as they; Nash his answers being like his books[2], which bore these titles, *An Almond for a Parrot*[3], *A Fig for my God-son, Come crack me this Nut*, and the like: so that his merry wit made some sport, and such a discovery of their absurdities, as

---

[1] [158$\frac{7}{8}$.]

[2] [The meaning seems to be, "Nash's answers being like his (Martin's) books: which (answers) bore, &c." Compare the titles at length of the pamphlets mentioned in the next note with the two following of Penry's. "O read over "Dr. John Bridges, for it is a "worthy work: or, An Epitome of "the first book of that right wor-"shipfull volume written against "the Puritans in the defence of the "noble clergie, by as worshipful a "priest, John Bridges, presbyter, "priest, or elder, doctor of divillitie, "and deane of Sarum. Wherein "the arguments of the Puritans "are wisely prevented, that when "they come to answer M. Doctor "they must needs say something "that hath been spoken. Compiled "for the behoofe and overthrow of "the parsons, fyckers, and currats, "that have learnt their catechisms "and are past grace. By the re-"verend and worthy Martin Mar-"prelate, gentleman, and dedicated "to the confocation house.... "Printed over sea in Europe, within "two furlongs of a bouncing priest, "at the cost and charge of M. Mar-"prelate, gentleman."

"Theses Martinianæ: i. e. cer-"tain demonstrative conclusions, 'set down and collected, as it "should seem, by that famous and "renowned clark, the reverend "Martin Marprelate the great; "serving as a sufficient and mani-"fest confutation of all that ever "the college of catercaps, with their "whole band of clergie priests, "have or can bring for the defence "of their ambitious and antichris-"tian prelacy. Published and set "forth as an after-birth of the "noble gentleman himself, by a "pretty stripling of his, Martin "Junior, and dedicated by him to "his good neame and nuncka, "maister John Kankerbury.... "Printed by the assigns of Martin "Junior, without any privilege of "the Cater-caps."]

[3] ["An Almond for a Parrot, "or Cuthbert Curryknave's Alms. "Fit for the knave Martin and the "rest of those impudent beggars, "that cannot be content to stay "their stomach with a benefice, "but they will needs break their "fast with our bishops. Imprinted "at a place, not far from a place, "by the assigns of Signior Some-"body, and are to be sold at his "shop in Trouble-knave Street, at "the sign of the Standish."

"Pappe with an Hatchet; alias, "A Fig for my Godson; or, Crack "me this Nut; or, A Country "Cuff, i. e. a sound box of the ear (which is strange) he put a greater stop to these malicious pamphlets, than a much wiser man had been able[1].

And now the reader is to take notice, that at the death of Father Alvie, who was master of the Temple, this Walter Travers was lecturer there for the evening sermons[2], which he preached with great approbation, especially of some citizens, and the younger gentlemen of that society; and for the most part approved by Mr. Hooker himself, in the midst of their oppositions: for he continued lecturer a part of his time: Mr. Travers being indeed a man of competent learning, of winning behaviour, and of a blameless life. But he had taken orders by the presbytery in Antwerp[3], (and with them some opinions, that could never be eradicated,) and if in any thing he was transported, it was in an extreme desire to set up that government in this nation: for the promoting of which he had a correspondence with Theodore Beza at Geneva[4], and others in Scotland[5]; and was one of the chiefest assistants to Mr. Cartwright in that design.

Mr. Travers had also a particular hope to set up this government in the Temple, and to that end used his most

---

"for the idiot Martin to hold his "peace, seeing the patch will take "no warning. Written by one that "dares call a dog a dog, and made "to prevent Martin's dog days. "Imprinted by John Anoke and "John Astile for the Bailiff of "Withernam, cum privilegio peren- "nitatis, and are to be sold at the "sign of the Crab-tree Cudgel in "Thwack-coat Lane."
'To give Pap with a Hatchet:' "a proverbial phrase, for doing a "kind thing in an unkind manner." Nares' Glossary. 'Pap.'
Watt, Biblioth. Brit. ascribes the pamphlet to Lilly, and not to Nash.]
[1] ["By his (Dr. Bancroft's) ad-"vice that course was taken, which "did principally stop Martin's and "his fellows' mouths; *viz.* to have "them answered after their own "vain writings." Abp. Whitgift, ap. Strype, Whitg. II. 387.]
[2] [Mr. Alvie himself appears to have been inclined to Puritanism, as his name occurs in "Troubles "at Frankfort," among the signa-tures to "the Discipline," 1557. Phœnix, vol. ii. 142. This may partly account for Travers's ap-pointment.]
[3] [Fuller, C. H. b. ix. p. 214, inserts the testimonial of his ordi-nation, bearing date May 14, 1578.]
[4] [Fuller, ibid. "Meeting with "some discontents in the college "after the death of Dr. Beaumont, "in whose time he was elected fel-"low, he took occasion to travel "beyond seas, and coming to Ge-"neva, contracted familiarity with "Mr. Beza and other foreign "divines, with whom he by letters "continued correspondency till the "day of his death."]
[5] [He and Cartwright were in-vited by Melvin and others to be readers in divinity at St. Andrew's: and the tone of the letter, given in Fuller, C. H. b. ix. p. 215, seems to imply previous acquaintance and correspondence.]

zealous endeavours to be master of it; and his being disappointed by Mr. Hooker's admittance, proved the occasion of a public opposition betwixt them in their sermons. Many of which were concerning the doctrine and ceremonies of this church: insomuch that as St. Paul withstood St. Peter to his face, so did they withstand each other in their sermons; for as one hath pleasantly exprest it, "The forenoon sermon spake "Canterbury, and the afternoon, Geneva[1]."

In these sermons there was little of bitterness, but each party brought all the reasons he was able, to prove his adversary's opinion erroneous. And thus it continued a long time, till the oppositions became so visible, and the consequences so dangerous, especially in that place, that the prudent archbishop put a stop to Mr. Travers his preaching by a positive prohibition; [and that chiefly because of his foreign ordination[2]:] against which Mr. Travers appealed, and petitioned her Majesty's Privy Council to have it recalled, where besides his patron the Earl of Leicester[3], he met also with many assisting friends; but they were not able to prevail with or against the archbishop, whom the Queen had entrusted with all church-power; and he had received so fair a testimony of Mr. Hooker's principles, and of his learning and moderation, that he withstood all solicitations.

But the denying this petition of Mr. Travers was unpleasant to divers of his party, and the reasonableness of it became at last to be so publicly magnified by them and many others of that party, as never to be answered: so that, intending the bishop's and Mr. Hooker's disgrace, they procured it to be privately printed[4], and scattered abroad; and then Mr. Hooker was forced to appear and make as public an answer: which

---

[1] [Fuller, Worthies of England, p. 264. "The pulpit spake pure "Canterbury in the morning, and "Geneva in the afternoon, until "Travers was silenced."]

[2] [The words in brackets were inserted by Strype. The Author of "M. Some laid open in his colours," p. 25, says, "I have heard that "M. Travers, when he was thrust "out of the Temple, was bidden by "my Lord of Canterbury to prove "his calling; alleging that he was "no minister: for what authority, "saith he in his choler, hath M. "Cartwright to make a minister?"]

[3] [Rather, lord Burghley, to whom Travers was domestic chaplain, as appears by a memorial of his in Strype, Whitg. I. 475. Fuller adds that he was tutor to Burghley's son Robert, afterwards Earl of Salisbury. C. H. b. ix. p. 214.]

[4] [Rather "copied out:" see Answer to Travers's Supplication, § 9. in vol. iii.]

he did, and dedicated it to the archbishop; and it proved so full an answer, an answer that had in it so much of clear reason, and writ with so much meekness and majesty of style, that the bishop began to have him in admiration[1], and to rejoice that he had appeared in his cause, and disdained not earnestly to beg his friendship, even a familiar friendship, with a man of so much *quiet learning* and *humility*[2].

To enumerate the many particular points, in which Mr. Hooker and Mr. Travers dissented, (all or most of which I have seen written,) would prove at least tedious: and therefore I shall impose upon my reader no more than two, which shall immediately follow, and by which he may judge of the rest.

Mr. Travers excepted against Mr. Hooker, for that in one of his sermons he declared, "That the assurance of what we "believe by the word of God is not to us so certain as that "which we perceive by sense." And Mr. Hooker confesseth he said so, and endeavours to justify it by the reasons following[3]:

"First, I taught, that the things which God promises "in his word are surer than what we touch, handle, or "see: but are we so sure and certain of them? If we be, "why doth God so often prove his promises to us as he "doth, by arguments drawn from our sensible experience? "For we must be surer of the proof, than of the things "proved; otherwise it is no proof. For example, how is it "that many men looking on the moon at the same time, "every one knoweth it to be the moon as certainly as the "other doth? But many believing one and the same pro- "mise, have not all the same fulness of persuasion. For "how falleth it out, that men being assured of any thing by "sense, can be no surer of it than they are; when as the "strongest in faith that liveth upon the earth hath always "need to labour, strive, and pray, that his assurance concern- "ing heavenly and spiritual things may grow, increase, and be "augmented?"

[1] [Originally "to wonder at the "man."]

[2] [Possibly the very words of the archbishop, in some letter or conversation, reported to Walton by the Cranmer family.]

[3] [Answer to Travers's Supplication, § 9.]

The sermon[1] that gave him the cause of this his justification, makes the case more plain, by declaring, "that there is "besides this certainty of evidence, a certainty of adherence." In which, having most excellently demonstrated what the certainty of adherence is, he makes this comfortable use of it: "Comfortable (he says) as to weak believers, who suppose "themselves to be faithless, not to believe, when notwith-"standing they have their adherence; the Holy Spirit hath "his private operations, and worketh secretly in them, and "effectually too, though they want the inward testimony "of it."

Tell this, saith he, to a man that hath a mind too much dejected by a sad sense of his sin; to one that by a too severe judging of himself, concludes that he wants faith, because he wants the comfortable assurance of it; and his answer will be, "Do not persuade me, against my know-"ledge, against what I find and feel in myself: I do not, "I know I do not, believe." Mr. Hooker's own words follow: "Well then, to favour such men a little in their "weakness, let that be granted which they do imagine; "be it, that they adhere not to God's promises, but are "faithless, and without belief: but are they not grieved "for their unbelief? They confess they are. Do they not "wish it might, and also strive that it may be otherwise? "We know they do. Whence cometh this, but from a "secret love and liking that they have of those things be-"lieved? For no man can love those things which in his "own opinion are not; and if they think those things to be, "which they shew they love, when they desire to believe "them; then must it be, that by desiring to believe, they "prove themselves true believers: for without faith no man "thinketh that things believed are: which argument all the "subtilties of infernal powers will never be able to dissolve." This is an abridgment of part of the reasons Mr. Hooker gives for his justification of this his opinion, for which he was excepted against by Mr. Travers.

Mr. Hooker was also accused by Mr. Travers, for that he in one of his sermons[2] had declared, "That he doubted not

[1] [On the Certainty and Perpetuity of Faith in the Elect.]
[2] [Of Justification.]

"but that God was merciful to many of our forefathers living "in popish superstition, forasmuch as they sinned igno- "rantly:" and Mr. Hooker in his answer professeth it to be his judgment, and declares his reasons for this charitable opinion to be as followeth.

But first[1] [because Travers's argument against this charitable opinion of Hooker was, that they could not be saved, because they sought to be justified by the merit of their works, and so overthrow the foundation of faith] he states the question about justification and works, and how the foundation of faith without works is overthrown; and then he proceeds to discover that way which natural men and some others have mistaken to be the way, by which they hope to attain true and everlasting happiness: and having discovered the mistaken, he proceeds to direct to that true way, by which, and no other, everlasting life and blessedness is attainable. And these two ways he demonstrates thus (they be his own words that follow): "That, the way of nature; "this, the way of grace: the end of that way, salvation "merited, presupposing the righteousness of men's works; "their righteousness, a natural ability to do them; that "ability, the goodness of God which created them in such "perfection. But the end of this way, salvation bestowed "upon men as a gift: presupposing not their righteousness, "but the forgiveness of their unrighteousness, justification; "their justification, not their natural ability to do good, "but their hearty sorrow for not doing, and unfeigned belief "in Him, for whose sake not doers are accepted, which is "their vocation; their vocation, the election of God, taking "them out of the number of lost children; their election, "a Mediator in whom to be elected; this mediation inexpli- "cable mercy; this mercy supposing their misery for whom "he vouchsafed to die, and make himself a Mediator."

And he also declareth, "there is no meritorious cause for "our justification but Christ; no effectual, but His mercy;" and says also, "we deny the grace of our Lord Jesus Christ, "we abuse, disannul, and annihilate the benefit of His pas- "sion, if by a proud imagination we believe we can merit "everlasting life, or can be worthy of it." This belief (he

---

[1] ["because....of faith," interpolated, apparently by Strype.]

declareth) is to destroy the very essence of our justification, and he makes all opinions that border upon this to be very dangerous. "Yet nevertheless" (and for this he was accused) "considering how many virtuous and just men, how "many saints and martyrs, have had their dangerous opin- "ions, amongst which this was one, that they hoped to "make God some part of amends, by voluntary punishments "which they laid upon themselves: because by [of?] this, "or the like erroneous opinions which do by consequence "overthrow the merits of Christ, shall man be so bold as to "write on their graves, 'Such men are damned, there is for "them no salvation!' St. Austin says, *Errare possum, hære-* "*ticus esse nolo.* And except we put a difference betwixt "them that err ignorantly, and them that obstinately persist "in it, how is it possible that any man should hope to be "saved? Give me a Pope or a Cardinal, whom great afflic- "tions have made to know himself; whose heart God hath "touched with true sorrow for all his sins, and filled with "a love of Christ and his Gospel; whose eyes are willingly "open to see the truth, and his mouth ready to renounce all "error, this one opinion of merit excepted, which he thinketh "God will require at his hands; and because he wanteth, "trembleth, and is discouraged, and yet can say, 'Lord, "cleanse me from all my secret sins!' shall I think, because "of this, or a like error, such men touch not so much as the "hem of Christ's garment? If they do, wherefore should "I doubt but that virtue may proceed from Christ to save "them? No, I will not be afraid to say to such a one, 'You "err in your opinion, but be of good comfort, you have to do "with a merciful God, who will make the best of that little "which you hold well, and not with a captious sophister, who "gathereth the worst out of every thing in which you are "mistaken.'

"But it will be said, (says Mr. Hooker,) 'The admittance "of merit in any degree, overthroweth the foundation, ex- "cludeth from the hope of mercy, from all possibility of sal- "vation.'" (And now Mr. Hooker's own words follow.)

"What, though they hold the truth sincerely in all other "parts of Christian faith; although they have in some mea- "sure all the virtues and graces of the Spirit; although

"they have all other tokens of God's children in them;
"although they be far from having any proud opinion that
"they shall be saved by the worthiness of their deeds;
"although the only thing that troubleth and molesteth them
"be a little too much dejection, somewhat too great a fear
"arising from an erroneous conceit, that God will require
"a worthiness in them, which they are grieved to find wanting
"in themselves? although they be not obstinate in this
"opinion? although they be willing and would be glad to
"forsake it, if any one reason were brought sufficient to
"disprove it? although the only cause why they do not
"forsake it ere they die, be their ignorance of that means by
"which it might be disproved? although the cause why the
"ignorance in this point is not removed, be the want of
"knowledge in such as should be able, and are not, to
"remove it? Let me die (says Mr. Hooker) if it be ever
"proved, that simply an error doth exclude a Pope or Car-
"dinal in such a case utterly from hope of life. Surely I must
"confess, that if it be an error to think that God may be mer-
"ciful to save men even when they err, my greatest comfort
"is my error: were it not for the love I bear to this error,
"I would never wish to speak or to live."

I was willing to take notice of these two points, as supposing them to be very material; and that as they are thus contracted, they may prove useful to my reader; as also, for that the answers be arguments of Mr. Hooker's great and clear reason, and equal charity. Other exceptions were also made against him by Mr. Travers, as, "That he prayed "before and not after his sermons; that in his prayers he "named bishops; that he kneeled both when he prayed and "when he received the Sacrament; and" (says Mr. Hooker in his defence) "other exceptions so like these, as but to "name, I should have thought a greater fault than to commit "them."

And it is not unworthy the noting, that in the manage of so great a controversy, a sharper reproof than this, and one like it, did never fall from the happy pen of this humble man. That like it was upon a like occasion of exceptions, to which his answer was, "Your next argument consists of "railing and of reasons: to your railing, I say nothing; to "your reasons, I say what follows[1]." And I am glad of this fair occasion, to testify the dovelike temper of this meek, this matchless man; and doubtless, if Almighty God had blessed the dissenters from the ceremonies and discipline of this church with a like measure of wisdom and humility, instead of their pertinacious zeal; then, Obedience and Truth had kissed each other; then peace and piety had flourished in our nation, and this church and state had been blessed like "Jerusalem that is at unity with itself;" but this can never be expected, till God shall bless the common people of this nation with a belief "*That schism is a sin, and, they not* "*fit to judge what is schism:*" and bless them also with a belief, "that there may be offences taken, which are not "given;" and, "that laws are not made for private men to "dispute, but to obey."

<small>J. S. The articles of false doctrines objected by Travers to Hooker.</small>

[Before we pass from these unhappy disceptations between Hooker and Travers, as we have heard two articles of pretended false doctrine objected by the one to the other, so it is pity the rest should be wholly lost, and for ever buried in silence: therefore, for the making this considerable part of the reverend man's life and history complete, and to retrieve whatsoever may be gotten of the pen and mind of so learned and judicious a person, take this further account, not only of two, but of all the articles that his before-mentioned adversary had marshalled up against him, collected from a sermon or sermons he had heard him preach at the Temple: together with his endeavoured confutation of them; and likewise Hooker's own vindication of himself to each of these articles. These articles seem to have been delivered by Travers to the Lord Treasurer. The same lord delivered them to Hooker to consider of, and to make his reply to. And of these articles the archbishop also was privy, and briefly declared his judgment and determination of them. I shall set all down exactly from an authentic manuscript.

---

[1] [Compare E. P. V. 30, 4. "Our answer therefore to their reasons "is, No: to their scoffs, Nothing."]

Doctrines delivered by Mr. Hooker, as they were set down and shewed by Mr. Travers, Mar. 30, 1585, under this title[1];

A short Note of sundry unsound Points of Doctrine at divers times delivered by Mr. Hooker in his public Sermons.

1. The church of Rome is a true church of Christ, and a church sanctified by profession of that truth, which God had revealed unto us by his Son, though not a pure and perfect church.

2. The fathers which lived and died in Popish superstition were saved, because they sinned ignorantly.

3. They which are of the church of Rome may be saved by such a faith as they have in Christ, and a general repentance of all their sins.

4. The church of Rome holdeth all men sinners, even the Blessed Virgin, though some of them think otherwise of her.

5. The church of Rome teacheth Christ's righteousness to be the only meritorious cause of taking away sin.

6. The Galatians which joined with faith in Christ, circumcision, as necessary unto salvation, notwithstanding be saved.

7. Neither the church of Rome, nor the Galatians, deny the foundation directly, but only by consequent: and therefore may be saved. Or else neither the Lutherans, nor whosoever hold any error (for every error by consequent denieth the foundation), may be saved.

---

[1] [In the Harleian MSS. No. 291. fol. 183–185, is a paper dated March 20, 1585, and headed, "Propositions taught and maintained by Mr. Hooker. The same briefly confuted by L. T. in a private Letter." And immediately following, "Doctrine preached by Mr. Hooker in the Temple the first of March 1585." These papers agree in substance, though not verbally with Strype's, as far as they go: for they do not contain either Hooker's answer or the archbishop's judgment on the disputed points. (L. T. was Lawrence Tomson. Dr. Bliss, in Ath. Oxon. I. 700. See an account of him in the same work, anno 1608, tom. II. p. 44. He was employed as a clerk by sir F. Walsingham. See a letter of his (Tomson's) at the end of Knewstub's Confutation of H. N. 1579.) It appears by Fuller, Ch. Hist. b. ix. p. 216, that notes of these sermons were taken by a great many persons. "Here might one on Sundays have "seen almost as many writers as "hearers. Not only young students, "but even the gravest benchers, "(such as Sir Edward Cook and "Sir James Altham then were) were "not more exact in taking instruc"tions from their clients, than in "writing notes from the mouths of "their ministers."]

8. An additament taketh not away that whereunto it is added, but confirmeth it. As he that saith of any, that he is a righteous man, saith, that he is a man: except it be privative; as when he saith, he is a dead man, then he denieth him to be a man: and of this sort of [privative] additaments neither are works, which are added to Christ by the Church of Rome; nor circumcision, added to him by the Galatians.

9. The Galatians' case is harder than the case of the church of Rome; for they added to Christ circumcision, which God had forbidden and abolished: but that which the church of Rome addeth, are works which God hath commanded.

10. No one sequel urged by the Apostle against the Galatians, for joining circumcision with Christ, but may be as well enforced against the Lutherans holding ubiquity.

11. A bishop or cardinal of the church of Rome, yea, the Pope himself, denying all other errors of popery, notwithstanding his opinion of justification by works, may be saved.

12. Predestination is not of the absolute will of God, but conditional.

13. The doings of the wicked are not of the will of God positive, but only permissive.

14. The reprobates are not rejected, but for the evil works which God did foresee they would commit.

15. The assurance of things which we believe by the Word, is not so sure, as of those which we perceive by sense.

Here follows an Account, given in by Mr. Hooker himself, of what he preached, March 28, 1585[1]. And then of what Travers in his Lectures excepted thereunto. And lastly, of Hooker's Reply and Vindication of himself and his Sermons.

<small>Hooker's own relation of his assertions, and vindication of</small> "I doubted not but that God was merciful to thousands "of our fathers, which lived in popish superstition: for "that *they* sinned ignorantly. But *we* have the light of "the truth.

[1] [Strype in his Life of Whitg. I. 476, makes the date 1586. But it is an oversight there, as is evident from the context.]

[1]"Which doctrine was withstood, because we are com-
"manded to depart out of Babylon, else we should be par-
"takers of those plagues there denounced against such as
"repent not of their superstitions: which they cannot who
"know them not.

them against Travers.

"I answered, that there were thousands in our days who
"hate sin, desiring to walk according to the will of God;
"and yet committing sin which they know not to be sin.
"I think, that they that desire forgiveness of secret sins,
"which they know not to be sins, and that are sorry for sins,
"that they know not to be sins, [such] do repent.

"It is replied, that without faith there is no repentance.
"Our fathers in desiring mercy did but as divers pagans;
"and had no true repentance.

"They thought they could not be saved by Christ without
"works, as the Galatians did: and so they denied the founda-
"tion of faith.

"I answered, although the proposition were true, that he
"who thinketh he cannot be saved by Christ without works,
"overthroweth the foundation; yet we may persuade our-
"selves that our forefathers might be saved. 1. Because
"many of them were ignorant of the dogmatical positions of
"the church of Rome. 2. Albeit they had divers positions
"of that church, yet it followeth not that they had this.
"3. Although they did generally hold this position, yet God
"might be merciful unto them. No exception hath been
"taken against any one of these assertions. 4. I add, that
"albeit all those, of whom we speak, did not only hold this
"generally, but as the scholars of Rome hold this position
"now, of joining works with Christ; whether doth that
"position overthrow the foundation directly, or only by con-
"sequence? If it doth overthrow the foundation directly, &c.

---

[1] ["Salvation belongeth to the
"Church of Christ. We may not
"think, that they could be capable
"of it, which lived in the errors
"held and maintained in the Church
"of Rome, that seat of Antichrist.
"Wherefore to his people God
"speaketh in this sort: 'Go out
"of Babylon, my people, go out of
"her, that you be not partaker of
"her sins, and that you taste not
"of her plagues.'
"The Galatians thinking that
"they could not be saved by Christ,
"except they were circumcised, did
"thereby exclude themselves from
"salvation. Christ did profit them
"nothing. So they which join their
"own works with Christ." *Travers's own Answer.*]

"To make all plain, these points are to be handled. First, "what is meant by the foundation. Secondly, what it is "to deny the foundation directly. Thirdly, whether the elect "may be so deceived, that they may come to this, to deny "the foundation directly. Fourthly, whether the Galatians "did directly deny it. Fifthly, whether the church of Rome, "by joining works with Christ in the matter of salvation, do "directly deny it.

I. To the first I answer: "The foundation is, that which "Peter, Nathaniel, and the Samaritans confessed; and that "which the Apostles expressly [affirm,] Acts iv. [12.] 'There "is none other name under heaven given among men, "whereby we must be saved.' It is, in fine, this, Salvation "is by Christ only. This word *only*, what doth it exclude? "[As when we say,] 'This judge shall *only* determine this "matter:' this *only* doth not exclude all other things, be-"sides the person of the judge; as, necessary witnesses, "the equity of the cause, &c. but *all persons:* and not all "persons from being present, but from determining the cause. "So when we say, 'Salvation *only* is by Christ,' we do not "exclude all other things. For then how could we say, that "faith were necessary? We exclude therefore not those means "whereby the benefits of Christ are applied to us; but all "other *persons*, for working any thing for our redemption.

"II. To the second point: We are said to deny the founda-"tion directly, when plainly and expressly we deny that "Christ only doth save. *By consequence* we deny the founda-"tion, when any such thing is defended, whereby it may be "inferred, that Christ doth not only save.

"III. To the third: The elect of God cannot so err that "they should deny directly the foundation: for that Christ "doth keep them from that extremity: and there is no "salvation to such as deny the foundation directly. There-"fore it is said, that they 'shall worship the beast, whose "names are not found in the book of life.' Antichrist may "prevail much against them [viz. the elect], and they may "receive the sign of the beast in the same degree, but not so "that they should directly deny the foundation.

"IV. To the fourth: Albeit the Galatians fell into error; "but not so that they lost salvation. If they had died before "they had known the doctrine of Paul, being before deceived "by those that they thought did teach the truth: what do "you think? should they have been damned? This we are "taught, that such errors [as are damning] shall not take "hold, but on those that love not the truth. The Galatians "had embraced the truth; and for it had suffered many "things, &c. There came among them seducers that required "circumcision. They being moved with a religious fear, "thought it to be the word of God, that they should be cir- "cumcised. The best of them might be brought into that "opinion; and dying before they could be otherwise in- "structed, they may not for that be excluded from salvation. "Circumcision being joined with Christ doth only by con- "sequence overthrow the foundation. To hold the founda- "tion by an additament is not to deny the foundation; unless "the additament be a privative. He is a just man, therefore "a man: but this followeth not; he is a dead man, therefore "he is a man. In the 15th chapter of the Acts they are "called *credentes* [i.e. such as believed] that taught the ne- "cessity of circumcision. That name could not have been "given unto them, if directly they had denied the foundation. "That which the Apostle doth urge against the Galatians, in "respect of circumcision, may be urged against the Lutherans "in respect of their consubstantiation. [But they do not "directly deny the foundation.] So neither did the Galatians "directly deny it.

"V. Lastly: Whether doth the church of Rome directly "deny the foundation, by joining Christ and works? There "is a difference between the papists and the Galatians: for "circumcision, which the Galatians joined with Christ, was "forbidden, and taken away by Christ. But works are "commanded, which the church of Rome doth join with "Christ. So that there is greater repugnancy to join circum- "cision with Christ, than to join works with him. But let "them be equal. As the Galatians only by consequent "denied the foundation, so do the Papists. (Zanchy, Calvin, "Mornay; I need not go so far as some of these.)[1] But

---

[1] [The words in ( ) appear to be a reference, crept by mistake into the text. The passages referred to are specified in the body of the sermon.]

"this I think, if the Pope, or any of the Cardinals, should
"forsake all other their corruptions, and yield up their souls,
"holding the foundation again but by a slender thread, and
"did but as it were touch the hem of Christ's garment,
"believing that which the Church of Rome doth in this
"point of doctrine, they may obtain mercy. For they have
"to deal with God, who is no captious sophister, and will not
"examine them in quiddities, but accept them if they plainly
"hold the foundation.

"This error is my only comfort as touching the salvation
"of our fathers. I follow Mr. Martyr. I know *Ignorantia
"non excusat in toto*, but *in tanto*. It maketh not a fault to
"be no fault, but that which is a fault to be a less one."

The Archbishop's judgment of those controversies.

At length, thus did the Archbishop of Canterbury discreetly and warily correct and moderate these articles between them both:

I. "Papists living and dying Papists may notwithstanding
"be saved. The reason; ignorance excused them. As the
"apostle allegeth, 1 Tim. i. 13. 'I obtained mercy because I
"did it ignorantly.'

The Archbishop's Judgment.

"Not *Papists*, but *our fathers*. Nor they *all*, but *many
"of them*. Nor *living and dying Papists*, but living in popish
"superstitions. Nor simply *might*, but *might by the mercy of
"God*, be saved. Ignorance did not excuse the fault to make
"it no fault: but the less their fault was, in respect of
"ignorance, the more hope we have, that God was merciful
"to them."

II. "Papists hold the foundation of faith: so that they
"may be saved, notwithstanding their opinion of merit."

Archbishop. "And Papists overthrow the foundation of
"faith, both by their doctrine of merit, and otherwise many
"ways. So that if they have, as their errors deserve, I do
"not see how they should be saved."

III. "General repentance may serve to their salvation,
"though they confess not their error of merit."

Archbishop. "General repentance will not serve any but
"the faithful man. Nor him, for any sin, but for such sins
"only as he doth not mark, nor know to be sin."

IV. "The Church of Rome is within the new covenant."

Archbishop. "The Church of Rome is not as the assemblies "of Turks, Jews, and Painims."

V. "The Galatians joining the law with Christ might have "been saved, before they received the Epistle."

Archbishop. "Of the Galatians, before they were told of "their error, what letteth us to think, as of our fathers, be- "fore the Church of Rome was admonished of her defection "from the truth?"]

And this also may be worthy of noting, that these exceptions of Mr. Travers against Mr. Hooker proved to be *felix error*, for they were the cause of his transcribing those few of his sermons, which we now see printed with his books; and of his Answer to Mr. Travers his Supplication: and of his most learned and useful Discourse of Justification, of Faith and Works; and by their transcription they fell into such hands as have preserved them from being lost, as too many of his other matchless writings were; and from these I have gathered many observations in this discourse of his life.

After the publication of his Answer to the Petition of Mr. Travers, Mr. Hooker grew daily into greater repute with the most learned and wise of the nation; but it had a contrary effect in very many of the Temple that were zealous for Mr. Travers and for his Church-discipline; insomuch, that though Mr. Travers left the place [1], yet the seeds of discontent could not be rooted out of that society, by the great reason, and as great meekness, of this humble man: for

---

[1] ["Adam Loftus, Archbishop of "Dublin, and Chancellor of Ire- "land, his ancient colleague in "Cambridge, invited him over to "be Provost of Trinity college in "Dublin. Embracing the motion, "over he went, accepting the place, "and continued some years therein, "till discomposed with the fear of "their civil wars, he returned into "England, and lived here many "years very obscurely, (though in "himself a shining light,) as to the "matter of outward maintenance. "Yet had he Agur's wish, neither "poverty nor riches, though his "'enough' seemed to be of shortest "size... When Archbishop Ussher, "brought up under him, proffered "money unto him for his relief, "Mr. Travers returned a thankful "refusal thereof. Sometimes he "did preach, rather when he durst, "than when he would; debarred "from all cure of souls by his non- "conformity. He lived and died "unmarried, and though leaving "many nephews (some eminent) "scholars, bequeathed all his books "of Oriental languages (wherein he "was exquisite) and plate worth "fifty pounds, to Sion college in "London." Fuller, C. H. IX. 218.]

though the chief benchers gave him much reverence and encouragement, yet he there met with many neglects and oppositions by those of Master Travers' judgment; insomuch that it turned to his extreme grief: and that he might unbeguile and win them, he designed to write a deliberate sober Treatise of the Church's power to make canons for the use of ceremonies, and by law to impose an obedience to them, as upon her children; and this he proposed to do in eight books of the Laws of Ecclesiastical Polity; intending therein to shew such arguments as should force an assent from all men, if reason delivered in sweet language, and void of any provocation, were able to do it: and that he might prevent all prejudice, he wrote before it a large Preface or Epistle to the Dissenting Brethren, wherein there were such bowels of love, and such a commixture of that love with reason, as was never exceeded but in Holy Writ; and particularly by that of St. Paul to his dear brother and fellow-labourer Philemon: than which, none was ever more like this Epistle of Mr. Hooker's: so that his dear friend and companion in his studies, Dr. Spenser, might after his death justly say[1], "What admirable height of learning and depth of judgment "dwelt in the lowly mind of this truly humble man, great "in all wise men's eyes except his own; with what gravity "and majesty of speech his tongue and pen uttered heavenly "mysteries; whose eyes, in the humility of his heart, were "always cast down to the ground: how all things that pro- "ceeded from him were breathed as from the spirit of love; "as if he, like the bird of the Holy Ghost, the Dove, had "wanted gall: let those that knew him not in his person, "judge by these living images of his soul, his writings."

The foundation of these books was laid in the Temple; but he found it no fit place to finish what he had there designed; and he therefore earnestly solicited the archbishop for a remove from that place, to whom he spake to this purpose: "My Lord, when I lost the freedom of my cell, "which was my college; yet, I found some degree of it in "my quiet country parsonage: but I am weary of the noise "and oppositions of this place, and indeed God and nature

---

[1] [In his Preface to the edition of 1604.]

"did not intend me for contentions, but for study and quiet-
"ness. My Lord, my particular contests with Mr. Travers
"here have proved the more unpleasant to me, because I
"believe him to be a good man[1]; and that belief hath occa-
"sioned me to examine mine own conscience concerning his
"opinions; and, to satisfy that, I have consulted the scrip-
"ture, and other laws both human and divine, whether the
"conscience of him and others of his judgment ought to
"be so far complied with as to alter our frame of Church-
"government, our manner of God's worship, our praising
"and praying to him, and our established ceremonies, as
"often as his and others' tender consciences shall require
"us: and, in this examination, I have not only satisfied
"myself, but have begun a Treatise, in which I intend[2] a
"justification of the Laws of our Ecclesiastical Polity; in
"which design God and his holy Angels shall at the last
"great day bear me that witness which my conscience now
"does; that my meaning is not to provoke any, but rather to
"satisfy all tender consciences, and I shall never be able to
"do this, but where I may study, and pray for God's blessing
"upon my endeavours, and keep myself in peace and pri-
"vacy, and behold God's blessing spring out of my mother

---

[1] ["In the very midst of the "paroxysm betwixt Hooker and "Travers, the latter still bare (and "none can challenge the other to "the contrary) a reverend esteem "of his adversary. And when an "unworthy aspersion, some years "after, was cast on Hooker, Mr. "Travers being asked of a private "friend what he thought of the "truth of that accusation: 'In "truth,' said he, 'I take Mr. Hooker "to be a holy man.'" Fuller, C. H. IX. 217.]

[2] [This paragraph originally stood as follows; "I have not only satis-"fied myself, but have begun a "Treatise in which I intend the "satisfaction of others, by a demon-"stration of the reasonableness of "our laws of Ecclesiastical Polity; "and therein laid a hopeful founda-"tion for the Church's peace; and, "so as not to provoke your ad-"versary Mr. Cartwright, nor Mr.

"Travers, whom I take to be mine, "(but not mine enemy,) God knows "this to be my meaning. To which "end, I have searched many books, "and spent many thoughtful hours; "and I hope, not in vain: for I "write to reasonable men. But, "my Lord, I shall never be able to "finish what I have begun, unless "I be removed into some quiet "country parsonage, where I may "see God's blessing spring out of "my mother earth, and eat mine "own bread in peace and privacy. "A place where I may, without "disturbance, meditate my ap-"proaching mortality, and that "great account, which all flesh "must at the last great day give to "the God of all spirits.

"This is my design; and, as "these are the desires of my heart, "so they shall, by God's assistance, "be the constant endeavours of the "uncertain remainder of my life."]

"earth, and eat my own bread without oppositions; and "therefore, if your Grace can judge me worthy of such a "favour, let me beg it, that I may perfect what I have "begun."

About this time the parsonage or rectory of Boscum, in the diocese of Sarum, and six miles from that city, became void. The Bishop of Sarum is patron of it: but in the vacancy of that see (which was three years betwixt the translation[1] of Bishop Pierce to the see of York, and Bishop Caldwell's admission into it) the disposal of that and all benefices belonging to that see during this said vacancy, came to be disposed of by the Archbishop of Canterbury; and he presented Richard Hooker to it, in the year 1591. And Richard Hooker was also in this said year instituted, July 17, to be a minor prebend of Salisbury, the corps to it being Nether-Havin[2], about ten miles from that city; which prebend was of no great value, but intended chiefly to make him capable of a better preferment in that church[3]. In this Boscum he continued till he had finished four of his eight proposed books of the Laws of Ecclesiastical Polity, and these were entered into the Register-book in Stationers'-hall, the 9th of

---

[1] [Originally "death of Bishop "Pierce." Strype, Whitg. II. 202, charges Walton with this mistake, not being aware that he had corrected it in a subsequent edition. Dr. John Peers, or Piers, was confirmed Archbishop of York, Feb. 19, 158⅘. Strype, Whitg. I. 548. Dr. John Coldwell, Dean of Rochester, was consecrated Bishop of Salisbury, Dec. 26, 1591. Id. ibid. II. 112.]

[2] [At the end of Dr. Bernard's Clavi Trabales, 1661, are some memoranda of subscriptions to the Thirty-nine Articles, by divines of high authority; "among whom," says the compiler, "it pleased me "to find the hand of the reverend "and learned Mr. Hooker thus "subscribing, 'Per me Richardum "Hooker clericum in artibus ma-"gistrum præsentatum ad Canoni-"catum et Præbendam de Neather-"Haven in Ecclesia cathedrali Sa-"rum. 17 Julii 1591.'" p. 147.]

[3] [He was at the same time made Subdean of Sarum. See that title in Le Neve's Fasti, 273. "1591, 33 "Eliz. Richard Hooker was col-"lated July 23, 1591. Void by the "resignation of Baldgey;" who succeeded Hooker at the Temple. The Subdean is not, as such, a Canon residentiary, and his emoluments are very scanty. In the Chapter books appear the following entries:

Subdeans of Sarum. Installed.
Ric. Hooker per Lit. mandat. Archiepi .... 23 Julii 1591.
Thos. Coldwell per Resign. Ric. Hooker .... 16 Feb. 1594.

Netheravon Prebend.
Ric. Hooker per Resign. Nic. Baldguy...23 Julii 1591.
Thos. Joy per Resign.   — Hooker ... 6 Feb. 1594. (16 Feb. ?)

March, 1592 [1], but not published [2] till the year 1594, and then were with the before-mentioned large and affectionate preface, which he directs "to them that seek (as they term it) "the Reformation of the Laws and Orders Ecclesiastical in "the Church of England;" of which books I shall yet say nothing more, but that he continued his laborious diligence to finish the remaining four during his life (of all which more properly hereafter) but at Boscum he finisht and publisht but only the first four, being then in the thirty-ninth year of his age.

He left Boscum in the year 1595, by a surrender of it into the hands of Bishop Caldwell, and he presented Benjamin Russel, who was instituted into it the 23d of June in the same year.

The parsonage of Bishopsborne in Kent, three miles from Canterbury, is in that archbishop's gift; but, in the latter end of the year 1594, Dr. William Redman the rector of it was made Bishop of Norwich [3]; by which means the power of presenting to it was *pro ea vice* in the Queen; and she presented Richard Hooker, whom she loved well, to this good living of Borne the 7th of July, 1595, in which living he

---

In Sir Thomas Phillips's Book of Wiltshire Institutions (taken from the Archives of the Registry) is the following entry, under the title, Registrum Johannis Coldwell:

1595	Patronus.	Clericus.
Eccl. Boscomb.	Ricardus Hooker, clericus.	Benjamin Russell per resign. dicti Ric. Hooker.

In this, the description of Hooker as patron is an error, unless he was so for one turn, as it is said in some other instances, "ex concessione Episcopi." The patronage of Boscomb has been in the bishop from the very earliest period. Between the years 1584 and 1591, Bishop Pierce's Register is lost: consequently Hooker's institution does not appear.

The above particulars were kindly communicated to the editor by a member of the Chapter. That Hooker was really the patron by concession *pro ea vice* seems the more probable, as the person presented had been a scholar of C.C.C. and possibly one of Hooker's own pupils. "Benj. Russell, discipulus. "Feb. 6, 1579." From the President's Register.]

[1 The true date is 29th January, 159$\frac{2}{3}$. Arber's Transcripts, II. 295.] 1886.

2 [Originally "printed." The change may be thought to be warranted by the letter to lord Burghley; for which see App. N°. V. although Mr. Strype (Whitg. II. 148.) conjectures the book to have been sent in a written copy rather than in print.]

3 [Consecrated 12 Jan. 159$\frac{4}{5}$, Strype, Whitg. II. 218.]

continued till his death, without any addition of dignity or profit[1].

And now having brought our Richard Hooker, from his birthplace to this where he found a grave, I shall only give some account of his books, and of his behaviour in this parsonage of Borne, and then give a rest both to myself and my reader.

His first four Books and large Epistle have been declared to be printed at his being at Boscum, anno 1594. Next, I am to tell, that at the end of these four Books, there was when he first printed them this Advertisement to the Reader: "I have for some causes thought it at this time more fit to "let go these first four Books by themselves, than to stay "both them and the rest, till the whole might together "be published. Such generalities of the cause in question "as are here handled, it will be perhaps not amiss to con- "sider apart, by way of introduction unto the books that "are to follow concerning particulars; in the mean time "the reader is requested to mend the printer's errors, as "noted underneath."

And I am next to declare, that his fifth Book (which is larger than his first four) was first also printed by itself anno 1597, and dedicated to his patron (for till then he chose none) the archbishop. These Books were read with an admiration of their excellency in this, and their just fame spread itself also into foreign nations. And I have been told more than forty years past, that either Cardinal Allen, or learned Dr. Stapleton[2] (both Englishmen, and in Italy

---

[1] [Mr. Wharton says (Def. of Plural. 192, 2d edition) that Hooker died possessed of very great preferments. But he offers no proof of this assertion; nor is any to be found in Le Neve's Fasti. Fulman, MSS. vol. x. near the end, says, "Heylin, Animadv. on Fuller's Ch. "Hist. p. 165, calls him Prebend "of Canterbury; I think, without "good ground." Dr. Heylyn's assertion is the less to be regarded, because in the same sentence he commits two other mistakes concerning Hooker: calling him "then "Master of the Temple," and dating the first publication of his great work 1595. Dr. Spenser in his preface expressly affirms "he neither "enjoyed nor expected any the least "dignity;" meaning at the time of his death.]

[2] [Stapleton is particularly mentioned as an admirer of Hooker, in Bishop King's letter to Walton. He died in 1598. Collier, E. H. II. 662. Cardinal Allen in 1594. Id. ibid. 643. This proves that the former must have been the person here meant.]

about the time when Hooker's four Books were first printed) meeting with this general fame of them, were desirous to read an author that both the reformed and the learned of their own Romish Church did so much magnify, and therefore caused them to be sent for to Rome; and after reading them, boasted to the Pope, (which then was Clement the Eighth,) " That though he had lately said he never met with " an English book whose writer deserved the name of an " author; yet there now appeared a wonder to them, and " it would be so to his Holiness, if it were in Latin; for a " poor obscure English priest had writ four such Books of " Laws and Church-Polity, and in a style that expressed " such a grave and so humble a majesty, with such clear " demonstration of reason, that in all their readings they had " not met with any that exceeded him;" and this begot in the Pope an earnest desire that Dr. Stapleton should bring the said four books, and looking on the English read a part of them to him in Latin; which Dr. Stapleton did, to the end of the first book; at the conclusion of which, the Pope spake to this purpose: " There is no learning that this " man hath not searcht into; nothing too hard for his under- " standing: this man indeed deserves the name of an author; " his books will get reverence by age, for there is in them " such seeds of eternity, that if the rest be like this, they " shall last till the last fire shall consume all learning."

Nor was this high, the only testimony and commendations given to his Books; for at the first coming of King James into this kingdom, he inquired of the Archbishop Whitgift for his friend Mr. Hooker that writ the Books of Church-Polity; to which the answer was, that he died a year before Queen Elizabeth, who received the sad news of his death with very much sorrow: to which the King replied, " And I receive it with no less, that I shall want the desired " happiness of seeing and discoursing with that man, from " whose Books I have received such satisfaction: indeed, " my Lord, I have received more satisfaction in reading a " leaf, or paragraph, in Mr. Hooker, though it were but about " the fashion of Churches, or Church-musick, or the like, " but especially of the Sacraments, than I have had in " the reading particular large treatises written but of one of

"those subjects by others, though very learned men; and, I
"observe there is in Mr. Hooker no affected language[1];
"but a grave, comprehensive, clear manifestation of reason;
"and that backed with the authority of the Scripture, the
"fathers and schoolmen, and with all law both sacred and
"civil. And though many others write well, yet in the
"next age they will be forgotten; but doubtless there is
"in every page of Mr. Hooker's book the picture of a divine
"soul, such pictures of Truth and Reason, and drawn in
"so sacred colours, that they shall never fade, but give an
"immortal memory to the author." And it is so truly true,
that the king thought what he spake, that as the most
learned of the nation have and still do mention Mr. Hooker
with reverence; so he also did never mention him but with
the epithet of *learned*, or *judicious*, or *reverend*, or *venerable*
Mr. Hooker.

Nor did his son, our late King Charles the First, ever

---

[1] [Chr. Letter, page 45. "Our "last scruple and demaund is this: "seeing your bookes be so long and "tedious, in a stile not usuall, and, "as we verilie thinke, the like harde "to be found, farre differing from "the simplicitie of holie scripture, "and nothing after the frame of "the writings of the reverend and "learned fathers of our Church, "as of Cranmer, Ridley, Latimer, "Jewell, Whitgift, Fox, Fulke, &c. ".... whether your meaning be to "show yourself some rare Demos- "thenes, or extraordinary rabbi, "&c." Hooker, MS. note: "The "dislike you have of me for not "thinking as some others doe "whom you love, hath drawñe you "into invectives against my stile, "and made you eloquent in accusing "me for that my maner of writing "is not such as other mens hath "bene. You might with as great "discretion find falt that I look "not like Calvin, Beza, Paulus "Fagius, P. Martyr, M. Luther. "For I hold it as possible to be "like all those in countenance, as "them in stile whom you have "mentioned. You that carry the "mind of a Phalaris towards your "adversary are not fit to exercise "the office of an Aristarchus. I "must looke as nature, speak as "custome, and think as God's "good Spirit hath taught me, judg "you howsoever either of my mynd, "or of my stile, or if you will of my "looke also." Again, Chr. Letter, p. 46. "In the booke of that most "learned and reverend Father D. "Whitgift wee finde the question "judicially (Hooker in margin. "'you would say, judiciously') sett "downe, his aunswere to the matter "in question sensible, his reasons ".... directly applied, so as such "poore men as wee be *may beare* "*away* what he saith .... but in "your writing we are mightily in- "combred."

Hooker, MS. note: "You *beare* "*it away*. I wish it did rather "cary you away from the errors "and vanities of your mind.

"But howsoever your part re- "quire you to speake heere, the "censure which all the pack of "you giveth both of my L. Grace "his writings, and of all other "mens that hath the same cause "is Ἀνέγνων, ἔγνων, κατέγνων."]

mention him but with the same reverence, enjoining his son [1], our now gracious King, to be studious in Mr. Hooker's books. And our learned antiquary Mr. Camden [2] mentioning the death, the modesty, and other virtues of Mr. Hooker, and magnifying his books, wisht "that for the honour of this, and " benefit of other nations, they were turned into the universal " language." Which work, though undertaken by many, yet they have been weary, and forsaken it; but the reader may now expect it, having been long since begun, and lately finisht by the happy pen of Dr. Earl, now Lord Bishop of Salisbury, of whom I may justly say, (and let it not offend him, because it is such a truth as ought not to be concealed from posterity, or those that now live, and yet know him not,) that since Mr. Hooker died, none have lived whom God hath blessed with more innocent wisdom, more sanctified learning, or a more pious, peaceable, primitive temper: so that this excellent person seems to be only like himself, and our venerable Richard Hooker; and only fit to make the learned of all nations happy, in knowing what hath been too long confined to the language of our little island [3].

---

[1] [Rather his daughter, the Lady Elisabeth. See her relation at the end of Εἰκὼν Βασιλικὴ, p. 261, ed. 1649. "He bid me read Bishop "Andrews' Sermons, Hooker's Ec-"clesiastical Polity, and Bishop " Laud's book against Fisher, which " would ground me against popery." Thus exprest by Gauden, in his Dedication of Hooker's Works to King Charles II. ed. 1662: "Your "Majesty's Royal Father, a few "days before he was crowned with "martyrdom, recommended to his "dearest children the diligent read-"ing of Mr. Hooker's Ecclesiastical " Polity, even next the Bible." (Why the last clause was inserted does not appear.) This seems to have been Walton's authority for saying that his Majesty gave the injunction to his son.]

[2] In his Annals of Eliz. 1599. [" Hoc anno animam cœlo reddidit " Richardus Hookerus ex Devonia " nobilium ingeniorum feraci oriun-"dus, Oxoniæ in Corporis Christi " collegio educatus, theologus mo-" destia, temperantia, mansuetudine " et cæteris virtutibus imitandus, et " supra multiplici eruditionis laude " celebris, quam libri de Ecclesias-"tica Politeia, patria lingua editi, " dignissimi qui Latine loquantur, " abunde testentur." t. II. p. 189. ed. 1627.]

[3] [Bishop Earle was tutor to Prince Charles, and attended him in his exile: (see Clarendon, III. 203, 752. ed. 1819.) Dean of Westminster, 1660, Bishop of Worcester 1662, Bishop of Salisbury 1663, died Nov. 17, 1665, at Oxford, and is buried in Merton college chapel. The following is part of his epitaph there: " Ille qui " Hookeri ingentis Politiam Eccle-"siasticam; ille qui Caroli Mar-"tyris Εἰκόνα Βασιλικὴν, volumen, " quo post Apocalypsin divinius " nullum, legavit orbi sic Latine " redditas, ut uterque unius Fidei " Defensor, patriam adhuc retineat " majestatem." April 26, 1662, in

There might be many more and just occasions taken to speak of his books, which none ever did or can commend too much; but I decline them, and hasten to an account of his Christian behaviour and death at Borne; in which place he continued his customary rules of mortification and self-denial; was much in fasting, frequent in meditation and prayers, enjoying those blessed returns, which only men of strict lives feel and know, and of which men of loose and godless lives cannot be made sensible; for, spiritual things are spiritually discerned.

At his entrance into this place, his friendship was much sought for by Dr. Hadrian Saravia, then or about that time made one of the prebends of Canterbury, a German by birth [1], and sometimes a pastor both in Flanders and Holland [2], where he had studied and well considered the controverted points concerning episcopacy and sacrilege, and in England had a just occasion to declare his judgment concerning both, unto his brethren ministers in the Low Countries; which was excepted against by Theodore Beza and others [3]; against whose exceptions, he rejoined [4], and thereby became the happy author of many learned tracts writ in Latin; especially of three; one of the Degrees of Ministers, and of

---

convocation, "the care of translating "the Book of Common Prayer into "Latin was committed to Dr. John "Earl, Dean of Westminster, and "Dr. John Pearson." Collier, E. H. II. 889. Bishop Burnet says, "He was the man of all the clergy, "for whom the King had the "greatest esteem. He had been "his sub-tutor, and had followed "him in all his exile, with so clear "a character, that the King could "never see or hear of any one "thing amiss in him. So he, who "had a secret pleasure in finding "out any thing that lessened a man "esteemed eminent for piety, yet "had a value for him beyond all "the men of his order." Hist. of his Own Times, I. 225, ed. 1724.]

[1] [" Natione Belgica, natus He-"dinæ Artesii." His epitaph in Canterbury cathedral, quoted by Strype, Wh. II. 210. " His father "a Spaniard, his mother one of "Artois: both protestants." Strype, An. I. ii. 224. The Belgic provinces were often spoken of under the title of Lower Germany; and are so in Saravia's own dedication of his three Treatises.]

[2] [At Ghent, before 1566. Strype, ibid. 226. In the dedication mentioned above, Dr. S. says, "Apud "meos fratres et collegas, et non-"nullos ex magistratu urbis Gan-"davi, &c." Thence he retired to England, and was sent by the council to Jersey, but was "evocatus ab "Ecclesiis Belgicis," and taught at Leyden for some ten years, ending 1587. Ibid. and in Baker's notes at the end of Strype, An. IV. 603.]

[3] [Especially Danæus: see Saravia's Answer to Beza; and Collier, E. H. II. 622.]

[4] [In 1594. Strype, An. I. ii. 224. Whitg. II. 207.]

the Bishop's Superiority above the Presbytery; a second against Sacrilege; and a third of Christian Obedience to Princes; the last being occasioned by Gretzerus the Jesuit[1]. And it is observable, that when in a time of church-tumults, Beza gave his reasons to the Chancellor of Scotland for the abrogation of episcopacy in that nation, partly by letters, and more fully in a treatise of a threefold episcopacy, (which he calls divine, human, and Satanical,) this Dr. Saravia had by the help of Bishop Whitgift made such an early discovery of their intentions[2], that he had almost as soon answered that

---

[1] [Strype, Whitg. II. 202, gives some account of Dr. Saravia's first publication; which contains three tracts: 1. De Diversis Ministrorum Evangelii Gradibus. 2. De Honore Præsulibus et Presbyteris debito. 3. De Sacrilegis et Sacrilegorum Pœnis. What Walton calls his *third* Tract is probably that which now stands *fifth*, (in his works collected and published in folio, 1611,) viz. "Responsio Hadriani Saraviæ "ad quasdam calumnias, Jesuiticas "nimirum illas Gretzeri in defen-"sione sua Bellarminiana." It is chiefly taken up with a comparison between papal primacy and regal supremacy. Walton perhaps confuses it with the incomplete work (four books out of seven) "De Im-"perandi Potestate, et Christiana "Obedientia:" which closes the volume abovementioned. But that was not written against Gretser.]

[2] ["Honoratus vir Dom. Gla-"mius, quondam regni Scotiæ Can-"cellarius, de deturbandis Episco-"pis gradu, quem ab Apostolorum "temporibus in hunc usque diem "ubique terrarum in Ecclesia tenu-"erunt, a D. Beza consilium, vel "(ut mihi videtur) potius suffra-"gium petivit; ut ejus rei, quam "animo perficere constituerat, illum "probatorem haberet et auctorem. "Epistolarum autem ipsorum nac-"tus exemplaria, mirari cœpi, tam "levibus rationibus quenquam ad "innovandam tanti momenti rem "potuisse moveri. Quando illud "argumentum contra eundem D. "Bezam pertractavi, hanc quoque "disputationem adjecissem, si ad "meas manus pervenissent. Et "ubi illas nactus sum, non statim "contra quidquam pervulgandum "existimavi, sed distuli in hunc "usque diem, expectans opportuni-"tatem, qua commodo Ecclesiarum "cum minima offensione prodire in "lucem posset." Saravia, Dedic. prefixed to his Examen Tractatus de Episcopatuum Triplici Genere. It appears from an epistle of Whitgift to Beza, in Strype, Wh. II. 166, that the letter of Beza, referred to here, was not written to Lord Glamis himself, but to James Lawson, who succeeded Knox as minister in Edinburgh, and of whom some account may be found in M'Crie's Life of Knox, II. 213, 293. It was dated 1580. (misprinted 1590 in Strype.) Whitgift intimates in his letter, that Beza's book, of a threefold episcopacy, had been "in 1580 sent to this island "and not much after also trans-"lated into the English tongue, and "privately printed; together with "his epistle to one *Lausanus*, a Scot, "written the same year." He speaks also of Saravia's book of Degrees in the Ministry, and of the care which he, Whitgift, and his brethren took to have the Church properly vindicated, in a way which indirectly much confirms the statement in the text. Only Walton seems to be wrong in what he says of the date of Saravia's Examen. The quotation from Saravia, just given, proves that work to have appeared a good while after Beza's. Probably Walton

treatise as it became publick, and he therein discovered how Beza's opinion did contradict that of Calvin and his adherents; leaving them to interfere with themselves in point of episcopacy[1]; but of these tracts it will not concern me to say more, than that they were most of them dedicated to his and the Church of England's watchful patron, John Whitgift, the archbishop, and printed about the time in which Mr. Hooker also appeared first to the world, in the publication of his first four Books of Ecclesiastical Polity[2].

---

had seen or heard of Whitgift's letter in the Antiquities of Canterbury, Cantuaria Sacra, App. xv. and had applied what is there said of the book of Degrees, &c. to the Examen. At the end of Clavi Trabales is a letter of Saravia to the ministers of Guernsey, in which, p. 144, he says, "I pass over what I "have myself written concerning it "(the Discipline) in my book, De "diversis Ministrorum Gradibus, "and in my defence against the "answer of Mr. Beza, and more "largely in my Confutation of his "book De Triplici Genere Episco- "porum. I cannot wonder enough "at the Scotchmen, who could be "persuaded to abolish and reject "the state of bishops, by reasons so "ill grounded, partly false, partly of "no moment at all, and altogether "unworthy a man of such fame. "If the Scots had not more sought "after the temporal means of bi- "shops than after true reformation, "never had Mr. Beza's book per- "suaded them to do what they have "done." Dr. Saravia had been, as this letter states, one of the first protestant ministers in the islands, and knew "which were the begin- "nings, and by what means and "occasions the preaching of God's "word was planted there." p. 137. "In those beginnings, at the pur- "suit" (the letter is from the French) "of Mr. John After, "Dean, I was sent by my Lords "of the Council to the islands, as "well in the school that was newly "erected," (Elisabeth college,) "as "to be a minister there." p. 138. Whenever Saravia's works are re-edited (they amply deserve it) it is to be hoped that this letter will not be forgotten: nor yet the masterly paper on Barret's recantation (i. e. on the Calvinistic controversy) in Strype, Whitg. III. 321.]

[1] [" D. Calvinus in tractatu de "necessitate reformandæ Ecclesiæ "testatur, se paratum fuisse subji- "cere se Hierarchiæ Ecclesiasticæ, "quæ Christo Domino subjici non "recusaret. Ejus verba hæc sunt. "'Talem nobis Hierarchiam exhi- "beant, in qua sic emineant Epi- "scopi, ut sub Christo esse non "recusent, ut ab illo tanquam "unico capite pendeant, et ad ip- "sum referantur; in qua sic inter "se fraternam societatem colant, ut "non alio modo quam ejus veritate "sint colligati: tum vero nullo non "anathemate dignos fateor, si qui "erunt, qui non eam revereantur, "summaque obedientia observent.' "Hic audivimus, quid de Episcopis, "et Episcoporum Hierarchia cen- "suerit D. Calvinus. Ab ejus sen- "tentia si D. Beza non recessisset, "hac disputatione nihil opus esset." Sarav. Prol. ad Exam. Tract. de Episc. Tripl. Gen.

[2] [The three tracts came out earlier, 1590, and were printed in English, 1591. In 1590 also Saravia was incorporated at Oxford, July 9, being before D.D. of the university of Leyden. Wood, Fasti, subjoined to the Athen. Oxon. I. 252. His preferments in England, after his return hither in 1587, were these, as far as appears. First, master of the school at Southampton: in which he was much distinguished, Nich. Fuller the orientalist being

This friendship being sought for by this learned doctor, you may believe was not denied by Mr. Hooker, who was by fortune so like him, as to be engaged against Mr. Travers, Mr. Cartwright, and others of their judgment, in a controversy too like Dr. Saravia's; so that in this year of 1595, and in this place of Borne, these two excellent persons began a holy friendship, increasing daily to so high and mutual affections, that their two wills seemed to be but one and the same: and, their designs both for the glory of God, and peace of the Church, still assisting and improving each other's virtues, and the desired comforts of a peaceable piety. Which I have willingly mentioned, because it gives a foundation to some things that follow.

This parsonage of Borne is from Canterbury three miles, and near to the common road that leads from that city to Dover: in which parsonage Mr. Hooker had not been twelve months, but his Books, and the innocency and sanctity of his life became so remarkable, that many turned out of the road, and others (scholars especially) went purposely to see the man, whose life and learning were so much admired; and alas! as our Saviour said of St. John Baptist, "What went "they out to see? a man clothed in purple and fine linen?" No, indeed; but[1] an "obscure, harmless man; a man in poor "clothes, his loins usually girt in a coarse gown, or canonical "coat; of a mean stature, and stooping, and yet more lowly "in the thoughts of his soul; his body worn out, not with "age, but study, and holy mortifications; his face full of heat-"pimples, begot by his unactivity and sedentary life." And to this true character of his person, let me add this of his

---

one of his pupils, (Ath. Oxon. II. 327), and Sir Tho. Lake, Secretary of State to King James, (Chalmers, Biog. Dict.) Then Dr. Saravia was successively Prebendary of Gloucester, (ibid.) Canterbury, Dec. 6, 1595, (Le Neve, p. 16.) Westminster, July 5, 1601, (id. 371,) in the room of Bishop Andrews, and Rector of Great Chart in Kent, Feb. 24, 160$\frac{9}{10}$. (Clavi Trab. 148.) In 1607 he was nominated one of the translators of the Bible, his name appearing third, after those of Andrews and Overall, in the Westminster committee, to whom was assigned the Old Testament, from Genesis to the second Book of Kings. (Fuller, C. H. X. 45.) His Hebrew learning probably, as well as his great discretion, led the archbishop to employ him in his communications with the "learned "though morose" Hugh Broughton. Strype, Whitg. II. 118. III. 370. He died aged 82, Jan. 15, 161$\frac{2}{3}$. (Ath. Oxon. ubi sup.)]

[1] [Probably the very words of Walton's informant.]

disposition and behaviour: God and nature blessed him with so blessed a bashfulness, that as in his younger days his pupils might easily look him out of countenance; so neither then, nor in his age, "did he ever willingly look any man in the "face; and was of so mild and humble a nature, that his poor "parish-clerk and he did never talk but with both their hats "on, or both off, at the same time:" and to this may be added, that though he was not purblind, yet he was short or weak-sighted; and where he fixt his eyes at the beginning of his sermon, there they continued till it was ended; and the reader has a liberty to believe, that his modesty and dim sight were some of the reasons why he trusted Mrs. Churchman to choose his wife.

This parish-clerk lived till the third or fourth year of the late long parliament: betwixt which time and Mr. Hooker's death, there had come many to see the place of his burial, and the monument dedicated to his memory by Sir William Cooper, (who still lives,) and the poor clerk had many rewards for shewing Mr. Hooker's grave-place, and his said monument, and did always hear Mr. Hooker mentioned with commendations and reverence; to all which, he added his own knowledge and observations of his humility and holiness; and in all which discourses, the poor man was still more confirmed in his opinion of Mr. Hooker's virtues and learning: but it so fell out, that about the said third or fourth year of the long parliament, the then present parson of Borne was sequestred, (you may guess why,) and a Genevian minister put into his good living. This, and other like sequestrations, made the clerk express himself in a wonder, and say, "They had sequestred so many good men, that he doubted, "if his good master Mr. Hooker had lived till now, they "would have sequestred him too."

It was not long, before this intruding minister had made a party in and about the said parish, that were desirous to receive the sacrament as in Geneva; to which end, the day was appointed for a select company, and forms and stools set about the altar or communion-table, for them to sit and eat, and drink; but when they went about this work, there was a want of some joint-stools, which the minister sent the clerk to fetch, and then to fetch cushions (but not to kneel upon). When the clerk saw them begin to sit down, he began to wonder; but the minister bade him "cease "wondering, and lock the church door;" to whom he replied, "Pray take you the keys, and lock me out: I will "never come more into this church; for all men will say, my "master Hooker was a good man, and a good scholar, and I "am sure it was not used to be thus in his days." And, report says, the old man went presently home, and died; I do not say died immediately, but within a few days after[1].

But let us leave this grateful clerk in his quiet grave, and return to Mr. Hooker himself, continuing our observations of his Christian behaviour in this place, where he gave a holy valediction to all the pleasures and allurements of earth, possessing his soul in a virtuous quietness, which he maintained by constant study, prayers, and meditations: his use was to preach once every Sunday, and he or his curate to catechise after the second lesson in the evening prayer; his sermons were neither long nor earnest, but uttered with a grave zeal, and an humble voice; his eyes always fixt on one place to prevent his imagination from wandering, insomuch that he seemed to study as he spake[2]; the design of his

[1] [Sampson Horton was buried May 9, 1648, having been parish clerk of Bishopsborne threescore years. Dr. Zouch, from the Parish Register.]

[2] ["Mr. Hooker his voice was "low, stature little, gesture none at "all.... Where his eye was left "fixed at the beginning, it was "found fixed at the end of his "sermon: in a word, the doctrine "he delivered had nothing but itself "to garnish it. His stile was long "and pithy, drawing on a whole "flock of several clauses before he "came to the close of a sentence. "So that when the copiousness of "his stile met not with proportion- "able capacity in his auditors, it "was unjustly censured, for per- "plext, tedious, and obscure. His "sermons followed the inclination "of his studies, and were for the "most part on controversies, and "deep points of school divinity. "Mr. Travers his utterance was "graceful, gesture plausible, matter "profitable, method plain, and his "stile carried in it *indolem pietatis*, "a genius of grace, flowing from "his sanctified heart. Some say, "that the congregation in the Tem- "ple *ebb'd in the forenoon and* "*flowed in the afternoon*, and that "the auditory of Mr. Travers was "far the more numerous, the first "occasion of emulation betwixt "them. But such as knew Mr. "Hooker, knew him too wise to take "exception at such trifles, the ra- "ther because the most judicious "is always the least part in all au- "ditories." Fuller, C. H. IX. 216. This work was published just before the Restoration. In his Worthies of England, 1662, the following occurs: "Hooker his stile was "prolix but not tedious, and such "who would patiently attend and "give him credit all the reading or "hearing of his sentences, had their "expectation ever paid at the close

sermons (as indeed of all his discourses) was to shew reasons for what he spake; and with these reasons, such a kind of rhetorick, as did rather convince and persuade, than frighten men into piety[1]; studying not so much for matter (which he never wanted) as for apt illustrations to inform and teach his unlearned hearers by familiar examples, and then make them better by convincing applications; never labouring by hard words, and then by needless distinctions and subdistinctions, to amuse his hearers, and get glory to himself; but glory only to God. Which intention, he would often say, was as discernible in a preacher, "as a natural from an artificial "beauty."

He never failed, the Sunday before every Ember week, to give notice of it to his parishioners, persuading them both to fast, and then to double their devotions for a learned and pious clergy; but especially the last; saying often, "That "the life of a pious clergyman was visible rhetorick, and so "convincing, that the most godless men (though they would "not deny themselves the enjoyment of their present lusts) "did yet secretly wish themselves like those of the strictest "lives." And to what he persuaded others, he added his own example of fasting and prayer; and did usually every Ember-week take from the parish-clerk the key of the church-door; into which place he retired every day, and lockt himself up for many hours; and did the like most Fridays, and other days of fasting.

He would by no means omit the customary time of *Procession*[2], persuading all both rich and poor, if they desired the

" thereof. He may be said to have
" made good music with his fiddle
" and stick alone, without any rosin,
" having neither pronunciation nor
" gesture to grace his matter." p. 264.]

[1] [" The Gospel, which Mr. " Hooker dispensed in so still a " voice and silent gesture, but with " potent demonstrations of scripture " and reason, which are the greatest " virtue and efficaciousness of a " preacher, whose mere Stentorian " noise and theatrick gesticulations " in a pulpit, serve more to amuse " and scare, or to decoy or *lowbel* " the gaping, sleeping, or frighted " people, than much to edify, in- " form, or amend them." Gauden's Life of Hooker, p. 36.

("*Low-bell;* a hand-bell used in "fowling, to make the birds lie " close, till, by a more violent noise, " and a light, they are alarmed, and " fly into the net.

'As timorous larks amazed are
'With light and with a low-bell.'

" Percy's Reliques, III. 321.") From Nares's Glossary.]

[2] [See in the 2d Book of Homilies, the "Exhortation to be spoken to " such parishes where they use their " Perambulation in Rogation week, " for the oversight of the bounds

preservation of love, and their parish-rights and liberties, to accompany him in his perambulation; and most did so: in which perambulation, he would usually express more pleasant discourse than at other times, and would then always drop some loving and facetious observations to be remembered against the next year, especially by the boys and young people; still inclining them and all his present parishioners, to meekness, and mutual kindnesses, and love; because "love "thinks not evil, but covers a multitude of infirmities."

He was diligent to inquire who of his parish were sick, or any ways distrest, and would often visit them, unsent for; supposing that the fittest time to discover to them those errors to which health and prosperity had blinded them; and having by pious reasons and prayers moulded them into holy resolutions for the time to come, he would incline them to confession, and bewailing their sins, with purpose to forsake them, and then to receive the Communion, both as a strengthening of those holy resolutions, and as a seal betwixt God and them of his mercies to their souls, in case that present sickness did put a period to their lives.

And as he was thus watchful and charitable to the sick, so he was as diligent to prevent lawsuits, still urging his parishioners and neighbours to bear with each other's infirmities, and live in love, because (as St. John says) "he that lives in "love lives in God, for God is love." And to maintain this holy fire of love constantly burning on the altar of a pure heart, his advice was to watch and pray, and always keep themselves fit to receive the Communion; and then to receive it often, for it was both a confirming and strengthening of their graces; this was his advice: and at his entrance or departure out of any house, he would usually speak to the whole family, and bless them by name; insomuch, that as he seemed in his youth to be taught of God, so he seemed in this place to teach his precepts, as Enoch did by walking with him, in all holiness and humility, making each day a step towards a blessed eternity. And though in this weak and declining age of the world, such examples are become

"and limits of their town." See also Bishop Sparrow's Rationale of Common Prayer, p. 160. It appears from Strype, Parker, I. 303—5, that this was one of the usages excepted against by the Puritans.]

barren, and almost incredible; yet let his memory be blest with this true recordation, because he that praises Richard Hooker praises God, who hath given such gifts to men; and let this humble and affectionate relation of him become such a pattern, as may invite posterity to imitate these his virtues.

This was his constant behaviour both at Borne and in all the places in which he lived: thus did he walk with God and tread the footsteps of primitive piety; and yet, as that great example of meekness and purity, even our blessed Jesus, was not free from false accusations, no more was this disciple of his, this most humble, most innocent, holy man; his was a slander parallel to that of chaste Susannah's by the wicked elders; or that against St. Athanasius, as it is recorded in his life[1], (for that holy man had heretical enemies,) a slander which this age calls *trepanning*[2]; the particulars need not a repetition; and that it was false, needs no other testimony than the public punishment of his accusers, and their open confession of his innocency. It was said that the accusation was contrived by a dissenting brother, one that endured not church-ceremonies, hating him for his Books' sake, which he was not able to answer; and his name hath been told me, but I have not so much confidence in the relation, as to make my pen fix a scandal on him to posterity; I shall rather leave it doubtful till the great day of revelation. But this is certain, that he lay under the great charge, and the anxiety of this accusation, and kept it secret to himself for many months; and being a helpless man, had lain longer under this heavy burden, but that the Protector of the innocent gave such an accidental occasion as forced him to make it known to his two dear friends, Edwin Sandys and George Cranmer: who were so sensible of their tutor's sufferings, that they gave themselves no rest, till by their disquisitions and diligence they had found out the fraud, and brought him the welcome news, that his accusers did confess they had wronged him, and begged his pardon: to which the good man's reply was to this purpose, "The Lord forgive them;" and, "The Lord

[1] [Sozomen, E. H. II. 25. Theodoret E. H. I. 30.]
[2] [Or "trapanning;" see Todd's edition of Johnson's Dictionary. No example of the word is there given of a date previous to the 17th century.]

"bless you for this comfortable news. Now I have a just
"occasion to say with Solomon, 'Friends are born for the
"days of adversity,' and such you have proved to me: and
"to my God I say, as did the mother of St. John Baptist,
"'Thus hath the Lord dealt with me, in the day wherein he
"looked upon me, to take away my reproach among men.'
"And, O my God, neither my life nor my reputation are
"safe in mine own keeping, but in thine, who didst take
"care of me, when I yet hanged upon my mother's breast:
"blessed are they that put their trust in thee, O Lord; for
"when false witnesses were risen up against me; when
"shame was ready to cover my face, when my nights were
"restless, when my soul thirsted for a deliverance, as the hart
"panteth after the rivers of waters; then thou, Lord, didst
"hear my complaints, pity my condition, and art now become
"my deliverer; and as long as I live I will hold up my hands
"in this manner, and magnify thy mercies, who didst not
"give me over as a prey to mine enemies, the net is broken
"and they are taken in it. O blessed are they that put their
"trust in thee; and no prosperity shall make me forget those
"days of sorrow, or to perform those vows that I have made
"to thee in the days of my affliction; for with such sacrifices,
"thou, O God, art well pleased; and I will pay them."

Thus did the joy and gratitude of this good man's heart break forth. And it is observable, that as the invitation to this slander was his meek behaviour and dovelike simplicity, for which he was remarkable; so his Christian charity ought to be imitated: for, though the spirit of revenge is so pleasing to mankind, that it is never conquered but by a supernatural grace, revenge being indeed so deeply rooted in human nature, that to prevent the excesses of it (for men would not know moderation) Almighty God allows not any degree of it to any man, but says, "Vengeance is mine:" and though this be said positively by God himself, yet this revenge is so pleasing, that man is hardly persuaded to submit the menage of it to the time, and justice, and wisdom of his Creator, but would hasten to be his own executioner of it: and yet nevertheless, if any man ever did wholly decline, and leave this pleasing passion to the time and measure of God alone, it was this Richard Hooker of whom I write; for when his slanderers were to suffer, he laboured to procure their pardon; and when that was denied him, his reply was, "That however he "would fast and pray, that God would give them repentance, "and patience to undergo their punishment." And his prayers were so far returned into his own bosom, that the first was granted, if we may believe a penitent behaviour, and an open confession. And it is observable, that after this time he would often say to Dr. Saravia, "O with what quiet-"ness did I enjoy my soul after I was free from the fears of "my slander! and how much more after a conflict and "victory over my desires of revenge!"

About the year 1600, and of his age forty-six, he fell into a long and sharp sickness, occasioned by a cold taken in his passage by water betwixt London and Gravesend; from the malignity of which he was never recovered; for, after that time till his death he was not free from thoughtful days and restless nights: but a submission to His will that makes the sick man's bed easy by giving rest to his soul, made his very languishment comfortable: and yet all this time he was solicitous in his study, and said often to Dr. Saravia, (who saw him daily, and was the chief comfort of his life,) "That "he did not beg a long life of God for any other reason, but "to live to finish his three remaining Books of Polity; and "then, Lord, let thy servant depart in peace;" which was his usual expression. And God heard his prayers, though he denied the Church the benefit of them, as completed by himself; and it is thought he hastened his own death, by hastening to give life to his Books. But this is certain, that the nearer he was to his death, the more he grew in humility, in holy thoughts and resolutions.

About a month before his death, this good man, that never knew, or at least never considered, the pleasures of the palate, became first to lose his appetite, and then, to have an averseness to all food, insomuch, that he seemed to live some intermitted weeks by the smell of meat only, and yet still studied and writ. And now his guardian Angel seemed to foretell him, that the day of his dissolution drew near; for which, his vigorous soul appeared to thirst.

In this time of his sickness, and not many days before his death, his house was robbed; of which he having notice, his question was, "Are my books and written papers safe?" and being answered, that they were, his reply was, "Then it matters not; for no other loss can trouble me."

About one day before his death, Dr. Saravia, who knew the very secrets of his soul, (for they were supposed to be confessors to each other,) came to him, and after a conference of the benefit, the necessity, and safety of the Church's absolution, it was resolved the doctor should give him both that and the Sacrament the day following. To which end, the doctor came, and after a short retirement and privacy, they two returned to the company; and then the doctor gave him and some of those friends which were with him, the blessed Sacrament of the body and blood of our Jesus. Which being performed, the doctor thought he saw a reverend gaiety and joy in his face; but it lasted not long; for his bodily infirmities did return suddenly, and became more visible; insomuch that the doctor apprehended death ready to seize him: yet, after some amendment, left him at night, with a promise to return early the day following; which he did, and then found him better in appearance, deep in contemplation, and not inclinable to discourse; which gave the doctor occasion to inquire his present thoughts: to which he replied, "That he was meditating the number and nature of "angels, and their blessed obedience and order, without "which, peace could not be in heaven; and oh that it might "be so on earth!" After which words he said, "I have lived "to see this world is made up of perturbations, and I have "been long preparing to leave it, and gathering comfort for "the dreadful hour of making my account with God, which "I now apprehend to be near; and, though I have by his "grace loved him in my youth, and feared him in mine age, "and laboured to have a conscience void of offence to him, "and to all men; yet, if thou, O Lord, be extreme to mark "what I have done amiss, who can abide it? And therefore, "where I have failed, Lord shew mercy to me, for I plead "not my righteousness, but the forgiveness of my unright- "eousness, for His merits who died to purchase pardon for "penitent sinners; and since I owe thee a death, Lord let it "not be terrible, and then take thine own time; I submit to "it! Let not mine, O Lord, but let thy will be done!" With which expression he fell into a dangerous slumber; dangerous, as to his recovery; yet recover he did, but it was to speak only these few words: "Good doctor, God hath heard my "daily petitions, for I am at peace with all men, and He is at "peace with me; and from that blessed assurance I feel that "inward joy, which this world can neither give nor take "from me: my conscience beareth me this witness, and this "witness makes the thoughts of death joyful. I could wish "to live to do the Church more service, but cannot hope it, "for my days are past as a shadow that returns not." More he would have spoken, but his spirits failed him; and after a short conflict betwixt nature and death, a quiet sigh put a period to his last breath, and so he fell asleep. And now he seems to rest like Lazarus in Abraham's bosom; let me here draw his curtain, till with the most glorious company of the Patriarchs and Apostles, the most noble army of Martyrs and Confessors, this most learned, most humble, holy man, shall also awake to receive an eternal tranquillity; and with it, a greater degree of glory than common Christians shall be made partakers of.

In the mean time, bless, O Lord, Lord bless his brethren, the clergy of this nation, with effectual endeavours to attain, if not to his great learning, yet to his remarkable Meekness, his godly Simplicity, and his Christian Moderation: for these will bring peace at the last! And, Lord, let his most excellent writings be blest with what he designed when he undertook them: which was, "Glory to thee, O God on high, "peace in thy Church, and good-will to mankind!"

Amen, Amen.
IZAAK WALTON.

The following epitaph was long since presented to the world, in memory of Mr. Hooker, by Sir William Cooper, who also built him a fair monument in Borne church, and acknowledges him to have been his spiritual father.

> THOUGH nothing can be spoke worthy his fame,
> Or the remembrance of that precious name,
> Judicious Hooker; though this cost be spent
> On him that hath a lasting monument

In his own Books, yet ought we to express,
If not his worth, yet our respectfulness.
Church ceremonies he maintained, then why
Without all ceremony should he die?
Was it because his life and death should be
Both equal patterns of humility?
Or that perhaps this only glorious one
Was above all to ask, why had he none?
Yet he that lay so long obscurely low
Doth now preferr'd to greater honours go.
Ambitious men, learn hence to be more wise;
Humility is the true way to rise:
And God in me this lesson did inspire,
To bid this humble man, Friend, sit up higher [1].

[1] ["Sir William Cowper, who "erected this monument, was the "great grandfather of William, the "first Earl Cowper. He suffered "imprisonment, the loss of his son, "and other great calamities, for his "fidelity to Charles I. He out-"lived all his troubles, residing at "his castle of Hertford, and famed "for his hospitality, charity, and "other Christian virtues." Zouch, I. 439.]

AN APPENDIX

TO

THE LIFE OF MR. RICHARD HOOKER.

AND now having by a long and laborious search satisfied myself, and I hope my reader, by imparting to him the true relation of Mr. Hooker's life: I am desirous also to acquaint him with some observations that relate to it, and which could not properly fall to be spoken till after his death; of which my reader may expect a brief and true account in the following Appendix.

And first it is not to be doubted, but that he died in the forty-seventh, if not in the forty-sixth year of his age; which I mention, because many have believed him to be more aged; but I have so examined it, as to be confident I mistake not; and for the year of his death, Mr. Camden, who, in his Annals of Queen Elizabeth, 1599, mentions him with a high commendation of his life and learning, declares him to die in the year 1599; and yet in that inscription of his monument set up at the charge of Sir William Cooper in Borne church, where Mr. Hooker was buried, his death is there said to be in *anno* 1603[1], but doubtless both mistaken; for I have it attested under the hand of William Somner the archbishop's register for the province of Canterbury, that Richard Hooker's

---

[1] ["The following is an accurate copy of the inscription on Hooker's "monument:
"SUNT MELIORA MIHI.
"RICHARDUS HOOKER EXONIENSIS SCHOLARIS SOCIUSQ: COLLEGII "CORP. XPI OXON. DEINDE LONDONIIS TEMPLI INTERIORIS IN SACRIS "MAGISTER RECTORQ HUJUS ECCLIÆ. SCRIPSIT VIII LIBROS POLITIÆ "ECCLESIASTICÆ ANGLICANÆ, QUORUM TRES DESIDERANTUR. OBIIT "ANº. DOM. MDCIII. ÆTATIS SUÆ L.
"POSUIT HOC PIISSIMO VIRO MONUMENTUM ANº. DOM. MDCXXXIII. "GULIELMUS COWPER ARMIGER IN CHRITO JESU QUEM GENUIT PER "EVANGELIUM. 1 Cor. iv. 15." Dr. Zouch.] [By the kindness of the Rev. T. Hirst, Rector of Bishopsbourne, Dr. Zouch's transcript, which has some inaccuracies, has been corrected for this edition. 1886.]

will[1] bears date Octob. 26th, in *anno* 1600, and that it was proved the third of December following[2]. And that at his death he left four daughters, Alice, Cicily, Jane, and Mar-

[1] [Zouch's Walton, I. 440. "The "following is extracted from the "Registry of the Archdeacon's "court of Canterbury. 'In the "name of God, Amen. This sixe "and twentieth of October, in the "yeare of our Lord one thousand "and sixe hundred, I Richard "Hooker of Bishopsborne, though "sicke in bodye, yet sounde in "minde, thankes be unto almightye "God, doe ordaine and make this "my last will and testament in "manner and forme followinge. "First, I bequeth my soule unto "allmightye God my Creator, "hopinge assuredly of my salva- "tion purchased thorough the death "of Christ Jesus, and my bodye to "the earth to be buried at the dis- "cretion of mine executor. *Item*, "I give and bequeth unto my "daughter Alice Hooker one hun- "dred pounds of lawfull Englishe "money, to be paide unto her at "the day of her marriage. *Item*, I "give and bequeth unto my daugh- "ter Cicilye Hooker one hundred "pounds of lawful Englishe moneye, "to be paid unto her at the daye of "her marriage. *Item*, I give and "bequethe unto my daughter Jane "Hooker one hundred pounds of "lawful Englishe money, to be "paid unto her at the day of her "marriage. *Item*, I give unto my "daughter Margaret Hooker one "hundred pounds of lawful Englishe "moneye, to be paid unto her at "the day of her marriage. And if "it shall happen any of my said "daughters to departe this life be- "fore the day of their said marriage, "then I will that her or their por- "tion so dieinge, shall be equally "divided among her or their sisters "survivinge. *Item*, I give and be- "queth unto the poor of the p'ishe "of Barhā five pounds of lawful "money, to be paid unto them by "mine executor. *Item*, I give unto "the poore of the p'ishe of Bishopes- "borne fiftye shillings of lawful "Englishe money, to be paid unto "them by mine executor. *Item*, I "give and bequeth three pounds of "lawful Englishe money towards "the buildinge and makeing of a "newe and sufficient pulpett in the "p'ishe church of Bishopesborne. "The residue of goods and chattells "whatsoever unbequethed, my fu- "neral, debts, and legacies, dis- "charged and paid, I give unto "Joane Hooker, my wel beloved "wife, whom I ordaine and make "sole executor of this my last will "and testament. And I ordaine, "and make my wel-beloved father, "Mr. John Churchman, and my "assured good frende, Mr. Edwin "Sandes, my overseers. By me, "Richard Hooker. Sealed and de- "livered in the presence of them, "whose names are subscribed; "Robert Rose, Daniel Nichols, "Avery Cheston. Proved the third "day of December, 1600, before "the Rev. James Bissel, clerk, "surr'ate to Rev. George Newman, "Doctor of Laws, Commissary "General of the city and diocese of "Canterbury, by the oath of Joane "Hooker, widow, the relict and "executrix named in the said will, "&c. THOS. BACKHOUSE, Re- "gistrar. Inventory, 1092*l*. 9*s*. 2*d*. "Ex. WM. CULLEN.'"

The churches of Barham and Bishopsbourne are consolidated, and the former is the most populous part of the cure. Cranmer's being then absent in Ireland will account for his not being named as "overseer."]

[2] And the reader may take notice, that since I first writ this Appendix to the Life of Mr. Hooker, Mr. Fulman, of Corpus Christi college, hath shewed me a good authority for the very day and hour of Mr. Hooker's death, in one of his Books of Polity, which had been Archbishop Laud's. In which book, beside many considerable marginal notes of some passages of his time, under the bishop's own hand, there

garet; that he gave to each of them an hundred pound; that he left Joan his wife his sole executrix; and that by his inventory, his estate (a great part of it being in books) came to 1092*l*. 9*s*. 2*d*. which was much more than he thought himself worth; and which was not got by his care, much less by the good housewifery of his wife, but saved by his trusty servant Thomas Lane, that was wiser than his master in getting money for him, and more frugal than his mistress in keeping of it: of which will of Mr. Hooker's I shall say no more, but that his dear friend Thomas, the father of George Cranmer, (of whom I have spoken, and shall have occasion to say more,) was one of the witnesses to it [1].

One of his elder daughters was married to one Chalinor, sometime a schoolmaster in Chichester, and are both dead long since. Margaret his youngest daughter was married unto Ezekiel Chark [2], bachelor in divinity, and rector of St. Nicholas in Harbledown near Canterbury, who died about sixteen years past, and had a son Ezekiel, now living, and in sacred orders, being at this time rector of Waldron in Sussex; she left also a daughter, with both whom I have spoken not many months past, and find her to be a widow in a condition that wants not, but very far from abounding; and these two attested unto me, that Richard Hooker their grandfather had a sister, by name Elizabeth Harvey, that lived to the age of 121 years, and died in the month of September, 1663 [3].

For his other two daughters, I can learn little certainty, but have heard they both died before they were marriageable; and for his wife, she was so unlike Jephtha's daughter, that she stayed not a comely time to bewail her widowhood; nor lived long enough to repent her second marriage, for which doubtless she would have found cause, if there had

---

is also written in the titlepage of that book (which now is Mr. Fulman's) this attestation:

"Ricardus Hooker vir summis "doctrinæ dotibus ornatus, de Ec- "clesia præcipue Anglicana optime "meritus, obiit Novemb. 2, circiter "horam secundam postmeridianam. "Anno 1600." [Buried Nov. 4th. Bishopsbourne Register. 1886.]

[1] [He might be present when the will was made, and Walton might learn as much from his daughter. But (as will have been seen) he was not a witness, technically speaking.]

[2] [William Chark, of Peterhouse college, Cambridge, was one of the leaders of the Puritanical party in Hooker's time: and was the first preacher at Lincoln's Inn, appointed 1581. Strype, Ann. III. i. 79.]

[3] [Whom Fuller had conversed with: see before, p. 1, note 4.]

been but four months betwixt Mr. Hooker's and her death. But she is dead, and let her other infirmities be buried with her.

Thus much briefly for his age, the year of his death, his estate, his wife, and his children. I am next to speak of his Books, concerning which I shall have a necessity of being longer, or shall neither do right to myself, or my reader, which is chiefly intended in this Appendix.

I have declared in his Life, that he proposed Eight Books, and that his first four were printed *anno* 1594, and his Fifth Book first printed, and alone, *anno* 1597, and that he lived to finish the remaining three of the proposed eight; but whether we have the last three as finisht by himself, is a just and material question; concerning which I do declare, that I have been told almost 40 years past, by one that very well knew Mr. Hooker, and the affairs of his family, that about a month after the death of Mr. Hooker, Bishop Whitgift, then Archbishop of Canterbury, sent one of his chaplains [1] to inquire of Mrs. Hooker for the three remaining Books of Polity, writ by her husband; of which she would not, or could not give any account: and that about three months after that time the bishop procured her to be sent for to London, and then by

---

[1] [The following letter, from Bishop Andrewes to Dr. Parry, was first printed in the 8vo. edition of Hooker, Oxford 1793.

"*Salutem in Christo.*

"I CANNOT choose but write "though you do not: I never failed "since I last saw you, but dayly "prayed for him till this very instant "you sent this heavie news. I have "hitherto prayed, *Serva nobis hunc:* "now must I, *Da nobis alium.* " Alas for our greate loss; and when " I say ours, though I meane yours "and myne, yet much more the "common: with [which?] the less "sense they have of so greate a "damage, the more sad wee neede "to bewayle them and ourselves, "who knowe his workes and his "worth to be such as behind him "he hath not (that I knowe) left "anie neere him. And whether I "shall live to knowe anie neere "him, I am in greate doubt, that I "care not how manie and myself

"had redeemed his longer life to "have done good in a better subject "then he had in hand, though that "were very good. Good brother, "have a care to deal with his exe- "cutrix or executor, or (him that is "like to have a greate stroke in it) "his father in lawe, that there be "special care and regard for pre- "serving such papers as he left, "besides the three last books ex- "pected. By preserving I meane, "that not only they be not em- "bezelled, and come to nothing, "but that they come not into greate "hands, whoe will only have use of "them *quatenus et quousque*, and "suppresse the rest, or unhappily "all: but rather into the hands of "some of them that unfeinedly "wished him well, though of the "meaner sort; who may upon good "assurance (very good assurance) "be trusted with them; for it is "pitie they should admit anie limit- "ation. Doe this, and doe it ma- "ture: it had bin more then time

his procurement she was to be examined, by some of her Majesty's council, concerning the disposal of those Books; but by way of preparation for the next day's examination, the bishop invited her to Lambeth; and, after some friendly questions, she confessed to him, "that one Mr. Charke, and "another minister that dwelt near Canterbury, came to her, "and desired that they might go into her husband's study, "and look upon some of his writings; and that there they "two burnt and tore many of them, assuring her, that they "were writings not fit to be seen; and that she knew nothing "more concerning them." Her lodging was then in King-street in Westminster, where she was found next morning dead in her bed, and her new husband suspected and questioned for it; but he was declared innocent of her death.

And I declare also, that Dr. John Spencer, (mentioned in the Life of Mr. Hooker,) who was of Mr. Hooker's college, and of his time there, and betwixt whom there was so friendly a friendship, that they continually advised together in all their studies, and particularly in what concerned these Books of Polity: this Dr. Spencer, the three perfect books being lost, had delivered into his hands (I think by Bishop Whitgift) the imperfect Books, or first rough draughts of them, to be made as perfect as they might be, by him, who both knew Mr. Hooker's handwriting, and was best acquainted with his intentions[1]. And a fair testimony of this may appear by an Epistle first and usually printed before Mr. Hooker's five Books (but omitted, I know not why, in the last impression of the eight printed together in *anno* 1662, in which the publishers seem to impose the three doubtful

"long since to have bin about it, if
"I had sooner knowne it. If my
"word or letter would doe anie good
"to Mr. Churchman, it should not
"want. But what cannot yourself
"or Mr. Sandys doe therein? For
"Mr. Cranmer is away; happie in
"that he shall gaine a weeke or two
"before he knowe of it. Almightie
"God comfort us over him! whose
"taking away I trust I shall no
"longer live then with grief I re-
"member; therefore with grief be-
"cause with inward and most just
"honour I ever honoured him since

"I knew him.
   "Your assured
     "Poore loving friend,
        "L. ANDREWES."
"At the Court, 7 Nov. 1600."

For some account of Dr. Parry, see p. 109, note 3. The Editor has not yet been able to meet with the above letter in the Bodleian library.] ["Copy, Rawl. MSS. D. 404. (112)." MS. note in Bodleian copy of ed. of 1793.] 1886.

[1] [See Bp. King's letter to Walton, infra, p. 100; and the note there from H. Jackson, p. 103.]

Books to be the undoubted Books of Mr. Hooker) with these two letters J. S. at the end of the said Epistle, which was meant for this John Spencer: in which Epistle the reader may find these very words, which may give some authority to what I have here written of his last three Books.

"And though Mr. Hooker hastened his own death by
"hastening to give life to his Books, yet he held out with
"his eyes to behold these Benjamins, these sons of his right
"hand, though to him they proved Benonies, sons of pain
"and sorrow[1]. But, some evil-disposed minds, whether of
"malice, or covetousness, or wicked blind zeal, it is uncer-
"tain, as soon as they were born, and their father dead,
"smothered them; and, by conveying the perfect copies, left
"unto us nothing but the old imperfect mangled draughts
"dismembered into pieces; no favour, no grace, not the
"shadow of themselves remaining in them. Had the father
"lived to behold them thus defaced, he might rightly have
"named them Benonies, the sons of sorrow; but being the
"learned will not suffer them to die and be buried, it is
"intended the world shall see them as they are: the learned
"will find in them some shadows of resemblances of their
"father's face. God grant, that as they were with their bre-
"thren dedicated to the Church for messengers of peace; so,
"in the strength of that little breath of life that remaineth
"in them, they may prosper in their work, and by satisfying
"the doubts of such as are willing to learn, they may help to
"give an end to the calamities of these our Civil Wars!
"J. S."

And next the reader may note, that this epistle of Dr. Spencer's was writ and first printed within four years after the death of Mr. Hooker, in which time all diligent search had been made for the perfect copies; and then granted not recoverable, and therefore endeavoured to be completed out of M. Hooker's rough draughts, as is exprest by the said D. Spencer, since whose death it is now 50 years[2].

[1] [Confirmed by Dr. Covel, in his Just and Temperate Defence of the Books of Ecclesiastical Policy, p. 149, 1603. "Concerning those three "Books of his, which from his own "mouth I am informed that they "were finished, I know not in whose "hands they are, nor whether the "Church shall ever be bettered by "so excellent a work."

[2] [Dr. Spenser died Apr. 3, 1614. Wood, Ath. Oxon. II. 146, says,

And I do profess by the faith of a Christian, that Dr. Spencer's wife (who was my aunt[1], and sister to George Cranmer, of whom I have spoken) told me forty years since, in these, or in words to this purpose, "that her husband "had made up, or finisht Mr. Hooker's last three Books; and "that upon her husband's death-bed, or in his last sickness, "he gave them into her hand, with a charge they should not "be seen by any man, but be by her delivered into the hands "of the then Archbishop of Canterbury, which was Dr. Abbot, "or unto Dr. King then Bishop of London, and that she did "as he enjoined her."

I do conceive, that from D. Spencer's, and no other copy, there have been divers transcripts, and I know that these were to be found in several places, as namely, Sir Thomas Bodlie's library, in that of D. Andrews, late Bishop of Winton, in the late Lord Conway's, in the Archbishop of Canterbury's, and in the Bishop of Armagh's, and in many

"Several years before his death, he "took extraordinary pains, together "with a most judicious and com- "plete divine, named R. Hooker, "before mentioned, about the com- "piling of a learned and profitable "work, which he published, (I "mean some of the Books of Eccle- "siastical Policy,) yet would not be "moved to put his name to; and "therefore it fell out, that 'tulit alter "honores.'" This statement is apparently taken from the Epistle Dedicatory, prefixed to "A learned and "gracious sermon, preached at "Paul's Cross, by that famous and "judicious divine, John Spenser, "D. of Divinity, and late President "of C.C.C. in Oxford. Published "for the benefit of Christ's Vine- "yard, by H. M. 1615." H. M. was Hamlet Marshall, Spenser's Curate. Athen. Oxon. II. 145. Mr. Marshall, however, does not name Hooker, nor his work. His words are, "When he had taken extra- "ordinary pains, together with a "most judicious and complete di- "vine in our church, about the com- "piling of a learned and profitable "work now extant, yet would he "not be moved to put his hand to "it, though he had a special hand "in it: and therefore," &c. These words are addressed to Bishop King, Spenser's most intimate friend, and the patron of his wife and children; and Mr. Marshall states himself to have "lived under Spenser's roof, "having been his minister for the "space of five years, penning and "observing his precious medita- "tions." If therefore the passage really refer to Hooker, it must be taken as sufficient authority for the fact, otherwise probable enough, that Spenser gave so much help in the composition of Hooker's great work, as to make his partial friends think he might almost be reckoned joint author of it. It is curious, that in the page just before, Mr. Marshall has appropriated, without acknowledgment, the remarkable passage, quoted by Walton from Spenser himself, supr. p. 66, and beginning, "What admirable height," &c.: this passage Mr. Marshall has inserted as though it were his own, making it part of his panegyric on Dr. Spenser.]

[1] [See note 2, p. 4.]

others [1]; and most of these pretended to be the author's own hand, but much disagreeing, being indeed altered and diminisht, as men have thought fittest to make Mr. Hooker's judgment suit with their fancies, or give authority to their corrupt designs; and for proof of a part of this, take these following testimonies.

Dr. Barnard, sometime chaplain to Dr. Usher, late Lord Archbishop of Armagh, hath declared in a late book called *Clavi Trabales*, printed by Richard Hodgkinson, *anno* 1661 [2],

---

[1] [Authority for this statement is to be found in the following notice, prefixed to the first edition of the 6th and 8th books, 1651 [1648. p. xxxiii]:

"The several copies compared before " publication.

" The copy that is in Sir Tho. " Bodley's library in Oxford.

" The copy that was in the Lord " Archbishop of Canterbury his li- " brary.

" The copy that was in Dr. An- " drews late Lord Bishop of Win- " chester his library.

" Two copies in the hands of the " Lord Archbishop of Armagh.

" The copy in the hands of the " Lord Viscount Conway."

In the titlepage the publication is described as a " work long expected, " and now published according to " the most authentic copies." The following is subjoined:

" To the Reader.

" Here is presented unto thee, " Two of the Three so long expected " and much desired Books of learned " Mr. Hooker's Ecclesiastical Po- " licy, viz. the Sixth and the Eighth, " as they were preserved in the " hands of those Mirrors of Learn- " ing, Dr. Andrews, late Lord Bishop " of Winchester, and the present Dr. " Usher, Lord Archbishop of Ar- " magh, with great hopes the Seventh " would have been recovered, that " they might have been published " to the world's view at once: but " endeavours used to that purpose " have hitherto proved fruitless. And " now fearing that some erroneous, if " not counterfeit copies might come " [are, 1648] abroad, hath occasioned

" the publishing of these, to prevent " as much as may be any addition of " abuses to the [abused, 1648] author; " and also that he which so much " desired the unity of the Church, " might have the divided members " of his labours united."]

[2] [" Clavi Trabales, or, Nails fast- " ened by some great masters of " assemblies," (alluding to Eccl. xii. 11,) " confirming the King's supre- " macy, and church government " under bishops. I. Two speeches " of the late Lord Primate Usher's: " the one of the King's supremacy, " the other of the duty of subjects " to supply the King's necessities. " II. His judgment and practice in " point of loyalty, episcopacy, li- " turgy, and constitutions of the " Church of England. III. Mr. " Hooker's judgment of the King's " power in matters of religion, ad- " vancement of bishops, &c. IV. " Bishop Andrews of church-go- " vernment, &c. both confirmed " and enlarged by the said Primate. " V. A letter of Dr. Hadrianus Sa- " ravia, of the like subjects. Unto " which is added" (at p. 21,) " a " sermon of regal power, and the " novelty of the doctrine of resist- " ance. Published by Nicholas Ber- " nard, D.D. and rector of Whit- " church, in Shropshire."

In the author's Preface is the following passage, after some account of Numbers I. and II. " Hereunto, " two other treatises have been " thought fit to be added, (men- " tioned in the foresaid vindication, " but then not intended to be pub- " lished,) which the eminent primate " had a hand in. The one, Mr.

that in his search and examination of the said bishop's manuscripts, he there found the three written Books, which were supposed the 6, 7, and 8, of Mr. Hooker's Books of Ecclesiastical Polity; and, that in the said three Books (now printed as Mr. Hooker's) there are so many omissions, that they amount to many paragraphs, and which cause many incoherencies;

"Hooker's Judgment, &c. left out of the common copies, enlarged and confirmed by the primate, all the marginal notes of the quotations out of the fathers, being under his own hand, are noted with this mark*. The other," &c.

Bishop Sanderson, in his Preface to the Reader, which follows, bears strong testimony to the good faith of this publication. "We hold ourselves religiously obliged to use all faithfulness and sincerity in the publishing of other men's works; by suffering every author to speak his own sense in his own words, nor taking the boldness to change a phrase or syllable therein, at least not without giving the reader both notice where, and some good account also why, we have so done. Such faithfulness and ingenuity the learned publisher of these treatises professeth himself to have used, in setting them forth neither better nor worse, but just as he found them in the reverend primate's papers, some perfect and some imperfect, according as they were, and still are, in the copies which are in his custody, and which he is ready upon all occasions to shew if need shall require." Then, speaking of Bishop Andrews's treatise, he says, "Whatever defects it may have for want of the author's last hand thereunto, the publisher in order to the public good, thought fit to join it with the rest in this edition, especially the learned primate having had it under his file, as by the notes and other additions written with the primate's own hand, (which I have seen and can testify,) doth plainly appear. *The same also is to be said of the three pieces of the renowned Hooker, and of what is written with the same hand in the margent of the*

"*MS. copy;* whereof some account is given p. 47." It should be p. 49, where Dr. Bernard states, "I have found among the primate's papers a MS. containing Mr. Hooker's judgment of these three things: 1. Of regal power in ecclesiastical affairs. 2. Of the King's power in the advancement of bishops unto the rooms of prelacy. 3. Of the King's exemption from censures and other judicial power. All which (as the primate notes with his own hand) are not found in the common copies of Mr. Hooker's MS., (though by what art, and upon what design, so much was expunged, I know not,) only thus far the primate hath joined his testimony with Mr. Hooker in these, (which seem to be the true,) that he hath corrected and perfected the copy throughout with his own hand: and not only found out the several quotations, and put them down in the margent, but added many of his own, with some other large annotations, by which his zeal for the defence of regal power is the more evident."

The above extracts contain all that Dr. Bernard has stated on this subject in the Clavi Trabales. They hardly amount to a declaration, that he had himself found the three written Books among the archbishop's MSS. It seems rather as if he had found a copy, made by or for the archbishop, (and that an unfinished one,) of certain portions of the treatise. The marginal notes appear to imply as much: of some paragraphs, Ussher having remarked that they are, of others, that they are not, "wanting, in the common Books of Mr. Hooker's MS." E. g. p. 65, of Cl. Trab. compared with p. 73.]

the omissions are by him set down at large in the said printed Book, to which I refer the reader for the whole; but think fit in this place to insert this following short part of some of the said omissions.

"First, as there could be in natural bodies no motion "of any thing, unless there were some first which moved "all things, and continued unmoveable; even so in politic "societies there must be some unpunishable, or else no man "shall suffer punishment; for such [sith] punishments pro "ceed always from superiors, to whom the administration "of justice belongeth, which administration must have ne "cessarily a fountain that deriveth it to all others, and "receiveth not from any, because otherwise the course of "justice should go infinitely in a circle, every superior "having his superior without end, which cannot be; there "fore, a well-spring, it followeth, there is, a supreme head "of justice whereunto all are subject, but itself in subjec "tion to none. Which kind of preeminency if some ought "to have in a kingdom, who but the king shall have it? "Kings therefore, or no man, can have lawful power to "judge[1].

"If private men offend, there is the magistrate over them "which judgeth; if magistrates, they have their prince; if "princes, there is Heaven, a tribunal, before which they "shall appear; on earth they are not accountable to any." "Here," says the doctor, "it breaks off abruptly[2]."

And I have these words also attested under the hand of Mr. Fabian Philips, a man of note for his useful books. "I "will make oath, if I shall be required, that Dr. Sanderson, "the late Bishop of Lincoln, did a little before his death "affirm to me, he had seen a manuscript affirmed to him to "be the handwriting of Mr. Richard Hooker, in which there "was no mention made of the king or supreme governors "being accountable to the people[3]; this I will make oath, "that that good man attested to me.

FABIAN PHILIPS."

[1] [The right reading is, "Kings "therefore no man can have lawful "power and authority to judge:" and so it appears in Clavi Trabales.]

[2] [Clavi Trabales, p. 94.]

[3] [It is hardly necessary to observe, that this attestation implies the MS. to have professedly contained the eighth Book of the Laws of Ecclesiastical Polity. The pas-

So that there appears to be both omissions and additions in the said last three printed Books; and this may probably be one reason why Dr. Sanderson, the said learned bishop (whose writings are so highly and justly valued) gave a strict charge near the time of his death, or in his last will, "that "nothing of his, that was not already printed, should be "printed after his death."

It is well known how high a value our learned King James put upon the Books writ by Mr. Hooker, as also that our late King Charles (the martyr for the Church) valued them the second of all books, testified by his commending them to the reading of his son Charles, that now is our gracious king[1]; and you may suppose that this Charles the First was not a stranger to the pretended three Books, because in a discourse with the Lord Say, in the time of the long parliament, when the said lord required the king to grant the truth of his argument, because it was the judgment of Mr. Hooker, (quoting him in one of the three written Books,) the king replied, "they were not allowed to be Mr. "Hooker's books;" but, however, "he would allow them to be "Mr. Hooker's, and consent to what his lordship proposed to "prove out of those doubtful Books, if he would but consent "to the judgment of Mr. Hooker in the other five that were "the undoubted Books of Mr. Hooker[2]."

[In this relation concerning these three doubtful Books of Mr. Hooker's, my purpose was to inquire, then set down what I observed and know, which I have done, not as an engaged person, but indifferently; and now, leave my reader

sage referred to may be that, in which Hooker explains at large his idea of the original dependency of kings, as of other supreme governors, on the whole body of the nation. But he is elsewhere very careful in distinguishing between this original theoretical dependency, and their being practically accountable afterwards. It is conceivable, therefore, that Bishop Sanderson may have referred not to the printed or to any particular copy, but to a current notion of what the MSS. contained: although Walton, by his inferring hence that there are "additions in "the last three printed books," evidently understood the bishop otherwise. Sanderson had probably seen the copy in the possession of his friend Dr. Barlow, now in the library of Queen's college: and not improbably that also, which Dr. Bernard used for his Clavi Trabales. See his (Sanderson's) preface to that work, as quoted above. Of F. Philips, see Wood, A. O. Fasti, 5.]

[1] [See note 1, p. 73.]
[2] [Dugdale, Short View of the late Troubles, p. 39.]

to give sentence, for their legitimation, as to himself; but so, as to leave others the same liberty of believing or disbelieving them to be Mr. Hooker's; and it is observable, that as Mr. Hooker advised with Dr. Spencer, in the design and manage of these books, so also, and chiefly with his dear pupil George Cranmer[1], (whose sister was the wife of Dr. Spencer,) of which this following letter may be a testimony; and doth also give authority to some things mentioned both in this Appendix and in the Life of Mr. Hooker, and is therefore added[2].

I. W.]

---

[1] [See also the notes on the sixth Book.]

[2] [The letter, relating wholly to the matter of Hooker's argument, and not at all to the events of his life, will be inserted in the present edition by way of Appendix to the fifth Book.]

FURTHER APPENDIX

TO

THE LIFE OF MR. RICHARD HOOKER.

NUMBER I.

The Copy of a Letter writ to Mr. Izaak Walton, by Dr. King, Lord Bishop of Chichester [1].

HONEST IZAAK,

THOUGH a familiarity of more than forty years' [2] continuance, and the constant experience of your love, even in the worst of the late sad times, be sufficient to endear our friendship; yet I must confess my affection much improved, not only by evidences of private respect to those very many that know and love you, but by your new demonstration of a public spirit, testified in a diligent, true, and useful collection, of so many material passages as you have now afforded me in the Life of venerable Mr. Hooker; of which, since desired by such a friend as yourself, I shall not deny to give the testimony of what I know concerning him and his learned Books; but shall first here take a fair occasion to tell you, that you have been happy in choosing to write the lives of three such persons, as posterity hath just cause to honour;

---

[1] [This letter has hitherto been *prefixed* to the Life of Hooker. But as it chiefly relates to the fate of the three last Books of the Laws of Ecclesiastical Polity, it was judged more convenient to transfer it to the Appendix.

According to Wood, Ath. Oxon. III. 839, Dr. Henry King was made Bishop of Chichester 1641, and died October 1669.]

[2] [On comparing this with note 1, p. 4 on the Introduction to the Life, it will appear that Walton's intimacy with the writer of this letter began about the time of his (Walton's) first marriage: Bishop King's family being most intimate with that of Mrs. Spencer, whose niece Walton married.]

which they will do the more for the true relation of them by your happy pen; of all which I shall give you my unfeigned censure.

I shall begin with my most dear and incomparable friend, Dr. Donne, late dean of St. Paul's church, who not only trusted me as his executor, but three days before his death delivered into my hands those excellent sermons of his now made public; professing before Dr. Winniff[1], Dr. Monford[2], and, I think, yourself, then present at his bed-side, that it was by my restless importunity that he had prepared them for the press; together with which (as his best legacy) he gave me all his sermon-notes, and his other papers, containing an extract of near fifteen hundred authors. How these were got out of my hands, you, who were the messenger for them[3], and how lost both to me and yourself, is not now seasonable to complain; but, since they did miscarry, I am glad that the general demonstration of his worth was so fairly preserved, and represented to the world by your pen in the history of his life; indeed so well, that, beside others, the best critic of our later time (Mr. John Hales, of Eton college) affirmed to me, "he had not seen a life written with more "advantage to the subject, or more reputation to the writer, "than that of Dr. Donne's."

After the performance of this task for Dr. Donne, you undertook the like office for our friend Sir Henry Wotton, betwixt which two there was a friendship begun in Oxford, continued in their various travels, and more confirmed in the religious friendship of age, and doubtless this excellent person had writ the life of Dr. Donne, if death had not prevented him: by which means, his and your precollections for that work fell to the happy menage of your pen: a work, which you would have declined, if imperious persuasions had not been stronger than your modest resolutions against it. And I am thus far glad, that the first life was so imposed upon you, because it gave an unavoidable cause of writing the second: if not, it is too probable we had wanted both, which had been

---

[1] ["Dr. Winniff, Bp. of Lincoln "1641, died 1654: see some ac- "count of him in Clarendon, Hist. "of Reb. b. iv. p. 423, ed. 1819." From Dr. Zouch in loc.]

[2] ["Dr. Thomas Mountfort, a "residentiary of St. Paul's, died "Feb. 27, 1632." Dr. Zouch.]

[3] [The word "know" seems to have dropped out of the copy.]

a prejudice to all lovers of honour and ingenious learning. And let me not leave my friend Sir Henry without this testimony added to yours, that he was a man of as florid a wit, and as elegant a pen, as any former (or ours which in that kind is a most excellent) age, hath ever produced.

And now having made this voluntary observation of our two deceased friends, I proceed to satisfy your desire concerning what I know and believe of the ever-memorable Mr. Hooker, who was *schismaticorum malleus*[1], so great a champion for the church of England's rights, against the factious torrent of Separatists that then ran high against Church Discipline, and in his unanswerable Books continues still to be so against the unquiet disciples of their schism, which now under other names still carry on their design; and who (as the proper heirs of their irrational zeal) would again rake into the scarce-closed wounds of a newly bleeding state and church.

And first, though I dare not say that I knew Mr. Hooker, yet, as our[2] ecclesiastical history reports to the honour of S. Ignatius, that he lived in the time of St. John, and had seen him in his childhood[3]; so, I also joy that in my minority I have often seen Mr. Hooker, with my father, who was after Lord Bishop of London[4]; from whom, and others, at that time, I have heard most of the material passages which you relate in the history of his life; and from my father received such a character of his learning, humility, and other virtues, that, like jewels of unvaluable price, they still cast such a lustre as envy or the rust of time shall never darken.

From my father I have also heard all the circumstances of the plot to defame him; and how Sir Edwin Sandys

---

[1] ["Petrus de Alliaco, circ. A.D. 1400, *Malleus a veritate aberrantium indefessus* appellari solitus." Wharton, App. ad Hist. Lit. p. 84.]

[2] ["our," spoken as by a churchman to a layman.]

[3] [Martyr. S. Ignat. in Coteler. Patr. Apost. II. 163, 169.]

[4] [Dr. John King was student of Ch. Ch. 1576, had the living of St. Anne and St. Agnes, London, 1580: of St. Andrew's, Holborn, 1597: was Dean of Ch. Ch. 1605: Bishop of London, 1611: died 1621. Wood's Ath. Oxon. II. 294. He was charged, after his death, with papistry: which charge his son, the writer of this letter, refuted in a sermon at St. Paul's Cross, which was published, and is extant.]

outwitted his accusers, and gained their confession; and I could give an account of each particular of that plot, but that I judge it fitter to be forgotten, and rot in the same grave with the malicious authors.

I may not omit to declare, that my father's knowledge of Mr. Hooker was occasioned by the learned Dr. John Spencer, who after the death of Mr. Hooker was so careful to preserve his unvaluable sixth, seventh, and eighth Books of Ecclesiastical Polity, and his other writings, that he procured Henry Jackson[1], then of Corpus Christi College, to transcribe for him all Mr. Hooker's remaining written papers[2]; many of which were imperfect; for his study had been rifled, or worse used, by Mr. Chark, and another, of principles too like his: but these papers were endeavoured to be completed by his dear friend, Dr. Spencer, who bequeathed them as a precious legacy to my father; after whose death they rested in my hand, till Dr. Abbot, then Archbishop of Canterbury, commanded them out of my custody, by authorizing Dr. John Barkham[3] to require and bring them to him to his palace in

---

[1] ["Henry Jackson, scholar of "C. C. C. Dec. 1, 1602, aged 16, "having for two years before been "clerk of the said house." Wood, A. O. III. 577. He was successively rector of Trent in Somersetshire, and of Meysey Hampton in Gloucestershire, where he died, June 4, and was buried, June 9, 1662. He was much employed in translating the treatises of the English reformers into Latin. Fulm. 10. 78. Wood says, "being a studious and "cynical person he never expected "or desired more preferment. He "was a great admirer of R. Hooker "and J. Reynolds, whose memories "being most dear to him, he did "for the sake of the first indus"triously collect and publish some "of his small treatises, and of the "latter, several of his epistles and "orations."]

[2] ["....si totus non essem in "poliendo libro octavo D. Richardi "Hookeri de Ecclesiastica Poli"teia, quem Præses Collegii nostri "mihi commendavit, aliquid ad te "misissem, ut tuum expiscarer ju"dicium an lucem necne merea-

"tur." 1612. H. Jackson, in a letter preserved by Fulman, X. 86. "..Jam "occupatus sum in conficiendo D. "Hookeri libri 8vo de Ecclesiastica "Politeia, qui est de regis dominio." Id. Septr. 1612. "Puto Præsidem "nostrum emissurum sub suo no"mine D. Hookeri librum octavum, "a me plane vitæ restitutum. 'Tulit "alter honores.'" Id. 1612, D. Thomæ Festo.]

[3] [Fuller, Worthies of England, p. 276, tit. Exeter. "John Bark"ham, born in this city, was bred "in Corpus Christi College in Ox"ford, whereof he was fellow, chap"lain afterwards to Archbishop "Bancroft, and parson of Bock"ing in Essex. Much his modesty "and no less his learning; who, "though never the public parent "of any, was the careful nurse "of many books, which had other"wise expired in their infancy had "not his care preserved them.... "A greater lover of coins than "money.... That excellent collec"tion in Oxford library was his "gift to the archbishop, before the "archbishop gave it to the uni-

Lambeth[1]; at which time, I have heard, they were put into the bishop's library, and that they remained there till the martyrdom of Archbishop Laud, and were then by the brethren of that faction given with all the library to Hugh Peters[2], as a reward for his remarkable service in those sad times of the Church's confusion: and though they could hardly fall into a fouler hand, yet there wanted not other endeavours to corrupt and make them speak that language, for which the faction then fought; which indeed was, " to " subject the sovereign power to the people."

But I need not strive to vindicate Mr. Hooker in this particular; his known loyalty to his prince whilst he lived, the sorrow expressed by King James at his death, the value our late Sovereign (of ever-blessed memory) put upon his works, and now the singular character of his worth by you given in the passages of his life, (especially in your Appendix to it,) do sufficiently clear him from that imputation: and I am glad you mention how much value Thomas Stapleton, Pope Clement the Eighth, and other eminent men of the Romish persuasion, have put upon his Books, having been told the same in my youth by persons of worth that have travelled Italy.

Lastly, I must again congratulate this undertaking of yours, as now more proper to you than any other person, by reason of your long knowledge and alliance to the worthy family of the Cranmers, (my old friends also,) who have been men of noted wisdom, especially Mr. George Cranmer, whose prudence, added to that of Sir Edwin Sandys, proved very useful in the completing of Mr. Hooker's matchless Books; one of their letters I herewith send you, to make use of, if you think

"versity. He died March 25, "1641."]

[1] [The same thing was done in the case of Dr. Reynolds. Fulman (IX. 225.) has "A note of "such MSS. &c. as it pleased my "L. grace to retayne, of those which "we were enjoyned to bring unto "him out of D. Rainolds' studie. "June 4, 1607...... Item, Travers "to the Lords in fol. Item, Divers "other papers, the titles whereof "we could not take." Reynolds died May 21.]

[2] [" Whereas formerly books, to " the value of an hundred pounds, " were bestowed upon Mr. Peters, " out of the Archbishop of Canter- " bury's particular private study : " and whereas the said study is " appraised at a matter of forty " pounds more than the said hun- " dred pounds : it is this day ordered, " that Mr. Peters shall have the " whole study of books freely be- " stowed upon him." Commons' Journals, June 27, 1644.]

fit[1]. And let me say further, you merit much from many of Mr. Hooker's best friends then living; namely, from the ever-renowned Archbishop Whitgift, of whose incomparable worth, with the character of the times, you have given us a more short and significant account than I have received from any other pen. You have done much for the learned Sir Henry Savile, his contemporary and familiar friend; amongst the surviving monuments of whose learning (give me leave to tell you so) two are omitted; his edition of Euclid[2]; but especially his translation of King James his Apology for the Oath of Allegiance, into elegant Latin[3]: which flying in that dress as far as Rome, was by the Pope and conclave sent to Salamanca unto Franciscus Suarez, (then residing there as President of that college,) with a command to answer it. And it is worth noting, that when he had perfected the work, (which he calls *Defensio Fidei Catholicæ,*) it was transmitted to Rome for a view of the inquisitors; who according to their custom blotted out what they pleased, and (as Mr. Hooker hath been used since his death) added whatsoever might advance the Pope's supremacy, or carry on their own interest: commonly coupling together *deponere et occidere,* the deposing and then killing of princes[4]; which cruel and unchristian language Mr. John Saltkell, the amanuensis to Suarez, when he wrote that answer, (but since a convert, and living long in my father's house,) often professed, the good old man (whose piety and charity Mr. Saltkell magnified much) not only disavowed, but detested. Not to trouble you further, your reader (if, according to your desire, my approbation of your

---

[1] [Bishop King could not mean Cranmer's Letter on the new Church Discipline, for that had been printed in 1642. He might mean the Notes by Cranmer and Sandys, on the sixth Book of Eccl. Polity; which notes Fulman received from Walton, and they are now preserved in the library of Corpus Christi college.]

[2] ["Prælectiones tresdecim in "principium Elementorum Euclidis "Oxoniæ habitæ, an. 1620. Oxon. "1621, 4to." Wood, A. O. II. 314.]

[3] [The original is in K. James's Works, p. 247, &c. The date of the translation is 1609.]

[4] [Lib. VI. c. 4. § 12—18. "Dicendum est, post sententiam "condemnatoriam regis de regni "privatione, latam per legitimam "potestatem; vel quod perinde est, "post sententiam declaratoriam cri-"minis habentis talem pœnam ipso "jure impositam; posse quidem "eum, qui sententiam tulerit, vel "cui ipse commiserit, regem privare "regno, etiam illum interficiendo, "si aliter non potuerit, vel si justa "sententia ad hanc etiam pœnam "extendatur."]

work carries any weight) will here find many just reasons to thank you for it; and possibly for this circumstance here mentioned (not known to many) may happily apprehend one to thank him, who is,

SIR,
Your ever faithful and affectionate old Friend,
HENRY CHICHESTER.

Chichester, Novem. 17, 1664.

NUMBER II.

[See before, p. 11, note 1.]

D. Johannes Rainoldus Georgio Cranmero [1].

*****tua paria [2], quæ vocas, mi Georgi, non probavi quidem, fateor; neque tamen tam ingratus mihi fuit conspectus amborum, in altero pari, quam unius in altero. Nam quamvis ad notitiam earum rerum quas scire cupis, aliquantum in Ramo, permultum in Vive, plurimum in Scaligero, te putem opis habiturum; tamen in Scoto et Aquinate non esse nihil quod inservire possit tuo studio promovendo, libens agnosco. Illud inter meum et tuum judicium discriminis intercedit, quod tu de iis videris honorificentius sentire, quam ego. Nam ego minus tribuo Scoto quam Aquinati [3], Aquinati quam Scaligero, immo vero pluris unum Scaligerum quam sexcentos Scotos et Aquinates facio. Verum tamen si speras te collecturum aurum ex Ennii sterquilino [4], nihil impedio; præsertim cum promittas te daturum operam, ne maculeris luto. In altero vero pari, quo Campianum conjungis Ciceroni, τὸ ἐπὶ τῇ φακῇ μύρον [5], multo magis a te dissentio, nec in eo tuum mihi vel affectum satis sobrium, vel judicium satis sanum esse

---

[1] [This letter, transcribed from Fulman, IX. 154—156, is inserted here, as furnishing some information concerning the literary and theological opinions of two of Hooker's most intimate friends.]

[2] [It should seem that Cranmer had written to his tutor, by way of rhetorical exercise, a pair of parallels: one between Scotus and Aquinas, another (which may be conjectured to have been more or less playful) between Cicero and the Jesuit Campion.]

[3] [Hooker did not quite agree with his tutor. For he calls Scotus "the wittiest of the school divines." E. P. I. 11, 5.]

[4] ["Cum is (Virgilius) aliquando "Ennium in manu haberet, roga- "returque quidnam faceret, respon- "dit, se aurum colligere de stercore "Ennii." Donat. in vit. Virgil. c. 18.]

[5] [Cic. ad Att. I. 19.]

visum, concedo. Nam qui te præ manibus habere semper
eum scribis, et laudas tanquam novum Æsculapii filium, et
(quasi parum esset esse proximum Ciceroni) in verbis, in
sententiis, in metaphoris, in figuris, denique in omni eloquentiæ munere perfectissimum[1] esse prædicas: negare non
possum quin et studiosius eum pervolutare, quam decuit, viru-
lentissimum hostem pietatis, et admirari vehementius, quam
calamistratum oportuit rhetorculum, mihi videare. Cæterum
de judicio tuo non judico. Sit Isocrate concinnior, acutior
Hyperide, nervosior Demosthene, subtilior Lysia, copiosior
Platone. Sit repertus nostro seculo, cui cedat Lactantius,
antiquitate judice, Christianus Cicero. Affectus mihi tuus
non placet, Georgi: qui tam libenter eum lectitas, a quo
veritas mendaciis, pietas convitiis, religio calumniis; veritatis,
pietatis, religionis cultores maledictis et contumeliis acerbis-
simis proscinduntur. At enim, "Sit," inquies, "in rebus
"impurior; exhauriam ego sentinam, et fæces, et inde puris-
"sima delibabo." At ex sentina pestilens odor exhalat,
infestissimus valetudini, præsertim corporis infirmi. Tune
tuis viribus ita præfidis ut nihil metuas periculi? Avunculus
quidem tuus, quum ei sciscitanti ut solet quid Georgius,
literas ostenderem; ingemuit. Timuit fortasse plusquam
necesse fuit, ut amor res solliciti plena est timoris; sed ingemuit. Faxit Deus, ut eventus illum potius nimis timidum,
quam te parum prudentem fuisse coarguat. Sed meminisse
debes prudenter dictum a Cicerone; "ut qui in sole ambulant,
"quamvis alia de causa ambulent;" nosti quid sequatur[2].
Ego vero Fabium existimo meritissimo interdixisse pueris
poetas qui nocent moribus[3]. Quid ita M. Fabi? quia mihi
potior bene vivendi, quam vel optime loquendi, ratio habetur.
Illi tanta ratio bene vivendi; tibi minor recte credendi? Illi,
"teneræ mentes, non solum quæ diserta, sed vel magis quæ

---

[1] ["Edmund Campion, formerly "a scholar of Oxford, about 1581 "set forth a book consisting of ten "reasons, written in a *terse, elegant* "Latin style, and dedicated to the "scholars of both Universities, in "vindication of what he had done "in returning to Rome, and ex- "hortatory to them to follow him, "slandering the Protestant religion "with false and unworthy impu- "tations. Care was taken privily "to disperse this book in the uni- "versities." Strype, Aylmer, 31.
"A book written by Campion, of "the History of Ireland. The "Archbp. [Parker, 1572.] *liked the* "*wit of the writer.*" P. II. 164.]

[2] [De Orat. II. 14.]

[3] [Quintil. I. 14.]

"honesta sunt, discant;" tibi, quamvis impia, tamen si diserta, teneris ediscenda mentibus placebunt? Quid? ne ipse quidem Campianus tuus persuadet tibi meliora? qui "bella sterqui-"linia spernenda" monet[1]? Spernito. Laudas ejus scripta, ut perdiserta; agnoscis res impuras, sentinam, fæces. Ergo bella sterquilinia, te ipso judice. Contemnito. Quanquam utinam essent tantummodo sterquilinia bella: sunt gladii liti melle, sunt venena mixta vino. Quare mihi prorsus displicet quod scribis: "Non res ab illo, sed voces postulo." Perinde quasi diceres de poculo venenato, "non venenum sed vinum "haurio." Non res ab illo, sed voces postulas. Atque adeo Augustinus, cum esset Manichæus, ut de seipso confitetur, "verbis" Ambrosii suspendebatur intentus; verum autem incuriosus et contemptor astabat. "Cum autem," inquit, "non satagerem discere quæ dicebat, sed tantum quemad-"modum dicebat, audire, veniebant in animum meum simul "cum verbis quæ diligebam, res etiam quas negligebam; "neque enim ea dirimere poteram[2]." Quod si Augustinus Manichæus cum audiret (non propter res sed propter voces) Ambrosium Catholicum, et rebus captus, et vocibus, evasit Catholicus; ignosce mihi si putem esse posse periculum, ne Cranmerus religiosus dum Campianum Pontificium (non propter res, sed propter voces) assidua versat manu, (avertat Deus omen; sed qui amant, metuunt,) ne quid contrahat contagionis. Nam sive te cogitas esse vel ingenio majore, vel judicio, quam fuit Augustinus, teipsum nimis amas; sive homines facilius a pravis ad recta flecti, quam a rectis ad prava, putas; laberis imprudentia. Quamobrem si me forsitan uti consultore, quam teipso, malis; nec in Græcis Julianum Apostatam cum Demosthene, nec in Latinis Campianum Papistam cum Cicerone, tanquam optimos magistros eloquentiæ conjunges. Vale, et tuum cole. Londini, ex ædibus D. Walsinghami, 15 Mart.

Tuus, amore parens, præceptor officio,

JOHANNES RAINOLDUS.

[1] ["Sunt quædam illecebræ Lu-"theranæ, quibus suum ille (Dia-"bolus) regnum amplificat, quibus "ille tendiculis hamatus multos "jam vestri ordinis inescavit. Quæ-"nam? Aurum, gloria, deliciæ, ve-"neres. Contemnite. Quid enim "aliud ista sunt, nisi terrarum ilia, "canorus aer, popina vermium, bella "sterquilinia? Spernite." Campion. sub fine Ration. x^{ma}. vid. "Doc-"trinæ Jesuiticæ præcipua Capita. "Rupellæ, 1585." p. 207.]

[2] [Confess. V. 13, 14.]

NUMBER III.

[These two letters, also preserved by Fulman, IX. 208, 210, are conjectured to be Hooker's on the following account. They were evidently written by a Hebrew scholar, a married man, having a residence in London, intimate with Reynolds and under obligations to him, and thoroughly entering into his character. All this, added to the initials R. H., may perhaps justify the insertion of the letters here. To the Editor they appear strongly marked by Hooker's peculiar vein of humour.]

To the worshipfull my verie loving frend Mr. D. Rainoldes at Queenes college [1] in Oxford.

S. Your excuse is so reasonable that if the falt had bene found in earnest yeat you have thereof fullie cleered your self. I wish your physick may this yeare so cure you that the next we maie see you heere [2], which I should be glad of. Mr. Parrie [3] is returned unto the citie this last night as I understand, but as yeat I have not seen him, and therefore what to answere you touching my self for the matter of lazines and Moses Maimonius I do not know. I have both. And trulie the one doth not suffer the other to doe me that pleasure which otherwise it might. But concerning bookes

---

[1] [In 1586, Sir F. Walsingham offered a stipend for a lecture of controversial divinity, for the purpose, as Heylyn says, of "making "the religion of the Church of "Rome more odious;" and Reynolds being employed to read it, with a stipend of xx*l.* resigned his fellowship, and retired to Queen's college, where he lived many years. Fulman, IX. 116, 136—140. Heylyn's Life of Laud, p. 50. "Some "marvelled at me, that I left a cer-"taintie for an uncertaintie, when I "resigned my fellowship in Corpus "Christi college. But indeede dis-"sensions and factions there did "make me so weary of the place, "that a woorse uncertaintie then so "noble and worthy a knighte as "Syr Francis Walsingham, would "have woon me from it." Reynolds to Barfoote, 1594, in Fulm. IX. 192.]

[2] [If the letter be Hooker's, this seems to imply that it was written before he had any certainty of vacating the Temple by his presentation to Boscomb, which took place July 17, 1591. Broughton was in Germany, 1590, but in 1591 he was in England again; probably coming over that he might make something of the controversy with Reynolds. Lightfoot, Preface to Broughton's Works.]

[3] [Henry Parry, scholar of C.C.C. 1576, Nov. 13, (three years junior to Hooker;) Chaplain to the Queen, at the time of her death; Bishop of Worcester, 1610. Wood, A. O. II. 192.]

which you saie you would often write of but that Cajetan hath hindered, there is no cause it should if all be considered which I my self should waigh though you doe not. Nevertheless because I will not anie waie have you hindered by such meanes, I am content to observe *legem Cinciam*[1]. Persons' Directory[2] when I can procure you shall have. Mine own I lent unto Mr. Sandes D. Chaloner's[3] neighbour. Otherwise that you should have to use till I get one for you. In the mean while I send you an English Jordanus Brunus[4], the price amounteth unto two whole pence. He is an earnest suter to the stationers for their hall to read his Concent in[5]. The report goeth here that he hath fullie satisfied you both by speech and letters and that you have now assented unto him[6]. What the question

---

[1] ["Fuit de donis et muneribus, "nequis ea ob causam orandam "caperet." Tac. Ann. XI. 5.
It seems as if Reynolds had desired him to procure Cajetan's works, and he had sent Reynolds the book for a present. The mention of "two whole pence," and the beginning of the other letter, confirm this conjecture.]

[2] ["The second part of a Christ-"ian Directory or Exercise guid-"ing men to Eternal Salvation," London, 1591, 12mo. See A. O. II. 70.]

[3] [".... my loving brother D. "Chaloner" — Reynolds to the Countess of W. (Warwick? See Nichols's Progresses of Q. E. II. A. D. 1596, p. 1.) in Fulm. IX. 183. See also fol. 186.]

[4] ["H. Broughton, ut vid." Fulman. For an account of him see Wordsworth, Eccl. Biog. IV. 150, Strype, Whitg. II. 113—118, An. IV. 105. Whitg. II. 220—226. 320—326; 355—361, III. 360, 367. II. 388, 389, 390, 406—415, 527. Broughton resembled Jordanus Brunus in his wild and roving tendencies, but not in his atheism. The name of the latter was familiar at that time in England, where he had resided from 1583 to 1586, and had dedicated a book to Sir Philip Sidney. Biogr. Univ.]

[5] ["About 1584 or 1585, he set "forth, and dedicated to the Queen, "'A Concent of Scripture'... But "Dr. Reynolds, about the year "1589, in his public readings .... "disputed against it... Broughton "wrote several tracts in vindication "of his own assertion. So that it "became at last a general discourse, "... not only in that University, "but in London and other parts of "the nation ... At length both of "them had a meeting ... At last "in 1591, he by a letter to the "Archbishop and the Bishop of "London, (Aylmer,) dated London, "Nov. 4, acquainted them with the "case." Strype, Whitg. II. 113, 114. "This opposition of his "Concent, as also the entreaty of "divers friends, put him on to read "in private for the explication of it: "and he had auditors to the number "of 80, 90, or 100, ... and they "met weekly. He first read in "Paul's, at the east end of the "church ...... then in a large "chamber in Cheapside; in Mark-"lane, and some other places." Lightfoot's Pref. to Broughton's Works, fol. 1662.]

[6] ["Oxford knoweth how I forced "D. R. to agree with me for the li-"mits of Daniel's sevens." Broughton, Works, 619.]

is I doe not know. But the report I accompt as true as the like concerning his confounding of the Jewes at Francford and their desyre to have had him read Hebrue unto them, which notwithstanding I assure you he seemeth a little himself contented to nourish by some wordes of his own in this pamphlet¹. The commentaries which he mentioneth I can assure you to be meere emptie names. For except those which are in the Venice Bibles², let any man in Christendome show me so manie as he speaketh of upon the book of Esther, and I dare make my self his bondman. And even for those in Bomberg edition of the Bible, I know not whether Ezra and Solomo be joygned there or no in any of those editions which are his. But that you shall quicklie see. I will know what that Sepher Juchasim is, and when I have known I will send you word³. I would spend one twentie poundes to find a man so skilfull in those writings as he would seeme. He sometime nameth Sephur Zohar as roundlie⁴ as if the book were familiar unto him. And yeat the book known to be such as scarce one Jew amongst thousandes doth by long studie attain tolerablie to understand. In summe if needes you must have adversaries I wish you had them which are more judicious and lesse vaine than this

---

¹ ["With one R. Ellis, in Frank-"fort synagogue, 1589, I drew all "the law to Christ, so that he "denied nothing—but still desired "to hear the matter enlarged." A Require of Consent. Works, 617. This, however, appears to be of later date than the pamphlet referred to by R. H.]

² [Namely, Bomberg's: of which there were at that time four editions. See Horne's Introd. II. 119.]

³ ["The Sepher Juchasim, of "which R. H. professes his igno-"rance, was not printed until 1566, "and that at Constantinople. The "author lived at the end of the "15th century."]

⁴ ["The Book Zohar from its "conciseness as well as from its "cabalistic language, is one of great "difficulty. Professor Tholuck has "translated selections from it: "which work being mentioned to "an eminent Jewish convert, he "expressed his conviction that none "but a child of Israel could tho-"roughly understand it. It is a "book of extreme value on account "of its Christian interpretation of "passages in the Old Testament, "and its approach to Christian "doctrines. So that although the "author was manifestly a Jew, one "can hardly help suspecting, that "in his descriptions of the office "and character of the Messias, who "was to come, he owed something "to his knowledge of Him who "was come. The author lived "probably about the 2d century. "The quotations of Broughton out "of this book which I have ob-"served are very uninteresting, and "imply any thing but a real know-"ledge of its character."]

man. But for this time enough unlesse my matter were of more importance. To Mr. Provost[1] my hartie commendations. Ours heer salute you. Have care of your health which I wish the Lord to continue.

Yo^{rs} ever,
R. H.

To the worshipfull my verie good frend Mr. D. Rainoldes at Queenes college in Oxford.

S. You doe amisse to make a law to take place in things past. It must stand for heereafter and I am verie well content it shall. Of your two jewels the one, but whether the better or no I know not, as it is you shall receyve heere again inclosed. I hope notwithstanding the man's modestie in detracting from himself still in the Latin tonge, that yeat he hath more knowledg that waie than in the Greek, which by this epistle[2] doth seeme no otherwise to flow from him nor to proceed lesse naturallie then what? you know the old comparison of hony out of a stockfish. And therefore there is no need he should κήδεσθαι καλλιεπείας εὐλέξιος ὡραιοκόμου. A phrase than which I dare saie Heliodorus[3] hath not a sleeker and a tricshier[4] one. But were it not trow you a great deal better to have fewer tongues and a litle more wisdome to guide them? For any thing I can discern by this small bit of write his judgment in things and wordes are much about one pitch. And therefore in my mind you have done very well in resolving not to

---

[1] [H. Robinson, chaplain to Abp. Grindal, was Provost of Queen's coll. from 1581 to 1599: Bp. of Carlisle, 1598. In a letter before quoted, Broughton tells Whitgift and Aylmer, that "he had written "to Dr. Robinson, Provost of "Queen's college, certain theses "which might end the cause:" adding divers complaints of Reynolds. Strype, Whitg. II. 114.]

[2] ["Broughton composed an "oration in Greek, which he sent "to Whitgift concerning our Sa-"viour's descent into hell." Strype, Whitg. II. 320. "In p. 390, he "reproaches Whitgift for his *Latin* "*studies*," insinuating that he knew no Greek.]

[3] ["Id confirmas Heliodori, "gravis scilicet authoris, judicio." Reynolds in a letter to Albericus Gentilis, subjoined to the "Overthrow of Stage Plays," p. 166. Oxford, 1629.]

[4] ["My tricksy spirit."
Tempest, V. 1.
"I do know
"A many fools . . . . . . that for
"a tricksy word
"Defy the matter."
Merch. of Venice, III. 5.]

troble yourself much with him[1]. Your lectures I should be marvelous glad to see published. But I fear least you be not able to perfect them still as you read. And if not then perhaps your revising them will be more then another reading, and by that meanes time will beguile both your purpose and other men's hope. Well, as God will, whome I beseech to direct and strengthen you for the best. We are now in the countrie. Yeat if there be ought which you would have to be done in London, there cometh everie daie lightlie some or other from thence. Mr. Parrye's suddain departure out of London caused your busines to be forgotten

---

[1] [Mr. Pusey, to whom the editor is indebted for notes 3 and 4, p. 111, writes on the subject of these letters, as follows: "I cannot "find any tract of Broughton's, "which corresponds better to the "references, than the Require of "Consent: although I do not see "in this the reference to the Sepher "Juchasim, nor that to the Com- "mentaries on Esther. Without "however verifying the minuter "points, one can see that R. H. "knew his subject, and that, pro- "bably, much better than Brough- "ton, who made so much display "of it. From H.'s way of speak- "ing, it seems to have been notori- "ous at the time, that Broughton's "confounding the Jews at Frank- "fort was a pure fiction of his own "vanity. He may have challenged "some Jews there to dispute, but "there seems to me internal evi- "dence enough in this tract alone "to shew that the dispute (if held "at all) was not such as he has "thought fit to publish. It appears "a mere trick, to throw odium on "his antagonists, by representing a "Jew as objecting to Christianity "just those points, which he (B.) "was urging against them. For "the most part too they are such "points as no Jew would urge by "way of objection: and he must "have been a most complaisant an- "tagonist, who selected for debate "against Broughton, the very theses "on which B. had been practising "all his life, merely as it were to "give him occasion of triumphantly "producing his favourite explana- "tions.

"On the whole, he seems to have "spoiled some learning by an inor- "dinate quantity of vanity, which "weakened his judgment and ren- "dered him unfit for important "works: and his exclusion from "them, e. g. from the translation "of the Bible, soured his temper. "The importance which he attri- "butes to some of the points in "which he differs from the transla- "tors, appears almost like a partial "insanity. At all times he betrays "a weak judgment, and could not "have been more happily charac- "terized than in R. H.'s words: "'pity he had not fewer tongues,' "&c.

"With regard to the only point "of importance in the question be- "tween Broughton and his oppo- "nents, the seventy weeks of Daniel, "he seems to have been as widely "wrong as Dr. Reynolds: for he "bent the chronology to his own "views, and having assumed that "the limits of the seventy weeks "were the time of the vision and "the death of Christ, he shortened "heathen chronology to make it "agree with his view.

"Lively, of whom Broughton "speaks so lightly, but whom Po- "cocke never mentions but with "great respect, was probably, next "to Pococke, the greatest of our "Hebraists."]

as I think. My self could not at that time goe to D. Turner, when I receyved your letter, and therefore I sent Benjamin unto him, and by his appointment thapothecarie hath delivered for you that which I hope is come ere this to your own handes. If he have not written unto you himself, then upon receipt of your next letter I will goe unto him or send, that he may be discharged, and you shall have word thereof. If my self had bene within when it was delivered, I had done it then. I left word it should be done. But they to whome I gave charge thereof were not in the waie or els their mindfulnes was not out of the waie[1]. My hartie commendations to Mr. Provost. Ours all unto your self. The Lord preserve blesse and keepe you. Enfield the vth of September

Yo*rs* ever,

R. H.

NUMBER IV.

A List, in order of time, of Letters preserved by Mr. Fulman, MSS. t. ix. relating to the disputes in C. C. C. which led to Hooker's temporary expulsion, A.D. 1580.

1. Reynolds to the Bishop of Winton (Horn) complaining of the appointment of John Spenser, B.A. then only nineteen, and of the county of Suffolk, (which had no place on the foundation,) to be Greek lecturer. 3 July, 1578. (fol. 188.)

2. Appeal to the same, by several fellows of C. C. C. (as appears,) Hooker probably being one. 16 July. (fol. 188, 9.)

3. Reasons confirming the appeal. 26 July. (fol. 189, 190.)

4. Fragment of a letter on the same subject apparently from Reynolds to Sir F. Walsingham, Aug. 2. (fol. 191.)

5. (If there be no error in the date) Memorial "from "D. Bickley, (Warden of Merton,) D. Floide," (probably Griffith Lloyd, then Principal of Jesus,) "D. Bush, D. Dunne, "the President of St. John's, the principal of Brodegates,

---

[1] [Meaning, perhaps, (if the negative be not, as seems likely, from a slip of the pen,) that their "mindfulness" was "nothing ex-"traordinary, nothing to wonder "at."]

"and to the number of a fourescore Masters of Art, to the "Earl of Warwick," (Leicester's brother,) remonstrating against the appointment of Barfoote to succeed Cole in the headship of C. C. C. Nov. 26, probably 1579. (fol. 182.)

6. Reynolds to Walsingham, inclosing part of a letter to the Earl of Warwick, in which he explains his reasons for opposing the proposed nomination of Barfoote. 9 March $15\frac{79}{80}$. (fol. 178, 179.)

7. Dr. Humfrey, Dr. James, and others, to the Earl of Leicester, recommending Reynolds in case of a vacancy at C. C. C. probably 15 March, $15\frac{79}{80}$. (fol. 170.)

8. The same, to Walsingham, in support of the above. Same date. (fol. 171.)

9. Walsingham and Wilson, in reply to the above, signifying that Leicester had withdrawn his support promised to Barfoote, and that the fellows might "use their liberty" in electing Reynolds. 20 March $15\frac{79}{80}$. (fol. 171.)

10. Reynolds to Walsingham, acknowledging the above and requesting him to use his influence with the Earl of Warwick, not to press the election of Barfoote. 6 Apr. 1580. (fol. 172.)

11. Walsingham and Wilson to Dr. Cole, President of C. C. C. requesting him to time his resignation so as to insure, if possible, Reynolds for his successor. 9 Apr. 1580. (fol. 172.)

12. Reynolds to Walsingham, thanking him for the above, and informing him that Cole is willing to continue president, for which purpose he solicits Walsingham's aid. May 11, 1580. (fol. 173.)

13. Reynolds to Walsingham, complaining of his expulsion. Oct. 9, probably 1580. (fol. 174.) See note 1, p. 20, on the Life of Hooker.

14. Reynolds to Knollis, the same date. See Life, p. 26. (fol. 180.)

15. Reynolds to Wilson, the same date, and to the same effect; adding a petition, that the Lord Treasurer might be prevailed on to intercede with the visitor for the expelled fellows. (fol. 180.)

16. Reynolds to Walsingham, stating that he had been advised by the Bishop of Winchester to endeavour to con-

ciliate the Earl of Warwick; and requesting his good offices thereto. In this letter he speaks very strongly against Barfoote's character and conduct, and intimates that he was still agitating to obtain the headship. 22 Oct. 1580. (fol. 174.)

17. The same to the same; thanking him for having been instrumental in disposing the Earl of Warwick to receive him kindly, and acquiescing in his advice, that he should resign all thoughts of the headship: adding however expressions of extreme anxiety lest Barfoote should obtain it. Oxford, Nov. 2, probably 1580. (fol. 175.)

18. Reynolds to Secretary Wilson, (as appears,) apologizing for not having called to thank him, before he left London: expressing satisfaction at his own and his friends' return, but alarm as to the future prospects of the college. No date.

[It may be questioned whether Nº. 5, (the Oxford memorial to Lord Warwick,) ought not to come in here, rather than in the preceding year, to which Mr. Fulman, though doubtingly, assigns it. If it be rightly placed here, one may conjecture, that it prevailed with Lord Warwick to withdraw his recommendation, and that the matter was then finally compromised, as Reynolds before wished, (see Letter 12,) by Cole's retaining the presidentship.]

NUMBER V.

[1] Mr. Richard Hooker to the Lord Treasurer, when he sent him the written copy of his Ecclesiastical Polity.

MSS. Burghlean. My duty in most humble maner remembered. So it is, my good Lord, that manitimes affection causeth those things to be don, which would rather be forborn, if men were wholly guided by judgment. Albeit therefore, I must needs in reason condemne my self of over-great boldness, for thus presuming to offer to your Lordship's view my poor and slender labours: yet, because that which moves me so to do, is a dutiful affection some way to manifest itself, and glad to take this present occasion, for want of other more worthy your Lordship's acceptation: I am in that behalf not out of hope,

---

[1] [From Strype, Life of Whitgift, III. 299.]

OF THE

LAWS OF ECCLESIASTICAL POLITY,

EIGHT BOOKS.

TO THE READER[1].

THIS unhappy controversy, about the received ceremonies and discipline of the Church of England, which hath so long time withdrawn so many of her ministers from their principal work, and employed their studies in contentious oppositions; hath by the unnatural growth and dangerous fruits thereof, made known to the world, that it never received blessing from the Father of peace. For whose experience doth not find, what confusion of order, and breach of the sacred bond of love, hath sprung from this dissension; how it hath rent the body of the church into divers parts, and divided her people into divers sects; how it hath taught the sheep to despise their pastors, and alienated the pastors from the love of their flocks; how it hath strengthened the irreligious in their impieties, and hath raised the hopes of the sacrilegious devourers of the remains of Christ's patrimony; and given way to the common adversary of God's truth, and our prosperity, to grow great in our land without resistance? who seeth not how it hath distracted the minds of the multitude, and shaken their faith, and scandalized their weakness, and hath generally killed the very heart of true piety, and religious devotion, by changing our zeal towards Christ's glory, into the fire of envy and malice, and heart-burning, and zeal to every man's private cause? This is the sum of all the gains which the tedious contentions of so many years have brought in, by the ruin of Christ's kingdom, the increase of Satan's, partly in superstition and partly in impiety. So much better were it in these our dwellings of peace, to endure any inconvenience whatsoever in the outward frame, than in desire of alteration,

[1] [Prefixed to the first five Books, as published in 1604, by Dr. John Spenser. This is printed from that edition.]

thus to set the whole house on fire. Which moved the religious heart of this learned writer, in zeal of God's truth, and in compassion to his church, the mother of us all, which gave us both the first breath of spiritual life, and from her breasts hath fed us unto this whatsoever measure of growth we have in Christ, to stand up and take upon him a general defence both of herself, and of her established laws; and by force of demonstration, so far as the nature of the present matter could bear, to make known to the world and these oppugners of her, that all those bitter accusations laid to her charge, are not the faults of her laws and orders, but either their own mistakes in the misunderstanding, or the abuses of men in the ill execution of them. A work subject to manifold reprehensions and oppositions, and not suitable to his soft and mild disposition, desirous of a quiet, private life, wherein he might bring forth the fruits of peace in peace. But the love of God and of his country, whose greatest danger grew from this division, made his heart hot within him, and at length the fire kindled, and amongst many other most reverend and learned men, he also presumed to speak with his pen. And the rather, because he saw that none of these ordinary objections of partialities could elevate the authority of his writing, who always affected a private state, and neither enjoyed, nor expected any the least dignity in our church. What admirable height of learning and depth of judgment dwelled within the lowly mind of this true humble man, great in all wise men's eyes, except his own; with what gravity and majesty of speech his tongue and pen uttered heavenly mysteries, whose eyes in the humility of his heart were always cast down to the ground; how all things that proceeded from him were breathed, as from the spirit of love, as if he like the bird of the Holy Ghost, the dove, had wanted gall; let them that knew him not in his person judge by these living images of his soul, his writings. For out of these, even those who otherwise agree not with him in opinion, do afford him the testimony of a mild and a loving spirit; and of his learning, what greater proof can we have than this, that his writings are most admired by those who themselves do most excel in judicious learning, and by them the more often they are read, the more highly they are extolled and desired?

which is the cause of this second[1] edition of his former books, and that without any addition or diminution whatsoever. For who will put a pencil to such a work, from which such a workman hath taken his? There is a purpose of setting forth the three last books also, their father's *Posthumi*. For as in the great declining of his body, spent out with study, it was his ordinary petition to Almighty God, that if he might live to see the finishing of these books, then, *Lord, let thy servant depart in peace*, (to use his own words,) so it pleased God to grant him his desire. For he lived till he saw them perfected; and though like Rachel he died as it were in the travail of them, and hastened death upon himself, by hastening to give them life: yet he held out to behold with his eyes, these *partus ingenii*, these *Benjamins*, sons of his right hand, though to him they were *Benonies*, sons of pain and sorrow. But some evil disposed minds, whether of malice, or covetousness, or wicked blind zeal, it is uncertain, as if they had been Egyptian midwives, as soon as they were born, and their father dead, smothered them, and by conveying away the perfect copies, left unto us nothing but certain old unperfect and mangled draughts, dismembered into pieces, and scattered like Medea's Absyrtus, no favour, no grace, not the shadows of themselves almost remaining in them. Had the father lived to see them brought forth thus defaced, he might rightfully have named them *Benonies*, the sons of sorrow.

But seeing the importunities of many great and worthy persons will not suffer them quietly to die and to be buried, it is intended that they shall see them as they are. The learned and judicious eye will yet perhaps delight itself in beholding the goodly lineaments of their well set bodies, and in finding out some shadows and resemblances of their father's face. God grant that as they were with their brethren dedicated to the church for messengers of peace, so in the strength of that little breath of life that remaineth in them, they may prosper in their work; and by satisfying the doubts of such as are willing to learn, may help to give an end to the calamities of these our civil wars.

J. S.[2]

[[1] So ed. 1604.]   [[2] T. S. 1604. Corrected in "fourth" ed. 1617.]

A PREFACE

TO THEM THAT SEEK (AS THEY TERM IT)

THE REFORMATION OF LAWS[1],

AND

ORDERS ECCLESIASTICAL,

IN THE

CHURCH OF ENGLAND.

THOUGH for no other cause, yet for this; that posterity may know we have not loosely through silence permitted things to pass away as in a dream, there shall be for men's information extant thus much concerning the present state of the Church of God established amongst us, and their careful endeavour which would have upheld the same[2]. At your hands, beloved in our Lord and Saviour Jesus Christ, (for in him the love which we bear unto all that would but seem to be born of him, it is not the sea of your gall and bitterness that shall ever drown,) I have no great cause to look for other than the selfsame portion and lot, which your manner hath been hitherto to lay on them that concur not in opinion and sentence with you[3].

The cause and occasion of handling these things, and what might be wished in them, for whose sakes so much pain is taken.

[1 So early edd. "the laws." K.]
[2 The same foreboding tone of thought is apparent in book v. 79, 16.]
[3 [Christ. Letter, &c. p. 4. "May "wee not trulie say, that under "the shewe of inveighing against "Puritanes, the chiefest pointes of "popish blasphemie are many times "and in many places by divers men "not obscurelie broached, both in "sermons and in writing .... and "verelie such a thing offered itselfe "unto our eyes, in reading your "bookes, and we had not skill "howe to judge otherwise of the "handling of your penne and of "the scope of your matter. Not-"withstanding because rash judge-"ment may prejudice honest "travailes, and faithfull labourers "may have their unadvised slippes, "and we could not tell how

Preface.
Ch. i. 2.

But our hope is, that the God of peace shall (notwithstanding man's nature too impatient of contumelious malediction) enable us quietly and even gladly to suffer all things, for that work sake which we covet to perform.

[2.] The wonderful zeal and fervour wherewith ye have withstood the received orders of this Church, was the first thing which caused me to enter into consideration, whether (as all your published books and writings peremptorily maintain) every Christian man, fearing God, stand bound to join with you for the furtherance of that which ye term the *Lord's Discipline*. Wherein I must plainly confess unto you, that before I examined your sundry declarations in that behalf, it could not settle in my head to think, but that undoubtedly such numbers of otherwise right well affected and most religiously inclined minds had some marvellous reasonable inducements, which led them with so great earnestness that way. But when once, as near as my slender ability would serve, I had with travail and care performed that part of the Apostle's advice and counsel in such cases, whereby he willeth to "try all things[1]," and was come at the length so far, that there remained only the other clause to be satisfied, wherein he concludeth that "what good is "must be held;" there was in my poor understanding no

"zeale, love, or glorie, might carie "a man of such towardlie and "excellent giftes, in the first shew-"ing of himselfe to the worlde; "or that an earnest striving and "bending yourselfe in heate of "disputation against the one side, "might dazell your eyes, and draw "your hand at unawares to farre "and too favourable to the other "side; or else peradventure we "might mistake your meaning, "and so wee should doe you wrong "against our willes. We thought "it therefore our parte, in regarde "of our dutie to the Church, and "most agreeing to charitie, both "for your credit and our ease, in "all Christian love to intreat you, "that as you tender the good es-"tate of Christe's Church among "us, and of thousands converted to "the gospel, you would in like "publike manner (but plainly and "directlie) show unto us and all "English protestants your owne "true meaning, and how your "wordes in divers thinges doe "agree with the doctrine established "among us." On which Hooker's note is, "That because they are loth "to prejudice honest travailes by "rash judgment, and it might be "they mistooke my meaning, they "thought it fittest in charity, in "great care of my credit, and in "all Christian love, to set abroad "their suspitions, and to give no-"tise of alarm throughout hir ma-"jestie's dominions, till such time "as my mind were explained unto "them for satisfaction in their "doubtes, whereby they might be "the better furnished to satisfy "others in my behalf."

[1] [1 Thess. v. 21.]

remedy, but to set down this as my final resolute persuasion: "Surely the present form of church-government "which the laws of this land have established is such, as "no law of God nor reason of man hath hitherto been "alleged of force sufficient to prove they do ill, who to "the uttermost of their power withstand the alteration "thereof." Contrariwise, "The other, which instead of it "we are required to accept, is only by error and misconceit "named the ordinance of Jesus Christ, no one proof as yet "brought forth whereby it may clearly appear to be so in "very deed." *Preface. Ch. ii. 1.*

[3.] The explication of which two things I have here thought good to offer into your own hands, heartily beseeching you even by the meekness of Jesus Christ, whom I trust ye love; that, as ye tender the peace and quietness of this church, if there be in you that gracious humility which hath ever been the crown and glory of a Christianly-disposed mind, if your own souls, hearts, and consciences (the sound integrity whereof can but hardly stand with the refusal of truth in personal respects) be, as I doubt not but they are, things most dear and precious unto you: let "not the faith which ye have in our Lord Jesus Christ" be blemished "with partialities[1];" regard not who it is which speaketh, but weigh only what is spoken. Think not that ye read the words of one who bendeth himself as an adversary against the truth which ye have already embraced; but the words of one who desireth even to embrace together with you the self-same truth, if it be the truth; and for that cause (for no other, God he knoweth) hath undertaken the burdensome labour of this painful kind of conference. For the plainer access whereunto, let it be lawful for me to rip up to the very bottom, how and by whom your Discipline was planted, at such time as this age we live in began to make first trial thereof.

II. [2] A founder it had, whom, for mine own part, I think incomparably the wisest man that ever the French Church did enjoy, since the hour it enjoyed him. His bringing *The first establishment of new disci-*

---

[1] James ii. 1.
[2] [Compare the second chapter of Abp. Bancroft's Survey of the pretended Holy Discipline: in which a similar sketch is given of Calvin's proceedings at Geneva.]

Preface.
Ch. ii. 1.

pline by Mr. Calvin's industry in the Church of Geneva; and the beginning of strife about it amongst ourselves.

up was in the study of the civil law. Divine knowledge he gathered, not by hearing or reading so much, as by teaching others. For, though thousands were debtors to him, as touching knowledge in that kind; yet he to none but only to God, the author of that most blessed fountain, the Book of Life, and of the admirable dexterity of wit, together with the helps of other learning which were his guides: till being occasioned to leave France, he fell at the length upon Geneva; which city the bishop and clergy thereof had a little before (as some do affirm) forsaken[1], being of likelihood frighted with the people's sudden attempt for abolishment of popish religion: the event of which enterprise they thought it not safe for themselves to wait

[A.D.1536.] for in that place. At the coming of Calvin thither[2], the form of their civil regiment was popular, as it continueth at this day: neither king, nor duke, nor nobleman of any authority or power over them, but officers chosen by the people yearly out of themselves, to order all things with public consent. For spiritual government, they had no laws at all agreed upon, but did what the pastors of their souls by persuasion could win them unto. Calvin, being admitted one of their preachers, and a divinity reader amongst them, considered how dangerous it was that the whole estate of that Church should hang still on so slender a thread as the liking of an ignorant multitude is, if it have power to change whatsoever itself listeth. Wherefore taking unto him two of the other ministers[3] for more countenance of the action, (albeit the rest were all against it,) they moved, and in the end persuaded[4] with much ado, the people to bind themselves by solemn oath, first never to admit the Papacy

---

[1] [Pierre de la Baume, of a noble family in France, was the last bishop acknowledged in Geneva. "Il "partit à la mi-Juillet [1533] pour "se ranger au party de Savoye "contre la Ville." Besides the agitation occasioned by the new opinions, he was at the time engaged in a dispute with the Syndics regarding the judicial prerogative. Spon, Hist. de Genève, I. 344. Aug. 27, 1535, Protestantism was established by ordinance of the Syndics. ibid. p. 366.]

[2] [Aug. 1536. He was on his way to Basle or Strasburgh, but went round by Geneva on account of the war, and was persuaded by Farel to remain. Spon, II. p. 14.]

[3] [Farel and Couraut. Beza, Vit. Calv. [first published 1564] prefixed to his Works. Gen. 1617: from which most of these particulars are taken.]

[4] [20 July, 1537.]

amongst them again; and secondly, to live in obedience unto such orders concerning the exercise of their religion, and the form of their ecclesiastical government, as those their true and faithful ministers of God's word had agreeably to scripture set down for that end and purpose.

Preface, Ch. ii. 2.

[2.] When these things began to be put in ure, the people also (what causes moving them thereunto, themselves best know) began to repent them of that they had done, and irefully to champ upon the bit they had taken into their mouths; the rather, for that they grew by means of this innovation into dislike with some Churches near about them, the benefit of whose good friendship their state could not well lack[1].

It was the manner of those times (whether through men's desire to enjoy alone the glory of their own enterprizes, or else because the quickness of their occasions required present despatch; so it was,) that every particular Church did that within itself, which some few of their own thought good, by whom the rest were all directed. Such number of Churches then being, though free within themselves, yet small, common conference beforehand might have eased them of much after trouble[2]. But a greater inconvenience it bred, that every later endeavoured to be certain degrees more removed from conformity with the Church of Rome, than the rest before had been[3]: whereupon grew marvellous great dissimilitudes, and by reason thereof, jealousies, heart-burnings, jars and

---

[1] ["Sous pretexte de conserver "les libertez de la ville, et de ce "qu'ils n'avoient pas voulu se con-"former à l'usage de Berne pour "la Communion, ils firent pronon-"cer un arrêt au Conseil," &c. Spon. II. 18.]

[2] [Chr. Letter, p. 39. "You "blame them, that in that trouble-"some time they wanted common "conference." Hooker, MS. note. "No man blamed for those de-"fects, which necessity casteth upon "him."]

[3] [Chr. Letter, p. 43. "The "Church of Rome favourablie "admitted to be of the house of "God; Calvin with the reformed "churches full of faults, and *most* "*of all they which indevoured to be*

"*most removed from conformitie* "*with the Church of Rome.*" Hooker, MS. note. "True. "For are not your Anabaptists, "Familists, Libertines, Arrians, and "other like extreme reformers of "popery grown by that very meanes "hatefull to the whole world? Are "not their heresies a thousand times "more execrable and hatefull than "popery?

"Is it then a matter heinous to "looke awry upon any man which "hath been earnest against the "Pope? As earnest men that way "as M. Calvin are nothing spared "by you and yours in any such "conflict. You honour Calvin as "the father of discipline; this is the "boil that will not be touched."]

Preface,
Ch. ii. 3.

discords amongst them. Which, notwithstanding, might have easily been prevented, if the orders, which each Church did think fit and convenient for itself, had not so peremptorily been established under that high commanding form, which tendered them unto the people, as things everlastingly required by the law of that Lord of lords, against whose statutes there is no exception to be taken. For by this mean it came to pass, that one Church could not but accuse and condemn another of disobedience to the will of Christ, in those things where manifest difference was between them: whereas the selfsame orders allowed, but yet established in more wary and suspense manner, as being to stand in force till God should give the opportunity of some general conference what might be best for every of them afterwards to do; this I say had both prevented all occasion of just dislike which others might take, and reserved a greater liberty unto the authors themselves of entering into farther consultation afterwards. Which though never so necessary they could not easily now admit, without some fear of derogation from their credit: and therefore that which once they had done, they became for ever after resolute to maintain.

[A.D. 1538.] Calvin therefore and the other two his associates, stiffly refusing to administer the holy Communion to such as would not quietly, without contradiction and murmur, submit themselves unto the orders which their solemn oath had bound them to obey, were in that quarrel banished the town[1].

[3.] A few years after[2] (such was the levity of that people) the places of one or two of their ministers being fallen void, they were not before so willing to be rid of their learned pastor, as now importunate to obtain him again from them who had given him entertainment, and which were loath to part with him, had not unresistable earnestness been used. One of the town ministers, that saw in what manner the people were bent for the revocation of Calvin, gave him notice of their affection in this sort[3].

---

[1] [MS. note on Chr. Letter, p. 39. "De Calvino vere quod Tullius de Q. Metel. 'De civitate decedere maluit quam de sententia.' "Orat. vol. III. p. 151. Oratione "pro Balbo." c. 5.]

[2] [1541, 1 May. Spon. II. 25.]

[3] Epist. Cal. 24, [p. 27, ed. Gen.

"The senate of two hundred being assembled, they all "crave Calvin. The next day a general convocation. They "cry in like sort again all, We will have Calvin, that "good and learned man, Christ's minister. This," saith he, "when I understood, I could not choose but praise "God, nor was I able to judge otherwise than that 'this "was the Lord's doing, and that it was marvellous in our "eyes,' and that 'the stone which the builders refused "was now made the head of the corner[1].'" The other two[2] whom they had thrown out, (together with Calvin,) they were content should enjoy their exile. Many causes might lead them to be more desirous of him. First, his yielding unto them in one thing might happily put them in hope, that time would breed the like easiness of condescending further unto them. For in his absence he had persuaded them, with whom he was able to prevail, that albeit himself did better like of common bread to be used in the Eucharist, yet the other they rather should accept, than cause any trouble in the church about it[3]. Again, they saw that the name of Calvin waxed every day greater abroad[4], and that together with his fame, their infamy was spread, which had so rashly and childishly ejected him. Besides, it was not unlikely but that his credit in the world might many ways stand the poor town in great stead: as the truth is, their minister's foreign estimation

Preface, Ch. ii. 3.

1617. "In crastinum Ducentorum "congregatur concilium, et omnes "petunt Calvinum: congregatur et "generale sequenti die, itidem cla-"mant omnes, Calvinum probum et "doctum virum Christi ministrum "volumus. Quod cum intellexis-"sem, non potui non laudare Deum, "aliterque [neque aliter?] judicare, "quam quod a Domino esset factum "istud, et esset mirabile in oculis "nostris: quodque lapidem quem "reprobarant ædificantes in caput "fieret anguli." Bernard to Calvin. 6 Feb. 1541.]

[1] Luke xx. 17. [Ps. cxviii. 22, 23.]

[2] [There seems to be a slight oversight here. Farel and Couraut (not Viret) were the two ejected with Calvin in 1538. Couraut died the same year. (Calv. Ep. p. 10.) Viret was before that time settled at Lausanne, but returned to Geneva for a time to assist Calvin in the new settlement, 1541; as did Farel from Neufchatel, where he had obtained an appointment. Bayle, art. Viret. Spon. II. 19, 25.]

[3] ["Calvinus bonos nonnullos "ista mutatione usque adeo offensos, "ut etiam a cœna sibi abstinendum "putarent, serio monuit, ne ob "istud ἀδιάφορον litem moverent." Beza. Vit. Calv.]

[4] [By his theological lectures at Strasburgh; his settlement of the church there; his defence of the church itself of Geneva against Cardinal Sadolet; his Institutes, Commentary on the Romans, and Book on the Lord's Supper.]

Preface,
Ch. ii. 4.

Sept. 13.

hitherto hath been the best stake in their hedge. But whatsoever secret respects were likely to move them, for contenting of their minds Calvin returned (as it had been another Tully) to his old home.

[4.] He ripely considered how gross a thing it were for men of his quality, wise and grave men, to live with such a multitude, and to be tenants at will under them, as their ministers, both himself and others, had been. For the remedy of which inconvenience, he gave them plainly to understand, that if he did become their teacher again, they must be content to admit a complete form of discipline, which both they and also their pastors should now be solemnly sworn to observe for ever after. Of which discipline the main and principal parts were these: A standing ecclesiastical court to be established; perpetual judges in that court to be their ministers; others of the people to be annually chosen (twice so many in number as they) to be judges together with them in the same court: these two sorts to have the care of all men's manners, power of determining all kind of ecclesiastical causes, and authority to convent, to control, to punish, as far as with excommunication, whomsoever they should think worthy, none either small or great excepted.

This device I see not how the wisest at that time living could have bettered, if we duly consider what the present estate of Geneva did then require. For their bishop and his clergy being (as it is said) departed from them by moonlight, or howsoever, being departed; to choose in his room any other bishop, had been a thing altogether impossible. And for their ministers to seek that themselves alone might have coercive power over the whole church, would perhaps have been hardly construed at that time. But when so frank an offer was made, that for every one minister there should be two of the people to sit and give voice in the ecclesiastical consistory, what inconvenience could they easily find which themselves might not be able always to remedy?

Howbeit (as evermore the simpler sort are, even when they see no apparent cause, jealous notwithstanding over the secret intents and purposes of wiser men) this proposition of his did somewhat trouble them. Of the ministers themselves which had stayed behind in the city when Calvin was gone, some, upon knowledge of the people's earnest intent to recall him to his place again, had beforehand written their letters of submission, and assured him of their allegiance for ever after, if it should like him to hearken unto that public suit. But yet misdoubting what might happen, if this discipline did go forward; they objected against it the example of other reformed churches living quietly and orderly without it. Some of chiefest place and countenance amongst the laity professed with greater stomach their judgments, that such a discipline was little better than Popish tyranny disguised and tendered unto them under a new form[1]. This sort, it may be[2],

[1] [Capito, of Basle, writes thus to Farel in Calvin's Epist. p. 6. "Auditis, 'Tyranni esse voluistis in liberam ecclesiam, voluistis novum Pontificatum revocare.' Beza: "Non deerant.... qui Papisticam tyrannidem sic revocari clamitarent."]

[2] Chr. Letter, p. 39. "After speaking of his restoring and reestablishing of discipline, you have in one place, 'Many things might lead them (to be more desirous of him'). And in another place, 'he rightelie considered,' &c. 'This devise I see not howe the wisest,' &c. Therefore we pray you to tell us how such 'might lead' and 'may bees,' such entring into his thought, and crosse commending that for his divise which he simply propounded as out of the scriptures of God, may not drop into your reader's heart such unheeded impressions, as may make him highly admire R. H. great gravitie and judicious wisedome, and J. Calvin's carnall policie, fine hipocrisie and peremptorie follie."

Hooker, MS. note. "Safer to discuss all the saincts in heaven than M. Calvin. Howe bold they are themselves with as great men as M. Calvin, namely, Chrysostome, Jerome, Ambrose, Austin. Calvin himself not hereby justifyed "from censuring both the deedes and writings of men which went before him.—The acts of every present age most sincerely judged of by posterity. While men are living the judgment of their friends is perverted with love, the verdict of their enemies corrupt through envie.

"That Calvin's bitternes was a great cause to augment his troble. His nature from a child observed by his own parents, as Beza noteth, was propense to sharpe and severe reprehension where he thought any falt was. ('Destinabat eum pater ab initio theologiæ studiis, ad quæ ultro illum inclinare ex eo colligebat, quod in illa etiam tenera ætate mirum in modum religiosus esset, et severus omnium in suis sodalibus vitiorum censor.') And this not to be misliked in him.

"But his maner of dealing against them which were in deed bad men was that which wrought him self much woe, and did them no good. His friends saw this, as appeareth by his 95 Epist. unto Farellus. [N. suo more rescripsisse non infitiatus est Bucerus. Nam hoc unum causatus est cur mihi non recitaret, quia nollet mihi frustra stomachum movere. Hinc collige quantum amarulentiæ fuerit, quod ille judicavit pro

Preface,
Ch. ii. 4.

had some fear, that the filling up of the seats in the consistory with so great a number of laymen was but to please the minds of the people, to the end they might think their own sway somewhat; but when things came to trial of practice, their pastors' learning would be at all times of force to over-persuade simple men, who knowing the time of their own presidentship to be but short would always stand in fear of their ministers' perpetual authority: and among the ministers themselves, one being so far in estimation above the rest, the voices of the rest were likely to be given for the most part respectively, with a kind of secret dependency and awe: so that in show a marvellous indifferently composed senate ecclesiastical was

"sua prudentia non posse a me sine graviore offensione transmitti." p. 388.] "His own wordes declaring how in his sermons he handled and delt with his adversaries, Epist. 15." ["Ita ejus impietatem palam et aperte etiam pro concione sugillabam, ut nihilo minus aut ipsi aut aliis dubius esset sermo, quam si vel nominasem, vel digito demonstrassem." p. 19. On his deathbed he thus expressed himself to the senators of Geneva: "Ultro certe agnosco me vobis hoc quoque nomine plurimum debere, quod vehementiam illam meam interdum immoderatam æquo animo tulistis." Beza.] "His usage of H. 8, hir M. father that now is. Such courses condemned by Beza in the fourth of his Epistles against one Adrian a Dutch minister, p. 42." ("Hoc certe non fuit vel prudentis vel boni etiam pastoris in illustrissimum illum Principem nominatim declamare.")

Id. note on p. 37. "Remember to make a comparison between Calvin and Beza, how different they were in naturall disposition, and yeat how linked in amity and concord, Calvin being of a stiff nature, Beza of a pliable, the one stern and severe, the other tractable and gentle. Both wise and discreet men. Whereby we see what it is for any one church or

"place of government to have two, one succeeding another, and both in theire waies excellent, although unlike. For Beza was one whom no man would displease, Calvin one whom no man durst. His dependants both abroad and at home; his intelligence from forrein churches; his correspondence every where with the chiefest; his industry in pursuing them which did at any time openly either withstand his proceedings or gainsay his opinions; his booke intitled, 'contra Nebulonem quendam;' his writing but of three lines in disgrace of any man as forcible as any proscription throughout all reformed churches; his rescripts and answeres of as great authority as decretall epistles. His grace in preaching the meanest of all other guifts in him, ['Facundiæ contemptor et verborum parcus.' Beza.] yeat even that way so had in honour and estimation, that an hearer of his being asked wherfore he came not sometime to other men's sermons as well as Calvin's, answered, That if Calvin and S. Paul himself should preach both at one hower, he would leave S. Paul to heare Calvin. Zanch. tom. VII. Epist. ante Miscell." This reference is from the C. C. C. Transcript.]

to govern, but in effect one only man should, as the spirit and soul of the residue, do all in all[1]. But what did these vain surmises boot? Brought they were now to so strait an issue, that of two things they must choose one: namely, whether they would to their endless disgrace, with ridiculous lightness dismiss him whose restitution they had in so impotent manner desired; or else condescend unto that demand, wherein he was resolute either to have it, or to leave them. They thought it better to be somewhat hardly yoked at home, than for ever abroad discredited. Wherefore in the end those orders were on all sides assented unto: with no less alacrity of mind than cities unable to hold out longer are wont to shew, when they take conditions such as it liketh him to offer them which hath them in the narrow straits of advantage.

Preface, Ch. ii. 5.

A.D. 1541.

[Nov. 20.]

[5.] Not many years were over-passed, before these twice-sworn men adventured to give their last and hottest assault to the fortress of the same discipline; childishly granting by common consent of their whole Senate, and that under their town seal, a relaxation to one Bertelier, whom the Eldership had excommunicated[2]: further also decreeing, with strange absurdity, that to the same Senate it should belong to give final judgment in matter of excommunication, and to absolve whom it pleased them: clean contrary to their own former deeds and oaths. The report of which decree being forthwith brought unto Calvin; "Before," saith he, "this decree take place, either my blood or banish-"ment shall sign it." Again, two days before the communion should be celebrated, his speech was publickly to like effect: "Kill me if ever this hand do reach forth the "things that are holy to them whom the Church hath "judged despisers[3]." Whereupon, for fear of tumult, the forenamed Bertelier was by his friends advised for that time not to use the liberty granted him by the Senate, nor to pre-

[1553.]

---

[1] [Compare Bancroft, Survey, p. 20.]
[2] [Calv. Epist. p. 163.]
[3] ["Inter concionandum, elata "voce ac manu, multa de sacris "mysteriis in eorum contemptores "locutus: 'At ego, inquit, Chry- "sostomum secutus vim quidem "non opponam, sed ultro me potius "occidi facile patiar, quam hæc "manus contemptoribus Dei, rite "judicatis, sancta Domini porri- "gat.'" Beza.]

Preface, Ch. ii. 6. sent himself in the church, till they saw somewhat further what would ensue. After the communion quietly ministered, and some likelihood of peaceable ending of these troubles without any more ado, that very day in the afternoon, besides all men's expectation, concluding his ordinary sermon, he telleth them, that because he neither had learned nor taught to strive with such as are in authority, "therefore," saith he, "the case so standing as now it doth, let me use "these words of the apostle unto you, 'I commend you unto "God and the word of his grace[1];'" and so bade them heartily all adieu[2].

[6.] It sometimes cometh to pass, that the readiest way which a wise man hath to conquer, is to fly. This voluntary and unexpected mention of sudden departure caused presently the Senate (for according to their wonted manner they still continued only constant in unconstancy) to gather themselves together, and for a time to suspend their own decree, leaving things to proceed as before till they had heard the judgment of four Helvetian cities[3] concerning the matter which was in strife. This to have done at the first before they gave assent unto any order had shewed some wit and discretion in them: but now to do it was as much as to say in effect, that they would play their parts on a stage. Calvin therefore dispatched with all expedition his letters unto some principal pastor in every of those cities, craving earnestly at their hands, to respect this cause as a thing whereupon the whole state of religion and piety in that church did so much depend, that God and all good men were now inevitably certain to be trampled under foot, unless those four cities by their good means might be brought to give sentence with the

---

[1] [Acts xx. 32.]

[2] ["Locum illum insignem Ac-"torum Apostolicorum forte trac-"tans, in quo Paulus Ecclesiæ Ephe-"sinæ valedicit, testatus se eum "non esse, qui adversus magistra-"tum pugnare sciret aut doceret, "cætumque multis verbis cohorta-"tus, ut in ea quam audivisset doc-"trina perseveraret, tandem, veluti "postremam hanc concionem Ge-"nevæ habiturus, 'Et quandoqui-"dem, inquit, ita se res habent, "liceat mihi quoque, fratres, apud "vos hæc Apostoli verba usurpare, "Commendo vos Deo et sermoni "gratiæ ipsius:' quæ voces tum "sceleratos illos mirifice percule-"runt, tum bonos etiam tanto magis "serio officii admonuerunt." Beza.]

[3] [Zurich, Berne, Schaffhausen, Basle. See the letters from Calvin to Viret and Bullinger, and the case submitted to the Church of Zurich, with Bullinger's answer, in Calvin's Epistles, p. 163-171.]

ministers of Geneva, when the cause should be brought before them: yea so to give it, that two things it might effectually contain; the one an absolute approbation of the discipline of Geneva as consonant unto the word of God, without any cautions, qualifications, ifs or ands; the other an earnest admonition not to innovate or change the same. His vehement request herein as touching both points was satisfied. For albeit the said Helvetian Churches did never as yet observe that discipline, nevertheless, the Senate of Geneva having required their judgment concerning these three questions: First, "After what manner, by God's commandment, "according to the scripture and unspotted religion, excom-"munication is to be exercised:" Secondly, "Whether it "may not be exercised some other way than by the Con-"sistory:" Thirdly, "What the use of their Churches was "to do in this case[1]:" answer was returned from the said Churches, "That they had heard already of those consistorial "laws, and did acknowledge them to be *godly* ordinances "*drawing towards* the prescript of the word of God; for "which cause they did not think it good for *the Church of* "*Geneva* by innovation to change the same, but rather to "keep them as they were[2]." Which answer, although not answering unto the former demands, but respecting what Master Calvin had judged requisite for them to answer, was notwithstanding accepted without any further reply: in as much as they plainly saw, that when stomach doth strive with wit, the match is not equal. And so the heat of their former contentions began to slake.

[7.] The present inhabitants of Geneva, I hope, will not take it in evil part, that the faultiness of their people heretofore is by us so far forth laid open, as their own learned guides and pastors have thought necessary to discover it unto the world. For out of their books and writings it is that I have collected this whole narration, to the end it might thereby appear in what sort amongst them that discipline was

Preface, Ch. ii. 7.

---

[1] Epist. 166.
[2] [Bullinger to Calvin, Epist. p. 170. "Dudum audivisse nos de "legibus istius Ecclesiæ Consisto-"rialibus, et agnoscere illas pias "esse, et accedere ad verbi Dei "præscriptum: ideoque non videri "admittendum ut per innovationem "mutentur." Calvin's own statement of the affair may be found in his correspondence, p. 163-172.]

Preface, Ch. ii. 7.

planted, for which so much contention is raised amongst ourselves. The reason which moved Calvin herein to be so earnest, was, as Beza himself testifieth[1], "For that he saw "how needful these bridles were, to be put in the jaws of "that city." That which by wisdom he saw to be requisite for that people, was by as great wisdom compassed.

But wise men are men, and the truth is truth. That which Calvin did for establishment of his discipline, seemeth more commendable than that which he taught for the countenancing of it established[2]. Nature worketh in us all a love to our own counsels. The contradiction of others is a fan to inflame that love. Our love set on fire to maintain that which once we have done, sharpeneth the wit to dispute, to argue, and by all means to reason for it. Wherefore a marvel it were if a man of so great capacity, having such incitements to make him desirous of all kind of furtherances unto his cause, could espy in the whole Scripture of God nothing which might breed at the least a probable opinion of likelihood, that divine authority itself was the same way somewhat inclinable. And

---

[1] "Quod eam urbem videret omnino his frenis indigere."

[2] [Chr. Letter, p. 42. "If such "bold and bare affirmations may go "for payment, why may wee not as "well heare and believe Maister "Harding, which calles all the "whole and pure doctrine beleeved "and professed in England, A "wicked new devise of Geneva?"

Hooker, MS. note. "Do not you "yourself call the discipline which "they use in Geneva, a new found "discipline? p. 45. If it be a new "found thing, and not found elswhere till Geneva had erected it, "yourself must say of discipline, It "is a new devise of Geneva: except "you recant your opinion concerning the newnes of it. For all the "world doth know that the first "practise thereof was in Geneva. "You grauntinge it to be but a new "found thing must either shew us "some author more ancient, or els "acknowledge it as we do to have "been there devised. If you excuse "the speech and say it is ironicall, "you betray yourself to be a favourer of that part, and confess "yourself an egregious dissembler.

"Because the anti-Trinitarians "doe say, that our doctrine of the "glorious and blessed Trinity is a "wicked new devise of the Pope, "will you say that this may as well "be believed as their speech which "say that sundry other things in the "papacie are both new and wicked? "Although I terme not their discipline wicked for mine owne part. "Only I hold it a new devise."

The passage referred to stands thus in p. 45 of the Chr. Letter: "Is that new found discipline so "nearlie seated with our English "creed, that such expert archers "ayming at the one must needes "hit the other?" On which Hooker's note is, "A new found discipline! who is able to endure such "blasphemy? You speake but in "jeast. Were it known that you "meane as you say, surely those "wordes might cost you dear. But "they are incident into your part, "and have in that respect their safe "conduct."]

all which the wit even of Calvin was able from thence to draw, by sifting the very utmost sentence and syllable, is no more than that certain speeches there are which to him did seem to intimate that all Christian churches ought to have their Elderships endued with power of excommunication, and that a part of those Elderships every where should be chosen out from amongst the laity, after that form which himself had framed Geneva unto. But what argument are ye able to shew, whereby it was ever proved by Calvin, that any one sentence of Scripture doth necessarily enforce these things, or the rest wherein your opinion concurreth with his against the orders of your own church?

[8.] We should be injurious unto virtue itself, if we did derogate from them whom their industry hath made great. Two things of principal moment there are which have deservedly procured him honour throughout the world: the one his exceeding pains in composing the Institutions of Christian religion; the other his no less industrious travails for exposition of holy Scripture according unto the same Institutions. In which two things whosoever they were that after him bestowed their labour, he gained the advantage of prejudice against them, if they gainsayed; and of glory above them, if they consented. His writings published after the question about that discipline was once begun omit not any the least occasion of extolling the use and singular necessity thereof. Of what account the Master of Sentences[1] was in the church of Rome, the same and more amongst the preachers of reformed churches Calvin had purchased; so that the perfectest divines were judged they, which were skilfullest in Calvin's writings. His books almost the very canon to judge both doctrine and discipline by[2]. French churches, both

Preface, Ch. ii. 8.

---

[1] [Peter Lombard. A.D. 1141. See Cave, Hist. Lit. I. 667, and Heumann ap. Brucker. Hist. Phil. III. 717. "Fastigium summum theo-"logiæ scholasticæ assecutus illi "ætati visus est, ejusque vestigiis "insistere pulchrum duxit ipsius "posteritas scholastica."]

[2] ["What should the world doe "with the old musty doctors? Al-"leage scripture, and shew it al-"leaged in the sense that Calvin "alloweth, and it is of more force "in any man's defense, and to the "proofe of any assertion, than if "ten thousand Augustines, Jeromes, "Chrysostomes, Cyprians, or who-"soever els were brought foorth. "Doe we not daily see that men are "accused of heresie for holding that "which the fathers held, and that "they never are cleere, if they find "not somewhat in Calvin to justify "themselves?" MS. note of Hooker

Preface,
Ch. ii. 9.

under others abroad and at home in their own country, all cast according to that mould which Calvin had made. The Church of Scotland in erecting the fabric of their reformation took the selfsame pattern. Till at length the discipline, which was at the first so weak, that without the staff of their approbation, who were not subject unto it themselves, it had not brought others under subjection, began now to challenge universal obedience[1], and to enter into open conflict with those very Churches, which in desperate extremity had been relievers of it.

[9.] To one of those churches which lived in most peaceable sort, and abounded as well with men for their learning in other professions singular, as also with divines whose equals were not elsewhere to be found, a church ordered by Gualter's discipline, and not by that which Geneva adoreth; unto this church, the Church of Heidelberg, there cometh one who craving leave to dispute publicly defendeth with open disdain of their government, that "to a minister with his Eldership "power is given by the law of God to excommunicate whom- "soever, yea even kings and princes themselves[2]." Here were the seeds sown of that controversy which sprang up between Beza and Erastus about the matter of excommunication, whether there ought to be in all churches an Eldership in the titlepage of "A Christian "Letter," &c.]

[1] ["Two things there are which "trouble greatly these later times: "one, that the Church of Rome "cannot, another, that Geneva will "not erre." MS. note of Hooker on Chr. Letter, p. 37.]

[2] ["Accidit, ut Anglus quidam, "qui propter rem vestiariam ex "Anglia ferebatur excessisse, doc- "toris titulo cuperet insigniri, et de "adiaphoris et vestibus disputa- "tionem proponeret. Hanc theo- "logi admittere noluerunt, ne scilicet "Anglos offenderent, ... ut autem "nostræ res turbarentur, pro nihilo, "ut videtur, duxerunt. Quare inter "alias hanc thesin proposuit; opor- "tere in quavis recte constituta "ecclesia hanc servari procuratio- "nem, in qua ministri cum suo de- "lecto ad eam rem presbyterio jus "teneant, quosvis peccantes, etiam "Principes, excommunicandi." Erastus, Præf. Thesium. The dispute occurred A.D. 1568. But the work was not published till after Erastus' death, 1589: the dispute having been quieted for the time by the interference of the Church of Zurich, and Frederic, Elector Palatine. Beza replied, 1590, by his tract "de vera "Excommunicatione et Christiano "Presbyterio;" in the Preface to which he charges the publisher of Erastus' work as follows, "An "boni et pii homines auctores tibi "fuerunt, ut clam ista excuderes? "ut pro Londini, vel alterius in "Anglia civitatis nomine, Pescla- "vium fictitium supponeres?" And in a letter to Whitgift, (Strype, Whitg. III. 302,) he intimates the same: and Whitgift in his reply (II. 168) allows it, though disclaiming all connivance at the publication on his own part.]

having power to excommunicate, and a part of that Eldership to be of necessity certain chosen out from amongst the laity for that purpose. In which disputation they have, as to me it seemeth, divided very equally the truth between them; Beza most truly maintaining the necessity of excommunication, Erastus as truly the non-necessity of lay elders to be ministers thereof.

Preface, Ch. ii. 10.

[10.] Amongst ourselves, there was in King Edward's days some question moved by reason of a few men's scrupulosity[1] touching certain things. And beyond seas, of them which fled in the days of Queen Mary, some contenting themselves abroad with the use of their own service-book at home authorized before their departure out of the realm, others liking better the Common Prayer-book of the Church of Geneva translated, those smaller contentions before begun were by this mean somewhat increased[2]. Under the happy reign of her Majesty which now is, the greatest matter a while contended for was the wearing of the cap and surplice[3], till there came Admonitions[4] directed unto the high court of Parliament, by men who concealing their names thought it

[1] [See Strype, Cranm. I. 302–309. Mem. II. i. 350–354. Burnet, Reform. II. 282. III. 349–351. Wordsworth's Eccl. Biog. II. 437–440.]

[2] [See Strype, Grind. 13–16. Mem. II. 404–411. Burnet II. 612, and especially "Troubles at Frankfort," (of which book vid. Strype, An. II. i. 482,) in Phœnix II. 44, &c.]

[3] [In the convocation of 1562, about half of the lower house were for concession in these and one or two other points. (Strype, Ann. I. i. 499–506.) In 1564, complaints having been made from different quarters of positive molestation given by the nonconformists, Archbishop Parker endeavoured to enforce conformity, but was checked by the interest of the Puritans with Lord Leicester; so that he could not obtain the royal sanction for the "Advertisements" then issued, (Str. Parker, I. 300–345. Ann. I. ii. 125–175,) until the following year; when they occasioned several deprivations in the diocese of London. (Parker I. 420–460. Grind. 142–146.) In 1567 this had led to the establishment of conventicles, (Parker I. 478. Grind. 168,) and more extensive reform began to be talked of, (Ann. I. ii. 349,) especially in 1570, at Cambridge, which caused Cartwright's expulsion (ibid. 372). In 1571, a bill of alterations was proposed in parliament, which occasioning the Queen's interference, had the effect, as it should seem, of preventing the adoption of the "Reformatio Legum Ecclesiasticarum," which the archbishop at the time had thoughts of, (Ann. II. i. 93–99. P. II. 62. 63.)]

[4] [The rejection of Mr. Strickland's bill above mentioned, by the parliament of 1571, led to the immediate publication of the first "Admonition to the Parliament." It was so eagerly read, that it went through four editions before the end of 1572, (Parker II. 110,) in which year Field and Wilcox were imprisoned for it. (Ann. II. i. 274. Parker II. 139.)]

Preface, Ch. ii. 10.

glory enough to discover their minds and affections, which now were universally bent even against all the orders and laws, wherein this church is found unconformable to the platform of Geneva¹. Concerning the Defender² of which Admonitions, all that I mean to say is but this: *there will come a time when three words uttered with charity and meekness shall receive a far more blessed reward than three thousand volumes written with disdainful sharpness of wit.* But the manner of men's writing must not alienate our hearts from the truth, if it appear they have the truth; as the followers of the same defender do think he hath; and in that persuasion they follow him, no otherwise than himself doth Calvin, Beza, and others, with the like persuasion that they in this cause had the truth. We being as fully persuaded otherwise, it resteth that some kind of trial be used to find out which part is in error.

---

¹ [Bishop Cooper, Adm. to the People of England, p. 160, takes the following view of the gradual advance of Puritanism. "At the beginning, some learned and godly preachers, for private respects in themselves, made strange to wear the surplice, cap, or tippet: but yet so that they declared themselves to think the thing indifferent, and not to judge evil of such as did use them." (He seems to mean Grindal, Sandys, Parkhurst, Nowel, and others, 1562.) "Shortly after rose up other," (Sampson, Humfrey, Lever, Whittingham, &c.) "defending that they were not things indifferent, but distained with antichristian idolatry, and therefore not to be suffered in the Church. Not long after came another sort," (Cartwright, Travers, Field, &c.) "affirming that those matters touching apparel were but trifles, and not worthy contention in the Church, but that there were greater things far of more weight and importance, and indeed touching faith and religion, and therefore meet to be altered in a church rightly reformed. As the Book of Common Prayer, the administration of the Sacraments, the government of the Church, the election of ministers, and a number of other like. Fourthly, now break out another sort," (the Brownists,) "earnestly affirming, and teaching, that we have no church, no bishops, no ministers, no sacraments; and therefore that all that love Jesus Christ ought with all speed to separate themselves from our congregations, because our assemblies are profane, wicked, and antichristian. Thus have you heard of four degrees for the overthrow of the state of the Church of England. Now lastly of all come in these men, that make their whole direction against the living of bishops and other ecclesiastical ministers: that they should have no temporal lands or jurisdiction."] [Cf. Bacon on Church Controversies, (1589,) Spedding Life, &c. i. 86.] 1886.

² [Thomas Cartwright. Whitgift's Answer to the Admonition was sent to Parker, Oct. 21, 1572, (Str. Whitg. I. 86,) and replied to by T. C. early the next year. For Whitgift was far advanced in his Defence, June 4, 1573: (Park. II. 254:) and it was sent to Lord Burghley, 5 Feb. 157¾, Cartwright's 2d Reply came out in two portions, 1575 and 1577.]

III. The first mean whereby nature teacheth men to judge good from evil, as well in laws as in other things, is the force of their own discretion. Hereunto therefore St. Paul referreth oftentimes his own speech, to be considered of by them that heard him. "I speak as to them "which have understanding, judge ye what I say[1]." Again afterward, "Judge in yourselves, is it comely that "a woman pray uncovered[2]?" The exercise of this kind of judgment our Saviour requireth in the Jews[3]. In them of Berea the Scripture commendeth it[4]. Finally, whatsoever we do, if our own secret judgment consent not unto it as fit and good to be done, the doing of it to us is sin, although the thing itself be allowable. St. Paul's rule therefore generally is, "Let every man in his own mind "be fully persuaded of that thing which he either alloweth "or doth[5]."

[2.] Some things are so familiar and plain, that truth from falsehood, and good from evil, is most easily discerned in them, even by men of no deep capacity. And of that nature, for the most part, are things absolutely unto all men's salvation necessary, either to be held or denied, either to be done or avoided. For which cause St. Augustine[6] acknowledgeth, that they are not only set down, but also plainly set down in Scripture; so that he which heareth or readeth may without any great difficulty understand. Other things also there are belonging (though in a lower degree of importance) unto the offices of Christian men: which, because they are more obscure, more intricate and hard to be judged of, therefore God hath appointed some to spend their whole time principally in the study of things divine, to the end that in these more doubtful cases their understanding might be a light to direct others. "If the "understanding power or faculty of the soul be" (saith the

Preface, Ch. iii. 2.

By what means so many of the people are trained unto the liking of that discipline.

---

[1] 1 Cor. x. 15.
[2] Ibid. xi. 13.
[3] Luke xii. 56, 57.
[4] Acts xvii. 11.
[5] Rom. xiv. 5.
[6] [De peccator. merit. et remiss. l. ii. § 59. t. x. p. 48, ed. Ant. 1700, where after mentioning a certain obscure subject, he adds, " Credo, " quod etiam hinc divinorum elo- " quiorum clarissima auctoritas es- " set si homo id sine dispendio " promissæ salutis ignorare non " posset." And the marginal note is, " Scripturæ claræ in his quæ ad " salutem necessaria sunt."]

Preface,
Ch. iii. 3.

grand physician[1]) "like unto bodily sight, not of equal "sharpness in all, what can be more convenient than that, "even as the dark-sighted man is directed by the clear "about things visible; so likewise in matters of deeper dis- "course the wise in heart do shew the simple where his way "lieth?" In our doubtful cases of law, what man is there who seeth not how requisite it is that professors of skill in that faculty be our directors? So it is in all other kinds of knowledge. And even in this kind likewise the Lord hath himself appointed, that "the priest's lips should preserve "knowledge, and that other men should seek the truth at "his mouth, *because* he is the messenger of the Lord of "hosts[2]." Gregory Nazianzen, offended at the people's too great presumption in controlling the judgment of them to whom in such cases they should have rather submitted their own, seeketh by earnest entreaty to stay them within their bounds: "Presume not ye that are sheep to make "yourselves guides of them that should guide you; neither "seek ye to overskip the fold which they about you have "pitched. It sufficeth for your part, if ye can well frame "yourselves to be ordered. Take not upon you to judge "your judges, nor to make them subject to your laws who "should be a law to you; for God is not a God of sedition "and confusion, but of order and of peace[3]."

[3.] But ye will say that if the guides of the people be blind, the common sort of men must not close up their own eyes and be led by the conduct of such[4]: if the priest be "partial in the law[5]," the flock must not therefore depart from the ways of sincere truth, and in simplicity

---

[1] Galen. de opt. docen. gen. [Εἰ δ' ἔστι μὲν, ὥσπερ ὀφθαλμος τῷ σώματι, τοιοῦτος ἐν τῇ ψυχῇ νοῦς, οὐ μὴν ἅπασί γε ὁμοίως ὀξὺς, ἐγχωρεῖ καθάπερ βλέπων ὀξύτερον ἐπάγει πρὸς τὸ θέαμα τὸν ἀμβλύτερον ὁρῶντα, κατὰ τὸν αὐτὸν τρόπον καὶ ἐπὶ τῶν νοημάτων, ὑπὸ τῶν φθασάντων ἰδεῖν ἐναργῶς τὸ νοητὸν ἐπάγεσθαι πρὸς τὴν θέασιν αὐτῆς τὸν ἀμβλύτατον. (qu. ἀμβλύτερον?) t. i. p. 8. Basil., 1538.]

[2] Mal. ii. 7.

[3] Greg. Nazian. Orat. qua se excusat. [p. 37, of Musculus's Latin Version, Basil, 1550, or Opp. t. i. p. 154. Paris, 1609. Τὰ πρόβατα μὴ ποιμαίνετε τοὺς ποιμενὰς, μηδὲ ὑπὲρ τοὺς ἑαυτῶν ὅρους ἐπαίρεσθε· ἀρκεῖ γὰρ ὑμῖν, ἂν καλῶς ποιμαίνησθε· μὴ κρίνετε τοὺς κριτὰς, μηδὲ νομοθετεῖτε τοῖς νομοθέταις. Οὐ γάρ ἐστι Θεὸς ἀκαταστασίας καὶ ἀταξίας, ἀλλ' εἰρήνης καὶ τάξεως. The second clause is in the Latin, "neque super terminos "*eorum* elevemini:" from which evidently Hooker translated.]

[4] Matt. xv. 14.

[5] Mal. ii. 9.

yield to be followers of him for his place sake and office over them. Which thing, though in itself most true, is in your defence notwithstanding weak; because the matter wherein ye think that ye see, and imagine that your ways are sincere, is of far deeper consideration than any one amongst five hundred of you conceiveth. Let the vulgar sort amongst you know, that there is not the least branch of the cause wherein they are so resolute, but to the trial of it a great deal more appertaineth than their conceit doth reach unto. I write not this in disgrace of the simplest that way given, but I would gladly they knew the nature of that cause wherein they think themselves throughly instructed and are not; by means whereof they daily run themselves, without feeling their own hazard, upon the dint of the Apostle's sentence against "evil-speakers as touching things "wherein they are ignorant [1]."

[4.] If it be granted a thing unlawful for private men, not called unto public consultation, to dispute which is the best state of civil polity[2], (with a desire of bringing in some other kind, than that under which they already live, for of such disputes I take it his meaning was;) if it be a thing confessed, that of such questions they cannot determine without rashness, inasmuch as a great part of them consisteth in special circumstances, and for one kind as many reasons may be brought as for another; is there any reason in the world, why they should better judge what kind of regiment ecclesiastical is the fittest? For in the civil state more insight, and in those affairs more experience a great deal must needs be granted them, than in this they can possibly have. When they which write in defence of your discipline and commend it unto the Highest not in the least cunning manner, are forced notwithstanding to acknowledge, "that with whom the truth is they know "not[3]," they are not certain; what certainty or knowledge can the multitude have thereof?

Preface, Ch. iii. 4.

---

[1] Jude 10; 2 Pet. ii. 12.
[2] Calvin. Instit. lib. iv. cap. xx. § 8. ["Sane valde otiosum esset, "quis potissimum sit politiæ in eo "quo vivunt loco futurus status, a "privatis hominibus disputari: qui-"bus de constituenda re aliqua pub-"lica deliberare non licet."]
[3] The Author of the Petition directed to her Majesty, p. 3. ["I "do not now write either to pull "down bishoprics, or erect presby-

Preface,
Ch. iii. 5, 6, 7.

[5.] Weigh what doth move the common sort so much to favour this innovation, and it shall soon appear unto you, that the force of particular reasons which for your several opinions are alleged is a thing whereof the multitude never did nor could so consider as to be therewith wholly carried; but certain general inducements are used to make saleable your cause in gross; and when once men have cast a fancy towards it, any slight declaration of specialties will serve to lead forward men's inclinable and prepared minds.

[6.] The method of winning the people's affection unto a general liking of "the cause" (for so ye term it) hath been this. First, In the hearing of the multitude, the faults especially of higher callings are ripped up with marvellous exceeding severity and sharpness of reproof[1]; which being oftentimes done begetteth a great good opinion of integrity, zeal, and holiness, to such constant reprovers of sin, as by likelihood would never be so much offended at that which is evil, unless themselves were singularly good.

[7.] The next thing hereunto is, to impute all faults and corruptions, wherewith the world aboundeth, unto the kind of ecclesiastical government established[2]. Wherein, as before

"teries. With whom the truth is I will not determine, for I know not. What seemeth most probable and true to me, that I know. How the truth should come to light, that is the question." This writer was Penry. Bancr. Surv. 342.]

[1] ["A certain writer for reformation .... writeth of noblemen and gentlemen .... 'Whereof came,' saith he, 'this division of such personages from others, seeing all men came of one man and one woman? Was it for their lusty hawking and hunting? for their nimble dicing, and cunning carding? for their singing and dancing? for their open bragging and swearing? for their false fleering and flattering? for their subtle killing and stealing? for their cruel polling and pilling, &c. No, no, there was no such thing.' You would be glad then, I am sure, to know what thing it was: indeed the same author doth not conceal it: in effect it is (though it be delivered in better words) viz. that their rebellion and treason against their governors procured them that prerogative with the people: 'Because,' saith he, 'they revenged and delivered the oppressed people out of the hands of their governors who abused their authority, and wickedly, cruelly, and tyrannously ruled over them; the people of a grateful and thankful mind gave them that estimation and honour.'" Bancr. Surv. p. 7, quoting "A Treatise of Obedience," p. 114, of which treatise, see Strype, An. I. i. 182, 185. It was written by Chr. Goodman against Q. Mary, and published at Geneva, 1558, with a recommendatory preface by Whittingham.]

[2] ["The necessity of the thing is many ways apparent, both in that it hath so plentiful warrant from God's own word .... and

by reproving faults they purchased unto themselves with the multitude a name to be virtuous; so by finding out this kind of cause they obtain to be judged wise above others: whereas in truth unto the form even of Jewish government, which the Lord himself (they all confess) did establish, with like shew of reason they might impute those faults which the prophets condemn in the governors of that commonwealth, as to the English kind of regiment ecclesiastical, (whereof also God himself though in other sort is author,) the stains and blemishes found in our state; which springing from the root of human frailty and corruption, not only are, but have been always more or less, yea and (for any thing we know to the contrary) will be till the world's end complained of, what form of government soever take place.

Preface,
Ch. iii. 8, 9.

[8.] Having gotten thus much sway in the hearts of men, a third step is to propose their own form of church-government, as the only sovereign remedy of all evils; and to adorn it with all the glorious titles that may be. And the nature, as of men that have sick bodies, so likewise of the people in the crazedness of their minds possessed with dislike and discontentment at things present, is to imagine that any thing, (the virtue whereof they hear commended,) would help them; but that most, which they least have tried.

[9.] The fourth degree of inducement is by fashioning the very notions and conceits of men's minds in such sort, that when they read the scripture, they may think that every thing soundeth towards the advancement of that discipline, and to the utter disgrace of the contrary. Pythagoras, by bringing up his scholars in the speculative knowledge of numbers, made their conceits therein so strong, that when they came to the contemplation of things natural, they imagined that in every particular thing they even beheld as it were with their eyes, how the elements of number gave essence and being to the works of nature. A thing in reason impossible; which notwithstanding, through their misfashioned

"also in that the gospel can take no "root, nor have any free passage, "for want of it: and the greatness "of your fault appeareth by this; "that in so doing you are the cause "of all the ignorance, atheism, "schisms, treasons, popery, and "ungodliness, that is to be found "in this land." Pref. to Demonstr. of Discipline.]

Preface, preconceit, appeared unto them no less certain, than if nature
Ch. iii. 9. had written it in the very foreheads of all the creatures of
God[1]. When they of the "Family of Love" have it once in
their heads, that Christ doth not signify any one person, but a
quality whereof many are partakers; that to be "raised" is
nothing else but to be regenerated, or endued with the said
quality; and that when separation of them which have it from
them which have it not is here made, this is "judgment:"
how plainly do they imagine that the Scripture every where
speaketh in the favour of that sect[2]? And assuredly, the very

---

[1] Arist. Metaph. lib. i. cap. 5. ["It is no hard thing for a man "that hath wit, and is strongly pos- "sest of an opinion, and resolute to "maintain it, to find some places of "scripture, which by good handling "will be woed to cast a favourable "countenance upon it. Pytha- "goras' Schollers having been bred "up in the doctrine of numbers, "when afterward they diverted "upon the studies of nature, fancied "in themselves somewhat in natural "bodies like unto numbers, and "thereupon fell into a conceit that "numbers were the principles of "them. So fares it with him that "to the reading of Scripture comes "fore-possest with some opinion." Hales's Golden Remains, p. 4, ed. 1658. See Diog. Laert. lib. viii. p. 220. ed. Pearson; Brucker, Hist. Phil. I. 1045, &c.]

[2] [The Family of Love, or Fami- lists, as they are sometimes called, originated with Henry Nicholas of Amsterdam, and afterwards of Emb- den, about the middle of the 16th century: and may be considered as a kind of offshoot from the German Anabaptists. For their progress in England see Strype, Ann. II. i. 556, ii. 282. Grindal, 383, Whitg. I. 421, III. 158. Christopher Vitel, a joiner of Colchester, was one of their chief propagandists here. See "The displaying of an horrible sect "of gross and wicked heretics, "naming themselves the Family of "Love: with the lives of the au- "thors, &c. by J. R." (John Rogers,) "1578, London." This writer says that H. N. had then as many as 1000 followers in England. From the number of their tracts, (he quotes about a dozen,) and from the attention which they appear to have attracted at the time, he would seem to have much underrated their numbers. Vitel replied to this pamphlet, and Rogers rejoined in 1579. (Both his pamphlets are in Bp. Atterbury's collection, in the library of Christ Church, Oxford, E. 522, 525.) The same year an ela- borate and scholarlike "Confutation "of certain monstrous and horrible "heresies taught by H. N." was published by J. Knewstubs, of Cam- bridge, afterwards one of the repre- sentatives of the Puritan party at the Hampton-court conference. He states, p. 32, "By the doctrine of "H. N. Christ is no one man, but "an estate and condition in man, "common unto so many as have "[so] received his doctrine that "they are grown thereby to perfec- "tion." And, p. 36, "H. N. his "Christ is not God, but an affection "or disposition in man, which, if "it were good, were yet no more "but godliness, not God himself." Which statements he abundantly confirms by quotations from various tracts, but refers to one which he had not seen, as being reported to contain the fullest development of the new doctrine. That work is "An Introduction to the holy un- "derstanding of the Glass of Right- "eousness; set forth by H. N." No printer's name nor date is given. The following passage may be taken

cause which maketh the simple and ignorant to think they even see how the word of God runneth currently on your side, is, that their minds are forestalled and their conceits perverted beforehand, by being taught, that an "elder" doth signify a layman admitted only to the office or rule of government in the Church; a "doctor," one which may only teach, and neither preach nor administer the Sacraments; a "deacon," one which hath charge of the alms-box, and of nothing else: that the "sceptre," the "rod," the "throne" and "kingdom" of Christ, are a form of regiment, only by pastors, elders, doctors,

Preface, Ch. iii. 9.

as a fair specimen of it. (c. 5. No. 28.) "Behold, this same holy being of "God is the true life of the Holy "Ghost, which heretofore God "wrought among his people Israel, "and likewise among the Gentiles "that feared his name.... 29. This "same being of God is indeed the "right food of the soul, and bread of "life, and is descended unto us from "heaven for a life to the man: and "was heretofore broken and distri- "buted to *the people of Israel* and the "disciples of Christ, to feed on in "their souls.... 31. This same bread "which is given unto them is the "true meat offering of Christ, viz. "His Body: and this cup which "is poured forth unto them is the "true shedding of His Blood, *the* "*which is the outflowing of the holy* "*word or Spirit* of Christ, upon all "believers of Christ, to everlasting "life.... 33. Behold, that same bread "or Body of Christ is the Word that "became flesh and it dwelt among "them.... 34. *And the same is the* "*New Testament*, which God in "those days made and appointed "with His people." Compare c. 18, No. 16, &c. And c. 22, 30. "Unto "all that believed was the resur- "rection from the dead, and ever- "lasting life, witnessed and pro- "mised through Jesus Christ. In "sure and firm hope whereof the "upright believers have rested in "the Lord Jesus Christ, till the "appearing of His coming, *which* "*is now, in this day of the Love,* "*revealed, out of the heavenly Being.*

"With which Jesus Christ the "former believers of Christ, who "were fallen asleep, rested, or died "in Him, *are now also manifested* "*in glory*. For Christ in the ap- "pearing of his coming *raiseth* "his deceased from the dead, to the "intent they should reign with Him "over all his enemies, and *condemn-* "*eth* all the ungodly who have not "liked of him."

"I remember," (says Strype, Ann. II. i. 561, writing in 1725,) "a "great admirer of this sect, within "less than twenty years ago, told "me, that there was then but one "of the Family of Love alive, and "he an old man." But their prin- ciples, unfortunately, were not ex- tinct. "I have now before me the "works (or part of them) of Henry "Nicholas, the Father of the Family "of Love: they were given to a "friend of mine by a Quaker, with "this encomium: that he believed "he would not find one word amiss, "or one superfluous, in the whole "book, and commended it, as an "excellent piece. It is not un- "likely that he took it for a Quaker "book; for there is not his name "at length, only H. N. to it; and "it has quite through the Quaker "phyz and mien, that twins are "not more alike. And though he "directs it, To the Family of Love, "yet an ignorant Quaker might "take that for his own family, and "apply it to the Quakers." Leslie's Works, II. 609, ed. 1721.]

Preface,
Ch. iii. 10.

and deacons¹; that by mystical resemblance Mount Sion and Jerusalem are the churches which admit, Samaria and Babylon the churches which oppugn the said form of regiment. And in like sort they are taught to apply all things spoken of repairing the walls and decayed parts of the city and temple of God, by Esdras, Nehemias, and the rest²; as if purposely the Holy Ghost had therein meant to foresignify, what the authors of Admonitions to the Parliament, of Supplications to the Council, of Petitions to her Majesty, and of such other like writs, should either do or suffer in behalf of this their cause.

[10.] From hence they proceed to an higher point, which is the persuading of men credulous and over-capable of such pleasing errors, that it is the special illumination of the Holy Ghost, whereby they discern those things in the word, which others reading yet discern them not. "Dearly beloved," saith St. John, "give not credit unto every spirit³." There are but two ways whereby the Spirit leadeth men into all truth; the one extraordinary, the other common; the one belonging but unto some few, the other extending itself unto all that are of God; the one, that which we call by a special divine excellency Revelation, the other Reason. If the Spirit by such revelation have discovered unto them the secrets of that discipline out of Scripture, they must profess themselves to be all (even men, women, and children) Prophets. Or if reason be the hand which the Spirit hath led them by; forasmuch as persuasions grounded upon reason are either weaker or stronger according to the force of those reasons whereupon the same are grounded, they must every of them from the greatest to the least be able for every several article to shew

---

¹ ["Having occasion to talk "upon a time with an artisan of "Kingston, about his refusal, after "the purest fashion, to be examined "upon his oath, because I saw how "peart he was, and rapt out text "upon text (full ignorantly, God "knoweth,) I was so bold as to "examine him in the second peti-"tion of the Lord's Prayer, de-"manding of him, what he thought "was meant by this word, 'king-"dom,' therein mentioned. Where-"unto he made in effect this "answer, without any staggering: "'We pray,' saith he, 'that our hea-"venly Father would at the last "grant unto us, that we might "have pastors, doctors, elders, and "deacons in every parish, and so "be governed by such elderships as "Christ's holy discipline doth re-"quire.'" Bancroft, Survey, &c. c. 31.]

² [T. C. Preface to 2d Reply, fol. 1. 2.]

³ 1 John iv. 1.

some special reason as strong as their persuasion therein is *Preface,* earnest. Otherwise how can it be but that some other sinews Ch. iii. 11, 12. there are from which that overplus of strength in persuasion doth arise? Most sure it is, that when men's affections do frame their opinions, they are in defence of error more earnest a great deal, than (for the most part) sound believers in the maintenance of truth apprehended according to the nature of that evidence which scripture yieldeth: which being in some things plain, as in the principles of Christian doctrine; in some things, as in these matters of discipline, more dark and doubtful; frameth correspondently that inward assent which God's most gracious Spirit worketh by it as by his effectual instrument. It is not therefore the fervent earnestness of their persuasion, but the soundness of those reasons whereupon the same is built, which must declare their opinions in these things to have been wrought by the Holy Ghost, and not by the fraud of that evil spirit, which is even in his illusions strong[1].

[11.] After that the fancy of the common sort hath once throughly apprehended the Spirit to be author of their persuasion concerning discipline; then is instilled into their hearts, that the same Spirit leading men into this opinion doth thereby seal them to be God's children; and that, as the state of the times now standeth, the most special token to know them that are God's own from others is an earnest affection that way. This hath bred high terms of separation between such and the rest of the world; whereby the one sort are named The brethren, The godly, and so forth; the other, worldlings, time-servers, pleasers of men not of God, with such like[2].

[12.] From hence, they are easily drawn on to think it exceeding necessary, for fear of quenching that good Spirit, to use all means whereby the same may be both strengthened in themselves, and made manifest unto others. This maketh them diligent hearers of such as are known that way to incline; this maketh them eager to take and to seek all

---

[1] 2 Thess. ii. 11.
[2] [The 22d art. of Charge against Cartwright in 1590 is, "That from "time to time, since his abode in "Warwick, by his practice and deal-"ing, he hath nourished a faction, "and heartburning of one inhabit-"ant there against another, severing "them in his own and his followers' "speeches, by the names of *The* "*godly*, or *Brethren favouring sin-*"*cerity*, and *The profane*." Fuller, C. H. b. ix. p. 200.]

occasions of secret conference with such; this maketh them glad to use such as counsellors and directors in all their dealings which are of weight, as contracts, testaments, and the like; this maketh them, through an unweariable desire of receiving instruction from the masters of that company, to cast off the care of those very affairs which do most concern their estate, and to think that then they are like unto Mary, commendable for making choice of the better part. Finally, this is it which maketh them willing to charge, yea, oftentimes even to overcharge themselves, for such men's sustenance and relief, lest their zeal to the cause should any way be unwitnessed. For what is it which poor beguiled souls will not do through so powerful incitements?

[13.] In which respect it is also noted, that most labour hath been bestowed to win and retain towards this cause them whose judgments are commonly weakest by reason of their sex[1]. And although not "women loden with sins[2]," as

---

[1] [For example: a copy of the Admonition to the Parliament, in the library of Christ Church, Oxford, has the following lines in MS. in the blank leaf at the beginning:

To Mrs. Catesbie my very frende.

Read and peruse this lytle booke
  with prayer to the Lorde
That all may yelde that therein looke
  to truthe with one accorde.
Whiche thoughe our troubles it hathe wrought
  it shall prevayle at laste,
And utterly confounde God's foes
  with his confoundinge blaste.
As Pope hath falne, so muste all popes
  and popelings every one,
So muste his lawes whereby he rulde,
  and God's worde stand alone.
Whiche is the scepter of the might
  of Chryste our Lorde and Kynge,
To whiche we must subject of right
  ourselves, and everye thinge.
        Yo^{rs} in the Lorde,
          Io. Feilde.

Field is mentioned by Archb. Bancroft (Survey, &c. p. 42) as one of the first planners of the Admonition. He was imprisoned the year it came out, (1572,) according to Strype, (Ann. II. i. 275,) for presenting a copy of it to the parliament. Bishop Sandys complained that when Field was in Newgate the people resorted to him "as in popery they were wont to run on pilgrimage." (Strype, Parker, II. 268.) He was a leader of the secret Puritan synod in 1580: and is constantly mentioned as one of the most busy and important among them.

See also Clarendon's Hist. of the Reb. I. 177, Oxford, 1819.]

[2] 2 Tim. iii. 6.

the apostle Saint Paul speaketh, but (as we verily esteem of them for the most part) women propense and inclinable to holiness be otherwise edified in good things, rather than carried away as captives into any kind of sin and evil by such as enter into their houses, with purpose to plant there a zeal and a love towards this kind of discipline: yet some occasion is hereby ministered for men to think, that if the cause which is thus furthered did gain by the soundness of proof whereupon it doth build itself, it would not most busily endeavour to prevail where least ability of judgment is: and therefore, that this so eminent industry in making proselytes more of that sex than of the other groweth, for that they are deemed apter to serve as instruments and helps in the cause. Apter they are through the eagerness of their affection, that maketh them, which way soever they take, diligent in drawing their husbands, children, servants, friends and allies the same way; apter through that natural inclination unto pity, which breedeth in them a greater readiness than in men to be bountiful towards their preachers who suffer want; apter through sundry opportunities, which they especially have, to procure encouragements for their brethren; finally, apter through a singular delight which they take in giving very large and particular intelligence, how all near about them stand affected as concerning the same cause.

Preface, Ch. iii. 14.

[14.] But be they women or be they men, if once they have tasted of that cup, let any man of contrary opinion open his mouth to persuade them, they close up their ears, his reasons they weigh not, all is answered with rehearsal of the words of John, "'We are of God; he that knoweth God heareth us[1]:' "as for the rest, ye are of the world; for this world's pomp "and vanity it is that ye speak, and the world, whose ye are, "heareth you." Which cloak sitteth no less fit on the back of their cause, than of the Anabaptists, when the dignity, authority and honour of God's magistrate is upheld against them. Shew these eagerly-affected men their inability to judge of such matters; their answer is, "God hath chosen the "simple[2]." Convince them of folly, and that so plainly, that very children upbraid them with it; they have their bucklers

---

[1] 1 John iv. 6.   [2] 1 Cor. i. 27.

<small>Preface,
Ch. iii. 15.</small> of like defence: "Christ's own apostle was accounted mad: "the best men evermore by the sentence of the world have "been judged to be out of their right minds[1]."

[15.] When instruction doth them no good, let them feel but the least degree of most mercifully-tempered severity[2], they fasten on the head of the Lord's vicegerents here on earth whatsoever they any where find uttered against the cruelty of bloodthirsty men, and to themselves they draw all the sentences which scripture hath in the favour of innocency persecuted for the truth; yea, they are of their due and deserved sufferings no less proud, than those ancient disturbers to whom Saint Augustine writeth, saying[3]: "Martyrs "rightly so named are they not which suffer for their "disorder, and for the ungodly breach they have made of "Christian unity, but which for righteousness' sake are "persecuted. For Agar also suffered persecution at the "hands of Sara, wherein, she which did impose was holy, "and she unrighteous which did bear the burden. In like "sort, with thieves was the Lord himself crucified; but they, "who were matched in the pain which they suffered[4], were "in the cause of their sufferings disjoined."...."If that must "needs be the true church which doth endure persecution,

---

[1] Acts xxvi. 24. Sap. v. 4. "We "fools thought his life madness." Merc. Tris. ad Æsculap. [lib. xv. fol. 43.] Οἱ ἐν γνώσει ὄντες οὔτε τοῖς πολλοῖς ἀρέσκουσι, οὔτε οἱ πολλοὶ αὐτοῖς· μεμηνέναι δὲ δοκοῦσι, καὶ γέλωτα ὀφλισκάνουσι. Vide Lactant. de Justit. lib. v. cap. 16.

[2] [This was written before either of the executions which took place in Queen Elizabeth's reign for disturbances on puritanical grounds. For Hooker's book was sent to Lord Burghley, March 13, 1592, (Strype, Whitg. III. 300,) Barrow and Greenwood were condemned, March 23, (ibid. II. 186,) Penry in May (ib. 176). Udall who had been convicted was pardoned, at Whitgift's intercession, June 1592, (ib. 102.)]

[3] Aug. Ep. 50. [al. 185, § 9. t. II. 64⁋. "Veri martyres illi sunt, "de quibus Dominus ait, Beati qui "persecutionem patiuntur propter "justitiam. Non ergo qui propter "iniquitatem, et propter Christianæ "unitatis impiam divisionem, sed "qui propter justitiam persecutio"nem patiuntur, hi martyres veri "sunt. Nam et Agar passa est perse"cutionem a Sara, et illa erat sancta "quæ faciebat, illa iniqua quæ patie"batur. Et ipse Dominus cum latro"nibus crucifixus est: sed quos pas"sio jungebat, causa separabat."]

[4] [Ibid. § 11. "Si Ecclesia vera "ipsa est, quæ persecutionem pati"tur, non quæ facit; quærant ab "Apostolo, quam Ecclesiam signifi"cabat Sara, quando persecutionem "faciebat ancillæ. Liberam quippe "matrem nostram, cœlestem Jeru"salem, id est veram Dei Ecclesiam, "in illa muliere dicit fuisse figura"tam, quæ affligebat ancillam. Si "autem melius discutiamus, magis "illa persequebatur Saram super"biendo, quam illam Sara coer"cendo."]

"and not that which persecuteth, let them ask of the apostle "what church Sara did represent, when she held her maid "in affliction. For even our mother which is free, the "heavenly Jerusalem, that is to say, the true Church of God, "was, as he doth affirm, prefigured in that very woman by "whom the bondmaid was so sharply handled. Although, if "all things be throughly scanned, she did in truth more "persecute Sara by proud resistance, than Sara her by "severity of punishment."

Preface, Ch. iii. 16. iv. 1.

[16.] These are the paths wherein ye have walked that are of the ordinary sort of men; these are the very steps ye have trodden, and the manifest degrees whereby ye are of your guides and directors trained up in that school: a custom of inuring your ears with reproof of faults especially in your governors; an use to attribute those faults to the kind of spiritual regiment under which ye live; boldness in warranting the force of their discipline for the cure of all such evils; a slight of framing your conceits to imagine that Scripture every where favoureth that discipline; persuasion that the cause why ye find it in Scripture is the illumination of the Spirit, that the same Spirit is a seal unto you of your nearness unto God, that ye are by all means to nourish and witness it in yourselves, and to strengthen on every side your minds against whatsoever might be of force to withdraw you from it.

IV. Wherefore to come unto you whose judgment is a lantern of direction for all the rest, you that frame thus the people's hearts, not altogether (as I willingly persuade myself) of a politic intent or purpose, but yourselves being first overborne with the weight of greater men's judgments: on your shoulders is laid the burden of upholding the cause by argument. For which purpose sentences out of the word of God ye allege divers: but so, that when the same are discussed, thus it always in a manner falleth out, that what things by virtue thereof ye urge upon us as altogether necessary, are found to be thence collected only by poor and marvellous slight conjectures. I need not give instance in any one sentence so alleged, for that I think the instance in any alleged otherwise a thing not easy to be given. A very strange thing sure it were, that such a discipline as ye speak

What hath caused so many of the learneder sort to approve the same discipline.

Preface,
Ch. iv. 2.

of should be taught by Christ and his apostles in the word of God, and no church ever have found it out, nor received it till this present time [1]; contrariwise, the government against which ye bend yourselves be observed every where throughout all generations and ages of the Christian world, no church ever perceiving the word of God to be against it. We require you to find out but one church upon the face of the whole earth, that hath been ordered by your discipline, or hath not been ordered by ours, that is to say, by episcopal regiment, sithence the time that the blessed Apostles were here conversant.

[2.] Many things out of antiquity ye bring, as if the purest times of the Church had observed the selfsame orders which you require; and as though your desire were that the churches of old should be patterns for us to follow, and even glasses, wherein we might see the practice of that which by you is gathered out of Scripture. But the truth is, ye mean nothing less. All this is done for fashion's sake only: for ye complain of it as of an injury, that men should be willed to seek for examples and patterns of government in any of those times that have been before [2]. Ye plainly hold, that from the very Apostles' time till this present age, wherein yourselves imagine ye have found out a right pattern of sound discipline, there never was any time safe to be followed. Which thing ye thus endeavour to prove. "Out of [3] "Egesippus" ye say that "Eusebius [4] writeth," how although "as long as the Apostles lived the Church did remain a pure

---

[1] [Bancroft, Sermon at S. Paul's Cross, 9 Feb. 158⅘, p. 10, 11, has the same affirmation and challenge almost in the same words. "A very "strange matter if it were true, that "Christ should erect a form of "government for the ruling of his "Church, to continue from his de-"parture out of the world until his "coming again; and that the same "should never be once thought of "or put in practice for the space of "1500 years: or at the least (to take "them at their best) that the govern-"ment and kingdom of Christ should "then be overthrown, when by all "men's confessions the divinity of "his Person, the virtue of his Priest-"hood, the power of his office as "He is a Prophet, and the honour "of his kingly Authority was so "godly, so learnedly, and so mightily "established."]

[2] T. C. lib. i. p. 97.

[3] [Id. ibid. and ii. 507–511.]

[4] Euseb. Hist. Eccles. lib. iii. cap. 32. iv. 22. ['Ο αὐτὸς ἀνὴρ ἐπιλέγει, ὡς ἄρα μέχρι τῶν τότε χρόνων παρθένος καθαρὰ καὶ ἀδιάφθορος ἔμεινεν ἡ ἐκκλησία, ἐν ἀδήλῳ που σκότει φωλευόντων εἰσέτι τότε, τῶν, εἰ καί τινες ὑπῆρχον, παραφθείρειν ἐπιχειρούντων τὸν ὑγιῆ κανόνα τοῦ σωτηρίου κηρύγματος. And in b. iv. 22, he cites the very words of Hegesippus, Διὰ τοῦτο ἐκάλουν τὴν ἐκκλησίαν παρ-

"virgin, yet after the death of the Apostles, and after they
"were once gone whom God vouchsafed to make hearers of
"the divine wisdom with their own ears, the placing of
"wicked error began to come into the Church. Clement
"also in a certain place, to confirm that there was corruption
"of doctrine immediately after the Apostles' time, allegeth
"the proverb, that 'There are few sons like their fathers[1].'
"Socrates saith of the churches of Rome and Alexandria[2],
"the most famous churches in the Apostles' times, that about
"the year 430, the Roman and Alexandrian bishops, leaving
"the sacred function, were degenerate to a secular rule or
"dominion[3]." Hereupon ye conclude, that it is not safe to
fetch our government from any other than the Apostles'
times.

[3.] Wherein by the way it may be noted, that in proposing
the Apostles' times as a pattern for the Church to follow,
though the desire of you all be one, the drift and purpose of
you all is not one. The chiefest thing which lay-reformers
yawn for is, that the clergy may through conformity in state
and condition be apostolical, poor as the Apostles of Christ
were poor. In which one circumstance if they imagine so
great perfection, they must think that Church which hath
such store of mendicant Friars, a church in that respect most
happy. Were it for the glory of God and the good of his
Church indeed that the clergy should be left even as bare as
the Apostles when they had neither staff nor scrip, that God,
which should lay upon them the condition of his Apostles,
would I hope endue them with the selfsame affection which
was in that holy Apostle, whose words concerning his own
right virtuous contentment of heart, "as well how to want,
"as how to abound[4]," are a most fit episcopal emprese.
The Church of Christ is a body mystical. A body cannot
stand, unless the parts thereof be proportionable. Let it
therefore be required on both parts, at the hands of the

θένον· οὔπω γὰρ ἔφθαρτο ἀκοαῖς μα-
ταίαις. See Dr. Routh's note, Reliquiæ Sacræ, i. 233.]
    [1] Lib. Strom. somewhat after the
beginning. [Ed. Potter. t. i. 322.]
['Ολίγοι δὲ οἱ πατράσιν ὅμοιοι; from
Hom. Od. ii. 276.]

[2] Hist. Eccles. lib. vii. cap. 11.
    [3] [Τῆς Ῥωμαίων ἐπισκοπῆς, ὁμοίως
τῇ Ἀλεξανδρέων, πέρα τῆς ἱερωσύνης,
ἐπὶ δυναστείαν ἤδη πάλαι προελθούσης.]
    [4] Phil. iv. 12. [For the word em-
prese or impress see Shakespeare,
Rich. II. act III. sc. 1.]

Preface,
Ch. iv. 4.

clergy, to be in meanness of state like the Apostles; at the hands of the laity, to be as they were who lived under the Apostles: and in this reformation there will be, though little wisdom, yet some indifferency.

[4.] But your reformation which are of the clergy (if yet it displease you not that I should say ye are of the clergy[1]) seemeth to aim at a broader mark. Ye think that he which will perfectly reform must bring the form of church-discipline unto the state which then it was at. A thing neither possible, nor certain, nor absolutely convenient.

Concerning the first, what was used in the Apostles' times, the Scripture fully declareth not; so that making their times the rule and canon of church-polity, ye make a rule, which being not possible to be fully known, is as impossible to be kept.

Again, sith the later even of the Apostles' own times had that which in the former was not thought upon; in this general proposing of the apostolical times, there is no certainty which should be followed: especially seeing that ye give us great cause to doubt how far ye allow those times[2]. For albeit "the loover of antichristian building were not," ye say, as then "set up, yet the foundations thereof were "secretly and under the ground laid in the Apostles' times[3]:" so that all other times ye plainly reject, and the Apostles' own times ye approve with marvellous great suspicion, leav-

---

[1] [T. C. iii. 219. "Those which "were baptized in their beds were "thereby made unapt to have any "place among the clergy (*as they* "*call them*).")

[2] [Penry, Brief Discovery, &c. p. 20. "We know Diotrephes to have "been in the Church even in the "Apostles' times.... and therefore "we cannot greatly marvel, though "even in their time there had been "a divers government from this of "the Lord's appointment, which we "labour for. For even in the Apo- "stles' time the mystery of iniquity "began to work."]

[3] [T. C. i. 97. The word "loover" is also used, T. C. ii. 621. "How "childishe is yt, after so long tra- "vaile to prove a bishop over the "ministers off a diocese,.... in the "ende to endevour to prove, that "there may be superioritie? as if "any man would denie this that "graunted the other: and yt is *to* "*set the fondacion upon the lover.*" "Louver, (from *l'ouvert*, Fr. an "opening:) an opening for the "smoke to go out at in the roof of "a cottage: in the north of Eng- "land, an opening at the top of a "dovecote. 'The ancient manner "of building in Cornwall was, to "set hearths in the midst of rooms "for chimneys, which vented the "smoke at a louver in the top.' "Carew, Survey of Cornwall. And "see Spenser's F. Q. vi. x. 42." Todd's Johnson's Dict.]

ing it intricate and doubtful, wherein we are to keep ourselves unto the pattern of their times.

Thirdly, whereas it is the error of the common multitude to consider only what hath been of old, and if the same were well, to see whether still it continue; if not, to condemn that presently which is, and never to search upon what ground or consideration the change might grow: such rudeness cannot be in you so well borne with, whom learning and judgment hath enabled much more soundly to discern how far the times of the Church and the orders thereof may alter without offence. True it is, the ancienter[1], the better ceremonies of religion are; howbeit, not absolutely true and without exception: but true only so far forth as those different ages do agree in the state of those things, for which at the first those rites, orders, and ceremonies, were instituted. In the Apostles' times that was harmless, which being now revived would be scandalous; as their *oscula sancta*[2]. Those feasts of charity[3], which being instituted by the Apostles, were retained in the Church long after, are not now thought any where needful. What man

Preface, Ch. iv. 4.

---

[1] "Antiquitas ceremoniis atque "fanis tantum sanctitatis tribuere "consuevit, quantum adstruxerit "vetustatis." Arno. p. 746. [The words are from Minutius Felix, p. 4, line 30, ed. Elmenhorst. In many former editions, and no doubt in that which Hooker used, the dialogue of Minutius is ascribed to Arnobius.]

[2] Rom. xvi. 16; 2 Cor. xiii. 12; 1 Thess. v. 26; 1 Pet. v. 14. In their meetings to serve God, their manner was, in the end to salute one another with a kiss; using these words, "Peace be with you." For which cause Tertullian doth call it, *signaculum orationis*, "the seal of "prayer." Lib. de Orat. [c. 14.]

[3] Epist. Jud. 12. Concerning which feasts, Saint Chrysostom saith, "Statis diebus mensas faciebant "communes, et peracta synaxi post "sacramentorum communionem in- "ibant convivium, divitibus quidem "cibos afferentibus, pauperibus au- "tem et qui nihil habebant etiam "vocatis." [Καθάπερ ἐπὶ τῶν τρισ- χιλίων τῶν ἐξ ἀρχῆς πιστευσάντων, κοινῇ πάντες εἰστιῶντο καὶ κοινὰ πάντα ἐκέκτηντο, οὕτω καὶ τότε ὅτε ταῦτα ἔγραψεν ὁ Ἀπόστολος ἐγίνετο, οὐχ οὕτω μὲν μετὰ ἀκριβείας, ὥσπερ δὲ τις ἀπόρροια τῆς κοινωνίας ἐκείνης ἐναπομείνασα καὶ εἰς τοὺς μετὰ ταῦτα κατέβη. Καὶ ἐπειδὰν συνέβαινε τοὺς μὲν πένητας εἶναι, τοὺς δὲ πλουσίους, τὰ μὲν ἑαυτῶν οὐ κατετίθεντο πάντα εἰς μέσον, κοινὰς δὲ ἐποιοῦντο τὰς τραπέζας ἐν ἡμέραις νενομισμέναις, ὡς εἰκὸς, καὶ τῆς συνάξεως ἀπαρτισθείσης μετὰ τὴν τῶν μυστηρίων κοινωνίαν ἐπὶ κοινὴν πάντες ᾔεσαν εὐωχίαν, τῶν μὲν πλουτούντων φερόντων τὰ ἐδέσματα, τῶν δὲ πενομένων καὶ οὐδὲν ἐχόντων ὑπ' αὐτῶν καλουμένων καὶ κοινῇ πάντων ἑστιωμένων. iii. 416.] In 1 Cor. xi. 17, Hom. xxvii. Of the same feasts in like sort, Tertullian. "Cœna "nostra de nomine rationem sui "ostendit. Vocatur enim ἀγάπη, id "quod est penes Græcos *dilectio*. "Quantiscunque sumptibus con- "stet, lucrum est pietatis nomine "facere sumptum." Apol. cap. 39.

is there of understanding, unto whom it is not manifest how the way of providing for the clergy by tithes, the device of almshouses for the poor, the sorting out of the people into their several parishes, together with sundry other things which the Apostles' times could not have, (being now established,) are much more convenient and fit for the Church of Christ, than if the same should be taken away for conformity's sake with the ancientest and first times?

[5.] The orders therefore, which were observed in the Apostles' times, are not to be urged as a rule universally either sufficient or necessary. If they be, nevertheless on your part it still remaineth to be better proved, that the form of discipline, which ye entitle apostolical, was in the Apostles' times exercised. For of this very thing ye fail even touching that which ye make most account of[1], as being matter of substance in discipline, I mean the power of your lay-elders, and the difference of your Doctors from the Pastors in all churches. So that in sum, we may be bold to conclude, that besides these last times, which for insolency, pride, and egregious contempt of all good order, are the worst, there are none wherein ye can truly affirm, that the complete form of your discipline, or the substance thereof, was practised.

[6.] The evidence therefore of antiquity failing you, ye fly to the judgments of such learned men, as seem by their writings to be of opinion, that all Christian churches should receive your discipline, and abandon ours. Wherein, as ye heap up the names of a number of men not unworthy to be had in honour; so there are a number whom when ye mention, although it serve you to purpose with the ignorant and vulgar sort, who measure by tale and not by weight, yet surely they who know what quality and value the men are of, will think ye draw very near the dregs. But were they all of as great account as the best and chiefest amongst them, with us notwithstanding neither are they, neither ought

---

[1] ["Tantum inter cæteros eminent Presbyteri isti non docentes, 'quantum lenta solent inter viburna cupressi:' tantumque præstare videntur reliquis, ut ipsorum nomine totus hic consessus Presbyterium dicatur. Quum igitur tota illa moles novæ disciplinæ.... hoc uno fundamento nitatur.... &c." Sutcliffe de Presbyt. p. 90.]

they to be of such reckoning, that their opinion or conjecture should cause the laws of the Church of England to give place. Much less when they neither do all agree in that opinion, and of them which are at agreement, the most part through a courteous inducement have followed one man as their guide, finally that one therein not unlikely to have swerved[1]. If any chance to say it is probable that in the Apostles' times there were lay-elders, or not to mislike the continuance of them in the Church, or to affirm that Bishops at the first were a name but not a power distinct from Presbyters, or to speak any thing in praise of those Churches which are without episcopal regiment, or to reprove the fault of such as abuse that calling; all these ye register for men persuaded as you are, that every Christian Church standeth bound by the law of God to put down Bishops, and in their rooms to elect an Eldership so authorized as you would have it for the government of each parish. Deceived greatly they are therefore, who think that all they whose names are cited amongst the favourers of this cause, are on any such verdict agreed[2].

Preface, Ch. iv. 7.

[7.] Yet touching some material points of your discipline, a kind of agreement we grant there is amongst many divines of reformed Churches abroad. For, first, to do as the Church of Geneva did the learned in some other Churches must needs be the more willing, who having used in like manner not the slow and tedious help of proceeding by public authority, but the people's more quick endeavour for alteration, in such an exigent I see not well how they could have stayed to deliberate about any other regiment than that which already was devised to their hands, that which in like case had been taken, that which was easiest to be established without delay, that which was likeliest to content the people by reason of some kind of sway which it giveth them. When therefore the example of one Church was thus at the first almost through a kind of constraint or necessity followed by many, their concurrence in persuasion about some material points belonging to the same polity is not strange. For we are not to marvel greatly, if they which

[1] ["Swarved"—and so always in 1st ed. 1594.]
[2] [Full evidence of this point may be seen in Whitgift's two works.]

Preface,
Ch. iv. 8. have all done the same thing, do easily embrace the same opinion as concerning their own doings.

[8.] Besides, mark I beseech you that which Galen in matter of philosophy noteth[1]; for the like falleth out even in questions of higher knowledge. It fareth many times with men's opinions as with rumours and reports. "That "which a credible person telleth is easily thought probable "by such as are well persuaded of him. But if two, or three, "or four, agree all in the same tale, they judge it then to "be out of controversy, and so are many times overtaken for "want of due consideration; either some common cause "leading them all into error, or one man's oversight deceiv-"ing many through their too much credulity and easiness "of belief." Though ten persons be brought to give testimony in any cause, yet if the knowledge they have of the thing whereunto they come as witnesses, appear to have grown from some one amongst them, and to have spread itself from hand to hand, they all are in force but as one testimony. Nor is it otherwise here where the daughter churches do speak their mother's dialect; here where so many sing one song, by reason that he is the guide of the choir[2], concerning whose deserved authority amongst even the gravest divines we have already spoken at large. Will ye ask what should move those many learned to be followers of one man's judgment, no necessity of argument forcing them thereunto? Your demand is answered by yourselves. Loth ye are to think that they, whom ye judge to have attained as sound knowledge in all points of doctrine as any since the Apostles' time, should mistake in discipline[3]. Such is natu-

---

[1] Galen. clas. 2, lib. de cujusque Anim. Peccat. Notitia atque Medela, [t. i. p. 366. Basil. 1538. —μηδενὶ ψευδῶς συγκαταθέμενον ἑαυτὸν, ὥσπερ ἑκάστης ἡμέρας ὁρῶ παμπόλλους τῶν φιλῶν, ἐνίους μὲν ἑνὶ τῶν εἰπόντων ὁτιοῦν πιστεύσαντας· .... προπετῶς δὲ καὶ ὃ τρίσιν ἢ τέσσαρσιν, ἄνευ τοῦ διορίσασθαι πότερον ἐνδέχεται πάντας αὐτοὺς ἐκ μιᾶς αἰτίας κοινῆς ἀληθεύειν, ἢ ψεύδεσθαι πάντας ἐκ μιᾶς αἰτίας κοινῆς.]

[2] ["quier," ed. 1594.]

[3] Petition to the Queen's Majesty, p. 14.—["It *may* be that they who "have attained to as sound know-"ledge in all points of doctrine as "any since the apostles' time should "mistake in discipline. It *may* be "that they whom the Spirit of truth "and wisdom hath directed in ex-"pounding the Scriptures should be "always forsaken of that Spirit "when they come to expound or "speak of a text concerning disci-"pline.. But.. men not partial will "still make scruples in these mat-"ters."]

rally our affection, that whom in great things we mightily *Preface,* admire, in them we are not persuaded willingly that any Ch. v. 1. thing should be amiss. The reason whereof is, "for that "as dead flies putrify the ointment of the apothecary[1], so "a little folly him that is in estimation for wisdom[2]." This in every profession hath too much authorized the judgments of a few. This with Germans hath caused Luther, and with many other Churches Calvin, to prevail in all things. Yet are we not able to define, whether the wisdom of that God, (who setteth before us in holy Scripture so many admirable patterns of virtue, and no one of them without somewhat noted wherein they were culpable, to the end that to Him alone it might always be acknowledged, "Thou only art holy, thou only art just[3];") might not permit those worthy vessels of his glory to be in some things blemished with the stain of human frailty, even for this cause, lest we should esteem of any man above that which behoveth.

V. Notwithstanding, as though ye were able to say a great deal more than hitherto your books have revealed to the world, earnest challengers[4] ye are of trial by some public disputation. Wherein if the thing ye crave be no more than only leave to dispute openly about those matters that are in question, the schools in universities (for any thing I know) are open unto you. They have their yearly

Their calling for trial by disputation.

---

[1] ["apoticarie," ed. 1594.]
[2] Eccles. x. 1.
[3] [ὅτι μόνος ὅσιος. Apoc. xv. 4. Σὺ μόνος Ἅγιος,—σὺ μόνος Κύριος. Morning Hymn in Apost. Constit. vii. 4, used by our Church in the Post-Communion.]
[4] ["Would to God that free con-"ference in these matters might be "had. For howsoever learned and "many they seeme to be, they should "and may in this realme finde inowe, "to matche them, and shame them "to, if they hold on as they have "begon." Address "to the godly "readers," prefixed to the first Admonition to the Parliament, p. 2. See also "A View of Popish Abuses," subjoined to the 1st Admonition, p. 18; and 2nd Adm. p. 36; and Petition to the Queen's Maj. p. 3. "There is a way devised and much "commended by learned men, as a "notable mean to compound con-"troversies, namely, private con-"ferences by advised writing, not "extemporal speaking, the question "agreed of. The arguments, the "answers, replies, and rejoinders "set down, till both parties had "fully said, all by-matters laid "aside. In fine the whole to be pub-"lished, that your Majesty, the "honourable counsellors and Par-"liament may judge thereof." And Pref. to Dem. of Disc. "Venture "your bishopricks upon a disputa-"tion, and we will venture our "lives: take the challenge if you "dare."]

Preface,
Ch. v. 2, 3.

Acts and Commencements, besides other disputations both ordinary and upon occasion, wherein the several parts of our own ecclesiastical discipline are oftentimes offered unto that kind of examination; the learnedest of you have been of late years noted seldom or never absent from thence at the time of those greater assemblies; and the favour of proposing there in convenient sort whatsoever ye can object (which thing myself have known them to grant of scholastical courtesy unto strangers) neither hath (as I think) nor ever will (I presume) be denied you.

[2.] If your suit be to have some great extraordinary confluence, in expectation whereof the laws that already are should sleep and have no power over you, till in the hearing of thousands ye all did acknowledge your error and renounce the further prosecution of your cause: haply[1] they whose authority is required unto the satisfying of your demand do think it both dangerous to admit such concourse of divided minds, and unmeet that laws, which being once solemnly established are to exact obedience of all men and to constrain thereunto, should so far stoop as to hold themselves in suspense from taking any effect upon you till some disputer can persuade you to be obedient[2]. A law is the deed of the whole body politic, whereof if ye judge yourselves to be any part, then is the law even your deed also. And were it reason in things of this quality to give men audience, pleading for the overthrow of that which their own very deed hath ratified? Laws that have been approved may be (no man doubteth) again repealed, and to that end also disputed against, by the authors thereof themselves. But this is when the whole doth deliberate what laws each part shall observe, and not when a part refuseth the laws which the whole hath orderly agreed upon.

[3.] Notwithstanding, forasmuch as the cause we maintain is (God be thanked) such as needeth not to shun any trial, might it please them on whose approbation the matter dependeth to condescend so far unto you in this behalf, I

---

[1] ["happily," and so usually in ed. 1594.]
[2] [See in Strype, Ann. IV. 239, 240, a petition of Barrow for a conference, with Archbishop Whitgift's reasons against it.]

wish heartily that proof were made even by solemn conference in orderly and quiet sort, whether you would yourselves be satisfied, or else could by satisfying others draw them to your part. Provided always, first, inasmuch as ye go about to destroy a thing which is in force, and to draw in that which hath not as yet been received ; to impose on us that which we think not ourselves bound unto, and to overthrow those things whereof we are possessed ; that therefore ye are not to claim in any such conference other than the plaintiff's or opponent's part, which must consist altogether in proof and confirmation of two things : the one, that our orders by you condemned we ought to abolish ; the other, that yours we are bound to accept in the stead thereof : secondly, because the questions in controversy between us are many, if once we descend unto particularities ; that for the easier and more orderly proceeding therein the most general be first discussed, nor any question left off, nor in each question the prosecution of any one argument given over and another taken in hand, till the issue whereunto by replies and answers both parts are come, be collected, read, and acknowledged as well on the one side as on the other to be the plain conclusion which they are grown unto: thirdly, for avoiding of the manifold inconveniences whereunto ordinary and extemporal disputes are subject ; as also because, if ye should singly dispute one by one as every man's own wit did best serve, it might be conceived by the rest that haply some other would have done more ; the chiefest of you do all agree in this action, that whom ye shall then choose your speaker, by him that which is publickly brought into disputation be acknowledged by all your consents not to be his allegation but yours, such as ye all are agreed upon, and have required him to deliver in all your names ; the true copy whereof being taken by a notary, that a reasonable time be allowed for return of answer unto you in the like form. Fourthly, whereas a number of conferences have been had in other causes with the less effectual success, by reason of partial and untrue reports published afterwards unto the world ; that to prevent this evil, there be at the first a solemn declaration made on both parts, of their agreement to have that very book and no other set abroad, wherein their present authorized notaries do write those things fully and

Preface, Ch. v. 3.

Preface,
Ch. vi. 2.

only, which being written and there read, are by their own open testimony acknowledged to be their own. Other circumstances hereunto belonging, whether for the choice of time, place, and language, or for prevention of impertinent and needless speech, or to any end and purpose else—they may be thought on when occasion serveth.

In this sort to broach my private conceit for the ordering of a public action I should be loth (albeit I do it not otherwise than under correction of them whose gravity and wisdom ought in such cases to overrule,) but that so venturous boldness I see is a thing now general; and am thereby of good hope, that where all men are licensed to offend, no man will shew himself a sharp accuser.

No end of contention, without submission of both parts unto some definitive sentence.

VI. What success God may give unto any such kind of conference or disputation, we cannot tell. But of this we are right sure, that nature, Scripture [1], and experience itself, have all taught the world to seek for the ending of contentions by submitting itself unto some judicial and definitive sentence, whereunto neither part that contendeth may under any pretence or colour refuse to stand. This must needs be effectual and strong. As for other means without this, they seldom prevail. I would therefore know, whether for the ending of these irksome strifes, wherein you and your followers do stand thus formally divided against the authorized guides of this church, and the rest of the people subject unto their charge; whether I say ye be content to refer your cause to any other higher judgment than your own, or else intend to persist and proceed as ye have begun, till yourselves can be persuaded to condemn yourselves. If your determination be this, we can be but sorry that ye should deserve to be reckoned with such, of whom God himself pronounceth, "The way of peace they have not known [2]."

[2.] Ways of peaceable conclusion there are, but these two certain: the one, a sentence of judicial decision given by authority thereto appointed within ourselves; the other, the like kind of sentence given by a more universal authority. The former of which two ways God himself in the Law

---

[1] [Hebr. vi. 16. "An oath for confirmation is to them an end of "all strife."]   [2] Rom. iii. 17.

prescribeth, and his Spirit it was which directed the very first Christian churches in the world to use the latter.

Preface, Ch. vi. 3.

The ordinance of God in the Law was this. "[1] If there "arise a matter too hard for thee in judgment, between blood "and blood, between plea, &c. then shalt thou arise, and go "up unto the place which the Lord thy God shall choose; "and thou shalt come unto the Priests of the Levites, and "unto the Judge that shall be in those days, and ask, and "they shall shew thee the sentence of judgment, and thou "shalt do according to that thing, which they of that place "which the Lord hath chosen shew thee, and thou shalt "observe to do according to all that they inform thee; "according to the law which they shall teach thee, and "according to the judgment which they shall tell thee, shalt "thou do; thou shalt not decline from the thing which they "shall shew thee to the right hand nor to the left. And that "man that will do presumptuously, not hearkening unto the "Priest (that standeth before the Lord thy God to minister "there) or unto the Judge, that man shall die, and thou shalt "take away evil from Israel."

When there grew in the Church of Christ a question, Whether the Gentiles believing might be saved, although they were not circumcised after the manner of Moses, nor did observe the rest of those legal rites and ceremonies whereunto the Jews were bound; after great dissension and disputation about it, their conclusion in the end was to have it determined by sentence at Jerusalem; which was accordingly done in a council there assembled for the same purpose[2]. Are ye able to allege any just and sufficient cause wherefore absolutely ye should not condescend in this controversy to have your judgments overruled by some such definitive sentence, whether it fall out to be given with or against you; that so these tedious contentions may cease?

[3.] Ye will perhaps make answer, that being persuaded already as touching the truth of your cause, ye are not to hearken unto any sentence, no not though Angels should define otherwise, as the blessed Apostle's own example teacheth[3]: again, that men, yea councils, may err; and that, unless the judgment given do satisfy your minds,

---

[1] Deut. xvii. 8. [2] Acts xv. [3] [Gal. i. 8.]

Preface, Ch. vi. 3. unless it be such as ye can by no further argument oppugn, in a word, unless you perceive and acknowledge it yourselves consonant with God's word; to stand unto it not allowing it were to sin against your own consciences.

But consider I beseech you first as touching the Apostle, how that wherein he was so resolute and peremptory, our Lord Jesus Christ made manifest unto him even by intuitive revelation, wherein there was no possibility of error. That which you are persuaded of, ye have it no otherwise than by your own only probable collection, and therefore such bold asseverations as in him were admirable, should in your mouths but argue rashness. God was not ignorant that the priests and judges, whose sentence in matters of controversy he ordained should stand, both might and oftentimes would be deceived in their judgment. Howbeit, better it was in the eye of His understanding, that sometime an erroneous sentence definitive should prevail, till the same authority perceiving such oversight, might afterwards correct or reverse it, than that strifes should have respite to grow, and not come speedily unto some end.

Neither wish we that men should do any thing which in their hearts they are persuaded they ought not to do, but this persuasion ought (we say) to be fully settled in their hearts; that in litigious and controversed causes of such quality, the will of God is to have them do whatsoever the sentence of judicial and final decision shall determine, yea, though it seem in their private opinion to swerve utterly from that which is right: as no doubt many times the sentence amongst the Jews did seem unto one part or other contending, and yet in this case, God did then allow them to do that which in their private judgment it seemed, yea and perhaps truly seemed, that the law did disallow. For if God be not the author of confusion but of peace, then can he not be the author of our refusal, but of our contentment, to stand unto some definitive sentence; without which almost impossible it is that either we should avoid confusion, or ever hope to attain peace. To small purpose had the Council of Jerusalem been assembled, if once their determination being set down, men might afterwards have defended their former opinions. When therefore they had given their definitive sentence, all controversy was at an end. Things were disputed before they came to be determined; men afterwards were not to dispute any longer, but to obey. The sentence of judgment finished their strife, which their disputes before judgment could not do. This was ground sufficient for any reasonable man's conscience to build the duty of obedience upon, whatsoever his own opinion were as touching the matter before in question. So full of wilfulness and self-liking is our nature, that without some definitive sentence, which being given may stand, and a necessity of silence on both sides afterward imposed, small hope there is that strifes thus far prosecuted will in short time quietly end.

[4.] Now it were in vain to ask you, whether ye could be content that the sentence of any court already erected should be so far authorized, as that among the Jews established by God himself, for the determining of all controversies: "That "man which will do presumptuously, not hearkening unto the "Priest that standeth before the Lord to minister there, nor "unto the Judge, let him die." Ye have given us already to understand, what your opinion is in part concerning her sacred Majesty's Court of High Commission; the nature whereof is the same with that amongst the Jews[1], albeit the power be not so great. The other way haply may like you better, because Master Beza, in his last book save one[2] written about these matters, professeth himself to be now weary of such combats and encounters, whether by word or writing, inasmuch as he findeth that "controversies thereby are made but brawls;" and therefore wisheth "that in some common lawful assembly "of churches all these strifes may at once be decided."

---

[1] [See George Cranmer's notes on B. vi.]

[2] Præf. Tract. de Presbyt. et Excom. ["Ab illis peto, ... ut me jam"pridem istarum concertationum "pertæsum, quibus in rixas evadere "potius quam mitigari, nedum ex"tingui controversias apparet, non "inviti patiantur vel partes istas "minus occupatis aliis fratribus re"linquere, si fuerit opus, obeundas; "vel tacitum expectare, donec aut "Ecclesiæ suæ sic domi et foris "vexatæ precibus hoc tribuat Do"minus, ut lites omnes istæ com"muni aliquo legitimo ecclesiarum "conventu decidantur; vel mihi "denique septuagesimum primum "jam annum in terris peregrinanti "portus ille beatæ et perennis qui"etis, ad quem totus anhelo, per "clementissimi Servatoris mei mi"sericordiam patefiat."] [Præf. sign. A. 7. Beza's pamphlet against Erastus, dated, "Genevæ à Duce Sabaudo, contra jus et fas omne circumvallatæ Kal. Mart. anno temporis ultimi 1590."] 1886.

Preface,
Ch. vi. 5, 6.

[5.] Shall there be then in the meanwhile no "doings?" Yes. There are the weightier matters of the law, "judgment, and "mercy, and fidelity[1]." These things we ought to do; and these things, while we contend about less, we leave undone. Happier are they whom the Lord when he cometh shall find "doing" in these things, than disputing about "Doctors, Elders, "and Deacons." Or if there be no remedy but somewhat needs ye must do which may tend to the setting forward of your discipline; do that which wise men, who think some statute of the realm more fit to be repealed than to stand in force, are accustomed to do before they come to parliament where the place of enacting is; that is to say, spend the time in re-examining more duly your cause, and in more throughly considering of that which ye labour to overthrow. As for the orders which are established, sith equity and reason, the law of nature, God and man, do all favour that which is in being, till orderly judgment of decision be given against it; it is but justice to exact of you, and perverseness in you it should be to deny, thereunto your willing obedience.

[6.] Not that I judge it a thing allowable for men to observe those laws which in their hearts they are steadfastly persuaded to be against the law of God: but your persuasion in this case ye are all bound for the time to suspend; and in otherwise doing, ye offend against God by troubling his Church without any just or necessary cause. Be it that there are some reasons inducing you to think hardly of our laws. Are those reasons demonstrative, are they necessary, or but mere probabilities only? An argument necessary and demonstrative is such, as being proposed unto any man and understood, the mind cannot choose but inwardly assent. Any one such reason dischargeth, I grant, the conscience, and setteth it at full liberty. For the public approbation given by the body of this whole church unto those things which are established, doth make it but probable that they are good. And therefore unto a necessary proof that they are not good it must give place. But if the skilfullest amongst you can shew that all the books ye have hitherto written be able to afford any one argument of this nature, let

[1] Matt. xxiii. 23.

the instance be given. As for probabilities, what thing was there ever set down so agreeable with sound reason, but some probable shew against it might be made? Is it meet that when publicly things are received, and have taken place, general obedience thereunto should cease to be exacted, in case this or that private person, led with some probable conceit, should make open protestation, "I Peter or John dis-"allow them, and pronounce them nought?" In which case your answer will be, that concerning the laws of our church, they are not only condemned in the opinion of "a private "man, but of thousands," yea and even "of those amongst "which divers are in public charge and authority[1]." As though when public consent of the whole hath established any thing, every man's judgment being thereunto compared were not private, howsoever his calling be to some kind of public charge. So that of peace and quietness there is not any way possible, unless the probable voice of every entire[2] society or body politic overrule all private of like nature in the same body. Which thing effectually proveth, that God, being author of peace and not of confusion in the church, must needs be author of those men's peaceable resolutions, who concerning these things have determined with themselves to think and do as the church they are of decreeth, till they see necessary cause enforcing them to the contrary.

Preface, Ch. vii. 1, 2.

VII. Nor is mine own intent any other in these several books of discourse, than to make it appear unto you, that for the ecclesiastical laws of this land, we are led by great reason to observe them, and ye by no necessity bound to impugn them. It is no part of my secret meaning to draw you hereby into hatred, or to set upon the face of this cause any fairer glass than the naked truth doth afford; but my whole endeavour is to resolve the conscience, and to shew as near as I can what in this controversy the heart is to think, if it will follow the light of sound and sincere judgment, without either cloud of prejudice, or mist of passionate affection.

The matter contained in these eight Books.

[2.] Wherefore seeing that laws and ordinances in particular, whether such as we observe, or such as yourselves would have established;—when the mind doth sift and

---

[1] T. C. lib. iii. p. 181.   [2] ["intier;" and so vii. 7. ed. 1594.]

<small>*Preface,*
Ch. vii. 3-5.</small>
examine them, it must needs have often recourse to a number of doubts and questions about the nature, kinds, and qualities of laws in general; whereof unless it be throughly informed, there will appear no certainty to stay our persuasion upon: I have for that cause set down in the first place an introduction on both sides needful to be considered: declaring therein what law is, how different kinds of laws there are, and what force they are of according unto each kind.

[3.] This done, because ye suppose the laws for which ye strive are found in Scripture, but those not, against which ye strive; and upon this surmise are drawn to hold it as the very main pillar of your whole cause, "That Scripture ought "to be the only rule of all our actions," and consequently that the church-orders which we observe being not commanded in Scripture, are offensive and displeasant unto God: I have spent the second Book in sifting of this point, which standeth with you for the first and chiefest principle whereon ye build.

[4.] Whereunto the next in degree is, That as God will have always a Church upon earth, while the world doth continue, and that Church stand in need of government; of which government it behoveth Himself to be both the Author and Teacher: so it cannot stand with duty that man should ever presume in any wise to change and alter the same; and therefore " that in Scripture there must of necessity be found some " particular form of Polity Ecclesiastical, the Laws whereof " admit not any kind of alteration."

[5.] The first three Books being thus ended, the fourth proceedeth from the general grounds and foundations of your cause unto your general accusations against us, as having in the orders of our Church (for so you pretend) " corrupted " the right form of church-polity with manifold popish rites " and ceremonies, which certain reformed Churches have " banished from amongst them, and have thereby given us " such example as " (you think) " we ought to follow." This your assertion hath herein drawn us to make search, whether these be just exceptions against the customs of our Church, when ye plead that they are the same which the Church of Rome hath, or that they are not the same which some other reformed Churches have devised.

[6.] Of those four Books which remain and are bestowed about the specialties of that cause which lieth in controversy, the first examineth the causes by you alleged, wherefore the public duties of Christian religion, as our prayers, our Sacraments, and the rest, should not be ordered in such sort as with us they are; nor that power, whereby the persons of men are consecrated unto the ministry, be disposed of in such manner as the laws of this church do allow. The second and third are concerning the power of jurisdiction: the one, whether laymen, such as your governing Elders are, ought in all congregations for ever to be invested with that power; the other, whether Bishops may have that power over other Pastors, and therewithal that honour, which with us they have? And because besides the power of order which all consecrated persons have, and the power of jurisdiction which neither they all nor they only have, there is a third power, a power of Ecclesiastical Dominion, communicable, as we think, unto persons not ecclesiastical, and most fit to be restrained unto the Prince or Sovereign commander over the whole body politic: the eighth book we have allotted unto this question, and have sifted therein your objections against those preeminences royal which thereunto appertain. Preface, Ch. vii. 6, 7. viii. 1.

[7.] Thus have I laid before you the brief of these my travails, and presented under your view the limbs of that cause litigious between us: the whole entire body whereof being thus compact, it shall be no troublesome thing for any man to find each particular controversy's resting-place, and the coherence it hath with those things, either on which it dependeth, or which depend on it.

VIII. The case so standing therefore, my brethren, as it doth, the wisdom of governors ye must not blame, in that they further also forecasting the manifold strange and dangerous innovations which are more than likely to follow, if your discipline should take place, have for that cause thought it hitherto a part of their duty to withstand your endeavours that way. The rather, for that they have seen already some small beginnings of the fruits thereof, in them who concurring with you in judgment about the necessity of that discipline, have adventured without more ado to separate themselves from the rest of the Church, and to put your speculations in *How just cause there is to fear the manifold dangerous events likely to ensue upon this intended reformation, if it did take place.*

Preface,
Ch. viii. 1.

execution[1]. These men's hastiness the warier sort of you doth not commend; ye wish they had held themselves longer in, and not so dangerously flown abroad before the feathers of the cause had been grown; their error with merciful terms ye reprove, naming them, in great commiseration of mind, your "poor brethren[2]." They on the contrary side more bitterly accuse you as their "false brethren;" and against you they plead, saying: "From your breasts it is that we "have sucked those things, which when ye delivered unto us "ye termed that heavenly, sincere, and wholesome milk of "God's word[3], howsoever ye now abhor as poison that which "the virtue thereof hath wrought and brought forth in us. "You sometime our companions, guides and familiars, with "whom we have had most sweet consultations[4], are now

---

[1] [See Strype, Whitg. II. 191; Ann. IV. 127, 136, 187-196, 197, 202, 239, 246. Bancroft, Survey, &c. 340-349. The head of this separation was Robert Browne. See his "Treatise of Reformation with-"out tarrying for any, and of the "wickedness of those Preachers, "which will not reform themselves "and their charge, because they "will tarry till the Magistrate com-"mand and compel them." Prefixed to "A Book which sheweth "the Life and Manners of all true "Christians." (Bodl. 4º. B. 8. Th. Seld.) Middleburgh, 1582. Also (Bodl. 4º. Crymes, 744.) "Green-"wood's Answer to Giffard," (who had written a short Treatise against the Donatists of England,) and in the same volume, 2. "A collection "of certain slanderous Articles given "out by the Bishops;" and 3. "A "Collection of certain Letters and "Conferences lately passed betwixt "certain Preachers and two Prison-"ers in the Fleet," (Barrow and Greenwood,) all 1590. In this latter, p. 7, we find the following portion of a dialogue between Barrow and Sperin, a Puritan minister. "Bar. "'Trow you, are none wicked in all "the land, with whom you stand "one body? for all are of your "church. Will you justify also all "the parishes of England?' Sper.

"'I will justify all those parishes that "have preaching ministers.' Bar. "'And what think you of those that "have unpreaching ministers?' Sper. "'*I think not such to be true churches*.' "(Mr. Sperin was here requested to "set down this under his hand, but "would not.") In "An Answer to "M. Cartwright his Letter for join-"ing with the English Churches," (which letter is subjoined in the same pamphlet, Bodl. 4º. S. 58. Th.) we read, p. 12, "Another proof is, "as though it were granted him, "*That where a preaching minister is, "there is a church.*"]

[2] [Penry, Preface to "A Brief "Discovery," (after speaking of Donatism,) "If any of our poor "brethren be carried away, to think "otherwise of the congregations of "England, which enjoy the word "truly preached and the right ad-"ministration of the sacraments: "we cease not to pray that the Lord "would reform their judgments. "But woe be unto our bishops, "which are the cause of this their "stumbling, and maintainers of their "error. For the poor brethren do "hold nothing in this point, but "that which the learned fathers, as "M. Bancroft calleth them, have "decreed."]

[3] 1 Pet. ii. 2.

[4] Psalm lv. 13.

"become our professed adversaries, because we think the
"statute-congregations in England to be no true Christian
"churches[1]; because we have severed ourselves from them;
"and because without their leave and license that are in civil
"authority, we have secretly framed our own churches ac-
"cording to the platform of the word of God. For of that
"point between you and us there is no controversy. Alas!
"what would ye have us to do? At such time as ye were
"content to accept us in the number of your own, your
"teachings we heard, we read your writings: and though
"we would, yet able we are not to forget with what zeal ye
"have ever professed, that in the English congregations (for
"so many of them as be ordered according unto their own
"laws) the very public service of God is fraught as touching
"matter with heaps of intolerable pollutions, and as concern-
"ing form, borrowed from the shop of Antichrist; hateful
"both ways in the eyes of the Most Holy; the kind of their
"government by bishops and archbishops antichristian; that
"discipline which Christ hath 'essentially tied,' that is to
"say, so united unto his Church, that we cannot account it
"really to be his Church which hath not in it the same disci-
"pline, that very discipline no less there despised, than in
"the highest throne of Antichrist[2]; all such parts of the

Preface,
Ch. viii. 1,

---

[1] [See the opinions charged on Barrow and Greenwood before the court of high commission, Nov. 1587, in Paule's Life of Whitgift; Wordsworth, E. B. IV. 356. One of them is, "That all the precise, "which refuse the ceremonies of the "Church, and yet preach in the same "Church, strain at a gnat and swal- "low a camel; and are close hypo- "crites, and walk in a left-handed "policy: as Master Cartwright, "Whiggington, &c." See the notes on Cranmer's letter to Hooker, vol. ii. book v. appendix 2.]

[2] Pref. against Dr. Bancr. [Pref. to "a Briefe Discovery of the Un- "truthes and Slanders (against the "true government of the Church of "Christ) contained in a Sermon, "preached the 8 of Februarie, 1588, "by D. Bancroft, and since that "time set forth in print, with addi- "tions by the said Author." By Penry, 1590. The passage referred to is, "The visible Church of "God, wheresoever it be, hath the "power of binding and loosing an- "nexed unto it, as our Saviour "Christ teacheth us, Matth. 18, "which authority is so essentially "tied unto the visible Church, that "wheresoever this power is to be "found, there the Church of Christ "is also visible, and wheresoever "there is a visible Church, there "this authority cannot be denied to "be.... Now the reader cannot be "ignorant, that our bishops will "never grant that the visible con- "gregations in England ought to "have this power of binding and "loosing... The crime therefore of "schism, and Donatism, which M. "Bancroft and the prelates would "fasten upon us, doth justly cleave

Preface, "word of God as do any way concern that discipline no less
Ch. viii. 1. "unsoundly taught and interpreted by all authorized English
"pastors, than by Antichrist's factors themselves; at baptism
"crossing, at the supper of the Lord kneeling, at both, a
"number of other the most notorious badges of Antichristian
"recognizance usual. Being moved with these and the like
"your effectual discourses, whereunto we gave most attentive
"ear, till they entered even into our souls, and were as fire
"within our bosoms; we thought we might hereof be bold to
"conclude, that sith no such Antichristian synagogue may be
"accounted a true church of Christ, you by accusing all con-
"gregations ordered according to the laws of England as
"Antichristian, did mean to condemn those congregations, as
"not being any of them worthy the name of a true Christian
"church. Ye tell us now it is not your meaning. But what
"meant your often threatenings of them, who professing
"themselves the inhabitants of Mount Sion, were too loth to
"depart wholly as they should out of Babylon? Whereat our
"hearts being fearfully troubled, we durst not, we durst not
"continue longer so near her confines, lest her plagues might
"suddenly overtake us, before we did cease to be partakers
"with her sins: for so we could not choose but acknow-
"ledge with grief that we were, when, they doing evil, we
"by our presence in their assemblies seemed to like thereof,
"or at leastwise not so earnestly to dislike, as became men
"heartily zealous of God's glory. For adventuring to erect
"the discipline of Christ without the leave of the Christian
"magistrate, haply ye may condemn us as fools, in that we
"hazard thereby our estates and persons further than you
"which are that way more wise think necessary: but of any
"offence or sin therein committed against God, with what
"conscience can you accuse us, when your own positions are,
"that the things we observe should every of them be dearer
"unto us than ten thousand lives; that they are the peremp-
"tory commandments of God; that no mortal man can dis-
"pense with them, and that the magistrate grievously sinneth

"unto themselves...... It shall be "wherewith the Church of God in a
"proved in the end, that they are "while (if they hold on their course)
"the schismatics and not we. It "can have no more to do, than in
"shall appear that they are growing "times past it had with the schis-
"to make a body of their own, "matical Donatists."]

"in not constraining thereunto? Will ye blame any man for "doing that of his own accord, which all men should be com-"pelled to do that are not willing of themselves? When God "commandeth, shall we answer that we will obey, if so be "Cæsar will grant us leave? Is discipline an ecclesiastical "matter or a civil? If an ecclesiastical, it must of necessity "belong to the duty of the minister. And the minister "(you say) holdeth all his authority of doing whatsoever "belongeth unto the spiritual charge of the house of God "even immediately from God himself, without dependency "upon any magistrate. Whereupon it followeth, as we sup-"pose, that the hearts of the people being willing to be "under the sceptre of Christ, the minister of God, into whose "hands the Lord himself hath put that sceptre, is without all "excuse if thereby he guide them not. Nor do we find that "hitherto greatly ye have disliked those churches abroad, "where the people with direction of their godly ministers "have even against the will of the magistrate brought in "either the doctrine or discipline of Jesus Christ. For "which cause we must now think the very same thing of "you, which our Saviour did sometime utter concerning "falsehearted Scribes and Pharisees, 'they say, and do not[1].'" Thus the foolish Barrowist deriveth his schism by way of conclusion, as to him it seemeth, directly and plainly out of your principles. Him therefore we leave to be satisfied by you from whom he hath sprung.

Preface, Ch. viii. 2.

[2.] And if such by your own acknowledgment be persons dangerous, although as yet the alterations which they have made are of small and tender growth; the changes likely to ensue throughout all states and vocations within this land, in case your desire should take place, must be thought upon.

First concerning the supreme power of the Highest, they are no small prerogatives, which now thereunto belonging the form of your discipline will constrain it to resign; as in the last book of this treatise we have shewed at large[2].

---

[1] Matth. xxiii. 3.
[2] [From this it would seem that the whole treatise was in a manner finished before 1594, when this preface was published.]

Preface,
Ch. viii. 3.

Again it may justly be feared whether our English nobility, when the matter came in trial, would contentedly suffer themselves to be always at the call, and to stand to the sentence of a number of mean persons assisted with the presence of their poor teacher[1], a man (as sometimes it happeneth) though better able to speak, yet little or no whit apter to judge, than the rest: from whom, be their dealings never so absurd, (unless it be by way of complaint to a synod,) no appeal may be made unto any one of higher power, inasmuch as the order of your discipline admitteth no standing inequality of courts, no spiritual judge to have any ordinary superior on earth, but as many supremacies as there are parishes and several congregations.

[3.] Neither is it altogether without cause that so many do fear the overthrow of all learning as a threatened sequel of this your intended discipline. For if "the world's preser-" "vation" depend upon "the multitude of the wise[2];" and of that sort the number hereafter be not likely to wax overgreat, "when" (that wherewith the son of Sirach professeth himself at the heart grieved) "men of understanding are" already so "little set by[3]:" how should their minds whom the love of so precious a jewel filleth with secret jealousy even in regard of the least things which may any way hinder the flourishing estate thereof, choose but misdoubt lest this discipline, which always you match with divine doctrine as her natural and true sister, be found unto all kinds of know-

---

[1] [Sutcliffe de Presbyt. 134 : "Le-"gibus nostris antiquatis, et ho-"minibus doctis ab Ecclesiæ clavo "(quam secundum leges et divinas "et humanas administrant) dimotis, "presbyteri se ad rem accingent, "Deus bone, quales et quanti ho-"mines ! accedent primo Pastores "quidam (si quales apud nos sunt "scire cupiatis) adolescentuli pleri-"que novi, rerum imperiti, cui pueros "male credideris, aut unum servu-"lum ; qui seipsos vix regunt, tan-"tum abest ut principes regere pos-"sint. Aderunt etiam (τὸ ἐπὶ τῇ φακῇ "μυρὸν) Presbyteri, viri bene barbati "et tetrici, quorum plurimæ sunt "species : eorum enim nonnulli ar-"tifices sunt, ut fabri, qui nobis arte "Vulcania disciplinam excudent : "coqui etiam aderunt, ut aliquid "sit in presbyterio insipido con-"dimenti : sutores, ut pugnantes "presbyterorum sententias sarci-"ant : sine cæmentariis, arx hæc "presbyteralis ædificari non potest : "adjungentur præterea aliquot agri-"colarum et mercatorum centuriæ : "pharmacopolæ vero non recte de-"siderabuntur, multo enim illis opus "erit helleboro. Atque istis ita con-"stitutis et consarcinatis, quis non "presbyterium istiusmodi omnibus "archiepiscopis, episcopis, et reli-"quis ecclesiæ Anglicanæ modera-"toribus præferat?"]

[2] Sap. vi. 24.

[3] Ecclus. xxvi. 28.

ledge a step-mother[1]; seeing that the greatest worldly hopes, which are proposed unto the chiefest kind of learning, ye seek utterly to extirpate as weeds, and have grounded your platform on such propositions as do after a sort undermine those most renowned habitations, where through the goodness of Almighty God all commendable arts and sciences are with exceeding great industry hitherto (and so may they for ever continue) studied, proceeded in, and professed[2]? To charge you as purposely bent to the overthrow of that, wherein so many of you have attained no small perfection, were injurious. Only therefore I wish that yourselves did well consider, how opposite certain your positions are unto the state of collegiate societies, whereon the two universities consist. Those degrees which their statutes bind them to take are by your laws taken away[3]; yourselves who have sought them ye so excuse, as that ye would have men to think ye judge them not allowable, but tolerable only, and to be borne with, for some help which ye find in them unto the furtherance of your purposes, till the corrupt estate of the Church may be better reformed. Your laws forbidding ecclesiastical persons utterly the exercise of civil power must needs deprive the Heads and Masters in the same colleges of all such authority as now they exercise, either at home, by punishing the faults of those, who not as children to their parents by the law of nature, but altogether by civil authority are subject unto them: or abroad by keeping courts amongst their tenants. Your laws making permanent equality amongst

Preface, Ch. viii. 3.

[1] ["By studying in corners, "many melancholy model-makers, "and church-cobblers may be made, "but not one sound divine: for "scholars profit by mutual con-"ference, disputation, exercise, mu-"tual emulation and example, as "much as by hearing and reading: "but those helps they lose that teach "in corners. There is but small "hope that they would make learned "men, or semblant that they mean "any such matter, when taking "away the livings of the clergy, and "hope of reward from the learned, "they turn men up to live upon "pensions, and to stand to the "courtesy of unlettered elders and "deacons, that think crusts too "good for learned men." Sutcliffe, False Semblant, &c. 134.]

[2] [Technical words, for the three degrees academical in the several faculties: including the faculty of arts; for masters of arts are all, properly speaking, professors or readers.]

[3] [Adm. 16: "The titles of oure "universitie, doctors, and bachelors "of divinitie, are not only for vayn "glory sought and graunted, but "there they are the names of course, "conferred rather by the prophane "judgments of them that know not "what office of the Church they "belong too," &c.]

Preface,
Ch. viii. 4.

ministers a thing repugnant to the word of God, enforce those colleges, the seniors whereof are all or any part of them ministers under the government of a master in the same vocation, to choose as oft as they meet together a new president. For if so ye judge it necessary to do in synods, for the avoiding of permanent inequality amongst ministers, the same cause must needs even in these collegiate assemblies enforce the like. Except peradventure ye mean to avoid all such absurdities, by dissolving those corporations, and by bringing the universities unto the form of the School of Geneva. Which thing men the rather are inclined to look for, inasmuch as the ministry, whereinto their founders with singular providence have by the same statutes appointed them necessarily to enter at a certain time, your laws bind them much more necessarily to forbear, till some parish abroad call for them[1].

[4.] Your opinion concerning the law civil is that the knowledge thereof might be spared, as a thing which this land doth not need[2]. Professors in that kind being few, ye are the bolder to spurn at them, and not to dissemble your minds as concerning their removal: in whose studies although myself have not much been conversant, nevertheless exceeding great cause I see there is to wish that thereunto more encouragement were given; as well for the singular treasures of wisdom therein contained, as also for the great use we have thereof, both in decision of certain kinds of causes arising daily within ourselves, and especially for commerce with nations abroad, whereunto that knowledge is most requisite. The reasons wherewith ye would persuade that Scripture is the only rule to frame all our actions by, are in every respect as effectual for proof that the same is the only law whereby to determine all our civil controversies. And then what doth let, but that as those men may have their

---

[1] [Decl. of Disc. transl. by T. C. p. 155.]
[2] Humb. Motion to the L. L. p. 50. ["As for the canon law, it is "no way hurtful, but good for the "state of this realm, if it were "abolished: being, as hereafter will "appear, not necessary but danger-"ous to the state.... As for the "maintaining of civilians, as the law "already maketh no great necessity "of them, having little other way "to set them on work, but by the "canon law: if such men's studies "were converted another way to "more profit, in the Church and "commonwealth, little or no loss or "inconvenience would follow."]

desire, who frankly broach it already that the work of refor- *Preface,* mation will never be perfect, till the law of Jesus Christ be Ch. viii. 5. received alone; so pleaders and counsellors may bring their books of the common law, and bestow them as the students of curious and needless arts [1] did theirs in the Apostles' time? I leave them to scan how far those words of yours may reach, wherein ye declare that, whereas now many houses lie waste through inordinate suits of law, "this one thing will shew the "excellency of discipline for the wealth of the realm, and "quiet of subjects; that the Church is to censure such a party "who is apparently troublesome and contentious, and without "*reasonable cause* upon a mere will and stomach doth vex "and molest his brother, and trouble the country [2]." For mine own part I do not see but that it might very well agree with your principles, if your discipline were fully planted, even to send out your writs of surcease unto all courts of England besides, for the most things handled in them [3].

[5.] A great deal further I might proceed and descend

---

[1] Acts xix. 19.
[2] Humb. Motion, p. 74.
[3] [Bp. Cooper, Adm. to the people of England, (1588,) p. 86: "The canon law must be utterly "taken away, with all offices to the "same belonging.... The use and "study of the civil law will be utterly "overthrown. For the civilians in "this realm live not by the use of "the civil law, but by the offices of "the canon law, and such things as "are within the compass thereof. "And if you take those offices and "functions away, and those matters "wherewith they deal in the canon "law, you must needs take away "the hope of reward, and by that "means their whole study." Sutcliffe, Remonstrance to the Demonstr. of Disc. p. 41: "That "which is needless, is unlawful. All "courts of record, as chancery "and common-pleas, &c. shall be "found needless, if the consistory "of presbyters and elders were set "up: which is only needful in the "church or congregation of the "faithful brethren, because they "may determine all matters wherein "any breach of charity may be; as "the admonitioner saith: *Ergo,* all "courts of record, as chancery, "common pleas, &c. by their reason "will be found unlawful:" and see p. 178, where, Udall having said, "Governors of the Church may "not meddle in matters ecclesiastical only,.. in deciding of controversies, in doctrine and manners, as far as appertaineth to the "conscience," Sutcliffe remarks: "This one limit of authority will "carry all causes (though most "civil in their nature and practice) "out of all courts in the land unto "their elderships. First, the chancery, that decideth matters of "controversy by conscience, is "clearly dammed up, and may go "pick paigles" (i. e. cowslips). "And are any other civil courts in "better case? No verily: for can "any controversy be betwixt man "and man, but it 'appertaineth to "conscience,' to give the matter "contended for unto him to whom "of right it is due?" See also "False Semblant," &c. page 132, 133.]

Preface,
Ch. viii. 6.

lower. But forasmuch as against all these and the like difficulties your answer is[1], that we ought to search what things are consonant to God's will, not which be most for our own ease; and therefore that your discipline being (for such is your error) the absolute commandment of Almighty God, it must be received although the world by receiving it should be clean turned upside down; herein lieth the greatest danger of all. For whereas the name of divine authority is used to countenance these things, which are not the commandments of God, but your own erroneous collections; on him ye must father whatsoever ye shall afterwards be led, either to do in withstanding the adversaries of your cause, or to think in maintenance of your doings. And what this may be, God doth know. In such kinds of error the mind once imagining itself to seek the execution of God's will, laboureth forthwith to remove both things and persons which any way hinder it from taking place; and in such cases if any strange or new thing seem requisite to be done, a strange and new opinion concerning the lawfulness thereof is withal received and broached under countenance of divine authority.

[6.] One example[2] herein may serve for many, to shew that false opinions, touching the will of God to have things done, are wont to bring forth mighty and violent practices against the hindrances of them; and those practices new opinions more pernicious than the first, yea most extremely sometimes opposite to that which the first did seem to intend. Where the people took upon them the reformation of the Church by casting out popish superstition, they having received from their pastors a general instruction "that whatsoever the heavenly Father hath not planted "must be rooted out[3]," proceeded in some foreign places so far that down went oratories and the very temples of God themselves. For as they chanced to take the compass of their commission stricter or larger, so their dealings

[1] Counterp. page 108: "His" (Cosins's) "first reasons are drawn "from the inconveniences, which "he thinketh will come into the "Church by this means; as re- "quiring rather (like a civilian not "a divine) what is safe, than what "is according to God his will."]

[2] [See Abp. Whitgift's Exhortation prefixed to the Answer to the Admonition. 1st ed. p. 13–16.]

[3] Matth. xv. 13. [See Brandt, Hist. of the Reform. in the Low Countries: B. ii. and vii.]

the Anabaptists: their affected Austerity.

were accordingly more or less moderate. Amongst others there sprang up presently one kind of men, with whose zeal and forwardness the rest being compared were thought to be marvellous cold and dull. These grounding themselves on rules more general; that whatsoever the law of Christ commandeth not, thereof Antichrist is the author: and that whatsoever Antichrist or his adherents did in the world, the true professors of Christ are to undo; found out many things more than others had done, the extirpation whereof was in their conceit as necessary as of any thing before removed. Hereupon they secretly made their doleful complaints every where as they went[1], that albeit the world did begin to profess some dislike of that which was evil in the kingdom of darkness, yet fruits worthy of a true repentance were not seen; and that if men did repent as they ought, they must endeavour to purge the earth of all manner evil, to the end there might follow a new world afterward, wherein righteousness only should dwell. Private repentance they said must appear by every man's fashioning his own life contrary unto the customs and orders of this present world, both in greater things and in less. To this purpose they had always in their mouths those greater things, charity, faith, the true fear of God, the cross, the mortification of the flesh[2]. All their exhortations were to set light

Preface, Ch. viii. 6.

---

[1] Guy de Brés contre l'Erreur des Anabaptistes, p. 3. ["La racine, source, et fondement des Anabaptistes ou Rebaptisez de nostre temps: avec tres ample refutation des arguments principaux, par lesquels ils ont accoustumé de troubler l'Eglise de nostre Seigneur Jesus Christ, et seduire les simples. Le tout reduit en trois livres, par Guy de Brés. Chez Pierre de S. Andre, MDXCV," small 4to pp. 903, no place of publication mentioned. [Originally published 1565. Biog. Univ.] The author was a pastor at Lille and Valenciennes, and with Saravia and three or four others was a principal author of "A Confession of Faith of the Reformed Churches of the Low Countries, 1561 or 1562," adopted by the States of Holland in 1622. "The said Saravia says in a certain letter, which I myself have seen, that 'Guido de Brés communicated this Confession to such ministers as he could find, desiring them to correct what they thought amiss in it; so that it was not to be considered as one man's work; but that none who were concerned in it ever designed it for a rule of faith to others, but only for a scriptural proof of what they themselves believed.'" Brandt's Hist. of the Reform. in the Low Countries, Eng. Transl. I. 142. De Brés was hanged at Valenciennes by the government of Philip II, in 1567. Ibid. p. 250. Anabaptism began by his account in Lower Saxony, about 1521.]

[2] P. 4.

of the things in this world, to count riches and honours vanity, and in token thereof not only to seek neither, but if men were possessors of both, even to cast away the one and resign the other, that all men might see their unfeigned conversion unto Christ[1]. They were solicitors of men to fasts[2], to often meditations of heavenly things, and as it were conferences in secret with God by prayers, not framed according to the frozen manner of the world, but expressing such fervent desires as might even force God to hearken unto them. Where they found men in diet, attire, furniture of house, or any other way, observers of civility and decent order, such they reproved as being carnally and earthly minded. Every word otherwise than severely and sadly uttered seemed to pierce like a sword through them[3]. If any man were pleasant, their manner was presently with deep sighs to repeat those words of our Saviour Christ, "Woe be to you which now laugh, for ye shall lament[4]." So great was their delight to be always in trouble, that such as did quietly lead their lives, they judged of all other men to be in most dangerous case. They so much affected to cross the ordinary custom in every thing, that when other men's use was to put on better attire, they would be sure to shew themselves openly abroad in worse: the ordinary names of the days in the week they thought it a kind of profaneness to use, and therefore accustomed themselves to make no other distinction than by numbers, the First, Second, Third day[5].

[7.] From this they proceeded unto public reformation, first ecclesiastical, and then civil. Touching the former, they boldly avouched that themselves only had the truth, which thing upon peril of their lives they would at all times defend; and that since the apostles lived, the same was never before in all points sincerely taught[6]. Wherefore that things might again be brought to that ancient integrity which Jesus Christ by his word requireth, they began to control the ministers of the gospel for attributing so much force and virtue unto the scriptures of God read, whereas the truth was, that when the word is said to engender faith in the heart, and to con-

---

[1] p. 16. [2] p. 118, 119. [3] p. 116, 120. [4] Luke vi. 25. [5] p. 117. [6] p. 40.

vert the soul of man, or to work any such spiritual divine effect, these speeches are not thereunto appliable as it is read or preached, but as it is ingrafted in us by the power of the Holy Ghost opening the eyes of our understanding, and so revealing the mysteries of God, according to that which Jeremy promised before should be, saying, "I will put my "law in their inward parts, and I will write it in their "hearts[1]." The Book of God they notwithstanding for the most part so admired, that other disputation against their opinions than only by allegation of Scripture they would not hear ; besides it they thought no other writings in the world should be studied ; insomuch as one of their great prophets exhorting them to cast away all respects unto human writings, so far to his motion they condescended, that as many as had any books save the Holy Bible in their custody, they brought and set them publicly on fire[2]. When they and their Bibles were alone together, what strange fantastical opinion soever at any time entered into their heads, their use was to think the Spirit taught it them. Their phrensies concerning our Saviour's incarnation, the state of souls departed, and suchlike[3], are things needless to be rehearsed. And forasmuch as they were of the same suit with those of whom the apostle speaketh, saying, "They are still learning, but never "attain to the knowledge of truth[4]," it was no marvel to see them every day broach some new thing, not heard of before. Which restless levity they did interpret to be their growing to spiritual perfection, and a proceeding from faith to faith[5]. The differences amongst them grew by this mean in a manner infinite, so that scarcely was there found any one of them, the forge of whose brain was not possessed with some special mystery. Whereupon, although their mutual contentions[6] were most fiercely prosecuted amongst themselves, yet when they came to defend the cause common to them all against the adversaries of their faction, they had ways to lick one another whole ; the sounder in his own persuasion excusing *the dear brethren*[7], which were not so far enlightened, and professing a charitable hope of the mercy of

Preface, Ch. viii. 7.

[1] Jer. xxxi. 33. [De Brés, p. 81, 92.]
[2] p. 27. [and 702.]
[3] [De Brés, l. ii. and iii.]
[4] 2 Tim. iii. 7, p. 65.
[5] p. 66.
[6] p. 135.
[7] p. 25.

Preface,
Ch. viii. 7.

God towards them notwithstanding their swerving from him in some things. Their own ministers they highly magnified as men whose vocation was from God [1]; the rest their manner was to term disdainfully Scribes and Pharisees [2], to account their calling an human creature, and to detain the people as much as might be from hearing them. As touching Sacraments [3], Baptism administered in the Church of Rome they judged to be but an execrable mockery and no baptism; both because the ministers thereof in the Papacy are wicked idolaters, lewd persons, thieves and murderers, cursed creatures, ignorant beasts; and also for that to baptize is a proper action belonging unto none but the Church of Christ, whereas Rome is Antichrist's synagogue. The custom of using godfathers and godmothers at christenings they scorned [4]. Baptizing of infants, although confessed by themselves to have been continued ever sithence the very Apostles' own times, yet they altogether condemned; partly because sundry errors are of no less antiquity [5]; and partly for that there is no commandment in the gospel of Christ which saith, "Baptize "infants [6];" but he contrariwise in saying, "Go preach "and baptize," doth appoint that the minister of baptism shall in that action first administer doctrine, and then baptism; as also in saying, "Whosoever doth believe and is baptized," he appointeth that the party to whom baptism is administered shall first believe and then be baptized; to the end that believing may go before this sacrament in the receiver, no otherwise than preaching in the giver; sith equally in both [7], the law of Christ declareth not only what things are required, but also in what order they are required. The Eucharist they received (pretending our Lord and Saviour's example) after supper; and for avoiding all those impieties which have been grounded upon the mystical words of Christ, "This is my "body, this is my blood," they thought it not safe to mention either body or blood in that sacrament, but rather to abrogate both, and to use no words but these, "Take, eat, declare the "death of our Lord: Drink, shew forth our Lord's death [8]." In rites and ceremonies their profession was hatred of all conformity with the Church of Rome: for which cause they

[1] p. 71.   [2] p. 124.   [3] p. 764.   [4] p. 748.   [5] p. 514.
[6] p. 722, 726, 688.   [7] p. 518.   [8] p. 38.

would rather endure any torment than observe the solemn festivals which others did, inasmuch as Antichrist (they said) was the first inventor of them[1].

Preface, Ch. viii. 8-10.

[8.] The pretended end of their civil reformation was that Christ might have dominion over all; that all crowns and sceptres might be thrown down at his feet; that no other might reign over Christian men but he, no regiment keep them in awe but his discipline, amongst them no sword at all be carried besides his, the sword of spiritual excommunication. For this cause they laboured with all their might in overturning the seats of magistracy[2], because Christ hath said, "Kings of nations[3];" in abolishing the execution of justice[4], because Christ hath said, "Resist not evil;" in forbidding oaths, the necessary means of judicial trial[5], because Christ hath said, "Swear not at all:" finally, in bringing in community of goods[6], because Christ by his apostles hath given the world such example, to the end that men might excel one another not in wealth the pillar of secular authority, but in virtue.

[9.] These men at the first were only pitied in their error, and not much withstood by any; the great humility, zeal, and devotion, which appeared to be in them, was in all men's opinion a pledge of their harmless meaning. The hardest that men of sound understanding conceived of them was but this, "O quam honesta voluntate miseri errant! With how good a "meaning these poor souls do evil[7]!" Luther made request unto Frederick duke of Saxony[8], that within his dominion they might be favourably dealt with and spared, for that (their error excepted[9]) they seemed otherwise right good men. By means of which merciful toleration they gathered strength, much more than was safe for the state of the commonwealth wherein they lived. They had their secret corner-meetings and assemblies in the night, the people flocked unto them by thousands[10].

[10.] The means whereby they both allured and retained so great multitudes were most effectual: first, a wonderful show

---

[1] p. 122. [2] p. 841. [3] [Luke xxii. 25.] [4] p. 833. [5] p. 849.
[6] p. 40. [7] Lactant. de Justit. lib. v. c. 19. [p. 480, ed. Oxon. 1684.]
[8] p. 6. [9] [So first edition: *exempted*, 1604, followed by later ones.] 1886.
[10] p. 4, 20, 41, 42.

Preface,
Ch. viii. 11.

of zeal towards God, wherewith they seemed to be even rapt in every thing they spake: secondly, an hatred of sin, and a singular love of integrity, which men did think to be much more than ordinary in them, by reason of the custom which they had to fill the ears of the people with invectives against their authorized guides, as well spiritual as civil: thirdly, the bountiful relief wherewith they eased the broken estate of such needy creatures, as were in that respect the more apt to be drawn away[1]: fourthly, a tender compassion which they were thought to take upon the miseries of the common sort, over whose heads their manner was even to pour down showers of tears, in complaining that no respect was had unto them, that their goods were devoured by wicked cormorants, their persons had in contempt, all liberty both temporal and spiritual taken from them[2], that it was high time for God now to hear their groans, and to send them deliverance: lastly, a cunning sleight which they had to stroke and smooth up the minds of their followers, as well by appropriating unto them all the favourable titles, the good words, and the gracious promises in Scripture; as also by casting the contrary always on the heads of such as were severed from that retinue. Whereupon the people's common acclamation unto such deceivers was, "These are verily the men of God, these are "his true and sincere prophets[3]." If any such prophet or man of God did suffer by order of law condign and deserved punishment, were it for felony, rebellion, murder, or what else, the people, (so strangely were their hearts enchanted,) as though blessed Saint Stephen had been again martyred, did lament that God took away his most dear servants from them[4].

[11.] In all these things being fully persuaded, that what they did, it was obedience to the will of God, and that all men should do the like; there remained, after speculation, practice, whereby the whole world thereunto (if it were possible) might be framed. This they saw could not be done but with mighty opposition and resistance; against which to strengthen themselves, they secretly entered into league of association[5]. And peradventure considering, that although they were many,

[1] p. 55.   [2] p. 6, 7.   [3] p. 7.   [4] p. 27.   [5] p. 6.

yet long wars would in time waste them out; they began to think whether it might not be that God would have them do, for their speedy and mighty increase, the same which sometime God's own chosen people, the people of Israel, did. Glad and fain they were to have it so; which very desire was itself apt to breed both an opinion of possibility, and a willingness to gather arguments of likelihood, that so God himself would have it. Nothing more clear unto their seeming, than that a new Jerusalem being often spoken of in Scripture, they undoubtedly were themselves that new Jerusalem, and the old did by way of a certain figurative resemblance signify what they should both be and do. Here they drew in a sea of matter, by applying all things unto their own company, which are any where spoken concerning divine favours and benefits bestowed upon the old commonwealth of Israel: concluding that as Israel was delivered out of Egypt, so they spiritually out of the Egypt of this world's servile thraldom unto sin and superstition; as Israel was to root out the idolatrous nations, and to plant instead of them a people which feared God; so the same Lord's good will and pleasure was now, that these new Israelites should, under the conduct of other Josuas, Samsons, and Gedeons, perform a work no less miraculous in casting out violently the wicked from the earth, and establishing the kingdom of Christ with perfect liberty: and therefore, as the cause why the children of Israel took unto one man many wives, might be lest the casualties of war should any way hinder the promise of God concerning their multitude from taking effect in them; so it was not unlike that for the necessary propagation of Christ's kingdom under the Gospel the Lord was content to allow as much.

Preface, Ch. viii. 12.

[12.] Now whatsoever they did in such sort collect out of Scripture, when they came to justify or persuade it unto others, all was the heavenly Father's appointment, his commandment, his will and charge. Which thing is the very point, in regard whereof I have gathered this declaration. For my purpose herein is to shew, that when the minds of men are once erroneously persuaded that it is the will of God to have those things done which they fancy, their opinions are as thorns in their sides, never suffering them to take rest

Preface,
Ch. viii. 13.

till they have brought their speculations into practice. The lets and impediments of which practice their restless desire and study to remove leadeth them every day forth by the hand into other more dangerous opinions, sometimes quite and clean contrary to their first pretended meanings: so as what will grow out of such errors as go masked under the cloak of divine authority, impossible it is that ever the wit of man should imagine, till time have brought forth the fruits of them: for which cause it behoveth wisdom to fear the sequels thereof, even beyond all apparent cause of fear. These men, in whose mouths at the first sounded nothing but only mortification of the flesh, were come at the length to think they might lawfully have their six or seven wives apiece; they which at the first thought judgment and justice itself to be merciless cruelty, accounted at the length their own hands sanctified with being embrued in Christian blood; they who at the first were wont to beat down all dominion, and to urge against poor constables, "Kings of nations;" had at the length both consuls and kings of their own erection amongst themselves: finally, they which could not brook at the first that any man should seek, no not by law, the recovery of goods injuriously taken or withheld from him, were grown at the last to think they could not offer unto God more acceptable sacrifice, than by turning their adversaries clean out of house and home, and by enriching themselves with all kind of spoil and pillage; which thing being laid to their charge, they had in a readiness their answer [1], that now the time was come, when according to our Saviour's promise, "the meek ones must inherit the "earth [2];" and that their title hereunto was the same which the righteous Israelites had unto the goods of the wicked Egyptians [3].

[13.] Wherefore sith the world hath had in these men so fresh experience, how dangerous such active errors are, it must not offend you, though, touching the sequel of your present mispersuasions, much more be doubted, than your own intents and purposes do haply aim at. And yet your words already are somewhat, when ye affirm, that your

---

[1] p. 41. [2] Matt. v. 5. [3] Exod. xi. 2.

Pastors, Doctors, Elders, and Deacons, ought to be in this Church of England, "whether her Majesty and our state "will or no[1];" when for the animating of your confederates ye publish the musters which ye have made of your own bands, and proclaim them to amount I know not to how many thousands[2]; when ye threaten, that sith neither your suits to the parliament, nor supplications to our convocation-house, neither your defences by writing, nor challenges of disputation in behalf of that cause are able to prevail, we must blame

Preface,
Ch. viii. 13.

---

[1] Mart. in his third Libel.

[2] [Second Adm. p. 59, (misprint for 65,) ed. 1617. "We beseech "you to pity this case, and to pro-"vide for it; it is the case already "of many a thousand in this land; "yea, it is the case of as many as "seek the Lord aright, and desire "to have his own orders restored. "Great troubles will come of it, if "it be not provided for; even the "same God that hath stirred me, a "man unknown, to speak, though "those poor men which are locked "up in Newgate, neither do, nor "can be suffered to speak, will daily "stir up more."

Str. Whitg. II. 18. (from a MS.) "One of our late libellers" [marg. Martyn] "braggeth of 100,000 "hands: and wisheth the parlia-"ment to bring in this reformation "though it be by withstanding the "Queen's Majesty."

Ibid. 191. In 1592, the Barrowists "were reckoned to amount to "20,000 by Sir W. Raleigh, in a "speech of his in the last parlia-"ment."

"You are too broad with Mar-"tin's brood, for he hath 100,000 "that will set their hands to his "articles, and shew the Queen." Pap with an Hatchet. (Of this pamphlet see before, in a note to the Life of Hooker.)

"Let the magistrate once con-"sider what pestilent and dangerous "beasts these wretches" (the Bishops) "are unto the civil state. "For either by their own confes-"sion they are the bishops of the "Devil, (and so by that means will "be the undoing of the state, if "they be continued therein,) or "else their places ought to be in "this commonwealth *whether her* "*Majesty and our State will or no,* "*because they are not* (as they say) "*the Bishops of man.* Are they "then the Bishops of God? that is, "have they such a calling as the "Apostles, Evangelists, &c. had? "that is, such a calling as ought "lawfully to be in a Christian com-"monwealth (unless the magistrate "would injury the Church, yea, "maim, deform, and make a mon-"ster of the Church) whether the "magistrate will or no." Ha' ye any Work for a Cooper? p. 28.

And in the Epitome, against Dr. Bridges, having quoted a passage from Bp. Aylmer's "Harborough "for faithful Subjects," in which the Bishop had commended "those "that in King Henry VIII. days "would not grant him that his pro-"clamations should have the force "of a statute," Penry proceeds, "I "assure you, brother John, you "have spoken many things worthy "the noting, and I would our par-"liament men would mark this ac-"tion done in K. Hen. VIII. days, "and follow it in bringing in re-"formation, and putting down Lord "Bishops, with all other points of "superstition. They may in your "judgment not only do any thing "against their King's or Queen's "mind (that is behovefull to the "honour of God and the good of "the commonwealth) but even "withstand the proceedings of their "sovereign."]

ourselves, if to bring in discipline some such means hereafter be used as shall cause all our hearts to ache[1]. "That "things doubtful are to be construed[2] in the better part," is a principle not safe to be followed in matters concerning the public state of a commonweal. But howsoever these and the like speeches be accounted as arrows idly shot at random, without either eye had to any mark, or regard to their lighting-place; hath not your longing desire for the practice of your discipline brought the matter already unto this demurrer amongst you, whether the people and their godly pastors that way affected ought not to make separation from the rest, and to begin the exercise of discipline without the license of civil powers, which license they have sought for, and are not heard? Upon which question as ye have now divided yourselves, the warier sort of you taking the one part, and the forwarder in zeal the other; so in case these earnest ones should prevail, what other sequel can any wise man imagine but this, that having first resolved that attempts for discipline without superiors are lawful, it will follow in the next place to be disputed what may be attempted against superiors which will not have the sceptre of that discipline to rule over them? Yea even by you which have stayed yourselves from running headlong with the other sort, somewhat notwithstanding there hath been done without the leave or liking of your lawful superiors, for the exercise of a part of your discipline amongst the clergy thereunto addicted[3]. And lest examination of prin-

Preface, Ch. viii. 13.

---

[1] Demonstr. in the Pref. ["We "have sought to advance the cause "of God, by humble suit to the "parliament, by supplication to "your convocation house, by writ-"ing in defence of it, and by chal-"lenging to dispute for it: seeing "none of these means used by us "have prevailed, if it come in by "that means, which will make all "your hearts to ache, blame your-"selves: for it must prevail, mau-"gre the malice of all that stand "against it; or such a judgment "must overtake this land, as shall "cause the ears that hear thereof to "tingle, and make us be a by word "to all that pass by us."]

[2] [constered, ed. 1594.]

[3] [In 1567, some of the ministers who had been silenced by the bishops for nonconformity began to set up separate assemblies, using the Geneva Prayer Book. Strype, Parker, I. 478–483. In 1577, the same party, by their "use "or rather abuse" (Bishop Cox to Burghley, in Str. Ann. II. ii. 611.) of prophesyings, caused the inhibition of those exercises, (Queen's letter to the Bishop of Lincoln, ibid. 612.) and the suspension of Archbishop Grindal.

Puritan notions regarding certain Oaths.

cipal parties therein should bring those things to light, which might hinder and let your proceedings; behold, for a bar against that impediment, one opinion ye have newly added unto the rest even upon this occasion, an opinion to exempt you from taking oaths which may turn to the molestation of your brethren in that cause[1]. The next neighbour opinion whereunto, when occasion requireth, may follow for dispensation with oaths already taken, if they afterwards be found to import a necessity of detecting ought which may bring such good men into trouble or damage, whatsoever the cause be[2]. O merciful God, what man's wit is there able to sound the depth of those dangerous and fearful evils, whereinto our weak and impotent nature is inclinable to sink itself, rather than to shew an acknowledgment of error in that which once we have unadvisedly taken upon us to defend, against the stream as it were of a contrary public resolution!

[14.] Wherefore if we any thing respect their error, who being persuaded even as you are have gone further upon that persuasion than you allow; if we regard the present state of the highest governor placed over us, if the quality and disposition of our nobles, if the orders and laws of our famous universities, if the profession of the civil or the practice of the common law amongst us, if the mischiefs whereinto even before our eyes so many others have fallen headlong from no less plausible and fair beginnings than yours are: there is in every of these considerations most just cause to fear lest our hastiness to embrace a thing of so perilous consequence

Preface, Ch. viii. 14.

(Grind. 342.) In 1585, they are charged with having established synods and classes in various counties, with reordination, unauthorized fast-days, and other schismatical acts. (Articles against Cartwright, in Fuller, C. H. IX. 200, 201, 202.) comp. in Strype's Whitg. III. 244-256, the bill exhibited against them in the Star Chamber.]

[1] [This seems to have been first started, in a formal and public way, by Cartwright and others, when cited before the ecclesiastical commission in 1590. Strype, Whitg. II. 19, 26, 28-32.]

[2] [The 31st article tendered to Cartwright, (Fuller, ubi sup.) contains this clause, "That they should "all teach .... that it is not lawful "to take any oath, whereby a man "may be driven to discover any "thing penal to himself or to his "brother; especially if he be persuaded the matter to be lawful, "for which the punishment is like "to be inflicted: or having taken "it in this case, need not discover "the very truth."]

Preface,
Ch. ix. 1-3.

The conclusion of all.

should cause posterity to feel those evils, which as yet are more easy for us to prevent than they would be for them to remedy.

IX. The best and safest way for you therefore, my dear brethren, is, to call your deeds past to a new reckoning, to reexamine the cause ye have taken in hand, and to try it even point by point, argument by argument, with all the diligent exactness ye can; to lay aside the gall of that bitterness wherein your minds have hitherto over-abounded, and with meekness to search the truth. Think ye are men, deem it not impossible for you to err; sift unpartially your own hearts, whether it be force of reason or vehemency of affection, which hath bred and still doth feed these opinions in you. If truth do any where manifest itself, seek not to smother it with glosing delusions, acknowledge the greatness thereof, and think it your best victory when the same doth prevail over you.

[2.] That ye have been earnest in speaking or writing again and again the contrary way, shall be no blemish or discredit at all unto you. Amongst so many so huge volumes as the infinite pains of St. Augustine have brought forth, what one hath gotten him greater love, commendation and honour, than the book[1] wherein he carefully collecteth his own oversights, and sincerely condemneth them? Many speeches there are of Job's whereby his wisdom and other virtues may appear; but the glory of an ingenuous mind he hath purchased by these words only, "[2] Behold, I will lay "mine hand on my mouth: I have spoken once, yet will I "not therefore maintain argument; yea twice, howbeit for "that cause further I will not proceed."

[3.] Far more comfort it were for us (so small is the joy we take in these strifes) to labour under the same yoke, as men that look for the same eternal reward of their labours, to be joined with you in bands of indissoluble love and amity, to live as if our persons being many our souls were but one, rather than in such dismembered sort to spend our few and wretched days in a tedious prosecuting of wearisome contentions: the end whereof, if they have not some speedy end,

---

[1] [viz. "Retractationum."]   [2] Job xl. 4, 5.

will be heavy even on both sides. Brought already we are even to that estate which Gregory Nazianzen mournfully describeth, saying[1], "My mind leadeth me" (sith there is no other remedy) "to fly and to convey myself into some "corner out of sight, where I may scape from this cloudy "tempest of maliciousness, whereby all parts are entered "into a deadly war amongst themselves, and that little "remnant of love which was, is now consumed to nothing. "The only godliness we glory in, is to find out somewhat "whereby we may judge others to be ungodly. Each other's "faults we observe as matter of exprobration and not of "grief. By these means we are grown hateful in the eyes "of the heathens themselves, and (which woundeth us the "more deeply) able we are not to deny but that we have "deserved their hatred. With the better sort of our own "our fame and credit is clean lost. The less we are to "marvel if they judge vilely of us, who although we did "well would hardly allow thereof. On our backs they also "build that are lewd, and what we object one against "another, the same they use to the utter scorn and disgrace "of us all. This we have gained by our mutual home-"dissensions. This we are worthily rewarded with, which "are more forward to strive than becometh men of virtuous "and mild disposition."

[4.] But our trust in the Almighty is, that with us contentions are now at their highest float, and that the day will come (for what cause of despair is there?) when the passions of former enmity being allayed, we shall with ten times redoubled tokens of our unfeignedly reconciled love,

Preface, Ch. ix. 4.

---

[1] Greg. Naz. in Apol. [p. 33, sq. ed. Par. 1609: Ἀγαπητὸν, ὁρῶντα τοὺς ἄλλους ἄνω καὶ κάτω φερομένους τε καὶ ταρασσομένους, φυγόντα φυγῇ ἐκ τοῦ μέσου, ὑπὸ σκέπην ἀναχωρήσαντα, λαθεῖν τοῦ Πονηροῦ τὴν ζάλην καὶ τὴν σκοτόμαιναν· ἡνίκα πολεμεῖ μὲν ἀλλήλοις τὰ μέλη, οἴχεται δὲ τῆς ἀγάπης εἰ καί τι ἦν λείψανον...... Πάντες δὲ ἐσμὲν εὐσεβεῖς, ἐξ ἑνὸς μόνου, τοῦ καταγινώσκειν ἄλλων ἀσέβειαν ... θηρῶμεν δὲ τὰς ἀλλήλων ἁμαρτίας, οὐκ ἵνα θρηνήσωμεν, ἀλλ' ἵνα ὀνειδίσωμεν ....Ἐκ δὲ τούτων, ὡς τὸ εἰκός, μισούμεθα μὲν ἐν τοῖς ἔθνεσι· καὶ, ὃ τούτου χαλεπώτερον, οὐδὲ εἰπεῖν ἔχομεν, ὡς οὐ δικαίως· διαβεβλήμεθα δὲ καὶ τῶν ἡμετέρων τοῖς ἐπιεικεστέροις· οὐδὲν γὰρ θαυμαστὸν, εἰ τοῖς πλείοσιν, οἳ μόλις ἄν τι καὶ τῶν καλῶν ἀποδέχοιντο· τεκταίνουσι δὲ ἐπὶ τῶν νώτων ἡμῶν οἱ ἁμαρτωλοὶ (Ps. cxxviii. 3, Sept.), καὶ ἃ κατ' ἀλλήλων ἐπινοοῦμεν, κατὰ πάντων ἔχουσι· καὶ γεγόναμεν θέατρον καινόν.....Ταῦτα ἡμῖν ὁ πρὸς ἀλλήλους πόλεμος· ταῦτα οἱ λίαν ὑπὲρ τοῦ ἀγαθοῦ καὶ πρᾴου μαχόμενοι. Hooker appears to have translated from Musculus' Latin, p. 18, 19.]

Preface,
Ch. ix. 4.

shew ourselves each towards other the same which Joseph and the brethren of Joseph were at the time of their interview in Egypt. Our comfortable expectation and most thirsty desire whereof what man soever amongst you shall any way help to satisfy, (as we truly hope there is no one amongst you but some way or other will,) the blessings of the God of peace, both in this world and in the world to come, be upon him moe than the stars of the firmament in number.

What Things are handled in the Books following:

Book the First, concerning Laws in general.

The Second, of the use of Divine Law contained in Scripture; whether that be the only Law which ought to serve for our direction in all things without exception.

The Third, of Laws concerning Ecclesiastical Polity; whether the form thereof be in Scripture so set down, that no addition or change is lawful.

The Fourth, of general exceptions taken against the Laws of our Polity, as being popish, and banished out of certain reformed churches.

The Fifth, of our Laws that concern the public religious duties of the Church, and the manner of bestowing that Power of Order, which enableth men in sundry degrees and callings to execute the same.

The Sixth, of the Power of Jurisdiction, which the reformed platform claimeth unto lay-elders, with others.

The Seventh, of the Power of Jurisdiction, and the honour which is annexed thereunto in Bishops.

The Eighth, of the power of Ecclesiastical Dominion or Supreme Authority, which with us the highest governor or Prince hath, as well in regard of domestical Jurisdictions, as of that other foreignly claimed by the Bishop of Rome.

OF THE

LAWS

OF

ECCLESIASTICAL POLITY.[1]

THE FIRST BOOK.
CONCERNING LAWS AND THEIR SEVERAL KINDS IN GENERAL.

THE MATTER CONTAINED IN THIS FIRST BOOK.

I. The cause of writing this general Discourse concerning Laws.
II. Of that Law which God from before the beginning hath set for himself to do all things by.
III. The Law which natural agents observe, and their necessary manner of keeping it.
IV. The Law which the Angels of God obey.
V. The Law whereby man is in his actions directed to the imitation of God.
VI. Men's first beginning to understand that Law.
VII. Of Man's Will, which is the first thing that Laws of action are made to guide.
VIII. Of the natural finding out of Laws by the light of Reason, to guide the Will unto that which is good.
IX. Of the benefit of keeping that Law which Reason teacheth.
X. How Reason doth lead men unto the making of human Laws, whereby politic Societies are governed, and to agreement about Laws whereby the fellowship or communion of independent Societies standeth.
XI. Wherefore God hath by Scripture further made known such supernatural Laws as do serve for men's direction.
XII. The cause why so many natural or rational Laws are set down in Holy Scripture.
XIII. The benefit of having divine Laws written.
XIV. The sufficiency of Scripture unto the end for which it was instituted.
XV. Of Laws positive contained in Scripture, the mutability of certain of them, and the general use of Scripture.
XVI. A Conclusion, shewing how all this belongeth to the cause in question.

[1] [Of this title it may not be improper to remark, that it by no means conveys the same idea with the phrase commonly substituted for it, Hooker's Ecclesiastical Polity. It does not profess to deliver a complete scheme or system, but only to contain a methodized course of observations on those portions of Church government, which seemed at the time most to require discussion.]

BOOK I.
Ch. i. 1, 2.

The cause of writing this general Discourse.

I. HE that goeth about to persuade a multitude, that they are not so well governed as they ought to be, shall never want attentive and favourable hearers; because they know the manifold defects whereunto every kind of regiment is subject, but the secret lets and difficulties, which in public proceedings are innumerable and inevitable, they have not ordinarily the judgment to consider. And because such as openly reprove supposed disorders of state are taken for principal friends to the common benefit of all, and for men that carry singular freedom of mind; under this fair and plausible colour whatsoever they utter passeth for good and current. That which wanteth in the weight of their speech, is supplied by the aptness of men's minds to accept and believe it. Whereas on the other side, if we maintain things that are established, we have not only to strive with a number of heavy prejudices deeply rooted in the hearts of men, who think that herein we serve the time, and speak in favour of the present state, because thereby we either hold or seek preferment; but also to bear such exceptions as minds so averted beforehand usually take against that which they are loth should be poured into them.

[2.] Albeit therefore much of that we are to speak in this present cause may seem to a number perhaps tedious, perhaps obscure, dark, and intricate; (for many talk of the truth, which never sounded the depth from whence it springeth; and therefore when they are led thereunto they are soon weary, as men drawn from those beaten paths wherewith they have been inured;) yet this may not so far prevail as to cut off that which the matter itself requireth, howsoever the nice humour of some be therewith pleased or no. They unto whom we shall seem tedious are in no wise injured[1] by us, because it is in their own hands to spare that labour which they are not willing to endure. And if any complain of obscurity, they must consider, that in these matters it cometh no otherwise to pass than in sundry the works both of art and also of nature, where that which hath greatest force in the very things we see is notwithstanding itself oftentimes not seen. The stateliness of houses, the goodliness

---

[1] [Injuried, ed. 1594.]

of trees, when we behold them delighteth the eye ; but that foundation which beareth up the one, that root which ministereth unto the other nourishment and life, is in the bosom of the earth concealed ; and if there be at any time occasion to search into it, such labour is then more necessary than pleasant, both to them which undertake it and for the lookers-on. In like manner, the use and benefit of good laws all that live under them may enjoy with delight and comfort, albeit the grounds and first original causes from whence they have sprung be unknown, as to the greatest part of men they are. But when they who withdraw their obedience pretend that the laws which they should obey are corrupt and vicious ; for better examination of their quality, it behoveth the very foundation and root, the highest wellspring and fountain of them to be discovered. Which because we are not oftentimes accustomed to do, when we do it the pains we take are more needful a great deal than acceptable, and the matters which we handle seem by reason of newness (till the mind grow better acquainted with them) dark, intricate, and unfamiliar. For as much help whereof as may be in this case, I have endeavoured throughout the body of this whole discourse, that every former part might give strength unto all that follow, and every later bring some light unto all before. So that if the judgments of men do but hold themselves in suspense as touching these first more general meditations, till in order they have perused the rest that ensue ; what may seem dark at the first will afterwards be found more plain, even as the later particular decisions will appear I doubt not more strong, when the other have been read before.

[3.] The Laws of the Church, whereby for so many ages together we have been guided in the exercise of Christian religion and the service of the true God, our rites, customs, and orders of ecclesiastical government, are called in question : we are accused as men that will not have Christ Jesus to rule over them, but have wilfully cast his statutes behind their backs, hating to be reformed and made subject unto the sceptre of his discipline. Behold therefore we offer the laws whereby we live unto the general trial and judgment of the whole world ; heartily beseeching Almighty God, whom we desire to serve according to his own will, that both we

BOOK I. and others (all kind of partial affection being clean laid aside)
Ch. ii. 1, 2. may have eyes to see and hearts to embrace the things that
in his sight are most acceptable.

And because the point about which we strive is the quality of our laws, our first entrance hereinto cannot better be made, than with consideration of the nature of law in general, and of that law which giveth life unto all the rest, which are commendable, just, and good; namely the law whereby the Eternal himself doth work. Proceeding from hence to the law, first of Nature, then of Scripture, we shall have the easier access unto those things which come after to be debated, concerning the particular cause and question which we have in hand.

Of that law II. All things that are, have some operation not violent or
which God casual. Neither doth any thing ever begin to exercise the
from before
the begin- same, without some fore-conceived end for which it worketh.
ning hath And the end which it worketh for is not obtained, unless
set for him-
self to do the work be also fit to obtain it by. For unto every end every
all things operation will not serve. That which doth assign unto each
by.
thing the kind, that which doth moderate the force and power, that which doth appoint the form and measure, of working, the same we term a *Law*. So that no certain end could ever be attained, unless the actions whereby it is attained were regular; that is to say, made suitable, fit and correspondent unto their end, by some canon, rule or law. Which thing doth first take place in the works even of God himself.

[2.] All things therefore do work after a sort, according to law: all other things according to a law, whereof some superior, unto whom they are subject, is author; only the works and operations of God have Him both for their worker, and for the law whereby they are wrought. The being of God is a kind of law to his working: for that perfection which God is, giveth perfection to that he doth. Those natural, necessary, and internal operations of God, the Generation of the Son, the Proceeding of the Spirit, are without the compass of my present intent: which is to touch only such operations as have their beginning and being by a voluntary purpose, wherewith God hath eternally decreed when and how they should be. Which eternal decree is that we term an eternal law.

Law of Subordination in the Most Holy Trinity. 201

Dangerous it were for the feeble brain of man to wade far into the doings of the Most High; whom although to know be life, and joy to make mention of his name; yet our soundest knowledge is to know that we know him not as indeed he is, neither can know him: and our safest eloquence concerning him is our silence, when we confess without confession that his glory is inexplicable, his greatness above our capacity and reach[1]. He is above, and we upon earth; therefore it behoveth our words to be wary and few[2].

BOOK I.
Ch. ii. 3.

Our God is one, or rather very *Oneness*, and mere unity, having nothing but itself in itself, and not consisting (as all things do besides God) of many things. In which essential Unity of God a Trinity personal nevertheless subsisteth, after a manner far exceeding the possibility of man's conceit. The works which outwardly are of God, they are in such sort of Him being one, that each Person hath in them somewhat peculiar and proper. For being Three, and they all subsisting in the essence of one Deity; from the Father, by the Son, through the Spirit, all things are. That which the Son doth hear of the Father, and which the Spirit doth receive of the Father and the Son, the same we have at the hands of the Spirit as being the last, and therefore the nearest unto us in order, although in power the same with the second and the first[3].

[3.] The wise and learned among the very heathens themselves have all acknowledged some First Cause, whereupon originally the being of all things dependeth. Neither have they otherwise spoken of that cause than as an Agent, which knowing *what* and *why* it worketh, observeth in working a most exact *order* or *law*. Thus much is signified by that which Homer mentioneth, Διὸς δ' ἐτελείετο βουλή[4]. Thus

---

[1] ["De quo nihil dici et exprimi "mortalium potis est significatione "verborum: qui, ut intelligaris, "tacendum est; atque, ut per um- "bram te possit errans investigare "suspicio, nihil est omnino muti- "endum." Arnob. Adv. Gentes, I. 31. See Davison on Prophecy, p. 672, first edit.]

[2] [Eccles. v. 2.]

[3] John xvi. 13-15. [Ὅταν δὲ ἔλθῃ ἐκεῖνος, τὸ Πνεῦμα τῆς ἀληθείας, ὁδηγήσει ὑμᾶς εἰς πᾶσαν τὴν ἀλήθειαν· οὐ γὰρ λαλήσει ἀφ' ἑαυτοῦ, ἀλλ' ὅσα ἂν ἀκούσῃ λαλήσει, ... Ἐκεῖνος ἐμὲ δοξάσει, ὅτι ἐκ τοῦ ἐμοῦ λήψεται, καὶ ἀναγγελεῖ ὑμῖν. Πάντα, ὅσα ἔχει ὁ Πατὴρ, ἐμά ἐστι· διὰ τοῦτο εἶπον, ὅτι ἐκ τοῦ ἐμοῦ λήψεται, καὶ ἀναγγελεῖ ὑμῖν. And c. xiv. 15: Πάντα, ἃ ἤκουσα παρὰ τοῦ Πατρός μου, ἐγνώρισα ὑμῖν.]

[4] Jupiter's *counsel* was accomplished. [Il. A. 5.]

much acknowledged by Mercurius Trismegistus, Τὸν πάντα κόσμον ἐποίησεν ὁ δημιουργὸς οὐ χερσὶν ἀλλὰ λόγῳ[1]. Thus much confest by Anaxagoras and Plato, terming the Maker of the world an *intellectual* Worker[2]. Finally the Stoics, although imagining the first cause of all things to be fire, held nevertheless, that the same fire having art, did ὁδῷ βαδίζειν ἐπὶ γενέσει κόσμου[3]. They all confess therefore in the working of that first cause, that Counsel is used, Reason followed, a Way observed; that is to say, constant Order and Law is kept; whereof itself must needs be author unto itself. Otherwise it should have some worthier and higher to direct it, and so could not itself be the first. Being the first, it can have no other than itself to be the author of that law which it willingly worketh by.

God therefore is a law both to himself, and to all other things besides. To himself he is a law in all those things, whereof our Saviour speaketh, saying, "My Father worketh "as yet, so I[4]." God worketh nothing without cause. All those things which are done by him have some end for which they are done; and the end for which they are done is a reason of his will to do them. His will had not inclined to create woman, but that he saw it could not be well if she were not created. *Non est bonum,* "It is not good man "should be alone; therefore let us make a helper for him[5]." That and nothing else is done by God, which to leave undone were not so good.

If therefore it be demanded, why God having power and ability infinite, the effects notwithstanding of that power are all so limited as we see they are: the reason hereof is the end which he hath proposed, and the law whereby his wisdom hath stinted the effects of his power in such sort, that it doth not work infinitely, but correspondently unto that end for which it worketh, even "all things χρηστῶς[6],

---

[1] [C. 7. § 1.] The Creator made the whole world not with hands, but by *reason*.

[2] Stob. in Eclog. Phys. [This seems to refer to the following: Ἀναξαγόρας, νοῦν κόσμου ποιὸν [κοσμοποιὸν] τὸν Θεόν. Stob. ed. Canter. p. 2 : Πλάτων.. "νοῦς ὁ Θεός.. "τούτου δὲ πατρὸς καὶ ποιητοῦ, τὰ "ἄλλα θεῖα ἔγγονα.".. Ibid. p. 5.]

[3] Proceed by a certain and a set *Way* in the making of the world. [οἱ στοικοὶ νοερὸν θεὸν ἀποφαίνονται, πῦρ τεχνικὸν, ὁδῷ βαδίζον ἐπὶ γενέσει κόσμου. Ibid. 5.]

[4] John v. 17.
[5] Gen. ii. 18.
[6] Sap. viii. 1; xi. 20.

God's Law or Counsel perfect, and unsearchable. 203

"in most decent and comely sort," all things in "Measure, Number, and Weight."

[4.] The general end of God's external working is the exercise of his most glorious and most abundant virtue. Which abundance doth shew itself in variety, and for that cause this variety is oftentimes in Scripture exprest by the name of *riches*[1]. "The Lord hath made all things for his "own sake[2]." Not that any thing is made to be beneficial unto him, but all things for him to shew beneficence and grace in them.

The particular drift of every act proceeding externally from God we are not able to discern, and therefore cannot always give the proper and certain reason of his works. Howbeit undoubtedly a proper and certain reason there is of every finite work of God, inasmuch as there is a law imposed upon it; which if there were not, it should be infinite, even as the worker himself is.

[5.] They err therefore who think that of the will of God to do this or that there is no reason besides his will. Many times no reason known to us; but that there is no reason thereof I judge it most unreasonable to imagine, inasmuch as he worketh all things κατὰ τὴν βουλὴν τοῦ θελήματος αὐτοῦ, not only according to his own will, but "the Counsel of his "own will[3]." And whatsoever is done with counsel or wise resolution hath of necessity some reason why it should be done, albeit that reason be to us in some things so secret, that it forceth the wit of man to stand, as the blessed Apostle himself doth, amazed thereat[4]: "O the depth of "the riches both of the wisdom and knowledge of God! how "unsearchable are his judgments," &c. That law eternal which God himself hath made to himself, and thereby worketh all things whereof he is the cause and author; that law in the admirable frame whereof shineth with most perfect beauty the countenance of that wisdom which hath testified concerning herself[5], "The Lord possessed me in the beginning of "his way, even before his works of old I was set up;" that law, which hath been the pattern to make, and is the card

---

[1] Ephes. i. 7; Phil. iv. 19; Col. ii. 3.
[2] Prov. xvi. 4.
[3] Ephes. i. 11.
[4] Rom. xi. 33.
[5] Prov. viii. 22.

to guide the world by; that law which hath been of God and with God everlastingly; that law, the author and observer whereof is one only God to be blessed for ever: how should either men or angels be able perfectly to behold? The book of this law we are neither able nor worthy to open and look into. That little thereof which we darkly apprehend we admire, the rest with religious ignorance we humbly and meekly adore.

[6.] Seeing therefore that according to this law He worketh, "of whom, through whom, and for whom, are all things[1];" although there seem unto us confusion and disorder in the affairs of this present world: "Tamen quoniam bonus "mundum rector temperat, recte fieri cuncta ne dubites[2]:" "let no man doubt but that every thing is well done, because "the world is ruled by so good a guide," as transgresseth not His own law, than which nothing can be more absolute, perfect, and just.

The law whereby He worketh is eternal, and therefore can have no show or colour of mutability: for which cause, a part of that law being opened in the promises which God hath made (because his promises are nothing else but declarations what God will do for the good of men) touching those promises the Apostle hath witnessed, that God may as possibly "deny himself[3]" and not be God, as fail to perform them. And concerning the counsel of God, he termeth it likewise a thing "unchangeable[4];" the counsel of God, and that law of God whereof now we speak, being one.

Nor is the freedom of the will of God any whit abated, let or hindered, by means of this; because the imposition of this law upon himself is his own free and voluntary act.

This law therefore we may name eternal, being "that "order which God before all ages hath set down with him- "self, for himself to do all things by."

The law which natural agents have given

III. I am not ignorant that by "law eternal" the learned for the most part do understand the order, not which God hath eternally purposed himself in all his works to observe,

---

[1] Rom. xi. 36.
[2] Boet. lib. iv. de Consol. Philos. [p. 105, ed. Lugd. Bat. 1656.] pros. 5.
[3] 2 Tim. ii. 13.
[4] Heb. vi. 17.

but rather that which with himself he hath set down as expedient to be kept by all his creatures, according to the several condition[1] wherewith he hath endued them. They who thus are accustomed to speak apply the name of Law unto that only rule of working which superior authority imposeth; whereas we somewhat more enlarging the sense thereof term any kind of rule or canon, whereby actions are framed, a law. Now that law which, as it is laid up in the bosom of God, they call *Eternal*, receiveth according unto the different kinds of things which are subject unto it different and sundry kinds of names. That part of it which ordereth natural agents we call usually *Nature's* law; that which Angels do clearly behold and without any swerving[2] observe is a law *Celestial* and heavenly; the law of *Reason*, that which bindeth creatures reasonable in this world, and with which by reason they may most plainly perceive themselves bound; that which bindeth them, and is not known but by special revelation from God, *Divine* law; *Human* law, that which out of the law either of reason or of God men probably gathering to be expedient, they make it a law. All things therefore, which are as they ought to be, are conformed unto *this second law eternal;* and even those things which to this eternal law are not conformable are notwithstanding in some sort ordered by *the first eternal law*. For what good or evil is there under the sun, what action correspondent or repugnant unto the law which God hath imposed upon his creatures, but in or upon it God doth work according to the law which himself hath eternally purposed to keep; that is to say, the *first law eternal?* So that a twofold law eternal being thus made, it is not hard to conceive how they both take place in all things[3].

BOOK I
Ch. iii. 1.

observe, them to observe, and their necessary manner of keeping it.

---

[1] [So edd. A, B, "conditions," K.] 1886.

[2] [Uniformly written "*swarve*" in the early edd.]

[3] "Id omne, quod in rebus crea-"tis fit, est materia legis æternæ." Th. I. 1, 2. q. 93, art. 4, 5, 6. [Thom. Aquin. Opp. xi. 202.] "Nullo modo "aliquid legibus summi Creatoris "ordinationique subtrahitur, a quo "pax universitatis administratur." August. de Civit. Dei, lib. xix. cap. 12. [t. VII. 556.] Immo et peccatum, quatenus a Deo juste permittitur, cadit in legem æternam. Etiam legi æternæ subjicitur peccatum, quatenus voluntaria legis transgressio pœnale quoddam incommodum animæ inserit, juxta illud Augustini, "Jussisti Domine, et sic est, ut "pœna sua sibi sit omnis animus "inordinatus." Confess. lib. i. cap. 12. [t. I. 77.] *Nec male scholastici*, "Quemadmodum," inquiunt,

BOOK I.
Ch. iii. 2.

[2.] Wherefore to come to the law of nature: albeit thereby we sometimes mean that manner of working which God hath set for each created thing to keep; yet forasmuch as those things are termed most properly natural agents, which keep the law of their kind unwittingly, as the heavens and elements of the world, which can do no otherwise than they do; and forasmuch as we give unto intellectual natures the name of *Voluntary* agents, that so we may distinguish them from the other; expedient it will be, that we sever the law of nature observed by the one from that which the other is tied unto. Touching the former, their strict keeping of one tenure, statute, and law, is spoken of by all, but hath in it more than men have as yet attained to know, or perhaps ever shall attain, seeing the travail of wading herein is given of God to the sons of men [1], that perceiving how much the least thing in the world hath in it more than the wisest are able to reach unto, they may by this means learn humility. Moses, in describing the work of creation, attributeth speech unto God: "God said, Let there "be light: let there be a firmament: let the waters under "the heaven be gathered together into one place: let the "earth bring forth: let there be lights in the firmament of "heaven." Was this only the intent of Moses, to signify the infinite greatness of God's power by the easiness of his accomplishing such effects, without travail, pain, or labour? Surely it seemeth that Moses had herein besides this a further purpose, namely, first to teach that God did not work as a

"videmus res naturales contingen-
"tes, hoc ipso quod a fine particulari
"suo atque adeo a lege æterna exorbi-
"tant, in eandem legem æternam in-
"cidere, quatenus consequuntur a-
"lium finem a lege etiam æterna ipsis
"in casu particulari constitutum; sic
"verisimile est homines, etiam cum
"peccant et desciscunt a lege æterna
"ut præcipiente, reincidere in ordi-
"nem æternæ legis ut punientis."

[1] [Eccles. III. 9, 10: "I have "seen the travail which God hath "given to the sons of men to be "exercised in it. He hath made "every thing beautiful in his time: "also he hath set the world in their "heart, so that no man can find "out the work that God maketh "from the beginning to the end."

Compare the use which Lord Bacon has made of the same text, Advancement of Learning, b. ii: "Knowledges are as pyramids, "whereof history is the basis. So "of natural philosophy, the basis is "natural history; the stage next the "basis is physic; the stage next "the vertical point is metaphysic. "As for the vertical point, *Opus*, "*quod operatur Deus a principio* "*usque ad finem*, the summary law "of nature, we know not whether "man's inquiry can attain unto "it." Works, I. p. 104, 8vo. London, 1803.]

necessary but a voluntary agent, intending beforehand and decreeing with himself that which did outwardly proceed from him: secondly, to shew that God did then institute a law natural to be observed by creatures, and therefore according to the manner of laws, the institution thereof is described, as being established by solemn injunction. His commanding those things to be which are, and to be in such sort as they are, to keep that tenure and course which they do, importeth the establishment of nature's law. This world's first creation, and the preservation since of things created, what is it but only so far forth a manifestation by execution, what the eternal law of God is concerning things natural? And as it cometh to pass in a kingdom rightly ordered, that after a law is once published, it presently takes effect far and wide, all states framing themselves thereunto; even so let us think it fareth in the natural course of the world: since the time that God did first proclaim the edicts of his law upon it, heaven and earth have hearkened unto his voice, and their labour hath been to do his will: He "made a law for "the rain [1];" He gave his "decree unto the sea, that the "waters should not pass his commandment [2]." Now if nature should intermit her course, and leave altogether though it were but for a while the observation of her own laws; if those principal and mother elements of the world, whereof all things in this lower world are made, should lose the qualities which now they have; if the frame of that heavenly arch erected over our heads should loosen and dissolve itself; if celestial spheres should forget their wonted motions, and by irregular volubility turn themselves any way as it might happen; if the prince of the lights of heaven, which now as a giant doth run his unwearied course [3], should as it were through a languishing faintness begin to stand and to rest himself; if the moon should wander from her beaten way, the times and seasons of the year blend themselves by disordered and confused mixture, the winds breathe out their last gasp, the clouds yield no rain, the earth be defeated of heavenly influence, the fruits of the earth pine away as children at the withered breasts of their mother no longer

---

[1] [Job xxviii. 26.]   [2] [Jer. v. 22.]   [3] Psalm xix. 5.

able to yield them relief[1]: what would become of man himself, whom these things now do all serve? See we not plainly that obedience of creatures unto the law of nature is the stay of the whole world?

[3.] Notwithstanding with nature it cometh sometimes to pass as with art. Let Phidias have rude and obstinate stuff to carve, though his art do that it should, his work will lack that beauty which otherwise in fitter matter it might have had. He that striketh an instrument with skill may cause notwithstanding a very unpleasant sound, if the string whereon he striketh chance to be uncapable of harmony. In the matter whereof things natural consist, that of Theophrastus taketh place, Πολὺ τὸ οὐχ ὑπακοῦον οὐδὲ δεχόμενον τὸ εὖ[2]. "Much of it is oftentimes such as will by no means "yield to receive that impression which were best and most "perfect." Which defect in the matter of things natural, they who gave themselves unto the contemplation of nature amongst the heathen observed often: but the true original cause thereof, divine malediction, laid for the sin of man upon these creatures which God had made for the use of man, this being an article of that saving truth which God hath revealed unto his Church, was above the reach of their merely natural

---

[1] [Hooker seems to have had in his mind the following passage:

"Postquam esse nomen in terris "Christianæ religionis occœpit, "quidnam inusitatum, quid incog- "nitum, quid contra leges princi- "paliter institutas aut sensit aut "passa est rerum ipsa quæ dicitur "appellaturque Natura? Nunquid "in contrarias qualitates prima illa "elementa mutata sunt, ex quibus "res omnes consensum est esse "concretas? Nunquid machinæ "hujus, et molis, qua universi "tegimur et continemur inclusi, "parte est in aliqua relaxata aut "dissoluta constructio? Nunquid "vertigo hæc mundi, primogenii "motus moderamen excedens, aut "tardius repere, aut præcipiti cœpit "volubilitate raptari? Nunquid ab "occiduis partibus attollere se astra, "atque in ortus fieri signorum "cœpta est inclinatio? Nunquid "ipse syderum sol princeps, cujus "omnia luce vestiuntur atque ani- "mantur, calore exarsit, intepuit, "atque in contrarios habitus moder- "aminis soliti temperamenta cor- "rupit? Nunquid luna desivit "redintegrare seipsam, atque in "veteres formas, novellarum sem- "per restitutione, traducere? Nun- "quid frigora, nunquid calores, "nunquid tepores medii, inæqua- "lium temporum confusionibus oc- "ciderunt? Nunquid longos ha- "bere dies bruma, et revocare tar- "dissimas luces nox cœpit æstatis? "Nunquid suas animas expiraverunt "venti? emortuisque flaminibus "neque cœlum coarctatur in nubila, "nec madidari ex imbribus arva "suescunt? Commendata semina "tellus recusat accipere? aut fron- "descere arbores nolunt?" Arnob. adv. Gent. I. 2.]

[2] Theophrast. in Metaph. [p. 271, l. 10, ed. Basil, 1541.]

capacity and understanding. But howsoever these swervings are now and then incident into the course of nature, nevertheless so constantly the laws of nature are by natural agents observed, that no man denieth but those things which nature worketh are wrought, either always or for the most part, after one and the same manner [1].

[4.] If here it be demanded what that is which keepeth nature in obedience to her own law, we must have recourse to that higher law whereof we have already spoken, and because all other laws do thereon depend, from thence we must borrow so much as shall need for brief resolution in this point. Although we are not of opinion therefore, as some are, that nature in working hath before her certain exemplary draughts or patterns, which subsisting in the bosom of the Highest, and being thence discovered, she fixeth her eye upon them, as travellers by sea upon the pole-star of the world, and that according thereunto she guideth her hand to work by imitation: although we rather embrace the oracle of Hippocrates [2], that "each thing both "in small and in great fulfilleth the task which destiny "hath set down;" and concerning the manner of executing and fulfilling the same, "what they do they know not, yet "is it in show and appearance as though they did know "what they do; and the truth is they do not discern the "things which they look on:" nevertheless, forasmuch as the works of nature are no less exact, than if she did both behold and study how to express some absolute shape or mirror always present before her; yea, such her dexterity and skill appeareth, that no intellectual creature in the world were able by capacity to do that which nature doth without capacity and knowledge; it cannot be but nature hath some director of infinite knowledge to guide her in all her ways. Who the guide of nature, but only the God of nature? "In him we live, move, and are [3]." Those things which nature is said to do, are by divine art performed,

---

[1] Arist. Rhet. i. cap. 39. [ἡ γὰρ αἰεὶ, ἢ ὡς ἐπιτοπολὺ ὡσαύτως ἀποβαίνει.]
[2] Τὴν πεπρωμένην μοίρην ἕκαστον ἐκπληροῖ καὶ ἐπὶ τὸ μέζον καὶ ἐπὶ τὸ μεῖον ... ὃ πρήσσουσιν οὐκ οἴδασιν, ὃ δὲ πρήσσουσι δοκέουσιν εἰδέναι, καί θ' ἃ μὲν ὁρῶσι οὐ γινώσκουσι. [p. 342, 48. ed. Genev. 1657. It need hardly be observed, that the beginning of the sentence alludes to Plato's doctrine.]
[3] Acts xvii. 28.

BOOK I.
Ch. iii. 4.

using nature as an instrument; nor is there any such art or knowledge divine in nature herself working, but in the Guide of nature's work.

Whereas therefore things natural which are not in the number of voluntary agents, (for of such only we now speak, and of no other,) do so necessarily observe their certain laws, that as long as they keep those forms[1] which give them their being, they cannot possibly be apt or inclinable to do otherwise than they do; seeing the kinds of their operations are both constantly and exactly framed according to the several ends for which they serve, they themselves in the meanwhile, though doing that which is fit, yet knowing neither what they do, nor why: it followeth that all which they do in this sort proceedeth originally from some such agent, as knoweth, appointeth, holdeth up, and even actually frameth the same.

The manner of this divine efficiency, being far above us, we are no more able to conceive by our reason than creatures unreasonable by their sense are able to apprehend after what manner we dispose and order the course of our affairs. Only thus much is discerned, that the natural generation and process of all things receiveth order of proceeding from the settled stability of divine understanding. This appointeth unto them their kinds of working; the disposition whereof in the purity of God's own knowledge and will is rightly termed by the name of Providence. The same being referred unto the things themselves here disposed by it, was wont by the ancient to be called natural Destiny. That law, the performance whereof we behold in things natural, is as it were an authentical or an original draught written in the bosom of God himself; whose Spirit being to execute the same useth every particular nature, every mere natural agent, only as an instrument created at the beginning, and ever since the beginning used, to work his own will and pleasure withal. Nature therefore is nothing else but God's instrument[2]: in the course whereof Dionysius perceiving

---

[1] Form in other creatures is a thing proportionable unto the soul in living creatures. Sensible it is not, nor otherwise discernible than only by effects. According to the diversity of inward forms, things of the world are distinguished into their kinds.

[2] Vide Thom. in Compend. Theol. cap. 3: "Omne quod movetur ab

God's natural Law regards the whole as a System.

some sudden disturbance is said to have cried out, "Aut "Deus naturæ patitur, aut mundi machina dissolvetur[1]:" "either God doth suffer impediment, and is by a greater than "himself hindered; or if that be impossible, then hath he "determined to make a present dissolution of the world; the "execution of that law beginning now to stand still, without "which the world cannot stand."

This workman, whose servitor nature is, being in truth but only one, the heathens imagining to be moe, gave him in the sky the name of Jupiter, in the air the name of Juno, in the water the name of Neptune, in the earth the name of Vesta and sometimes of Ceres, the name of Apollo in the sun, in the moon the name of Diana, the name of Æolus and divers other in the winds; and to conclude, even so many guides of nature they dreamed of, as they saw there were kinds of things natural in the world. These they honoured, as having power to work or cease accordingly as men deserved of them. But unto us there is one only[2] Guide of all agents natural, and he both the Creator and the Worker of all in all, alone to be blessed, adored and honoured by all for ever.

[5.] That which hitherto hath been spoken concerneth natural agents considered in themselves. But we must further remember also, (which thing to touch in a word shall suffice,) that as in this respect they have their law, which law directeth them in the means whereby they tend to their own perfection: so likewise another law there is, which toucheth them as they are sociable parts united into one body; a law which bindeth them each to serve unto other's good, and all to prefer the good of the whole before whatsoever their own particular; as we plainly see they do, when things natural in that regard forget their ordinary natural wont; that which is heavy mounting sometime upwards of

---

"aliquo est quasi instrumentum "quoddam primi moventis. Ridi- "culum est autem, etiam apud in- "doctos, ponere, instrumentum mo- "veri non ab aliquo principali "agente." [t. xvii. fol. 10.]

[1] [Vid. Breviar. Roman. 9 Oct. "Dionysius... unus ex Areopagitis "... cum adhuc in Gentilitatis errore "versaretur, eo die quo Christus "Dominus cruci affixus est, solem "præter naturam defecisse animad- "vertens, exclamasse traditur :. 'aut "Deus,' &c." Suidas (in Dionysio) makes him say, Ἡ τὸ Θεῖον πάσχει, ἢ τῷ πάσχοντι συμπάσχει. Michael Syngelus in Encomio; Ὁ ἄγνωστος, ἔφη, σαρκὶ πάσχει Θεός. Apud Opp. S. Dionys. II. 213. See also, p. 91, 253-259.]

[2] [Suggested by 1 Cor. viii. 6. ἡμῖν εἷς Θεός, ὁ Πατήρ.]

BOOK I.
Ch. iv. 1.

The law which angels do work by.

it[1] own accord, and forsaking the centre of the earth which to itself is most natural, even as if it did hear itself commanded to let go the good it privately wisheth, and to relieve the present distress of nature in common.

IV. But now that we may lift up our eyes (as it were) from the footstool to the throne of God, and leaving these natural, consider a little the state of heavenly and divine creatures: touching Angels, which are spirits[2] immaterial and intellectual, the glorious inhabitants of those sacred palaces, where nothing but light and blessed immortality, no shadow of matter for tears, discontentments, griefs, and uncomfortable passions to work upon, but all joy, tranquillity, and peace, even for ever and ever doth dwell: as in number and order they are huge, mighty, and royal armies[3], so likewise in perfection of obedience unto that law, which the Highest, whom they adore, love, and imitate, hath imposed upon them, such observants they are thereof, that our Saviour himself being to set down the perfect *idea* of that which we are to pray and wish for on earth, did not teach to pray or wish for more than only that here it might be with us, as with them it is in heaven[4]. God which moveth mere natural agents as an efficient only, doth otherwise move intellectual creatures, and especially his holy angels: for beholding the face of God[5], in admiration of so great excellency they all adore him; and being rapt with the love of his beauty, they cleave inseparably for ever unto him. Desire to resemble him in goodness maketh them unweariable and even unsatiable in their longing to do by all means all manner good unto all the creatures of God[6], but especially unto the children of

---

[1] [So all the early edd. On *It*, possessive, v. Morris, Spec. Early English, p. xxxi.] 1886.   [2] Psalm civ. 4; Heb. i. 7; Ephes. iii. 10.
[3] Dan. vii. 10; Matt. xxvi. 53; Heb. xii. 22; Luke ii. 13.
[4] Matt. vi. 10.   [5] Matt. xviii. 10.
[6] ["How oft do they their silver bowers leave,
 "To come to succour us, that succour want!
 "How oft do they with golden pinions cleave
 "The flitting skies, like flying pursuivant,
 "Against foul fiends to aid us militant!
 "They for us fight, they watch and duly ward,
 "And their bright squadrons round about us plant,
 "And all for love, and nothing for reward—
"O why should heavenly God to men have such regard?"
Fairy Queen, II. viii. 2. The three first books of the Fairy Queen were published 1590. Spenser died 1598.]

men[1]: in the countenance of whose nature, looking downward, they behold themselves beneath themselves; even as upward, in God, beneath whom themselves are, they see that character which is no where but in themselves and us resembled. Thus far even the paynims have approached; thus far they have seen into the doings of the angels of God; Orpheus confessing, that "the fiery throne of God is attended "on by those most industrious angels, careful how all things "are performed amongst men[2];" and the Mirror of human wisdom plainly teaching, that God moveth angels, even as that thing doth stir man's heart, which is thereunto presented amiable[3]. Angelical actions may therefore be reduced unto these three general kinds: first, most delectable love arising from the visible apprehension of the purity, glory, and beauty of God, invisible saving only unto spirits that are pure[4]: secondly, adoration grounded upon the evidence of the greatness of God, on whom they see how all things depend[5]; thirdly, imitation[6], bred by the presence of his exemplary goodness, who ceaseth not before them daily to fill heaven and earth with the rich treasures of most free and undeserved grace.

[2.] Of angels, we are not to consider only what they are and do in regard of their own being, but that also which concerneth them as they are linked into a kind of corporation amongst themselves, and of society or fellowship with men. Consider angels each of them severally in himself, and their law is that which the prophet David mentioneth, "All ye "his angels praise him[7]." Consider the angels of God associated, and their law is that which disposeth them as an army, one in order and degree above another[8]. Consider finally the angels as having with us that communion which the apostle to the Hebrews noteth, and in regard whereof

[1] Psalm xci. 11, 12; Luke xv. 7; Heb. i. 14; Acts x. 3; Dan. ix. 23; Matt. xviii. 10; Dan. iv. 13.
[2] Σῷ δὲ θρόνῳ πυρόεντι παρεστᾶσιν πολύμοχθοι
Ἄγγελοι, οἷσι μέμηλε βροτοῖς ὡς πάντα τελεῖται. [Fragm. iii. ex Clem. Alex. Strom. V. p. 824, 8 = 724. Potter.]
[3] Arist. Metaph. l. xii, c. 7. ["Movet ut amatum: moto vero, "alia moventur." Ap. Thom. Aquin. t. IV. fol. 159, ed. Venet. 1593.]
[4] Job xxxviii. 7; Matt. xviii. 10.
[5] Psalm cxlviii. 2; Heb. i. 6; Isa. vi. 3.
[6] This is intimated wheresoever we find them termed "the sons of "God," as Job i. 6, and xxxviii. 7.
[7] Ps. cxlviii. 2.
[8] Luke ii. 13. Matt. xxvi. 53.

BOOK I.
Ch. iv. 3.

angels have not disdained to profess themselves our "fellow-servants;" from hence there springeth up a third law, which bindeth them to works of ministerial employment[1]. Every of which their several functions are by them performed with joy.

[3.] A part of the angels of God notwithstanding (we know) have fallen[2], and that their fall hath been through the voluntary breach of that law, which did require at their hands continuance in the exercise of their high and admirable virtue. Impossible it was that ever their will should change or incline to remit any part of their duty, without some object having force to avert their conceit from God, and to draw it another way; and that before they attained that high perfection of bliss, wherein now the elect angels[3] are without possibility of falling. Of any thing more than of God they could not by any means like, as long as whatsoever they knew besides God they apprehended it not in itself without dependency upon God; because so long God must needs seem infinitely better than any thing which they so could apprehend. Things beneath them could not in such sort be presented unto their eyes, but that therein they must needs see always how those things did depend on God. It seemeth therefore that there was no other way for angels to sin, but by reflex of their understanding upon themselves; when being held with admiration of their own sublimity and honour, the memory of their subordination unto God and their dependency on him was drowned in this conceit; whereupon their adoration, love, and imitation of God could not choose but be also interrupted. The fall of angels therefore was pride[4]. Since their fall, their practices have been the clean contrary unto those before mentioned[5]. For being dis-

---

[1] Heb. xii. 22; Apoc. xxii. 9.   [2] 2 Pet. ii. 4; Jude 6.   [3] [1 Tim. v. 21.]
[4] ["But pride, impatient of long resting peace,
"Did puff them up with greedy bold ambition,
"That they gan cast their state how to increase
"Above the fortune of their first condition,
"And sit in God's own seat without commission:
"The brightest angel, even the child of light,
"Drew millions more against their God to fight."
          Spenser's Hymn on Heavenly Love, published 1596.]
[5] John viii. 44; 1 Pet. v. 8; Apoc. ix. 11; Gen. iii. 15; 1 Chron. xxi. 1; Job i. 7. and ii. 2; John xiii. 27; Acts v. 3; Apoc. xx. 8.

persed, some in the air, some on the earth, some in the water, some among the minerals, dens, and caves, that are under the earth; they have by all means laboured to effect an universal rebellion against the laws, and as far as in them lieth utter destruction of the works of God. These wicked spirits the heathens honoured instead of gods, both generally under the name of *Dii inferi*, "gods infernal;" and particularly, some in oracles, some in idols, some as household gods, some as nymphs: in a word, no foul and wicked spirit which was not one way or other honoured of men as God, till such time as light appeared in the world and dissolved the works of the devil. Thus much therefore may suffice for angels, the next unto whom in degree are men.

V. God alone excepted, who actually and everlastingly is whatsoever he may be, and which cannot hereafter be that which now he is not[1]; all other things besides are somewhat in possibility, which as yet they are not in act. And for this cause there is in all things an appetite or desire, whereby they incline to something which they may be; and when they are it, they shall be perfecter than now they are. All which perfections are contained under the general name of Goodness. And because there is not in the world any thing whereby another may not some way be made the perfecter, therefore all things that are, are good.

The law whereby man is in his actions directed to the imitation of God.

[2.] Again, sith there can be no goodness desired which proceedeth not from God himself, as from the supreme cause of all things; and every effect doth after a sort contain, at leastwise resemble, the cause from which it proceedeth: all things in the world are said in some sort to seek the highest, and to covet more or less the participation of God himself[2]. Yet this doth no where so much appear as it doth in man, because there are so many kinds of perfections which man seeketh. The first degree of goodness is that general perfection which all things do seek, in desiring the continuance of their being. All things therefore coveting as much as may be to be like unto God in being ever, that which cannot here-

---

[1] ["Let him know, that I have "considered, *that God only is what* "*he would be;* and that I am by "his grace become now so like him, "as to be pleased with what pleaseth "him." Walton's Life of Herbert, p. 321. ed. 1675.]

[2] Πάντα γὰρ ἐκείνου ὀρέγεται. Arist. de An. lib. ii. cap. 4. [Opp. I. 390. ed. Lugd. 1590.]

unto attain personally doth seek to continue itself another way, that is by offspring and propagation. The next degree of goodness is that which each thing coveteth by affecting resemblance with God in the constancy and excellency of those operations which belong unto their kind. The immutability of God they strive unto, by working either always or for the most part after one and the same manner; his absolute exactness they imitate, by tending unto that which is most exquisite in every particular. Hence have risen a number of axioms in philosophy[1], showing how "the "works of nature do always aim at that which cannot be "bettered."

[3.] These two kinds of goodness rehearsed are so nearly united to the things themselves which desire them, that we scarcely perceive the appetite to stir in reaching forth her hand towards them. But the desire of those perfections which grow externally is more apparent; especially of such as are not expressly desired unless they be first known, or such as are not for any other cause than for knowledge itself desired. Concerning perfections in this kind; that by proceeding in the knowledge of truth, and by growing in the exercise of virtue, man amongst the creatures of this inferior world aspireth to the greatest conformity with God; this is not only known unto us, whom he himself hath so instructed[2], but even they do acknowledge, who amongst men are not judged the nearest unto him. With Plato what one thing more usual, than to excite men unto the love of wisdom, by shewing how much wise men are thereby exalted above men; how knowledge doth raise them up into heaven; how it maketh them, though not gods, yet as gods, high, admirable, and divine? And Mercurius Trismegistus speaking of the virtues of a righteous soul[3], "Such spirits" (saith he) "are never cloyed "with praising and speaking well of all men, with doing good "unto every one by word and deed, because they study to frame "themselves according to *the pattern* of the Father of spirits."

---

[1] Ἐν τοῖς φύσει δεῖ τὸ βέλτιον, ἐὰν ἐνδέχηται, ὑπάρχειν μᾶλλον· ἡ φύσις ἀεὶ ποιεῖ τῶν ἐνδεχομένων τὸ βέλτιστον. Arist. 2. de coel. cap. 5. [t. i. p. 283.]

[2] Matt. v. 48; Sap. vii. 27.

[3] Ἡ δὲ τοιαύτη ψυχὴ κόρον οὐδέποτε ἔχει ὑμνοῦσα εὐφημοῦσά τε πάντας ἀνθρώπους, καὶ λόγοις καὶ ἔργοις πάντας [πάντως] εὐποιοῦσα, μιμουμένη αὐτῆς τὸν πατέρα. [c. 10. §. 21.] lib. iv. f. 12.

VI. In the matter of knowledge, there is between the angels of God and the children of men this difference: angels already have full and complete knowledge in the highest degree that can be imparted unto them; men, if we view them in their spring, are at the first without understanding or knowledge at all[1]. Nevertheless from this utter vacuity they grow by degrees, till they come at length to be even as the angels themselves are. That which agreeth to the one now, the other shall attain unto in the end; they are not so far disjoined and severed, but that they come at length to meet. The soul of man being therefore at the first as a book, wherein nothing is and yet all things may be imprinted; we are to search by what steps and degrees it riseth unto perfection of knowledge.

Men's first beginning to grow to the knowledge of that law which they are to observe.

[2.] Unto that which hath been already set down concerning natural agents this we must add, that albeit therein we have comprised as well creatures living as void of life, if they be in degree of nature beneath men; nevertheless a difference we must observe between those natural agents that work altogether unwittingly, and those which have though weak yet some understanding what they do, as fishes, fowls, and beasts have. Beasts are in sensible capacity as ripe even as men themselves, perhaps more ripe. For as stones, though in dignity of nature inferior unto plants, yet exceed them in firmness of strength or durability of being; and plants, though beneath the excellency of creatures endued with sense, yet exceed them in the faculty of vegetation and of fertility: so beasts, though otherwise behind men, may notwithstanding in actions of sense and fancy go beyond them; because the endeavours of nature, when it hath a higher perfection to seek, are in lower the more remiss, not esteeming thereof so much as those things do, which have no better proposed unto them.

[3.] The soul of man therefore being capable of a more divine perfection, hath (besides the faculties of growing unto sensible knowledge which is common unto us with beasts) a further ability, whereof in them there is no show at all, the ability of reaching higher than unto sensible things[2]. Till

---

[1] Vide Isa. vii. 16.

[2] Ὁ δὲ ἄνθρωπος εἰς τὸν οὐρανὸν ποία μὲν ἐστιν αὐτῷ [*leg.* αὐτοῦ] ἀναβαίνει, καὶ μετρεῖ αὐτὸν, καὶ οἶδε

BOOK I.
Ch. vi. 4.

we grow to some ripeness of years, the soul of man doth only store itself with conceits of things of inferior and more open quality, which afterwards do serve as instruments unto that which is greater; in the meanwhile above the reach of meaner creatures it ascendeth not. When once it comprehendeth any thing above this, as the differences of time, affirmations, negations, and contradictions in speech, we then count it to have some use of natural reason. Whereunto if afterwards there might be added the right helps of true art and learning (which helps, I must plainly confess, this age of the world, carrying the name of a learned age, doth neither much know nor greatly regard), there would undoubtedly be almost as great difference in maturity of judgment between men therewith inured, and that which now men are, as between men that are now and innocents. Which speech if any condemn, as being over hyperbolical, let them consider but this one thing. No art is at the first finding out so perfect as industry may after make it. Yet the very first man that to any purpose knew the way we speak of [1] and followed it, hath alone thereby performed more very near in all parts of natural knowledge, than sithence in any one part thereof the whole world besides hath done.

[4.] In the poverty of that other new devised aid [2] two

ὑψηλὰ, ποῖα δὲ ταπεινὰ, καὶ τὰ ἄλλα πάντα ἀκριβῶς μανθάνει. Καὶ τὸ πάντων μεῖζον, οὐδὲ τὴν γῆν καταλιπὼν ἄνω γίνεται. Merc. Tris. [c. 10 fin.] lib. iv. f. 12.

[1] Aristotelical Demonstration.
[2] Ramistry. [Peter Ramus was born in Picardy, 1515. He was a kind of self-taught person, who rose to eminence in the university of Paris. In 1543, he published "Institutiones Dialecticæ," and about the same time "Animadversiones Aristotelicæ." He was silenced after disputation, but allowed the next year to lecture in Rhetoric, and in 1552 was made Professor of Eloquence and Philosophy, probably through the Cardinal of Lorraine's influence. In 1562 he was ejected, and continued more or less unsettled till 1572, when he lost his life in the massacre of St. Bartholomew. (Brucker, Hist. Phil. v. 548-585.

Lips. 1766.) Strype, Ann. III. i. 500, says, "About this time (1585) "and somewhat before, another "great contest arose in both uni-"versities, concerning the two phi-"losophers, Aristotle and Ramus, "then chiefly read, and which of "them was rather to be studied." See also Ann. II. ii. 405. (1580.) "Everard Digby had writ somewhat "dialogue-wise against Ramus's "*Unica Methodus*, which in those "times prevailed much; and per-"haps brought into that college "(St. John's, Cambridge) to be read; "the rather, Ramus being a pro-"testant as well as a learned man." His institutes of Logic, expanded and illustrated, may be seen in Milton's Prose Works, by Symmons, VI. 195-353. He seems to have fallen into the common error of confounding rhetorical arrangement with logic. Of the value of his

things there are notwithstanding singular. Of marvellous quick despatch it is, and doth shew them that have it as much almost in three days, as if it dwell threescore years with them. Again, because the curiosity of man's wit doth many times with peril wade farther in the search of things than were convenient; the same is thereby restrained unto such generalities as every where offering themselves are apparent unto men of the weakest conceit that need be. So as following the rules and precepts thereof, we may define it to be, an Art which teacheth the way of speedy discourse, and restraineth the mind of man that it may not wax over-wise.

BOOK I.
Ch. vi. 5.
vii. 1.

[5.] Education and instruction are the means, the one by use, the other by precept, to make our natural faculty of reason both the better and the sooner able to judge rightly between truth and error, good and evil. But at what time a man may be said to have attained so far forth the use of reason, as sufficeth to make him capable of those Laws, whereby he is then bound to guide his actions; this is a great deal more easy for common sense to discern, than for any man by skill and learning to determine; even as it is not in philosophers, who best know the nature both of fire and of gold, to teach what degree of the one will serve to purify the other, so well as the artisan, who doth this by fire, discerneth by sense when the fire hath that degree of heat which sufficeth for his purpose.

VII. By reason man attaineth unto the knowledge of things that are and are not sensible. It resteth therefore that we search how man attaineth unto the knowledge of such things unsensible as are to be known that they may be done. Seeing then that nothing can move unless there be

Of man's Will, which is the thing that Laws of action are made to guide.

theory the following was Bacon's opinion: "De Unica Methodo, et "dichotomiis perpetuis nihil attinet "dicere: fuit enim nubecula quæ- "dam doctrinæ, quæ cito transiit; "res simul et levis et scientiis dam- "nosissima. Etenim hujusmodi "homines, cum methodi suæ legi- "bus res torqueant, et quæcumque "in dichotomias illas non apte ca- "dunt, aut omittant, aut præter "naturam inflectant, hoc efficiunt, "ut quasi nuclei et grana scientia- "rum exsiliant, ipsi aridas tantum "et desertas siliquas stringant." Further on in the same chapter he specifies Ramus as the patron of the method alluded to. De Augm. Scient. VI. 2. In his Impetus Philosophici, c. 2, he says, " Nullum "mihi commercium cum hoc igno- "rantiæ latibulo, perniciosissima "literarum tinea, compendiorum "patre," &c. Works, IX. 304. 8°. Lond. 1803. Andrew Melvin was a pupil of Ramus. Zouch's Walton, II. 134.]

some end, the desire whereof provoketh unto motion; how should that divine power of the soul, that "spirit of our "mind[1]," as the apostle termeth it, ever stir itself unto action, unless it have also the like spur? The end for which we are moved to work, is sometimes the goodness which we conceive of the very working itself, without any further respect at all; and the cause that procureth action is the mere desire of action, no other good besides being thereby intended. Of certain turbulent wits it is said, "Illis quieta "movere magna merces videbatur[2]:" they thought the very disturbance of things established an hire sufficient to set them on work. Sometimes that which we do is referred to a further end, without the desire whereof we would leave the same undone; as in their actions that gave alms to purchase thereby the praise of men[3].

[2.] Man in perfection of nature being made according to the likeness of his Maker resembleth him also in the manner of working: so that whatsoever we work as men, the same we do wittingly work and freely; neither are we according to the manner of natural agents any way so tied, but that it is in our power to leave the things we do undone. The good which either is gotten by doing, or which consisteth in the very doing itself, causeth not action, unless apprehending it as good we so like and desire it: that we do unto any such end, the same we choose and prefer before the leaving of it undone. Choice there is not, unless the thing which we take be so in our power that we might have refused and left it. If fire consume the stubble, it chooseth not so to do, because the nature thereof is such that it can do no other. To choose is to will one thing before another. And to will is to bend our souls to the having or doing of that which they see to be good. Goodness is seen with the eye of the understanding. And the light of that eye, is reason. So that two principal fountains there are of human action, Knowledge and Will; which Will, in things tending towards any end, is termed Choice[4]. Concerning Knowledge, "Be- "hold, (saith Moses[5],) I have set before you this day good "and evil, life and death." Concerning Will, he addeth

---

[1] Eph. iv. 23.   [2] Sallust. [Cat. 21.]   [3] Matt. vi. 2.
[4] [See Arist. Eth. III. 2, 3. VI. 2.]   [5] Deut. xxx. 19.

immediately, "Choose life;" that is to say, the things that tend unto life, them choose.

[3.] But of one thing we must have special care, as being a matter of no small moment; and that is, how the Will, properly and strictly taken, as it is of things which are referred unto the end that man desireth, differeth greatly from that inferior natural desire which we call Appetite. The object of Appetite is whatsoever sensible good may be wished for; the object of Will is that good which Reason doth lead us to seek. Affections, as joy, and grief, and fear, and anger, with such like, being as it were the sundry fashions and forms of Appetite, can neither rise at the conceit of a thing indifferent, nor yet choose but rise at the sight of some things. Wherefore it is not altogether in our power, whether we will be stirred with affections or no: whereas actions which issue from the disposition of the Will are in the power thereof to be performed or stayed. Finally, Appetite is the Will's solicitor, and the Will is Appetite's controller; what we covet according to the one by the other we often reject; neither is any other desire termed properly Will, but that where Reason and Understanding, or the show of Reason, prescribeth the thing desired.

It may be therefore a question, whether those operations of men are to be counted voluntary, wherein that good which is sensible provoketh Appetite, and Appetite causeth action, Reason being never called to counsel; as when we eat or drink, and betake ourselves unto rest, and such like. The truth is, that such actions in men having attained to the use of Reason are voluntary. For as the authority of higher powers hath force even in those things, which are done without their privity, and are of so mean reckoning that to acquaint them therewith it needeth not; in like sort, voluntarily we are said to do that also, which the Will if it listed might hinder from being done, although about the doing thereof we do not expressly use our reason or understanding, and so immediately apply our wills thereunto. In cases therefore of such facility, the Will doth yield her assent as it were with a kind of silence, by not dissenting; in which respect her force is not so apparent as in express mandates or prohibitions, especially upon advice and consultation going before.

BOOK I.
Ch. vii. 4-6.

[4.] Where understanding therefore needeth, in those things Reason is the director of man's Will by discovering in action what is good. For the Laws of well-doing are the dictates of right Reason. Children, which are not as yet come unto those years whereat they may have; again, innocents, which are excluded by natural defect from ever having; thirdly, madmen, which for the present cannot possibly have the use of right Reason to guide themselves, have for their guide the Reason that guideth other men, which are tutors over them to seek and to procure their good for them. In the rest there is that light of Reason, whereby good may be known from evil, and which discovering the same rightly is termed right.

[5.] The Will notwithstanding doth not incline to have or do that which Reason teacheth to be good, unless the same do also teach it to be possible. For albeit the Appetite, being more general, may wish any thing which seemeth good, be it never so impossible[1]; yet for such things the reasonable Will of man doth never seek. Let Reason teach impossibility in any thing, and the Will of man doth let it go; a thing impossible it doth not affect, the impossibility thereof being manifest.

[6.] There is in the Will of man naturally that freedom, whereby it is apt to take or refuse any particular object whatsoever being presented unto it[2]. Whereupon it followeth,

---

[1] O mihi præteritos referat si Jupiter annos! [Virg. Æn. viii. 560.]

[2] [Chr. Letter, p. 11: "Heere "we pray your helpe to teach us, "how will is *apt* (as you say) freelie "to take or refuse anie particular "object whatsoever, and that reason "by diligence is able to find out any "good concerning us: if it be true "that the Church of England pro- "fesseth, that without the prevent- "ing and helping grace of God, we "can will and doe nothing pleasing "to God."

Hooker, MS. note. "There are "certaine wordes, as Nature, Rea- "son, Will, and such like, which "wheresoever you find named, you "suspect them presently as bugs "wordes*, because what they mean "you do not indeed as you ought "apprehend. You have heard "that man's Nature is corrupt, his "Reason blind, his Will perverse. "Whereupon under coulour of con- "demning corrupt Nature, you con- "demn Nature, and so in the rest."

"Vide Hilarium, p. 31." (Ed. Basil. 1570; p. 822. ed. Bened.) "Vide et Philon. p. 33." (Ed. Paris, 1552.) "et Dionys. p. 338." (Par. 1562.)

"Voluntas hominis natura sua "non ligatur, sed vi vitiositatis quæ "naturæ accessit.

"'Apt,' originaliter apta, *able*. Ra- "tio divinis instructa auxiliis potest "omne bonum necessarium invenire,

* ["These are bugs words." Beaum. and Fletch., Tamer tamed, Act. I. Sc. 3.]

that there is no particular object so good, but it may have the shew of some difficulty or unpleasant quality annexed to it, in respect whereof the Will may shrink and decline it; contrariwise (for so things are blended) there is no particular evil which hath not some appearance of goodness whereby to insinuate itself. For evil as evil cannot be desired[1]: if that be desired which is evil, the cause is the goodness which is or seemeth to be joined with it. Goodness doth not move by being, but by being apparent; and therefore many things are neglected which are most precious, only because the value of them lieth hid. Sensible Goodness is most apparent, near, and present; which causeth the Appetite to be therewith strongly provoked. Now pursuit and refusal in the Will do follow, the one the affirmation the other the negation of goodness, which the understanding apprehendeth[2], grounding itself upon sense, unless some higher Reason do chance to teach the contrary. And if Reason have taught it rightly to be good, yet not so apparently that the mind receiveth it with utter impossibility of being otherwise, still there is place left for the Will to take or leave. Whereas therefore amongst so many things as are to be done, there are so few, the goodness whereof Reason in such sort doth or easily can discover, we are not to marvel at the choice of evil even then when the contrary is probably known. Hereby it cometh to pass that custom inuring the mind by long practice, and so leaving there a sensible impression, prevaileth more than reasonable

"destituta nullum. Habet tamen "omne bonum satis quidem in se "quo probare se possit homini se- "dulo diligenterque attendenti. Sed "nostra nos alio segnities avertit, "donec studium virtutis Spiritus "Sanctus excitat. Vide Cyprianum "de sua conversione." (Ad Donatum, Opp. p. 3. ed. Fell.) "Item ea "quæ Sapientia de se profitetur in li- "bro Proverbiorum atque alibi. Est "itaque segnis humana ratio propter "summam bonarum rerum investi- "gandarum difficultatem. Eam dif- "ficultatem tollit lumen divinæ gra- "tiæ. Hinc alacres efficimur, alioqui "a labore ad libidinem prociives. "Habet virtus vitio et plura et "fortiora quæ hominem alliciant.

"Sed ea latent maximam partem "hominum. Quid ita? Quia Ratio, "quæ est oculus mentis, alto in nobis "somno sepulta jacet otiose. At ex- "citata et illuminata Sancti Spiritus "virtute omnia dijudicat, et quæ "prius ignota fastidio fuerunt, ea "nunc perspecta modis omnibus "amplectenda decernit."]

[1] Εἰ δέ τις ἐπὶ κακίαν ὁρμᾷ, πρῶτον μὲν οὐχ ὡς ἐπὶ κακίαν αὐτὴν ὁρμήσει, ἀλλ' ὡς ἐπ' ἀγαθόν. Paulo post: 'Ἀδύνατον γὰρ ὁρμᾶν ἐπὶ κακὰ βουλόμενον ἔχειν αὐτά, οὔτε ἐλπίδι ἀγαθοῦ οὔτε φόβῳ μείζονος κακοῦ. Alcin. de Dog. Plat. [c. 38. ed. Oxon. 1667.]

[2] [Arist. Eth. Nic. VI. 2: Ὅπερ ἐν διανοίᾳ κατάφασις καὶ ἀπόφασις, τοῦτο ἐν ὀρέξει δίωξις καὶ φυγή.]

persuasion what way soever. Reason therefore may rightly discern the thing which is good, and yet the Will of man not incline itself thereunto, as oft as the prejudice of sensible experience doth oversway.

[7.] Nor let any man think that this doth make any thing for the just excuse of iniquity. For there was never sin committed, wherein a less good was not preferred before a greater, and that wilfully; which cannot be done without the singular disgrace of Nature, and the utter disturbance of that divine order, whereby the preeminence of chiefest acceptation is by the best things worthily challenged. There is not that good which concerneth us, but it hath evidence enough for itself, if Reason were diligent to search it out. Through neglect thereof, abused we are with the show of that which is not; sometimes the subtilty of Satan inveigling us as it did Eve[1], sometimes the hastiness of our Wills preventing the more considerate advice of sound Reason, as in the Apostles[2], when they no sooner saw what they liked not, but they forthwith were desirous of fire from heaven; sometimes the very custom of evil making the heart obdurate against whatsoever instructions to the contrary, as in them over whom our Saviour spake weeping[3], "O Jerusalem, how often, and "thou wouldest not!" Still therefore that wherewith we stand blameable, and can no way excuse it, is, In doing evil, we prefer a less good before a greater, the greatness whereof is by reason investigable and may be known. The search of knowledge is a thing painful; and the painfulness of knowledge is that which maketh the Will so hardly inclinable thereunto. The root hereof, divine malediction; whereby the instruments[4] being weakened wherewithal the soul (especially in reasoning) doth work, it preferreth rest in ignorance before wearisome labour to know. For a spur of diligence therefore we have a natural thirst after knowledge ingrafted in us. But by reason of that original weakness in the instruments, without which the understanding part is not

---

[1] 2 Cor. xi. 3.   [2] Luke ix. 54.
[3] Matt. xxiii. 37.
[4] "A corruptible body is heavy "unto the soul, and the earthly "mansion keepeth down the mind "that is full of cares. And hardly "can we discern the things that are "upon earth, and with great labour "find we out the things which are "before us. Who can then seek "out the things that are in heaven?" Sap. ix. 15, 16.

able in this world by discourse to work, the very conceit of painfulness is as a bridle to stay us. For which cause the Apostle, who knew right well that the weariness of the flesh is an heavy clog to the Will, striketh mightily upon this key, "Awake thou that sleepest; Cast off all which presseth "down; Watch; Labour; Strive to go forward, and to "grow in knowledge[1]."

BOOK I.
Ch. viii. 1.

VIII. Wherefore to return to our former intent of discovering the natural way, whereby rules have been found out concerning that goodness wherewith the Will of man ought to be moved in human actions; as every thing naturally and necessarily doth desire the utmost good and greatest perfection whereof Nature hath made it capable, even so man. Our felicity therefore being the object and accomplishment of our desire, we cannot choose but wish and covet it. All particular things which are subject unto action, the Will doth so far forth incline unto, as Reason judgeth them the better for us, and consequently the more available to our bliss. If Reason err, we fall into evil, and are so far forth deprived of the general perfection we seek. Seeing therefore that for the framing of men's actions the knowledge of good from evil is necessary, it only resteth that we search how this may be had. Neither must we suppose that there needeth one rule to know the good and another the evil by[2]. For he that knoweth what is straight doth even thereby discern what is crooked, because the absence of straightness in bodies capable thereof is crookedness. Goodness in actions is like unto straightness; wherefore that which is done well we term *right*. For as the straight way is most acceptable to him that travelleth, because by it he cometh soonest to his journey's end; so in action, that which doth lie the evenest between us and the end we desire must needs be the fittest for our use. Besides which fitness for use, there is also in rectitude, beauty; as contrariwise in obliquity, deformity. And that which is good in the actions of men, doth not only delight as profitable, but as amiable also. In which consideration the Grecians most divinely have given to the active perfection of

Of the natural way of finding out Laws by Reason to guide the Will unto that which is good.

---

[1] Eph. v. 14; Heb. xii. 1, 12; 1 Cor. xvi. 13; Prov. ii. 4; Luke xiii. 24.
[2] Τῷ εὐθεῖ καὶ αὐτὸ καὶ τὸ καμ- πύλον γινώσκομεν· κριτὴς γὰρ ἀμ- φοῖν ὁ κανών. Arist. de An. lib. i. [cap. 3. t. 85.]

VOL. I. Q

BOOK I.
Ch. viii. 2, 3.

men a name expressing both beauty and goodness[1], because goodness in ordinary speech is for the most part applied only to that which is beneficial. But we in the name of goodness do here imply both.

[2.] And of discerning goodness there are but these two ways; the one the knowledge of the causes whereby it is made such; the other the observation of those signs and tokens, which being annexed always unto goodness, argue that where they are found, there also goodness is, although we know not the cause by force whereof it is there. The former of these is the most sure and infallible way, but so hard that all shun it, and had rather walk as men do in the dark by haphazard, than tread so long and intricate mazes for knowledge' sake. As therefore physicians are many times forced to leave such methods of curing as themselves know to be the fittest, and being overruled by their patients' impatiency are fain to try the best they can, in taking that way of cure which the cured will yield unto; in like sort, considering how the case doth stand with this present age full of tongue and weak of brain, behold we yield to the stream thereof; into the causes of goodness we will not make any curious or deep inquiry; to touch them now and then it shall be sufficient, when they are so near at hand that easily they may be conceived without any far-removed discourse: that way we are contented to prove, which being the worse in itself, is notwithstanding now by reason of common imbecility the fitter and likelier to be brooked[2].

[3.] Signs and tokens to know good by are of sundry kinds; some more certain and some less. The most certain token of evident goodness is, if the general persuasion of all men do so account it. And therefore a common received error is never utterly overthrown, till such time as we go from signs unto causes, and shew some manifest root or fountain thereof common unto all, whereby it may clearly appear how it hath come to pass that so many have been overseen. In which case surmises and slight probabilities will not serve, because the universal consent of men is the perfectest and strongest in this kind, which comprehendeth

---

[1] Καλοκαγαθία.
[2] [Arist. Eth. Nic. I. 4, 5. ed.

Cardwell: Ἴσως οὖν ἡμῖν γε ἀρκτέον ἀπὸ τῶν ἡμῖν γνωρίμων.]

only the signs and tokens of goodness. Things casual do vary, and that which a man doth but chance to think well of cannot still have the like hap. Wherefore although we know not the cause, yet thus much we may know; that some necessary cause there is, whensoever the judgments of all men generally or for the most part run one and the same way, especially in matters of natural discourse. For of things necessarily and naturally done there is no more affirmed but this, "They keep "either always or for the most part one tenure[1]." The general and perpetual voice of men is as the sentence of God himself[2]. For that which all men have at all times learned, Nature herself must needs have taught[3]; and God being the author of Nature, her voice is but his instrument. By her from Him we receive whatsoever in such sort we learn. Infinite duties there are, the goodness whereof is by this rule sufficiently manifested, although we had no other warrant besides to approve them. The Apostle St. Paul having speech concerning the heathen saith of them[4], "They are a law unto "themselves." His meaning is, that by force of the light of Reason, wherewith God illuminateth every one which cometh into the world, men being enabled to know truth from false-

[1] *Ἡ ἀεὶ ἢ ὡς ἐπὶ τὸ πολὺ ὡσαύτως ἀποβαίνει. Arist. Rhet. l. i. [c. 10.]
[2] ["Vox populi, vox Dei." The origin of the saying is obscure. It was current in the middle ages, as "*Scriptura:*" v. Eadmer, Hist. Nov. i. 42.]
[3] "Non potest error contingere "ubi omnes idem [ita] opinantur." Monticat.* in 1. Polit. [p. 3] "Quic- "quid in omnibus individuis unius "speciei communiter inest, id cau- "sam communem habeat oportet, "quæ est eorum individuorum spe- "cies et natura." Idem. "Quod "a tota aliqua specie fit, universalis "particularisque naturæ fit in- "stinctu." ["Meminisse debemus "vaticinium illud, Quod a tota aliqua "animalium specie fit, quia univer- "salis particularisque fit instinctu, "verum existere."] Ficin. de Christ.

Rel. [cap. 1.] "Si proficere cupis, "primo firme id verum puta, quod "sana mens omnium hominum "attestatur." Cusa in Compend. cap. 1. [D. Nicolai de Cusa Cardinalis, utriusque juris Doctoris, omnique philosophia incomparabilis viri Opera. Basil. 1565. Compendium; Directio veritatis, p. 239. See Cave Hist. Lit. t. I. App. 130.] "Non licet naturale universaleque "hominum judicium falsum va- "numque existimare." Teles. [Bernardi Telesii, Consentini, de Rerum Natura juxta propria principia Libri ix, Neapoli 1586. On this writer's method of philosophizing see a dissertation in Bacon's works, ix. 332.] Ὁ γὰρ πᾶσι δοκεῖ, τοῦτο εἶναι φαμέν. Ὁ δὲ ἀναιρῶν ταύτην τὴν πίστιν οὐ πάνυ πιστότερα ἐρεῖ. Arist. Eth. lib. x. cap. 2.   [4] Rom. ii. 14.

* [Antonio Montecatini, Professor of Civil Law at Ferrara (1568-1597), published Comm. on Aristot. Politics. Ferrara, 1587. Marsilius Ficinus, Florentine Platonist (1433-1499). *De religione Christiana.* Flor. 1474. Cardinal Nicolas Cusa (1401-1464). Bernardino Telesio of Cosenza (1509-1588), a reformer of natural philosophy.]

hood, and good from evil, do thereby learn in many things what the will of God is; which will himself not revealing by any extraordinary means unto them, but they by natural discourse attaining the knowledge thereof, seem the makers of those Laws which indeed are his, and they but only the finders of them out.

[4.] A law therefore generally taken, is a directive rule unto goodness of operation. The rule of divine operations outward, is the definitive appointment of God's own wisdom set down within himself. The rule of natural agents that work by simple necessity, is the determination of the wisdom of God, known to God himself the principal director of them, but not unto them that are directed to execute the same. The rule of natural agents which work after a sort of their own accord, as the beasts do, is the judgment of common sense or fancy concerning the sensible goodness of those objects wherewith they are moved. The rule of ghostly or immaterial natures, as spirits and angels, is their intuitive intellectual judgment concerning the amiable beauty and high goodness of that object, which with unspeakable joy and delight doth set them on work. The rule of voluntary agents on earth is the sentence that Reason giveth concerning the goodness of those things which they are to do. And the sentences which Reason giveth are some more some less general, before it come to define in particular actions what is good.

[5.] The main principles of Reason are in themselves apparent. For to make nothing evident of itself unto man's understanding were to take away all possibility of knowing any thing. And herein that of Theophrastus is true, "They "that seek a reason of all things do utterly overthrow "Reason[1]." In every kind of knowledge some such grounds there are, as that being proposed the mind doth presently embrace them as free from all possibility of error, clear and manifest without proof. In which kind axioms or principles more general are such as this, "that the greater "good is to be chosen before the less." If therefore it should be demanded what reason there is, why the Will of Man, which doth necessarily shun harm and covet whatso-

---

[1] Ἀπάντων ζητοῦντες λόγον, ἀναιροῦσι λόγον. Theoph. in Metaph. [p. 270. 23.]

ever is pleasant and sweet, should be commanded to count the pleasures of sin gall, and notwithstanding the bitter accidents wherewith virtuous actions are compassed, yet still to rejoice and delight in them: surely this could never stand with Reason, but that wisdom thus prescribing groundeth her laws upon an infallible rule of comparison; which is, "That small difficulties, when exceeding great good is sure "to ensue, and on the other side momentany benefits, when "the hurt which they draw after them is unspeakable, are not "at all to be respected." This rule is the ground whereupon the wisdom of the Apostle buildeth a law, enjoining patience unto himself[1]; "The present lightness of our affliction worketh "unto us even with abundance upon abundance an eternal "weight of glory; while we look not on the things which are "seen, but on the things which are not seen: for the things "which are seen are temporal, but the things which are not "seen are eternal:" therefore Christianity to be embraced, "whatsoever calamities in those times it was accompanied withal. Upon the same ground our Saviour proveth the law most reasonable, that doth forbid those crimes which men for gain's sake fall into. "For a man to win the world if it be "with the loss of his soul, what benefit or good is it[2]?" Axioms less general, yet so manifest that they need no further proof, are such as these, "God to be worshipped;" "parents to "be honoured;" "others to be used by us as we ourselves "would by them." Such things, as soon as they are alleged, all men acknowledge to be good; they require no proof or further discourse to be assured of their goodness.

Notwithstanding whatsoever such principle there is, it was at the first found out by discourse, and drawn from out of the very bowels of heaven and earth. For we are to note, that things in the world are to us discernible, not only so far forth as serveth for our vital preservation, but further also in a twofold higher respect. For first if all other uses were utterly taken away, yet the mind of man being by nature speculative and delighted with contemplation in itself, they were to be known even for mere knowledge and understanding's sake. Yea further besides this, the knowledge of every the least

BOOK I.
Ch. viii. 5.

---

[1] 2 Cor. iv. 17. [2] Matt. xvi. 26.

thing in the whole world hath in it a second peculiar benefit unto us, inasmuch as it serveth to minister rules, canons, and laws, for men to direct those actions by, which we properly term human. This did the very heathens themselves obscurely insinuate, by making *Themis*, which we call *Jus*, or Right, to be the daughter of heaven and earth [1].

[6.] We know things either as they are in themselves, or as they are in mutual relation one to another. The knowledge of that which man is in reference unto himself, and other things in relation unto man, I may justly term the mother of all those principles, which are as it were edicts, statutes, and decrees, in that Law of Nature, whereby human actions are framed. First therefore having observed that the best things, where they are not hindered, do still produce the best operations, (for which cause, where many things are to concur unto one effect, the best is in all congruity of reason to guide the residue, that it prevailing most, the work principally done by it may have greatest perfection:) when hereupon we come to observe in ourselves, of what excellency our souls are in comparison of our bodies, and the diviner part in relation unto the baser of our souls; seeing that all these concur in producing human actions, it cannot be well unless the chiefest do command and direct the rest [2]. The soul then ought to conduct the body, and the spirit of our minds [3] the soul. This is therefore the first Law, whereby the highest power of the mind requireth general obedience at the hands of all the rest concurring with it unto action.

[7.] Touching the several grand mandates, which being imposed by the understanding faculty of the mind must be obeyed by the Will of Man, they are by the same method found out, whether they import our duty towards God or towards man.

Touching the one, I may not here stand to open, by what degrees of discourse the minds even of mere natural men have attained to know, not only that there is a God, but also what power, force, wisdom, and other properties that God hath, and how all things depend on him. This being therefore presupposed, from that known relation which God hath

---

[1] [Hesiod. Theog. 126, 133, 135.]   [2] Arist. Pol. i. cap. 5.   [3] [Eph. iv. 23.]

The Love of God and of our Neighbour. 231

unto us as unto children[1], and unto all good things as unto effects whereof himself is the principal cause[2], these axioms and laws natural concerning our duty have arisen, "that in all "things we go about his aid is by prayer to be craved[3]:" "that "he cannot have sufficient honour done unto him, but the "utmost of that we can do to honour him we must[4];" which is in effect the same that we read[5], "Thou shalt love the Lord "thy God with all thy heart, with all thy soul, and with all thy "mind:" which Law our Saviour doth term[6] "The first and "the great commandment."

BOOK I.
Ch. viii. 7.

Touching the next, which as our Saviour addeth is "like "unto this," (he meaneth in amplitude and largeness, inasmuch as it is the root out of which all Laws of duty to menward have grown, as out of the former all offices of religion towards God,) the like natural inducement hath brought men to know that it is their duty no less to love others than themselves. For seeing those things which are equal must needs all have one measure; if I cannot but wish to receive all good, even as much at every man's hand as any man can wish unto his own soul, how should I look to have any part of my desire herein satisfied, unless myself be careful to satisfy the like desire which is undoubtedly in other men, we all being of one and the same nature? To have any thing offered them repugnant to this desire must needs in all respects grieve them as much as me: so that if I do harm I must look to suffer; there being no reason that others should shew greater measure of love to me than they have by me shewed unto them. My desire therefore to be loved of my equals in nature as much as possible may be, imposeth upon me a natural duty of bearing to them-ward fully the like affection. From which relation of equality between ourselves and them that are as ourselves, what several rules and canons natural Reason hath drawn for direction of life no man is ignorant; as namely, "That because we would take no harm, we must

---

[1] Οὐδεὶς Θεὸς δύσνους ἀνθρώποις. Plat. in Theæt. [t. i. 151. ed. Serrani.]
[2] Ὅ τε γὰρ Θεὸς δοκεῖ τὸ αἴτιον πᾶσιν εἶναι καὶ ἀρχή τις. Arist. Metaph. lib. i. cap. 2. [t. ii. 485.]
[3] Ἀλλ', ὦ Σώκρατες, τοῦτό γε δὴ πάντες, ὅσοι καὶ κατὰ βραχὺ σωφροσύνης μετέχουσιν, ἐπὶ πάσῃ ὁρμῇ καὶ σμικροῦ καὶ μεγάλου πράγματος Θεὸν ἀεί που καλοῦσι. Plat. in Tim. [t. iii. 27.]
[4] Arist. Ethic. lib. iii. cap. ult.
[5] Deut. vi. 5.
[6] Matt. xxii. 38.

BOOK I.
Ch. viii. 8.

"therefore do none;" "That sith we would not be in any "thing extremely dealt with, we must ourselves avoid all "extremity in our dealings;" "That from all violence and "wrong we are utterly to abstain[1];" with such like; which further to wade in would be tedious, and to our present purpose not altogether so necessary, seeing that on these two general heads already mentioned all other specialities are dependent[2].

[8.] Wherefore the natural measure whereby to judge our doings, is the sentence of Reason, determining and setting down what is good to be done. Which sentence is either mandatory, shewing what must be done; or else permissive, declaring only what may be done; or thirdly admonitory, opening what is the most convenient for us to do. The first taketh place, where the comparison doth stand altogether between doing and not doing of one thing which in itself is absolutely good or evil; as it had been for Joseph[3] to yield or not to yield to the impotent desire of his lewd mistress, the one evil the other good simply. The second is, when of divers things evil, all being not evitable, we are permitted to take one; which one saving only in case of so great urgency were not otherwise to be taken; as in the matter of divorce amongst the Jews[4]. The last, when of divers things good, one is principal and most eminent; as in their act who sold their possessions and laid the price at the Apostles' feet[5]; which possessions they might have retained unto themselves without sin: again, in the Apostle St. Paul's own choice[6] to maintain himself by his own labour; whereas in living by the Church's maintenance, as others did, there had been no offence committed[7]. In Goodness therefore there is a latitude or extent, whereby it cometh to pass that even of good actions some are better than other some; whereas

---

[1] "Quod quis in se approbat, in "alio reprobare non posse." L. *in arenam*, C. de inof. test. [Cod. Just. p. 254. ed. Lugd. 1553.] "Quod quisque juris in alium sta-"tuerit, ipsum quoque eodem uti "debere." L. *quod quisque*. [Digest. lib. ii. tit. 2. tom. 1. p. 60. Lugd. 1552.] "Ab omni penitus "injuria atque vi abstinendum." L. i. sect. 1. *Quod vi, aut clam.*

[Ibid. lib. xliii. tit. 23. tom. 3. p. 335.]
[2] "On these two commandments "hangeth the whole Law." Matt. xxii. 40.
[3] Gen. xxxix. 9.
[4] Mark x. 4.
[5] Acts iv. 37; v. 4.
[6] 2 Thess. iii. 8.
[7] [See note, b. ii. c. 8. § 5.]

otherwise one man could not excel another, but all should be either absolutely good, as hitting jump that indivisible point or centre wherein goodness consisteth ; or else missing it they should be excluded out of the number of well-doers. Degrees of well-doing there could be none, except perhaps in the seldomness and oftenness of doing well. But the nature of Goodness being thus ample, a Law is properly that which Reason in such sort defineth to be good that it must be done. And the Law of Reason or human Nature is that which men by discourse of natural Reason have rightly found out themselves to be all for ever bound unto in their actions.

[9.] Laws of Reason have these marks to be known by. Such as keep them resemble most lively in their voluntary actions that very manner of working which Nature herself doth necessarily observe in the course of the whole world. The works of Nature are all behoveful, beautiful, without superfluity or defect; even so theirs, if they be framed according to that which the Law of Reason teacheth. Secondly, those Laws are investigable by Reason, without the help of Revelation supernatural and divine. Finally, in such sort they are investigable, that the knowledge of them is general, the world hath always been acquainted with them ; according to that which one in Sophocles observeth concerning a branch of this Law, "It is no child of to-day's or yesterday's birth, "but hath been no man knoweth how long sithence[1]." It is not agreed upon by one, or two, or few, but by all. Which we may not so understand, as if every particular man in the whole world did know and confess whatsoever the Law of Reason doth contain ; but this Law is such that being proposed no man can reject it as unreasonable and unjust. Again, there is nothing in it but any man (having natural perfection of wit and ripeness of judgment) may by labour and travail find out. And to conclude, the general principles thereof are such, as it is not easy to find men ignorant of them, Law rational therefore, which men commonly use to call the Law of Nature, meaning thereby the Law which human Nature knoweth itself in reason universally bound unto, which also

[1] Οὐ γάρ τι νῦν γε κἀχθὲς, ἀλλ' ἀεί ποτε
Ζῇ ταῦτα, κοὐδεὶς οἶδεν ἐξ ὅτου 'φάνη.
                Soph. Antig. [v. 456.]

for that cause may be termed most fitly the Law of Reason; this Law, I say, comprehendeth all those things which men by the light of their natural understanding evidently know, or at leastwise may know, to be beseeming or unbeseeming, virtuous or vicious, good or evil for them to do.

[10.] Now although it be true, which some have said [1], that "whatsoever is done amiss, the Law of Nature and "Reason thereby is transgressed," because even those offences which are by their special qualities breaches of supernatural laws, do also, for that they are generally evil, violate in general that principle of Reason, which willeth universally to fly from evil: yet do we not therefore so far extend the Law of Reason, as to contain in it all manner laws whereunto reasonable creatures are bound, but (as hath been shewed) we restrain it to those only duties, which all men by force of natural wit either do or might understand to be such duties as concern all men. "Certain half-waking "men there are" (as Saint Augustine noteth [2]), "who neither "altogether asleep in folly, nor yet throughly awake in the "light of true understanding, have thought that there is not "at all any thing just and righteous in itself; but look, "wherewith nations are inured, the same they take to be "right and just. Whereupon their conclusion is, that seeing "each sort of people hath a different kind of right from other, "and that which is right of its own nature must be every-"where one and the same, therefore in itself there is nothing "right. These good folk," saith he, ("that I may not trouble "their wits with rehearsal of too many things,) have not "looked so far into the world as to perceive that, 'Do as thou "wouldest be done unto,' is a sentence which all nations

---

[1] Th. 1. 2. q. 94. art. 3. [tom. xi. 204.] "Omnia peccata sunt in "universum contra rationem et "naturæ legem." Aug. de Civit. Dei, l. xii. cap. 1. "Omne vitium "naturæ nocet, ac per hoc contra "naturam est." [tom. vii. 301.]

[2] De Doctr. Christ. l. iii. c. 14. [tom. iii. 51. "Quidam dormi-"tantes, ut ita dicam, qui neque 'alto somno stultitiæ sopiebantur, "nec in sapientiæ lucem poterant "evigilare, putaverunt nullam esse "justitiam per se ipsam, sed uni-"cuique genti consuetudinem suam "justam videri; quæ cum sit di-"versa omnibus gentibus, debeat "autem incommutabilis manere "justitia, fieri manifestum, nullam "usquam esse justitiam. Non in-"tellexerunt, (ne multa commemo-"rem,) 'Quod tibi fieri non vis, alii "ne feceris,' nullo modo posse ulla "eorum gentili diversitate variari. "Quæ sententia cum refertur ad "dilectionem Dei, omnia flagitia "moriuntur; cum ad proximi, om-"nia facinora."]

Law of Reason transgressed through ill Custom. 235

"under heaven are agreed upon. Refer this sentence to the "love of God, and it extinguisheth all heinous crimes; refer "it to the love of thy neighbour, and all grievous wrongs it "banisheth out of the world." Wherefore as touching the Law of Reason, this was (it seemeth) Saint Augustine's judgment: namely, that there are in it some things which stand as principles universally agreed upon; and that out of those principles, which are in themselves evident, the greatest moral duties we owe towards God or man may without any great difficulty be concluded.

[11.] If then it be here demanded, by what means it should come to pass (the greatest part of the Law moral being so easy for all men to know) that so many thousands of men notwithstanding have been ignorant even of principal moral duties, not imagining the breach of them to be sin: I deny not but lewd and wicked custom, beginning perhaps at the first amongst few, afterwards spreading into greater multitudes, and so continuing from time to time, may be of force even in plain things to smother the light of natural understanding; because men will not bend their wits to examine whether things wherewith they have been accustomed be good or evil. For example's sake, that grosser kind of heathenish idolatry, whereby they worshipped the very works of their own hands, was an absurdity to reason so palpable, that the Prophet David comparing idols and idolaters together maketh almost no odds between them, but the one in a manner as much without wit and sense as the other; "They that make them are like unto them, and so are all "that trust in them[1]." That wherein an idolater doth seem so absurd and foolish is by the Wise Man thus exprest[2], "He is not ashamed to speak unto that which hath no life, "he calleth on him that is weak for health, he prayeth for "life unto him which is dead, of him which hath no expe- "rience he requireth help, for his journey he sueth to him "which is not able to go, for gain and work and success in "his affairs he seeketh furtherance of him that hath no "manner of power." The cause of which senseless stupidity is afterwards imputed to custom[3]. "When a father mourned "grievously for his son that was taken away suddenly, he

---

[1] Psal. cxxxv. 18.   [2] Wisd. xiii. 17.   [3] Wisd. xiv. 15, 16.

BOOK I.
Ch. viii. 11.

"made an image for him that was once dead, whom now he "worshippeth as a god, ordaining to his servants ceremonies "and sacrifices. Thus by process of time this wicked custom "prevailed, and was kept as a law;" the authority of rulers, the ambition of craftsmen, and such like means thrusting forward the ignorant, and increasing their superstition.

Unto this which the Wise Man hath spoken somewhat besides may be added. For whatsoever we have hitherto taught, or shall hereafter, concerning the force of man's natural understanding, this we always desire withal to be understood; that there is no kind of faculty or power in man or any other creature, which can rightly perform the functions allotted to it, without perpetual aid and concurrence of that Supreme Cause of all things. The benefit whereof as oft as we cause God in his justice to withdraw, there can no other thing follow than that which the Apostle noteth, even men endued with the light of reason to walk notwithstanding[1] "in the vanity of their mind, having their cogitations dark-"ened, and being strangers from the life of God through the "ignorance which is in them, because of the hardness of "their hearts." And this cause is mentioned by the prophet Esay[2], speaking of the ignorance of idolaters, who see not how the manifest Law of Reason condemneth their gross iniquity and sin. "They have not in them," saith he, "so "much wit as to think, 'Shall I bow to the stock of a tree?' "All knowledge and understanding is taken from them; for "God hath shut their eyes that they cannot see."

That which we say in this case of idolatry serveth for all other things, wherein the like kind of general blindness hath prevailed against the manifest Laws of Reason. Within the compass of which laws we do not only comprehend whatsoever may be easily known to belong to the duty of all men, but even whatsoever may possibly be known to be of that quality, so that the same be by *necessary* consequence deduced out of clear and manifest principles. For if once we descend unto probable collections what is convenient for men, we are then in the territory where free and arbitrary determinations, the territory where Human Laws take place; which laws are after to be considered.

[1] Ephes. iv. 17, 18. [2] Isa. xliv. 18, 19.

IX. Now the due observation of this Law which Reason teacheth us cannot but be effectual unto their great good that observe the same. For we see the whole world and each part thereof so compacted, that as long as each thing performeth only that work which is natural unto it, it thereby preserveth both other things and also itself. Contrariwise, let any principal thing, as the sun, the moon, any one of the heavens or elements, but once cease or fail, or swerve, and who doth not easily conceive that the sequel thereof would be ruin both to itself and whatsoever dependeth on it? And is it possible, that Man being not only the noblest creature in the world, but even a very world in himself, his transgressing the Law of his Nature should draw no manner of harm after it? Yes[1], "tribulation and anguish "unto every soul that doeth evil." Good doth follow unto all things by observing the course of their nature, and on the contrary side evil by not observing it; but not unto natural agents that good which we call Reward, not that evil which we properly term Punishment. The reason whereof is, because amongst creatures in this world, only Man's observation of the Law of his Nature is Righteousness, only Man's transgression Sin. And the reason of this is the difference in his manner of observing or transgressing the Law of his Nature. He doth not otherwise than voluntarily the one or the other. What we do against our wills, or constrainedly, we are not properly said to do it, because the motive cause of doing it is not in ourselves, but carrieth us, as if the wind should drive a feather in the air, we no whit furthering that whereby we are driven. In such cases therefore the evil which is done moveth compassion; men are pitied for it, as being rather miserable in such respect than culpable. Some things are likewise done by man, though not through outward force and impulsion, though not against, yet without their wills; as in alienation of mind, or any the like inevitable utter absence of wit and judgment. For which cause, no man did ever think the hurtful actions of furious men and innocents to be punishable. Again, some things we do neither against nor without, and yet not simply and merely with our wills, but with our wills in such sort moved, that

BOOK I.
Ch. ix. 1.

The benefit of keeping that Law which Reason teacheth.

[1] Rom. ii. 9.

BOOK I.
Ch. ix. 2.

albeit there be no impossibility but that we might, nevertheless we are not so easily able to do otherwise. In this consideration one evil deed is made more pardonable than another. Finally, that which we do being evil, is notwithstanding by so much more pardonable, by how much the exigence of so doing or the difficulty of doing otherwise is greater; unless this necessity or difficulty have originally risen from ourselves. It is no excuse therefore unto him, who being drunk committeth incest, and allegeth that his wits were not his own; inasmuch as himself might have chosen whether his wits should by that mean have been taken from him. Now rewards and punishments do always presuppose something willingly done well or ill; without which respect though we may sometimes receive good or harm, yet then the one is only a benefit and not a reward, the other simply an hurt not a punishment. From the sundry dispositions of man's Will, which is the root of all his actions, there groweth variety in the sequel of rewards and punishments, which are by these and the like rules measured: "Take away the will, and all acts are equal: That which we "do not, and would do, is commonly accepted as done[1]." By these and the like rules men's actions are determined of and judged, whether they be in their own nature rewardable or punishable.

[2.] Rewards and punishments are not received, but at the hands of such as being above us have power to examine and judge our deeds. How men come to have this authority one over another in external actions, we shall more diligently examine in that which followeth. But for this present, so much all do acknowledge, that sith every man's heart and conscience doth in good or evil, even secretly committed and known to none but itself, either like or disallow itself, and accordingly either rejoice, very nature exulting (as it were) in certain hope of reward, or else grieve (as it were) in a sense of future punishment; neither of which can in this case be looked for from any other, saving only from Him who discerneth and judgeth the very secrets of all hearts:

---

[1] "Voluntate sublata, omnem ac-"tum parem esse." L. *fœdissi-mam*, c. *de adult.* [Cod. Justin. 968.]

"Bonam voluntatem plerumque pro "facto reputari." L. *si quis in testament.* [Ibid. 732.]

therefore He is the only rewarder and revenger of all such BOOK I. actions; although not of such actions only, but of all whereby Ch. x. 1. the Law of Nature is broken whereof Himself is author. For which cause, the Roman laws, called The Laws of the Twelve Tables, requiring offices of inward affection which the eye of man cannot reach unto, threaten the neglecters of them with none but divine punishment[1].

X. That which hitherto we have set down is (I hope) How Reasufficient to shew their brutishness, which imagine that religion and virtue are only as men will account of them; that we might make as much account, if we would, of the contrary, without any harm unto ourselves, and that in nature they are as indifferent one as the other. We see then how nature itself teacheth laws and statutes to live by. The laws which have been hitherto mentioned do bind men absolutely even as they are men, although they have never any settled fellowship, never any solemn agreement amongst themselves what to do or not to do[2]. But forasmuch as we are not by ourselves sufficient to furnish ourselves with competent store of things needful for such a life as our nature doth desire, a life fit for the dignity of man; therefore to supply those defects and imperfections which are in us living single and solely by ourselves, we are naturally induced to seek communion and fellowship with others. This was the cause of men's uniting themselves at the first in politic Societies, which societies could not be without Government, nor Government without a distinct kind of Law from that which hath been already declared. Two foundations there are which bear up public societies; the one, a natural inclination, whereby all men desire sociable life and fellowship; the other, an order expressly or secretly agreed upon touching the manner of their union in living together. The latter is that which we call the Law of a Commonweal, the very soul of a politic body, the parts whereof are by law animated, held together, and set on work in such actions, as the common good requireth. Laws politic, ordained for external order and regiment amongst men, are never framed as they

How Reason doth lead men unto the making of human laws whereby politic Societies are governed; and to agreement about laws whereby the fellowship or communion of independent societies standeth.

[1] "Divos caste adeunto, pietatem "adhibento: qui secus faxit, Deus "ipse vindex erit." [Cic. de Leg. II. 8.]

[2] Ἔστι γὰρ, ὃ μαντεύονταί τι πάντες φύσει κοινὸν δίκαιον καὶ ἄδικον, κἂν μηδεμία κοινωνία πρὸς ἀλλήλους ᾖ μηδὲ συνθήκη. Arist. Rhet. i. [c. 13.]

BOOK I.
Ch. x. 2.

should be, unless presuming the will of man to be inwardly obstinate, rebellious, and averse from all obedience unto the sacred laws of his nature; in a word, unless presuming man to be in regard of his depraved mind little better than a wild beast, they do accordingly provide notwithstanding so to frame his outward actions, that they be no hindrance unto the common good for which societies are instituted: unless they do this, they are not perfect. It resteth therefore that we consider how nature findeth out such laws of government as serve to direct even nature depraved to a right end.

[2.] All men desire to lead in this world a happy life. That life is led most happily, wherein all virtue is exercised without impediment or let. The Apostle[1], in exhorting men to contentment although they have in this world no more than very bare food and raiment, giveth us thereby to understand that those are even the lowest of things necessary; that if we should be stripped of all those things without which we might possibly be, yet these must be left; that destitution in these is such an impediment, as till it be removed suffereth not the mind of man to admit any other care. For this cause, first God assigned Adam maintenance of life, and then appointed him a law to observe[2]. For this cause, after men began to grow to a number, the first thing we read they gave themselves unto was the tilling of the earth and the feeding of cattle. Having by this mean whereon to live, the principal actions of their life afterward are noted by the exercise of their religion[3]. True it is, that the kingdom of God must be the first thing in our purposes and desires[4]. But inasmuch as righteous life presupposeth life; inasmuch as to live virtuously it is impossible except we live; therefore the first impediment, which naturally we endeavour to remove, is penury and want of things without which we cannot live. Unto life many implements are necessary; moe, if we seek (as all men naturally do) such a life as hath in it joy, comfort, delight, and pleasure. To this end we see how quickly sundry arts mechanical were found out, in the very prime of the world[5]. As things of greatest

[1] 1 Tim. vi. 8. [2] Gen. i. 29; ii. 17. [3] Gen. iv. 2, 26.
[4] Matt. vi. 33. [5] Gen. iv. 20, 21, 22.

necessity are always first provided for, so things of greatest dignity are most accounted of by all such as judge rightly. Although therefore riches be a thing which every man wisheth, yet no man of judgment can esteem it better to be rich, than wise, virtuous, and religious. If we be both or either of these, it is not because we are so born. For into the world we come as empty of the one as of the other, as naked in mind as we are in body. Both which necessities of man had at the first no other helps and supplies than only domestical; such as that which the Prophet implieth, saying, "Can a mother forget her child[1]?" such as that which the Apostle mentioneth, saying, "He that careth not for his "own is worse than an infidel[2];" such as that concerning Abraham, "Abraham will command his sons and his house-"hold after him, that they keep the way of the Lord[3]."

[3.] But neither that which we learn of ourselves nor that which others teach us can prevail, where wickedness and malice have taken deep root. If therefore when there was but as yet one only family in the world, no means of instruction human or divine could prevent effusion of blood[4]; how could it be chosen but that when families were multiplied and increased upon earth, after separation each providing for itself, envy, strife, contention and violence must grow amongst them? For hath not Nature furnished man with wit and valour, as it were with armour, which may be used as well unto extreme evil as good? Yea, were they not used by the rest of the world unto evil; unto the contrary only by Seth, Enoch, and those few the rest in that line[5]? We all make complaint of the iniquity of our times: not unjustly; for the days are evil. But compare them with those times wherein there were no civil societies, with those times wherein there was as yet no manner of public regiment established, with those times wherein there were not above eight persons righteous living upon the face of the earth[6]; and we have surely good cause to think that God hath blessed us exceedingly, and hath made us behold most happy days.

[4.] To take away all such mutual grievances, injuries, and wrongs, there was no way but only by growing unto com-

---

[1] Isa. xlix. 15. [2] 1 Tim. v. 8. [3] Gen. xviii. 19.
[4] Gen. iv. 8. [5] Gen. vi. 5; Gen. v. [6] 2 Pet. ii. 5.

BOOK I.
Ch. x. 4.

position and agreement amongst themselves, by ordaining some kind of government public, and by yielding themselves subject thereunto; that unto whom they granted authority to rule and govern, by them the peace, tranquillity, and happy estate of the rest might be procured. Men always knew that when force and injury was offered they might be defenders of themselves; they knew that howsoever men may seek their own commodity, yet if this were done with injury unto others it was not to be suffered, but by all men and by all good means to be withstood; finally they knew that no man might in reason take upon him to determine his own right, and according to his own determination proceed in maintenance thereof, inasmuch as every man is towards himself and them whom he greatly affecteth partial; and therefore that strifes and troubles would be endless, except they gave their common consent all to be ordered by some whom they should agree upon: without which consent there were no reason that one man should take upon him to be lord or judge over another; because, although there be according to the opinion of some very great and judicious men a kind of natural right in the noble, wise, and virtuous, to govern them which are of servile disposition[1]; nevertheless for manifestation of this their right, and men's more peaceable contentment on both sides, the assent of them who are to be governed seemeth necessary.

To fathers within their private families Nature hath given a supreme power; for which cause we see throughout the world even from the foundation thereof, all men have ever been taken as lords and lawful kings in their own houses. Howbeit over a whole grand multitude having no such dependency upon any one, and consisting of so many families as every politic society in the world doth, impossible it is that any should have complete lawful power, but by consent of men, or immediate appointment of God; because not having the natural superiority of fathers, their power must needs be either usurped, and then unlawful; or, if lawful, then either granted or consented unto by them over whom they exercise the same, or else given extraordinarily from God, unto whom all the world is subject. It is no improbable opinion therefore which the arch-philosopher was of, that as the chiefest person

[1] Arist. Polit. lib. iii. et iv.

in every household was always as it were a king, so when numbers of households joined themselves in civil society together, kings were the first kind of governors amongst them[1]. Which is also (as it seemeth) the reason why the name of *Father* continued still in them, who of fathers were made rulers; as also the ancient custom of governors to do as Melchisedec, and being kings to exercise the office of priests, which fathers did at the first, grew perhaps by the same occasion.

Howbeit not this the only kind of regiment that hath been received in the world. The inconveniences of one kind have caused sundry other to be devised. So that in a word all public regiment of what kind soever seemeth evidently to have risen from deliberate advice, consultation, and composition between men, judging it convenient and behoveful; there being no impossibility in nature considered by itself, but that men might have lived without any public regiment. Howbeit, the corruption of our nature being presupposed, we may not deny but that the Law of Nature doth now require of necessity some kind of regiment, so that to bring things unto the first course they were in, and utterly to take away all kind of public government in the world, were apparently to overturn the whole world.

[5.] The case of man's nature standing therefore as it doth, some kind of regiment the Law of Nature doth require; yet the kinds thereof being many, Nature tieth not to any one, but leaveth the choice as a thing arbitrary. At the first when some certain kind of regiment was once approved, it may be that nothing was then further thought upon for the manner of governing, but all permitted unto their wisdom and discretion which were to rule[2]; till by experience they found this for all parts very inconvenient, so as the thing which they had devised for a remedy did indeed but increase the sore which it should have cured. They saw that to live by one man's will became the cause of all men's misery. This constrained

---

[1] Arist. Polit. lib. i. cap. 2. Vide et Platonem in 3. de Legibus. [t. ii. 680.]

[2] "Cum premeretur initio multitudo ab iis qui majores opes habebant, ad unum aliquem confugiebant virtute præstantem, qui cum prohiberet injuria tenuiores, æquitate constituenda summos cum infimis pari jure retinebat. Cum id minus contingeret, leges sunt inventæ." Cic. Offic. lib. ii. [c. 12.]

BOOK I.
Ch. x. 6, 7.

them to come unto laws, wherein all men might see their duties beforehand, and know the penalties of transgressing them. If things be simply good or evil, and withal universally so acknowledged, there needs no new law to be made for such things[1]. The first kind therefore of things appointed by laws human containeth whatsoever being in itself naturally good or evil, is notwithstanding more secret than that it can be discerned by every man's present conceit, without some deeper discourse and judgment. In which discourse because there is difficulty and possibility many ways to err, unless such things were set down by laws, many would be ignorant of their duties which now are not, and many that know what they should do would nevertheless dissemble it, and to excuse themselves pretend ignorance and simplicity, which now they cannot[2].

[6.] And because the greatest part of men are such as prefer their own private good before all things, even that good which is sensual before whatsoever is most divine; and for that the labour of doing good, together with the pleasure arising from the contrary, doth make men for the most part slower to the one and proner to the other, than that duty prescribed them by law can prevail sufficiently with them: therefore unto laws that men do make for the benefit of men it hath seemed always needful to add rewards, which may more allure unto good than any hardness deterreth from it, and punishments, which may more deter from evil than any sweetness thereto allureth. Wherein as the generality is natural, *virtue rewardable and vice punishable;* so the particular determination of the reward or punishment belongeth unto them by whom laws are made. Theft is naturally punishable, but the kind of punishment is positive, and such lawful as men shall think with discretion convenient by law to appoint.

[7.] In laws, that which is natural bindeth universally, that which is positive not so. To let go those kind of positive

---

[1] Τὸ γονέας τιμᾶν καὶ φίλους εὐποιεῖν καὶ τοῖς εὐεργέταις χάριν ἀποδιδόναι, ταῦτα καὶ τὰ τούτοις ὅμοια οὐ προστάττουσι τοῖς ἀνθρώποις οἱ γεγραμμένοι νόμοι ποιεῖν, ἀλλ' εὐθὺς ἀγράφῳ καὶ κοινῷ νόμῳ νομίζεται. Arist. Rhet. ad Alex. [c. 2.]

[2] "Tanta est enim vis voluptatum, ut et ignorantiam protelet in tum, ut et conscientiam corrumpat in dissimulationem." Tertull. lib. de Spectacul. [c. 1.]

laws which men impose upon themselves, as by vow unto God, contract with men, or such like; somewhat it will make unto our purpose, a little more fully to consider what things are incident into the making of the positive laws for the government of them that live united in public society. Laws do not only teach what is good, but they enjoin it, they have in them a certain constraining force. And to constrain men unto any thing inconvenient doth seem unreasonable. Most requisite therefore it is that to devise laws which all men shall be forced to obey none but wise men be admitted. Laws are matters of principal consequence; men of common capacity and but ordinary judgment are not able (for how should they?) to discern what things are fittest for each kind and state of regiment. We cannot be ignorant how much our obedience unto laws dependeth upon this point. Let a man though never so justly oppose himself unto them that are disordered in their ways, and what one amongst them commonly doth not stomach at such contradiction, storm at reproof, and hate such as would reform them? Notwithstanding even they which brook it worst that men should tell them of their duties, when they are told the same by a law, think very well and reasonably of it. For why? They presume that the law doth speak with all indifferency; that the law hath no side-respect to their persons; that the law is as it were an oracle proceeded from wisdom and understanding [1].

[8.] Howbeit laws do not take their constraining force from the quality of such as devise them, but from that power which doth give them the strength of laws. That which we spake before concerning the power of government must here be applied unto the power of making laws whereby to govern; which power God hath over all: and by the natural law, whereunto he hath made all subject, the lawful power of making laws to command whole politic societies of men belongeth so properly unto the same entire societies, that for any prince or potentate of what kind soever upon earth to exercise the same of himself, and not either by express commission immediately and personally received from God, or else by authority derived at the first from

[1] [Arist. Eth. Nic. x. c. ix. 12.]

their consent upon whose persons they impose laws, it is no better than mere tyranny.

Laws they are not therefore which public approbation hath not made so. But approbation not only they give who personally declare their assent by voice sign or act, but also when others do it in their names by right originally at the least derived from them. As in parliaments, councils, and the like assemblies, although we be not personally ourselves present, notwithstanding our assent is by reason of others agents there in our behalf. And what we do by others, no reason but that it should stand as our deed, no less effectually to bind us than if ourselves had done it in person. In many things assent is given, they that give it not imagining they do so, because the manner of their assenting is not apparent. As for example, when an absolute monarch commandeth his subjects that which seemeth good in his own discretion, hath not his edict the force of a law whether they approve or dislike it? Again, that which hath been received long sithence and is by custom now established, we keep as a law which we may not transgress; yet what consent was ever thereunto sought or required at our hands?

Of this point therefore we are to note, that sith men naturally have no full and perfect power to command whole politic multitudes of men, therefore utterly without our consent we could in such sort be at no man's commandment living. And to be commanded we do consent, when that society whereof we are part hath at any time before consented, without revoking the same after by the like universal agreement. Wherefore as any man's deed past is good as long as himself continueth; so the act of a public society of men done five hundred years sithence standeth as theirs who presently are of the same societies, because corporations are immortal; we were then alive in our predecessors, and they in their successors do live still. Laws therefore human, of what kind soever, are available by consent.

[9.] If here it be demanded how it cometh to pass that this being common unto all laws which are made, there should be found even in good laws so great variety as there is; we must note the reason hereof to be the sundry particular ends, whereunto the different disposition of that subject or matter, for which laws are provided, causeth them to have especial respect in making laws. A law there is mentioned amongst the Grecians whereof Pittacus is reported to have been author; and by that law it was agreed, that he which being overcome with drink did then strike any man, should suffer punishment double as much as if he had done the same being sober[1]. No man could ever have thought this reasonable, that had intended thereby only to punish the injury committed according to the gravity of the fact: for who knoweth not that harm advisedly done is naturally less pardonable, and therefore worthy of the sharper punishment? But forasmuch as none did so usually this way offend as men in that case, which they wittingly fell into, even because they would be so much the more freely outrageous; it was for their public good where such disorder was grown to frame a positive law for remedy thereof accordingly. To this appertain those known laws of making laws; as that law-makers must have an eye to the place where, and to the men amongst whom; that one kind of laws cannot serve for all kinds of regiment; that where the multitude beareth sway, laws that shall tend unto preservation of that state must make common smaller offices to go by lot, for fear of strife and division likely to arise; by reason that ordinary qualities sufficing for discharge of such offices, they could not but by many be desired, and so with danger contended for, and not missed without grudge and discontentment, whereas at an uncertain lot none can find themselves grieved, on whomsoever it lighteth; contrariwise the greatest, whereof but few are capable, to pass by popular election, that neither the people may envy such as have those honours, inasmuch as themselves bestow them, and that the chiefest may be kindled with desire to exercise all parts of rare and beneficial virtue, knowing they shall not lose their labour by growing in fame and estimation amongst the people: if the helm of chief government be in the hands of a few of the wealthiest, that then laws providing for continuance thereof must make the punishment of contumely and wrong offered

[1] Arist. Polit. lib. ii. cap. ult.

BOOK I.
Ch. x. 10.

unto any of the common sort sharp and grievous, that so the evil may be prevented whereby the rich are most likely to bring themselves into hatred with the people, who are not wont to take so great offence when they are excluded from honours and offices, as when their persons are contumeliously trodden upon. In other kinds of regiment the like is observed concerning the difference of positive laws, which to be every where the same is impossible and against their nature.

[10.] Now as the learned in the laws[1] of this land observe, that our statutes sometimes are only the affirmation or ratification of that which by common law was held before; so here it is not to be omitted that generally all laws human, which are made for the ordering of politic societies, be either such as establish some duty whereunto all men by the law of reason did before stand bound; or else such as make that a duty now which before was none. The one sort we may for distinction's sake call "mixedly," and the other "merely" human. That which plain or necessary reason bindeth men unto may be in sundry considerations expedient to be ratified by human law. For example, if confusion of blood in marriage, the liberty of having many wives at once, or any other the like corrupt and unreasonable custom doth happen to have prevailed far, and to have gotten the upper hand of right reason with the greatest part; so that no way is left to rectify such foul disorder without prescribing by law the same things which reason necessarily *doth* enforce but is not *perceived* that so it doth; or if many be grown unto that which the Apostle did lament in some, concerning whom he writeth, saying, that "even what things they naturally know, "in those very things as beasts void of reason they corrupted "themselves[2];" or if there be no such special accident, yet forasmuch as the common sort are led by the sway of their

---

[1] Staundf. Preface to the Pleas of the Crown. ["Citavi non pauca e "Bractono et Britono, vetustis le-"gum scriptoribus, hoc nimirum "consilio: ut cum leges coronæ "magna ex parte jure statutario "constant, ponatur ante legentis "oculos commune jus, quod fuit "ante ea statuta condita. Nam ea "res maxime conducit recte inter-"pretandis statutis. Id enim intel-"ligenti statim occurrunt mala quæ "commune jus contraxit. Pervidet "autem ille quotæ illorum malorum "parti medetur, et quotæ non; et "sitne hujusmodi statutum nova-"tum jus per se, an nihil aliud "quam communis juris affirmatio." Ed. 1574.]

[2] Jude 10.

sensual desires, and therefore do more shun sin for the sensible evils which follow it amongst men, than for any kind of sentence which reason doth pronounce against it[1]: this very thing is cause sufficient why duties belonging unto each kind of virtue, albeit the Law of Reason teach them, should notwithstanding be prescribed even by human law. Which law in this case we term *mixed*, because the matter whereunto it bindeth is the same which reason necessarily doth require at our hands, and from the Law of Reason it differeth in the manner of binding only. For whereas men before stood bound in conscience to do as the Law of Reason teacheth, they are now by virtue of human law become constrainable, and if they outwardly transgress, punishable. As for laws which are *merely* human, the matter of them is any thing which reason doth but probably teach to be fit and convenient; so that till such time as law hath passed amongst men about it, of itself it bindeth no man. One example whereof may be this. Lands are by human law in some places after the owner's decease divided unto all his children, in some all descendeth to the eldest son. If the Law of Reason did necessarily require but the one of these two to be done, they which by law have received the other should be subject to that heavy sentence, which denounceth against all that decree wicked, unjust, and unreasonable things, *woe*[2]. Whereas now whichsoever be received there is no Law of Reason transgressed; because there is probable reason why either of them may be expedient, and for either of them more than probable reason there is not to be found.

[11.] Laws whether mixedly or merely human are made by politic societies: some, only as those societies are civilly united; some, as they are spiritually joined and make such a body as we call the Church. Of laws human in this latter kind we are to speak in the third book following. Let it therefore suffice thus far to have touched the force wherewith Almighty God hath graciously endued our nature, and thereby enabled the same to find out both those laws which all men generally are for ever bound to observe, and also such

---

[1] [Arist. Eth. Nic. X. 10: Οἱ πολλοὶ ἀνάγκῃ μᾶλλον ἢ λόγῳ πειθαρχοῦσι, καὶ ζημίαις ἢ τῷ καλῷ.]   [2] Isaiah x. 1.

as are most fit for their behoof, who lead their lives in any ordered state of government.

[12.] Now besides that law which simply concerneth men as men, and that which belongeth unto them as they are men linked with others in some form of politic society, there is a third kind of law which toucheth all such several bodies politic, so far forth as one of them hath public commerce with another. And this third is the Law of Nations. Between men and beasts there is no possibility of sociable communion, because the well-spring of that communion is a natural delight which man hath to transfuse from himself into others, and to receive from others into himself especially those things wherein the excellency of his kind doth most consist. The chiefest instrument of human communion therefore is speech, because thereby we impart mutually one to another the conceits of our reasonable understanding[1]. And for that cause seeing beasts are not hereof capable, forasmuch as with them we can use no such conference, they being in degree, although above other creatures on earth to whom nature hath denied sense, yet lower than to be sociable companions of man to whom nature hath given reason; it is of Adam said that amongst the beasts "he found not for "himself any meet companion[2]." Civil society doth more content the nature of man than any private kind of solitary living, because in society this good of mutual participation is so much larger than otherwise. Herewith notwithstanding we are not satisfied, but we covet (if it might be) to have a kind of society and fellowship even with all mankind. Which thing Socrates intending to signify professed himself a citizen, not of this or that commonwealth, but of the world[3]. And an effect of that very natural desire in us (a manifest token that we wish after a sort an universal fellowship with all men) appeareth by the wonderful delight men have, some to visit foreign countries, some to discover nations not heard of in former ages, we all to know the affairs and dealings of other people, yea to be in league of amity with them: and this not only for traffick's sake, or to the end that when many are confederated each may make other the more strong, but

---

[1] Arist. Polit. i. cap. 2.
[2] Gen. ii. 20.
[3] Cic. Tusc. v. [c. 37.] et i. de Legib. [c. 12.]

for such cause also as moved the Queen of Saba to visit Salomon[1]; and in a word, because nature doth presume that how many men there are in the world, so many gods as it were there are, or at leastwise such they should be towards men[2].

[13.] Touching laws which are to serve men in this behalf; even as those Laws of Reason, which (man retaining his original integrity) had been sufficient to direct each particular person in all his affairs and duties, are not sufficient but require the access of other laws, now that man and his offspring are grown thus corrupt and sinful; again, as those laws of polity and regiment, which would have served men living in public society together with that harmless disposition which then they should have had, are not able now to serve, when men's iniquity is so hardly restrained within any tolerable bounds: in like manner, the national laws of mutual[3] commerce between societies of that former and better quality might have been other than now, when nations are so prone to offer violence, injury, and wrong. Hereupon hath grown in every of these three kinds that distinction between Primary and Secondary laws; the one grounded upon sincere, the other built upon depraved nature. Primary laws of nations are such as concern embassage, such as belong to the courteous entertainment of foreigners and strangers, such as serve for commodious traffick, and the like. Secondary laws in the same kind are such as this present unquiet world is most familiarly acquainted with; I mean laws of arms, which yet are much better known than kept. But what matter the Law of Nations doth contain I omit to search.

The strength and virtue of that law is such that no particular nation can lawfully prejudice the same by any their several laws and ordinances, more than a man by his private resolutions the law of the whole commonwealth or state wherein he liveth. For as civil law, being the act of a whole body politic, doth therefore overrule each several part of the same body; so there is no reason that any one commonwealth of itself should to the prejudice of another

---

[1] 1 Kings x. 1; 2 Chron. ix. 1; Matt. xii. 42; Luke xi. 31.
[2] ["Ἄνθρωπος ἀνθρώπῳ δαιμόνιον— *Homo homini deus*: Erasm. Adag. Chil. 1. cent. 1. 69. Cf. Bacon, N. Org. i. 129.] 1886.
[3] [So 1st and 2nd edd. 'natural,' 4th ed. 1617, and so K.] 1886.

BOOK I.
Ch. x. 14.

annihilate that whereupon the whole world hath agreed. For which cause, the Lacedæmonians forbidding all access of strangers into their coasts, are in that respect both by Josephus and Theodoret deservedly blamed [1], as being enemies to that hospitality which for common humanity's sake all the nations on earth should embrace.

[14.] Now as there is great cause of communion, and consequently of laws for the maintenance of communion, amongst nations; so amongst nations Christian the like in regard even of Christianity hath been always judged needful.

And in this kind of correspondence amongst nations the force of general councils doth stand. For as one and the same law divine, whereof in the next place we are to speak, is unto all Christian churches a rule for the chiefest things; by means whereof they all in that respect make one church, as having all but "one Lord, one faith, and one baptism [2]:" so the urgent necessity of mutual communion for preservation of our unity in these things, as also for order in some other things convenient to be every where uniformly kept, maketh it requisite that the Church of God here on earth have her laws of spiritual commerce between Christian nations; laws by virtue whereof all churches may enjoy freely the use of those reverend, religious, and sacred consultations, which are termed Councils General. A thing whereof God's own blessed Spirit was the author [3]; a thing practised by the holy Apostles themselves; a thing always afterwards kept and observed throughout the world; a thing never otherwise than most highly esteemed of, till pride, ambition, and tyranny began by factious and vile endeavours to abuse that divine invention unto the furtherance of wicked purposes. But as the just authority of civil courts and parliaments is not therefore to be abolished, because sometime there is cunning used to frame them according to the private intents of men over potent in the commonwealth; so the grievous abuse which hath been of councils should rather cause men to study how so gracious a thing may again be reduced to that first perfection, than in regard of stains and blemishes sithence growing be held for ever in extreme disgrace.

[1] Joseph. lib. ii. contra Apion. Græc. Aff. [p. 611. t. iv. ed. Par. 1642.] [c. 36.] Theod. lib. ix. de sanand.   [2] Ephes. iv. 5.   [3] Acts xv. 28.

Laws supernatural relate to Man's chief Good.

To speak of this matter as the cause requireth would require very long discourse. All I will presently say is this: whether it be for the finding out of any thing whereunto divine law bindeth us, but yet in such sort that men are not thereof on all sides resolved; or for the setting down of some uniform judgment to stand touching such things, as being neither way matters of necessity, are notwithstanding offensive and scandalous when there is open opposition about them; be it for the ending of strifes, touching matters of Christian belief, wherein the one part may seem to have probable cause of dissenting from the other; or be it concerning matters of polity, order, and regiment in the church; I nothing doubt but that Christian men should much better frame themselves to those heavenly precepts, which our Lord and Saviour with so great instancy gave[1] as concerning peace and unity, if we did all concur in desire to have the use of ancient councils again renewed, rather than these proceedings continued, which either make all contentions endless, or bring them to one only determination, and that of all other the worst[2], which is by sword.

[15.] It followeth therefore that a new foundation being laid, we now adjoin hereunto that which cometh in the next place to be spoken of; namely, wherefore God hath himself by Scripture made known such laws as serve for direction of men.

XI. All things, (God only excepted,) besides the nature which they have in themselves, receive externally some perfection from other things, as hath been shewed. Insomuch as there is in the whole world no one thing great or small, but either in respect of knowledge or of use it may unto our perfection add somewhat. And whatsoever such perfection there is which our nature may acquire, the same we properly term our Good; our Sovereign Good or Blessedness, that wherein the highest degree of all our perfection consisteth, that which being once attained unto there can rest nothing further to be desired; and therefore with it our souls are fully content and satisfied, in that they have they rejoice, and thirst for no more. Wherefore of good things desired some are such that for themselves we covet them not, but only because they serve as instruments unto that for which we are

---
[1] John xiv. 27.   [2] So B.; 'worse,' A.] 1886.

BOOK I.
Ch. xi. 2.

to seek: of this sort are riches. Another kind there is, which although we desire for itself, as health, and virtue, and knowledge, nevertheless they are not the last mark whereat we aim, but have their further end whereunto they are referred, so as in them we are not satisfied as having attained the utmost we may, but our desires do still proceed. These things are linked and as it were chained one to another; we labour to eat, and we eat to live, and we live to do good, and the good which we do is as seed sown with reference to a future harvest[1]. But we must come at length to some pause. For, if every thing were to be desired for some other without any stint, there could be no certain end proposed unto our actions, we should go on we know not whither; yea, whatsoever we do were in vain, or rather nothing at all were possible to be done. For as to take away the first efficient of our being were to annihilate utterly our persons, so we cannot remove the last final cause of our working, but we shall cause whatsoever we work to cease. Therefore something there must be desired for itself simply and for no other. That is simply for itself desirable, unto the nature whereof it is opposite and repugnant to be desired with relation unto any other. The ox and the ass desire their food, neither propose they unto themselves any end wherefore; so that of them this is desired for itself; but why? By reason of their imperfection which cannot otherwise desire it; whereas that which is desired simply for itself, the excellency thereof is such as permitteth it not in any sort to be referred to a further end.

[2.] Now that which man doth desire with reference to a further end, the same he desireth in such measure as is unto that end convenient; but what he coveteth as good in itself, towards that his desire is ever infinite. So that unless the last good of all, which is desired altogether for itself, be also infinite, we do evil in making it our end; even as they who placed their felicity in wealth or honour or pleasure or any thing here attained; because in desiring any thing as our final perfection which is not so, we do amiss[2]. Nothing

---

[1] "He that soweth to the Spirit shall of the Spirit reap life everlasting." Gal. vi. 8.
[2] Vide Arist. Ethic. lib. x. c. 10. [c. 7.] et Metaph. l. xii. c. 6. ["Est "aliquid, quod non motum movet; "quod æternum, et substantia, et "actus est."] et c. 4, ['Præter hæc "item [est] cuncta movens, tan- "quam omnium primum."] et c. 30.

may be infinitely desired but that good which indeed is infinite; for the better the more desirable; that therefore most desirable wherein there is infinity of goodness: so that if any thing desirable may be infinite, that must needs be the highest of all things that are desired. No good is infinite but only God; therefore he our felicity and bliss. Moreover, desire tendeth unto union with that it desireth. If then in Him we be blessed, it is by force of participation and conjunction with Him. Again, it is not the possession of any good thing can make them happy which have it, unless they enjoy the thing wherewith they are possessed. Then are we happy therefore when fully we enjoy God, as an object wherein the powers of our souls are satisfied even with everlasting delight; so that although we be men, yet by being unto God united we live as it were the life of God.

[3.] Happiness therefore is that estate whereby we attain, so far as possibly may be attained, the full possession of that which simply for itself is to be desired, and containeth in it after an eminent sort the contentation of our desires, the highest degree of all our perfection. Of such perfection capable we are not in this life. For while we are in the world, subject we are unto sundry imperfections[1], griefs of body, defects of mind; yea the best things we do are painful, and the exercise of them grievous, being continued without intermission; so as in those very actions whereby we are especially perfected in this life we are not able to persist; forced we are with very weariness, and that often, to interrupt them: which tediousness cannot fall into those operations that are in the state of bliss, when our union with God is complete. Complete union with him must be according unto every power and faculty of our minds apt to receive so glorious an object. Capable we are of God both by understanding and will: by understanding, as He is that sovereign Truth which comprehendeth the rich treasures of all wisdom; by will, as He is that sea of Goodness whereof whoso tasteth

BOOK I.
Ch. xi. 3.

---

[1] Μόνον, ὦ Ἀσκλήπιε, τὸ ὄνομα τοῦ ἀγαθοῦ ἐν ἀνθρώποις, τὸ δὲ ἔργον οὐδαμοῦ.... Τὸ μὴ λίαν κακὸν, ἐνθάδε τὸ ἀγαθόν ἐστι. Τὸ δὲ ἐνθάδε ἀγαθὸν, μόριον τοῦ κακοῦ τὸ ἐλάχιστον. Ἀδύνατον οὖν τὸ ἀγαθὸν ἐνθάδε καθαρεύειν τῆς κακίας.... Κἀγὼ δὲ χάριν ἔχω τῷ Θεῷ τῷ εἰς νοῦν μοι βαλόντι περὶ τῆς γνώσεως τοῦ ἀγαθοῦ, ὅτι ἀδύνατόν ἐστιν αὐτὸ ἐν τῷ κόσμῳ εἶναι· ὁ γὰρ κόσμος πλήρωμά ἐστι τῆς κακίας, ὁ δὲ Θεὸς τοῦ ἀγαθοῦ, ἢ τὸ ἀγαθὸν τοῦ Θεοῦ. Merc. Tris. [lib. vi. f. 14.]

BOOK I.
Ch. xi. 4.

shall thirst no more. As the will doth now work upon that object by desire, which is as it were a motion towards the end as yet unobtained; so likewise upon the same hereafter received it shall work also by love. "Appetitus inhiantis fit "amor fruentis," saith St. Augustine: "The longing dis-"position of them that thirst is changed into the sweet affec-"tion of them that taste and are replenished[1]." Whereas we now love the thing that is good, but good especially in respect of benefit unto us; we shall then love the thing that is good, only or principally for the goodness of beauty in itself. The soul being in this sort, as it is active, perfected by love of that infinite good, shall, as it is receptive, be also perfected with those supernatural passions of joy, peace, and delight. All this endless and everlasting[2]. Which perpetuity, in regard whereof our blessedness is termed "a crown which "withereth not[3]," doth neither depend upon the nature of the thing itself, nor proceed from any natural necessity that our souls should so exercise themselves for ever in beholding and loving God, but from the will of God, which doth both freely perfect our nature in so high a degree, and continue it so perfected. Under Man, no creature in the world is capable of felicity and bliss. First, because their chiefest perfection consisteth in that which is best for them, but not in that which is simply best, as ours doth. Secondly, because whatsoever external perfection they tend unto, it is not better than themselves, as ours is. How just occasion have we therefore even in this respect with the Prophet to admire the goodness of God! "Lord, what is man, that thou shouldst "exalt him above the works of thy hands[4]," so far as to make thyself the inheritance of his rest and the substance of his felicity?

[4.] Now if men had not naturally this desire to be happy, how were it possible that all men should have it? All men have. Therefore this desire in man is natural. It is not in our power not to do the same; how should it then be in our power to do it coldly or remissly? So that our desire being

---

[1] Aug. de Trin. lib. ix. c. ult. [Verbatim, "Appetitus, quo inhiatur rei "cognoscendæ, fit amor cognitæ." viii. 888.]
[2] "The just shall go into life ever-"lasting." Matt. xxv. [46.] "They "shall be as the angels of God." Matt. xxii. [30.]
[3] 2 Tim. iv. 8; 1 Pet. v. 4.
[4] Psalm viii. 4.

natural is also in that degree of earnestness whereunto nothing can be added. And is it probable that God should frame the hearts of all men so desirous of that which no man may obtain? It is an axiom of nature that natural desire cannot utterly be frustrate[1]. This desire of ours being natural should be frustrate, if that which may satisfy the same were a thing impossible for man to aspire unto. Man doth seek a triple perfection[2]: first a sensual, consisting in those things which very life itself requireth either as necessary supplements, or as beauties and ornaments thereof; then an intellectual, consisting in those things which none underneath man is either capable of or acquainted with; lastly a spiritual and divine, consisting in those things whereunto we tend by supernatural means here, but cannot here attain unto them. They that make the first of these three the scope of their whole life, are said by the Apostle[3] to have no god but only their belly, to be earthly-minded men. Unto the second they bend themselves, who seek especially to excel in all such knowledge and virtue as doth most commend men. To this branch belongeth the law of moral and civil perfection. That there is somewhat higher than either of these two, no other proof doth need than the very process of man's desire, which being natural should be frustrate, if there were not some farther thing wherein it might rest at the length contented, which in the former it cannot do. For man doth not seem to rest satisfied, either with fruition of that wherewith his life is preserved, or with performance of such actions as advance him most deservedly in estimation; but doth further covet, yea oftentimes manifestly pursue with great sedulity and earnestness, that which cannot stand him in any stead for vital use; that which exceedeth the reach of sense; yea somewhat above capacity of reason, somewhat divine and heavenly, which with hidden exultation it rather surmiseth than conceiveth; somewhat it seeketh, and what that is directly it knoweth not, yet very intentive desire thereof doth so incite it, that all other known delights and pleasures are

---

[1] [Thom. Aq.] Comment. in Prœm. ii. Metaph. ["Si comprehensio esset "impossibilis, tunc desiderium esset "otiosum: et concessum est ab om- "nibus, quod nulla res est otiosa in "fundamento naturæ et creaturæ." t. viii. p. 14, ed. Venet. 1552.]
[2] [Arist. Eth. Nic. I. v. 2.]
[3] Phil. iii. 19.

BOOK I.
Ch. xi. 5.

laid aside, they give place to the search of this but only suspected desire. If the soul of man did serve only to give him being in this life, then things appertaining unto this life would content him, as we see they do other creatures; which creatures enjoying what they live by seek no further, but in this contentation do shew a kind of acknowledgment that there is no higher good which doth any way belong unto them. With us it is otherwise. For although the beauties, riches, honours, sciences, virtues, and perfections of all men living, were in the present possession of one; yet somewhat beyond and above all this there would still be sought and earnestly thirsted for. So that Nature even in this life doth plainly claim and call for a more divine perfection than either of these two that have been mentioned.

[5.] This last and highest estate of perfection whereof we speak is received of men in the nature of a Reward[1]. Rewards do always presuppose such duties performed as are rewardable. Our natural means therefore unto blessedness are our works; nor is it possible that Nature should ever find any other way to salvation than only this. But examine the works which we do, and since the first foundation of the world what one can say, My ways are pure? Seeing then all flesh is guilty of that for which God hath threatened eternally to punish, what possibility is there this way to be saved? There resteth therefore either no way unto salvation, or if any, then surely a way which is supernatural, a way which could never have entered into the heart of man as much as once to conceive or imagine, if God himself had not revealed it extraordinarily. For which cause we term it the Mystery or secret way of salvation. And therefore St. Ambrose in this matter appealeth justly from man to God[2], "Cœli mysterium "doceat me Deus qui condidit, non homo qui seipsum igno-"ravit:—Let God himself that made me, let not man that "knows not himself, be my instructor concerning the mystical "way to heaven." "When men of excellent wit," saith Lactantius, "had wholly betaken themselves unto study, after "farewell bidden unto all kind as well of private as public "action, they spared no labour that might be spent in the

[1] "Rejoice and be glad, for great "is your reward in heaven." Matt. v. 12. "Summa merces est ut "ipso perfruamur." Aug. de Doct. Christ. cap. 6. [I. 32. t. iii. 16.]
[2] Ambros. contra Sym. [Ep. 18, § 7. t. ii. 835.]

"search of truth; holding it a thing of much more price to
"seek and to find out the reason of all affairs as well divine as
"human, than to stick fast in the toil of piling up riches and
"gathering together heaps of honours. Howbeit, they both
"did fail of their purpose, and got not as much as to quite [1]
"their charges; because truth which is the secret of the Most
"High God, whose proper handy-work all things are, cannot
"be compassed with that wit and those senses which are our
"own. For God and man should be very near neighbours,
"if man's cogitations were able to take a survey of the coun-
"sels and appointments of that Majesty everlasting. Which
"being utterly impossible, that the eye of man by itself should
"look into the bosom of divine Reason; God did not suffer
"him being desirous of the light of wisdom to stray any
"longer up and down, and with bootless expense of travail to
"wander in darkness that had no passage to get out by. His
"eyes at the length God did open, and bestow upon him the
"knowledge of the truth by way of Donative, to the end that
"man might both be clearly convicted of folly, and being
"through error out of the way, have the path that leadeth
"unto immortality laid plain before him [2]." Thus far Lactantius Firmianus, to shew that God himself is the teacher of
the truth, whereby is made known the supernatural way of
salvation and law for them to live in that shall be saved. In
the natural path of everlasting life the first beginning is that

---

[1] [So A. and B.: '*quit*,' 1617, sqq. —Cf. variation in Shakesp. Rich. II. 5. 1. 43. Qq. Rom. and Jul. 2. 4. 204, Fol. Pericl. 3. 2. 18, Qq. '*quite*,' where edd. read '*quit*.'] 1886.

[2] "Magno et excellenti ingenio "viri, cum se doctrinæ penitus de-"didissent, quicquid laboris poterat "impendi (contemptis omnibus et "privatis et publicis actionibus) ad "inquirendæ veritatis studium con-"tulerunt, existimantes multo esse "præclarius humanarum divinarum-"que rerum investigare ac scire "rationem, quam struendis opibus "aut cumulandis honoribus inhæ-"rere. Sed neque adepti sunt id "quod volebant, et operam simul "atque industriam perdiderunt: "quia veritas, id est arcanum summi "Dei qui fecit omnia, ingenio ac "propriis sensibus non potest com-"prehendi. Alioqui nihil inter "Deum hominemque distaret, si "consilia et dispositiones illius ma-"jestatis æternæ cogitatio asseque-"retur humana. Quod quia fieri "non potuit ut homini per seipsum "ratio divina notesceret, non est "passus hominem Deus lumen "sapientiæ requirentem diutius "aberrare, ac sine ullo laboris "effectu vagari per tenebras inex-"tricabiles. Aperuit oculos ejus "aliquando, et notionem veritatis "munus suum fecit, ut et huma-"nam sapientiam nullam esse mon-"straret, et erranti ac vago viam "consequendæ immortalitatis osten-"deret." Lactant. lib. i. cap. 1.

ability of doing good, which God in the day of man's creation endued him with; from hence obedience unto the will of his Creator, absolute righteousness and integrity in all his actions; and last of all the justice of God rewarding the worthiness of his deserts with the crown of eternal glory. Had Adam continued in his first estate, this had been the way of life unto him and all his posterity. Wherein I confess notwithstanding with the wittiest of the school-divines [1], "That if we speak of "strict justice, God could no way have been bound to requite "man's labours in so large and ample a manner as human "felicity doth import; inasmuch as the dignity of this "exceedeth so far the other's value. But be it that God "of his great liberality had determined in lieu of man's "endeavours to bestow the same by the rule of that justice "which best beseemeth him, namely, the justice of one that "requiteth nothing mincingly, but all with pressed and "heaped and even over-enlarged measure; yet could it never "hereupon necessarily be gathered, that such justice should "add to the nature of that reward the property of everlasting "continuance; sith possession of bliss, though it should be "but for a moment, were an abundant retribution." But we are not now to enter into this consideration, how gracious and bountiful our good God might still appear in so rewarding the sons of men, albeit they should exactly perform whatsoever duty their nature bindeth them unto. Howsoever God did propose this reward, we that were to be rewarded must have done that which is required at our hands; we failing in the one, it were in nature an impossibility that the other should be looked for. The light of nature is never able to find out any way of obtaining the reward of bliss, but by performing exactly the duties and works of righteousness.

[6.] From salvation therefore and life all flesh being

---

[1] Scot. lib. iv. Sent. dist. 49, 6. "Loquendo de stricta justitia, Deus "nulli nostrum propter quæcunque "merita est debitor perfectionis "reddendæ tam intensæ, propter "immoderatum excessum illius per-"fectionis ultra illa merita. Sed "esto quod ex liberalitate sua deter-"minasset meritis conferre actum "tam perfectum tanquam præmium, "tali quidem justitia qualis decet "eum, scilicet supererogantis in "præmiis: tamen non sequitur ex "hoc necessario, quod per illam "justitiam sit reddenda perfectio "perennis tanquam præmium, imo "abundans fieret retributio in beati-"tudine unius momenti." [p. 168. Venet. 1598.]

excluded this way, behold how the wisdom of God hath excluded this way, behold how the wisdom of God hath revealed a way mystical and supernatural, a way directing unto the same end of life by a course which groundeth itself upon the guiltiness of sin, and through sin desert of condemnation and death. For in this way the first thing is the tender compassion of God respecting us drowned and swallowed up in misery; the next is redemption out of the same by the precious death and merit of a mighty Saviour, which hath witnessed of himself, saying[1], "I am the way," the way that leadeth us from misery into bliss. This supernatural way had God in himself prepared before all worlds. The way of supernatural duty which to us he hath prescribed, our Saviour in the Gospel of St. John doth note, terming it by an excellency, The Work of God[2], "This is the work of God, "that ye believe in him whom he hath sent." Not that God doth require nothing unto happiness at the hands of men saving only a naked belief (for hope and charity we may not exclude[3]); but that without belief all other things are as nothing, and it the ground of those other divine virtues.

Concerning Faith, the principal object whereof is that eternal Verity which hath discovered the treasures of hidden wisdom in Christ; concerning Hope, the highest object whereof is that everlasting Goodness which in Christ doth quicken the dead; concerning Charity, the final object whereof is that incomprehensible Beauty which shineth in the countenance of Christ the Son of the living God: concerning these virtues, the first of which beginning here with a weak apprehension of things not seen, endeth with the intuitive vision of God in the world to come; the second beginning here with a trembling expectation of things far removed and as yet but only heard of, endeth with real and actual fruition of that which no tongue can express; the third beginning here with a weak inclination of heart towards him unto whom we are not able to approach, endeth with endless union, the

---

[1] John xiv. 6.
[2] John vi. 29.
[3] [Chr. Letter, p. 13. "Tell us ".. whether you thinke that *not* "*faith alone*, but faith, hope, and "love, be the formall cause of our "righteousness."
Hooker, MS. note. "Is faith then "the formall cause of justification? "And faith alone a cause in this "kind? Who hath taught you this "doctrine? Have you been tampering so long with Pastors, Doctors, "Elders, Deacons; that the first "principles of your religion are now "to learn?"]

BOOK I.
Ch. xii. 1.

mystery whereof is higher than the reach of the thoughts of men; concerning that Faith, Hope, and Charity, without which there can be no salvation, was there ever any mention made saving only in that law which God himself hath from heaven revealed? There is not in the world a syllable muttered with certain truth concerning any of these three, more than hath been supernaturally received from the mouth of the eternal God.

Laws therefore concerning these things are supernatural, both in respect of the manner of delivering them, which is divine; and also in regard of the things delivered, which are such as have not in nature any cause from which they flow, but were by the voluntary appointment of God ordained besides the course of nature, to rectify nature's obliquity withal.

The cause why so many natural or rational Laws are set down in Holy Scripture.

XII. When supernatural duties are necessarily exacted, natural are not rejected as needless. The law of God therefore is, though principally delivered for instruction in the one, yet fraught with precepts of the other also. The Scripture is fraught even with laws of Nature; insomuch that Gratian [1] defining Natural Right, (whereby is meant the right which exacteth those general duties that concern men naturally even as they are men,) termeth "Natural Right, that which the "Books of the Law and the Gospel do contain." Neither is it vain that the Scripture aboundeth with so great store of laws in this kind: for they are either such as we of ourselves could not easily have found out, and then the benefit is not small to have them readily set down to our hands; or if they be so clear and manifest that no man endued with reason can lightly be ignorant of them, yet the Spirit as it were borrowing them from the school of Nature, as serving to prove things less manifest, and to induce a persuasion of somewhat which were in itself more hard and dark, unless it should in such sort be cleared, the very applying of them unto cases particular is not without most singular use and profit many ways for men's instruction. Besides, be they plain of themselves or obscure, the evidence of God's own testimony added to the natural assent of reason concerning the certainty of them, doth not a little comfort and confirm the same.

[1] "Jus naturale est, quod in Lege et Evangelio continetur." p. 1, d. 1. [Corp. Jur. Can. p. 2. Lugd. 1584.]

[2.] Wherefore inasmuch as our actions are conversant about things beset with many circumstances, which cause men of sundry wits to be also of sundry judgments concerning that which ought to be done; requisite it cannot but seem the rule of divine law should herein help our imbecility, that we might the more infallibly understand what is good and what evil. The first principles of the Law of Nature are easy; hard it were to find men ignorant of them. But concerning the duty which Nature's law doth require at the hands of men in a number of things particular, so far hath the natural understanding even of sundry whole nations been darkened, that they have not discerned no not gross iniquity to be sin[1]. Again, being so prone as we are to fawn upon ourselves, and to be ignorant as much as may be of our own deformities, without the feeling sense whereof we are most wretched, even so much the more, because not knowing them we cannot so much as desire to have them taken away: how should our festered sores be cured, but that God hath delivered a law as sharp as the two-edged sword, piercing the very closest and most unsearchable corners of the heart[2], which the Law of Nature can hardly, human laws by no means possible, reach unto? Hereby we know even secret concupiscence to be sin, and are made fearful to offend though it be but in a wandering cogitation. Finally, of those things which are for direction of all the parts of our life needful, and not impossible to be discerned by the

---

[1] Joseph. lib. secundo contra Apion. [c. 37.] "Lacedæmonii quo-"modo non sunt ob inhospitalita-"tem reprehendendi, fœdumque ne-"glectum nuptiarum? Elienses vero "et Thebani ob coitum cum mascu-"lis plane impudentem et contra "naturam, quem recte et utiliter "exercere putabant? Cumque hæc "omnino perpetrarunt, etiam suis "legibus miscuere." Vid. Th. 1, 2, q. 94, 4, 5, 6. "Lex naturæ sic "corrupta fuit apud Germanos, ut "latrocinium non reputarent pecca-"tum." [t. xi. 204.] August. (aut quisquis auctor est) lib. de quæst. Nov. et Vet. Test. "Quis nesciat quid "bonæ vitæ conveniat, aut ignoret "quia quod sibi fieri non vult aliis "minime debeat facere? At vero "ubi naturalis lex evanuit oppressa "consuetudine delinquendi, tunc "oportuit manifestari scriptis, ut "Dei judicium omnes audirent "[legem manifestari, ut in Judæis "omnes homines audirent:] non "quod penitus obliterata est, sed "quia maxima ejus auctoritate care-"bant, idololatriæ studebatur, timor "Dei in terris non erat, fornicatio "operabatur, circa rem proximi "avida erat concupiscentia. Data "[danda] ergo lex erat, ut et quæ "sciebantur auctoritatem haberent, "et quæ latere cœperant manifesta-"rentur." Quæst. iv. [t. iii. App. 44.]

[2] Heb. iv. 12.

BOOK I.
Ch. xii. 3.
xiii. 1.

light of Nature itself; are there not many which few men's natural capacity, and some which no man's, hath been able to find out? They are, saith St. Augustine[1], but a few, and they endued with great ripeness of wit and judgment, free from all such affairs as might trouble their meditations, instructed in the sharpest and the subtlest points of learning, who have, and that very hardly, been able to find out but only the immortality of the soul. The resurrection of the flesh what man did ever at any time dream of, having not heard it otherwise than from the school of Nature? Whereby it appeareth how much we are bound to yield unto our Creator, the Father of all mercy, eternal thanks, for that he hath delivered his law unto the world, a law wherein so many things are laid open, clear, and manifest, as a light which otherwise would have been buried in darkness, not without the hazard, or rather not with the hazard but with the certain loss, of infinite thousands of souls most undoubtedly now saved.

[3.] We see, therefore, that our sovereign good is desired naturally; that God the author of that natural desire had appointed natural means whereby to fulfil it; that man having utterly disabled his nature unto those means hath had other revealed from God, and hath received from heaven a law to teach him how that which is desired naturally must now supernaturally be attained. Finally, we see that because those latter exclude not the former quite and clean as unnecessary, therefore together with such supernatural duties as could not possibly have been otherwise known to the world, the same law that teacheth them, teacheth also with them such natural duties as could not by light of Nature easily have been known.

The benefit of having divine laws written.

XIII. In the first age of the world God gave laws unto our fathers, and by reason of the number of their days their memories served instead of books; whereof the manifold imperfections and defects being known to God, he mercifully relieved the same by often putting them in mind of that whereof it behoved them to be specially mindful. In which respect we see how many times one thing hath been iterated unto sundry even of the best and wisest amongst them. After

---

[1] ["Humanis argumentationibus "haec invenire conantes, vix pauci "magno praediti ingenio, abundan- "tes otio, doctrinisque subtilissimis "eruditi, ad indagandam solius "animae immortalitatem pervenire "potuerunt." De Trin. lib. xiii. c. 12. tom. viii. 935.]

that the lives of men were shortened, means more durable to preserve the laws of God from oblivion and corruption grew in use, not without precise direction from God himself. First therefore of Moyses[1] it is said, that he "wrote all the words "of God[2];" not by his own private motion and device: for God taketh this act to himself[3], "I have written." Furthermore, were not the Prophets following commanded also to do the like? Unto the holy evangelist St. John, how often express charge is given, "*Scribe*," "Write these things[4]." Concerning the rest of our Lord's disciples, the words of St. Augustine are[5], "Quicquid ille de suis factis et dictis nos legere voluit, "hoc scribendum illis tanquam suis manibus imperavit."

[2.] Now, although we do not deny it to be a matter merely accidental unto the law of God to be written; although writing be not that which addeth authority and strength thereunto; finally, though his laws do require at our hands the same obedience howsoever they be delivered; his providence, notwithstanding, which hath made principal choice of this way to deliver them, who seeth not what cause we have to admire and magnify? The singular benefit that hath grown unto the world, by receiving the laws of God even by his own appointment committed unto writing, we are not able to esteem as the value thereof deserveth. When the question therefore is, whether we be now to seek for any revealed law of God otherwhere than only in the sacred Scripture; whether we do now stand bound in the sight of God to yield to traditions urged by the Church of Rome the same obedience and reverence we do to his written law, honouring equally and adoring both as divine: our answer is, No. They that so earnestly plead for the authority of tradition, as if nothing were more safely conveyed than that which spreadeth itself by report, and descendeth by relation of former generations unto the ages that succeed, are not all of them (surely a miracle it were if they should be) so simple as thus to persuade themselves; howsoever, if the simple

---

[1] [Hooker writes both *Moses* and *Moyses*, the Vulgate form, which is preserved in the French *Moïse*: *Moses*, generally in books i–iv. *Moyses*, towards the end of book v.] 1886.

[2] Exod. xxiv. 4.

[3] Hos. viii. 12. [and Exod. xxiv. 12.]

[4] Apoc. i. 11; xiv. 13.

[5] Aug. lib. i. de Cons. Evang. cap. ult. [t. iii. pars 2. p. 26.]

BOOK I.
Ch. xiii. 3.

were so persuaded, they could be content perhaps very well to enjoy the benefit, as they account it, of that common error. What hazard the truth is in when it passeth through the hands of report, how maimed and deformed it becometh, they are not, they cannot possibly be ignorant. Let them that are indeed of this mind consider but only that little of things divine, which the [1] heathen have in such sort received. How miserable had the state of the Church of God been long ere this, if wanting the sacred Scripture we had no record of his laws, but only the memory of man receiving the same by report and relation from his predecessors?

[3.] By Scripture it hath in the wisdom of God seemed meet to deliver unto the world much but personally expedient to be practised of certain men; many deep and profound points of doctrine, as being the main original ground whereupon the precepts of duty depend; many prophecies, the clear performance whereof might confirm the world in belief of things unseen; many histories to serve as looking-glasses to behold the mercy, the truth, the righteousness of God towards all that faithfully serve, obey, and honour him; yea many entire meditations of piety, to be as patterns and precedents in cases of like nature; many things needful for explication, many for application unto particular occasions, such as the providence of God from time to time hath taken to have the several books of his holy ordinance written. Be it then that together with the principal necessary laws of God there are sundry other things written, whereof we might haply be ignorant and yet be saved: what? shall we hereupon think them needless? shall we esteem them as riotous branches wherewith we sometimes behold most pleasant vines overgrown? Surely no more than we judge our hands or our eyes superfluous, or what part soever, which if our bodies did want, we might notwithstanding any such defect retain still the complete being of men. As therefore a complete

[1] I mean those historical matters concerning the ancient state of the first world, the deluge, the sons of Noah, the children of Israel's deliverance out of Egypt, the life and doings of Moses their captain, with such like: the certain truth whereof delivered in Holy Scripture is of the heathen, which had them only by report, so intermingled with fabulous vanities, that the most which remaineth in them to be seen is the show of dark and obscure steps, where some part of the truth hath gone.

it contains all Things necessary to Salvation. 267

man is neither destitute of any part necessary, and hath some BOOK I.
parts whereof though the want could not deprive him of his Ch. xiv. 1.
essence, yet to have them standeth him in singular stead in
respect of the special uses for which they serve; in like sort
all those writings which contain in them the Law of God, all
those venerable books of Scripture, all those sacred tomes and
volumes of Holy Writ, they are with such absolute perfection
framed, that in them there neither wanteth any thing the lack
whereof might deprive us of life, nor any thing in such wise
aboundeth, that as being superfluous, unfruitful, and altogether
needless, we should think it no loss or danger at all if we did
want it.

XIV. Although the Scripture of God therefore be stored The sufficiency of
with infinite variety of matter in all kinds, although it Scripture
abound with all sorts of laws, yet the principal intent of unto the
Scripture is to deliver the laws of duties supernatural. Often-which it
times it hath been in very solemn manner disputed, whether was instituted.
all things necessary unto salvation be necessarily set down
in the Holy Scriptures or no[1]. If we define that necessary
unto salvation, whereby the way to salvation is in any sort
made more plain, apparent, and easy to be known; then
is there no part of true philosophy, no art of account, no
kind of science rightly so called, but the Scripture must
contain it. If only those things be necessary, as surely none
else are, without the knowledge and practice whereof it is
not the will and pleasure of God to make any ordinary grant
of salvation; it may be notwithstanding and oftentimes hath
been demanded, how the books of Holy Scripture contain
in them all necessary things, when of things necessary the
very chiefest is to know what books we are bound to esteem
holy; which point is confessed impossible for the Scripture
itself to teach. Whereunto we may answer with truth, that
there is not in the world any art or science, which proposing
unto itself an end (as every one doth some end or other)
hath been therefore thought defective, if it have not delivered
simply whatsoever is needful to the same end; but all kinds
of knowledge have their certain bounds and limits; each

[1] "Utrum cognitio supernaturalis necessaria viatori sit sufficienter tradita in sacra Scriptura?" This question proposed by Scotus is affirmatively concluded. [In Sent. lib. i. p. 10, D. et Resp. p. 2, K.]

of them presupposeth many necessary things learned in other sciences and known beforehand. He that should take upon him to teach men how to be eloquent in pleading causes, must needs deliver unto them whatsoever precepts are requisite unto that end; otherwise he doth not the thing which he taketh upon him. Seeing then no man can plead eloquently unless he be able first to speak; it followeth that ability of speech is in this case a thing most necessary. Notwithstanding every man would think it ridiculous, that he which undertaketh by writing to instruct an orator should therefore deliver all the precepts of grammar; because his profession is to deliver precepts necessary unto eloquent speech, yet so that they which are to receive them be taught beforehand so much of that which is thereunto necessary, as comprehendeth the skill of speaking. In like sort, albeit Scripture do profess to contain in it all things that are necessary unto salvation; yet the meaning cannot be simply of all things which are necessary, but all things that are necessary in some certain kind or form; as all things which are necessary, and either could not at all or could not easily be known by the light of natural discourse; all things which are necessary to be known that we may be saved, but known with presupposal of knowledge concerning certain principles whereof it receiveth us already persuaded, and then instructeth us in all the residue that are necessary. In the number of these principles one is the sacred authority of Scripture. Being therefore persuaded by other means that these Scriptures are the oracles of God, themselves do then teach us the rest, and lay before us all the duties which God requireth at our hands as necessary unto salvation.

[2.] Further, there hath been some doubt likewise, whether *containing in Scripture* do import express setting down in plain terms, or else *comprehending* in such sort that by reason we may from thence conclude all things which are necessary. Against the former of these two constructions instance hath sundry ways been given. For our belief in the Trinity, the co-eternity of the Son of God with his Father, the proceeding of the Spirit from the Father and the Son, the duty of baptizing infants: these with such other principal points, the necessity whereof is by none denied, are notwithstanding in Scripture nowhere to be found by express literal mention, only deduced they are out of Scripture by collection. This kind of comprehension in Scripture being therefore received, still there is doubt how far we are to proceed by collection, before the full and complete measure of things necessary be made up. For let us not think that as long as the world doth endure the wit of man shall be able to sound the bottom of that which may be concluded out of the Scripture; especially if "things "contained by collection" do so far extend, as to draw in whatsoever may be at any time out of Scripture but probably and conjecturally surmised. But let *necessary* collection be made requisite, and we may boldly deny, that of all those things which at this day are with so great necessity urged upon this church under the name of reformed church-discipline, there is any one which their books hitherto have made manifest to be contained in the Scripture. Let them, if they can, allege but one properly belonging to their cause, and not common to them and us, and shew the deduction thereof out of Scripture to be necessary.

[3.] It hath been already shewed, how all things necessary unto salvation in such sort as before we have maintained must needs be possible for men to know; and that many things are in such sort necessary, the knowledge whereof is by the light of Nature impossible to be attained. Whereupon it followeth that either all flesh is excluded from possibility of salvation, which to think were most barbarous; or else that God hath by supernatural means revealed the way of life so far forth as doth suffice. For this cause God hath so many times and ways spoken to the sons of men. Neither hath he by speech only, but by writing also, instructed and taught his Church. The cause of writing hath been to the end that things by him revealed unto the world might have the longer continuance, and the greater certainty of assurance, by how much that which standeth on record hath in both those respects preeminence above that which passeth from hand to hand, and hath no pens but the tongues, no books but the ears of men to record it. The several books of Scripture having had each some several occasion and particular purpose which

BOOK I.
Ch. xiv. 4.

caused them to be written, the contents thereof are according to the exigence of that special end whereunto they are intended. Hereupon it groweth that every book of Holy Scripture doth take out of all kinds of truth, natural[1], historical[2], foreign[3], supernatural[4], so much as the matter handled requireth.

Now forasmuch as there hath been reason alleged sufficient to conclude, that all things necessary unto salvation must be made known, and that God himself hath therefore revealed his will, because otherwise men could not have known so much as is necessary; his surceasing to speak to the world, since the publishing of the Gospel of Jesus Christ and the delivery of the same in writing, is unto us a manifest token that the way of salvation is now sufficiently opened, and that we need no other means for our full instruction than God hath already furnished us withal.

[4.] The main drift of the whole New Testament is that which St. John setteth down as the purpose of his own history; [5] "These things are written, that ye might believe "that Jesus is Christ the Son of God, and that in believing "ye might have life through his name." The drift of the Old that which the Apostle mentioneth to Timothy, [6] "The "Holy Scriptures are able to make thee wise unto salvation." So that the general end both of Old and New is one; the difference between them consisting in this, that the Old did make wise by teaching salvation through Christ that should come, the New by teaching that Christ the Saviour is come, and that Jesus whom the Jews did crucify, and whom God did raise again from the dead, is he. When the Apostle therefore affirmeth unto Timothy, that the Old was able to make him wise to salvation, it was not his meaning that the Old alone can do this unto us which live sithence the publication of the New. For he speaketh with presupposal of the doctrine of Christ known also unto Timothy; and therefore first it is said, [7] "Continue thou in those things "which thou hast learned and art persuaded, knowing of "whom thou hast been taught them." Again, those Scrip-

---

[1] Eph. v. 29.   [2] 2 Tim. iii. 8.   [3] Tit. i. 12.   [4] 2 Pet. ii. 4.
[5] John xx. 31.   [6] 2 Tim. iii. 15.   [7] 2 Tim. iii. 14.

and of both with the Light of Nature. 271

tures he granteth were able to make him wise to salvation; but he addeth, [1]"through the faith which is in Christ." Wherefore without the doctrine of the New Testament teaching that Christ hath wrought the redemption of the world, which redemption the Old did foreshew he should work, it is not the former alone which can on our behalf perform so much as the Apostle doth avouch, who presupposeth this when he magnifieth that so highly. And as his words concerning the books of ancient Scripture do not take place but with presupposal of the Gospel of Christ embraced; so our own words also, when we extol the complete sufficiency of the whole entire body of the Scripture, must in like sort be understood with this caution, that the benefit of nature's light be not thought excluded as unnecessary, because the necessity of a diviner light is magnified.

[5.] There is in Scripture therefore no defect, but that any man, what place or calling soever he hold in the Church of God, may have thereby the light of his natural understanding so perfected, that the one being relieved by the other, there can want no part of needful instruction unto any good work which God himself requireth, be it natural or supernatural, belonging simply unto men as men, or unto men as they are united in whatsoever kind of society. It sufficeth therefore that Nature and Scripture do serve in such full sort, that they both jointly, and not severally either of them, be so complete, that unto everlasting felicity we need not the knowledge of any thing more than these two may easily furnish our minds with on all sides[2]; and therefore they which add traditions, as a part of supernatural necessary truth, have not the truth, but are in error. For they only plead, that whatsoever God revealeth as necessary for all

---

[1] Verse 15.

[2] [Christ. Letter, p. 7: "Although you exclude traditions as a part of supernaturall trueth, yet you infer that the light of nature teacheth some knowledge naturall whiche is necessarie to salvation." And p. 8: "What scripture approveth such a saying,.. that cases and matters of salvation bee determinable by any other lawe then of holy Scripture." Hooker, MS. note: "Remember here to show the use of the law of nature in handling matters of religion. Are there not cases of salvation wherein a man may have controversie with infidels which believe not the Scriptures? And even with them which believe Scripture the law of nature notwithstanding is not without force, that any man to whom it is alleaged can cast it of as a thing impertinent."]

BOOK I.
Ch. xv. 1.

Christian men to do or believe, the same we ought to embrace, whether we have received it by writing or otherwise; which no man denieth: when that which they should confirm, who claim so great reverence unto traditions, is, that the same traditions are necessarily to be acknowledged divine and holy. For we do not reject them only because they are not in the Scripture, but because they are neither in Scripture, nor can otherwise sufficiently by any reason be proved to be of God. That which is of God, and may be evidently proved to be so, we deny not but it hath in his kind, although unwritten, yet the selfsame force and authority with the written laws of God. It is by ours acknowledged, "that "the Apostles did in every church institute and ordain some "rites and customs serving for the seemliness of church-"regiment, which rites and customs they have not committed "unto writing[1]." Those rites and customs being known to be apostolical, and having the nature of things changeable, were no less to be accounted of in the Church than other things of the like degree; that is to say, capable in like sort of alteration, although set down in the Apostles' writings. For both being known to be apostolical, it is not the manner of delivering them unto the Church, but the author from whom they proceed, which doth give them their force and credit.

Of laws positive contained in Scripture; the mutability of certain of them, and the general use of Scripture.

XV. Laws being imposed either by each man upon himself, or by a public society upon the particulars thereof, or by all the nations of men upon every several society, or by the Lord himself upon any or every of these; there is not amongst these four kinds any one but containeth sundry both natural and positive laws. Impossible it is but that they should fall into a number of gross errors, who only take such laws for positive as have been made or invented of men, and holding this position hold also, that all positive and none but positive laws are mutable. Laws natural do always bind; laws positive not so, but only after they have been expressly and

[1] Whitakerus adversus Bellarmin. quæst. 6, cap. 6. ["Fatemur "Apostolos in singulis ecclesiis ritus "aliquos atque consuetudines, or-"dinis et decori causa, sanxisse, "non autem scripsisse: quia hi "ritus non fuerunt perpetui futuri, "sed liberi, qui pro commodo et "temporum ratione mutari pos-"sent." Controv. adv. Bellarmin. Opp. I. 372. Controv. I. quæst. 6, cap. 6. Genev. 1610.]

wittingly imposed. Laws positive there are in every of those kinds before mentioned. As in the first kind the promises which we have passed unto men, and the vows we have made unto God; for these are laws which we tie ourselves unto, and till we have so tied ourselves they bind us not. Laws positive in the second kind are such as the civil constitutions peculiar unto each particular commonweal. In the third kind the law of Heraldry in war is positive: and in the last all the judicials which God gave unto the people of Israel to observe. And although no laws but positive be mutable, yet all are not mutable which be positive. Positive laws are either permanent or else changeable, according as the matter itself is concerning which they were first made. Whether God or man be the maker of them, alteration they so far forth admit, as the matter doth exact.

[2.] Laws that concern supernatural duties are all positive[1], and either concern men supernaturally as men, or else as parts of a supernatural society, which society we call the Church. To concern men as men supernaturally is to concern them as duties which belong of necessity to all, and yet could not have been known by any to belong unto them, unless God had opened them himself, inasmuch as they do not depend upon any natural ground at all out of which they may be deduced, but are appointed of God to supply the defect of those natural ways of salvation, by which we are not now able to attain thereunto. The Church being a supernatural society doth differ from natural societies in this, that the persons unto whom we associate ourselves, in the one are men simply considered as men, but they to whom we be joined in the other, are God, Angels, and holy men. Again the Church being both a society and a society supernatural, although as it is a society it have the selfsame original

---

[1] [To prevent any misapplication of this principle, it may be useful to compare Butler's Analogy, p. ii. c. 1. § 2; where moral precepts and duties are contrasted with positive in a manner which may at first appear inconsistent with Hooker's language. But the appearance of discrepancy will perhaps be removed, if it is considered that Hooker opposes the term Positive to Natural, in regard of our ability or inability to *obtain the knowledge* of a law without express revelation: Butler on the other hand opposes Positive to Moral, in regard of our ability or inability to *discern the reasonableness* of a law *made known* to us by revelation or otherwise.]

BOOK I.
Ch. xv. 3.

grounds which other politic societies have, namely, the natural inclination which all men have unto sociable life, and consent to some certain bond of association, which bond is the law that appointeth what kind of order they shall be associated in: yet unto the Church as it is a society supernatural this is peculiar, that part of the bond of their association which belong to the Church of God must be a law supernatural, which God himself hath revealed concerning that kind of worship which his people shall do unto him. The substance of the service of God therefore, so far forth as it hath in it any thing more than the Law of Reason doth teach, may not be invented of men, as it is amongst the heathens [1], but must be received from God himself, as always it hath been in the Church, saving only when the Church hath been forgetful of her duty.

[3.] Wherefore to end with a general rule concerning all the laws which God hath tied men unto: those laws divine that belong, whether naturally or supernaturally, either to men as men, or to men as they live in politic society, or to men as they are of that politic society which is the Church, without any further respect had unto any such variable accident as the state of men and of societies of men and of the Church itself in this world is subject unto; all laws that so belong unto men, they belong for ever, yea although they be Positive Laws, unless being positive God himself which made them alter them. The reason is, because the subject or matter of laws in general is thus far forth constant: which matter is that for the ordering whereof laws were instituted, and being instituted are not changeable without cause, neither can they have cause of change, when that which gave them their first institution remaineth for ever one and the same. On the other side, laws that were made for men or societies or churches, in regard of their being such as they do not always continue, but may perhaps be clean otherwise a while after, and so may require to be otherwise ordered than before; the laws of God himself which are of this nature, no man endued with common sense will ever deny to be of a different constitution from the former, in respect of the one's

[1] "Their fear towards me was taught by the precept of men." Lea. xxix. 13.

constancy and the mutability of the other. And this doth seem to have been the very cause why St. John doth so peculiarly term the doctrine that teacheth salvation by Jesus Christ, [1]*Evangelium æternum,* " an eternal Gospel ; " because there can be no reason wherefore the publishing thereof should be taken away, and any other instead of it proclaimed, as long as the world doth continue : whereas the whole law of rites and ceremonies, although delivered with so great solemnity, is notwithstanding clean abrogated, inasmuch as it had but temporary cause of God's ordaining it.

[4.] But that we may at the length conclude this first general introduction unto the nature and original birth, as of all other laws, so likewise of those which the sacred Scripture containeth, concerning the Author whereof even infidels have confessed that He can neither err nor deceive[2]: albeit about things easy and manifest unto all men by common sense there needeth no higher consultation ; because as a man whose wisdom is in weighty affairs admired would take it in some disdain to have his counsel solemnly asked about a toy, so the meanness of some things is such, that to search the Scripture of God for the ordering of them were to derogate from the reverend authority and dignity of the Scripture, no less than they do by whom Scriptures are in ordinary talk very idly applied unto vain and childish trifles : yet better it were to be superstitious than profane; to take from thence our direction even in all things great or small, than to wade through matters of principal weight and moment, without ever caring what the law of God hath either for or against our designs. Concerning the custom of the very Painims, thus much Strabe witnesseth : " Men that are civil do lead their lives after one " common law appointing them what to do. For that other-" wise a multitude should with harmony amongst themselves " concur in the doing of one thing, (for this is civilly to live,) " or that they should in any sort manage community of life, " it is not possible. Now laws or statutes are of two sorts. " For they are either received from gods, or else from men.

---

[1] Apoc. xiv. 6.
[2] Κομιδῇ ἄρα ὁ Θεὸς ἁπλοῦν καὶ ἀληθὲς ἔν τε ἔργῳ καὶ ἐν λόγῳ, καὶ οὔτε αὐτὸς μεθίσταται οὔτε ἄλλους ἐξαπατᾷ, οὔτε κατὰ φαντασίας οὔτε κατὰ λόγους οὔτε κατὰ σημείων πομπὰς, οὔθ' ὕπαρ οὔτ' ὄναρ. Plat. in fine 2 Polit. [p. 382 E.]

BOOK I.
Ch. xv. 4.

"And our ancient predecessors did surely most honour and
"reverence that which was from the gods; for which cause
"consultation with oracles was a thing very usual and frequent
"in their times[1]." Did they make so much account of the
voice of their gods, which in truth were no gods; and shall
we neglect the precious benefit of conference with those
oracles of the true and living God, whereof so great store is
left to the Church, and whereunto there is so free, so plain,
and so easy access for all men? "By thy commandments[2]"
(this was David's confession unto God) "thou hast made me
"wiser than mine enemies." Again, "I have had more
"understanding than all my teachers, because thy testimonies
"are my meditations." What pains would not they have
bestowed in the study of these books, who travelled sea and
land to gain the treasure of some few days' talk with men
whose wisdom the world did make any reckoning of? That
little which some of the heathens did chance to hear, concerning such matter as the sacred Scripture plentifully containeth, they did in wonderful sort affect; their speeches[3] as
oft as they make mention thereof are strange, and such as
themselves could not utter as they did other things, but still
acknowledged that their wits, which did every where else
conquer hardness, were with profoundness here over-matched.
Wherefore seeing that God hath endued us with sense, to the
end that we might perceive such things as this present life
doth need; and with reason, lest that which sense cannot
reach unto, being both now and also in regard of a future
estate hereafter necessary to be known, should lie obscure;
finally, with the heavenly support of prophetical revelation,
which doth open those hidden mysteries that reason could
never have been able to find out[4], or to have known the

---

[1] Πολιτικοὶ ὄντες ἀπὸ προστάγματος κοινοῦ ζῶσιν. Ἄλλως γὰρ οὐχ οἷόν τε τοὺς πολλοὺς ἕν τι κατὰ ταὐτὸ ποιεῖν ἡρμοσμένως ἀλλήλοις (ὅπερ ἦν τὸ πολιτεύεσθαι), καὶ ἄλλως πως νέμειν βίον κοινόν. Τὸ δὲ πρόσταγμα διττόν· ἢ γὰρ παρὰ θεῶν, ἢ παρὰ ἀνθρώπων. Καὶ οἵ γε ἀρχαῖοι τὸ παρὰ τῶν θεῶν ἐπρέσβευον μᾶλλον καὶ ἐσέμνυνον· καὶ διὰ τοῦτο καὶ ὁ χρηστηριαζόμενος ἦν τότε πολύς. Strab. Geogr. lib. xvi. [c. 38. t. vi. p. 361, Lips. 1811.]

[2] Psalm cxix. 98.

[3] Vide Orphei Carmina. [Cf. quotation in iv. 1. and fragments in Justin M. ad Gentes. 15, Euseb. Prop. xiii. 12, Proclus in Timæum, &c., printed in the Tauchnitz ed. of the Orphica, 1829, pp. 133-139.—1886.]

[4] Ὧν γὰρ ὁ νοῦς ἀπολείπεται, πρὸς ταῦθ' ἡ προφητεία φθάνει. Philo de Mos. [lib. ii. in init. p. 655. Paris, 1640.]

necessity of them unto our everlasting good: use we the precious gifts of God unto his glory and honour that gave them, seeking by all means to know what the will of our God is; what righteous before him; in his sight what holy, perfect, and good, that we may truly and faithfully do it.

XVI. Thus far therefore we have endeavoured in part to open, of what nature and force laws are, according unto their several kinds; the law which God with himself hath eternally set down to follow in his own works; the law which he hath made for his creatures to keep; the law of natural and necessary agents; the law which angels in heaven obey; the law whereunto by the light of reason men find themselves bound in that they are men; the law which they make by composition for multitudes and politic societies of men to be guided by; the law which belongeth unto each nation; the law that concerneth the fellowship of all; and lastly the law which God himself hath supernaturally revealed. It might peradventure have been more popular and more plausible to vulgar ears, if this first discourse had been spent in extolling the force of laws, in shewing the great necessity of them when they are good, and in aggravating their offence by whom public laws are injuriously traduced. But forasmuch as with such kind of matter the passions of men are rather stirred one way or other, than their knowledge any way set forward unto the trial of that whereof there is doubt made; I have therefore turned aside from that beaten path, and chosen though a less easy yet a more profitable way in regard of the end we propose. Lest therefore any man should marvel whereunto all these things tend, the drift and purpose of all is this, even to shew in what manner, as every good and perfect gift, so this very gift of good and perfect laws is derived from the Father of lights[1]; to teach men a reason why just and reasonable laws are of so great force, of so great use in the world; and to inform their minds with some method of reducing the laws whereof there is present controversy unto their first original causes, that so it may be in every particular ordinance thereby the better discerned, whether the same be reasonable, just, and righteous, or no. Is there any thing which can either be throughly understood or soundly judged of, till the very first causes and principles from which originally

BOOK I. Ch. xvi. 1.

A conclusion shewing how all this belongeth to the cause in question.

[1] James i. 17.

BOOK I.
Ch. xvi. 2.

it springeth be made manifest? If all parts of knowledge have been thought by wise men to be then most orderly delivered and proceeded in, when they are drawn to their first original[1]; seeing that our whole question concerneth the quality of ecclesiastical laws, let it not seem a labour superfluous that in the entrance thereunto all these several kinds of laws have been considered, inasmuch as they all concur as principles, they all have their forcible operations therein, although not all in like apparent and manifest manner. By means whereof it cometh to pass that the force which they have is not observed of many.

[2.] Easier a great deal it is for men by law to be taught what they ought to do, than instructed how to judge as they should do of law: the one being a thing which belongeth generally unto all, the other such as none but the wiser and more judicious sort can perform. Yea, the wisest are always touching this point the readiest to acknowledge, that soundly to judge of a law is the weightiest thing which any man can take upon him[2]. But if we will give judgment of the laws under which we live; first let that law eternal be always before our eyes, as being of principal force and moment to breed in religious minds a dutiful estimation of all laws, the use and benefit whereof we see; because there can be no doubt but that laws apparently good are (as it were) things copied out of the very tables of that high everlasting law; even as the book of that law hath said concerning itself, "By me kings reign, and "by me "princes "decree justice[3]." Not as if men did behold that book and accordingly frame their laws; but because it worketh in them, because it discovereth and (as it were) readeth itself to the world by them, when the laws which they make are righteous. Furthermore, although we perceive not the goodness of laws made, nevertheless sith things in themselves may have that which we peradventure discern not, should not this breed a fear in our hearts, how we speak or judge in the worse part concerning that, the unadvised

---

[1] Arist. Phys. lib. i. cap. 1. [τὸ εἰδέναι καὶ τὸ ἐπίστασθαι συμβαίνει περὶ πάσας τὰς μεθόδους, ὧν εἰσιν ἀρχαὶ ἢ αἴτια ἢ στοιχεῖα, ἐκ τοῦ ταῦτα γνωρίζειν· τότε γὰρ οἰόμεθα γιγνώσκειν ἕκαστον, ὅταν τὰ αἴτια γνωρίσωμεν τὰ πρῶτα, καὶ τὰς ἀρχὰς τὰς πρώτας, καὶ μέχρι τῶν στοιχείων.]

[2] Arist. Ethic. x. [c. 10.] Τὸ κρῖναι ὀρθῶς μέγιστον. Intelligit de legum qualitate judicium.

[3] Prov. viii. 15.

disgrace whereof may be no mean dishonour to Him, towards whom we profess all submission and awe? Surely there must be very manifest iniquity in laws, against which we shall be able to justify our contumelious invectives. The chiefest root whereof, when we use them without cause, is ignorance how laws inferior are derived from that supreme or highest law.

[3.] The first that receive impression from thence are natural agents. The law of whose operations might be haply thought less pertinent, when the question is about laws for human actions, but that in those very actions which most spiritually and supernaturally concern men, the rules and axioms of natural operations have their force. What can be more immediate to our salvation than our persuasion concerning the law[1] of Christ towards his Church? What greater assurance of love towards his Church, than the knowledge of that mystical union, whereby the Church is become as near unto Christ as any one part of his flesh is unto other? That the Church being in such sort his he must needs protect it, what proof more strong than if a manifest law so require, which law it is not possible for Christ to violate? And what other law doth the Apostle for this allege, but such as is both common unto Christ with us, and unto us with other things natural; "No man hateth his own flesh, but doth "love and cherish it[2]?" The axioms of that law therefore, whereby natural agents are guided, have their use in the moral, yea, even in the spiritual actions of men, and consequently in all laws belonging unto men howsoever.

[4.] Neither are the Angels themselves so far severed from us in their kind and manner of working, but that between the law of their heavenly operations and the actions of men in this our state of mortality such correspondence there is, as maketh it expedient to know in some sort the one, for the other's more perfect direction. Would Angels acknowledge

---

[1] [The context leads to the suspicion that Hooker wrote "the *love* of "Christ." But the original edition reads "lawe," and the list of errata at the end, which is carefully made, as appears, by the author himself, offers no correction: neither does Dr. Spenser's edition, at least the reprint of it in 1632.—Spenser's ed. 1604, reads as the first ed. "lawe." It is no doubt the right reading.—1886.]

[2] Ephes. v. 29.

BOOK I.
Ch. xvi. 5.

themselves "fellow-servants[1]" with the sons of men, but that both having one Lord, there must be some kind of law which is one and the same to both, whereunto their obedience being perfecter is to our weaker both a pattern and a spur? Or would the Apostles, speaking of that which belongeth unto saints as they are linked together in the bond of spiritual society[2], so often make mention how Angels therewith are delighted, if in things publicly done by the Church we are not somewhat to respect what the Angels of heaven do? Yea, so far hath the Apostle Saint Paul proceeded, as to signify[3], that even about the outward orders of the Church which serve but for comeliness, some regard is to be had of Angels, who best like us when we are most like unto them in all parts of decent demeanour. So that the law of Angels we cannot judge altogether impertinent unto the affairs of the Church of God.

[5.] Our largeness of speech how men do find out what things reason bindeth them of necessity to observe, and what it guideth them to choose in things which are left as arbitrary; the care we have had to declare the different nature of laws which severally concern all men, from such as belong unto men either civilly or spiritually associated, such as pertain to the fellowship which nations, or which Christian nations, have amongst themselves, and in the last place such as concerning every or any of these God himself hath revealed by his Holy Word: all serveth but to make manifest, that as the actions of men are of sundry distinct kinds, so the laws thereof must accordingly be distinguished. There are in men operations, some natural, some rational, some supernatural, some politic, some finally ecclesiastical: which if we measure not each by his own proper law, whereas the things themselves are so different, there will be in our understanding and judgment of them confusion.

As that first error sheweth, whereon our opposites in this cause have grounded themselves. For as they rightly maintain that God must be glorified in all things, and that the actions of men cannot tend unto his glory unless they be framed after his law; so it is their error to think that the only law which God hath appointed unto men in that behalf

---

[1] Apoc. xix. 10. [2] 1 Pet. i. 12; Ephes. iii. 10; 1 Tim. v. 21.
[3] 1 Cor. xi. 10.

is the sacred Scripture. By that which we work naturally, BOOK I. as when we breathe, sleep, move, we set forth the glory of Ch. xvi. 5. God as natural agents do[1], albeit we have no express purpose to make that our end, nor any advised determination therein to follow a law, but do that we do (for the most part) not as much as thinking thereon. In reasonable and moral actions another law taketh place; a law by the observation whereof[2] we glorify God in such sort, as no creature else under man is able to do; because other creatures have not judgment to examine the quality of that which is done by them, and therefore in that they do they neither can accuse nor approve themselves. Men do both, as the Apostle teacheth; yea, those men which have no written law of God to shew what is good or evil, carry written in their hearts the universal law of mankind, the Law of Reason, whereby they judge as by a rule which God hath given unto all men for that purpose[3]. The law of reason doth somewhat direct men how to honour God as their Creator; but how to glorify God in such sort as is required, to the end he may be an everlasting Saviour, this we are taught by divine law, which law both ascertaineth the truth and supplieth unto us the want of that other law. So that in moral actions, divine law helpeth exceedingly the law of reason to guide man's life; but in supernatural it alone guideth.

Proceed we further; let us place man in some public society with others, whether civil or spiritual; and in this case there is no remedy but we must add yet a further law. For although even here likewise the laws of nature and reason be of necessary use, yet somewhat over and besides them is necessary, namely human and positive law, together with that law which is of commerce between grand societies, the law of nations, and of nations Christian. For which cause the law of God hath likewise said, "Let every soul be "subject to the higher powers[4]." The public power of all societies is above every soul contained in the same societies. And the principal use of that power is to give laws unto all that are under it; which laws in such case we must obey, unless there be reason shewed which may necessarily enforce that the law of Reason or of God doth enjoin the contrary.

[1] Psalm cxlviii. 7, 8, 9.   [2] Rom. i. 21.   [3] Rom. ii. 15.   [4] Rom. xiii. 1.

BOOK I.]
Ch. xvi. 6, 7.

Because except our own private and but probable resolutions be by the law of public determinations overruled, we take away all possibility of sociable life in the world. A plainer example whereof than ourselves we cannot have. How cometh it to pass that we are at this present day so rent with mutual contentions, and that the Church is so much troubled about the polity of the Church? No doubt if men had been willing to learn how many laws their actions in this life are subject unto, and what the true force of each law is, all these controversies might have died the very day they were first brought forth.

[6.] It is both commonly said, and truly, that the best men otherwise are not always the best in regard of society. The reason whereof is, for that the law of men's actions is one, if they be respected only as men; and another, when they are considered as parts of a politic body. Many men there are, than whom nothing is more commendable when they are singled; and yet in society with others none less fit to answer the duties which are looked for at their hands[1]. Yea, I am persuaded, that of them with whom in this cause we strive, there are whose betters amongst men would be hardly found, if they did not live amongst men, but in some wilderness by themselves. The cause of which their disposition so unframable unto societies wherein they live, is, for that they discern not aright what place and force these several kinds of laws ought to have in all their actions. Is there question either concerning the regiment of the Church in general, or about conformity between one church and another, or of ceremonies, offices, powers, jurisdictions in our own church? Of all these things they judge by that rule which they frame to themselves with some show of probability, and what seemeth in that sort convenient, the same they think themselves bound to practise; the same by all means they labour mightily to uphold; whatsoever any law of man to the contrary hath determined they weigh it not. Thus by following the law of private reason, where the law of public should take place, they breed disturbance.

[7.] For the better inuring therefore of men's minds with

---

[1] Πολλοὶ γὰρ ἐν μὲν τοῖς οἰκείοις πρὸς ἕτερον ἀδυνατοῦσι. Arist. Ethic. τῇ ἀρετῇ δύνανται χρῆσθαι, ἐν δὲ τοῖς lib. v. cap. 3.

the true distinction of laws, and of their several force according to the different kind and quality of our actions, it shall not peradventure be amiss to shew in some one example how they all take place. To seek no further, let but that be considered, than which there is not any thing more familiar unto us, our food.

What things are food and what are not we judge naturally by sense[1]; neither need we any other law to be our director in that behalf than the selfsame which is common unto us with beasts.

But when we come to consider of food, as of a benefit which God of his bounteous goodness hath provided for all things living[2]; the law of Reason doth here require the duty of thankfulness at our hands, towards him at whose hands we have it. And lest appetite in the use of food should lead us beyond that which is meet, we owe in this case obedience to that law of Reason, which teacheth mediocrity in meats and drinks. The same things divine law teacheth also, as at large we have shewed it doth all parts of moral duty, whereunto we all of necessity stand bound, in regard of the life to come[3].

---

[1] Job xxxiv. 3.
[2] Psalm cxlv. 15, 16.
[3] [Chr. Letter, p. 13: "If from "sound and sincere virtues (as you "say) full joy and felicitie ariseth, "and that we all of necessitie stand "bound unto all partes of morall "duetie in regarde of life to come, "and God requireth more at the "handes of men unto happines, then "such a naked beleefe, as Christ "calleth the worke of God : alas "what shall we poore sinful wretches "doe, &c." Hooker, MS. note : "Repent, and believe." And again, Chr. Letter, ib.: "Tell us ... whether "there bee not other sufficient causes "to induce a Christian to godlines "and honestie of life, such as is the "glorie of God our Father; his great "mercies in Christ ; his love to us ; "example to others, but that we "must do it to merit or to make "perfitt that which Christ hath done "for us." Hooker, MS. note : "Your godfathers and godmothers "have much to answere unto God "for not seing you better cate- "chised.

"A thing necessarie as you graunt "that by good workes we shold "seeke God's glory, shew ourselves "thankfull for his mercyes in Christ, "answer his loving kindnes to- "wardes us, and give other men "good example. If then these things "be necessarie unto eternall life, "and workes necessarily to be done "for these ends, how should workes "bee but necessary unto the last "end, seing the next and neerest "cannot be attained without them ?

"And is there neither heaven nor "hell, neither reward nor punish- "ment hereafter, to be respected "here in the leading of our lives ? "When thapostle doth deterre from "sinne, are his arguments only "these ? only these his reasons when "he stirreth unto workes of right- "eousness ?

"See Euseb. Emisenus where "he speaketh of Dorcas hir gar- "ments made for the poor." (De Init. Quadrag. Bibl. Patr. Colon. 1618, v. 551. "'Orationibus,' in- "quit, 'et eleemosynis purgantur "peccata:' per utramque ergo rem, "sed maxime per eleemosynam, Dei "misericordia requirenda est. Opor-

284 Distinctions of Laws exemplified in Laws regarding Diet.

BOOK I.
Ch. xvi. 7.

But of certain kinds of food the Jews sometime had, and we ourselves likewise have, a mystical, religious, and supernatural use, they of their paschal lamb and oblations, we of our bread and wine in the Eucharist; which use none but divine law could institute.

Now as we live in civil society, the state of the commonwealth wherein we live both may and doth require certain laws concerning food[1]; which laws, saving only that we are members of the commonwealth where they are of force, we should not need to respect as rules of action, whereas now in their place and kind they must be respected and obeyed.

Yea, the selfsame matter is also a subject wherein sometime ecclesiastical laws have place; so that unless we will be

"tet itaque ut sibi res utraque consentiat: illa rogat, hæc impetrat; illa quodammodo judicis audientiam deprecatur, hæc gratiam promeretur; illa ostium pulsat, hæc aperit; illa prodit desiderium, hæc desiderii procurat effectum: illa supplicat, sed supplicantem ista commendat. Sic laudabilis Tabitha, quæ in Actibus Apostolorum interpretata dicitur *Dorcas*, in operibus bonis vitæ diem claudens, evolante anima corpus relinquens, cum jam omnibus et operationis et vitæ renuntiasset officiis, flentes accurrunt viduæ, pauperes adgregantur tunicas et vestes quas faciebat illis Dorcas cœlo ostendentes, conveniunt Deum: testimonia meritorum clamant; defuncta operatrice, vox operum bona: quæ in sæculo gesserat consequuntur animam in aliud sæculum; consequuntur et revolvuntur; reditque de loco mortis ad vitam præstitam. Itaque indumenta pauperculis hic ostenduntur, illic operantur; hic adhuc præbent usum, illic jam tribuunt præmium: quam mira et pretiosa merita largitatis! Hic adhuc utentium algentes humeros calefaciebant, etiam illic largitricis animam refrigerabant. Unde et nos, charissimi, animas nostras morti obnoxias piis operibus suscitemus. Dabunt absque dubio æternam vitam, quæ aliquoties etiam temporariam reddiderunt." Who was author of this Homily is uncertain: evidently not Eusebius of Emesa. It might be Salvian, Eucherius of Lyons, or some other Father of the Gallican Church in the fourth or fifth century. See Cave, Hist. Lit. i. 157, and E. P. B. vi.)

On this whole subject Hooker says, "Looke S. Augustin's booke, "'De Fide et Operibus.'" (of which the following is a specimen: "Hoc est enim evangelizare Christum, non tantum dicere quæ sunt credenda de Christo, sed etiam quæ observanda ei qui accedit ad compagem corporis Christi; immo vero cuncta dicere quæ sunt credenda de Christo, non solum cujus sit filius, unde secundum divinitatem, unde secundum carnem genitus, quæ perpessus et quare, quæ sit virtus resurrectionis ejus, quod donum Spiritus promisit dederitque fidelibus; sed etiam qualia membra, quibus sit caput, quærat, instituat, diligat, liberet, atque ad æternam vitam honoremque perducat. Hæc cum dicuntur, aliquando brevius atque constrictius, aliquando latius et uberius, Christus evangelizatur; et tamen non solum quod ad fidem, verum etiam quod ad mores fidelium pertinet, non prætermittitur." t. vi. 172, F. c. ix. see also c. x.–xiv.)]

[1] [See 5 Eliz. c. 5. § 14, 15; 27 Eliz. c. 11; 35 Eliz. c. 7. § 22.]

Conclusion: Reverence due to Law generally.

authors of confusion in the Church, our private discretion, which otherwise might guide us a contrary way, must here submit itself to be that way guided, which the public judgment of the Church hath thought better. In which case that of Zonaras concerning fasts may be remembered. "Fastings "are good, but let good things be done in good and con-"venient manner. He that transgresseth in his fasting the "orders of the holy fathers," the positive laws of the Church of Christ, must be plainly told, "that good things do lose the "grace of their goodness, when in good sort they are not "performed[1]."

And as here men's private fancies must give place to the higher judgment of that Church which is in authority a mother over them; so the very actions of whole churches have, in regard of commerce and fellowship with other churches, been subject to laws concerning food, the contrary unto which laws had else been thought more convenient for them to observe; as by that order of abstinence from strangled and blood[2] may appear; an order grounded upon that fellowship which the churches of the Gentiles had with the Jews.

Thus we see how even one and the selfsame thing is under divers considerations conveyed through many laws; and that to measure by any one kind of law all the actions of men were to confound the admirable order, wherein God hath disposed all laws, each as in nature, so in degree, distinct from other.

[8.] Wherefore that here we may briefly end: of Law there can be no less acknowledged, than that her seat is the bosom of God, her voice the harmony of the world: all things in heaven and earth do her homage, the very least as feeling her care, and the greatest as not exempted from her power, both[3] Angels and men and creatures of what condition soever, though each in different sort and manner, yet all with uniform consent, admiring her as the mother of their peace and joy.

---

[1] [Καλὸν μὲν ἡ νηστεία· τὰ δὲ καλὰ καλῶς γινέσθω. Εἰ δέ τις θεσμοὺς ἀποστολικοὺς ἢ πατέρων ἁγίων παραβαίνων νηστεύει, ἀκούσεται] ὅτι οὐ καλὸν τὸ καλόν, ὅταν μὴ καλῶς γίνηται. Zonar. in Can. Apost. 66. p. 34. [ap. Beverig. Synod. t. i. p. 43.] Probably Hooker has here respect to the schismatical fasts which were practised by many of the Puritans.]

[2] Acts xv. 20.

[3] "But," 1st ed., corrected in Spenser's ed. 1604 to "both." 1886.

THE SECOND BOOK.

CONCERNING THEIR FIRST POSITION WHO URGE REFORMATION IN THE CHURCH OF ENGLAND: NAMELY, THAT SCRIPTURE IS THE ONLY RULE OF ALL THINGS WHICH IN THIS LIFE MAY BE DONE BY MEN.

THE MATTER CONTAINED IN THIS SECOND BOOK.

I. An answer to their first proof brought out of Scripture, Prov. ii. 9.
II. To their second, 1 Cor. x. 31.
III. To their third, 1 Tim. iv. 5.
IV. To their fourth, Rom. xiv. 23.
V. To their proofs out of Fathers, who dispute negatively from authority of Holy Scripture.
VI. To their proof by the Scripture's custom of disputing from divine authority negatively.
VII. An examination of their opinion concerning the force of arguments taken from human authority for the ordering of men's actions and persuasions.
VIII. A declaration what the truth is in this matter.

AS that which in the title hath been proposed for the matter whereof we treat, is only the ecclesiastical law whereby we are governed; so neither is it my purpose to maintain any other thing than that which therein truth and reason shall approve. For concerning the dealings of men who administer government, and unto whom the execution of that law belongeth; they have their Judge who sitteth in heaven, and before whose tribunal-seat they are accountable for whatsoever abuse or corruption, which (being worthily misliked in this church) the want either of care or of conscience in them hath bred. We are no patrons of those things therefore, the best defence whereof is speedy redress and amendment. That which is of God we defend, to the uttermost of that ability which he hath given; that which is otherwise, let it wither even in the root from whence it hath sprung[1]. Wherefore all these abuses being severed and set apart,

---

[1] [Acts v. 38, 39.]

First Puritan Principle: Scripture the only Rule. 287

which rise from the corruption of men and not from the laws themselves; come we to those things which in the very whole entire form of our church polity have been (as we persuade ourselves) injuriously blamed by them, who endeavour to overthrow the same, and instead thereof to establish a much worse; only through a strong misconceit they have, that the same is grounded on divine authority.

Now whether it be that through an earnest longing desire to see things brought to a peaceable end, I do but imagine the matters whereof we contend to be fewer than indeed they are; or else for that in truth they are fewer when they come to be discussed by reason, than otherwise they seem when by heat of contention they are divided into many slips, and of every branch an heap is made: surely, as now we have drawn them together, choosing out those things which are requisite to be severally all discussed, and omitting such mean specialties as are likely (without any great labour) to fall afterwards of themselves; I know no cause why either the number or the length of these controversies should diminish our hope of seeing them end with concord and love on all sides; which of his infinite love and goodness the Father of all peace and unity grant.

[2.] Unto which scope that our endeavour may the more directly tend, it seemeth fittest that first those things be examined, which are as seeds from whence the rest that ensue have grown. And of such the most general is that wherewith we are here to make our entrance: a question not moved (I think) any where in other churches, and therefore in ours the more likely to be soon (I trust) determined. The rather, for that it hath grown from no other root, than only a desire to enlarge the necessary use of the Word of God; which desire hath begotten an error enlarging it further than (as we are persuaded) soundness of truth will bear. For whereas God hath left sundry kinds of laws unto men, and by all those laws the actions of men are in some sort directed; they hold that one only law, the Scripture, must be the rule to direct in all things, even so far as to the "taking up of a rush or "straw[1]." About which point there should not need any

[1] T. C. l. ii. p. 59, 60. [The words are (p. 59,) "When he seeth "that St. Paul speaketh here of "civil, private, and indifferent ac-

BOOK II.
Ch. i. 3.

question to grow, and that which is grown might presently end, if they did yield but to these two restraints: the first is, not to extend the actions whereof they speak so low as that instance doth import of taking up a straw, but rather keep themselves at the least within the compass of moral actions, actions which have in them vice or virtue: the second, not to exact at our hands for every action the knowledge of some place of Scripture out of which we stand bound to deduce it, as by divers testimonies they seek to enforce; but rather as the truth is, so to acknowledge, that it sufficeth if such actions be framed according to the law of Reason; the general axioms, rules, and principles of which law being so frequent in Holy Scripture, there is no let but in that regard even out of Scripture such duties may be deduced by some kind of consequence, (as by long circuit of deduction it may be that even all truth out of any truth may be concluded [1],) howbeit no man bound in such sort to deduce all his actions out of Scripture, as if either the place be to him unknown whereon they may be concluded, or the reference unto that place not presently considered of, the action shall in that respect be condemned as unlawful. In this we dissent, and this we are presently to examine.

The first pretended proof of the first position out of Scripture, Prov. ii. 9.

[3.] In all parts of knowledge rightly so termed things most general are most strong. Thus it must be, inasmuch as the certainty of our persuasion touching particulars dependeth altogether upon the credit of those generalities out of which they grow. Albeit therefore every cause admit not such infallible evidence of proof, as leaveth no possibility of doubt or scruple behind it; yet they who claim the general assent

"tions, as of eating this or that kind of meat (than which there can be nothing more indifferent) he might easily have seen that the sentence of the Apostle reacheth even to his case, of taking up a straw." Which refers to Whitg. Def. 85: "It is not true that whatsoever cannot be proved in the word of God is not of faith, for then to take up a straw... were against faith, and so deadly sin, because it is not found in the Law of God." Again, T. C. ii. 60. "Seemeth it so strange a thing unto him that a man should not take up a straw but for some purpose, and for some good purpose?" &c.]

[1] [So Bishop Butler, Analogy, part I, ch. vii: "Things seemingly the most insignificant imaginable are perpetually observed to be necessary conditions to other things of the greatest importance; so that any one thing whatever may, for ought we know to the contrary, be a necessary condition to any other." p. 182. ed. 1736.]

of the whole world unto that which they teach, and do not fear to give very hard and heavy sentence upon as many as refuse to embrace the same, must have special regard that their first foundations and grounds be more than slender probabilities. This whole question which hath been moved about the kind of church regiment, we could not but for our own resolution's sake endeavour to unrip and sift; following therein as near as we might the conduct of that judicial method which serveth best for invention of truth. By means whereof, having found this the head theorem of all their discourses, who plead for the change of ecclesiastical government in England, namely, "That the Scripture of God is "in such sort the rule of human actions, that simply what-"soever we do and are not by it directed thereunto, the "same is sin;" we hold it necessary that the proofs hereof be weighed. Be they of weight sufficient or otherwise, it is not ours to judge and determine; only what difficulties there are which as yet withhold our assent, till we be further and better satisfied, I hope no indifferent amongst them will scorn or refuse to hear.

[4.] First therefore whereas they allege, "That Wisdom" doth teach men "every good way [1];" and have thereupon inferred that no way is good in any kind of action unless wisdom do by Scripture lead unto it; see they not plainly how they restrain the manifold ways which wisdom hath to teach men by, unto one only way of teaching, which is by Scripture? The bounds of wisdom are large, and within them much is contained. Wisdom was Adam's instructor in Paradise; wisdom endued the fathers who lived before the law with the knowledge of holy things; by the wisdom of the law of God David attained to excel others in understanding [2]; and Salomon likewise to excel David by the selfsame wisdom of God teaching him many things besides the law. The ways of well-doing are in number even as

---

[1] T. C. l. i. p. 20: "I say, that "the word of God containeth what-"soever things can fall into any "part of man's life. For so Salomon "saith in the second chapter of the "Proverbs, 'My son, if thou receive "my words, &c. then thou shalt "understand justice, and judgment, "and equity, and every good way." [In T. C. literally it is, "The word "of God containeth the direction "of all things pertaining to the "Church, yea, of whatsoever things "can fall into any part of man's "life." (p. 14.)]

[2] Psalm cxix. 99.

BOOK II. many as are the kinds of voluntary actions; so that whatso-
Ch. ii. 1. ever we do in this world and may do it ill, we shew ourselves therein by well-doing to be wise. Now if wisdom did teach men by Scripture not only all the ways that are right and good in some certain kind, according to that of St. Paul[1] concerning the use of Scripture, but did simply without any manner of exception, restraint, or distinction, teach every way of doing well; there is no art, but Scripture should teach it, because every art doth teach the way how to do something or other well. To teach men therefore wisdom professeth, and to teach them every good way; but not every good way by one way of teaching. Whatsoever either men on earth or the Angels of heaven do know, it is as a drop of that unemptiable fountain of wisdom; which wisdom hath diversely imparted her treasures unto the world. As her ways are of sundry kinds, so her manner of teaching is not merely one and the same. Some things she openeth by the sacred books of Scripture; some things by the glorious works of Nature: with some things she inspireth them from above by spiritual influence; in some things she leadeth and traineth them only by worldly experience and practice. We may not so in any one special kind admire her, that we disgrace her in any other; but let all her ways be according unto their place and degree adored.

The second II. That "all things be done to the glory of God[2]," the
proof out of blessed Apostle (it is true) exhorteth. The glory of God is
Scripture.
1 Cor. x. 31. the admirable excellency of that virtue divine, which being made manifest, causeth men and Angels to extol his greatness,

---

[1] 2 Tim. iii. 16. "The whole "Scripture is given by inspiration "of God, and is profitable to teach, "to improve, to correct, and to in-"struct in righteousness, that the "man of God may be absolute, "being made perfect unto all good "works." He meaneth all and only those good works, which belong unto us as we are men of God, and which unto salvation are necessary. Or if we understand by *men of God*, God's ministers, there is not required in them an universal skill of every good work or way, but an ability to teach whatsoever men are bound to do that they may be saved. And with this kind of knowledge the Scripture sufficeth to furnish them as touching matter.

[2] T. C. l. i. p. 26. [14.] "St. "Paul saith, 'That whether we eat "or drink, or whatsoever we do, we "must do it to the glory of God.' "But no man can glorify God in "any thing but by obedience; and "there is no obedience but in respect "of the commandment and word of "God: therefore it followeth that "the word of God directeth a man "in all his actions."

and in regard thereof to fear him. By "being glorified" it is not meant that he doth receive any augmentation of glory at our hands, but his name we glorify when we testify our acknowledgment of his glory. Which albeit we most effectually do by the virtue of obedience; nevertheless it may be perhaps a question, whether St. Paul did mean that we sin as oft as ever we go about any thing, without an express intent and purpose to obey God therein. He saith of himself, "I do in all things please all men, seeking not mine own "commodity but" rather the good "of many, that they may "be saved[1]." Shall it hereupon be thought that St. Paul did not move either hand or foot, but with express intent even thereby to further the common salvation of men? We move, we sleep, we take the cup at the hand of our friend, a number of things we oftentimes do, only to satisfy some natural desire, without present, express, and actual reference unto any commandment of God. Unto his glory even these things are done which we naturally perform, and not only that which morally and spiritually we do. For by every effect proceeding from the most concealed instincts of nature His power is made manifest. But it doth not therefore follow that of necessity we shall sin, unless we expressly intend this in every such particular.

[2.] But be it a thing which requireth no more than only our general presupposed willingness to please God in all things, or be it a matter wherein we cannot so glorify the name of God as we should without an actual intent to do him in that particular some special obedience; yet for any thing there is in this sentence alleged to the contrary, God may be glorified by obedience, and obeyed by performance of his will, and his will be performed with an actual intelligent desire to fulfil that law which maketh known what his will is, although no special clause or sentence of Scripture be in every such action set before men's eyes to warrant it. For Scripture is not the only law whereby God hath opened his will touching all things that may be done, but there are other kinds of laws which notify the will of God, as in the former book hath been proved at large: nor is there any law of God, whereunto he doth not account our obedience his glory. " Do therefore all

[1] 1 Cor. x. 33.

BOOK II.
Ch. ii. 3.
iii. 1.

"things unto the glory of God (saith the Apostle), be inoffensive both to Jews and Grecians and the Church of God; even as I please all men in all things, not seeking mine own commodity, but many's, that they may be saved." In the least thing done disobediently towards God, or offensively against the good of men, whose benefit we ought to seek for as for our own, we plainly shew that we do not acknowledge God to be such as indeed he is, and consequently that we glorify him not. This the blessed Apostle teacheth; but doth any Apostle teach, that we cannot glorify God otherwise, than only in doing what we find that God in Scripture commandeth us to do?

[3.] The churches dispersed amongst the heathen in the east part of the world are by the Apostle St. Peter exhorted to have their "conversation honest amongst the Gentiles, that "they which spake evil of them as of evil-doers might by the "good works which they should see glorify God in the day "of visitation[1]." As long as that which Christians did was good, and no way subject unto just reproof, their virtuous conversation was a mean to work the heathen's conversion unto Christ. Seeing therefore this had been a thing altogether impossible, but that infidels themselves did discern, in matters of life and conversation, when believers did well and when otherwise, when they glorified their heavenly Father and when not; it followeth that some things wherein God is glorified may be some other way known than only by the sacred Scripture; of which Scripture the Gentiles being utterly ignorant did notwithstanding judge rightly of the quality of Christian men's actions. Most certain it is that nothing but only sin doth dishonour God. So that to glorify him in all things is to do nothing whereby the name of God may be blasphemed[2]; nothing whereby the salvation of Jew or Grecian or any in the Church of Christ may be let or hindered[3]; nothing whereby his law is transgressed[4]. But the question is, whether only Scripture do shew whatsoever God is glorified in?

The third Scripture proof, 1 Tim. iv. 5.

III. And though meats and drinks be said to be sanctified by the word of God and by prayer[5], yet neither is this a

[1] 1 Pet. ii. 12.
[3] 1 Cor. x. 32.
[2] Rom. ii. 24.
[4] Rom. ii. 23.
[5] "And that which St. Paul said "of meats and drinks, that they are

reason sufficient to prove, that by Scripture we must of necessity be directed in every light and common thing which is incident into any part of man's life. Only it sheweth that unto us the word, that is to say the Gospel of Christ, having not delivered any such difference of things clean and unclean, as the Law of Moses did unto the Jews, there is no cause but that we may use indifferently all things, as long as we do not (like swine) take the benefit of them without a thankful acknowledgment of His liberality and goodness by whose providence they are enjoyed. And therefore the Apostle gave warning beforehand to take heed of such as should enjoin to "abstain from meats, which God hath created to be received "with thanksgiving by them which believe and know the "truth. For every creature of God is good, and nothing to "be refused, if it be received with thanksgiving, because it is "sanctified by the Word of God and prayer[1]." The Gospel, by not making many things unclean, as the Law did, hath sanctified those things generally to all, which particularly each man unto himself must sanctify by a reverend and holy use. Which will hardly be drawn so far as to serve their purpose, who have imagined the Word in such sort to sanctify all things, that neither food can be tasted, nor raiment put on, nor in the world any thing done, but this deed must needs be sin in them which do not first know it appointed unto them by Scripture before they do it.

IV. But to come unto that which of all other things in Scripture is most stood upon; that place of St. Paul they say is "of all other most clear, where speaking of those things "which are called indifferent, in the end he concludeth, "That 'whatsoever is not of faith is sin.' But faith is not "but in respect of the Word of God. Therefore whatsoever "is not done by the Word of God is sin." Whereunto we answer, that albeit the name of Faith being properly and strictly taken, it must needs have reference unto some uttered word as the object of belief: nevertheless sith the ground of credit is the credibility of things credited; and things are made credible, either by the known condition and quality of

BOOK II.
Ch. iv. 1.

The fourth Scripture proof, Rom. xiv. 23.
T. C. l. i. p. 27.
[p. 14.]

"sanctified unto us by the word of "God, the same is to be under-"standed of all things else whatso-"ever we have the use of." T. C. l. i. p. 26. [14.]
[1] 1 Tim. iv. 3, 4.

BOOK II.
Ch. iv. 2.

the utterer[1], or by the manifest likelihood of truth which they have in themselves; hereupon it riseth that whatsoever we are persuaded of, the same we are generally said to believe. In which generality the object of faith may not so narrowly be restrained, as if the same did extend no further than to the only Scriptures of God. "Though," saith our Saviour, "ye "believe not me, believe my works, that ye may know and "believe that the Father is in me and I in him[2]." "The "other disciples said unto Thomas, We have seen the Lord;" but his answer unto them was, "Except I see in his hands "the print of the nails, and put my finger into them, I will not "believe[3]." Can there be any thing more plain than that which by these two sentences appeareth, namely, that there may be a certain belief grounded upon other assurance than Scripture: any thing more clear, than that we are said not only to believe the things which we know by another's relation, but even whatsoever we are certainly persuaded of, whether it be by reason or by sense?

[2.] Forasmuch therefore as it is granted that St. Paul doth mean nothing else by Faith, but only "a full persuasion "that that which we do is well done[4];" against which kind of faith or persuasion as St. Paul doth count it sin to enterprise any thing, so likewise "some of the very heathen "have taught[5], as Tully, 'That nothing ought to be done "whereof thou doubtest whether it be right or wrong[6];' "whereby it appeareth that even those which had no know-

---

[1] Psalm xix. 8; Apoc. iii. 14; 2 Cor. i. 18.
[2] John x. 38.
[3] John xx. 25.
[4] "And if any will say that St. "Paul meaneth there a full πληροφο-"ρίαν and persuasion that that which "he doth is well done, I grant it. "But from whence can that spring "but from faith? How can we per-"suade and assure ourselves that "we do well, but whereas we have "the word of God for our warrant?" T. C. l. i. p. 27. [14.]
[5] "What also that some even of "those heathen men have taught, "that nothing ought to be done "whereof thou doubtest whether it "be right or wrong. Whereby it "appeareth that even those which "had no knowledge of the word of "God did see much of the equity of "this which the Apostle requireth "of a Christian man: and that the "chiefest difference is, that where "they sent men for the difference of "good and evil to the light of Rea-"son, in such things the Apostle "sendeth them to the school of "Christ in his word, which only is "able through faith to give them "assurance and resolution in their "doings." T. C. l. ii. p. 60.
[6] [De Offic. i. 9: "Bene præci-"piunt, qui vetant quidquam agere, "quod dubites æquum sit an ini-"quum."]

"ledge of the word of God did see much of the equity of this which the Apostle requireth of a Christian man;" I hope we shall not seem altogether unnecessarily to doubt of the soundness of their opinion, who think simply that nothing but only the word of God can give us assurance in any thing we are to do, and resolve us that we do well. For might not the Jews have been fully persuaded that they did well to think (if they had so thought) that in Christ God the Father was, although the only ground of this their faith had been the wonderful works they saw him do? Might not, yea, did not Thomas fully in the end persuade himself, that he did well to think that body which now was raised to be the same which had been crucified? That which gave Thomas this assurance was his sense; "Thomas, because "thou hast seen, thou believest," saith our Saviour[1]. What Scripture had Tully for this assurance? Yet I nothing doubt but that they who allege him think he did well to set down in writing a thing so consonant unto truth. Finally, we all believe that the Scriptures of God are sacred, and that they have proceeded from God; ourselves we assure that we do right well in so believing. We have for this point a demonstration sound and infallible. But it is not the word of God which doth or possibly can assure us, that we do well to think it his word. For if any one book of Scripture did give testimony to all, yet still that Scripture which giveth credit to the rest would require another Scripture to give credit unto it, neither could we ever come unto any pause whereon to rest our assurance this way; so that unless beside Scripture there were something which might assure us that we do well, we could not think we do well, no not in being assured that Scripture is a sacred and holy rule of well-doing.

[3.] On which determination we might be contented to stay ourselves without further proceeding herein, but that we are drawn on into larger speech by reason of their so great earnestness, who beat more and more upon these last alleged words, as being of all other most pregnant.

Whereas therefore they still argue, "That wheresoever "faith is wanting, there is sin;" and, "in every action not

[1] John xx. 29.

"commanded faith is wanting;" *ergo*, "in every action not commanded, there is sin¹:" I would demand of them first, forasmuch as the nature of things indifferent is neither to be commanded nor forbidden, but left free and arbitrary; how there can be any thing indifferent, if for want of faith sin be committed when any thing not commanded is done. So that of necessity they must add somewhat, and at leastwise thus set it down: in every action not commanded of God or permitted with approbation, faith is wanting, and for want of faith there is sin.

[4.] The next thing we are to inquire is, What those things be which God permitteth with approbation, and how we may know them to be so permitted. When there are unto one end sundry means; as for example, for the sustenance of our bodies many kinds of food, many sorts of raiment to clothe our nakedness, and so in other things of like condition: here the end itself being necessary, but not so any one mean thereunto; necessary that our bodies should be both fed and clothed, howbeit no one kind of food or raiment necessary; therefore we hold these things free in their own nature and indifferent. The choice is left to our own discretion, except a principal bond of some higher duty remove the indifferency that such things have in themselves. Their indifferency is removed, if either we take away our own liberty, as Ananias did², for whom to have sold or held his possessions it was indifferent, till his solemn vow and promise unto God had strictly bound him one only way; or if God himself have precisely abridged the same, by restraining us unto or by barring us from some one or moe things of many, which otherwise were in themselves altogether indifferent. Many fashions of priestly attire there were, whereof Aaron and his sons might have had their free choice without sin, but that God expressly tied them unto one³. All meats indifferent unto the Jew, were it not that God by name excepted some, as swine's flesh⁴. Impossible therefore it is we should otherwise think, than that what things God doth neither command nor forbid, the same he permitteth with approbation either to be done or left undone.

¹ T. C. l. ii. p. 58.
² Acts v. 4.
³ Exod. xxviii. 4, 43; xxxix.
⁴ Lev. xi.

"All things are lawful unto me," saith the Apostle[1], speaking as it seemeth in the person of the Christian Gentile for maintenance of liberty in things indifferent; whereunto his answer is, that nevertheless "all things are not expedient;" in things indifferent there is a choice, they are not always equally expedient.

[5.] Now in things although not commanded of God yet lawful because they are permitted, the question is, what light shall shew us the conveniency which one hath above another. For answer, their final determination is, that[2] "Whereas the "Heathen did send men for the difference of good and evil "to the light of Reason, in such things the Apostle sendeth "us to the school of Christ in his word, which only is able "through faith to give us assurance and resolution in our "doings." Which word *only*, is utterly without possibility of ever being proved. For what if it were true concerning things indifferent, that unless the word of the Lord had determined of the free use of them, there could have been no lawful use of them at all: which notwithstanding is untrue; because it is not the Scripture's setting down such things as indifferent, but their not setting down as necessary, that doth make them to be indifferent: yet this to our present purpose serveth nothing at all. We inquire not now, whether any thing be free to be used which Scripture hath not set down as free: but concerning things known and acknowledged to be indifferent, whether particularly in choosing any one of them before another we sin, if any thing but Scripture direct us in this our choice. When many meats are set before me, all are indifferent, none unlawful, I take one as most convenient. If Scripture require me so to do, then is not the thing indifferent, because I must do what Scripture requireth. They are all indifferent, I might take any, Scripture doth not require of me to make any special choice of one: I do notwithstanding make choice of one, my discretion teaching me so to do. A hard case, that hereupon I should be justly condemned of sin. Nor let any man think that following the judgment of natural discretion in such cases we can have no assurance that we please God. For to the Author and God of our nature, how shall any

[1] 1 Cor. vi. 12.   [2] [T. C. ii. 60.]

operation proceeding in natural sort be in that respect unacceptable? The nature which himself hath given to work by he cannot but be delighted with, when we exercise the same any way without commandment of his to the contrary.

[6.] My desire is to make this cause so manifest, that if it were possible, no doubt or scruple concerning the same might remain in any man's cogitation. Some truths there are, the verity whereof time doth alter: as it is now true that Christ is risen from the dead; which thing was not true at such time as Christ was living on earth, and had not suffered. It would be known therefore, whether this which they teach concerning the sinful stain of all actions not commanded of God, be a truth that doth now appertain unto us only, or a perpetual truth, in such sort that from the first beginning of the world unto the last consummation thereof, it neither hath been nor can be otherwise. I see not how they can restrain this unto any particular time, how they can think it true now and not always true, that in every action not commanded there is for want of faith sin. Then let them cast back their eyes unto former generations of men, and mark what was done in the prime of the world. Seth, Enoch, Noah, Sem, Abraham, Job, and the rest that lived before any syllable of the law of God was written, did they not sin as much as we do in every action not commanded? That which God is unto us by his sacred word, the same he was unto them by such like means as Eliphaz in Job describeth[1]. If therefore we sin in every action which the Scripture commandeth us not, it followeth that they did the like in all such actions as were not by revelation from Heaven exacted at their hands. Unless God from heaven did by vision still shew them what to do, they might do nothing, not eat, not drink, not sleep, not move.

[7.] Yea, but even as in darkness candlelight may serve to guide men's steps, which to use in the day were madness; so when God had once delivered his law in writing, it may be they are of opinion that then it must needs be sin for men to do any thing which was not there commanded them to do,

---

[1] Job iv. 12. ["A thing was secretly brought to me, and mine ear received a little thereof; in thoughts from the visions of the night, when deep sleep falleth on men," &c.]

whatsoever they might do before. Let this be granted, and it shall hereupon plainly ensue, either that the light of Scripture once shining in the world, all other light of Nature is therewith in such sort drowned, that now we need it not, neither may we longer use it; or if it stand us in any stead, yet as Aristotle speaketh of men whom Nature hath framed for the state of servitude, saying, "They have reason so far "forth as to conceive when others direct them[1], but little or "none in directing themselves by themselves;" so likewise our natural capacity and judgment must serve us only for the right understanding of that which the sacred Scripture teacheth. Had the Prophets who succeeded Moses, or the blessed Apostles which followed them, been settled in this persuasion, never would they have taken so great pains in gathering together natural arguments, thereby to teach the faithful their duties. To use unto them any other motive than *Scriptum est*, "Thus it is written," had been to teach them other grounds of their actions than Scripture; which I grant they allege commonly, but not only. Only Scripture they should have alleged, had they been thus persuaded, that so far forth we do sin as we do any thing otherwise directed than by Scripture. St. Augustine was resolute in points of Christianity to credit none, how godly and learned soever he were, unless he confirmed his sentence by the Scriptures, *or by some reason not contrary to them*[2]. Let them therefore with St. Augustine reject and condemn that which is not grounded either on the Scripture, or on some reason not contrary to Scripture, and we are ready to give them our hands in token of friendly consent with them.

V. But against this it may be objected, and is, That the Fathers do nothing more usually in their books, than draw

---

[1] Arist. Pol. i. c. 5. ['Ο κοινωνῶν λόγου τοσοῦτον ὅσον αἰσθάνεσθαι ἀλλὰ μὴ ἔχειν.]

[2] August. Ep. 19. [al. 82. t. ii. 190. "Ego enim fateor caritati "tuæ" (he is writing to St. Jerome,) "solis eis Scripturarum libris, qui "jam canonici appellantur, didici "hunc timorem honoremque deferre, "ut nullum eorum auctorem scri- "bendo aliquid errasse firmissime "credam. Ac si aliquid in eis "offendero literis quod videatur "contrarium veritati, nihil aliud, "quam vel mendosum esse codicem, "vel interpretem non assecutum "esse quod dictum est, vel me "minime intellexisse, non ambigam. "Alios autem ita lego, ut quanta- "libet sanctitate doctrinaque præ- "polleant, non ideo verum putem, "quia ipsi ita senserunt, sed quia "mihi vel per illos auctores ca- "nonicos, vel probabili ratione, "quod a vero non abhorreat per- "suadere potuerunt."]

BOOK II.
Ch. v. 2.

ed to be proved by the use of taking arguments negatively from the authority of Scripture: which kind of disputing is usual in the Fathers.

arguments from the Scripture negatively in reproof of that which is evil; "Scriptures teach it not, avoid it therefore:" these disputes with the Fathers are ordinary, neither is it hard to shew that the Prophets themselves have so reasoned. Which arguments being sound and good, it should seem that it cannot be unsound or evil to hold still the same assertion against which hitherto we have disputed. For if it stand with reason thus to argue, "such a thing is not taught us in Scripture, therefore we may not receive or allow it;" how should it seem unreasonable to think, that whatsoever we may lawfully do, the Scripture by commanding it must make it lawful? But how far such arguments do reach, it shall the better appear by considering the matter wherein they have been urged.

[2.] First therefore this we constantly deny, that of so many testimonies as they are able to produce for the strength of negative arguments, any one doth generally (which is the point in question) condemn either all opinions as false, or all actions as unlawful, which the Scripture teacheth us not. The most that can be collected out of them is only that in some cases a negative argument taken from Scripture is strong, whereof no man endued with judgment can doubt. But doth the strength of some negative argument prove this kind of negative argument strong, by force whereof all things are denied which Scripture affirmeth not, or all things which Scripture prescribeth not condemned? The question between us is concerning matter of action, what things are lawful or unlawful for men to do. The sentences alleged out of the Fathers are as peremptory and as large in every respect for matter of opinion as of action: which argueth that in truth they never meant any otherwise to tie the one than the other unto Scripture, both being thereunto equally tied, as far as each is required in the same kind of necessity unto salvation. If therefore it be not unlawful to know and with full persuasion to believe much more than Scripture alone doth teach; if it be against all sense and reason to condemn the knowledge of so many arts and sciences as are otherwise learned than in Holy Scripture, notwithstanding the manifest speeches of ancient Catholic Fathers, which seem to close up within the bosom thereof all manner good and lawful knowledge; wherefore should their words be thought more effectual to shew that we may not in deeds and practice, than they are to prove that in speculation and knowledge we ought not to go any farther than the Scripture? Which Scripture being given to teach matters of belief no less than of action, the Fathers must needs be and are even as plain against credit besides the relation, as against practice without the injunction of the Scripture.

[3.] St. Augustine hath said [1], "Whether it be question of "Christ, or whether it be question of his Church, or of what "thing soever the question be; I say not, if we, but if an "angel from heaven shall tell us any thing beside that you "have received in the Scripture under the Law and the Gos- "pel, let him be accursed [2]." In like sort Tertullian [3], "We "may not give ourselves this liberty to bring in any thing of "our will, nor choose any thing that other men bring in of "their will; we have the Apostles themselves for authors, "which themselves brought nothing of their own will, but "the discipline which they received of Christ they delivered "faithfully unto the people." In which place the name of Discipline importeth not as they who allege it would fain have it construed, but as any man who noteth the circumstance of the place and the occasion of uttering the words will easily acknowledge, even the selfsame thing it signifieth which the name of Doctrine doth, and as well might the one as the other there have been used. To help them farther, doth not St. Jerome [4] after the selfsame manner dispute, "We believe it

---

[1] Aug. cont. Liter. Petil. lib. iii. c. 6. [t. ix. 301 : "Sive de Christo, "sive de ejus Ecclesia, sive de "quacunque alia re quæ pertinet ad "fidem vitamque vestram, non di- "cam nos, nequaquam comparandi "ei qui dixit, *Licet si nos,* sed "omnino quod secutus adjecit, *Si* "*angelus de cœlo vobis annuncia-* "*verit præter quam quod* in Scrip- "*turis legalibus et evangelicis ac-* "*cepistis, anathema sit.*"]

[2] T. C. l. ii. p. 80 : "Augustine "saith, Whether it be question of "Christ, or whether it be question "of his Church, &c. And lest the an- "swerer should restrain the general "saying of Augustine unto the Doc- "trine of the Gospel, so that he "would thereby shut out the Disci-

"pline;" [Here T. C. alleges the passage ascribed to St. Cyprian, quoted by Hooker in the next note;] "even Tertullian himself, before he "was imbrued with the heresy of "Montanus, giveth testimony unto "the discipline in these words, "'We may not give ourselves,' &c."

[3] Tertull. de Præscript. [c. 6 : "Nobis vero nihil ex nostro arbitrio "inducere licet, sed nec eligere quod "aliquis de arbitrio suo induxerit. "Apostolos Domini habemus auc- "tores, qui nec ipsi quicquam ex "suo arbitrio, quod inducerent, ele- "gerunt: sed acceptam a Christo "disciplinam fideliter nationibus ad- "signaverunt."]

[4] Hieron. contra Helvid. ["Ut "hæc quæ scripta sunt non nega-

BOOK II.
Ch. v. 4.

"not, because we read it not?" Yea, "We ought not so much as to know the things which the Book of the Law "containeth not," saith St. Hilary. Shall we hereupon then conclude, that we may not take knowledge of or give credit unto any thing, which sense or experience or report or art doth propose, unless we find the same in Scripture? No; it is too plain that so far to extend their speeches is to wrest them against their true intent and meaning. To urge any thing upon the Church, requiring thereunto that religious assent of Christian belief, wherewith the words of the holy prophets are received; to urge any thing as part of that supernatural and celestially revealed truth which God hath taught, and not to shew it in Scripture; this did the ancient Fathers evermore think unlawful, impious, execrable. And thus, as their speeches were meant, so by us they must be restrained.

[4.] As for those alleged words of Cyprian [1], "The Christ-"ian Religion shall find, that out of this Scripture rules of "all doctrines have sprung, and that from hence doth spring "and hither doth return whatsoever the ecclesiastical disci-"pline doth contain:" surely this place would never have been brought forth in this cause, if it had been but once read over in the author himself out of whom it is cited. For the words are uttered concerning that one principal commandment of love; in the honour whereof he speaketh after this sort [2]: "Surely this commandment containeth the law and

"mus, ita ea quæ non sunt scripta "renuimus. Natum Deum esse de "virgine credimus, quia legimus: "Mariam nupsisse post partum non "credimus, quia non legimus." t. ii. 13.] Hilar. in Ps. cxxxii. [§ 6. pag. 463: "Quæ libro legis non "continentur, ea nec nosse debe-"mus." He is speaking of an apocryphal tradition, that the angels supposed by some to be mentioned in Genesis vi. 1, 4. used to haunt Mount Hermon especially.]

[1] "Let him hear what Cyprian "saith, The Christian Religion (saith "he) shall find, that," &c. T. C. l. ii. p. 80.

[2] "Vere hoc mandatum legem "complectitur et prophetas, et in "hoc verbo omnium Scriptura-"rum volumina coarctantur. Hoc "natura, hoc ratio, hoc, Domine, "verbi tui clamat auctoritas, hoc ex "ore tuo audivimus, hic invenit "consummationem omnis religio. "Primum est hoc mandatum et ul-"timum; hoc in libro vitæ conscrip-"tum indeficientem et hominibus et "angelis exhibet lectionem. Legat "hoc unum verbum et in hoc man-"dato meditetur Christiana religio, "et inveniet ex *hac* Scriptura omni-"um doctrinarum regulas emanasse, "et hinc nasci et huc reverti quic-"quid ecclesiastica continet disci-"plina, et in omnibus irritum esse "et frivolum quicquid dilectio non "confirmat." [Arnold. Carnotens. de Baptismo Christi, ad calc. S. Cyprian. ed. Fell. pag. 33. Udall in his Demonstration of Discipline having quoted the same passage, Sutcliffe, Remonstrance to the Demonstration, page 17, meets it with

"the Prophets, and in this one word is the abridgment of all
"the volumes of Scripture. This nature and reason and the
"authority of thy word, O Lord, doth proclaim; this we have
"heard out of thy mouth; herein the perfection of all religion
"doth consist. This is the first commandment and the last:
"this being written in the Book of Life is (as it were) an
"everlasting lesson both to Men and Angels. Let Christian
"religion read this one word, and meditate upon this com-
"mandment, and out of this Scripture it shall find the rules
"of all learning to have sprung, and from hence to have risen
"and hither to return whatsoever the ecclesiastical discipline
"containeth, and that in all things it is vain and bootless
"which charity confirmeth not." Was this a sentence (trow
you) of so great force to prove that Scripture is the only rule
of all the actions of men? Might they not hereby even as
well prove, that one commandment of Scripture is the only
rule of all things, and so exclude the rest of the Scripture, as
now they do all means beside Scripture? But thus it fareth,
when too much desire of contradiction causeth our speech
rather to pass by number than to stay for weight.

[5.] Well, but Tertullian doth in this case speak yet more
plainly[1]: "The Scripture," saith he, "denieth what it
"noteth not;" which are indeed the words of Tertullian[2].
But what? the Scripture reckoneth up the kings of Israel,
and amongst those kings David; the Scripture reckoneth up
the sons of David, and amongst those sons Salomon. To
prove that amongst the kings of Israel there was no David
but only one, no Salomon but one in the sons of David;
Tertullian's argument will fitly prove. For inasmuch as the
Scripture did propose to reckon up all, if there were moe it
would have named them. In this case "the Scripture doth

---

the following, which occurs just before in the same tract: "Magister "bone, libenter te audio, et cum ad- "versaris mihi, etiam in plagis et "doloribus intelligo disciplinam, nec "latet me, *te docente*, ad siccandas "corruptionum mearum putredines "prodesse cauterium, et mundare "cicatrices veteres salem *disciplinæ* "tuæ, Evangelio tuo medente infu- "sum.... You see, that which he "first called Doctrine, he after, "ἐξηγητικῶς, calleth Discipline."]

[1] Tertull. lib. de Monog. [c. 4: "Semel vim passa institutio Dei "per Lamechum, constitit postea in "finem usque gentis illius. Secun- "dus Lamech nullus extitit, quomo- "do duabus maritatus. Negat Scrip- "tura quod non notat." p. 671.]

[2] "And in another place Tertul- "lian saith, That the Scripture de- "nieth that which it noteth not." T. C. l. ii. p. 81.

BOOK II.
Ch. v. 6.

"deny the thing it noteth not." Howbeit I could not but think that man to do me some piece of manifest injury, which would hereby fasten upon me a general opinion, as if I did think the Scripture to deny the very reign of King Henry the Eighth, because it nowhere noteth that any such King did reign. Tertullian's speech is probable concerning such matter as he there speaketh of. "There was," saith Tertullian, "no second Lamech like to him that had two wives; "the Scripture denieth what it noteth not." As therefore it noteth one such to have been in that age of the world; so had there been moe, it would by likelihood as well have noted many as one. What infer we now hereupon? "There "was no second Lamech; the Scripture denieth what it "noteth not." Were it consonant unto reason to divorce these two sentences, the former of which doth shew how the later is restrained, and not marking the former to conclude by the later of them, that simply whatsoever any man at this day doth think true is by the Scripture denied, unless it be there affirmed to be true? I wonder that a cause so weak and feeble hath been so much persisted in.

[6.] But to come unto those their sentences wherein matters of action are more apparently touched: the name of Tertullian is as before so here again pretended[1]; who writing unto his wife two books, and exhorting her in the one to live a widow, in case God before her should take him unto his mercy; and in the other, if she did marry, yet not to join herself to an infidel, as in those times some widows Christian had done for the advancement of their estate in this present world, he urged very earnestly St. Paul's words, "only in the Lord[2]:"

[1] T. C. l. ii. p. 80: "And that "in indifferent things it is not "enough that they be not against "the word, but that they be according to the word, it may appear by "other places, where he saith, 'That "whatsoever pleaseth not the Lord, "displeaseth him, and with hurt is "received,'" lib. ii. ad Uxorem.

[2] 1 Cor. vii. 39. Ad Uxor. l. ii. c. 2. ["Cum dicit, Tantum in Domino, jam non suadet, sed exserte "jubet.... Igitur cum quædam istis "diebus nuptias suas de Ecclesia "tolleret, id est, Gentili conjungeretur; idque ab aliis retro factum "recordarer; miratus aut ipsarum petulantiam, aut consiliariorum prævaricationem, quod nulla Scriptura ejus facti licentiam "proferrent, 'Numquid,' inquam, "'de illo capitulo sibi blandiuntur "primæ ad Corinthios, ubi scriptum "est, Siquis frater infidelem habet "uxorem, et illa matrimonio consentit, ne dimittat eam,' &c. Hanc "monitionem forsan fidelibus injunctis simpliciter intelligendam putent, (etiam infidelibus nubere licere,) qui ita interpretantur." p. 198.]

whereupon he demandeth of them that think they may do the contrary, what Scripture they can shew where God hath dispensed and granted license to do against that which the blessed Apostle so strictly doth enjoin[1]. And because in defence it might perhaps be replied, " Seeing God doth will "that couples which are married when both are infidels, if "either party chance to be after converted unto Christianity, "this should not make separation between them, as long as "the unconverted was willing to retain the other on whom "the grace of Christ had shined; wherefore then should "that let the making of marriage, which doth not dissolve "marriage being made?" after great reasons shewed why God doth in converts being married allow continuance with infidels, and yet disallow that the faithful when they are free should enter into bonds of wedlock with such, [he] concludeth in the end concerning those women that so marry, "They "that please not the Lord do even thereby offend the Lord; "they do even thereby throw themselves into evil[2];" that is to say, while they please him not by marrying in him, they do that whereby they incur his displeasure; they make an offer of themselves into the service of that enemy with whose servants they link themselves in so near a bond. What one syllable is there in all this prejudicial any way to that which we hold? For the words of Tertullian as they are by them alleged are two ways misunderstood; both in the former part, where that is extended generally to "all things" in the neuter gender, which he speaketh in the feminine gender of women's persons; and in the latter, where "received with hurt" is put instead of "wilful incurring that which is evil." And so in sum Tertullian doth neither mean nor say as is pretended, "What-"soever pleaseth not the Lord displeaseth him, and with hurt "is received;" but, "Those women that please not the Lord" by their kind of marrying "do even thereby offend the Lord, "they do even thereby throw themselves into evil."

BOOK II.
Ch. v. 7.

[7.] Somewhat more show there is in a second place of Tertullian, which notwithstanding when we have examined it

---

[1] [This is Hooker's division (A, and B.). It implies the insertion of the pronoun before "concludeth." Mr. Keble's punctuation carries on the pronoun from "he demandeth," line 1.] 1886.

[2] "Quæ Domino non placent, "utique Dominum offendunt, utique "Malo se inferunt." [Tertull. ad Uxor. lib. ii. c. 7.]

BOOK II.
Ch. v. 7.

will be found as the rest are[1]. The Roman emperor's custom was at certain solemn times to bestow on his soldiers a donative; which donative they received wearing garlands upon their heads. There were in the time of the emperors Severus and Antoninus[2] many, who being soldiers had been converted unto Christ, and notwithstanding continued still in that military course of life. In which number, one man there was amongst all the rest, who at such a time coming to the tribune of the army to receive his donative, came but with a garland in his hand, and not in such sort as others did. The tribune offended hereat demandeth what this great singularity should mean. To whom the soldier, *Christianus sum,* "I am a Christian." Many there were so besides him which yet did otherwise at that time; whereupon grew a question, whether a Christian soldier might herein do as the unchristian did, and wear as they wore. Many of them which were very sound in Christian belief did rather commend the zeal of this man than approve his action.

Tertullian was at the same time a Montanist, and an enemy unto the church for condemning that prophetical spirit which Montanus and his followers did boast they had received, as if in them Christ had performed his last promise; as if to them he had sent the Spirit that should be their perfecter and final instructor in the mysteries of Christian truth. Which exulceration of mind made him apt to take all occasions of contradiction. Wherefore in honour of that action, and to gall their minds who did not so much commend it, he wrote his book *De Corona Militis,* not dissembling the stomach where-

---

[1] T. C. lib. ii. p. 81. "And to come "yet nearer, where he disputeth "against the wearing of crown or "garland, (which is indifferent of "itself,) to those which objecting "asked, where the Scripture saith "that a man might not wear a "crown, he answereth by asking, "where the Scripture saith that they "may wear. And unto them re- "plying that 'it is permitted which "is not forbidden,' he answereth, "that 'it is forbidden which is not "permitted.' Whereby appeareth "that the argument of the Scrip- "tures negatively holdeth not only "in the doctrine and ecclesiastical "discipline, but even in matters ar- "bitrary, and variable by the advice "of the Church. Where it is not "enough that they be not forbidden, "unless there be some word which "doth permit the use of them; it "is not enough that the Scripture "speaketh not against them, un- "less it speak for them; and finally, "where it displeaseth the Lord "which pleaseth him not: we [one] "must of necessity have the word "of his mouth to declare his plea- "sure."

[2] [Caracalla.]

with he wrote it. For first, the man he commendeth as "one more constant than the rest of his brethren, who pre-"sumed," saith he, "that they might well enough serve two "Lords¹." Afterwards choler somewhat more rising with him, he addeth, "It doth even remain that they should also "devise how to rid themselves of his martyrdoms, towards "the prophecies of whose Holy Spirit they have already "shewed their disdain. They mutter that their good and "long peace is now in hazard. I doubt not but some of them "send the Scriptures before, truss up bag and baggage, make "themselves in a readiness that they may fly from city to "city. For that is the only point of the Gospel which they "are careful not to forget. I know even their pastors very "well what men they are; in peace lions, harts in time "of trouble and fear²." Now these men, saith Tertullian, "they must be answered, where we do find it written in "Scripture that a Christian man may not wear a garland³."

And as men's speeches uttered in heat of distempered affection have oftentimes much more eagerness than weight, so he that shall mark the proofs alleged and the answers to things objected in that book will now and then perhaps espy the like imbecility. Such is that argument whereby they that wore on their heads garlands are charged as transgressors of nature's law⁴, and guilty of sacrilege against God the Lord of nature, inasmuch as flowers in such sort worn can neither be smelt nor seen well by those that wear them; and God made flowers sweet and beautiful, that being seen and smelt

---

¹ Tert. de Coron. Milit. c. 1. ["Dei miles cæteris constantior "fratribus, qui se duobus dominis "servire non posse præsumpserat, "solus libero capite, coronamento "in manu otioso." The reading before Pamelius was "servire pos-"se præsumpserant." (So Oehler. 1853.)]

² ["Plane superest ut etiam mar-"tyria recusare meditentur, qui "prophetias ejusdem Sp. Sancti re-"spuerunt. Mussitant denique tam "bonam et longam sibi pacem peri-"clitari. Nec dubito quosdam "Scripturas emigrare, sarcinas ex-"pedire, fugæ accingi de civitate in "civitatem. Nullam enim aliam "Evangelii memoriam curant. Novi "et pastores eorum in pace leones, "in prœlio cervos." p. 205.]

³ [Quatenus illud opponunt, "Ubi autem prohibemur coronari? "hanc magis localem substantiam "causæ præsentis aggrediar." ibid.]

⁴ [Ibid. c. 5. "In capite quis "sapor floris? quis coronæ sensus, "nisi vinculi tantum? quia neque "color cernitur, neque odor ducitur, "nec teneritas commendatur. Tam "contra naturam est florem capite "sectari, quam cibum aure, quam "sonum nare. Omne autem quod "contra naturam est monstri me-"retur notam penes omnes, penes "nos vero etiam elogium sacrilegii, "in Deum naturæ Dominum et "auctorem."]

BOOK II
Ch. v. 7.

unto they might so delight. Neither doth Tertullian bewray this weakness in striking only, but also in repelling their strokes with whom he contendeth. They ask, saith he, "What Scripture is there which doth teach that we should "not be crowned? And what Scripture is there which doth "teach that we should? For in requiring on the contrary "part the aid of Scripture, they do give sentence beforehand "that their part ought also by Scripture to be aided[1]." Which answer is of no great force. There is no necessity, that if I confess I ought not to do that which the Scripture forbiddeth me, I should thereby acknowledge myself bound to do nothing which the Scripture commandeth me not. For many inducements besides Scripture may lead me to that, which if Scripture be against, they all give place and are of no value, yet otherwise are strong and effectual to persuade.

Which thing himself well enough understanding, and being not ignorant that Scripture in many things doth neither command nor forbid, but use silence; his resolution in fine is, that in the church a number of things are strictly observed, whereof no law of Scripture maketh mention one way or other[2]; that of things once received and confirmed by use, long usage is a law sufficient; that in civil affairs, when there is no other law, custom itself doth stand for law[3]; that inasmuch as law doth stand upon reason, to allege reason serveth as well as to cite Scripture[4]; that whatsoever is reasonable, the same is lawful whosoever is author of it; that the authority

---

[1] [Ibid. c. 2. "Facile est statim "exigere, ubi scriptum sit, ne coro-"nemur? At enim ubi scriptum est, "ut coronemur? Expostulantes "enim Scripturæ patrocinium in "parte diversa, præjudicant suæ quo-"que parti Scripturæ patrocinium "adesse debere. Nam si ideo dicetur "coronari licere, quia non prohibeat "Scriptura, æque retorquebitur ideo "coronari non licere, quia Scriptura "non jubeat."]

[2] [Ibid. c. 3. "Etiam in tradi-"tionis obtentu exigenda est, inquis, "auctoritas scripta. Ergo quæra-"mus an et traditio non scripta "non debeat recipi? Plane nega-"bimus recipiendam, si nulla ex-"empla præjudicent aliarum obser-"vationum, quas sine ullius Scrip-"turæ instrumento, solius traditionis "titulo, exinde consuetudinis patro-"cinio vindicamus." He then instances in the customs of interrogatories in baptism, of trine immersion, and several other Church usages.]

[3] [Ibid. c. 4. "His igitur exem-"plis renunciatum erit, posse etiam "non scriptam traditionem in ob-"servatione defendi, confirmatam "consuetudine.... Consuetudo au-"tem etiam in civilibus rebus pro "lege suscipitur, cum deficit lex."]

[4] [Ibid. "Nec differt, Scriptura "an ratione consistat, quando et "legem ratio commendet. Porro "si lex ratione constat, lex erit omne "jam quod ratione constiterit *a* "*quocunque productum.*"]

of custom is great[1]; finally, that the custom of Christians was then and had been a long time not to wear garlands, and therefore that undoubtedly they did offend who presumed to violate such a custom by not observing that thing, the very inveterate observation whereof was a law sufficient to bind all men to observe it, unless they could shew some higher law, some law of Scripture, to the contrary[2]. This presupposed, it may stand then very well with strength and soundness of reason, even thus to answer, "Whereas they ask what Scripture for-"biddeth them to wear a garland; we are in this case rather "to demand what Scripture commandeth them. They cannot "here allege that it is permitted which is not forbidden them: "no, that is forbidden them which is not permitted." For long-received custom forbidding them to do as they did, (if so be it did forbid them,) there was no excuse in the world to justify their act, unless in the Scripture they could shew some law, that did license them thus to break a received custom.

Now whereas in all the books of Tertullian besides there is not so much found as in that one, to prove not only that we may do, but that we ought to do, sundry things which the Scripture commandeth not; out of that very book these sentences are brought to make us believe that Tertullian was of a clean contrary mind. We cannot therefore hereupon yield; we cannot grant, that hereby is made manifest the argument of Scripture negatively to be of force, not only in doctrine and ecclesiastical discipline, but even in matters arbitrary. For Tertullian doth plainly hold even in that book, that neither the matter which he intreateth of was arbitrary but necessary, inasmuch as the received custom of the Church

---

[1] [Ibid. "Hanc (rationem di-"vinam) nunc expostula, salvo tra-"ditionis respectu, *quocunque tradi-*"*tore censetur:* nec auctorem re-"spicias, sed auctoritatem: et in-"primis consuetudinis ipsius, quæ "propterea colenda est, ne non sit "rationis interpres, ut si hanc Deus "dederit, tunc discas, cur nam obser-"vanda sit tibi consuetudo."]

[2] [Ibid. c. 2. "Neminem dico "fidelium coronam capite nosse "alias, extra tempus tentationis "ejusmodi. Omnes ita observant "a catechumenis usque ad confes-"sores et martyres, vel negatores. "Viderint, unde auctoritas moris, de "qua cum maxime quæritur. Porro "cum quæritur [cur] quid observetur, "observari interim constat. Ergo "nec nullum nec incertum videri "potest delictum, quod committitur "in observationem suo jam nomine "vindicandam, et satis auctoratam "consensus patrocinio." And c. 3, " Habentes observationem invete-"ratam, quæ præveniendo statum "fecit."]

BOOK II. did tie and bind them not to wear garlands as the heathens
Ch. vi. 1. did; yea, and further also he reckoneth up particularly a
number of things, whereof he expressly concludeth, "Harum
"et aliarum ejusmodi disciplinarum si legem expostules Scrip-
"turarum, nullam invenies[1];" which is as much as if he had
said in express words, "Many things there are which con-
"cern the discipline of the Church and the duties of men,
"which to abrogate and take away the Scripture negatively
"urged may not in any case persuade us, but they must be
"observed, yea, although no Scripture be found which
"requireth any such thing." Tertullian therefore undoubtedly
doth not in this book shew himself to be of the same mind
with them by whom his name is pretended.

The first assertion endeavoured to be confirmed by the Scripture's custom of disputing from divine authority negatively.

VI.[2] But sith the sacred Scriptures themselves afford oftentimes such arguments as are taken from divine authority both one way and other; "The Lord hath commanded, "therefore it must be;" and again in like sort, "He hath "not, therefore it must not be;" some certainty concerning this point seemeth requisite to be set down.

God himself can neither possibly err, nor lead into error.

---

[1] Ibid. c. 4.

[2] T. C. l. ii. p. 48. "It is not "hard to shew that the Prophets "have reasoned negatively. As "when in the person of the Lord "the Prophet saith, *Whereof I* "*have not spoken*, Jer. xix. 5. *And* "*which never entered into my heart*, "Jer. vii. 31. And where he "condemneth them because they "have not asked counsel at the "mouth of the Lord, Isai. xxx. 2. "And it may be shewed that the "same kind of argument hath been "used in things which are not of "the substance of salvation or dam-"nation, and whereof there was no "commandment to the contrary, "(as in the former there was. Levit. "xviii. 21; and xx. 3; Deut. xvii. "16.) In Josua the children of "Israel are charged by the Prophet "that they asked not counsel at the "mouth of the Lord, when they "entered into covenant with the "Gibeonites, Josh. ix. 14. And yet "that covenant was not made con-"trary unto any commandment of "God. Moreover, we read that when "David had taken this counsel, to "build a temple unto the Lord, "albeit the Lord had revealed "before in his word that there "should be such a standing-place, "where the ark of the covenant and "the service should have a certain "abiding; and albeit there was no "word of God which forbade David "to build the temple; yet the Lord "(with commendation of his good "affection and zeal he had to the "advancement of his glory) con-"cludeth against David's resolution "to build the temple with this rea-"son, namely, that he had given "no commandment of this who "should build it. 1 Chron. xvii. 6." [The first part of this extract, from "It is not hard" to "Isai. xxx. 2." is from T. C. i. 13, 14. The parenthesis ("As in the former.... Deut. "xvii. 16.") seems to be a note of Hooker's. The latter part from "Moreover" is from T. C. ii. 49.]

must be limited by the known Scope of the Place.

BOOK II.
Ch. vi. 2.

For this cause his testimonies, whatsoever he affirmeth, are always truth and most infallible certainty[1].

Yea further, because the things that proceed from him are perfect without any manner of defect or maim; it cannot be but that the words of his mouth are absolute, and lack nothing which they should have for performance of that thing whereunto they tend. Whereupon it followeth, that the end being known whereunto he directeth his speech, the argument even negatively is evermore[2] strong and forcible concerning those things that are apparently requisite unto the same end. As for example: God intending to set down sundry times that which in Angels is most excellent, hath not any where spoken so highly of them as he hath of our Lord and Saviour Jesus Christ; therefore they are not in dignity equal unto him. It is the Apostle St. Paul's argument[3].

[2.] The purpose of God was to teach his people, both unto whom they should offer sacrifice, and what sacrifice was to be offered. To burn their sons in fire unto Baal he did not command them, he spake no such thing, neither came it into his mind; therefore this they ought not to have done. Which argument the Prophet Jeremy useth more than once, as being so effectual and strong, that although the thing he reproveth were not only not commanded but forbidden them[4], and that expressly; yet the Prophet chooseth rather to charge them with the fault of making a law unto themselves, than with the crime of transgressing a law which God had made[5]. For when the Lord hath once himself precisely set down a form of executing that wherein we are to serve him; the fault appeareth greater to do that which we are not, than not to do that which we are commanded. In this we seem to charge the law of God with hardness only, in that with foolishness; in this we shew ourselves weak and unapt to be doers of his will, in that we take upon us to be controllers of his wisdom; in this we fail to perform the thing which God seeth meet,

---

[1] 1 John i. 5. "God is light, "and there is in him no darkness "at all." Heb. vi. 18. "It is im-"possible that God should lie." Numb. xxiii. 19. "God is not as "man that he should lie."

[2] ["Ever more" (in two words) 1st ed. "Ever-more," Spencer. 1604.] 1886.

[3] [Heb. i. 5–13; ii. 5–8.]

[4] Levit. xviii. 21; xx. 3; Deut. xviii. 10.

[5] [See Whitgift, Defence, &c. p. 78.]

BOOK II.
Ch. vi. 3.

convenient, and good, in that we presume to see what is meet and convenient better than God himself. In those actions therefore the whole form whereof God hath of purpose set down to be observed, we may not otherwise do than exactly as he hath prescribed; in such things negative arguments are strong.

[3.] Again, with a negative argument David is pressed concerning the purpose he had to build a temple unto the Lord; "Thus saith the Lord, Thou shalt not build me a "house to dwell in. Wheresoever I have walked with all "Israel, spake I one word to any of the judges of Israel, "whom I commanded to feed my people, saying, Why have "ye not built me an house[1]?" The Jews urged with a negative argument touching the aid which they sought at the hands of the King of Egypt; "Woe to those rebellious "children, saith the Lord, which walk forth to go down "into Egypt, and have not asked counsel at my mouth; to "strengthen themselves with the strength of Pharao[2]." Finally, the league of Joshua with the Gabeonites is likewise with a negative argument touched. It was not as it should be: and why? the Lord gave them not that advice; "They "sought not counsel at the mouth of the Lord[3]."

By the virtue of which examples if any man shall suppose the force of negative arguments approved, when they are taken from Scripture in such sort as we in this question are pressed therewith, they greatly deceive themselves. For unto which of all these was it said that they had done amiss, in purposing to do or in doing any thing at all which "the Scripture" commanded them not? Our question is, Whether all be sin which is done without direction by Scripture, and not, Whether the Israelites did at any time amiss by following their own minds without asking counsel of God. No, it was that people's singular privilege, a favour which God vouchsafed them above the rest of the world, that in the affairs of their estate which were not determinable one way or other by the Scripture, himself gave them extraordinarily direction and counsel as oft as they sought it at his hands. Thus God did first by speech unto Moses, after by Urim and Thummim unto priests, lastly by dreams and visions unto prophets, from whom in such cases they were to receive the answer of God.

[1] 1 Chron. xvii. 6.   [2] Isaiah xxx. 1, 2.   [3] Josh. ix. 14.

Concerning Josua therefore, thus spake the Lord unto Moses, saying, "He shall stand before Eleazar the priest, who "shall ask counsel for him by the judgment of Urim before "the Lord[1];" whereof had Josua been mindful, the fraud of the Gabeonites could not so smoothly have passed unespied till there was no help.

The Jews had prophets to have resolved them from the mouth of God himself whether Egyptian aids should profit them, yea or no; but they thought themselves wise enough, and him unworthy to be of their counsel. In this respect therefore was their reproof though sharp yet just, albeit there had been no charge precisely given them that they should always take heed of Egypt.

But as for David, to think that he did evil in determining to build God a temple, because there was in Scripture no commandment that he should build it, were very injurious: the purpose of his heart was religious and godly, the act most worthy of honour and renown; neither could Nathan choose but admire his virtuous intent, exhort him to go forward, and beseech God to prosper him therein[2]. But God saw the endless troubles which David should be subject unto during the whole time of his regiment, and therefore gave charge to defer so good a work to the days of tranquillity and peace, wherein it might without interruption be performed. David supposed that it could not stand with the duty which he owed unto God, to set himself in a house of cedar-trees, and to behold the ark of the Lord's covenant unsettled. This opinion the Lord abateth, by causing Nathan to shew him plainly, that it should be no more imputed unto him for a fault than it had been unto the Judges of Israel before him, his case being the same which theirs was, their times not more unquiet than his, not more unfit for such an action.

Wherefore concerning the force of negative arguments so taken from the authority of Scripture as by us they are denied, there is in all this less than nothing.

[4.] And touching that which unto this purpose is borrowed from the controversy sometime handled between M. Harding[3]

---

[1] Numb. xxvii. 21.
[2] 1 Chron. xvii. 2.
[3] T. C. l. ii. p. 50: "M. Harding "reproacheth the Bishop of Salis- "bury with this kind of reasoning; "unto whom the Bishop answereth,

BOOK II.
Ch. vi. 4.

and the worthiest divine that Christendom hath bred for the space of some hundreds of years[1], who being brought up together in one University[2], it fell out in them which was spoken of two others, "They learned in the same that which "in contrary camps they did practise[3]:" of these two the one objecting that with us arguments taken from authority negatively are over common, the Bishop's answer hereunto is, that "[4] This kind of argument is thought to be good, "whensoever proof is taken of God's word; and is used not "only by us, but also by St. Paul, and by many of the Catholic "Fathers. St. Paul saith, God said not unto Abraham, 'In "thy seeds all the nations of the earth shall be blessed:' but, "'In thy seed, which is Christ:' and thereof he thought he "made a good argument[5]. Likewise, saith Origen, 'The "bread which the Lord gave unto his disciples, saying unto

"'The argument of authority negatively is taken to be good, whensoever proof is taken of God's word; and is used not only by us, but also by many of the Catholic Fathers.' A little after he sheweth the reason why the argument of authority of the Scripture negatively is good; namely, 'For that the word of God is perfect.' In another place unto M. Harding casting him in the teeth with negative arguments, he allegeth places out of Irenæus, Chrysostom, Leo, which reasoned negatively of the authority of the Scriptures. The places which he alledgeth be very full and plain in generality, without any such restraints as the Answerer imagineth; as they are there to be seen."

[1] [Vaughan in his Life of Dr. Thos. Jackson, prefixed to his (Jackson's) works, p. 8, says of him, "I shall willingly associate him to "those other worthies, his predecessors in the same college, (all "living at the same time:) to the "invaluable Bishop Jewel, *Theologorum quos orbis Christianus per aliquot annorum centenarios produxit maximo:* as grave Bishop "Goodwin hath described him. To "the famous Mr. Hooker, who for "his solid writings was sirnamed, "The Judicious, and entitled by "the same, *Theologorum Oxonium;* "'The Oxford of Divines:' as one "calls Athens, 'The Greece of "Greece itself.' To the learned Dr. "Reinolds, who managed the government of the same college with "the like care, honour and integrity, "although not with the same austerities" as Dr. Jackson. Bishop Godwin borrowed the expression referred to (De Præsul. Angl. p. 354, ed. 1743,) from Hooker: and adds concerning him, that he was "*a magno Theologo Literarum Oxonium appellatus.*"]

[2] [According to Camden, they were bred in the same grammar school also. "Out of this town's "school" (he is speaking of Barnstaple) "there issued two right "learned men and most renowned "divines, John Jewell Bishop of "Sarisbury, and T. Hardinge." Britannia, transl. by Holland, p. 208.]

[3] Vell. Paterc. "Jugurtha ac "Marius sub eodem Africano militantes, in iisdem castris didicere "quæ postea in contrariis facerent." [l. ii. c. 9.]

[4] [Reply to M. Harding's Answer.] Art. i. Divis. 29. [p. 51, ed. 1611.]

[5] Gal. iii. 16.

"them, Take and eat, he deferred not, nor commanded to be
"reserved till the next day¹.' Such arguments Origen and
"other learned Fathers thought to stand for good, whatsoever
"misliking Master Harding hath found in them. This kind
"of proof is thought to hold in God's commandments, for
"that they be full and perfect: and God hath specially
"charged us, that we should neither put to them nor take
"from² them; and therefore it seemeth good unto them that
"have learned of Christ, *Unus est Magister vester, Christus*³,
"and have heard the voice of God the Father from heaven,
"*Ipsum audite*⁴. But unto them that add to the word of
"God what them listeth, and make God's will subject unto
"their will, and break God's commandments for their own
"tradition's sake, unto them it seemeth not good."

Again, the English Apology alleging the example of the Greeks, how they have neither private masses, nor mangled sacraments, nor purgatories, nor pardons; it pleaseth Master Harding to jest out the matter, to use the help of his wits where strength of truth failed him, and to answer with scoffing at negatives. The Bishop's defence in this case is⁵, "The "ancient learned Fathers having to deal with impudent "heretics, that in defence of their errors avouched the judg- "ment of all the old bishops and doctors that had been before "them, and the general consent of the primitive and whole "universal Church, and that with as good regard of truth "and as faithfully as you do now; the better to discover the "shameless boldness and nakedness of their doctrine, were "oftentimes likewise forced to use the negative, and so to "drive the same heretics, as we do you, to prove their affirm- "atives, which thing to do it was never possible. The "ancient father Irenæus thus stayed himself, as we do, by "the negative⁶, 'Hoc neque Prophetæ prædicaverunt, neque "Dominus docuit, neque Apostoli tradiderunt;' 'This thing "neither did the Prophets publish, nor our Lord teach, nor "the Apostles deliver.' By a like negative Chrysostom saith⁷,

---

¹ Orig. in Levit. Hom. 5. [t. ii. 211. ed. Bened.]
² ["fro:" edd. 1, 2, 4.] 1886.
³ Matt. xxiii. 8. 10.
⁴ Matt. xvii. 5.
⁵ Defens. par. v. cap. 15, divis. 1.
⁶ Lib. i. cap. 1.
⁷ De incomp. nat. Dei, Hom. 3. t. vi. 403. ["Hanc arborem non "Paulus plantavit, non Apollos ri- "gavit, non Deus auxit."]

"'This tree neither Paul planted, nor Apollos watered, nor God increased.' In like sort Leo saith[1], 'What needeth it to believe that thing that neither the Law hath taught, nor the Prophets have spoken, nor the Gospel hath preached, nor the Apostles have delivered?' And again[2], 'How are the new devices brought in that our Fathers never knew?' St. Augustine, having reckoned up a great number of the Bishops of Rome, by a general negative saith thus[3]; 'In all this order of succession of bishops there is not one bishop found that was a Donatist.' St. Gregory being himself a Bishop of Rome, and writing against the title of *Universal Bishop*, saith thus[4], ' None of all my predecessors ever consented to use this ungodly title; no Bishop of Rome ever took upon him this name of singularity.' By such negatives, M. Harding, we reprove the vanity and novelty of your religion; we tell you, none of the catholic ancient learned Fathers either Greek or Latin, ever used either your private mass, or your half communion, or your barbarous unknown prayers. Paul never planted them, Apollos never watered them, God never increased them; they are of yourselves, they are not of God."

In all this there is not a syllable which any way crosseth us. For concerning arguments negative even taken from human authority, they are here proved to be in some cases very strong and forcible. They are not in our estimation idle reproofs, when the authors of needless innovations are opposed with such negatives as that of Leo, "How are these new devices brought in which our Fathers never knew?" When their grave and reverend superiors do reckon up unto them as Augustine did unto the Donatists, large catalogues of Fathers wondered at for their wisdom, piety, and learning[5], amongst

---

[1] Epist. xciii. c. 12. [p. 167, ed. Paris. 1639: "Quid opus est in cor admittere quod lex non docuit, quod prophetia non cecinit, quod Evangelii veritas non prædicavit, quod Apostolica doctrina non tradidit?"]

[2] Epist. xcvii. c. 5. ["Quomodo ... nova inducuntur, quæ nostri nunquam sensere majores?" Quoted by S. Leo from S. Ambrose, de Incarn. Dom. c. 6.]

[3] Epist. clxv. [al. 53. t. ii. 121. "In hoc ordine successionis nullus Donatista episcopus invenitur."]

[4] Lib. iv. Ep. 32. ["Nemo decessorum meorum hoc tam profano vocabulo uti consensit: nullus Romanorum Pontificum hoc singularitatis nomen assumpsit."]

[5] [S. Aug. Ep. 53. (al. 165.) § 2. "Si ordo episcoporum sibi succedentium considerandus est, quanto certius et vere salubriter ab ipso Petro numeramus, cui totius Ecclesiæ figuram gerenti

whom for so many ages before us no one did ever so think of the Church's affairs as now the world doth begin to be persuaded; surely by us they are not taught to take exception hereat, because such arguments are negative. Much less when the like are taken from the sacred authority of Scripture, if the matter itself do bear them. For in truth the question is not, whether an argument from Scripture negatively may be good, but whether it be so generally good, that in all actions men may urge it. The Fathers I grant do use very general and large terms, even as Hiero the king did in speaking of Archimedes, "From henceforward, whatsoever Archimedes "speaketh, it must be believed[1]." His meaning was not that Archimedes could simply in nothing be deceived, but that he had in such sort approved his skill, that he seemed worthy of credit for ever after in matters appertaining unto the science he was skilful in. In speaking thus largely it is presumed that men's speeches will be taken according to the matter whereof they speak. Let any man therefore that carrieth indifferency of judgment peruse the bishop's speeches, and consider well of those negatives concerning Scripture, which he produceth out of Irenæus, Chrysostom and Leo[2];

"Dominus ait, 'Super hanc petram "ædificabo Ecclesiam meam, et "portæ inferorum non vincent eam.' "Petro enim successit Linus; Lino, "Clemens; Clementi, Anacletus; "Anacleto, Evaristus; Evaristo, "Alexander; Alexandro, Sixtus; "Sixto, Telesphorus; Telesphoro, "Iginus; Igino, Anicetus; Aniceto, "Pius; Pio, Soter; Soteri, Eleuthe- "rius; Eleutherio, Victor; Victori, "Zephirinus; Zephirino, Calixtus: "Calixto, Urbanus; Urbano, Pon- "tianus; Pontiano, Antherus; An- "thero, Fabianus; Fabiano, Cor- "nelius; Cornelio, Lucius; Lucio, "Stephanus; Stephano, Xystus; "Xysto, Dionysius; Dionysio, Felix; "Felici, Eutychianus; Eutychiano, "Gaius; Gaio, Marcellinus; Mar- "cellino, Marcellus; Marcello, Eu- "sebius; Eusebio, Miltiades; Mil- "tiadi, Sylvester; Sylvestro, Marcus; "Marco, Julius; Julio, Liberius; "Liberio, Damasus; Damaso, Si- "ricius; Siricio, Anastasius. In hoc "ordine successionis nullus Dona-

"tista Episcopus invenitur."]
[1] [Proclus in Euclid, II. 3. Montucla, Hist. des Mathématiques, I. 230.]
[2] [S. Irenæus, I. 1. 15, (after a minute exposition of the Valentinian doctrine of Æons:) Τοιαύτης δὲ τῆς ὑποθέσεως αὐτῶν οὔσης, ἣν οὔτε Προφῆται ἐκήρυξαν, οὔτε ὁ Κύριος ἐδίδαξεν, οὔτε Ἀπόστολοι παρέδωκαν, ἣν περὶ τῶν ὅλων αὐχοῦσι πλεῖον τῶν ἄλλων ἐγνωκέναι, ἐξ ἀγράφων ἀναγινώσκοντες, καὶ τὸ δὴ λεγόμενον, ἐξ ἄμμου σχοινία πλέκειν ἐπιτηδεύοντες· ἀξιοπίστως προσαρμόζειν πειρῶνται τοῖς εἰρημένοις ἤτοι παραβολὰς κυριακὰς, ἢ ῥήσεις προφητικὰς, ἢ λόγους Ἀποστολικοὺς, ἵνα τὸ πλάσμα αὐτῶν μὴ ἀμάρτυρον εἶναι δοκῇ.
S. Chrysostom, VI. p. 402, 3, (speaking of one of the most offensive modifications of Arianism;) Ἡ τῶν Ἀνομοίων ἐρημωθεῖσα ψυχὴ, καὶ τῆς ἀπὸ τῶν γραφῶν ἐπιμελείας οὐκ ἀπολαύσασα, οἴκοθεν καὶ παρ' ἑαυτῆς τὴν ἀγρίαν ταύτην καὶ ἀνήμερον ἐξέβρασεν αἵρεσιν· τοῦτο γὰρ τὸ δέν-

which three are chosen from amongst the residue, because the sentences of the others (even as one of theirs also) do make for defence of negative arguments taken from human authority, and not from divine only. They mention no more restraint in the one than in the other; yet I think themselves will not hereby judge, that the Fathers took both to be strong, without restraint unto any special kind of matter wherein they held such arguments forcible. Nor doth the bishop either say or prove any more, than that an argument in some kinds of matter may be good, although taken negatively from Scripture.

Their opinion concerning the force of arguments taken from human authority for the ordering of men's actions or persuasions.

VII. An earnest desire to draw all things unto the determination of bare and naked Scripture hath caused here much pains to be taken in abating the estimation and credit of man. Which if we labour to maintain as far as truth and reason will bear, let not any think that we travail about a matter not greatly needful. For the scope of all their pleading against man's authority is, to overthrow such orders, laws, and constitutions in the Church, as depending thereupon if they should therefore be taken away, would peradventure leave neither face nor memory of Church to continue long in the world, the world especially being such as now it is. That which they have in this case spoken I would for brevity's sake let pass, but that the drift of their speech being so dangerous, their words are not to be neglected.

[2.] Wherefore to say that simply an argument taken from man's authority doth hold no way, "neither affirmatively nor "negatively[1]," is hard. By a man's authority we here understand the force which his word hath for the assurance of another's mind that buildeth upon it; as the Apostle somewhat did upon their report of the house of Chloe[2]; and the

δρον οὐ Παῦλος ἐφύτευσεν, οὐκ Ἀπολλὼς ἐπότισεν, οὐχ ὁ Θεὸς ηὔξησεν· ἀλλ' ἐφύτευσε μὲν λογισμῶν ἄκαιρος περιεργία, ἐπότισε δὲ ἀπονοίας τῦφος, ηὔξησε δὲ φιλοδοξίας ἔρως.
S. Leo, as before, Ep. xciii. c. 12.]

[1] T. C. lib. i. p. 25. [13.] "When "the question is of the authority of "a man, it holdeth neither affirm- "atively nor negatively. The reason "is, because the infirmity of man "can neither attain to the perfection "of any thing whereby he might "speak all things that are to be "spoken of it, neither yet be free "from error in those things which "he speaketh or giveth out. And "therefore this argument neither "affirmatively nor negatively com- "pelleth the hearer, but only in- "duceth him to some liking or dis- "liking of that for which it is "brought, and is rather for an ora- "tor to persuade the simpler sort "than for a disputer to enforce him "that is learned."

[2] 1 Cor. i. 11.

Samaritans in a matter of far greater moment upon the report of a simple woman. For so it is said in St. John's Gospel, "Many of the Samaritans of that city believed in him for the "saying of the woman, which testified, He hath told me all "things that ever I did [1]."

The strength of man's authority is affirmatively such that the weightiest affairs in the world depend thereon. In judgment and justice are not hereupon proceedings grounded? Saith not the Law that "in the mouth of two or three wit- "nesses every word shall be confirmed [2]?" This the law of God would not say, if there were in a man's testimony no force at all to prove any thing.

And if it be admitted that in matter of fact there is some credit to be given to the testimony of man, but not in matter of opinion and judgment; we see the contrary both acknowledged and universally practised also throughout the world. The sentences of wise and expert men were never but highly esteemed. Let the title of a man's right be called in question; are we not bold to rely and build upon the judgment of such as are famous for their skill in the laws of this land? In matter of state the weight many times of some one man's authority is thought reason sufficient, even to sway over whole nations.

And this not only "with the simpler sort;" but the learneder and wiser we are, the more such arguments in some cases prevail with us. The reason why the simpler sort are moved with authority is the conscience of their own ignorance; whereby it cometh to pass that having learned men in admiration, they rather fear to dislike them than know wherefore they should allow and follow their judgments. Contrariwise with them that are skilful authority is much more strong and forcible; because they only are able to discern how just cause there is why to some men's authority so much should be attributed. For which cause the name of Hippocrates (no doubt) were more effectual to persuade even such men as Galen himself, than to move a silly empiric. So that the very selfsame argument in this kind which doth but induce the vulgar sort to like, may constrain the wiser to yield. And therefore not orators only with the people, but even the very

---

[1] iv. 39. [2] Deut. xix. 15; Matt. xviii. 16.

BOOK II.
Ch. vii. 3.

profoundest disputers in all faculties have hereby often with the best learned prevailed most.

As for arguments taken from human authority and that negatively; for example sake, if we should think the assembling of the people of God together by the sound of a bell, the presenting of infants at the holy font by such as commonly we call their godfathers, or any other the like received custom, to be impious, because some men of whom we think very reverently have in their books and writings nowhere mentioned or taught that such things should be in the Church; this reasoning were subject unto just reproof, it were but feeble, weak, and unsound. Notwithstanding even negatively an argument from human authority may be strong, as namely thus: The Chronicles of England mention no moe than only six kings bearing the name of Edward since the time of the last conquest; therefore it cannot be there should be moe. So that if the question be of the authority of a man's testimony, we cannot simply avouch either that affirmatively it doth not any way hold; or that it hath only force to induce the simpler sort, and not to constrain men of understanding and ripe judgment to yield assent; or that negatively it hath in it no strength at all. For unto every of these the contrary is most plain.

[3.] Neither doth that which is alleged concerning the infirmity of men overthrow or disprove this. Men are blinded with ignorance and error; many things may escape them, and in many things they may be deceived; yea, those things which they do know they may either forget, or upon sundry indirect considerations let pass; and although themselves do not err, yet may they through malice or vanity even of purpose deceive others. Howbeit infinite cases there are wherein all these impediments and lets are so manifestly excluded, that there is no show or colour whereby any such exception may be taken, but that the testimony of man will stand as a ground of infallible assurance. That there is a city of Rome, that Pius Quintus and Gregory the Thirteenth and others have been Popes of Rome, I suppose we are certainly enough persuaded. The ground of our persuasion, who never saw the place nor persons beforenamed, can be nothing but man's testimony. Will any man here notwithstanding allege those mentioned human infirmities, as reasons why these things should be mistrusted or doubted of?

Yea, that which is more, utterly to infringe the force and strength of man's testimony were to shake the very fortress of God's truth. For whatsoever we believe concerning salvation by Christ, although the Scripture be therein the ground of our belief; yet the authority of man is, if we mark it, the key which openeth the door of entrance into the knowledge of the Scripture. The Scripture could not teach us the things that are of God, unless we did credit men who have taught us that the words of Scripture do signify those things. Some way therefore, notwithstanding man's infirmity, yet his authority may enforce assent.

[4.] Upon better advice and deliberation so much is perceived, and at the length confest; that arguments taken from the authority of men may not only so far forth as hath been declared, but further also be of some force in "human sci-"ences;" which force be it never so small, doth shew that they are not utterly naught. But in "matters divine" it is still maintained stiffly, that they have no manner force at all [1]. Howbeit, the very selfsame reason, which causeth to yield that they are of some force in the one, will at the length constrain also to acknowledge that they are not in the other altogether unforcible. For if the natural strength of man's wit may by experience and study attain unto such ripeness in the knowledge of things human, that men in this respect may

---

[1] T. C. lib. ii. p. 19: "Although "that kind of argument of authority "of men is good neither in human "nor divine sciences; yet it hath "some small force in human sci-"ences, (forasmuch as naturally, and "in that he is a man, he may come "to some ripeness of judgment in "those sciences,) which in divine "matters hath no force at all; as "of him which naturally, and as he "is a man, can no more judge of "them than a blind man of colours. "Yea so far is it from drawing credit, "if it be barely spoken without rea-"son and testimony of Scripture, "that it carrieth also a suspicion of "untruth whatsoever proceedeth "from him; which the Apostle did "well note, when, to signify a thing "corruptly spoken, and against the "truth, he saith, that 'it is spoken "according to man,' Rom. iii. He "saith not, 'as a wicked and lying "man,' but simply, 'as a man.' "And although this corruption be "reformed in many, yet for so much "as in whom the knowledge of the "truth is most advanced there re-"maineth both ignorance and dis-"ordered affections (whereof either "of them turneth him from speak-"ing of the truth), no man's au-"thority, with the Church espe-"cially and those that are called and "persuaded of the authority of the "Word of God, can bring any as-"surance unto the conscience."

presume to build somewhat upon their judgment; what reason have we to think but that even in matters divine, the like wits furnished with necessary helps, exercised in Scripture with like diligence, and assisted with the grace of Almighty God, may grow unto so much perfection of knowledge, that men shall have just cause, when any thing pertinent unto faith and religion is doubted of, the more willingly to incline their minds towards that which the sentence of so grave, wise, and learned in that faculty shall judge most sound? For the controversy is of the weight of such men's judgments. Let it therefore be suspected; let it be taken as gross, corrupt, repugnant unto the truth, whatsoever concerning things divine above nature shall at any time be spoken as out of the mouths of mere natural men, which have not the eyes wherewith heavenly things are discerned. For this we contend not. But whom God hath endued with principal gifts to aspire unto knowledge by; whose exercises, labours, and divine studies he hath so blessed that the world for their great and rare skill that way hath them in singular admiration; may we reject even their judgment likewise, as being utterly of no moment? For mine own part, I dare not so lightly esteem of the Church, and of the principal pillars therein.

[5.] The truth is, that the mind of man desireth evermore to know the truth according to the most infallible certainty which the nature of things can yield. The greatest assurance generally with all men is that which we have by plain aspect and intuitive beholding. Where we cannot attain unto this, there what appeareth to be true by strong and invincible demonstration, such as wherein it is not by any way possible to be deceived, thereunto the mind doth necessarily assent, neither is it in the choice thereof to do otherwise. And in case these both do fail, then which way greatest probability leadeth, thither the mind doth evermore incline. Scripture with Christian men being received as the Word of God; that for which we have probable, yea, that which we have necessary reason for, yea, that which we see with our eyes, is not thought so sure as that which the Scripture of God teacheth; because we hold that his speech revealeth there what himself seeth, and therefore the strongest proof of all, and the most necessarily assented unto by us (which do thus receive the Scripture) is the Scripture. Now it is not required or can be exacted at our hands, that we should yield unto any thing other assent, than such as doth answer the evidence which is to be had of that we assent unto. For which cause even in matters divine, concerning some things we may lawfully doubt and suspend our judgment, inclining neither to one side nor other; as namely touching the time of the fall both of man and angels: of some things we may very well retain an opinion that they are probable and not unlikely to be true, as when we hold that men have their souls rather by creation than propagation, or that the Mother of our Lord lived always in the state of virginity as well after his birth as before (for of these two the one, her virginity before, is a thing which of necessity we must believe; the other, her continuance in the same state always, hath more likelihood of truth than the contrary); finally in all things then are our consciences best resolved, and in most agreeable sort unto God and nature settled, when they are so far persuaded as those grounds of persuasion which are to be had will bear.

Which thing I do so much the rather set down, for that I see how a number of souls are for want of right information in this point oftentimes grievously vexed. When bare and unbuilded conclusions are put into their minds, they finding not themselves to have thereof any great certainty, imagine that this proceedeth only from lack of faith, and that the Spirit of God doth not work in them as it doth in true believers; by this means their hearts are much troubled, they fall into anguish and perplexity: whereas the truth is, that how bold and confident soever we may be in words, when it cometh to the point of trial, such as the evidence is which the truth hath either in itself or through proof, such is the heart's assent thereunto; neither can it be stronger, being grounded as it should be.

I grant that proof derived from the authority of man's judgment is not able to work that assurance which doth grow by a stronger proof; and therefore although ten thousand general councils would set down one and the same definitive sentence concerning any point of religion whatsoever, yet one demonstrative reason alleged, or one manifest testimony cited from the mouth of God himself to the contrary, could not choose but overweigh them all; inasmuch as for them to have been deceived it is not impossible; it is, that demonstrative reason or testimony divine should deceive. Howbeit in defect of proof infallible, because the mind doth rather follow probable persuasions than approve the things that have in them no likelihood of truth at all; surely if a question concerning matter of doctrine were proposed, and on the one side no kind of proof appearing, there should on the other be alleged and shewed that so a number of the learnedest divines in the world have ever thought; although it did not appear what reason or what Scripture led them to be of that judgment, yet to their very bare judgment somewhat a reasonable man would attribute, notwithstanding the common imbecilities which are incident into our nature.

[6.] And whereas it is thought, that especially with "the "Church, and those that are called and persuaded of the "authority of the Word of God, man's authority" with them especially "should not prevail;" it must and doth prevail even with them, yea with them especially, as far as equity requireth; and farther we maintain it not[1]. For men to be

---

[1] T. C. lib. ii. p. 21: "Of divers "sentences of the Fathers them-"selves (whereby some have likened "them to brute beasts without "reason which suffer themselves to "be led by the judgment and au-"thority of others, some have pre-"ferred the judgment of one simple "rude man alleging reason unto "companies of learned men) I will "content myself at this time with "two or three sentences. Irenæus "saith, Whatsoever is to be shewed "in the Scripture cannot be shewed "but out of the Scriptures them-"selves. lib. iii. cap. 12. Jerome "saith, 'No man be he never so "holy or eloquent hath any authority "after the Apostles:' in Ps. lxxxvi. "Augustine saith, 'That he will "believe none how godly and learn-"ed soever he be, unless he confirm "his sentence by the Scriptures, or "by some reason not contrary to "them.' Ep. 18." [al. 82. t. ii. p. 190.] "And in another place, Hear "this, the Lord saith; Hear not "this, Donatus saith, Rogatus saith, "Vincentius saith, Hilarius saith, "Ambrose saith, Augustine saith, "but hearken unto this, The Lord "saith. Ep. 48." [al. 93. c. 6. Opp. t. ii. p. 239. It may be questioned whether this place is at all relevant to Cartwright's purpose. *Glorificatum est nomen meum in gentibus, dicit Dominus.* Audi, *dicit Dominus;* non, dicit Donatus, aut Rogatus, aut Vincentius, aut Hilarius, aut Ambrosius, aut Augustinus; sed, *dicit Dominus;* cum legitur, *Et benedicentur in eo omnes tribus terræ....Et replebitur gloria ejus omnis terra, fiat, fiat.* Et tu sedes Cartennis, et cum decem Rogatistis, qui remansistis, dicis, *Non fiat, non fiat.*] "And again, having to do "with an Arian, he affirmeth that "neither he ought to bring forth "the Council of Nice, nor the other "the Council of Arimine, thereby "to bring prejudice each to other; "neither ought the Arian to be "holden by the authority of the one "nor himself by the authority of "the other, but by the Scriptures,

tied and led by authority, as it were with a kind of captivity of judgment, and though there be reason to the contrary not to listen unto it, but to follow like beasts the first in the herd, they know not nor care not whither, this were brutish. Again, that authority of men should prevail with men either against or above Reason, is no part of our belief. "Com- "panies of learned men" be they never so great and reve- rend, are to yield unto Reason; the weight whereof is no whit prejudiced by the simplicity of his person which doth allege it, but being found to be sound and good, the bare opinion of men to the contrary must of necessity stoop and give place.

Irenæus[1], writing against Marcion, which held one God author of the Old Testament and another of the New, to prove that the Apostles preached the same God which was known before to the Jews, he copiously allegeth sundry their sermons and speeches uttered concerning that matter and recorded in Scripture. And lest any should be wearied with such store of allegations, in the end he concludeth, "While " we labour for these demonstrations out of Scripture, and do " summarily declare the things which many ways have been

"which are witnesses proper to "neither but common to both, "matter with matter, cause with "cause, reason with reason, ought "to be debated. Cont. Max. Arian. "lib. iii. c. 14." [al. lib. ii. c. 14. § 3. t. viii. 704. Nec nunc ego Nicænum, nec tu debes Ariminense tanquam præjudicaturus proferre concilium. Nec ego hujus auctoritate, nec tu illius detineris. Scripturarum auc- toritatibus, non quorumque propriis, sed utrisque communibus testibus, res cum re, causa cum causa, ratio cum ratione concertet.] "And in "another place against Petilian the " Donatist he saith, Let not these " words be heard between us, I say, "You say; let us hear this, Thus " saith the Lord. And by and by " speaking of the Scriptures he saith, "There let us seek the Church, "there let us try the cause. De " Unit. Eccles. cap. 5." [cap. 2, 3. Inter nos et Donatistas quæstio est, ubi sit hoc corpus: i.e. ubi sit Ec- clesia. Quid ergo facturi sumus? in verbis nostris eam quæsituri; an in verbis capitis sui, Domini nostri Jesu Christi? Puto, quod in illius potius verbis eam quærere debemus, qui Veritas est, et optime novit corpus suum.... In verbis nostris Eccle- siam quæri nolumus ... c. 5. Non audiamus, " Hæc dicis, hoc dico," sed audiamus, " Hæc dicit Domi- "nus." Sunt certe libri Dominici, quorum auctoritati utrique consen- timus, utrique cedimus, utrique ser- vimus: ibi quæramus Ecclesiam, ibi discutiamus causam nostram.] " Hereby [here] it is manifest that "the argument of the authority of "man affirmatively is nothing " worth."

[1] [P. 230. ed. Grabe. "Nobis "autem conlaborantibus his osten- "sionibus quæ ex Scripturis sunt, "et quæ multifarie dicta sunt bre- "viter et compendiose annunti- "antibus, et tu cum magnanimitate "attende eis, et non longiloquium "puta; hoc intelligens: quoniam," &c.]

BOOK II.
Ch. vii. 6.

"spoken, be contented quietly to hear, and do not think my "speech tedious: Quoniam ostensiones quæ sunt in Scriptu-"ris non possunt ostendi nisi ex ipsis Scripturis; Because "demonstrations that are in Scripture may not otherwise be "shewed than by citing them out of the Scriptures themselves "where they are." Which words make so little unto the purpose, that they seem as it were offended at him which hath called them thus solemnly forth to say nothing.

And concerning the verdict of Jerome[1]; if no man, be he never so well learned, have after the Apostles any authority to publish new doctrine as from heaven, and to require the world's assent as unto truth received by prophetical revelation; doth this prejudice the credit of learned men's judgments in opening that truth, which by being conversant in the Apostles' writings they have themselves from thence learned?

St. Augustine exhorteth not to hear men, but to hearken what God speaketh. His purpose is not (I think) that we should stop our ears against his own exhortation, and therefore he cannot mean simply that audience should altogether be denied unto men, but either that if men speak one thing and God himself teach another, then he not they to be obeyed; or if they both speak the same thing, yet then also man's speech unworthy of hearing, not simply, but in comparison of that which proceedeth from the mouth of God.

"Yea, but we doubt what the will of God is." Are we in this case forbidden to hear what men of judgment think it to be? If not, then this allegation also might very well have been spared.

In that ancient strife which was between the catholic Fathers and Arians, Donatists, and others of like perverse and froward disposition, as long as to Fathers or councils alleged on the one side the like by the contrary side were opposed, impossible it was that ever the question should by this means grow unto any issue or end. The Scripture they both believed: the Scripture they knew could not give

[1] [viii. 127. C. sup. Psalm. 86. v. 6. "'Dominus narrabit in scrip-"tura populorum et principum, "horum qui fuerunt in ea.' 'Prin-"cipum:' hoc est, Apostolorum et "Evangelistarum. 'Horum qui "fuerunt in ea.' Videte quid dicat: "'Qui fuerunt,' non 'qui sunt:' "ut exceptis Apostolis, quodcunque "aliud postea dicetur, abscindatur: "non habeat postea auctoritatem, "Quamvis ergo sanctus sit aliquis "post Apostolos, quamvis disertus "sit, non habet auctoritatem."]

sentence on both sides; by Scripture the controversy between them was such as might be determined. In this case what madness was it with such kinds of proofs to nourish their contention, when there were such effectual means to end all controversy that was between them! Hereby therefore it doth not as yet appear, that an argument of authority of man affirmatively is in matters divine nothing worth.

Which opinion being once inserted into the minds of the vulgar sort, what it may grow unto God knoweth. Thus much we see, it hath already made thousands so headstrong even in gross and palpable errors, that a man whose capacity will scarce serve him to utter five words in sensible manner blusheth not in any doubt concerning matter of Scripture to think his own bare *Yea* as good as the *Nay* of all the wise, grave, and learned judgments that are in the whole world: which insolency must be repressed, or it will be the very bane of Christian religion.

[7.] Our Lord's disciples marking what speech he uttered unto them, and at the same time calling to mind a common opinion held by the Scribes, between which opinion and the words of their Master it seemed unto them that there was some contradiction, which they could not themselves answer with full satisfaction of their own minds; the doubt they propose to our Saviour, saying, "Why then say the Scribes "that Elias must first come [1]?" They knew that the Scribes did err greatly, and that many ways even in matters of their own profession. They notwithstanding thought the judgment of the very Scribes in matters divine to be of some value; some probability they thought there was that Elias should come, inasmuch as the Scribes said it. Now no truth can contradict any truth; desirous therefore they were to be taught how both might stand together; that which they knew could not be false, because Christ spake it; and this which to them did seem true, only because the Scribes had said it. For the Scripture, from whence the Scribes did gather it, was not then in their heads. We do not find that our Saviour reproved them of error, for thinking the judgment of the Scribes to be worth the objecting, for esteeming it to be of any moment or value in matters concerning God.

[1] [S. Matt. xvii. 10.]

BOOK II.
Ch. vii 8, 9.

[8.] We cannot therefore be persuaded that the will of God is, we should so far reject the authority of men as to reckon it nothing. No, it may be a question, whether they that urge us unto this be themselves so persuaded indeed[1]. Men do sometimes bewray that by deeds, which to confess they are hardly drawn. Mark then if this be not general with all men for the most part. When the judgments of learned men are alleged against them, what do they but either elevate their credit, or oppose unto them the judgments of others as learned? Which thing doth argue that all men acknowledge in them some force and weight, for which they are loath the cause they maintain should be so much weakened as their testimony is available. Again, what reason is there why alleging testimonies as proofs, men give them some title of credit, honour, and estimation, whom they allege, unless beforehand it be sufficiently known who they are; what reason hereof but only a common ingrafted persuasion, that in some men there may be found such qualities as are able to countervail those exceptions which might be taken against them, and that such men's authority is not lightly to be shaken off?

[9.] Shall I add further, that the force of arguments drawn from the authority of Scripture itself, as Scriptures commonly are alleged, shall (being sifted) be found to depend upon the strength of this so much despised and debased authority of man? Surely it doth, and that oftener than we are aware of. For although Scripture be of God, and therefore the proof which is taken from thence must needs be of all other most invincible; yet this strength it hath not, unless it avouch the selfsame thing for which it is brought. If there be either undeniable appearance that so it doth, or reason such as cannot deceive, then Scripture-proof (no

---

[1] [Christ. Letter, p. 8: "We "pray you to explane your owne "meaning, whether you thinke "that there be anie naturall light, "teaching knowledge of things ne- "cessarie to salvation, which know- "ledge is not contayned in holy "Scripture." Hooker, MS. note: "They are matters of salvation I "think which you handle in this "booke. If therefore determinable "only by Scripture, why presse "you me so often with humane "authorities? Why alleage you "the Articles of Religion as the "voice of the Church aganst me? "Why cite you so many commen- "taries, bookes and sermons, partly "of Bishops, partly of others?"]

doubt) in strength and value exceedeth all. But for the most part, even such as are readiest to cite for one thing five hundred sentences of holy Scripture; what warrant have they, that any one of them doth mean the thing for which it is alleged? Is not their surest ground most commonly, either some probable conjecture of their own, or the judgment of others taking those Scriptures as they do? Which notwithstanding to mean otherwise than they take them, it is not still altogether impossible. So that now and then they ground themselves on human authority, even when they most pretend divine. Thus it fareth even clean throughout the whole controversy about that discipline which is so earnestly urged and laboured for. Scriptures are plentifully alleged to prove that the whole Christian world for ever ought to embrace it. Hereupon men term it *The discipline of God*. Howbeit examine, sift and resolve their alleged proofs, till you come to the very root from whence they spring, the heart wherein their strength lieth; and it shall clearly appear unto any man of judgment, that the most which can be inferred upon such plenty of divine testimonies is only this, That *some things* which they maintain, as far as *some men* can *probably conjecture*, do *seem* to have been out of Scripture *not absurdly* gathered. Is this a warrant sufficient for any man's conscience to build such proceedings upon, as have been and are put in ure for the stablishment of that cause?

[10.] But to conclude, I would gladly understand how it cometh to pass, that they which so peremptorily do maintain that human authority is nothing worth are in the cause which they favour so careful to have the common sort of men persuaded, that the wisest, the godliest and the best learned in all Christendom are that way given, seeing they judge this to make nothing in the world for them. Again how cometh it to pass they cannot abide that authority should be alleged on the other side, if there be no force at all in authorities on one side or other? Wherefore labour they to strip their adversaries of such furniture as doth not help? Why take they such needless pains to furnish also their own cause with the like? If it be void and to no purpose that the names of men are so frequent in their books,

BOOK II.
Ch. viii. 1.

what did move them to bring them in, or doth to suffer them there remaining? Ignorant I am not how this is salved, "They do it not but after the truth made manifest first "by reason or by Scripture: they do it not but to control "the enemies of the truth, who bear themselves bold upon "human authority making not for them but against them "rather[1]." Which answers are nothing: for in what place or upon what consideration soever it be they do it, were it in their own opinion of no force being done, they would undoubtedly refrain to do it.

A declaration what the truth is in this matter.

VIII. But to the end it may more plainly appear what we are to judge of their sentences, and of the cause itself wherein they are alleged: first it may not well be denied, that all actions of men endued with the use of reason are generally either good or evil. For although it be granted that no action is properly termed good or evil unless it be voluntary; yet this can be no let to our former assertion, That all actions of men endued with the use of reason are generally either good or evil; because even those things are done voluntarily by us which other creatures do naturally, inasmuch as we might stay our doing of them if we would. Beasts naturally do take their food and rest when it offereth itself unto them. If men did so too, and could not do otherwise of themselves, there were no place for any such reproof as that of our Saviour Christ unto his disciples[2], "Could ye "not watch with me one hour?" That which is voluntarily performed in things tending to the end, if it be well done, must needs be done with deliberate consideration of some reasonable cause wherefore we rather should do it than not. Whereupon it seemeth, that in such actions only those are said to be good or evil which are capable of deliberation: so that many things being hourly done by men, wherein they need not use with themselves any manner of consultation at all, it may perhaps hereby seem that well or ill-doing belongeth only to our

---

[1] "If at any time it happened "unto Augustine (as it did against "the Donatists and others) to al-"lege the authority of the ancient "Fathers which had been before "him; yet this was not done be-"fore he had laid a sure foundation "of his cause in the Scriptures, and "that also being provoked by the "adversaries of the truth, who bare "themselves high of some council, "or of some man of name that had "favoured that part." T. C. lib. ii. p. 22.

[2] Matt. xxvi. 40.

weightier affairs, and to those deeds which are of so great importance that they require advice. But thus to determine were perilous, and peradventure unsound also. I do rather incline to think, that seeing all the unforced actions of men are voluntary, and all voluntary actions tending to the end have choice, and all choice presupposeth the knowledge of some cause wherefore we make it: where the reasonable cause of such actions so readily offereth itself that it needeth not to be sought for; in those things though we do not deliberate, yet they are of their nature apt to be deliberated on, in regard of the will, which may incline either way, and would not any one way bend itself, if there were not some apparent motive to lead it. Deliberation actual we use, when there is doubt what we should incline our wills unto. Where no doubt is, deliberation is not excluded as impertinent unto the thing, but as needless in regard of the agent, which seeth already what to resolve upon. It hath no apparent absurdity therefore in it to think, that all actions of men endued with the use of reason are generally either good or evil.

[2.] Whatsoever is good, the same is also approved of God: and according unto the sundry degrees of goodness, the kinds of divine approbation are in like sort multiplied. Some things are good, yet in so mean a degree of goodness, that men are only not disproved nor disallowed of God for them. "No man hateth his own flesh[1]." "If ye do good "unto them that do so to you, the very publicans themselves "do as much[2]." "They are worse than infidels that have no "care to provide for their own[3]." In actions of this sort, the very light of Nature alone may discover that which is so far forth in the sight of God allowable.

[3.] Some things in such sort are allowed, that they be also required as necessary unto salvation, by way of direct immediate and proper necessity final; so that without performance of them we cannot by ordinary course be saved, nor by any means be excluded from life observing them. In actions of this kind our chiefest direction is from Scripture, for Nature is no sufficient teacher what we should do that

---

[1] Ephes. v. 29. [2] Matt. v. 46. [3] 1 Tim. v. 8.

we may attain unto life everlasting. The unsufficiency of the light of Nature is by the light of Scripture so fully and so perfectly herein supplied, that further light than this hath added there doth not need unto that end.

[4.] Finally some things, although not so required of necessity that to leave them undone excludeth from salvation, are notwithstanding of so great dignity and acceptation with God, that most ample reward in heaven is laid up for them. Hereof we have no commandment either in Nature or Scripture which doth exact them at our hands; yet those motives there are in both which draw most effectually our minds unto them. In this kind there is not the least action but it doth somewhat make to the accessory augmentation of our bliss. For which cause our Saviour doth plainly witness, that there shall not be as much as a cup of cold water bestowed for his sake without reward[1]. Hereupon dependeth whatsoever difference there is between the states of saints in glory; hither we refer whatsoever belongeth unto the highest perfection of man by way of service towards God; hereunto that fervour and first love of Christians did bend itself, causing them to sell their possessions, and lay down the price at the blessed Apostles' feet[2]. Hereat St. Paul undoubtedly did aim in so far abridging his own liberty, and exceeding that which the bond of necessary and enjoined duty tied him unto[3].

[5.] Wherefore seeing that in all these several kinds of actions there can be nothing possibly evil which God approveth; and that he approveth much more than he doth command[4]; and that his very commandments in some kind,

---

[1] Matt. x. 42.
[2] Acts iv. 34, 35.
[3] 1 Thess. ii. 7, 9.
[4] [Chr. Letter, p. 15: "Whether "we may not justly judge, that in "thus speaking you sow the seede "of that doctrine which leadeth "men to those arrogant workes of "supererogation."

Hooker, MS. note: "Did God "command Paul not to marry, or "not to receyve his daily mainte-"nance from the Church? He re-"frained both without command-"ment, but not without approba-"tion from God. Yea, he himself "doth counsell that which he doth "not command, and they that fol-"lowed his counsell did well, al-"though they did it not by way of "necessary obedience, but of volun-"tarie choice.

"Was the sale of Ananias his "land allowed in God's sight? I "hope you will graunt it was, sith "the Holy Ghost commendeth "sundry others which did the like. "His purpose in selling was good, "but his fraud irreligious and wicked "in withholding the price which

as namely his precepts comprehended in the law of nature, may be otherwise known than only by Scripture; and that to do them, howsoever we know them, must needs be acceptable in his sight[1]: let them with whom we have hitherto disputed consider well, how it can stand with reason to make the bare mandate of sacred Scripture the only rule of all good and evil in the actions of mortal men. The testimonies of God are true, the testimonies of God are perfect, the testimonies of God are all sufficient unto that end for which they were given. Therefore accordingly we do receive them, we do not think that in them God hath omitted any thing needful unto his purpose, and left his intent to be accomplished by our devisings. What the Scripture purposeth, the same in all points it doth perform.

Howbeit that here we swerve not in judgment, one thing especially we must observe, namely that the absolute perfection of Scripture is seen by relation unto that end whereto it tendeth. And even hereby it cometh to pass, that first such as imagine the general and main drift of the body of sacred Scripture not to be so large as it is, nor that God did

"he pretended to give whole. Yeat did not God command Ananias or the rest to make any such sale. For then how should Peter have said it was free for Ananias to have reteined it in his handes? God did therefore approve what he did not command in that action.

"Had not the Law as well free offerings, which were approved, as necessary, which were commanded of God?

"If I should ask, have you sinned in not setting your name to your book, I am very sure you will answere, no, but that you have done what God alloweth. Yeat hath not God I think commaunded that you should conceale your name: and so you have shewed yourself heere a Papist by doing a work of supererogation, if every thing done and not commanded be such a work. The like might be said although you had put your name thereto. For the case is like in all workes indifferent.

"But as for supererogation in poperie, it belongeth unto satisfactory actions, and not unto meritorious. Whereas therefore with them workes not commanded are chiefly meritorious, and in merit no supererogation held, you do ill to say that he which maketh any thing not commanded allowable establisheth workes of supererogation."

Chr. Letter, p. 15. "You appeare to us to scatter the prophane graines of poperie."

Hooker, MS. note. "It is not I that scatter, but you that gather more than ever was let fall."]

[1] [Hooker, MS. note on Chr. Letter, p. 14. "De imperfectione bonorum operum vide Hier. contra Lucifer. cap. 6." (p. 142, D. "Conveniat unusquisque cor suum, et in omni vita inveniet, quam rarum sit fidelem animam inveniri, ut nihil ob gloriæ cupiditatem, nihil ob rumusculos hominum faciat, &c.") "and Genebrard. in Symb. Athanas. p. 306."]

thereby intend to deliver, as in truth he doth, a full instruction in all things unto salvation necessary, the knowledge whereof man by nature could not otherwise in this life attain unto: they are by this very mean induced either still to look for new revelations from heaven, or else dangerously to add to the word of God uncertain tradition, that so the doctrine of man's salvation may be complete; which doctrine, we constantly hold in all respects without any such thing added to be so complete, that we utterly refuse as much as once to acquaint ourselves with any thing further. Whatsoever to make up the doctrine of man's salvation is added, as in supply of the Scripture's unsufficiency, we reject it. Scripture purposing this, hath perfectly and fully done it.

Again the scope and purpose of God in delivering the Holy Scripture such as do take more largely than behoveth, they on the contrary side, racking and stretching it further than by him was meant, are drawn into sundry as great inconveniences. These pretending the Scripture's perfection infer thereupon, that in Scripture all things lawful to be done must needs be contained. We count those things perfect which want nothing requisite for the end whereto they were instituted. As therefore God created every part and particle of man exactly perfect, that is to say in all points sufficient unto that use for which he appointed it; so the Scripture, yea, every sentence thereof, is perfect, and wanteth nothing requisite unto that purpose for which God delivered the same. So that if hereupon we conclude, that because the Scripture is perfect, therefore all things lawful to be done are comprehended in the Scripture; we may even as well conclude so of every sentence, as of the whole sum and body thereof, unless we first of all prove that it was the drift, scope, and purpose of Almighty God in Holy Scripture to comprise all things which man may practise.

[6.] But admit this, and mark, I beseech you, what would follow. God in delivering Scripture to his Church should clean have abrogated amongst them the law of nature; which is an infallible knowledge imprinted in the minds of all the children of men, whereby both general principles for directing of human actions are comprehended, and conclusions derived from them; upon which conclusions groweth in particularity the choice of good and evil in the daily affairs of this life. Admit this, and what shall the Scripture be but a snare and a torment to weak consciences, filling them with infinite perplexities, scrupulosities, doubts insoluble, and extreme despairs[1]? Not that the Scripture itself doth cause any such thing, (for it tendeth to the clean contrary, and the fruit thereof is resolute assurance and certainty in that it teacheth,) but the necessities of this life urging men to do that which the light of nature, common discretion and judgment of itself directeth them unto; on the other side, this doctrine teaching them that so to do were to sin against their own souls, and that they put forth their hands to iniquity whatsoever they go about and have not first the sacred Scripture of God for direction; how can it choose but bring the simple a thousand times to their wits' end? how can it choose but vex and amaze them? For in every action of common life to find out some sentence clearly and infallibly setting before our eyes what we ought to do, (seem we in Scripture never so expert,) would trouble us more than we are aware. In weak and tender minds we little know what misery this strict opinion would breed, besides the stops it would make in the whole course of all men's lives and actions. Make all things sin which we do by direction of nature's light, and by the rule of common discretion, without thinking at all upon Scripture; admit this position, and parents shall cause their children to sin, as oft as they cause them to do any thing, before they come to years of capacity and be ripe for knowledge in the Scripture: admit this, and it shall not be with masters as it was with him in the Gospel, but servants being commanded to go[2] shall stand still, till they have their errand warranted unto them by Scripture. Which as it standeth with Christian duty in some cases, so in common affairs to require it were most unfit.

BOOK II. Ch. viii. 7.

[7.] Two opinions therefore there are concerning sufficiency of Holy Scripture, each extremely opposite unto the other, and both repugnant unto truth. The schools of Rome teach

[1] "Where this doctrine is accused "of bringing men to despair, it "hath wrong. For when doubting "is the way to despair, against "which this doctrine offereth the "remedy, it must need be that it "bringeth comfort and joy to the "conscience of man." T. C. lib. ii. p. 61.
[2] Luke vii. 8.

Scripture to be so unsufficient, as if, except traditions were added, it did not contain all revealed and supernatural truth, which absolutely is necessary for the children of men in this life to know that they may in the next be saved. Others justly condemning this opinion grow likewise unto a dangerous extremity, as if Scripture did not only contain all things in that kind necessary, but all things simply, and in such sort that to do any thing according to any other law were not only unnecessary but even opposite unto salvation, unlawful and sinful. Whatsoever is spoken of God or things appertaining to God otherwise than as the truth is, though it seem an honour it is an injury. And as incredible praises given unto men do often abate and impair the credit of their deserved commendation; so we must likewise take great heed, lest in attributing unto Scripture more than it can have, the incredibility of that do cause even those things which indeed it hath most abundantly to be less reverently esteemed. I therefore leave it to themselves to consider, whether they have in this first point or not overshot themselves; which God doth know is quickly done, even when our meaning is most sincere, as I am verily persuaded theirs in this case was.

THE THIRD BOOK.

CONCERNING THEIR SECOND ASSERTION, THAT IN SCRIPTURE THERE MUST BE OF NECESSITY CONTAINED A FORM OF CHURCH POLITY, THE LAWS WHEREOF MAY IN NOWISE BE ALTERED.

THE MATTER CONTAINED IN THIS THIRD BOOK.

I. What the Church is, and in what respect Laws of Polity are thereunto necessarily required.

II. Whether it be necessary that some particular Form of Church Polity be set down in Scripture, sith the things that belong particularly to any such Form are not of necessity to Salvation.

III. That matters of Church Polity are different from matters of Faith and Salvation, and that they themselves so teach which are our reprovers for so teaching.

IV. That hereby we take not from Scripture any thing which thereunto with the soundness of truth may be given.

V. Their meaning who first urged against the Polity of the Church of England, that nothing ought to be established in the Church more than is commanded by the Word of God.

VI. How great injury men by so thinking should offer unto all the Churches of God.

VII. A shift notwithstanding to maintain it, by interpreting *commanded*, as though it were meant that greater things only ought to be found set down in Scripture particularly, and lesser framed by the general rules of Scripture.

VIII. Another device to defend the same, by expounding *commanded*, as if it did signify *grounded* on Scripture, and were opposed to things found out by light of natural reason only.

IX. How Laws for the Polity of the Church may be made by the advice of men, and how those Laws being not repugnant to the Word of God are approved in his sight.

X. That neither God's being the Author of Laws, nor yet his committing of them to Scripture, is any reason sufficient to prove that they admit no addition or change.

XI. Whether Christ must needs intend Laws unchangeable altogether, or have forbidden any where to make any other Law than himself did deliver.

BOOK II. **I.** ALBEIT the substance of those controversies whereinto we have begun to wade be rather of outward things appertaining to the Church of Christ, than of any thing wherein the nature and being of the Church consisteth, yet because the subject or matter which this position concerneth is, *A Form of Church Government* or *Church Polity*, it therefore behoveth us so far forth to consider the nature of the Church, as is requisite for men's more clear and plain understanding in what respect Laws of Polity or Government are necessary thereunto.

Ch. i. 1, 2.

What the Church is, and in what respect Laws of Polity are thereunto necessarily required.

[2.] That Church of Christ, which we properly term his body mystical, can be but one; neither can that one be sensibly discerned by any man, inasmuch as the parts thereof are some in heaven already with Christ, and the rest that are on earth (albeit their natural persons be visible) we do not discern under this property, whereby they are truly and infallibly of that body. Only our minds by intellectual conceit are able to apprehend, that such a real body there is, a body collective, because it containeth an huge multitude; a body mystical, because the mystery of their conjunction is removed altogether from sense. Whatsoever we read in Scripture concerning the endless love and the saving mercy which God sheweth towards his Church, the only proper subject thereof is this Church. Concerning this flock it is that our Lord and Saviour hath promised, "I give unto them eternal life, and "they shall never perish, neither shall any pluck them out "of my hands[1]." They who are of this society have such marks and notes of distinction from all others, as are not object unto our sense; only unto God, who seeth their hearts and understandeth all their secret cogitations, unto him they are clear and manifest. All men knew Nathanael to be an Israelite. But our Saviour piercing deeper giveth further testimony of him than men could have done with such certainty as he did, "Behold indeed an Israelite in whom is "no guile[2]." If we profess, as Peter did[3], that we love the Lord, and profess it in the hearing of men, charity is prone to believe all things, and therefore charitable men are likely to think we do so, as long as they see no proof to the contrary.

[1] John x. 28. [2] John i. 47. [3] John xxi. 15.

The Church Visible: its Unity.

But that our love is sound and sincere, that it cometh from "a pure heart and a good conscience and a faith unfeigned[1]," who can pronounce, saving only the Searcher of all men's hearts, who alone intuitively doth know in this kind who are His?

[3.] And as those everlasting promises of love, mercy, and blessedness belong to the mystical Church; even so on the other side when we read of any duty which the Church of God is bound unto, the Church whom this doth concern is a sensibly known company. And this visible Church in like sort is but one, continued from the first beginning of the world to the last end. Which company being divided into two moieties, the one before, the other since the coming of Christ; that part, which since the coming of Christ partly hath embraced and partly shall hereafter embrace the Christian Religion, we term as by a more proper name the Church of Christ. And therefore the Apostle affirmeth plainly of all men Christian[2], that be they Jews or Gentiles, bond or free, they are all incorporated into one company, they all make but *one body*[3]. The unity of which visible body and Church of Christ consisteth in that uniformity which all several persons thereunto belonging have, by reason of that *one Lord* whose servants they all profess themselves, that *one Faith* which they all acknowledge, that *one Baptism* wherewith they are all initiated[4].

[4.] The visible Church of Jesus Christ is therefore one, in outward profession of those things, which supernaturally appertain to the very essence of Christianity, and are necessarily required in every particular Christian man. "Let all "the house of Israel know for certainty," saith Peter, "that "God hath made him both Lord and Christ, even this Jesus "whom you have crucified[5]." Christians therefore they are not, which call not him their Master and Lord[6]. And from hence it came that first at Antioch, and afterwards throughout the whole world, all that are of the Church visible were

---

[1] 1 Tim. i. 5.
[2] 1 Cor. xii. 13.
[3] "That he might reconcile both "unto God in one body." Ephes. ii. 16. "That the Gentiles should "be inheritors also, and of the same "body." Ephes. iii. 6. Vide Th. p. 3. q. 7. art. 3. [should it not be "q. 8. art. 3?"]
[4] [Ephes. iv. 5.]
[5] Acts ii. 36.
[6] John xiii. 13; Col. iii. 24. iv. 1.

called Christians even amongst the heathen. Which name unto them was precious and glorious, but in the estimation of the rest of the world even Christ Jesus himself was execrable[1]; for whose sake all men were so likewise which did acknowledge him to be their Lord. This himself did foresee, and therefore armed his Church, to the end they might sustain it without discomfort. "All these things they will do unto you "for my name's sake; yea, the time shall come, that whoso-"ever killeth you will think that he doth God good service[2]." "These things I tell you, that when the hour shall come, "ye may then call to mind how I told you beforehand of "them[3]."

[5.] But our naming of Jesus Christ the Lord is not enough to prove us Christians, unless we also embrace that faith, which Christ hath published unto the world. To shew that the angel of Pergamus continued in Christianity, behold how the Spirit of Christ speaketh, "Thou keepest "my name, and thou hast not denied my faith[4]." Concerning which faith, "the rule thereof," saith Tertullian, "is "one alone, immovable, and no way possible to be better "framed anew[5]." What rule that is he sheweth by rehearsing those few articles of Christian belief. And before Tertullian, Ireney; "The Church though scattered through the whole "world unto the utmost borders of the earth, hath from "the Apostles and their disciples received belief[6]." The

---

[1] I Cor. i. 23. Vide et Tacitum, lib. Annal. xv. [c. 44.] "Nero quæ-"sitissimis pœnis affecit quos per "flagitia invisos vulgus Christianos "appellabat. Auctor nominis ejus "Christus, qui Tiberio imperitante "per procuratorem Pontium Pila-"tum supplicio affectus erat. Re-"pressaque in præsens exitiabilis "superstitio rursus erumpebat, non "modo per Judæam, originem ejus "mali, sed per urbem etiam, quo "cuncta undique atrocia aut pu-"denda confluunt celebranturque."

[2] John xv. 21.

[3] John xvi. 2. 4.

[4] Apoc. ii. 13.

[5] Tertull. de Virgin. Veland. [c. 1: "Regula quidem fidei una om-"nino est, sola immobilis et irre-"formabilis."]

[6] Iren. advers. Hæres. lib. i. cap. 2 et 3. [Ἡ μὲν ἐκκλησία, καίπερ καθ' ὅλης τῆς οἰκουμένης ἕως περάτων τῆς γῆς διεσπαρμένη, παρὰ δὲ τῶν Ἀποστόλων καὶ τῶν ἐκείνων μαθητῶν παραλαβοῦσα τὴν ... πίστιν ...

And c. iii: Ταύτην τὴν πίστιν, ὡς προέφαμεν, ἡ ἐκκλησία, καίπερ ἐν ὅλῳ τῷ κόσμῳ διεσπαρμένη, ἐπιμελῶς φυλάσσει, ὡς ἕνα οἶκον οἰκοῦσα· καὶ ὁμοίως πιστεύει τούτοις, ὡς μίαν ψυχὴν καὶ τὴν αὐτὴν ἔχουσα καρδίαν· καὶ συμφώνως ταῦτα κηρύσσει καὶ διδάσκει καὶ παραδίδωσιν, ὡς ἐν στόμα κεκτημένη .... καὶ οὔτε ὁ πάνυ δυνατὸς ἐν λόγῳ τῶν ἐν ταῖς ἐκκλησίαις προεστώτων ἕτερα τούτων ἐρεῖ.... οὔτε ὁ ἀσθενὴς ἐν τῷ λόγῳ ἐλαττώσει τὴν παράδοσιν.]

parts of which belief he also reciteth, in substance the very same with Tertullian, and thereupon inferreth, "This faith "the Church being spread far and wide preserveth as if one "house did contain them: these things it equally embraceth, "as though it had even one soul, one heart, and no more: "it publisheth, teacheth and delivereth these things with "uniform consent, as if God had given it but one only "tongue wherewith to speak. He which amongst the guides "of the Church is best able to speak uttereth no more than "this, and less than this the most simple doth not utter," when they make profession of their faith.

[6.] Now although we know the Christian faith and allow of it, yet in this respect we are but entering; entered we are not into the visible Church before our admittance by the door of Baptism. Wherefore immediately upon the acknowledgment of Christian faith, the Eunuch (we see) was baptized by Philip[1], Paul by Ananias[2], by Peter an huge multitude containing three thousand souls[3], which being once baptized were reckoned in the number of souls added to the visible Church.

[7.] As for those virtues that belong unto moral righteousness and honesty of life, we do not mention them, because they are not proper unto Christian men, as they are Christian, but do concern them as they are men. True it is, the want of these virtues excludeth from salvation[4]. So doth much

---

[1] Acts viii. 38.
[2] Acts xxii. 16.
[3] Acts ii. 41.
[4] [Chr. Letter, p. 8: "Whether "you mean....that morall virtues "are any where rightlie taught but "in holy Scripture: *or that where-* "*soever they be taught, they be of* "*such necessitie, that the wante of* "*them exclude from salvation, and* "*what Scripture approveth such a* "*saying?*"
  Hooker, MS. note: "A doctrine "which would well have pleased "Caligula, Nero, and such other "monsters to hear. Had the apo- "stles taught this it might have ad- "vanced them happily to honour. "The contrary doctrine hath cost "many saints and martyrs their "lives."

Ibid. p. 13: "The very cause "why good workes cannot justify "is for that evell workes do exclude "from salvation: and the most "righteous in some things offend. "Vid. Philon. p. 205." ($εἰ γὰρ$ βουληθείη ὁ θεὸς δικάσαι τῷ θνητῷ χωρὶς ἐλέου, τὴν καταδικάζουσαν ψῆφον οἴσει, μηδενὸς ἀνθρώπων τὸν ἀπὸ γενέσεως μέχρι τελευτῆς βίον ἄπταιστον ἐξ ἑαυτοῦ δραμόντος, ἀλλὰ τοῦ μὲν ἑκουσίοις, τοῦ δὲ ἀκουσίοις χρησαμένου τοῖς ἐν ποσὶν ὀλισθήμασιν.)
  And again, ibid.: "The workes "of heathen men not acceptable "*propter pravum agendi principium.* "Vide Eucher." ("Licet dicere, Phi- "losophiæ alios nomen usurpasse, "nos vitam. Etenim, qualia ab his "dari possunt præcepta vivendi?

more the absence of inward belief of heart; so doth despair and lack of hope; so emptiness of Christian love and charity. But we speak now of the visible Church, whose children are signed with this mark, "One Lord, one Faith, one Baptism." In whomsoever these things are, the Church doth acknowledge them for her children; them only she holdeth for aliens and strangers, in whom these things are not found. For want of these it is that Saracens, Jews, and Infidels are excluded out of the bounds of the Church. Others we may not deny to be of the visible Church, as long as these things are not wanting in them. For apparent it is, that all men are of necessity either Christians or not Christians. If by external profession they be Christians, then are they of the visible Church of Christ: and Christians by external profession they are all, whose mark of recognizance hath in it those things which we have mentioned, yea, although they be impious idolaters, wicked heretics, persons excommunicable, yea, and cast out for notorious improbity. Such withal we deny not to be the imps and limbs of Satan, even as long as they continue such.

[8.] Is it then possible, that the selfsame men should belong both to the synagogue of Satan and to the Church of Jesus Christ? Unto that Church which is his mystical body, not possible; because that body consisteth of none but only true Israelites, true sons of Abraham, true servants and saints of God. Howbeit of the visible body and Church of Jesus Christ those may be and oftentimes are, in respect of the main parts of their outward profession, who in regard of their inward disposition of mind, yea, of external conversation, yea, even of some parts of their very profession, are most worthily both hateful in the sight of God himself, and in the eyes of the sounder parts of the visible Church most execrable. Our Saviour therefore compareth the kingdom of

"Causam nesciunt: ignorantes "enim Deum, et statim ab exordio "justitiæ declinantes, consequenti "in cætera feruntur errore. Sic "fit postea, ut studiorum talium "finis sit vanitas. Siqui apud illos "honestiora definiunt, huic jactan- "tiæ deserviunt, huic laborant: ita "apud eos non est vacua vitiis ab- "stinentia vitiorum." Epist. ad Valerian. in Bibl. Patr. Colon. 1618. t. iv. p. 777.)

And again, ibid.: "Morall "workes done in faith, hope and "charitie are accepted and rewarded "with God, the want thereof pun- "ished with eternal death. Noe "fornicator, adulterer, &c."]

The Visible Church, as in Israel, may be corrupt. 343

heaven to a net, whereunto all which cometh neither is nor seemeth fish[1]: his Church he compareth unto a field, where tares manifestly known and seen by all men do grow intermingled with good corn[2], and even so shall continue till the final consummation of the world. God hath had ever and ever shall have some Church visible upon earth. When the people of God worshipped the calf in the wilderness[3]; when they adored the brazen serpent[4]; when they served the gods of nations; when they bowed their knees to Baal[5]; when they burnt incense and offered sacrifice unto idols[6]: true it is, the wrath of God was most fiercely inflamed against them, their prophets justly condemned them, as an adulterous seed[7] and a wicked generation of miscreants, which had forsaken the living God[8], and of him were likewise forsaken[9], in respect of that singular mercy wherewith he kindly and lovingly embraceth his faithful children. Howbeit retaining the law of God and the holy seal of his covenant, the sheep of his visible flock they continued even in the depth of their disobedience and rebellion[10]. Wherefore not only *amongst* them God always had his Church, because he had thousands which never bowed their knees to Baal[11]; but whose knees were bowed unto Baal, even they were also of the visible Church of God. Nor did the Prophet so complain, as if that Church had been quite and clean extinguished; but he took it as though there had not been remaining in the world any besides himself, that carried a true and an upright heart towards God with care to serve him according unto his holy will.

[9.] For lack of diligent observing the difference, first between the Church of God mystical and visible, then between the visible sound and corrupted, sometimes more, sometimes less, the oversights are neither few nor light that have been committed. This deceiveth them, and nothing else, who think that in the time of the first world the family of Noah did contain all that were of the visible Church of God.

---

[1] Matt. xiii. 47.
[2] Matt. xiii. 24.
[3] Exod. xxxii; Ps. cvi. 19, 20.
[4] 2 Kings xviii. 4.
[5] Jer. xi. 13.
[6] 2 Kings xxii. 17.
[7] Isa. lvii. 3.
[8] Isa. i. 4.
[9] Isa. lx. 15.
[10] Jer. xiii. 11.
[11] 1 Kings xix. 18.

BOOK III. From hence it grew, and from no other cause in the world,
Ch. i. 9. that the African bishops in the council of Carthage[1], knowing how the administration of baptism belongeth only to the Church of Christ, and supposing that heretics which were apparently severed from the sound believing Church could not possibly be of the Church of Jesus Christ, thought it utterly against reason, that baptism administered by men of corrupt belief should be accounted as a sacrament. And therefore in maintenance of rebaptization their arguments are built upon the fore-alleged ground[2], "That heretics are "not at all any part of the Church of Christ. Our Saviour "founded his Church on a rock, and not upon heresy[3]. " Power of baptizing he gave to his Apostles, unto heretics "he gave it not[4]. Wherefore they that are without the "Church, and oppose themselves against Christ, do but "scatter His sheep and flock, without the Church baptize "they cannot." Again, "Are heretics Christians or are they "not? If they be Christians, wherefore remain they not "in God's Church? If they be no Christians, how make they "Christians? Or to what purpose shall those words of the "Lord serve: 'He which is not with me is against me;' "and, 'He which gathereth not with me scattereth[5]?' "Wherefore evident it is, that upon misbegotten children and "the brood of Antichrist without rebaptization the Holy "Ghost cannot descend[6]." But none in this case so earnest as Cyprian[7]: "I know no baptism but one, and that in the

[1] [A.D. 256.]
[2] Fortunat. in Concil. Car. [" Jesus Christus, Dominus et Deus "noster, Dei Patris et Creatoris "Filius, super petram ædificavit "Ecclesiam suam, non super hæ-"resin; et potestatem baptizandi "Episcopis dedit, non hæreticis. "Quare qui extra Ecclesiam sunt, "et contra Christum stantes oves "ejus et gregem spargunt, bapti-"zare foris non possunt." t. i. 233. ed. Fell]
[3] Matt. vii. 24. xvi. 18.
[4] Matt. xxviii. 19.
[5] Matt. xii. 30.
[6] Secundinus in eodem Concil. [ibid. p. 234: "Hæretici Christiani "sunt, an non? Si Christiani sunt, "cur in Ecclesia Dei non sunt? Si "Christiani non sunt, quomodo "Christianos faciunt? aut quo "pertinebit sermo Domini dicentis, "Qui non est mecum adversus me "est, et qui non mecum colligit "spargit? Unde constat, super filios "alienos et soboles Antichristi Spi-"ritum Sanctum per manus imposi-"tionem tantummodo non posse "descendere."]

[7] [Not Cyprian, but another Cæcilius, Bishop of Bilta in Mauritania, ibid. 230: "Ego unum bap-"tisma in Ecclesia sola scio, et "extra Ecclesiam nullum. Hic erit "unum, ubi spes vera est et fides "certa. Sic enim scriptum est: "'Una fides, una spes, unum bap-"tisma,' non apud hæreticos, ubi "spes nulla est, et fides falsa, ubi

led to the Error of Rebaptization.

"Church only; none without the Church, where he that "doth cast out the devil hath the devil: he doth examine "about belief whose lips and words do breathe forth a canker; "the faithless doth offer the articles of faith; a wicked "creature forgiveth wickedness; in the name of Christ "Antichrist signeth; he which is cursed of God blesseth; "a dead carrion promiseth life; a man unpeaceable giveth "peace; a blasphemer calleth upon the name of God; a "profane person doth exercise priesthood; a sacrilegious "wretch doth prepare the altar; and in the neck of all "these that evil also cometh, the Eucharist a very bishop of "the devil doth presume to consecrate." All this was true, but not sufficient to prove that heretics were in no sort any part of the visible church of Christ, and consequently their baptism no baptism. This opinion therefore was afterwards both condemned by a better advised council[1], and also revoked by the chiefest of the authors thereof themselves.

[10.] What is it but only the selfsame error and misconceit,

"omnia per mendacium aguntur, "ubi exorcizat dæmoniacus; sacra- "mentum interrogat cujus os et "verba cancer emittunt: fidem dat "infidelis; veniam delictorum tri- "buit sceleratus; in nomine Christi "tingit Antichristus; benedicit a "Deo maledictus; vitam pollicetur "mortuus; pacem dat impacificus; "Deum invocat blasphemus; sa- "cerdotium administrat prophanus; "ponit altare sacrilegus. Ad hæc "omnia accedit et illud malum, ut "antistites Diaboli audeant Eucha- "ristiam facere."]

[1] In Concilio Nicæno. Vide Hieron. Dial. adv. Lucifer. [ii. 146. The genuine canons of the council of Nice contain no express general enactment on this point: only the 8th canon exempts the Novatians from rebaptization, the 19th imposes it on the followers of Paul of Samosata. The principle however, for which Hooker contends, is plainly implied in these two enactments. See Routh, Scriptorum Ecclesiasticorum Opuscula, p. 359, 366. The 7th canon of Constantinople is more express: but its genuineness is doubted: however it may safely be appealed to for the practice of the orthodox church in that age, ibid. 379, 450. The passage from St. Jerome is as follows: "Conatus est "beatus Cyprianus contritos lacus "fugere, nec bibere de aqua aliena; "et idcirco hæreticorum baptisma "reprobans, ad Stephanum tunc "Romanæ urbis Episcopum, qui a "beato Petro vigesimus sextus fuit, "super hac re Africanam synodum "direxit: sed conatus ejus frustra "fuit. Denique illi ipsi episcopi, qui "rebaptizandos hæreticos cum eo "statuerant, ad antiquam consuetu- "dinem revoluti, novum emisere "decretum." (But see the viiith canon of the council of Arles, (A. D. 314.) as quoted by Dr. Routh, Reliquiæ Sacræ, III. 137. and his note there, which seems to prove that St. Jerome did not mean a formal repeal of St. Cyprian's rule, but a discontinuance of it in practice, sanctioned as we know by St. Augustin, who was Jerome's contemporary.) And p. 147. A. "Syn-"odus quoque Nicæna......omnes "hæreticos suscepit, exceptis Pauli "Samosateni discipulis."]

wherewith others being at this day likewise possessed, they ask us where our Church did lurk, in what cave of the earth it slept for so many hundreds of years together before the birth of Martin Luther? As if we were of opinion that Luther did erect a New Church of Christ. No, the Church of Christ which was from the beginning is and continueth unto the end: of which Church all parts have not been always equally sincere and sound. In the days of Abia it plainly appeareth that Judah was by many degrees more free from pollution than Israel, as that solemn oration sheweth wherein he pleadeth for the one against the other in this wise[1]: "O Jeroboam and all Israel hear you me: have ye "not driven away the priests of the Lord, the sons of Aaron "and the Levites, and have made you priests like the people "of nations? Whosoever cometh to consecrate with a young "bullock and seven rams, the same may be a priest of them "that are no gods. But we belong unto the Lord our God, "and have not forsaken him; and the priests the sons of "Aaron minister unto the Lord every morning and every "evening burnt-offerings and sweet incense, and the bread is "set in order upon the pure table, and the candlestick of gold "with the lamps thereof to burn every evening; for we keep "the watch of the Lord our God, but ye have forsaken him[2]." In St. Paul's time the integrity of Rome was famous; Corinth many ways reproved; they of Galatia much more out of square[3]. In St. John's time Ephesus and Smyrna in far better state than Thyatira and Pergamus were[4]. We hope therefore that to reform ourselves, if at any time we have done amiss, is not to sever ourselves from the Church we were of

---

[1] 2 Chron. xiii. 4, 9, 10, 11.

[2] [See the conclusion of Hooker's first sermon on part of St. Jude.]

[3] [Rom. i. 8; 1 Cor. i. iii-vi; Gal. i. 6.]

[4] Apoc. ii. Vide S. Hieron. [ubi sup. 146. "Apostolis adhuc in sæ-"culo superstitibus, adhuc apud "Judæam Christi sanguine recenti, "phantasma Domini corpus assere-"batur: Galatas ad observationem "legis traductos Apostolus iterum "parturit: Corinthios resurrec-"tionem carnis non credentes pluri-"bus argumentis ad verum iter tra-"here conatur.....Plurimi (hære-"ticorum) vivente adhuc Joanne "Apostolo eruperunt.....Angelo "Ephesi deserta charitas imputa-"tur: in angelo Pergamenæ Ec-"clesiæ, idolothytorum esus, et "Nicolaitarum doctrina reprehen-"ditur: item apud angelum Thyati-"rorum, Hiezabel Prophetissa, et "simulacrorum escæ, et fornica-"tiones increpantur. Et tamen om-"nes hos ad pœnitentiam Domi-"nus hortatur...non autem cogeret "pœnitere, si non esset pœnitenti"bus veniam concessurus."]

before. In the Church we were, and we are so still. Other difference between our estate before and now we know none but only such as we see in Juda; which having sometime been idolatrous became afterwards more soundly religious by renouncing idolatry and superstition. If Ephraim "be joined "unto idols," the counsel of the Prophet is, "Let him alone." "If Israel play the harlot, let not Juda sin[1]." "If it seem "evil unto you," saith Josua[2], "to serve the Lord, choose "you this day whom ye will serve; whether the gods whom "your fathers served beyond the flood, or the gods of the "Amorites in whose land ye dwell: but I and mine house "will serve the Lord." The indisposition therefore of the Church of Rome to reform herself must be no stay unto us from performing our duty to God; even as desire of retaining conformity with them could be no excuse if we did not perform that duty.

Notwithstanding so far as lawfully we may, we have held and do hold fellowship with them. For even as the Apostle doth say of Israel that they are in one respect enemies but in another beloved of God[3]; in like sort with Rome we dare not communicate concerning sundry her gross and grievous abominations, yet touching those main parts of Christian truth wherein they constantly still persist, we gladly acknowledge them to be of the family of Jesus Christ; and our hearty prayer unto God Almighty is, that being conjoined so far forth with them, they may at the length (if it be his will) so yield to frame and reform themselves, that no distraction remain in any thing, but that we "all may with one heart "and one mouth glorify God the Father of our Lord and "Saviour[4]," whose Church we are.

As there are which make the Church of Rome utterly no Church at all, by reason of so many, so grievous errors in their doctrines; so we have them amongst us, who under pretence of imagined corruptions in our discipline do give even as hard a judgment of the Church of England itself[5].

[11.] But whatsoever either the one sort or the other teach, we must acknowledge even heretics themselves to be, though a maimed part, yet a part of the visible Church. If an infidel

---

[1] Hos. iv. 17, 15. [2] Josh. xxiv. 15. [3] Rom. xi. 28. [4] Rom. xv. 6.
[5] [See Pref. c. viii. 1.]

should pursue to death an heretic professing Christianity, only for Christian profession's sake, could we deny unto him the honour of martyrdom? Yet this honour all men know to be proper unto the Church. Heretics therefore are not utterly cut off from the visible Church of Christ.

If the Fathers do any where, as oftentimes they do, make the true visible Church of Christ and heretical companies opposite; they are to be construed as separating heretics, not altogether from the company of believers, but from the fellowship of sound believers. For where professed unbelief is, there can be no visible Church of Christ; there may be, where sound belief wanteth. Infidels being clean without the Church deny directly and utterly reject the very principles of Christianity; which heretics embrace, and err only by misconstruction: whereupon their opinions, although repugnant indeed to the principles of Christian faith, are notwithstanding by them held otherwise, and maintained as most consonant thereunto. Wherefore being Christians in regard of the general truth of Christ which they openly profess, yet they are by the Fathers every where spoken of as men clean excluded out of the right believing Church, by reason of their particular errors, for which all that are of a sound belief must needs condemn them.

[12.] In this consideration, the answer of Calvin unto Farel concerning the children of Popish parents doth seem crazed[1]. "Whereas," saith he, "you ask our judgment about a matter, "whereof there is doubt amongst you, whether ministers of " our order professing the pure doctrine of the Gospel may "lawfully admit unto baptism an infant whose father is a "stranger unto our Churches, and whose mother hath fallen "from us unto the Papacy, so that both the parents are "popish: thus we have thought good to answer; namely, " that it is an absurd thing for us to baptize them which " cannot be reckoned members of our body. And sith Papists'

---

[1] Calvin. Epist. 149. [p. 173. ed. Genev. 1617. "Rogas, liceatne or-"dinis nostri ministris, qui puram "evangelii doctrinam profitentur, ad "baptismum admittere infantem, "cujus pater ab ecclesiis nostris "alienus est, mater vero ad Papatum "defecit, ita ut parentes ambo sint "Papistæ: ita respondendum cen-"suimus; absurdum esse ut eos "baptizemus, qui corporis nostri "membra censeri nequeunt. Quum "in hoc ordine sint Papistarum "liberi, quomodo baptismum illis "administrare liceat, non vide-"mus."]

"children are such, we see not how it should be lawful to "minister baptism unto them." Sounder a great deal is the answer of the ecclesiastical college of Geneva unto Knox, who having signified unto them, that himself did not think it lawful to baptize bastards or the children of idolaters (he meaneth Papists) or of persons excommunicate, till either the parents had by repentance submitted themselves unto the Church, or else their children being grown unto the years of understanding should come and sue for their own baptism : " For thus "thinking," saith he, "I am thought to be over-severe, and " that not only by them which are popish, but even in their "judgments also who think themselves maintainers of the " truth [1]." Master Knox's oversight herein they controlled. Their sentence was, " Wheresoever the profession of Christ-" ianity hath not utterly perished and been extinct, infants " are beguiled of their right, if the common seal be denied " them [2]." Which conclusion in itself is sound, although it seemeth the ground is but weak whereupon they built it. For the reason which they yield of their sentence, is this ; " The " promise which God doth make to the faithful concerning " their seed reacheth unto a thousand generations ; it resteth " not only in the first degree of descent. Infants therefore " whose great-grandfathers have been holy and godly, do in " that respect belong to the body of the church, although the " fathers and grandfathers of whom they descend have been " apostates [3]: because the tenure of the grace of God which " did adopt them three hundred years ago or more in their " ancient predecessors, cannot with justice be defeated and " broken off by their parents' impiety coming between [4]."

---

[1] Epist. 283. [Ibid. p. 441. "An "ad baptismum admitti debeant "spurii, idololatrarum et excommu-"nicatorum filii, priusquam vel pa-"rentes per resipiscentiam sese sub-"diderint Ecclesiæ, vel ii qui ex hu-"jusmodi prognati sunt, baptismum "petere possint. Quia nego, plus "æquo severus judicor, non a solis "Papisticis, verum etiam ab iis qui "sibi veritatis patroni videntur."]

[2] Epist. 285. [Ibid. p. 442. " Ubicunque non prorsus intercidit, "vel extincta fuit Christianismi pro-"fessio, fraudantur jure suo infantes, "si a communi symbolo arcentur."

[3] ["Apostataes," A.—changed to "Apostates" in Spenser's ed. 1604, and subsequent ones.] 1886.

[4] Calv. ubi supra. "Imprimis "expendere convenit, quos Deus "sua voce ad baptismum invitet. " Promissio autem non sobolem "tantum cujusque fidelium in pri-"mo gradu comprehendit, sed in "mille generationes extenditur.... " Nobis ergo minime dubium est, " quin soboles ex piis et sanctis

BOOK III.
Ch. i. 13.

By which reason of theirs although it seem that all the world may be baptized, inasmuch as no man living is a thousand descents removed from Adam himself, yet we mean not at this time either to uphold or to overthrow it: only their alleged conclusion we embrace, so it be construed in this sort; "That forasmuch as men remain in the visible Church, till "they utterly renounce the profession of Christianity, we may "not deny unto infants their right by withholding from them "the public sign of holy baptism, if they be born where the "outward acknowledgment of Christianity is not clean gone "and extinguished." For being in such sort born, their parents are within the Church, and therefore their birth doth give them interest and right in baptism.

[13.] Albeit not every error and fault, yet heresies and crimes which are not actually repented of and forsaken, exclude quite and clean from that salvation which belongeth unto the mystical body of Christ; yea, they also make a separation from the visible sound Church of Christ; altogether from the visible Church neither the one nor the other doth sever. As for the act of excommunication, it neither shutteth out from the mystical, nor clean from the visible, but only from fellowship with the visible in holy duties. With what congruity then doth the Church of Rome deny, that her enemies, whom she holdeth always for heretics, do at all appertain to the Church of Christ; when her own do freely grant, that albeit the Pope (as they say) cannot teach heresy nor propound error, he may notwithstanding himself worship idols, think amiss concerning matters of faith[1], yea, give himself unto acts diabolical, even being Pope? How exclude they us from being any part of the Church of Christ under the colour and pretence of heresy, when they cannot but grant it possible even for him to be as touching his own personal persuasion

"atavis progenita, quamvis apostatæ "fuerint avi et parentes, ad Eccle- "siæ tamen corpus pertineant.... "Quia iniquum est, cum Deus ante "annos trecentos vel plures adopti- "one sua eos dignatus fuerit, ut "quæ deinde secuta est parentum "impietas cælestis gratiæ cursum "abrumpat." The former letter was dated 1553, this 1559.]

[1] [Harding ap. Jewel. Def. of Apol. 632. ed. 1611. "The Pope "may err by personed error, in his "own private judgment, as a man; "and as a particular Doctor in his "own opinion: yet as he is Pope.. "in public judgment, in delibera- "tion, and definitive sentence, he "never erreth nor ever erred."]

heretical[1], who in their opinion not only is of the Church, but holdeth the chiefest place of authority over the same? But of these things we are not now to dispute. That which already we have set down, is for our present purpose sufficient.

[14.] By the Church therefore in this question we understand no other than only the visible Church. For preservation of Christianity there is not any thing more needful, than that such as are of the visible Church have mutual fellowship and society one with another. In which consideration, as the main body of the sea being one, yet within divers precincts hath divers names; so the Catholic Church is in like sort divided into a number of distinct Societies, every of which is termed a Church within itself. In this sense the Church is always a visible society of men; not an assembly, but a society. For although the name of the Church be given unto Christian assemblies, although any multitude of Christian men congregated may be termed by the name of a Church, yet assemblies properly are rather things that belong to a Church. Men are assembled for performance of public actions; which actions being ended, the assembly dissolveth itself and is no longer in being, whereas the Church which was assembled doth no less continue afterwards than before. "Where but "three are, and they of the laity also (saith Tertullian), yet "there is a Church[2]:" that is to say, a Christian assembly. But a Church, as now we are to understand it, is a Society; that is, a number of men belonging unto some Christian fellowship, the place and limits whereof are certain. That wherein they have communion is the public exercise of such duties as those mentioned in the Apostles' Acts, *Instruction, Breaking of Bread,* and *Prayers*[3]. As therefore they that are of the mystical body of Christ have those inward graces and virtues,

---

[1] [Alphonsus de Castro, a Spanish Franciscan, who came with Philip II. to England † 1558, "un des plus "célèbres théologiens espagnols du "16me siècle" (Biog. Univ.). His great work, *adv. omnes hæreses*, was printed ten times in 26 years) de Hær. i. 4, ap. Jewel. 633. "Non dubitamus "an hæreticum esse, et Papam esse, "coire in unum possint...... Non "enim credo aliquem esse adeo "impudentem Papæ assentatorem, "ut ei tribuere hoc velit, ut nec "errare, nec in interpretatione sacra- "rum literarum hallucinari possit." This passage (in the first ed. 1534) was omitted in the later editions of the work. See Laud's Conf. with Fisher, p. 263, 264. ed. 1639.]

[2] Tertull. Exhort. ad Castit. [c. 7.] "Ubi tres, Ecclesia est, licet Laici."

[3] Acts ii. 42.

BOOK III.
Ch. ii. 1.

whereby they differ from all others, which are not of the same body; again, whosoever appertain to the visible body of the Church, they have also the notes of external profession, whereby the world knoweth what they are: after the same manner even the several societies of Christian men, unto every of which the name of a Church is given with addition betokening severalty, as the Church of Rome, Corinth, Ephesus, England, and so the rest, must be endued with correspondent general properties belonging unto them as they are public Christian societies. And of such properties common unto all societies Christian, it may not be denied that one of the very chiefest is Ecclesiastical Polity.

Which word I therefore the rather use, because the name of Government, as commonly men understand it in ordinary speech, doth not comprise the largeness of that whereunto in this question it is applied. For when we speak of Government, what doth the greatest part conceive thereby, but only the exercise of superiority peculiar unto rulers and guides of others? To our purpose therefore the name of Church-Polity will better serve, because it containeth both government and also whatsoever besides belongeth to the ordering of the Church in public. Neither is any thing in this degree more necessary than Church-Polity, which is a form of ordering the public spiritual affairs of the Church of God.

Whether it be necessary that some particular form of Church-Polity be set down in Scripture, sith the things that belong particularly unto any such form are not of necessity to salvation.

II. But we must note, that he which affirmeth speech to be necessary amongst all men throughout the world, doth not thereby import that all men must necessarily speak one kind of language. Even so the necessity of polity and regiment in all Churches may be held without holding any one certain form to be necessary in them all. Nor is it possible that any form of polity, much less of polity ecclesiastical, should be good, unless God himself be author of it[1]. "Those "things that are not of God" (saith Tertullian), "they can "have no other than God's adversary for their author." Be it whatsoever in the Church of God, if it be not of God, we hate it. Of God it must be; either as those things sometime were, which God supernaturally revealed, and so delivered them unto Moses for government of the commonwealth of Israel; or else as those things which men find

[1] Tertull. de habitu mul. [c. 8.] "Æmuli sint necesse est, quæ Dei "non sunt."

it must be of God, but need not be in Scripture.

out by help of that light which God hath given them unto that end[1]. The very Law of Nature itself, which no man can deny but God hath instituted, is not of God, unless that be of God, whereof God is the author as well this later way as the former. But forasmuch as no form of Church-Polity is thought by them to be lawful, or to be of God, unless God be so the author of it that it be also set down in Scripture; they should tell us plainly, whether their meaning be that it must be there set down in whole or in part. For if wholly, let them shew what one form of Polity ever was so. Their own to be so taken out of Scripture they will not affirm; neither deny they that in part even this which they so much oppugn is also from thence taken. Again they should tell us, whether only that be taken out of Scripture which is actually and particularly there set down; or else that also which the general principles and rules of Scripture potentially contain. The one way they cannot as much as pretend, that all the parts of their own discipline are in Scripture: and the other way their mouths are stopped, when they would plead against all other forms besides their own; seeing the general principles are such as do not particularly prescribe any one, but sundry may equally be consonant unto the general axioms of the Scripture.

[2.] But to give them some larger scope and not to close them up in these straits: let their allegations be considered, wherewith they earnestly bend themselves against all which deny it necessary that any one complete form of Church-Polity should be in Scripture. First therefore whereas it hath been told them[2] that matters of faith, and in general matters necessary unto salvation, are of a different nature from ceremonies, order, and the kind of church government; and that the one is necessary to be expressly contained in the word of God, or else manifestly collected out of the same, the other not so; that it is necessary not to receive the one, unless there be something in Scripture for them; the other free, if nothing against them may thence be alleged; although there do not appear any just or reasonable cause to reject

---

[1] Rom. ii. 15. "Ille legis hujus "inventor, disceptator, lator." Cic. iii. de Repub. [ap. Lact. vi. 8. and Opp. vii. 906. Ed. Ernesti.]

[2] [In Whitgift's Answer to the Admon. 20, 21. See Defence 76, &c.]

BOOK III. or dislike of this, nevertheless as it is not easy to speak to
Ch. ii. 2. the contentation of minds exulcerated in themselves, but
that somewhat there will be always which displeaseth; so
herein for two things we are reproved. [1]The first is *mis-
distinguishing*, because matters of discipline and church government are (as they say) "matters necessary to salvation and of
"faith," whereas we put a difference between the one and the
other. Our second fault is, *injurious dealing* with the Scripture
of God, as if it contained only "the principal points of religion,
"some rude and unfashioned matter of building the Church,
"but had left out that which belongeth unto the form and
"fashion of it; as if there were in the Scripture no more than
"only to cover the Church's nakedness, and not chains,
"bracelets, rings, jewels, to adorn her; sufficient to quench her
"thirst, to kill her hunger, but not to minister a more liberal,
"and (as it were) a more delicious and dainty diet." In which
case[2] our apology shall not need to be very long.

[1] Two things misliked; the one that we distinguish matters of discipline or church government from matters of faith and necessary unto salvation: the other, that we are injurious to the Scripture of God in abridging the large and rich contents thereof. Their words are these: "You which distinguish "between these, and say, that mat-"ters of faith and necessary unto "salvation may not be tolerated in "the Church, unless they be ex-"pressly contained in the word of "God, or manifestly gathered; but "that ceremonies, order, discipline, "government in the Church, may "not be received against the word "of God, and consequently may be "received if there be no word "against them, although there be "none for them: you (I say) dis-"tinguishing or dividing after this "sort do prove yourself an evil "divider. As though matters of "discipline and kind of government "were not matters necessary to sal-"vation and of faith." [This sentence ("as though....of faith") is transposed by Hooker to this place, from where it occurs in T. C. a few lines above.] "It is no small "injury which you do unto the "word of God to pin it in so narrow "room, as that it should be able to "direct us but in the principal points "of our religion; or as though the "substance of religion, or some rude "and unfashioned matter of build-"ing of the Church were uttered in "them; and those things were left "out that should pertain to the form "and fashion of it; or as if there "were in the Scriptures only to "cover the Church's nakedness, and "not also chains and bracelets and "rings and other jewels to adorn "her and set her out; or that, to "conclude, there were sufficient to "quench her thirst and kill her "hunger, but not to minister unto "her a more liberal and (as it were) "a more delicious and dainty diet. "These things you seem to say, "when you say, that matters neces-"sary to salvation and of Faith are "contained in Scripture: especially "when you oppose these things to "Ceremonies, Order, Discipline, "and Government." T. C. lib. i. p. 26. [14.]

[2] [cause?]

III. The mixture of those things by speech which by nature are divided, is the mother of all error. To take away therefore that error which confusion breedeth, distinction is requisite. Rightly to distinguish is by conceit of mind to sever things different in nature, and to discern wherein they differ. So that if we imagine a difference where there is none, because we distinguish where we should not, it may not be denied that we misdistinguish. The only trial whether we do so, yea or no, dependeth upon comparison between our conceit and the nature of things conceived.

Ch. iii. 1-3. That matters of discipline are different from matters of faith and salvation; and that they themselves so teach which are our reprovers.

[2.] Touching matters belonging unto the Church of Christ this we conceive, that they are not of one suit. Some things are *merely* of faith, which things it doth suffice that we know and believe; some things not only to be known but done, because they concern the actions of men. Articles about the Trinity are matters of *mere* faith, and must be believed. Precepts concerning the works of charity are matters of action; which to know, unless they be practised, is not enough. This being so clear to all men's understanding, I somewhat marvel that they especially should think it absurd to oppose Church-government, a plain matter of action, unto matters of faith, who know that themselves divide the Gospel into Doctrine and Discipline[1]. For if matters of discipline be rightly by them distinguished from matters of doctrine, why not matters of government by us as reasonably set against matters of faith? Do not they under doctrine comprehend the same which we intend by matter of faith? Do not they under discipline comprise the regiment of the Church? When they blame that in us which themselves follow, they give men great cause to doubt that some other thing than judgment doth guide their speech.

[3.] What the Church of God standeth bound to know or do, the same in part nature teacheth. And because nature can teach them but only in part, neither so fully as is requisite for man's salvation, nor so easily as to make the way plain and expedite enough that many may come to the knowledge

---

[1] T. C. l. ii. p. 1. "We offer "to shew the Discipline to be a "part of the Gospel." And again, p. 5. "I speak of the Discipline as "of a part of the Gospel." If the Discipline be one part of the Gospel, what other part can they assign but Doctrine to answer in division to the Discipline? [See also lib. i. p. 32.]

of it, and so be saved; therefore in Scripture hath God both collected the most necessary things that the school of nature teacheth unto that end, and revealeth also whatsoever we neither could with safety be ignorant of, nor at all be instructed in but by supernatural revelation from him. So that Scripture containing all things that are in this kind any way needful for the Church, and the principal of the other sort, this is the next thing wherewith we are charged as with an error: we teach that whatsoever is unto salvation termed *necessary* by way of excellency, whatsoever it standeth all men upon to know or do that they may be saved, whatsoever there is whereof it may truly be said, "This not to believe "is eternal death and damnation," or, "This every soul that "will live must duly observe;" of which sort the articles of Christian faith and the sacraments of the Church of Christ are: all such things if Scripture did not comprehend, the Church of God should not be able to measure out the length and the breadth of that way wherein for ever she is to walk, heretics and schismatics never ceasing some to abridge, some to enlarge, all to pervert and obscure the same. But as for those things that are accessory hereunto, those things that so belong to the way of salvation, as to alter them is no otherwise to change that way, than a path is changed by altering only the uppermost face thereof; which be it laid with gravel, or set with grass, or paved with stone, remaineth still the same path; in such things because discretion may teach the Church what is convenient, we hold not the Church further tied herein unto Scripture, than that against Scripture nothing be admitted in the Church, lest that path which ought always to be kept even, do thereby come to be overgrown with brambles and thorns.

[4.] If this be unsound, wherein doth the point of unsoundness lie? It is not that we make some things *necessary*, some things *accessory* and appendent only: for our Lord and Saviour himself doth make that difference, by terming judgment and mercy and fidelity with other things of like nature, "the greater and weightier matters of the law[1]." Is it then in that we account ceremonies, (wherein we do not comprise sacraments, or any other the like substantial duties in the

[1] Matt. xxiii. 23.

exercise of religion, but only such external rites as are usually annexed unto Church actions,) is it an oversight that we reckon these things and matters[1] of government in the number of things accessory, not things necessary in such sort as hath been declared? Let them which therefore think us blameable consider well their own words. Do they not plainly compare the one unto garments which cover the body of the Church; the other unto rings, bracelets, and jewels, that only adorn it; the one to that food which the Church doth live by, the other to that which maketh her diet liberal, "dainty," and more "delicious"[2]? Is dainty fare a thing necessary to the sustenance, or to the clothing of the body rich attire? If not, how can they urge the necessity of that which themselves resemble by things not necessary? or by what construction shall any man living be able to make those comparisons true, holding that distinction untrue, which putteth a difference between things of external regiment in the Church and things necessary unto salvation?

BOOK III.
Ch. iv. 1.

IV. Now as it can be to nature no injury that of her we say the same which diligent beholders of her works have observed; namely, that she provideth for all living creatures nourishment which may suffice; that she bringeth forth no kind of creature whereto she is wanting in that which is needful[3]: although we do not so far magnify her exceeding bounty, as to affirm that she bringeth into the world the sons of men

That we do not take from Scripture any thing which may be thereunto given with soundness of truth.

---

[1] The government of the Church of Christ granted by Fenner himself to be thought a matter of great moment, yet not of the substance of religion. Against D. Bridges, pag. 121: if it be Fenner which was the author of that book. ["A Defence "of the Ecclesiastical Discipline "ordayned of God to be used in "His Church, against a Reply of "Maister Bridges to 'a briefe and "plain Declaration' of it, which was "printed an. 1584." 4°. 1588, p. 120, 121. "Our Saviour is sayde "with charge and commaundement "that they should be observed, to "have delivered to His Disciples "such things, as for the space of "fourtie days He declared unto "them concerning his kingdome. "A part whereof (it hathe bin "alreadie shewed) must needes be "understoode to have bin of the "government of His Church, "which necessarilie *dependeth on* "His kingdome."]

[2] ["Mirum videri debet...... "doctrina evangelica tanquam bona "valetudine contentos, de disciplina, "qua eandem tueantur, ac vires "simul et colorem acquirant, non "esse solicitos." Eccl. Disc. fol. 2. "Medicis contenta, qui salutem "procurassent, aliptas ad colorem "et vires acquirendas non adhibuit." fol. 3.]

[3] Arist. Pol. lib. i. cap. 8. et Plato in Menex. [t. ii. 237. E. ed. Serrani. πᾶν γὰρ τὸ τεκὸν τροφὴν ἔχει ἐπιτήδειαν ὧν ἂν τέκῃ.] Arist. lib. iii. de Animal. c. 4, 5.

adorned with gorgeous attire, or maketh costly buildings to spring up out of the earth for them: so I trust that to mention what the Scripture of God leaveth unto the Church's discretion in some things, is not in any thing to impair the honour which the Church of God yieldeth to the sacred Scripture's perfection. Wherein seeing that no more is by us maintained, than only that Scripture must needs teach the Church whatsoever is in such sort necessary as hath been set down; and that it is no more disgrace for Scripture to have left a number of other things free to be ordered at the discretion of the Church, than for nature to have left it unto the wit of man to devise his own attire, and not to look for it as the beasts of the field have theirs: if neither this can import, nor any other proof sufficient be brought forth, that we either will at any time or ever did affirm the sacred Scripture to comprehend no more than only those bare necessaries; if we acknowledge that as well for particular application to special occasions, as also in other manifold respects, infinite treasures of wisdom are over and besides abundantly to be found in the Holy Scripture; yea, that scarcely there is any noble part of knowledge, worthy the mind of man, but from thence it may have some direction and light; yea, that although there be no necessity it should of purpose prescribe any one particular form of church government, yet touching the manner of governing in general the precepts that Scripture setteth down are not few, and the examples many which it proposeth for all church governors even in particularities to follow; yea, that those things finally which are of principal weight in the very particular form of church polity (although not that form which they imagine, but that which we against them uphold) are in the selfsame Scriptures contained: if all this be willingly granted by us which are accused "to pin the word of God in so narrow room, " as that it should be able to direct us but in principal points of " our religion; or as though the substance of religion or some " rude and unfashioned matter of building the Church were " uttered in them, and those things left out that should pertain " to the form and fashion of it;" let the cause of the accused be referred to the accusers' own conscience, and let that judge whether this accusation be deserved where it hath been laid.

V. But so easy it is for every man living to err, and so hard to wrest from any man's mouth the plain acknowledgment of error, that what hath been once inconsiderately defended, the same is commonly persisted in, as long as wit by whetting itself is able to find out any shift, be it never so slight, whereby to escape out of the hands of present contradiction. So that it cometh herein to pass with men unadvisedly fallen into error, as with them whose state hath no ground to uphold it, but only the help which by subtle conveyance they draw out of casual events arising from day to day, till at length they be clean spent. They which first gave out, that "nothing ought to be established in the "Church which is not commanded by the word of God," thought this principle plainly warranted by the manifest words of the Law[1], "Ye shall put nothing unto the word "which I command you, neither shall you take aught there- "from, that ye may keep the commandments of the Lord "your God, which I command you." Wherefore having an eye to a number of rites and orders in the Church of England, as marrying with a ring, crossing in the one sacrament, kneeling at the other, observing of festival days moe than only that which is called the Lord's day, enjoining abstinence at certain times from some kinds of meat, churching of women after childbirth, degrees taken by divines in universities, sundry church offices, dignities, and callings, for which they found no commandment in the Holy Scripture, they thought by the one only stroke of that axiom to have cut them off. But that which they took for an oracle being sifted was repelled. True it is concerning the word of God, whether it be by misconstruction of the sense or by falsification of the words, wittingly to endeavour that any thing may seem divine which is not, or any thing not seem which is, were plainly to abuse, and even to falsify divine evidence; which injury offered but unto men, is most worthily counted heinous. Which point I wish they did well observe, with whom nothing is more familiar than to plead in these causes, "the law of "God," "the word of the Lord;" who notwithstanding when

BOOK III.
Ch. v. 1.

Their meaning who first did plead against the Polity of the Church of England, urging that "nothing "ought to "be esta-"blished "in the "Church "which is "not com-"manded "by the "word of "God;" and what Scripture they thought they might ground this assertion upon.

---

[1] "Whatsoever I command you, "take heed you do it. Thou shalt "put nothing thereto, nor take "aught therefrom." Deut. iv. 2. and xii. 32. [Adm. p. 3. See also Answ. 59, 60, 61. T. C. i. 21, 22. Eccl. Disc. fol. 5.]

BOOK III.
Ch. vi. 1.

they come to allege what word and what law they mean, their common ordinary practice is to quote by-speeches in some historical narration or other, and to urge them as if they were written in most exact form of law. What is to add to the law of God if this be not? When that which the word of God doth but deliver historically, we construe[1] without any warrant as if it were legally meant, and so urge it further than we can prove that it was intended; do we not add to the laws of God, and make them in number seem moe than they are? It standeth us upon to be careful in this case. For the sentence of God is heavy against them that wittingly shall presume thus to use the Scripture[2].

The same assertion we cannot hold without doing wrong unto all Churches.

VI. But let that which they do hereby intend be granted them; let it once stand as consonant to reason, that because we are forbidden to add to the law of God any thing, or to take aught from it, therefore we may not for matters of the Church make any law more than is already set down in Scripture: who seeth not what sentence it shall enforce us to give against all Churches in the world, inasmuch as there is not one, but hath had many things established in it, which though the Scripture did never command, yet for us to condemn were rashness? Let the Church of God even in the time of our Saviour Christ serve for example unto all the rest. In their domestical celebration of the passover, which supper they divided (as it were) into two courses; what Scripture did give commandment that between the first and the second he that was chief should put off the residue of his garments, and keeping on his feast-robe[3] only wash the feet of them that were with him? What Scripture did command them never to lift up their hands unwashed in prayer unto God? which custom Aristeas (be the credit of the author more or less) sheweth wherefore they did so religiously observe[4]. What Scripture did command the Jews every festival-day to fast till the sixth hour? the custom both

---

[1] ["conster," and so viii. 1. IV. xl. 7. and elsewhere, 1st ed. but not uniformly.] 1886.

[2] [Rev. xxii. 18.]

[3] John xiii. Cœnatorium: de quo Matt. xxii. 12. Ibi de Cœnatorio nuptiali.

[4] [De LXX. Interpretibus, ad calc. Josephi, Colon. 1691, p. 33, ἐπερώτησαν δὲ καὶ τοῦτο᾽ τίνος χάριν ἀπονιζόμενοι τὰς χεῖρας, τὸ τηνικαῦτα εὔχονται; διεσάφουν δὲ, ὅτι μαρτύριόν ἐστι τοῦ μηδὲν εἰργάσθαι κακόν᾽ πᾶσα γὰρ ἐνέργεια διὰ τῶν χειρῶν γίνεται.]

mentioned by Josephus in the history of his own life[1], and by the words of Peter signified[2]. Tedious it were to rip up all such things as were in that church established, yea by Christ himself and by his Apostle observed, though not commanded any where in Scripture.

BOOK III.
Ch. vii. 1, 2.

VII. Well, yet a gloss there is to colour that paradox, and notwithstanding all this, still to make it appear in show not to be altogether unreasonable. And therefore till further reply come, the cause is held by a feeble distinction; that the commandments of God being either general or special, although there be no express word for every thing in specialty, yet there are general commandments for all things, to the end, that even such cases as are not in Scripture particularly mentioned, might not be left to any to order at their pleasure, only with caution, that nothing be done against the word of God: and that for this cause the Apostle hath set down in Scripture four general rules, requiring such things alone to be received in the Church as do best and nearest agree with the same rules, that so all things in the Church may be appointed, not only *not against*, but *by* and *according to* the word of God. The rules are these, "Nothing scandalous or offensive unto any, especially unto the Church of God[3];" "All things in order and with seemliness[4];" "All unto edification[5];" finally, "All to the glory of God[6]." Of which kind how many might be gathered out of the Scripture, if it were necessary to take so much pains? Which rules they that urge, minding thereby to prove that nothing may be done in the Church but what Scripture commandeth, must needs hold that they tie the Church of Christ no otherwise than only because we find them there set down by the finger of the Holy Ghost. So that unless the Apostle by writing had delivered those rules to the Church, we should by observing them have sinned, as now by not observing them.

A shift to maintain, that nothing ought to be established in the Church which is not commanded in the word of God: namely, that commandments are of two sorts: and that all things lawful in the Church are commanded, if not by special precepts, yet by general rules in the word.

[2.] In the Church of the Jews is it not granted[7], that the appointment of the hour for daily sacrifices; the building of synagogues throughout the land to hear the word of God and

---

[1] [c. 54. τὴν σύνοδον διέλυσεν ἐπελθοῦσα ἕκτη ὥρα, καθ' ἣν τοῖς σάββασιν ἀριστοποιεῖσθαι νόμιμόν ἐστιν ἡμῖν. Cf. Acts x. 9.]
[2] [Acts ii. 15.]
[3] 1 Cor. x. 32.
[4] 1 Cor. xiv. 40.
[5] 1 Cor. xiv. 26.
[6] Rom. xiv. 6, 7. [and 1 Cor. x. 31. see T. C. i. 27.]
[7] T. C. lib. i. p. 35. [21.]

to pray in, when they came not up to Jerusalem, the erecting of pulpits and chairs to teach in, the order of burial, the rites of marriage, with such-like, being matters appertaining to the Church, yet are not any where prescribed in the law, but were by the Church's discretion instituted? What then shall we think? Did they hereby add to the law, and so displease God by that which they did? None so hardly persuaded of them. Doth their law deliver unto them the selfsame general rules of the Apostle, that framing thereby their orders they might in that respect clear themselves from doing amiss? St. Paul would then of likelihood have cited them out of the Law, which we see he doth not. The truth is, they are rules and canons of that law which is written in all men's hearts; the Church had for ever no less than now stood bound to observe them, whether the Apostles had mentioned them or no.

Seeing therefore those canons do bind as they are edicts of nature, which the Jews observing as yet unwritten, and thereby framing such church orders as in their law were not prescribed, are notwithstanding in that respect unculpable: it followeth that sundry things may be lawfully done in the Church, so as they be not done against the Scripture, although no Scripture do command them, but the Church only following the light of reason judge them to be in discretion meet.

[3.] Secondly, unto our purpose and for the question in hand, whether the commandments of God in Scripture be general or special, it skilleth not: for if being particularly applied they have in regard of such particulars a force constraining us to take some one certain thing of many, and to leave the rest; whereby it would come to pass, that any other particular but that one being established, the general rules themselves in that case would be broken; then is it utterly impossible that God should leave any thing great or small free for the Church to establish or not.

[4.] Thirdly, if so be they shall grant, as they cannot otherwise do, that these rules are no such laws as require any one particular thing to be done, but serve rather to direct the Church in all things which she doth; so that free and lawful it is to devise any ceremony, to receive any order, and to authorize any kind of regiment, no special commandment being thereby violated, and the same being thought such by them, to whom the judgment thereof appertaineth, as that it is not scandalous, but decent, tending unto edification, and setting forth the glory of God ; that is to say, agreeable unto the general rules of Holy Scripture: this doth them no good in the world for the furtherance of their purpose. That which should make for them must prove that men ought not to make laws for church regiment, but only keep those laws which in Scripture they find made. The plain intent of the Book of Ecclesiastical Discipline[1] is to shew that men may not devise laws of church government, but are bound for ever to use and to execute only those which God himself hath already devised and delivered in the Scripture. The selfsame drift the Admonitioners also had, in urging that nothing ought to be done in the Church according unto any law of man's devising, but all according to that which God in his word hath commanded. Which not remembering, they gather out of Scripture general rules to be followed in making laws ; and so in effect they plainly grant that we ourselves may lawfully make laws for the Church, and are not bound out of Scripture only to take laws already made, as they meant who first alleged that principle whereof we speak. One particular platform it is which they respected, and which they laboured thereby to force upon all Churches ; whereas these general rules do not let but that there may well enough be sundry. It is the particular order established in the Church of England, which thereby they did intend to alter, as being not commanded of God ; whereas unto those general rules they know we do not defend that we may hold any thing unconformable. Obscure it is not what meaning they had, who first gave out that grand axiom ; and according unto that meaning it doth prevail far and wide with the favourers of that part. Demand of them, wherefore they conform not themselves unto the order of our Church, and in every particular their answer for the most part is, "We find no such thing commanded in the word:" whereby they plainly require some special commandment for that which is exacted at their hands ; neither are they content

BOOK III.
Ch. vii. 4.

---

[1] [By Travers, Geneva 1580.]

BOOK III. to have matters of the Church examined by general rules
Ch. vii. 5. and canons.
viii. 1, 2.

[5.] As therefore in controversies between us and the Church of Rome, that which they practise is many times even according to the very grossness of that which the vulgar sort conceiveth; when that which they teach to maintain it is so nice and subtle that hold can very hardly be taken thereupon; in which cases we should do the Church of God small benefit by disputing with them according unto the finest points of their dark conveyances, and suffering that sense of their doctrine to go uncontrolled, wherein by the common sort it is ordinarily received and practised: so considering what disturbance hath grown in the Church amongst ourselves, and how the authors thereof do commonly build altogether on this as a sure foundation, "Nothing ought to be established in the Church which "in the word of God is not commanded;" were it reason that we should suffer the same to pass without controlment in that current meaning whereby every where it prevaileth, and stay till some strange construction were made thereof, which no man would lightly have thought on but being driven thereunto for a shift?

Another answer in defence of the former assertion, whereby the meaning thereof is opened in this sort. All Church orders must be commanded in the word, that is to say, grounded upon the word, and made according at the leastwise unto the general rules of Holy Scripture. As

VIII. The last refuge in maintaining this position is thus to construe it, "Nothing ought to be established in the Church, "but that which is commanded in the word of God;" that is to say, all Church orders must be "grounded upon the word "of God[1];" in such sort grounded upon the word, not that being found out by some "star, or light of reason, or learning, "or other help," they may be received, so they be not against the word of God; but according at leastwise unto the general rules of Scripture they must be made. Which is in effect as much as to say, "We know not what to say well in defence "of this position; and therefore lest we should say it is false, "there is no remedy but to say that in some sense or other it "may be true, if we could tell how."

[2.] First, that scholy had need of a very favourable reader and a tractable, that should think it plain construction, when to be *commanded in the word* and *grounded upon the word* are made all one. If when a man may live in the state of matrimony, seeking that good thereby which nature principally

[1] [T. C. ii. 56.]

Pleas in Disparagement of Human Reason. 365

desireth[1], he make rather choice of a contrary life in regard of St. Paul's judgment[2]; that which he doth is manifestly *grounded* upon the word of God, yet not *commanded* in his word, because without breach of any commandment he might do otherwise.

BOOK III Ch. viii. 3, 4.

for such things as are found out by any star or light of reason, and are in that respect received so they be not against the word of God, all such things it holdeth unlawfully received.

[3.] Secondly, whereas no man in justice and reason can be reproved for those actions which are framed according unto that known will of God, whereby they are to be judged; and the will of God which we are to judge our actions by, no sound divine in the world ever denied to be in part made manifest even by light of nature, and not by Scripture alone: if the Church being directed by the former of these two (which God hath given who gave the other, that man might in different sort be guided by them both), if the Church I say do approve and establish that which thereby it judgeth meet, and findeth not repugnant to any word or syllable of holy Scripture; who shall warrant our presumptuous boldness controlling herein the Church of Christ?

[4.] But so it is, the name of the light of nature is made hateful with men; the "star of reason and learning," and all other such like helps, beginneth no otherwise to be thought of than if it were an unlucky comet; or as if God had so accursed it, that it should never shine or give light in things concerning our duty any way towards him, but be esteemed as that star in the Revelation[3] called *Wormwood*, which being fallen from heaven, maketh rivers and waters in which it falleth so bitter, that men tasting them die thereof. A number there are, who think they cannot admire as they ought the power and authority of the word of God, if in things divine they should attribute any force to man's reason. For which cause they never use reason so willingly as to disgrace reason. Their usual and common discourses are unto this effect. First, "the natural man perceiveth not the things of the Spirit of "God: for they are foolishness unto him: neither can he "know them, because they are spiritually discerned[4]." Secondly, it is not for nothing that St. Paul giveth charge to "beware of philosophy[5]," that is to say, such knowledge as men by natural reason attain unto. Thirdly, consider them

[1] Arist. Pol. i. 2.   [2] 1 Cor. vii. 8. 26.   [3] Apoc. viii. 10.
[4] 1 Cor. ii. 14.   [5] Col. ii. 8.

BOOK III.
Ch. viii. 5.

that have from time to time opposed themselves against the Gospel of Christ, and most troubled the Church with heresy. Have they not always been great admirers of human reason? Hath their deep and profound skill in secular learning made them the more obedient to the truth, and not armed them rather against it? Fourthly, they that fear God will remember how heavy his sentences are in this case: "I will destroy "the wisdom of the wise, and will cast away the understand-"ing of the prudent. Where is the wise? where is the "scribe? where is the disputer of this world? hath not God "made the wisdom of this world foolishness? Seeing the "world by wisdom knew not God in the wisdom of God, it "pleased God by the foolishness of preaching to save be-"lievers[1]." Fifthly, the word of God in itself is absolute, exact and perfect. The word of God is a two-edged sword[2]; as for the weapons of natural reason, they are as the armour of Saul[3], rather cumbersome about the soldier of Christ than needful. They are not of force to do that which the Apostles of Christ did by the power of the Holy Ghost: "My preaching," therefore saith Paul, "hath not been in the "enticing speech of man's wisdom, but in plain evidence of "the Spirit and of power, that your faith might not be in the "wisdom of men, but in the power of God[4]." Sixthly, if I believe the Gospel, there needeth no reasoning about it to persuade me; if I do not believe, it must be the Spirit of God and not the reason of man that shall convert my heart unto him. By these and the like disputes an opinion hath spread itself very far in the world, as if the way to be ripe in faith were to be raw in wit and judgment; as if reason were an enemy unto religion, childish simplicity the mother of ghostly and divine wisdom.

[5.] The cause why such declamations prevail so greatly, is, for that men suffer themselves in two respects to be deluded; one is, that the wisdom of man being debased either in comparison with that of God, or in regard of some special thing exceeding the reach and compass thereof, it seemeth to them (not marking so much) as if simply it were condemned: another, that learning, knowledge or wisdom, falsely so termed, usurping a name whereof they are not worthy, and being

[1] 1 Cor. i. 19. [2] [Heb. iv. 12.] [3] [1 Sam. xvii. 39.] [4] 1 Cor. ii. 4.

under that name controlled; their reproof is by so much the more easily misapplied, and through equivocation wrested against those things whereunto so precious names do properly and of right belong. This, duly observed, doth to the former allegations itself make sufficient answer. Howbeit, for all men's plainer and fuller satisfaction:

BOOK III.
Ch. viii. 6, 7.

[6.] First, Concerning the inability of reason to search out and to judge of things divine, if they be such as those properties of God and those duties of men towards him, which may be conceived by attentive consideration of heaven and earth; we know that of mere natural men the Apostle testifieth[1], how they knew both God, and the Law of God. Other things of God there be which are neither so found, nor though they be shewed can never be approved without the *special* operation of God's good grace and Spirit. Of such things sometime spake the Apostle St. Paul, declaring how Christ had called him to be a witness of his death and resurrection from the dead, according to that which the Prophets and Moses had foreshewed. Festus, a mere natural man, an infidel, a Roman, one whose ears were unacquainted with such matter, heard him, but could not reach unto that whereof he spake; the suffering and the rising of Christ from the dead he rejecteth as idle superstitious fancies not worth the hearing[2]. The Apostle that knew them by the Spirit, and spake of them with power of the Holy Ghost, seemed in his eyes but learnedly mad[3]. Which example maketh manifest what elsewhere the same Apostle teacheth, namely, that nature hath need of grace[4], whereunto I hope we are not opposite, by holding that grace hath use of nature.

[7.] Secondly, Philosophy we are warned to take heed of: not that philosophy, which is true and sound knowledge attained by natural discourse of reason; but that philosophy, which to bolster heresy or error casteth a fraudulent show of reason upon things which are indeed unreasonable, and by that mean as by a stratagem spoileth the simple which are not able to withstand such cunning. "Take heed lest any "spoil you through philosophy and vain deceit[5]." He that exhorteth to beware of an enemy's policy doth not give

[1] Rom. i. 21, 32. [2] Acts xxv. 19. [3] Acts xxvi. 24.
[4] 1 Cor. ii. 14. [5] Col. ii. 8.

BOOK III.
Ch. viii. 8.

counsel to be impolitic, but rather to use all provident foresight and circumspection, lest our simplicity be overreached by cunning sleights. The way not to be inveigled by them that are so guileful through skill, is thoroughly to be instructed in that which maketh skilful against guile, and to be armed with that true and sincere philosophy, which doth teach, against that deceitful and vain, which spoileth.

[8.] Thirdly, But many great philosophers have been very unsound in belief. And many sound in belief, have been also great philosophers. Could secular knowledge bring the one sort unto the love of Christian faith? Nor Christian faith the other sort out of love with secular knowledge. The harm that heretics did, they did it unto such as were unable to discern between sound and deceitful reasoning; and the remedy against it was ever the skill which the ancient Fathers had to descry and discover such deceit. Insomuch that Cresconius the heretic complained greatly of St. Augustine, as being too full of logical subtilties[1]. Heresy prevaileth only by a counterfeit show of reason; whereby notwithstanding it becometh invincible, unless it be convicted of fraud by manifest remonstrance clearly true and unable to be withstood. When therefore the Apostle requireth ability to convict heretics[2], can we think he judgeth it a thing unlawful, and not rather needful, to use the principal instrument of their conviction, the light of reason? It may not be denied but that in the Fathers' writings there are sundry sharp invectives against heretics, even for their very philosophical reasonings. The cause whereof Tertullian confesseth not to have been any dislike conceived against the kind of such reasonings, but the end[3]. "We may," saith he, "even in matters of God

---

[1] [S. Aug. contr. Crescon. i. 16. t. ix. 397. "Quid est aliud Dialectica, quam peritia disputandi? Quod ideo aperiendum putavi, quia etiam ipsam mihi objicere voluisti, quasi 'Christianæ non congruat veritati, et ideo me doctores vestri, velut hominem dialecticum, merito fugiendum potius et cavendum, quam refellendum revincendumque censuerint.' Quod cum tibi non persuaserint, nam te adversus nos etiam scribendo disputare non piguit, tu tamen in me dialecticam criminatus es, quo falleres imperitos, eosque laudares qui disputando mecum congredi noluerant. Sed tu videlicet non dialectica uteris, cum contra nos scribis?"]

[2] Tit. i. 9, 11.

[3] Tert. de Resur. Carnis. [c. 3. "Est quidem et de communibus sensibus sapere in Dei rebus, sed in testimonium veri, non in adjutorium falsi; quod sit secundum divinam, non contra divinam dispositionem. Quædam enim et

"be made wiser by reasons drawn from the public persua-
"sions, which are grafted in men's minds: so they be used to
"further the truth, not to bolster error; so they make with,
"not against, that which God hath determined. For there
"are some things even known by nature, as the immortality
"of the soul unto many, our God unto all. I will therefore
"myself also use the sentence of some such as Plato, pronounc-
"ing every soul immortal. I myself too will use the secret
"acknowledgment of the commonalty [1], bearing record of the
"God of gods. But when I hear men allege, 'That which
"is dead is dead;' and, 'While thou art alive be alive;' and,
"'After death an end of all, even of death itself;' then will
"I call to mind both that the heart of the people with God
"is accounted dust [2], and that the very wisdom of the world
"is pronounced folly [3]. If then an heretic fly also unto such
"vicious popular and secular conceits, my answer unto him
"shall be, 'Thou heretic, avoid the heathen; although in this
"ye be one, that ye both belie God, yet thou that doest this
"under the name of Christ, differest from the heathen, in that
"thou seemest to thyself a Christian. Leave him therefore
"his conceits, seeing that neither will he learn thine. Why
"dost thou having sight trust to a blind guide; thou which
"hast put on Christ take raiment of him that is naked? If
"the Apostle have armed thee, why dost thou borrow a
"stranger's shield? Let him rather learn of thee to ac-
"knowledge, than thou of him to renounce the resurrection
"of the flesh.'" In a word, the Catholic Fathers did good

"natura nota sunt, ut immortalitas
"animæ penes plures, ut Deus
"noster penes omnes. Utar ergo
"et sententia Platonis alicujus pro-
"nunciantis, 'Omnis anima immor-
"talis.' Utar et conscientia populi,
"contestantis Deum Deorum... At
"cum aiunt, 'Mortuum quod mor-
"tuum,' et, 'Vive dum vivis,' et
"'Post mortem omnia finiuntur,
"etiam ipsa:' tunc meminero, et
"cor vulgi cinerem a Deo deputa-
"tum, et ipsam sapientiam sæculi
"stultitiam pronunciatam. Tunc
"si et hæreticus ad vulgi vitia, vel
"sæculi ingenia confugerit, 'Dis-
"cede,' dicam, 'ab ethnico, hære-
"tice; etsi unum estis omnes qui
"Deum fingitis; dum hoc tamen
"in Christi nomine facis, dum
"Christianus tibi videris, alius ab
"ethnico es. Redde illi suos sensus,
"quia nec ille de tuis instruitur.
"Quid cæco duci inniteris, si vides?
"Quid vestiris a nudo*, si Chris-
"tum induisti? Quid alieno uteris
"clypeo, si ab Apostolo armatus es?
"Ille potius a te discat carnis resur-
"rectionem confiteri, quam tu ab
"illo diffiteri.'"]

[1] ["communaltie," A. B.]
[2] [Isai. xliv. 20.]
[3] [1 Cor. iii. 19.]

[* "mundo," Keble's note by mistake. There is no various reading.] 1886.

unto all by that knowledge, whereby heretics hindering the truth in many, might have furthered therewith themselves, but that obstinately following their own ambitious or otherwise corrupted affections, instead of framing their wills to maintain that which reason taught, they bent their wits to find how reason might seem to teach that which their wills were set to maintain. For which cause the Apostle saith of them justly, that they are for the most part αὐτοκατάκριτοι, men condemned even in and of themselves[1]. For though they be not all persuaded that it is truth which they withstand, yet that to be error which they uphold they might undoubtedly the sooner a great deal attain to know, but that their study is more to defend what once they have stood in, than to find out sincerely and simply what truth they ought to persist in for ever.

[9.] Fourthly, There is in the world no kind of knowledge, whereby any part of truth is seen, but we justly account it precious; yea, that principal truth, in comparison whereof all other knowledge is vile, may receive from it some kind of light; whether it be that Egyptian and Chaldean wisdom mathematical, wherewith Moses and Daniel were furnished[2]; or that natural, moral, and civil wisdom, wherein Salomon excelled all men[3]; or that rational and oratorial wisdom of the Grecians, which the Apostle St. Paul brought from Tarsus; or that Judaical, which he learned in Jerusalem sitting at the feet of Gamaliel[4]: to detract from the dignity thereof were to injury[5] even God himself, who being that light which none can approach unto, hath sent out these lights whereof we are capable, even as so many sparkles resembling the bright fountain from which they rise.

But there are that bear the title of wise men and scribes and great disputers of the world, and are nothing in deed less than what in show they most appear. These being wholly addicted unto their own wills, use their wit, their learning, and all the wisdom they have, to maintain that which their

---

[1] Tit. iii. 11.
[2] Acts vii. 22; Dan. i. 17.
[3] 1 Kings iv. 29, 30.
[4] Acts xxii. 3.
[5] ["To injury, v. for 'to injure.' "'Those that are in authority, and "princes themselves, ought to take "great heed how they *injury* any "man by word or deed, and whom "they *injury*.' Danet's Comines. "lib. iii." Nares's Glossary. "I am strangely *injuried* by the "Archbishop." Hugh Broughton in Strype's Whitg. iii. 367. Cf. infra, V. xvi. 1.]

obstinate hearts are delighted with, esteeming in the frantic[1] error of their minds the greatest madness in the world to be wisdom, and the highest wisdom foolishness. Such were both Jews and Grecians, which professed the one sort legal, and the other secular skill, neither enduring to be taught the mystery of Christ: unto the glory of whose most blessed name, whoso study to use both their reason and all other gifts, as well which nature as which grace hath endued them with, let them never doubt but that the same God who is to destroy and confound utterly that wisdom falsely so named in others, doth make reckoning of them as of true Scribes, Scribes by wisdom instructed to the kingdom of heaven[2], not Scribes against that kingdom hardened in a vain opinion of wisdom; which in the end being proved folly, must needs perish, true understanding, knowledge, judgment and reason continuing for evermore.

[10.] Fifthly, Unto the word of God, being in respect of that end for which God ordained it perfect, exact, and absolute in itself, we do not add reason as a supplement of any maim or defect therein, but as a necessary instrument, without which we could not reap by the Scripture's perfection that fruit and benefit which it yieldeth. "The word of God is a twoedged "sword[3]," but in the hands of reasonable men; and reason as the weapon that slew Goliath, if they be as David was that use it. Touching the Apostles, He which gave them from above such power for miraculous confirmation of that which they taught, endued them also with wisdom from above to teach that which they so did confirm. Our Saviour made choice of twelve simple and unlearned men, that the greater their lack of natural wisdom was, the more admirable that might appear which God supernaturally endued them with from heaven. Such therefore as knew the poor and silly estate wherein they had lived, could not but wonder to hear the wisdom of their speech, and be so much the more attentive unto their teaching. They studied for no tongue, they spake with all[4]; of themselves they were rude, and knew not so much as how to premeditate; the Spirit gave them speech and eloquent utterance.

But because with St. Paul it was otherwise than with the

---

[1] ["phrentique," A. B.; "frantique," 1617.] 1886.
[2] Matt. xii.
[3] Heb. iv. 12.
[4] [So A. "withall" (one word) B. 1617, &c.] 1886.

BOOK III.
Ch. viii. 10.

rest, inasmuch as he never conversed with Christ upon earth as they did; and his education had been scholastical altogether, which theirs was not; hereby occasion was taken by certain malignants, secretly to undermine his great authority in the Church of Christ, as though the gospel had been taught him by others than by Christ himself, and as if the cause of the Gentiles' conversion and belief through his means had been the learning and skill which he had by being conversant in their books; which thing made them so willing to hear him, and him so able to persuade them; whereas the rest of the Apostles prevailed, because God was with them, and by miracle from heaven confirmed his word in their mouths. They were mighty in *deeds:* as for him, being absent, his writings had some force; in presence, his power not like unto theirs. In sum, concerning his preaching, their very byword was, λόγος ἐξουθενημένος, *addle speech, empty talk*[1]: his writings full of great words, but in the power of miraculous operations his presence not like the rest of the Apostles.

Hereupon it riseth that St. Paul was so often driven to make his apologies. Hereupon it riseth that whatsoever time he had spent in the study of human learning, he maketh earnest protestation to them of Corinth, that the gospel which he had preached amongst them did not by other means prevail with them, than with others the same gospel taught by the rest of the Apostles of Christ. "My preaching," saith he, " hath not been in the persuasive speeches of human wisdom, " but in demonstration of the Spirit and of power: that your "faith may not be in the wisdom of men, but in the power of "God [2]." What is it which the Apostle doth here deny? Is it denied that his speech amongst them had been *persuasive?* No: for of him the sacred history plainly testifieth, that for the space of a year and a half he spake in their synagogue every Sabbath[3], and *persuaded* both Jews and Grecians[4]. How then is the speech of men made persuasive? Surely there can be but two ways to bring this to pass, the one human, the other divine. Either St. Paul did *only* by art and natural industry cause his own speech to be credited; or else God by

[1] 2 Cor. x. 10.
[2] 1 Cor. ii. 4, 5.
[3] ["Saboth," 1st ed. So in III. xi. 8, IV. xiii. 1, V. c. 70–72 (1597) passim, Saboth or Sabboth. Compare *Sabaoth*, for *Sabbath*, in Spenser and Bacon.] 1886.
[4] Acts xviii. 4. 11.

miracle did authorize it, and so bring credit thereunto, as to the speech of the rest of the Apostles. Of which two, the former he utterly denieth. For why? if the preaching of the rest had been effectual by miracle, his *only* by force of his own learning; so great inequality between him and the other Apostles in this thing had been enough to subvert their faith. For might they not with reason have thought, that if he were sent of God as well as they, God would not have furnished them and not him with the power of the Holy Ghost? Might not a great part of them being simple haply have feared, lest their assent had been cunningly gotten unto his doctrine, rather through the weakness of their own wits than the certainty of that truth which he had taught them? How unequal had it been that all believers through the preaching of other Apostles should have their faith strongly built upon the evidence of God's own miraculous approbation, and they whom he had converted should have their persuasion built only upon his skill and wisdom who persuaded them?

As therefore calling from men may authorize us to teach, although it could not authorize him to teach as other Apostles did: so although the wisdom of man had not been sufficient to enable him such a teacher as the rest of the apostles were, unless God's miracles had strengthened both the one and the other's doctrine; yet unto our ability both of teaching and learning the truth of Christ, as we are but mere Christian men, it is not a little which the wisdom of man may add [1].

[1] [Chr. Letter, p. 43. "In all "your bookes, although we finde "manie good things, manie trueths "and fine points bravely handled, "yet in all your discourse, for the "most parte, Aristotle the patriarch "of philosophers (with divers other "humane writers) and the ingenuous "schoolemen, almost in all points "have some finger: reason is highlie "sett up against Holie Scripture, "and reading against preaching."

Hooker, MS. note. "If Aristotle "and the schoolmen be such peril-"ous creatures, you must needes "think yourself an happie man, "whome God hath so fairely blest "from too much knowledg in them.

"Remember heer S. Jerome's "Epistle in his own defense." (To Magnus, t. ii. 326. He pleads precedent, scriptural and ecclesiastical, for his use of profane learning.) "Forget not Picus Mirandula's "judgment of the schoolemen;" (Opp. i. 79. "Ut a nostris, ad "quos postremo philosophia perve-"nit, nunc exordiar; est in Joanne "Scoto vegetum quiddam atque "discussum, in Thoma solidum et "æquabile, in Ægidio tersum et ex-"actum, in Francisco acre et acu-"tum, in Alberto priscum, amplum, "et grande, in Henrico, ut mihi ".visum est, semper sublime et "venerandum.") "Beza's judgment "of Aristotle. (For his opinion of the use of logic, see Epist. 67.) "As also Calvin's judgment of phi-"losophie. Epist. 90, ad Buce-

BOOK III.
Ch. viii. 11, 12.

[11.] Sixthly, Yea, whatsoever our hearts be to God and to his truth, believe we or be we as yet faithless, for our conversion or confirmation the force of natural reason is great. The force whereof unto those effects is nothing without grace. What then? To our purpose it is sufficient, that whosoever doth serve, honour, and obey God, whosoever believeth in Him, that man would no more do this than innocents and infants do, but for the light of natural reason that shineth in him, and maketh him apt to apprehend those things of God, which being by grace discovered, are effectual to persuade reasonable minds and none other, that honour, obedience, and credit, belong of right unto God. No man cometh unto God to offer him sacrifice, to pour out supplications and prayers before him, or to do him any service, which doth not first believe him both to be, and to be a rewarder of them who in such sort seek unto him[1]. Let men be taught this either by revelation from heaven, or by instruction upon earth; by labour, study, and meditation, or by the only secret inspiration of the Holy Ghost; whatsoever the mean be they know it by, if the knowledge thereof were possible without discourse of natural reason, why should none be found capable thereof but only men; nor men till such time as they come unto ripe and full ability to work by reasonable understanding? The whole drift of the Scripture of God, what is it but only to teach Theology? Theology, what is it but the science of things divine? What science can be attained unto without the help of natural discourse and reason? "Judge you of that which I speak[2]," saith the Apostle. In vain it were to speak any thing of God, but that by reason men are able somewhat to judge of that they hear, and by discourse to discern how consonant it is to truth.

[12.] Scripture indeed teacheth things above nature, things

"rum." (p. 110. "Et philosophia "præclarum est Dei donum; et qui "omnibus sæculis extiterunt docti "viri, eos Deus ipse excitavit, ut ad ve-"ri notitiam mundo prælucerent.")
Again, Chr. Letter, ibid. "Shall "we doe you wronge to suspect.... "that you esteeme the preaching "and writing of all the reverend "Fathers of our Church, and the "bookes of holy Scripture to bee at "the least of no greater moment than

"*Aristotle and the schoolemen?*"
Hooker, MS. note: "I think of "the Scripture of God as reverently "as the best of the purified crew in "the world. I except not any, no "not the founders themselves and "captaines of that faction. In "which mind I hope by the grace "of Almighty God that I shall both "live and die."]
[1] Heb. xi. 6.
[2] 1 Cor. x. 15.

which our reason by itself could not reach unto. Yet those things also we believe, knowing by reason that the Scripture is the word of God. In the presence of Festus a Roman, and of King Agrippa a Jew, St. Paul omitting the one, who neither knew the Jews' religion nor the books whereby they were taught it, speaketh unto the other of things foreshewed by Moses and the Prophets and performed in Jesus Christ; intending thereby to prove himself so unjustly accused, that unless his judges did condemn both Moses and the Prophets, him they could not choose but acquit[1], who taught only that fulfilled, which they so long since had foretold. His cause was easy to be discerned; what was done their eyes were witnesses; what Moses and the Prophets did speak their books could quickly shew; it was no hard thing for him to compare them, which knew the one, and believed the other. "King Agrippa, believest thou the Pro- "phets? I know thou dost[2]." The question is how the books of the Prophets came to be credited of King Agrippa. For what with him did authorize the Prophets, the like with us doth cause the rest of the Scripture of God to be of credit.

[13.] Because we maintain that in Scripture we are taught all things necessary unto salvation; hereupon very childishly it is by some demanded, what Scripture can teach us the sacred authority of the Scripture, upon the knowledge whereof our whole faith and salvation dependeth[3]? As though there were any kind of science in the world which leadeth men into knowledge without presupposing a number of things already known. No science doth make known the first principles whereon it buildeth, but they are always either taken as plain and manifest in themselves, or as proved and granted already, some former knowledge having made them evident. Scripture teacheth all supernatural revealed truth, without the knowledge whereof salvation cannot be attained. The main principle whereupon our belief of all things therein contained dependeth, is, that the Scriptures are the oracles of God himself. This in itself we cannot say is evident. For then all men that hear it would acknowledge it in heart, as they do when they hear that "every whole is more than any "part of that whole," because this in itself is evident. The

---

[1] ["acquite," A. B.] 1886.   [2] Acts xxvi. 27.
[3] [Compare II. iv. 2.] 1886.

other we know that all do not acknowledge when they hear it. There must be therefore some former knowledge presupposed which doth herein assure the hearts of all believers. Scripture teacheth us that saving truth which God hath discovered unto the world by revelation, and it presumeth us taught otherwise that itself is divine and sacred.

[14.] The question then being by what means we are taught this; some answer that to learn it we have no other way than only tradition; as namely that so we believe because both we from our predecessors and they from theirs have so received. But is this enough? That which all men's experience teacheth them may not in any wise be denied. And by experience we all know, that the first outward motive leading men so to esteem of the Scripture is the authority of God's Church[1]. For when we know the whole Church of God hath that opinion of the Scripture, we judge it even at the first an impudent thing for any man bred and brought up in the Church to be of a contrary mind without cause. Afterwards the more we bestow our labour in reading or hearing the mysteries thereof, the more we find that the thing itself doth answer our received opinion concerning it. So that the former inducement prevailing somewhat with us before, doth now much more prevail, when the very thing hath ministered farther reason. If infidels or atheists

---

[1] [Chr. Letter, p. 9, 10. "Have "we not here good cause to suspect "the underpropping of a popish "principle concerning the Churches "authoritie above the Holie Scrip-"ture, to the disgrace of the Eng-"lish Church?"

Hooker, MS. note. "You have "already done your best to make a "jarre between nature and Scrip-"ture. Your next endeavour is to "doe the like betweene Scripture "and the Church. Your delight in "conflicts doth make you dreame of "them where they are not."

Again, Christ. Letter, p. 10. "We "pray you to expound, either by "experience or otherwise; Whether "the worde of God was receaved in "the world, and beleeved by men, "by the virtue and authoritie of the "witnesses, either Prophets or Apo-"stles, or the holy Church; or "that such were not esteemed for "the wordes sake."

Hooker, MS. note. "I am sorie "to see you in the groundes and "elements of your religion so sclen-"derly instructed.

"Fides nititur authoritate docentis. "Docens autem confirmatam habet "authoritatem personæ virtute mi-"raculorum. Id quod omnino ne-"cessarium est propter ea quæ docet "supra et præter naturalem ratio-"nem: qua omnis probatio argu-"mentosa nititur, quæ fidem facit. "Atque hoc Apostolus de se testatur, "cum efficacem fuisse sermonem "suum asserit non vi humanæ per-"suasionis, sed assistentis Spiritus "ad opera miraculosa perficienda. "Vide Tertullian. contra Gent. p. "637."]

chance at any time to call it in question, this giveth us occasion to sift what reason there is, whereby the testimony of the Church concerning Scripture, and our own persuasion which Scripture itself hath confirmed, may be proved a truth infallible. In which case the ancient Fathers being often constrained to shew, what warrant they had so much to rely upon the Scriptures, endeavoured still to maintain the authority of the books of God by arguments such as unbelievers themselves must needs think reasonable, if they judged thereof as they should. Neither is it a thing impossible or greatly hard, even by such kind of proofs so to manifest and clear that point, that no man living shall be able to deny it, without denying some apparent principle such as all men acknowledge to be true.

Wherefore if I believe the Gospel, yet is reason of singular use, for that it confirmeth me in this my belief the more: if I do not as yet believe, nevertheless to bring me to the number of believers except reason did somewhat help, and were an instrument which God doth use unto such purposes, what should it boot to dispute with infidels or godless persons for their conversion and persuasion in that point?

[15.] Neither can I think that when grave and learned men do sometime hold, that of this principle there is no proof but by the testimony of the Spirit, which assureth our hearts therein, it is their meaning to exclude utterly all force which any kind of reason may have in that behalf; but I rather incline to interpret such their speeches, as if they had more expressly set down, that other motives and inducements, be they never so strong and consonant unto reason, are notwithstanding uneffectual of themselves to work faith concerning this principle, if the special grace of the Holy Ghost concur not to the enlightening of our minds. For otherwise I doubt not but men of wisdom and judgment will grant, that the Church, in this point especially, is furnished with reason, to stop the mouths of her impious adversaries; and that as it were altogether bootless to allege against them what the Spirit hath taught us, so likewise that even to our ownselves it needeth caution and explication how the testimony of the Spirit may be discerned, by what means it may be known; lest men think that the Spirit of God doth testify those things

BOOK III.
Ch. viii. 16.
which the Spirit of error suggesteth. The operations of the Spirit, especially these ordinary which be common unto all true Christian men, are as we know things secret and undiscernible even to the very soul where they are, because their nature is of another and an higher kind than that they can be by us perceived in this life. Wherefore albeit the Spirit lead us into all truth and direct us in all goodness, yet because these workings of the Spirit in us are so privy and secret, we therefore stand on a plainer ground, when we gather by reason from the quality of things believed or done, that the Spirit of God hath directed us in both, than if we settle ourselves to believe or to do any certain particular thing, as being moved thereto by the Spirit.

[16.] But of this enough. To go from the books of Scripture to the sense and meaning thereof: because the sentences which are by the Apostles recited out of the Psalms[1], to prove the resurrection of Jesus Christ, did not prove it, if so be the Prophet David meant them of himself; this exposition therefore they plainly disprove, and shew by manifest reason, that of David the words of David could not possibly be meant. Exclude the use of natural reasoning about the sense of Holy Scripture concerning the articles of our faith, and then that the Scripture doth concern the articles of our faith who can assure us? That, which by right exposition buildeth up Christian faith, being misconstrued breedeth error: between true and false construction, the difference reason must shew. Can Christian men perform that which Peter requireth at their hands; is it possible they should both believe and be able, without the use of reason, to render "a reason of "their belief[2]," a reason sound and sufficient to answer them that demand it, be they of the same faith with us or enemies thereunto? may we cause our faith without reason to appear reasonable in the eyes of men? This being required even of learners in the school of Christ, the duty of their teachers in bringing them unto such ripeness must needs be somewhat more, than only to read the sentences of Scripture, and then paraphrastically to scholy them: to vary them with sundry forms of speech, without arguing or disputing about any thing which they contain. This method of teaching may

[1] Acts xiii. 36; ii. 34. [2] 1 Pet. iii. 15.

commend itself unto the world by that easiness and facility which is in it: but a law or a pattern it is not, as some do imagine, for all men to follow that will do good in the Church of Christ.

[17.] Our Lord and Saviour himself did hope by disputation to do some good, yea by disputation not only of but against, the truth, albeit with purpose for the truth. That Christ should be the son of David was truth; yet against this truth our Lord in the gospel objecteth, "If Christ be the son of "David, how doth David call him Lord[1]?" There is as yet no way known how to dispute, or to determine of things disputed, without the use of natural reason.

If we please to add unto Christ their example, who followed him as near in all things as they could; the sermon of Paul and Barnabas set down in the Acts[2], where the people would have offered unto them sacrifice; in that sermon what is there but only natural reason to disprove their act? "O men, why "do you these things? We are men even subject to the "selfsame passions with you: we preach unto you to leave "these vanities and to turn to the living God, the God that "hath not left himself without witness, in that he hath done "good to the world, giving rain and fruitful seasons, filling "our heart with joy and gladness."

Neither did they only use reason in winning such unto Christian belief as were yet thereto unconverted, but with believers themselves they followed the selfsame course. In that great and solemn assembly of believing Jews how doth Peter prove that the Gentiles were partakers of the grace of God as well as they, but by reason drawn from those effects, which were apparently known amongst them? "God which knoweth "hearts hath borne them witness in giving unto them the "Holy Ghost as unto us[3]."

The light therefore, which the "star of natural reason" and wisdom casteth, is too bright to be obscured by the mist of a word or two uttered to diminish that opinion which justly hath been received concerning the force and virtue thereof, even in matters that touch most nearly the principal duties of men and the glory of the eternal God.

[18.] In all which hitherto hath been spoken touching the

---

[1] Matt. xxii. 43.   [2] Acts xiv. 15.   [3] Acts xv. 8.

BOOK III.
Ch. ix. 1.

force and use of man's reason in things divine, I must crave that I be not so understood or construed, as if any such thing by virtue thereof could be done without the aid and assistance of God's most blessed Spirit. The thing we have handled according to the question moved about it; which question is, whether the light of reason be so pernicious, that in devising laws for the Church men ought not by it to search what may be fit and convenient. For this cause therefore we have endeavoured to make it appear, how in the nature of reason itself there is no impediment, but that the selfsame Spirit, which revealeth the things that God hath set down in his law, may also be thought to aid and direct men in finding out by the light of reason what laws are expedient to be made for the guiding of his Church, over and besides them that are in Scripture. Herein therefore we agree with those men, by whom human laws are defined to be ordinances, which such as have lawful authority given them for that purpose do probably draw from the laws of nature and God, by discourse of reason aided with the influence of divine grace. And for that cause, it is not said amiss touching ecclesiastical canons, that "by instinct of the Holy Ghost they have been made, and "consecrated by the reverend acceptation of all the world[1]."

How laws for the regiment of the Church may be made by the advice of men following therein the light of reason, and how those laws being not repugnant to the word of God are approved in his sight.

IX. Laws for the Church are not made as they should be, unless the makers follow such direction as they ought to be guided by: wherein that Scripture standeth not the Church of God in any stead, or serveth nothing at all to direct, but may be let pass as needless to be consulted with, we judge it profane, impious, and irreligious to think. For although it were in vain to make laws which the Scripture hath already made, because what we are already there commanded to do, on our parts there resteth nothing but only that it be executed; yet because both in that which we are commanded, it concerneth the duty of the Church by law to provide, that the looseness and slackness of men may not cause the commandments of God to be unexecuted; and a number of things there are for which the Scripture hath not provided by any law,

---

[1] Violatores, 25. q. i. [Decret. Gratian. caus. xxv. quæst. i. c. 6. in Corp. Jur. Canon. Paris. 1618. p. 313. "Violatores canonum volun- "tarii graviter a sanctis patribus ju- "dicantur, et a Sancto Spiritu (in- "stinctu cujus, et dono dictati sunt) "damnantur."]

but left them unto the careful discretion of the Church; we are to search how the Church in these cases may be well directed to make that provision by laws which is most convenient and fit. And what is so in these cases, partly Scripture and partly reason must teach to discern. Scripture comprehending examples and laws, laws some natural and some positive: examples there neither are for all cases which require laws to be made, and when there are, they can but direct as precedents only. Natural laws direct in such sort, that in all things we must for ever do according unto them; Positive so, that against them in no case we may do any thing, as long as the will of God is that they should remain in force. Howbeit when Scripture doth yield us precedents, how far forth they are to be followed; when it giveth natural laws, what particular order is thereunto most agreeable; when positive, which way to make laws unrepugnant unto them; yea though all these should want, yet what kind of ordinances would be most for that good of the Church which is aimed at, all this must be by reason found out. And therefore, " to refuse the conduct " of the light of nature," saith St. Augustine, " is not folly alone " but accompanied with impiety[1]."

[2.] The greatest amongst the School-divines, studying how to set down by exact definition the nature of an human law, (of which nature all the Church's constitutions are,) found not which way better to do it than in these words: " Out of the " precepts of the law of nature, as out of certain common and " undemonstrable principles, man's reason doth necessarily " proceed unto certain more particular determinations; which " particular determinations being found out according unto the " reason of man, they have the names of human laws, so that " such other conditions be therein kept as the making of laws " doth require[2]," that is, if they whose authority is thereunto required do establish and publish them as laws. And

---

[1] "Luminis naturalis ducatum " repellere non modo stultum est sed " et impium." August. lib. iv. de Trin. cap. 6. [The editor has not been able to verify this quotation.]

[2] Tho. Aqui. 1, 2. q. 91, art. 3. [t. xi. p. i. 199.] "Ex præceptis "legis naturalis, quasi ex quibus- "dam principiis communibus et in- "demonstrabilibus, necesse est quod " ratio humana procedat ad aliqua " magis particulariter disponenda. " Et istæ particulares dispositiones " adinventæ secundum rationem " humanam dicuntur *leges humanæ*, " observatis aliis conditionibus quæ " pertinent ad rationem legis."

BOOK III.
Ch. ix. 3.

the truth is, that all our controversy in this cause concerning the orders of the Church is, what particulars the Church may appoint. That which doth find them out is the force of man's reason. That which doth guide and direct his reason is first the general law of nature; which law of nature and the moral law of Scripture are in the substance of law all one. But because there are also in Scripture a number of laws particular and positive, which being in force may not by any law of man be violated; we are in making laws to have thereunto an especial eye. As for example, it might perhaps seem reasonable unto the Church of God, following the general laws concerning the nature of marriage, to ordain in particular that cousin-germans shall not marry. Which law notwithstanding ought not to be received in the Church, if there should be in Scripture a law particular to the contrary, forbidding utterly the bonds of marriage to be so far forth abridged. The same Thomas therefore whose definition of human laws we mentioned before, doth add thereunto this caution concerning the rule and canon whereby to make them [1]: *human laws are measures* in respect of men whose actions they must direct; howbeit such measures they are, as have also their higher rules to be measured by, *which rules are two, the law of God, and the law of nature.* So that laws human must be made according to the general laws of nature, and without contradiction unto any positive law in Scripture. Otherwise they are ill made.

[3.] Unto laws thus made and received by a whole church, they which live within the bosom of that church must not think it a matter indifferent either to yield or not to yield obedience. Is it a small offence to despise the Church of God [2]? "My son keep thy father's commandment," saith Salomon, "and forget not thy mother's instruction: bind "them both always about thine heart [3]." It doth not stand with the duty which we owe to our heavenly Father, that to the ordinances of our mother the Church we should shew ourselves disobedient. Let us not say we keep the commandments of the one, when we break the law of the other: for

---

[1] Quæst. 95. Art. 3. [t. xi. p. i. 206. "Lex humana... est quædam "regula, vel mensura, regulata, vel "mensurata quadam superiori men-"sura; quæ quidem est duplex, "scil. divina lex, et lex naturæ, ut "ex supradictis patet."]
[2] 1 Cor. xi. 22.
[3] Prov. vi. 20.

unless we observe both, we obey neither. And what doth let but that we may observe both, when they are not the one to the other in any sort repugnant? For of such laws only we speak, as being made in form and manner already declared, can have in them no contradiction unto the laws of Almighty God. Yea that which is more, the laws thus made God himself doth in such sort authorize, that to despise them is to despise in them Him. It is a loose and licentious opinion which the Anabaptists have embraced, holding that a Christian man's liberty is lost, and the soul which Christ hath redeemed unto himself injuriously drawn into servitude under the yoke of human power, if any law be now imposed besides the Gospel of Jesus Christ: in obedience whereunto the Spirit of God and not the constraint of man is to lead us, according to that of the blessed Apostle, "Such as are led by "the Spirit of God they are the sons of God[1]," and not such as live in thraldom unto men. Their judgment is therefore that the Church of Christ should admit no law-makers but the Evangelists. The author of that which causeth another thing to be, is author of that thing also which thereby is caused. The light of natural understanding, wit, and reason, is from God; he it is which thereby doth illuminate every man entering into the world[2]. If there proceed from us any thing afterwards corrupt and naught, the mother thereof is our own darkness, neither doth it proceed from any such cause whereof God is the author. He is the author of all that we think or do by virtue of that light, which himself hath given. And therefore the laws which the very heathens did gather to direct their actions by, so far forth as they proceeded from the light of nature, God himself doth acknowledge to[3] have proceeded even from himself, and that he was the writer of them in the tables of their hearts. How much more then he the author of those laws, which have been made by his saints, endued further with the heavenly grace of his Spirit, and directed as much as might be with such instructions as his sacred word doth yield! Surely if we have unto those laws that dutiful regard which their dignity doth require, it will not greatly need that we should be exhorted to live in obedience unto them. If they have God himself for their

---

[1] Rom. viii. 14.   [2] John i. 9.   [3] Rom. i. 19, ii. 15.

BOOK III. author, contempt which is offered unto them cannot choose
Ch. x. 1. but redound unto him. The safest and unto God the most
acceptable way of framing our lives therefore is, with all
humility, lowliness, and singleness of heart, to study, which
way our willing obedience both unto God and man may be
yielded even to the utmost of that which is due.

That neither God's being the author of laws, nor his committing them to Scripture, nor the continuance of the end for which they were instituted, is any reason sufficient to prove that they are unchangeable.

X. Touching the mutability of laws that concern the regiment and polity of the Church; changed they are, when either altogether abrogated, or in part repealed, or augmented with farther additions. Wherein we are to note, that this question about the changing of laws concerneth only such laws as are positive, and do make that now good or evil by being commanded or forbidden, which otherwise of itself were not simply the one or the other. Unto such laws it is expressly sometimes added, how long they are to continue in force. If this be nowhere express, then have we no light to direct our judgments concerning the changeableness or immutability of them, but by considering the nature and quality of such laws. The nature of every law must be judged of by the end for which it was made, and by the aptness of things therein prescribed unto the same end. It may so fall out that the reason why some laws of God were given is neither opened nor possible to be gathered by wit of man. As why God should forbid Adam that one tree, there was no way for Adam ever to have certainly understood. And at Adam's ignorance of this point Satan took advantage, urging the more securely a false cause because the true was unto Adam unknown. Why the Jews were forbidden to plough their ground with an ox and an ass, why to clothe themselves with mingled attire of wool and linen[1], both it was unto them and to us it remaineth obscure. Such laws perhaps cannot be abrogated saving only by whom they were made: because the intent of them being known unto none but the author, he alone can judge how long it is requisite they should endure. But if the reason why things were instituted may be known, and being known do appear manifestly to be of perpetual necessity; then are those things also perpetual, unless they

---

[1] Deut. xxii. 10, 11. (Spencer (de Legg. Hebræor. lib. ii. c. 31, 33.) conjectures, but without direct evidence, that these were prohibitions of Sabæan ceremonies.]

cease to be effectual unto that purpose for which they were at the first instituted. Because when a thing doth cease to be available unto the end which gave it being, the continuance of it must then of necessity appear superfluous. And of this we cannot be ignorant, how sometimes that hath done great good, which afterwards, when time hath changed the ancient course of things, doth grow to be either very hurtful, or not so greatly profitable and necessary. If therefore the end for which a law provideth be perpetually necessary, and the way whereby it provideth perpetually also most apt, no doubt but that every such law ought for ever to remain unchangeable.

[2.] Whether God be the author of laws by authorizing that power of men whereby they are made, or by delivering them made immediately from himself, by word only, or in writing also, or howsoever; notwithstanding the authority of their Maker, the mutability of that end for which they are made doth also make them changeable. The law of ceremonies came from God: Moses had commandment to commit it unto the sacred records of Scripture, where it continueth even unto this very day and hour: in force still, as the Jew surmiseth, because God himself was author of it, and for us to abolish what he hath established were presumption most intolerable. But (that which they in the blindness of their obdurate hearts are not able to discern) sith the end for which that law was ordained is now fulfilled, past and gone; how should it but cease any longer to be, which hath no longer any cause of being in force as before? "That which necessity "of some special time doth cause to be enjoined bindeth no "longer than during that time, but doth afterwards become "free [1]."

Which thing is also plain even by that law which the Apostles assembled at the council of Jerusalem did from thence deliver unto the Church of Christ, the preface whereof to authorize it was, "To the Holy Ghost and to us it hath "seemed good [2]:" which style they did not use as matching themselves in power with the Holy Ghost, but as testifying

---

[1] "Quod pro necessitate temporis statutum est, cessante necessitate, debet cessare pariter quod urgebat." i. q. 1. Quod pro necessit. [i. e. Decr. Gratiani, pars 1. causa 1. qu. 1. c. 41. in Corp. Jur. Canon. 116.]

[2] Acts xv. 28.

BOOK III. the Holy Ghost to be the author, and themselves but only
Ch. x. 3. utterers of that decree. This law therefore to have proceeded
from God as the author thereof no faithful man will deny. It
was of God, not only because God gave them the power
whereby they might make laws, but for that it proceeded even
from the holy motion and suggestion of that secret divine
Spirit, whose sentence they did but only pronounce. Notwithstanding, as the law of ceremonies delivered unto the Jews, so
this very law which the Gentiles received from the mouth of
the Holy Ghost, is in like respect abrogated by decease of the
end for which it was given.

[3.] But such as do not stick at this point, such as grant
that what hath been instituted upon any special cause needeth
not to be observed[1], that cause ceasing, do notwithstanding
herein fail; they judge the laws of God only by the author
and main end for which they were made, so that for us to
change that which he hath established, they hold it execrable
pride and presumption, if so be the end and purpose for
which God by that mean provideth be permanent. And upon
this they ground those ample disputes concerning orders and
offices, which being by him appointed for the government of
his Church, if it be necessary always that the Church of Christ
be governed, then doth the end for which God provided remain still; and therefore in those means which he by law did
establish as being fittest unto that end, for us to alter any
thing is to lift up ourselves against God, and as it were to
countermand him. Wherein they mark not that laws are instruments to rule by, and that instruments are not only to
be framed according unto the general end for which they
are provided, but even according unto that very particular,
which riseth out of the matter whereon they have to work.

---

[1] Counterp. p. 8. [Cosin in his "Answer to the Abstract," had produced the change of time in celebrating the Eucharist, from the evening after supper, to the morning before the first meal, as an instance of the authority left with the Church to vary matters of discipline. The author of the Counter-poison replies, "As it is a mere circumstance of "time, so the alteration hath ground "in the Scripture, because one and "the same time is not always kept. "Acts iii. 42; xx. 7, 11, &c. Neither "can that be said to be according to "the institution, which *being done* "*upon a particular cause* (as all di- "vines agree) *should not be observed* "*where that cause ceaseth.*" T. C. ii. 465. "Neither any man, nor all "men in the world, could have put "down the temporal ministeries of "Apostles, Evangelists, &c. which "the Lord ordained, unless the "Lord himself had withdrawn "them."]

The end wherefore laws were made may be permanent, and those laws nevertheless require some alteration, if there be any unfitness in the means which they prescribe as tending unto that end and purpose. As for example, a law that to bridle theft doth punish thieves with a quadruple restitution hath an end which will continue as long as the world itself continueth. Theft will be always, and will always need to be bridled. But that the mean which this law provideth for that end [1], namely the punishment of quadruple restitution, that this will be always sufficient to bridle and restrain that kind of enormity no man can warrant. Insufficiency of laws doth sometimes come by want of judgment in the makers. Which cause cannot fall into any law termed properly and immediately divine, as it may and doth into human laws often. But that which hath been once most sufficient may wax otherwise by alteration of time and place; that punishment which hath been sometime forcible to bridle sin may grow afterwards too weak and feeble.

[4.] In a word, we plainly perceive by the difference of those three laws which the Jews received at the hands of God, the moral, ceremonial, and judicial, that if the end for which and the matter according whereunto God maketh his laws continue always one and the same, his laws also do the like; for which cause the moral law cannot be altered: secondly, that whether the matter whereon laws are made continue or continue not, if their end have once ceased, they cease also to be of force; as in the law ceremonial it fareth: finally, that albeit the end continue, as in that law of theft specified and in a great part of those ancient judicials it doth; yet forasmuch as there is not in all respects the same subject or matter remaining for which they were first instituted, even this is sufficient cause of change: and therefore laws, though both ordained of God himself, and the end for which they were ordained continuing, may notwithstanding cease, if by alteration of persons or times they be found unsufficient to attain unto that end. In which respect why may we not presume that God doth even call for such change or alteration as the very condition of things themselves doth make necessary?

---

[1] [Exod. xxii. 1 ; 2 Sam. xii. 6.]

BOOK III.
Ch. x. 5, 6, 7.

[5.] They which do therefore plead the authority of the law-maker as an argument, wherefore it should not be lawful to change that which he hath instituted, and will have this the cause why all the ordinances of our Saviour are immutable; they which urge the wisdom of God as a proof, that whatsoever laws he hath made they ought to stand, unless himself from heaven proclaim them disannulled, because it is not in man to correct the ordinance of God; may know, if it please them to take notice thereof, that we are far from presuming to think that men can better any thing which God hath done, even as we are from thinking that men should presume to undo some things of men, which God doth know they cannot better. God never ordained any thing that could be bettered. Yet many things he hath that have been changed, and that for the better. That which succeedeth as better now when change is requisite, had been worse when that which now is changed was instituted. Otherwise God had not then left this to choose that, neither would now reject that to choose this, were it not for some new-grown occasion making that which hath been better worse. In this case therefore men do not presume to change God's ordinance, but they yield thereunto requiring itself to be changed.

[6.] Against this it is objected, that to abrogate or innovate the Gospel of Christ if men or angels should attempt, it were most heinous and cursed sacrilege. And the Gospel (as they say) containeth not only doctrine instructing men how they should believe, but also precepts concerning the regiment of the Church. Discipline therefore is "a part of the Gospel[1];" and God being the author of the whole Gospel, as well of discipline as of doctrine, it cannot be but that both of them "have a common cause." So that as we are to believe for ever the articles of evangelical doctrine, so the precepts of discipline we are in like sort bound for ever to observe.

[7.] Touching points of doctrine, as for example, the Unity

---

[1] "We offer to shew the disci-"pline to be a part of the Gospel, "and therefore to have a common "cause; so that in the repulse of "the discipline the Gospel receives "a check." And again, "I speak "of the discipline as of a part of the "Gospel, and therefore neither under "nor above the Gospel, but the "Gospel." T. C. lib. ii. p. 1, 4. [These latter words are in p. 5, but in p. 4 are the following: "The "discipline being, as it is propound-"ed, and offered to be proved, a "part of the Gospel, must needs arm "the Lord against the refuser."]

of God, the Trinity of Persons, salvation by Christ, the resurrection of the body, life everlasting, the judgment to come, and such like, they have been since the first hour that there was a Church in the world, and till the last they must be believed. But as for matters of regiment, they are for the most part of another nature. To make new articles of faith and doctrine no man thinketh it lawful; new laws of government what commonwealth or church is there which maketh not either at one time or another? "The rule of "faith[1]," saith Tertullian, "is but one, and that alone "immoveable and impossible to be framed or cast anew." The law of outward order and polity not so[2]. There is no reason in the world wherefore we should esteem it as necessary always to do, as always to believe, the same things; seeing every man knoweth that the matter of faith is constant, the matter contrariwise of action daily changeable, especially the matter of action belonging unto church polity. Neither can I find that men of soundest judgment have any otherwise taught, than that articles of belief, and things which all men must of necessity do to the end they may be saved, are either expressly set down in Scripture, or else plainly thereby to be gathered. But touching things which belong to discipline and outward polity, the Church hath authority to make canons, laws, and decrees, even as we read that in the Apostles' times it did[3]. Which kind of laws (forasmuch as they are not in themselves necessary to salvation) may after they are made be also changed as the difference of times or places shall require. Yea, it is not denied I am sure by themselves, that certain things in discipline are of that nature, as they may be varied by times, places, persons, and other the like circumstances. Whereupon I demand, are those changeable points of discipline commanded in the word of God or no? If they be not commanded and yet may be

[1] Tert. de Veland. Virg. c. 1.
[2] Mart. [i. e. Peter Martyr] in 1 Sam. xiv. ["Positum sit, licere "Ecclesiæ scribere sibi aut ca- "nones, aut leges, aut decreta, aut "sanctiones, aut quocunque ea velis "nomine appellari. Est enim Ec- "clesia cœtus, et regi debet verbo "Dei, præsertim quod attinet ad "salutem ipsius, et cultum Dei. "Sed sunt alia, quæ tantum perti- "nent ad externam disciplinam... "Istarum legum finis esse debet "ædificatio et εὐταξία. Quoniam "autem necessariæ non sunt, pro "temporum et locorum ratione mu- "tari possunt."]
[3] Acts xv.

received in the Church, how can their former position stand, condemning all things in the Church which in the word are not commanded? If they be commanded and yet may suffer change, how can this latter stand, affirming all things immutable which are commanded of God? Their distinction touching matters of substance and of circumstance, though true, will not serve. For be they great things or be they small, if God have commanded them in the Gospel, and his commanding them in the Gospel do make them unchangeable, there is no reason we should more change the one than we may the other. If the authority of the maker do prove unchangeableness in the laws which God hath made, then must all laws which he hath made be necessarily for ever permanent, though they be but of circumstance only and not of substance. I therefore conclude, that neither God's being author of laws for government of his Church, nor his committing them unto Scripture, is any reason sufficient wherefore all churches should for ever be bound to keep them without change.

[8.] But of one thing we are here to give them warning by the way. For whereas in this discourse we have oftentimes profest that many parts of discipline or church polity are delivered in Scripture, they may perhaps imagine that we are driven to confess their discipline to be delivered in Scripture, and that having no other means to avoid it, we are fain to argue for the changeableness of laws ordained even by God himself, as if otherwise theirs of necessity should take place, and that under which we live be abandoned. There is no remedy therefore but to abate this error in them, and directly to let them know, that if they fall into any such conceit, they do but a little flatter their own cause. As for us, we think in no respect so highly of it. Our persuasion is, that no age ever had knowledge of it but only ours; that they which defend it devised it; that neither Christ nor his Apostles at any time taught it, but the contrary. If therefore we did seek to maintain that which most advantageth our own cause, the very best way for us and the strongest against them were to hold even as they do, that in Scripture there must needs be found some particular form of church polity which God hath instituted, and which for that very cause belongeth to all churches, to all times[1]. But with any such partial eye to respect ourselves, and by cunning to make those things seem the truest which are the fittest to serve our purpose, is a thing which we neither like nor mean to follow. Wherefore that which we take to be generally true concerning the mutability of laws, the same we have plainly delivered, as being persuaded of nothing more than we are of this, that whether it be in matter of speculation or of practice, no untruth[2] can possibly avail the patron and defender long, and that things most truly are likewise most behovefully spoken.

BOOK III.
Ch. xi. 1, 2.

XI. This we hold and grant for truth, that those very laws which of their own nature are changeable, be notwithstanding uncapable of change, if he which gave them, being of authority so to do, forbid absolutely to change them; neither may they admit alteration against the will of such a law-maker. Albeit therefore we do not find any cause why of right there should be necessarily an immutable form set down in holy Scripture; nevertheless if indeed there have been at any time a church polity so set down, the change whereof the sacred Scripture doth forbid, surely for men to alter those laws which God for perpetuity hath established were presumption most intolerable.

Whether Christ have forbidden all change of those laws which are set down in Scripture.

[2.] To prove therefore that the will of Christ was to establish laws so permanent and immutable that in any sort to alter them cannot but highly offend God, thus they reason. First[3], if Moses, being but a servant in the house of God,

---

[1] "Disciplina est Christianæ Ec-"clesiæ Politia, a Deo ejus recte "administrandæ causa constituta, "ac propterea ex ejus verbo petenda, "et ob eandem causam omnium "ecclesiarum communis et omnium "temporum." Lib. de Eccles. Discip. in Anal. [See also p. 9, Cartwright's Translation.]

[2] 'Εοίκασιν οὖν οἱ ἀληθεῖς τῶν λόγων οὐ μόνον πρὸς τὸ εἰδέναι χρησιμώτατοι εἶναι, ἀλλὰ καὶ πρὸς τὸν βίον. Συνῳδοὶ γὰρ ὄντες ἔργοις, πιστεύονται. Arist. Ethic. lib. x. cap. I.

[3] Heb. iii. 6. "Either that com-"mendation of the son before the "servant is a false testimony, or the "son ordained a permanent govern-"ment in the Church. If perma-"nent, then not to be changed. "What then do they, that [not only] "hold it may be changed at the "magistrate's pleasure, but advise "the magistrate by his positive "laws to proclaim, that it is his "will, that if there shall be a "church within his dominions, he "will maim and deform the same?" M. M. [Martin Marprelate, "Ha' "ye any work for a Cooper?"] p. 16. "He that was as faithful as "Moses, left as clear instruction for "the government of the Church: "But Christ was as faithful as "Moses: Ergo." Demonst. of Discip. cap. i. [p. 3. See also Theses Martinianæ, 5th Thesis. "If Christ did not ordain a church

BOOK III. did therein establish laws of government for perpetuity, laws
Ch. xi. 3. which they that were of the household might not alter;
shall we admit into our thoughts, that the Son of God hath
in providing for this his household declared himself less faithful than Moses? Moses delivering unto the Jews such laws
as were durable, if those be changeable which Christ hath
delivered unto us, we are not able to avoid it, but (that which
to think were heinous impiety) we of necessity must confess
even the Son of God himself to have been less faithful than
Moses. Which argument shall need no touchstone to try it
by but some other of the like making. Moses erected in the
wilderness a tabernacle which was moveable from place to
place; Salomon a sumptuous and stately temple which was
not moveable: therefore Salomon was faithfuller than Moses,
which no man endued with reason will think. And yet by
this reason it doth plainly follow.

He that will see how faithful the one or the other was,
must compare the things which they both did unto the charge
which God gave each of them. The Apostle in making comparison between our Saviour and Moses attributeth faithfulness unto both, and maketh this difference between them;
Moses *in*, but Christ *over* the house of God; Moses in that
house which was *his by charge and commission*, though to
govern it, yet to govern it *as a servant;* but Christ over this
house as being *his own entire possession*.

[3.] Our Lord and Saviour doth make protestation, " I
" have given unto them the words which thou gavest me [1]."
Faithful therefore he was, and concealed not any part of his
Father's will. But did any part of that will require the
immutability of laws concerning church polity? They answer,
Yea. For else God should less favour us than the Jews [2].
God would not have their church guided by any laws but his

"government which at the pleasure
"of man cannot be changed, then
"he is inferior unto Moses: for the
"government placed by him might
"no man alter, and thereto might
"no man add any thing. Heb. iii.
"2, 3." Eccl. Disc. fol. 7. "Ne
"illum aliqua parte prophetici mu-
"neris spoliemus, aut servum,
"quantumvis fidelem, unigenito
"Filio, et tanquam Eliezerum

"Isaaco in paterna domo præfera-
"mus." Counterpoison, p. 9. Penry's Appellation to the High Court
of Parliament, p. 18.]

[1] John xvii. 8.

[2] "Either God hath left a pre-
" script form of government now,
" or else he is less careful under the
" New Testament than under the
" Old." Demonst. of Disc. cap. i.
[T. C. i. 62. ap. Whitg. Def. 304.]

own. And seeing this did so continue even till Christ, now to ease God of that care, or rather to deprive the Church of his patronage, what reason have we? Surely none to derogate any thing from the ancient love which God hath borne to his Church. An heathen philosopher [1] there is, who considering how many things beasts have which men have not, how naked in comparison of them, how impotent, and how much less able we are to shift for ourselves a long time after we enter into this world, repiningly concluded hereupon, that nature being a careful mother for them, is towards us a hard-hearted stepdame. No, we may not measure the affection of our gracious God towards his by such differences. For even herein shineth his wisdom, that though the ways of his providence be many, yet the end which he bringeth all at the length unto is one and the selfsame.

[4.] But if such kind of reasoning were good, might we not even as directly conclude the very same concerning laws of secular regiment? Their own words are these: "In the "ancient church of the Jews, God did command and Moses "commit unto writing all things pertinent as well to the "civil as to the ecclesiastical state [2]." God gave them laws of civil regiment, and would not permit their commonweal to be governed by any other laws than his own. Doth God less regard our temporal estate in this world, or provide for it

---

[1] [Philemon. Fragm. Incert. xliii. ed. Cler.=p. 841. Meineke, 1847.

πολύ γ' ἐστὶ πάντων ζῷον ἀθλιώτατον
ἄνθρωπος, εἴ τις ἐξετάζοι κατὰ τρόπον.
τὸν γὰρ βίον περίεργον εἰς τὰ πάντ' ἔχων,
ἀπορεῖ τὰ πλεῖστα διὰ τέλους, πονεῖ τ' ἀεί.
καὶ τοῖς μὲν ἄλλοις πᾶσιν ἡ γῆ θηρίοις
ἑκοῦσα παρέχει τὴν καθ' ἡμέραν τροφὴν,
αὐτὴ πορίζουσ', οὐ λαβοῦσα· πάνυ μόλις
ὥσπερ τὸ κατὰ χρέος κεφάλαιον ἐκτίει
τὸ σπέρμα, τοὺς τόκους ἀνευρίσκουσ' ἀεὶ
πρόφασίν τιν' αὐχμὸν, ἢ πάγην, ἵν' ἀποστερῇ (πάχνην ἀποστερεῖ).] K.*

[2] Ecclesiast. Disc. lib. i. [fol. 5. "statum [pertinent].... diligenter "In vetere Ecclesia Judæorum omnia "descripta sunt, et a Deo præcepta, "quæ ad regendum non modo "a Mose literis commendata."] "civilem sed etiam ecclesiasticum

[* Hooker more probably refers to Pliny, Nat. Hist. vii. 1: "Principium jure "tribuetur homini, cujus causa videtur cuncta alia genuisse natura, magna sæva "mercede contra tanta sua munera: non sit ut satis æstimare, parens melior "homini, an tristior noverca fuerit. Ante omnia, unum animantium cunctorum, "alienis velat opibus: cæteris varie tegumenta tribuit, testas, cortices, coria, "spinas.... Hominem tantum nudum (Lucret. v. 224) et in nuda humo natali "die abjicit ab vagitus statim et ploratum."] 1886.

worse than for theirs? To us notwithstanding he hath not as to them delivered any particular form of temporal regiment, unless perhaps we think, as some do, that the grafting of the Gentiles[1] and their incorporating into Israel[2] doth import that we ought to be subject unto the rites and laws of their whole polity. We see then how weak such disputes are, and how smally they make to this purpose.

[5.] That Christ did not mean to set down particular positive laws for all things in such sort as Moses did, the very different manner of delivering the laws of Moses and the laws of Christ doth plainly shew. Moses had commandment to gather the ordinances of God together distinctly, and orderly to set them down according unto their several kinds, for each public duty and office the laws that belong thereto, as appeareth in the books themselves, written of purpose for that end. Contrariwise the laws of Christ we find rather mentioned by occasion in the writings of the Apostles, than any solemn thing directly written to comprehend them in legal sort.

[6.] Again, the positive laws which Moses gave, they were given for the greatest part with restraint to the land of Jewry: "Behold," saith Moses, "I have taught you ordinances "and laws, as the Lord my God commanded me, that ye "should do even so within the land whither ye go to possess "it[3]." Which laws and ordinances positive he plainly distinguisheth afterward from the laws of the Two Tables which were moral[4]. "The Lord spake unto you out of the "midst of the fire; ye heard the voice of the words, but saw "no similitude, only a voice. Then he declared unto you "his covenant which he commanded you to do, the Ten "Commandments, and wrote them upon two tables of stone. "And the Lord commanded me that same time, that I should "teach you ordinances and laws which ye should observe "in the land whither ye go to possess it." The same difference is again set down in the next chapter following. For rehearsal being made of the Ten Commandments, it followeth immediately[5], "These words the Lord spake unto all your "multitude in the mount out of the midst of the fire, the "cloud, and the darkness, with a great voice, and added no

---

[1] Rom. xi. 17. [2] Ephes. ii. 12–16. [3] Deut. iv. 5.
[4] Deut. iv. 12–14. [5] Deut. v. 22.

"more; and wrote them upon two tables of stone, and "delivered them unto me." But concerning other laws, the people give their consent to receive them at the hands of Moses[1]: "Go thou near, and hear all that the Lord our God "saith, and declare thou unto us all that the Lord our God "saith unto thee, and we will hear it and do it." The people's alacrity herein God highly commendeth with most effectual and 'hearty speech[2]: "I have heard the voice of the "words of this people; they have spoken well. O that there "were such an heart in them to fear me, and to keep all my "commandments always, that it might go well with them "and with their children for ever! Go, say unto them, "'Return you to your tents;' but stand thou here with me, "and I will tell thee all the commandments and the ordinances "and the laws which thou shalt teach them, that they may "do them in the land which I have given them to possess." From this later kind the former are plainly distinguished in many things. They were not both at one time delivered, neither both after one sort, nor to one end. The former uttered by the voice of God himself in the hearing of six hundred thousand men; the former written with the finger of God; the former termed by the name of a Covenant; the former given to be kept without either mention of time how long, or of place where. On the other side, the later given after, and neither written by God himself, nor given unto the whole multitude immediately from God, but unto Moses, and from him to them both by word and writing; the later termed Ceremonies, Judgments, Ordinances, but no where Covenants; finally, the observation of the later restrained unto the land where God would establish them to inhabit.

The laws positive are not framed without regard had to the place and persons for which they are made. If therefore Almighty God in framing their laws had an eye unto the nature of that people, and to the country where they were to dwell; if these peculiar and proper considerations were respected in the making of their laws, and must be also regarded in the positive laws of all other nations besides: then seeing that nations are not all alike, surely the giving of one kind of positive laws unto one only people, without any liberty to

---

[1] Deut. v. 27.   [2] Deut. v. 28-31.

BOOK III.
Ch. xi. 7, 8.

alter them, is but a slender proof, that therefore one kind should in like sort be given to serve everlastingly for all.

[7.] But that which most of all maketh for the clearing of this point is, that the Jews[1], who had laws so particularly determining and so fully instructing them in all affairs what to do, were notwithstanding continually inured with causes exorbitant, and such as their laws had not provided for. And in this point much more is granted us than we ask, namely, that for one thing which we have left to the order of the Church, they had twenty which were undecided by the express word of God; and that as their ceremonies and sacraments were multiplied above ours, even so grew the number of those cases which were not determined by any express word. So that if we may devise one law, they by this reason might devise twenty; and if their devising so many were not forbidden, shall their example prove us forbidden to devise as much as one law for the ordering of the Church? We might not devise no not one, if their example did prove that our Saviour had utterly forbidden all alteration of his laws; inasmuch as there can be no law devised, but needs it must either take away from his, or add thereunto more or less, and so make some kind of alteration. But of this so large a grant we are content not to take advantage. Men are oftentimes in a sudden passion more liberal than they would be if they had leisure to take advice. And therefore so bountiful words of course and frank speeches we are contented to let pass, without turning them unto advantage with too much rigour.

[8.] It may be they had rather be listened unto, when they commend the kings of Israel "which attempted nothing in "the government of the Church without the express word of "God[2];" and when they urge[3] that God left nothing in his word "undescribed," whether it concerned the worship of God or outward polity, nothing unset down, and therefore

---

[1] "Whereas you say, that they "(the Jews) had nothing but what "was determined by the law, and "we have many things undeter- "mined and left to the order of the "Church; I will offer, for one that "you shall bring that we have left "to the order of the Church, to shew "you that they had twenty which "were undecided by the express "word of God." T. C. lib. i. p. 35. [22.]

[2] T. C. in the table to his second book.

[3] "If he will needs separate the "worship of God from the external "polity, yet as the Lord set forth "the one, so he left nothing un- "described in the other." T. C. lib. ii. p. 446.

charged them strictly to keep themselves unto that, without any alteration. Howbeit, seeing it cannot be denied, but that many things there did belong unto the course of their public affairs, wherein they had no express word at all to shew precisely what they should do; the difference between their condition and ours in these cases will bring some light unto the truth of this present controversy. Before the fact of the son of Shelomith, there was no law which did appoint any certain punishment for blasphemers[1]. That wretched creature being therefore deprehended in that impiety, was held in ward, till the mind of the Lord were known concerning his case. The like practice is also mentioned upon occasion of a breach of the Sabbath[2] day. They find a poor silly creature gathering sticks in the wilderness, they bring him unto Moses and Aaron and all the congregation, they lay him in hold, because it was not declared what should be done with him, till God had said unto Moses, "This man shall die the death[3]." The law required to keep the Sabbath; but for the breach of the Sabbath what punishment should be inflicted it did not appoint. Such occasions as these are rare. And for such things as do fall scarce once in many ages of men, it did suffice to take such order as was requisite when they fell. But if the case were such as being not already determined by law were notwithstanding likely oftentimes to come in question, it gave occasion of adding laws that were not before. Thus it fell out in the case of those men polluted[4], and of the daughters of Zelophehad[5], whose causes Moses having brought before the Lord, received laws to serve for the like in time to come. The Jews to this end had the Oracle of God, they had the Prophets: and by such means God himself instructed them from heaven what to do, in all things that did greatly concern their state and were not already set down in the Law. Shall we then hereupon argue even against our own experience and knowledge? Shall we seek to persuade men that of necessity it is with us as it was with them; that because God is ours in all respects as much as theirs, therefore either no such way of direction hath been at any time, or if it have been, it doth still continue in the Church; or if the same

[1] Levit. xxiv. 12. [2] ["Sabboth," A. B.] [3] Numb. xv. 33-35.
[4] Numb. ix. [5] Numb. xxvii.

BOOK III. do not continue, that yet it must be at the least supplied by
Ch. xi. 9. some such mean as pleaseth us to account of equal force?
A more dutiful and religious way for us were to admire the
wisdom of God, which shineth in the beautiful variety of all
things, but most in the manifold and yet harmonious dissimilitude of those ways, whereby his Church upon earth is guided
from age to age, throughout all generations of men.

[9.] The Jews were necessarily to continue till the coming
of Christ in the flesh, and the gathering of nations unto him.
So much the promise made unto Abraham[1] did import. So
much the prophecy of Jacob at the hour of his death did foreshew[2]. Upon the safety therefore of their very outward state
and condition for so long, the after-good of the whole world
and the salvation of all did depend. Unto their so long
safety, for two things it was necessary to provide; namely,
the preservation of their state against foreign resistance, and
the continuance of their peace within themselves.

Touching the one, as they received the promise of God
to be the rock of their defence, against which whoso did
violently rush should but bruise and batter themselves; so
likewise they had his commandment in all their affairs that
way to seek direction and counsel from him. Men's consultations are always perilous. And it falleth out many times
that after long deliberation those things are by their wit even
resolved on, which by trial are found most opposite to public
safety. It is no impossible thing for states, be they never so well
established, yet by oversight in some one act or treaty between
them and their potent opposites[3] utterly to cast away themselves for ever. Wherefore lest it should so fall out to them upon
whom so much did depend, they were not permitted to enter into
war, nor conclude any league of peace, nor to wade through
any act of moment between them and foreign states, unless
the Oracle of God or his Prophets were first consulted with.

And lest domestical disturbance should waste them within
themselves, because there was nothing unto this purpose more
effectual, than if the authority of their laws and governors
were such, as none might presume to take exception against
it, or to shew disobedience unto it, without incurring the

---

[1] Gen. xviii. 18.   [2] Gen. xlix. 10.
[3] [Comp. Hamlet, v. 2. 62, "mighty opposites."] 1886.

hatred and detestation of all men that had any spark of the fear of God; therefore he gave them even their positive laws from heaven, and as oft as occasion required chose in like sort rulers also to lead and govern them. Notwithstanding some desperately impious there were, which adventured to try what harm it could bring upon them, if they did attempt to be authors of confusion, and to resist both governors and laws. Against such monsters God maintained his own by fearful execution of extraordinary judgment upon them.

By which means it came to pass, that although they were a people infested and mightily hated of all others throughout the world, although by nature hard-hearted, querulous, wrathful, and impatient of rest and quietness; yet was there nothing of force either one way or other to work the ruin and subversion of their state, till the time before-mentioned was expired. Thus we see that there was not no cause of dissimilitude in these things between that one only people before Christ, and the kingdoms of the world since.

[10.] And whereas it is further alleged[1] that albeit "in "civil matters and things pertaining to this present life God "hath used a greater particularity with them than amongst "us, framing laws according to the quality of that people and "country; yet the leaving of us at greater liberty in things "civil is so far from proving the like liberty in things pertain- "ing to the kingdom of heaven, that it rather proves a straiter "bond. For even as when the Lord would have his favour "more appear by temporal blessings of this life towards the "people under the Law than towards us, he gave also politic "laws most exactly, whereby they might both most easily "come into and most steadfastly remain in possession of those "earthly benefits: even so at this time, wherein he would "not have his favour so much esteemed by those outward "commodities, it is required, that as his care in prescribing "laws for that purpose hath somewhat fallen in leaving them "to men's consultations which may be deceived, so his care "for conduct and government of the life to come should (if it "were possible) rise, in leaving less to the order of men than "in times past." These are but weak and feeble disputes for the inference of that conclusion which is intended. For

[1] T. C. lib. ii. p. 440.

saving only in such consideration as hath been shewed, there is no cause wherefore we should think God more desirous to manifest his favour by temporal blessings towards them than towards us. Godliness had unto them, and it hath also unto us, the promises both of this life and the life to come. That the care of God hath fallen in earthly things, and therefore should rise as much in heavenly; that more is left unto men's consultations in the one, and therefore less must be granted in the other; that God, having used a greater particularity with them than with us for matters pertaining unto this life, is to make us amends by the more exact delivery of laws for government of the life to come: these are proportions, whereof if there be any rule, we must plainly confess that which truth is, we know it not. God which spake unto them by his Prophets, hath unto us by his only-begotten Son; those mysteries of grace and salvation which were but darkly disclosed unto them, have unto us most clearly shined. Such differences between them and us the Apostles of Christ have well acquainted us withal. But as for matter belonging to the outward conduct or government of the Church, seeing that even in sense it is manifest that our Lord and Saviour hath not by positive laws descended so far into particularities with us as Moses with them, neither doth by extraordinary means, oracles, and prophets, direct us as them he did in those things which rising daily by new occasions are of necessity to be provided for; doth it not hereupon rather follow, that although not to them, yet to us there should be freedom and liberty granted to make laws?

[11.] Yea, but the Apostle St. Paul doth fearfully charge Timothy[1], even " in the sight of God who quickeneth all,

---

[1] [See Eccl. Disc. fol. 10. " Sed " universum hunc locum de disci- " plina a Deo profecta, et prophetica " immobili atque perpetua, et om- " nium ecclesiarum communi, gra- " vissima illa Pauli ad Timotheum " de eadem conservanda obtestatione " concludamus. Qui quum disci- " pulum suum omnem domus Dei, " quæ est Ecclesia, administrandæ " rationem docuisset, ' Denuncio,' " inquit, ' tibi, in conspectu Dei " illius qui vivificat omnia, et Jesu " Christi, qui præclaram illam con- " fessionem Pontio Pilato professus " est, ut hæc mandata sine labe et " sine reprehensione custodias usque " ad apparitionem Domini nostri " Jesu Christi :' &c. quæ gravissimis " verbis Apostolus persecutus est. " Unde primo colligimus, disciplinæ " quam ea epistola Paulus tradidisset, " Deum omnipotentem auctorem " esse, et Servatorem nostrum Jesum " Christum : ut qui ejusdem violatæ " ultores et vindices significantur. " Tum constantem esse atque immu- " tabilem, quæ nulla hominum neque " gratia variari, neque auctoritate " frangi debeat : cum non solum " ἐντολὴ καὶ παραγγελία appelletur, " sed jubeatur etiam ἄσπιλος καὶ

it does not relate to the Detail of Polity.

"and of Jesus Christ who witnessed that famous confession
"before Pontius Pilate[1], to keep what was commanded him
"safe and sound till the appearance of our Lord Jesus
"Christ[2]." This doth exclude all liberty of changing the
laws of Christ, whether by abrogation or addition, or howsoever. For in Timothy the whole Church of Christ receiveth
charge concerning her duty; and that charge is to keep the
Apostle's commandment; and his commandment did contain
the laws that concerned church government; and those laws
he straitly requireth to be observed without breach or blame,
till the appearance of our Lord Jesus Christ.

In Scripture we grant every one man's lesson to be the
common instruction of all men, so far forth as their cases are
like; and that religiously to keep the Apostle's commandments in whatsoever they may concern us we all stand bound.
But touching that commandment which Timothy was charged
with, we swerve undoubtedly from the Apostle's precise
meaning if we extend it so largely, that the arms thereof
shall reach unto all things which were commanded him by the
Apostle. The very words themselves do restrain themselves
unto some one especial commandment among many. And
therefore it is not said, "Keep the ordinances, laws, and
"constitutions, which thou hast received;" but τὴν ἐντολὴν,
"that great commandment, which doth principally concern
"thee and thy calling;" that commandment which Christ did
so often inculcate unto Peter[3]; that commandment unto the
careful discharge whereof they of Ephesus are exhorted,
"Attend to yourselves, and to all the flock wherein the Holy
"Ghost hath placed you Bishops, to feed the Church of God,
"which he hath purchased by his own blood[4];" finally that
commandment which unto the same Timothy is by the same
Apostle even in the same form and manner afterwards again
urged, "I charge thee in the sight of God and the Lord
"Jesus Christ, which will judge the quick and dead at his
"appearance and in his kingdom, *preach the word of God*[5]."

"ἀνεπίληπτος conservari. Postremo
"non certi alicujus temporis præ-
"ceptum esse, sed perpetuum, et
"quod ad omnia Ecclesiæ tempora
"pertineat: quum tam diserte præ-
"ceptum sit, ut usque in adventum

"Domini nostri Jesu Christi con-
"servetur."]
[1] John xviii. 36, 37.
[2] 1 Tim. vi. 13, 14.
[3] John xxi. 15.   [4] Acts xx. 28.
[5] 2 Tim. iv. 1.

BOOK III.
Ch. xi. 11.

When Timothy was instituted into the office, then was the credit and trust of this duty committed unto his faithful care. The doctrine of the Gospel was then given him, "as the pre-"cious talent or treasure of Jesus Christ[1];" then received he for performance of this duty "the special gift of the Holy "Ghost[2]." "To keep this commandment immaculate and "blameless" was to teach the Gospel of Christ without mixture of corrupt and unsound doctrine, such as a number did even in those times intermingle with the mysteries of Christian belief. "Till the appearance of Christ to keep it so," doth not import the time wherein it should be kept, but rather the time whereunto the final reward for keeping it was reserved: according to that of St. Paul concerning himself, "I have kept the faith; for the residue there is laid up for "me a crown of righteousness, which the Lord the righteous "shall in that day render unto me[3]." If they that labour in this harvest should respect but the present fruit of their painful travel, a poor encouragement it were unto them to continue therein all the days of their life. But their reward is great in heaven; the crown of righteousness which shall be given them in that day is honourable. The fruit of their industry then shall they reap with full contentment and satisfaction, but not till then. Wherein the greatness of their reward is abundantly sufficient to countervail the tediousness of their expectation. Wherefore till then, they that are in labour must rest in hope. "O Timothy, keep that which is "committed unto thy charge; that great commandment which "thou hast received keep, till the appearance of our Lord "Jesus Christ."

In which sense although we judge the Apostle's words to have been uttered, yet hereunto we do not require them to yield, that think any other construction more sound. If therefore it be rejected, and theirs esteemed more probable which hold, that the last words do import perpetual observation of the Apostle's commandment imposed necessarily for ever upon the militant Church of Christ; let them withal consider, that then his commandment cannot so largely be taken, as to comprehend whatsoever the Apostle did command Timothy. For themselves do not all bind the Church unto

[1] 1 Tim. vi. 20. τὴν παρακαταθήκην.   [2] 1 Tim. iv. 14.   [3] 2 Tim. iv. 7, 8.

The Puritans allow additional Church Laws. 403

some things whereof Timothy received charge, as namely unto that precept concerning the choice of widows[1]. So as they cannot hereby maintain that all things positively commanded concerning the affairs of the Church were commanded for perpetuity. And we do not deny that certain things were commanded to be though positive yet perpetual in the Church.

[12.] They should not therefore urge against us places that seem to forbid change, but rather such as set down some measure of alteration, which measure if we have exceeded, then might they therewith charge us justly: whereas now they themselves both granting, and also using liberty to change, cannot in reason dispute absolutely against all change. Christ delivered no inconvenient or unmeet laws: sundry of ours they hold inconvenient: therefore such laws they cannot possibly hold to be Christ's: being not his, they must of necessity grant them added unto his. Yet certain of those very laws so added they themselves do not judge unlawful; as they plainly confess both in matter of prescript attire and of rites appertaining to burial. Their own protestations are, that they plead against the inconvenience, not the unlawfulness of popish apparel[2]; and against the inconvenience not the unlawfulness of ceremonies in burial. Therefore they hold it a thing not unlawful to add to the laws of Jesus Christ; and so consequently they yield that no law of Christ forbiddeth addition unto church laws.

[13.] The judgment of Calvin being alleged[3] against them,

---

[1] [1 Tim. v. 9. See T. C. i. 153. al. 191. Whitg. Def. 693.]

[2] "My reasons do never conclude "the unlawfulness of these ceremo- "nies of burial, but the inconve- "nience and inexpedience of them." T. C. lib. iii. p. 241. And in the table. "Of the inconvenience, not "of the unlawfulness, of popish ap- "parel and ceremonies in burial."

[3] [By Archbishop Whitgift: see Answer, p. 25-29, and Def. 109- 113. The passage from Calvin is the following: "Quia Dominus... "quicquid ad salutem necessarium "erat, sacris suis oraculis tum "fideliter complexus est, tum per- "spicue enarravit, in his solus ma- "gister est audiendus. Quia autem "in externa disciplina et ceremoniis

"non voluit sigillatim præscribere "quid sequi debeamus, quod istud "penderet a temporum conditione "prævideret, neque judicaret unam "sæculis omnibus formam conve- "nire, confugere hic oportet ad ge- "nerales, quas dedit, regulas; ut "ad eas exigantur, quæcunque ad "ordinem et decorum præcipi ne- "cessitas Ecclesiæ postulabit." In- stit. c. xiii. § 31, ed. 1550, or lib. iv. c. x. § 30, according to the present arrangement. All Whitgift's quo- tations from the Institution specify *chapter* and *section* only. The di- vision of the work into books first took place in the edition of 1559: and Whitgift used an earlier copy. See Def. 391. 508.]

BOOK III. to whom of all men they attribute most[1]; whereas his words
Ch. xi. 13. be plain, that for ceremonies and external discipline the
Church hath power to make laws: the answer which hereunto they make is, that indefinitely the speech is true, and that so it was meant by him; namely, that some things belonging unto external discipline and ceremonies are in the power and arbitrement of the Church; but neither was it meant, neither is it true generally, that all external discipline and all ceremonies are left to the order of the Church, inasmuch as the sacraments of Baptism and the Supper of the Lord are ceremonies, which yet the Church may not therefore abrogate. Again, Excommunication is a part of external discipline, which might also be cast away, if all external discipline were arbitrary and in the choice of the Church.

By which their answer it doth appear, that touching the names of ceremony and external discipline they gladly would have us so understood, as if we did herein contain a great deal more than we do. The fault which we find with them is, that they overmuch abridge the Church of her power in these things. Whereupon they recharge us, as if in these things we gave the Church a liberty which hath no limits or bounds; as if all things which the name of discipline containeth were of the Church's free choice; so that we might either have church governors and government or want them, either retain or reject church censures as we list. They wonder at us, as at men which think it so indifferent what the Church doth in matter of ceremonies, that it may be feared lest we judge the very Sacraments themselves to be held at the Church's pleasure.

---

[1] "Upon the indefinite speaking "of M. Calvin, saying, 'ceremonies "and external discipline,' without "adding 'all' or 'some,' you go "about subtlely to make men be-"lieve, that M. Calvin had placed "the whole external discipline in "the power and arbiterment of the "Church. For if all external disci-"pline were arbitrary, and in the "choice of the Church, excommuni-"cation also (which is a part of it) "might be cast away; which I think "you will not say." And in the very next words before: "Where you "would give to understand that "ceremonies and external discipline "are not prescribed particularly by "the word of God, and therefore "left to the order of the Church: "you must understand that all ex-"ternal discipline is not left to the "order of the Church, being particu-"larly prescribed in the Scriptures: "no more than all ceremonies are "left to the order of the Church, as "the Sacrament of Baptism, and "Supper of the Lord." T. C. lib. i. p. 32. [and 33, al. 19. Whitgf. Def. 111.]

No, the name of ceremonies we do not use in so large a meaning as to bring Sacraments within the compass and reach thereof, although things belonging unto the outward form and seemly administration of them are contained in that name, even as we use it. For the name of ceremonies we use as they themselves do, when they speak after this sort: "The doctrine and discipline of the Church, as the "weightiest things, ought especially to be looked unto; but "the ceremonies also, as mint and cummin, ought not to be "neglected[1]." Besides, in the matter of external discipline or regiment itself, we do not deny but there are some things whereto the church is bound till the world's end. So as the question is only how far the bounds of the Church's liberty do reach. We hold, that the power which the Church hath lawfully to make laws and orders for itself doth extend unto sundry things of ecclesiastical jurisdiction, and such other matters, whereto their opinion is that the Church's authority and power doth not reach. Whereas therefore in disputing against us about this point, they take their compass a great deal wider than the truth of things can afford; producing reasons and arguments by way of generality, to prove that Christ hath set down all things belonging any way unto the form of ordering his Church, and hath absolutely forbidden change by addition or diminution, great or small: (for so their manner of disputing is:) we are constrained to make our defence, by shewing that Christ hath not deprived his Church so far of all liberty in making orders and laws for itself, and that they themselves do not think he hath so done. For are they able to shew that all particular customs, rites, and orders of reformed churches have been appointed by Christ himself? No: they grant that in matter of circumstance they alter that which they have received[2], but in things of substance, they keep the laws of Christ without change. If we say the same in our own behalf (which surely we may do with a great deal more truth) then must they cancel all that hath been before alleged, and begin to inquire afresh, whether we retain the

BOOK III. Ch. xi. 13.

---

[1] T. C. lib. iii. p. 171.
[2] "We deny not but certain "things are left to the order of the "Church, because they are of the "nature of those which are varied " by times, places, persons, and " other circumstances, and so could " not at once be set down and " established for ever." T. C. lib. i. p. 27. [15.]

laws that Christ hath delivered concerning matters of substance, yea or no. For our constant persuasion in this point is as theirs, that we have no where altered the laws of Christ farther than in such particularities only as have the nature of things changeable according to the difference of times, places, persons, and other the like circumstances. Christ hath commanded prayers to be made, sacraments to be ministered, his Church to be carefully taught and guided. Concerning every of these somewhat Christ hath commanded which must be kept till the world's end. On the contrary side, in every of them somewhat there may be added, as the Church shall judge it expedient. So that if they will speak to purpose, all which hitherto hath been disputed of they must give over, and stand upon such particulars only as they can shew we have either added or abrogated otherwise than we ought, in the matter of church polity. Whatsoever Christ hath commanded for ever to be kept in his Church, the same we take not upon us to abrogate; and whatsoever our laws have thereunto added besides, of such quality we hope it is as no law of Christ doth any where condemn.

[14.] Wherefore that all may be laid together and gathered into a narrower room: First, so far forth as the Church is the mystical body of Christ and his invisible spouse, it needeth no external polity. That very part of the law divine which teacheth faith and works of righteousness is itself alone sufficient for the Church of God in that respect. But as the Church is a visible society and body politic, laws of polity it cannot want [1].

[15.] Secondly: Whereas therefore it cometh in the second place to be inquired, what laws are fittest and best for the Church; they who first embraced that rigorous and strict opinion, which depriveth the Church of liberty to make any kind of law for herself, inclined as it should seem thereunto, for that they imagined all things which the Church doth without commandment of Holy Scripture subject to that reproof which the Scripture itself useth in certain cases [2] when divine authority ought alone to be followed. Hereupon they thought it enough for the cancelling of any kind of order whatsoever, to say, "The word of God teacheth it not, it is a device of

---

[1] [See above, ch. i.]   [2] Isa. xxix. 14; Col. ii. 22.

"the brain of man, away with it therefore out of the Church¹." St. Augustine was of another mind, who speaking of fasts on the Sunday saith², "That he which would choose out that "day to fast on, should give thereby no small offence to the "Church of God, which had received a contrary custom. "For in these things, whereof the Scripture appointeth no "certainty, the use of the people of God or the ordinances of "our fathers must serve for a law. In which case if we will "dispute, and condemn one sort by another's custom, it will "be but matter of endless contention ; where, forasmuch as "the labour of reasoning shall hardly beat into men's heads "any certain or necessary truth, surely it standeth us upon "to take heed, lest with the tempest of strife the brightness "of charity and love be darkened."

If all things must be commanded of God which may be practised of his Church, I would know what commandment the Gileadites had to erect that altar which is spoken of in the Book of Josua³. Did not congruity of reason induce them thereunto, and suffice for defence of their fact? I would know what commandment the women of Israel had yearly to mourn and lament in the memory of Jephtha's daughter⁴; what commandment the Jews had to celebrate their feast of Dedication, never spoken of in the law, yet solemnized even by our Saviour himself⁵; what commandment finally they had for the ceremony of odours used about the bodies of the dead, after which custom notwithstanding (sith it was their custom) our Lord was contented that his own most precious body should be entombed⁶. Wherefore to reject all orders of the Church which men have established, is to think worse of the laws of men in this respect, than either the judgment of wise men alloweth, or the law of God itself will bear.

[16.] Howbeit they which had once taken upon them to

---

¹ [See above, ch. ii. 1.]
² August. Ep. 86. [al. 36, t. ii. 68. "Quisquis hunc diem jejunio decer-"nendum putaverit, ... non parvo "scandalo erit Ecclesiæ : nec im-"merito. In his enim rebus de "quibus nihil certi statuit Scriptura "divina, mos populi Dei, vel insti-"tuta majorum pro lege tenenda "sunt. De quibus si disputare "voluerimus, et ex aliorum consue-"tudine alios improbare, orietur "interminata luctatio : quæ labore "sermocinationis cum certa docu-"menta nulla veritatis insinuet, "utique cavendum est, ne tempes-"tate contentionis serenitatem cari-"tatis obnubilet."]
³ Josh. xxii. 10.
⁴ Judges xi. 40.
⁵ John x. 22.
⁶ John xix. 40.

BOOK III.
Ch. xi. 16.
condemn all things done in the Church and not commanded of God to be done, saw it was necessary for them (continuing in defence of this their opinion) to hold that needs there must be in Scripture set down a complete particular form of church polity, a form prescribing how all the affairs of the Church must be ordered, a form in no respect lawful to be altered by mortal men [1]. For reformation of which oversight and error in them, there were that thought it a part of Christian love and charity to instruct them better [2], and to open unto them the difference between matters of perpetual necessity to all men's salvation, and matters of ecclesiastical polity: the one both fully and plainly taught in holy Scripture, the other not necessary to be in such sort there prescribed; the one not capable of any diminution or augmentation at all by men, the other apt to admit both. Hereupon the authors of the former opinion were presently seconded by other wittier and better learned [3], who being loth that the form of church polity which they sought to bring in should be otherwise than in the highest degree accounted of, took [4] first an exception against the difference between church polity and matters of necessity unto salvation [5]; secondly, against the restraint of Scripture, which they say receiveth injury at our hands, when we teach that it teacheth not as well matters of polity as of faith and salvation [6]. Thirdly, Constrained hereby we have been therefore both to maintain that distinction, as a thing not only true in itself, but by them likewise so acknowledged, though unawares [7]; Fourthly, and to make manifest that from Scripture we offer not to derogate the least thing that truth thereunto doth claim, inasmuch as by us it is willingly confest, that the Scripture of God is a storehouse abounding with inestimable

[1] [1 Admon. to the Parl. fol. 1. ap. Whitg. Def. 76. "Seeing that "nothing in this mortal life is more "diligently to be sought for, and "carefully to be looked unto, than "the restitution of true religion, "and reformation of God's Church: "it shall be your parts (dearly be-"loved) in this present parliament "assembled, as much as in you lieth "to promote the same, and to em-"ploy your whole labour and study "not only in abandoning all popish "remnants both in ceremonies and "regiment, but also in bringing in "and placing in God's Church those "things only, which the Lord him-"self in his word commandeth."]

[2] [Vide Whitgift's Answer to the Admonition, p. 20-29.]

[3] [By this it should seem that Hooker did not consider Cartwright himself as one of the authors of the Admonition.]

[4] [See above, ch. ii. 2.]

[5] [T. C. 1 Reply, p. 14.]

[6] [T. C. ibid.]

[7] [In ch. iii.]

treasures of wisdom and knowledge in many kinds, over and above things in this one kind barely necessary; yea, even that matters of ecclesiastical polity are not therein omitted, but taught also, albeit not so taught as those other things before mentioned [1]. For so perfectly are those things taught, that nothing can ever need to be added, nothing ever cease to be necessary; these on the contrary side, as being of a far other nature and quality, not so strictly nor everlastingly commanded in Scripture, but that unto the complete form of church polity much may be requisite which the Scripture teacheth not, and much which it hath taught become unrequisite, sometime because we need not use it, sometime also because we cannot. In which respect for mine own part, although I see that certain reformed churches, the Scottish especially and French, have not that which best agreeth with the sacred Scripture [2], I mean the government that is by Bishops, inasmuch as both those churches are fallen under a different kind of regiment; which to remedy it is for the one altogether too late, and too soon for the other during their present affliction and trouble [3]: this their defect and imperfection I had rather lament in such case than exagitate, considering that men oftentimes without any fault of their own may be driven to want that kind of polity or regiment which is best, and to content themselves with that, which either the irremediable error of former times, or the necessity of the present hath cast upon them.

---

[1] [In ch. iv.]
[2] [Saravia, De diversis Ministrorum Gradibus, Prol. ad Lect. "De hoc novo Ecclesiæ regendæ modo idem censeo, quod alii de Episcoporum regimine judicant; nempe quod sit humanus et ferendus, ubi alius melior obtineri non potest: et contra ille qui improbatur tanquam humanus mihi videtur esse divinus; utpote qui tam in Veteri quam in Novo Testamento a Deo sit institutus." Sutcliffe, False Semblant of counterfeit Discipline detected, p. 8. "We say, that so much as Christ hath appointed to be observed, as that there be pastors to teach, and a certain government, and such like discipline, is diligently to be kept. Where

"He hath left it free, there the governors of the Church, i. e. Christian princes and bishops, may set orders and see the same executed: and the orders appointed by Christ, and canons and customs of the Church, we call ecclesiastical discipline: and this we account to be changeable so far forth as is not by Christ commanded to be kept."]
[3] [The first part of Hooker's work was licensed to the press, March 9, 1592-3. The affliction meant is therefore the civil war in France, not the secession from protestantism of Henry IV: which was not made known till after June that year. Davila, lib. xiii. p. 697, comp. p. 692. Venice, 1692.]

BOOK III.
Ch. xi. 17.

[17.] Fifthly, Now because that position first-mentioned, which holdeth it necessary that all things which the Church may lawfully do in her own regiment be commanded in holy Scripture, hath by the later defenders thereof been greatly qualified; who, though perceiving it to be over extreme, are notwithstanding loth to acknowledge any oversight therein, and therefore labour what they may to salve it by construction; we have for the more perspicuity delivered what was thereby meant at the first[1]: sixthly, how injurious a thing it were unto all the churches of God for men to hold it in that meaning[2]: seventhly, and how imperfect their interpretations are who so much labour to help it, either by dividing commandments of Scripture into two kinds, and so defending that all things must be commanded, if not in special yet in general precepts[3]; eighthly, or by taking it as meant, that in case the Church do devise any new order, she ought therein to follow the direction of Scripture only, and not any starlight of man's reason[4]. Ninthly, both which evasions being cut off, we have in the next place declared after what sort the Church may lawfully frame to herself laws of polity, and in what reckoning such positive laws both are with God and should be with men[5]. Tenthly, furthermore, because to abridge the liberty of the Church in this behalf, it hath been made a thing very odious, that when God himself hath devised some certain laws and committed them to sacred Scripture, man by abrogation, addition, or any way, should presume to alter and change them; it was of necessity to be examined, whether the authority of God in making, or his care in committing those his laws unto Scripture, be sufficient arguments to prove that God doth in no case allow they should suffer any such kind of change[6]. Eleventhly, the last refuge for proof that divine laws of Christian church polity may not be altered by extinguishment of any old or addition of new in that kind, is partly a marvellous strange discourse, that Christ (unless he should shew himself not so faithful as Moses, or not so wise as Lycurgus and Solon[7]) must needs have set down in holy

---

[1] [In ch. v.]   [2] [In ch. vi.]
[3] [In ch. vii.] [4] [In ch. viii.]
[5] [In ch. ix.]   [6] [In ch. x.]
[7] "Nisi reip. suæ statum omnem "constituerit, magistratus ordinarit,

"singulorum munera potestatem-
"que descripserit, quæ judiciorum
"forique ratio habenda, quomodo
"civium finiendæ lites: non solum
"minus Ecclesiæ Christianæ pro-

Scripture some certain complete and unchangeable form of polity[1]: and partly a coloured show of some evidence where change of that sort of laws may seem expressly forbidden, although in truth nothing less be done[2].

[18.] I might have added hereunto their more familiar and popular disputes, as, The Church is a city, yea the city of the great King; and the life of a city is polity: The Church is the house of the living God; and what house can there be without some order for the government of it? In the royal house of a prince there must be officers for government, such as not any servant in the house but the prince whose the house is shall judge convenient. So the house of God must have orders for the government of it, such as not any of the household but God himself hath appointed. It cannot stand with the love and wisdom of God to leave such order untaken as is necessary for the due government of his Church. The numbers, degrees, orders, and attire of Salomon's servants, did shew his wisdom; therefore he which is greater than Salomon hath not failed to leave in his house such orders for government thereof, as may serve to be a looking-glass for his providence, care, and wisdom, to be seen in[3]. That little spark of the light of nature which remaineth in us may serve us for the affairs of this life. "But as in all other matters "concerning the kingdom of heaven, so principally in this "which concerneth the very government of that kingdom, "needful it is we should be taught of God. As long as men "are persuaded of any order that it is only of men, they pre- "sume of their own understanding, and they think to devise "another not only as good, but better than that which they

"vidit quam Moses olim Judaicæ, "sed quam a Lycurgo, Solone, Nu- "ma, civitatibus suis prospectum "sit." Lib. de Ecclesiast. Discip. [fol. 8, or p. 10 of T. C.'s translation.]
[1] [In ch. xi. 1–8.]
[2] [Ch. xi. 9.]
[3] [Eccl. Disc. fol. 143. "Chris- "tianæ Ecclesiæ, tanquam domus "Dei (ut a Paulo appellatur) οἰκο- "νομίαν qui attentius et accuratius "consideraverit, animadvertet pro- "fecto incredibilem quandam illam "in omnibus ejus partibus et di- "vinam sapientiam, ac tanto quidem "illa Salomonis in sacra historia "magis admirabilem, quanto sapi- "entior Salomone fuerit qui omnem "hujus domus ordinem rationemque "descripsit. Sive enim ministro- "rum ordines, sive accubitus, sive "varium pro cujusque dignitate or- "natum et habitum consideremus, "quod ad Ecclesiæ non modo salu- "tem conservandam, sed etiam dig- "nitatem illustrandam ornandam- "que aut prudenter excogitari, aut "cum judicio atque ratione disponi "collocarique potuerit: quid in hac "οἰκονομίᾳ requiratur?"]

"have received. By severity of punishment this presumption
"and curiosity may be restrained. But that cannot work
"such cheerful obedience as is yielded where the conscience
"hath respect to God as the author of laws and orders. This
"was it which countenanced the laws of Moses, made con-
"cerning outward polity for the administration of holy things.
"The like some lawgivers of the heathens did pretend, but
"falsely; yet wisely discerning the use of this persuasion.
"For the better obedience' sake therefore it was expedient
"that God should be author of the polity of his Church."

[19.] But to what issue doth all this come? A man would think that they which hold out with such discourses were of nothing more fully persuaded than of this, that the Scripture hath set down a complete form of church polity, universal, perpetual, altogether unchangeable. For so it would follow, if the premises were sound and strong to such effect as is pretended. Notwithstanding, they which have thus formally maintained argument in defence of the first oversight, are by the very evidence of truth themselves constrained to make this in effect their conclusion, that the Scripture of God hath many things concerning church polity; that of those many some are of greater weight, some of less; that what hath been urged as touching immutability of laws, it extendeth in truth no farther than only to laws wherein things of greater moment are prescribed. Now those things of greater moment, what are they? Forsooth[1], "doctors, pastors, lay-elders, elderships "compounded of these three; synods, consisting of many "elderships; deacons, women-church-servants or widows; "free consent of the people unto actions of greatest moment, "after they be by churches or synods orderly resolved." All "this form" of polity (if yet we may term that a form of building, when men have laid a few rafters together, and those not all of the soundest neither) but howsoever, all this form they conclude is prescribed in such sort, that to add to it any thing as of like importance (for so I think they mean) or to abrogate of it any thing at all, is unlawful. In which resolution if they will firmly and constantly persist, I see not but that concerning the points which hitherto have been disputed of, they must agree that they have molested the Church

[1] The Defence of Godly Ministers against D. Bridges, p. 133.

with needless opposition, and henceforward as we said before betake themselves wholly unto the trial of particulars, whether every of those things which they esteem as principal, be either so esteemed of, or at all established for perpetuity in holy Scripture; and whether any particular thing in our Church polity be received other than the Scripture alloweth of, either in greater things or in smaller.

[20.] The matters wherein Church polity is conversant are the public religious duties of the Church, as the administration of the word and sacraments, prayers, spiritual censures, and the like. To these the Church standeth always bound. Laws of polity, are laws which appoint in what manner these duties shall be performed.

In performance whereof because all that are of the Church cannot jointly and equally work, the first thing in polity required is a difference of persons in the Church, without which difference those functions cannot in orderly sort be executed. Hereupon we hold that God's clergy are a state, which hath been and will be, as long as there is a Church upon earth, necessary by the plain word of God himself; a state whereunto the rest of God's people must be subject as touching things that appertain to their souls' health. For where polity is, it cannot but appoint some to be leaders of others, and some to be led by others. "If the blind lead the "blind, they both perish[1]." It is with the clergy, if their persons be respected, even as it is with other men; their quality many times far beneath that which the dignity of their place requireth. Howbeit according to the order of polity, they being the "lights of the world[2]," others (though better and wiser) must that way be subject unto them.

Again, forasmuch as where the clergy are any great multitude, order doth necessarily require that by degrees they be distinguished; we hold there have ever been and ever ought to be in such case at leastwise two sorts of ecclesiastical persons, the one subordinate unto the other; as to the Apostles in the beginning, and to the Bishops always since, we find plainly both in Scripture and in all ecclesiastical records, other ministers of the word and sacraments have been.

Moreover, it cannot enter into any man's conceit to think

[1] Luke vi. 39.   [2] Matt. v. 14.

it lawful, that every man which listeth should take upon him charge in the Church; and therefore a solemn admittance is of such necessity, that without it there can be no church-polity.

A number of particularities there are, which make for the more convenient being of these principal and perpetual parts in ecclesiastical polity, but yet are not of such constant use and necessity in God's Church. Of this kind are, times and places appointed for the exercise of religion; specialties belonging to the public solemnity of the word, the sacraments, and prayer; the enlargement or abridgment of functions ministerial depending upon those two principal before-mentioned; to conclude, even whatsoever doth by way of formality and circumstance concern any public action of the Church. Now although that which the Scripture hath of things in the former kind be for ever permanent: yet in the later both much of that which the Scripture teacheth is not always needful; and much the Church of God shall always need which the Scripture teacheth not.

So as the form of polity by them set down for perpetuity is three ways faulty: faulty in omitting some things which in Scripture are of that nature, as namely the difference that ought to be of Pastors when they grow to any great multitude: faulty in requiring Doctors, Deacons, Widows, and such like, as things of perpetual necessity by the law of God, which in truth are nothing less: faulty also in urging some things by Scripture immutable, as their Lay-elders, which the Scripture neither maketh immutable nor at all teacheth, for any thing either we can as yet find or they have hitherto been able to prove. But hereof more in the books that follow.

[21.] As for those marvellous discourses whereby they adventure to argue that God must needs have done the thing which they imagine was to be done; I must confess I have often wondered at their exceeding boldness herein. When the question is whether God have delivered in Scripture (as they affirm he hath) a complete, particular, immutable form of church polity, why take they that other both presumptuous and superfluous labour to prove he should have done it; there being no way in this case to prove the deed of God, saving only by producing that evidence wherein he hath done it? But if there be no such thing apparent upon record, they do as if one should demand a legacy by force and virtue of some written testament, wherein there being no such thing specified, he pleadeth that there it must needs be, and bringeth arguments from the love or goodwill which always the testator bore him; imagining, that these or the like proofs will convict a testament to have that in it which other men can no where by reading find. In matters which concern the actions of God, the most dutiful way on our part is to search what God hath done, and with meekness to admire that, rather than to dispute what he in congruity of reason ought to do. The ways which he hath whereby to do all things for the greatest good of his Church are moe in number than we can search, other in nature than that we should presume to determine which of many should be the fittest for him to choose, till such time as we see he hath chosen of many some one; which one we then may boldly conclude to be the fittest, because he hath taken it before the rest. When we do otherwise, surely we exceed our bounds; who and where we are we forget; and therefore needful it is that our pride in such cases be controlled, and our disputes beaten back with those demands of the blessed Apostle, " How unsearchable are his judgments, and his ways past " finding out! Who hath known the mind of the Lord, or " who was his counsellor[1]?"

[1] Rom. xi. 33, 34.

THE FOURTH BOOK.

CONCERNING THEIR THIRD ASSERTION, THAT OUR FORM OF CHURCH POLITY IS CORRUPTED WITH POPISH ORDERS, RITES, AND CEREMONIES, BANISHED OUT OF CERTAIN REFORMED CHURCHES, WHOSE EXAMPLE THEREIN WE OUGHT TO HAVE FOLLOWED.

THE MATTER CONTAINED IN THIS FOURTH BOOK.

I. How great use Ceremonies have in the Church.
II. The first thing they blame in the kind of our Ceremonies is, that we have not in them ancient apostolical simplicity, but a greater pomp and stateliness.
III. The second, that so many of them are the same which the Church of Rome useth; and the reasons which they bring to prove them for that cause blame-worthy.
IV. How when they go about to expound what Popish Ceremonies they mean, they contradict their own arguments against Popish Ceremonies.
V. An answer to the argument whereby they would prove, that sith we allow the customs of our fathers to be followed, we therefore may not allow such customs as the Church of Rome hath, because we cannot account of them which are of that Church as of our fathers.
VI. To their allegation, that the course of God's own wisdom doth make against our conformity with the Church of Rome in such things.
VII. To the example of the eldest Churches which they bring for the same purpose.
VIII. That it is not our best polity (as they pretend it is) for establishment of sound religion, to have in these things no agreement with the Church of Rome being unsound.
IX. That neither the Papists upbraiding us as furnished out of their store, nor any hope which in that respect they are said to conceive, doth make any more against our ceremonies than the former allegations have done.
X. The grief which they say godly brethren conceive at such ceremonies as we have common with the Church of Rome.
XI. The third thing for which they reprove a great part of our ceremonies is, for that as we have them from the Church of Rome, so that Church had them from the Jews.
XII. The fourth, for that sundry of them have been (they say) abused unto idolatry, and are by that mean become scandalous.

XIII. The fifth, for that we retain them still, notwithstanding the example of certain Churches reformed before us, which have cast them out.

XIV. A declaration of the proceedings of the Church of England for the establishment of things as they are.

I. SUCH was the ancient simplicity and softness of spirit which sometimes prevailed in the world, that they whose words were even as oracles amongst men, seemed evermore loth to give sentence against any thing publicly received in the Church of God, except it were wonderful apparently evil; for that they did not so much incline to that severity which delighteth to reprove the least things it seeth amiss, as to that charity which is unwilling to behold any thing that duty bindeth it to reprove. The state of this present age, wherein zeal hath drowned charity, and skill meekness, will not now suffer any man to marvel, whatsoever he shall hear reproved by whomsoever. Those rites and ceremonies of the Church therefore, which are the selfsame now that they were when holy and virtuous men maintained them against profane and deriding adversaries, her own children have at this day in derision. Whether justly or no, it shall then appear, when all things are heard which they have to allege against the outward received orders of this church. Which inasmuch as themselves do compare unto "mint and cummin[1]," granting them to be no part of those things which in the matter of polity are weightier, we hope that for small things their strife will neither be earnest nor long.

[2.] The sifting of that which is objected against the orders of the Church in particular, doth not belong unto this place. Here we are to discuss only those general exceptions, which have been taken at any time against them.

First therefore to the end that their nature and the use whereunto they serve may plainly appear, and so afterwards their quality the better be discerned; we are to note, that in every grand or main public duty which God requireth at the

BOOK IV. Ch. i. 1, 2.

How great use Ceremonies have in the Church.

---

[1] Matt. xxiii. 23. "The doctrine "and discipline of the Church, as "the weightiest things, ought especially to be looked unto: but the "ceremonies also, as 'mint and "cummin,' ought not to be neglected." T. C. l. iii. p. 171.

BOOK IV.
Ch. i. 3.

hands of his Church, there is, besides that matter and form wherein the essence thereof consisteth, a certain outward fashion whereby the same is in decent sort administered. The substance of all religious actions is delivered from God himself in few words. For example's sake in the sacraments [1]. "Unto the element let the word be added, and they both do "make a sacrament," saith St. Augustine. Baptism is given by the element of water, and that prescript form of words which the Church of Christ doth use; the sacrament of the body and blood of Christ is administered in the elements of bread and wine, if those mystical words be added thereunto. But the due and decent form of administering those holy sacraments doth require a great deal more.

[3.] The end which is aimed at in setting down the outward form of all religious actions is the edification of the Church. Now men are edified, when either their understanding is taught somewhat whereof in such actions it behoveth all men to consider, or when their hearts are moved with any affection suitable thereunto; when their minds are in any sort stirred up unto that reverence, devotion, attention, and due regard, which in those cases seemeth requisite. Because therefore unto this purpose not only speech but sundry sensible means besides have always been thought necessary, and especially those means which being object to the eye, the liveliest and the most apprehensive sense of all other, have in that respect seemed the fittest to make a deep and a strong impression: from hence have risen not only a number of prayers, readings, questionings, exhortations, but even of visible signs also; which being used in performance of holy actions, are undoubtedly most effectual to open such matter, as men when they know and remember carefully, must needs be a great deal the better informed to what effect such duties serve. We must not think but that there is some ground of reason even in nature, whereby it cometh to pass that no nation under heaven either doth or ever did suffer public actions

---

[1] [In Joan. Tract. 80. § 3. t. iii. pars ii. 703. "'Jam vos mundi estis "propter verbum quod locutus sum "vobis.' Quare non ait, 'mundi "estis propter baptismum quo loti "estis,' nisi quia et in aqua verbum "mundat? Detrahe verbum, et quid "est aqua nisi aqua? Accedit ver- "bum ad elementum, et fit sacra- "mentum, etiam ipsum tanquam "visibile verbum."]

which are of weight, whether they be civil and temporal or else spiritual and sacred, to pass without some visible solemnity: the very strangeness whereof and difference from that which is common, doth cause popular eyes to observe and to mark the same. Words, both because they are common, and do not so strongly move the fancy of man, are for the most part but slightly heard: and therefore with singular wisdom it hath been provided, that the deeds of men which are made in the presence of witnesses should pass not only with words, but also with certain sensible actions, the memory whereof is far more easy and durable than the memory of speech can be.

The things which so long experience of all ages hath confirmed and made profitable, let not us presume to condemn as follies and toys, because we sometimes know not the cause and reason of them. A wit disposed to scorn whatsoever it doth not conceive, might ask wherefore Abraham should say to his servant, "Put thy hand under my thigh and swear[1]:" was it not sufficient for his servant to shew the religion of an oath by naming the Lord God of heaven and earth, unless that strange ceremony were added? In contracts, bargains, and conveyances, a man's word is a token sufficient to express his will. Yet "this was the ancient manner in "Israel concerning redeeming and exchanging, to establish "all things; a man did pluck off his shoe and gave it his "neighbour; and this was a sure witness in Israel[2]." Amongst the Romans in their making of a bondman free, was it not wondered wherefore so great ado should be made? The master to present his slave in some court, to take him by the hand, and not only to say in the hearing of the public magistrate, "I will that this man become free," but after these solemn words uttered, to strike him on the cheek, to turn him round, the hair of his head to be shaved off, the magistrate to touch him thrice with a rod, in the end a cap and a white garment to be given him. To what purpose all this circumstance[3]? Amongst the Hebrews how strange and in outward appearance almost against reason, that he which was minded to make himself a perpetual servant, should not only testify

---

[1] Gen. xxiv. 2.
[2] Ruth iv. 7.
[3] [See Persius, Sat. v. 75, &c. Festus, voc. "manumitti." Isidor. Orig. ix. 4.]

so much in the presence of the judge, but for a visible token thereof have also his ear bored through with an awl[1]! It were an infinite labour to prosecute these things so far as they might be exemplified both in civil and religious actions. For in both they have their necessary use and force. "The sen-"sible things which religion hath hallowed, are resemblances "framed according to things spiritually understood, whereunto "they serve as a hand to lead, and a way to direct[2]."

[4.] And whereas it may peradventure be objected, that to add to religious duties such rites and ceremonies as are significant, is to institute new Sacraments[3]; sure I am they will not say that Numa Pompilius did ordain a sacrament, a significant ceremony he did ordain, in commanding the priests "to execute the work of their divine service with their hands "as far as to the fingers covered; thereby signifying that "fidelity must be defended, and that men's right hands are "the sacred seat thereof[4]." Again we are also to put them in mind, that themselves do not hold all significant ceremonies for sacraments, insomuch as imposition of hands they deny to be a sacrament, and yet they give thereunto a forcible signification; for concerning it their words are these: "The party ordained "by this ceremony was put in mind of his separation to the "work of the Lord, that remembering himself to be taken as it "were with the hand of God from amongst others, this might "teach him not to account himself now his own, nor to do "what himself listeth, but to consider that God hath set him "about a work, which if he will discharge and accomplish, he "may at the hands of God assure himself of reward; and if "otherwise, of revenge[5]." Touching significant ceremonies,

---

[1] Exod. xxi. 6.

[2] Τὰ μὲν αἰσθητῶς ἱερὰ τῶν νοητῶν ἀπεικονίσματα, καὶ ἐπ᾽ αὐτὰ χειραγωγία καὶ ὁδός. Dionys. p. 121. [de Eccl. Hierarch. c. 2. no. 3. § 2. t. i. 255. Antverp. 1634.]

[3] [See Beza's Letter to Grindal in Adm. 5. "They sinned righte "greevously, as often as they "brought any Sacramentalles (that "is to say, any ceremonies to im-"port signification of spiritual "things) into the Church of God."]

[4] "Manu ad digitos usque invo-"luta rem divinam facere, signifi-"cantes fidem tutandam, sedemque "ejus etiam in dextris sacratam "esse." Liv. lib. i. [c. 21.]

[5] Eccles. disc. fol. 51. ["Designatus hac ceremonia monebatur se "ad opus Domini separari, et e reli-"quo populo ad illam procurationem "Dei ipsius manu quasi decerpi at-"que delibari: ut jam non amplius "se sui juris esse sciret, ut agat quod "velit, sed a Deo ad opus suum ad-"hibitum, cujus illum perfecti atque "absoluti remuneratorem, contempti "autem et neglecti ultorem atque "vindicem habiturus esset."]

some of them are sacraments, some as sacraments only. Sacraments are those which are signs and tokens of some general promised grace, which always really descendeth from God unto the soul that duly receiveth them; other significant tokens are only as Sacraments, yet no Sacraments: which is not our distinction, but theirs. For concerning the Apostles' imposition of hands these are their own words; " manuum " signum hoc et quasi Sacramentum usurparunt;" "they used " this sign, or as it were sacrament [1]."

BOOK IV.
Ch. ii. 1, 2.

II. Concerning rites and ceremonies there may be fault, either in the kind or in the number and multitude of them. The first thing blamed about the kind of ours is, that in many things we have departed from the ancient simplicity of Christ and his Apostles; we have embraced more outward stateliness, we have not those orders in the exercise of religion, which they who best pleased God and served him most devoutly never had. For it is out of doubt that the first state of things was best, that in the prime of Christian religion faith was soundest, the Scriptures of God were then best understood by all men, all parts of godliness did then most abound; and therefore it must needs follow, that customs, laws, and ordinances devised since are not so good for the Church of Christ, but the best way is to cut off later inventions, and to reduce things unto the ancient state wherein at the first they were [2]. Which rule or canon we hold to be either uncertain or at leastwise unsufficient, if not both [3].

The first thing they blame in the kind of our ceremonies is that we have not in them ancient apostolical simplicity, but a greater pomp and stateliness.

[2.] For in case it be certain, hard it cannot be for them to shew us, where we shall find it so exactly set down, that we may say without all controversy, "these were the orders of " the Apostles' times, these wholly and only, neither fewer " nor moe than these." True it is that many things of this nature be alluded unto, yea many things declared, and many things necessarily collected out of the Apostles' writings. But is it necessary that all the orders of the Church which were then in use should be contained in their books? Surely no. For if the tenor of their writings be well observed, it shall unto any man easily appear, that no more of them are there touched than were needful to be spoken of, sometimes

---

[1] Fol. 52.
[2] Lib. Eccles. Disc. et T. C. lib. iii. p. 181.
[3] [See before, Preface, iv. 4.]

by one occasion and sometimes by another. Will they allow then of any other records besides? Well assured I am they are far enough from acknowledging that the Church ought to keep any thing as apostolical, which is not found in the Apostles' writings, in what other records soever it be found. And therefore whereas St. Augustine affirmeth that those things which the whole Church of Christ doth hold, may well be thought to be apostolical although they be not found written[1]; this his judgment they utterly condemn. I will not here stand in defence of St. Augustine's opinion, which is, that such things are indeed apostolical, but yet with this exception, unless the decree of some general council have haply caused them to be received[2]: for of positive laws and orders received throughout the whole Christian world, St. Augustine could imagine no other fountain save these two. But to let pass St. Augustine; they who condemn him herein must needs confess it a very uncertain thing what the orders of the Church were in the Apostles' times, seeing the Scriptures do not mention them all, and other records thereof besides they utterly reject. So that in tying the Church to the orders of the Apostles' times, they tie it to a marvellous uncertain rule; unless they require the observation of no orders but only those which are known to be apostolical by the Apostles' own writings. But then is not this their rule of such sufficiency, that we should use it as a touchstone to try the orders of the Church by for ever.

[3.] Our end ought always to be the same; our ways and means thereunto not so. The glory of God and the good of His Church was the thing which the Apostles aimed at, and therefore ought to be the mark whereat we also level. But seeing those rites and orders may be at one time more which

---

[1] Tom. vii. de Bapt. contra Donatist. lib. v. cap. 23. [t. ix. 156. "Apostoli nihil exinde præceperunt: "sed consuetudo illa quæ opponebatur Cypriano ab eorum traditione exordium sumpsisse credenda est, sicut sunt multa quæ universa tenet Ecclesia, et ob hoc ab Apostolis præcepta bene credentur, quanquam scripta non reperiantur."] T. C. l. i. p. 31. [18.] "If this judgment of St. Augustine "be a good judgment and sound, "then there be some things commanded of God which are not in "the Scriptures; and therefore there "is no sufficient doctrine contained "in Scripture whereby we may be "saved. For all the commandments of God and of the Apostles "are needful for our salvation."

[2] Vide Ep. 118. [al. 54. t. ii. 124. A.]

at another are less available unto that purpose, what reason is there in these things to urge the state of one only age as a pattern for all to follow? It is not I am right sure their meaning, that we should now assemble our people to serve God in close and secret meetings; or that common brooks or rivers should be used for places of baptism; or that the Eucharist should be ministered after meat; or that the custom of church feasting should be renewed; or that all kind of standing provision for the ministry should be utterly taken away, and their estate made again dependent upon the voluntary devotion of men. In these things they easily perceive how unfit that were for the present, which was for the first age convenient enough. The faith, zeal, and godliness of former times is worthily had in honour; but doth this prove that the orders of the Church of Christ must be still the selfsame with theirs, that nothing may be which was not then, or that nothing which then was may lawfully since have ceased? They who recall the Church unto that which was at the first, must necessarily set bounds and limits unto their speeches. If any thing have been received repugnant unto that which was first delivered, the first things in this case must stand, the last give place unto them. But where difference is without repugnancy, that which hath been can be no prejudice to that which is.

[4.] Let the state of the people of God when they were in the house of bondage, and their manner of serving God in a strange land, be compared with that which Canaan and Jerusalem did afford, and who seeth not what huge difference there was between them? In Egypt it may be they were right glad to take some corner of a poor cottage, and there to serve God upon their knees, peradventure covered in dust and straw sometimes. Neither were they therefore the less accepted of God, but he was with them in all their afflictions, and at the length by working their admirable deliverance did testify, that they served him not in vain. Notwithstanding in the very desert they are no sooner possest of some little thing of their own, but a tabernacle is required at their hands. Being planted in the land of Canaan, and having David to be their king, when the Lord had given him rest from all his enemies, it grieved his religious mind to consider the growth of his own estate and dignity, the affairs of religion continuing still in their former manner: "Behold now I dwell in an "house of cedar-trees, and the ark of God remaineth still "within curtains¹." What he did purpose it was the pleasure of God that Salomon his son should perform, and perform it in manner suitable unto their present, not their ancient estate and condition. For which cause Salomon writeth unto the king of Tyrus, "The house which I build is great and won- "derful, for great is our God above all gods²." Whereby it clearly appeareth that the orders of the Church of God may be acceptable unto him, as well being framed suitable to the greatness and dignity of later, as when they keep the reverend simplicity of ancienter times. Such dissimilitude therefore between us and the Apostles of Christ in the order of some outward things is no argument of default.

Our orders and ceremonies blamed, in that so many of them are the same which the Church of Rome useth.

III. Yea, but we have framed ourselves to the customs of the church of Rome; our orders and ceremonies are papistical. It is espied that our church founders were not so careful as in this matter they should have been, but contented themselves with such discipline as they took from the church of Rome³. Their error we ought to reform by abolishing all popish orders. There must be no communion nor fellowship with Papists, *neither in doctrine, ceremonies, nor government*. It is not enough that we are divided from the church of Rome by the single wall of doctrine, retaining as we do part of their ceremonies and almost their whole government⁴; but government or ceremonies or whatsoever it be which is popish, away with it. This is the thing they require in us, the utter relinquishment of all things popish.

Wherein to the end we may answer them according unto their plain direct meaning, and not take advantage of doubtful speech, whereby controversies grow always endless; their main position being this, that "nothing should be placed "in the Church but what God in his word hath com-

---

¹ 2 Sam. vii. 2.
² 2 Chron. ii. 5.
³ Eccles. Disc. fol. 12. ["Video "architectos Ecclesiæ nostræ in ea "restauranda soli doctrinæ intentos, "de disciplina non laborasse, et ta- "lem fere qualem a Papistis acce- "perint retinere."] T. C. lib. i. p. 131. [102. Whitg. Def. 474.]
⁴ T. C. i. 20. [al. 8, 9. ap. Def. 54. "Judge whether they be more "joined with the Papists which "would have no communion with "them, neither in ceremonies, nor "doctrine, nor government; or they "which forsaking their doctrine re- "tain part of their ceremonies and "almost all their government: that "is, they that separate themselves "by three walls or by one."]

"manded[1]," they must of necessity hold all for popish which the church of Rome hath over and besides this. By popish orders, ceremonies, and government, they must therefore mean in every of these so much as the Church of Rome hath embraced without commandment of God's word: so that whatsoever such thing we have, if the church of Rome hath it also, it goeth under the name of those things that are popish, yea although it be lawful, although agreeable to the word of God. For so they plainly affirm, saying[2], "Although the "forms and ceremonies which they" (the church of Rome) "used were not unlawful, and that they contained nothing "which is not agreeable to the word of God, yet notwith- "standing neither the word of God, nor reason, nor the ex- "amples of the eldest churches both Jewish and Christian do "permit us to use the same forms and ceremonies, being "neither commanded of God, neither such as there may not "as good as they, and rather better, be established." The question therefore is, whether we may follow the church of Rome in those orders, rites, and ceremonies, wherein we do not think them blameable, or else ought to devise others, and to have no conformity with them, no not so much as in these things. In this sense and construction therefore as they affirm, so we deny, that whatsoever is popish we ought to abrogate.

[2.] Their arguments to prove that generally all popish orders and ceremonies ought to be clean abolished, are in sum these: [3] "First, whereas we allow the judgment of "St. Augustine, that touching those things of this kind which "are not commanded or forbidden in the Scripture, we are "to observe the custom of the people of God and decree of "our forefathers[4]; how can we retain the customs and "constitutions of the papists in such things, who were "neither the people of God nor our forefathers?" Secondly[5], "although the forms and ceremonies of the church of Rome "were not unlawful, neither did contain any thing which is "not agreeable to the word of God, yet neither the word "of God, nor the examples of the eldest churches of God, "nor reason, do permit us to use the same, *they being heretics*

---

[1] T. C. i. 25. [al. 13. Def. 76. from Answ. 20.]
[2] T. C. lib. i. p. 131. [102.]
[3] T. C. lib. i. p. 30. [17.]
[4] [Ep. 36. 2. t. ii. 68.]
[5] T. C. lib. i. p. 131. [102.]

BOOK IV.
Ch. iii. 2.

"*and so near about us,* and their orders being neither com-"manded of God, nor yet such but that as good or rather "better may be established." It is against the word of God to have conformity with the church of Rome in such things, as appeareth in that "the wisdom of God hath thought it "a good way to keep his people from infection of idolatry "and superstition, by severing them from idolaters in out-"ward ceremonies, and therefore hath forbidden them to do "things which are in themselves very lawful to be done." And further, "whereas the Lord was careful to sever them "by ceremonies from other nations, yet was he not so careful "to sever them from any as from the Egyptians amongst "whom they lived, and from those nations which were next "neighbours unto them, because from them was the greatest "fear of infection." So that following the course which the wisdom of God doth teach[1], "it were more safe for us to "conform our indifferent ceremonies to the Turks which are "far off, than to the papists which are so near."

Touching the example of the eldest churches of God; in one council it was decreed, "that[2] Christians should not "deck their houses with bay leaves and green boughs, be-"cause the Pagans did use so to do; and that they should "not rest from their labours those days that the Pagans did; "that they should not keep the first day of every month as they "did. [3] Another council decreed that Christians should not

---

[1] T. C. lib. i. p. 132. [103. and Eccl. Disc. fol. 100. "A quibus nos "tanto magis recedere et abhorrere "debueramus, quanto gravius pe-"riculum nobis ab illis quam ab "aliis hæreticis, quod inter eos ver-"samur, immineat. Qua ratione "etiam Dominus in Cananæos atro-"cius quam in reliquos idololatras "sæviri voluit."]

[2] Tom. ii. [Ed. Surii.] Braca. 73. [Capitula Martini Episc. Bracar. A.D. 572. in Concil. t. v. 913. "Non "liceat iniquas observationes agere "Kalendarum, et otiis vacare gen-"tilibus, neque lauro aut viriditate "arborum cingere domos. Omnis "hæc observatio paganismi est." This is not a decree of either of the councils of Braga, but one of a collection of oriental canons made by Martin archbishop of Braga (the reformer of the Gallician church from Arianism) and sent to the archbishop of Lugo, then the second see in the province, and to his provincial council. The oriental original of the seventy-third canon does not appear.]

[3] Con. Afric. cap. 27. ["Illud "etiam petendum," (scil. ab imperatoribus) "ut quæ contra præ-"cepta divina convivia multis in "locis exercentur, quæ ab errore "gentili attracta sunt, (ita ut nunc "a Paganis Christiani ad hæc cele-"branda agantur, ex qua re temporibus Christianorum imperato-"rum persecutio altera fieri occulta "videatur) vetari talia jubeant, et "de civitatibus et de possessionibus "imposita poena prohiberi: maxime,

"celebrate feasts on the birthdays of the martyrs, because it "was the manner of the heathen." "'O!' saith Tertullian, "'better is the religion of the heathen: for they use no "solemnity of the Christians, neither the Lord's day[1], neither "the Pentecost; and if they knew them they would have "nothing to do with them: for they would be afraid lest they "should seem Christians; but we are not afraid to be called "heathen[2].'" The same Tertullian would not have Christians to sit after they have prayed, because the idolaters did so[3]. Whereby it appeareth, that both of particular men and of councils, in making or abolishing of ceremonies, heed hath been taken that the Christians should not be like the idolaters, no not in those things which of themselves are most indifferent to be used or not used.

The same conformity is not less opposite unto reason; first inasmuch as "contraries must be cured by their contraries, "and therefore popery being anti-christianity is not healed, "but by establishment of orders thereunto opposite. The "way to bring a drunken man to sobriety is to carry him as "far from excess of drink as may be. To rectify a crooked

["cum etiam in natalibus beatissi-
"morum martyrum per nonnullas
"civitates, et in ipsis locis sacris,
"talia committere non reformident.
"Quibus diebus etiam (quod pu-
"doris est dicere) saltationes scele-
"ratissimas per vicos atque plateas
"exercent, ut matronalis honor, et
"innumerabilium fœminarum pu-
"dor, devote venientium ad sacra-
"tissimum diem, injuriis lascivi-
"entibus appetatur; ut etiam ipsius
"sanctæ religionis pœne fugiatur
"accessus." Concil. ii. 1649. The exact date of this canon seems to be uncertain: but it clearly refers not to Christians having feasts of their own as the Gentiles had, but to the danger they were in of being tempted to join with the Gentiles in *their* feasts, especially when happening on our sacred days. It is one of several canons, which imply a kind of evil something similar to what Christians living in India now experience.

The following is the summary of it given by Aristænus: Τὰ Ἑλληνικὰ συμπόσια παυέσθω, διὰ τὴν οἰκείαν ἀσχημοσύνην, καὶ τὸ πολλοὺς ἀφέλκεσθαι Χριστιανῶν, καὶ ἐν ἡμέραις μνήμης μαρτύρων γίνεσθαι. Beveridge, Synodicon, i. 598.]

[1] Lib. de Idololatria, [c. 14. "O "melior fides nationum in suam "sectam: quæ nullam solennitatem "Christianorum sibi vindicat, non "Dominicum diem, non Pente- "costen: etiam si nossent, nobiscum "non communicassent; timerent "enim, ne Christiani viderentur; "nos, ne Ethnici pronunciemur, non "veremur."] He seemeth to mean the feast of Easter-day, celebrated in the memory of our Saviour's resurrection, and for that cause termed the Lord's day.

[2] [T. C. i. 103.]

[3] Lib. de Anima. [a mistake in Cartwright's reference, for "de Ora- "tione." c. 16. (The error is noted by Whitgift, Def. 480.) "Quum "perinde faciant nationes, adoratis "sigillaribus suis residendo, vel "propterea in nobis reprehendi me- "retur, quod apud idola celebra- "tur."]

BOOK IV.
Ch. iv. 1.

"stick we bend it on the contrary side, as far as it was at the "first on that side from whence we draw it, and so it cometh "in the end to a middle between both, which is perfect "straightness[1]. Utter inconformity therefore with the church "of Rome in these things is the best and surest policy "which the Church can use. While we use their ceremo- "nies they take occasion to blaspheme, saying, that our "religion cannot stand by itself, unless it lean upon the staff "of their ceremonies. They hereby conceive great hope of "having the rest of their popery in the end, which hope "causeth them to be more frozen in their wickedness. Nei- "ther is it without cause that they have this hope, considering "that which Master Bucer noteth upon the eighteenth of St. "Matthew[2], that where these things have been left, popery "hath returned; but on the other part in places which have "been cleansed of these things, it hath not yet been seen that "it hath had any entrance[3]. None make such clamours "for these ceremonies, as the papists and those whom they "suborn; a manifest token how much they triumph and joy "in these things. They breed grief of mind in a number, that "are godly-minded and have anti-christianity in such detes- "tation, that their minds are martyred with the very sight of "them in the Church[4]. Such godly brethren we ought not "thus to grieve with unprofitable ceremonies, yea, ceremonies "wherein there is not only no profit, but also danger of great "hurt, that may grow to the Church by infection, which "popish ceremonies are means to breed[5]."

This in effect is the sum and substance of that which they bring by way of opposition against those orders which we have common with the church of Rome; these are the reasons wherewith they would prove our ceremonies in that respect worthy of blame.

That whereas they who blame us

IV. Before we answer unto these things, we are to cut off that whereunto they from whom these objections proceed do oftentimes fly for defence and succour, when the force and

[1] [Abridged from T. C. i. 103.]
[2] [P. 144. ed. 1553. "His certe "hodie debemus ut in multis locis, "ubi diu prædicatum Evangelium "fuit, adversa sint restituta omnia: "quum id nusquam, ubi serio et "pure prædicato Christo etiam ad "ipsius verbum reformatæ ceremo- "niæ sunt, accidisse videamus."]
[3] T. C. lib. iii. p. 178.
[4] Ibid. p. 179.
[5] Ibid. p. 180.

Cartwright's Way of qualifying the Charge of Papistry. 429

strength of their arguments is elided. For the ceremonies in use amongst us being in no other respect retained, saving only for that to retain them is to our seeming good and profitable, yea, so profitable and so good, that if we had either simply taken them clean away, or else removed them so as to place in their stead others, we had done worse: the plain and direct way against us herein had been only to prove, that all such ceremonies as they require to be abolished are retained by us to the hurt of the Church, or with less benefit than the abolishment of them would bring. But forasmuch as they saw how hardly they should be able to perform this, they took a more compendious way, traducing the ceremonies of our church under the name of being popish. The cause why this way seemed better unto them was, for that the name of popery is more odious than very paganism amongst divers of the more simple sort, so as whatsoever they hear named popish, they presently conceive deep hatred against it, imagining there can be nothing contained in that name but needs it must be exceeding detestable. The ears of the people they have therefore filled with strong clamour: "The Church of England is "fraught with popish ceremonies: they that favour the cause "of reformation maintain nothing but the sincerity of the "Gospel of Jesus Christ: all such as withstand them fight "for the laws of his sworn enemy, uphold the filthy relics of "Antichrist, and are defenders of that which is popish." These are the notes wherewith are drawn from the hearts of the multitude so many sighs; with these tunes their minds are exasperated against the lawful guides and governors of their souls; these are the voices that fill them with general discontentment, as though the bosom of that famous church wherein they live were more noisome than any dungeon. But when the authors of so scandalous incantations are examined, and called to account how can they justify such their dealings; when they are urged directly to answer, whether it be lawful for us to use any such ceremonies as the church of Rome useth, although the same be not commanded in the word of God; being driven to see that the use of some such ceremonies must of necessity be granted lawful, they go about to make us believe that they are just of the same opinion, and that they only think such ceremonies are not to be used when they are

BOOK IV.
Ch. iv. 1.

in this behalf when reason evicteth that all such ceremonies are not to be abolished, make answer, that when they condemn popish ceremonies, their meaning is of ceremonies unprofitable, or ceremonies, instead whereof as good or better may be devised: they cannot hereby get out of the briars, but contradict and gainsay themselves; inasmuch as their usual manner is to prove that ceremonies uncommanded of God, and yet used in the church of Rome, are for this very cause unprofitable to us, and not so good as others in their place would be.

unprofitable, or "when as good or better may be established[1]." Which answer is both idle in regard of us, and also repugnant to themselves.

[2.] It is in regard of us very vain to make this answer, because they know that what ceremonies we retain common unto the church of Rome, we therefore retain them, for that we judge them to be profitable, and to be such that others instead of them would be worse. So that when they say that we ought to abrogate such Romish ceremonies as are unprofitable, or else might have other more profitable in their stead, they trifle and they beat the air about nothing which toucheth us; unless they mean that we ought to abrogate all Romish ceremonies which in their judgment have either no use or less use than some other might have. But then must they shew some commission, whereby they are authorized to sit as judges, and we required to take their judgment for good in this case. Otherwise their sentences will not be greatly regarded, when they oppose their *methinketh* unto the orders of the Church of England: as in the question about surplices one of them doth[2]; "If we look to the colour, black methinketh is more "decent; if to the form, a garment down to the foot hath a "great deal more comeliness in it." If they think that we ought to prove the ceremonies commodious which we have retained, they do in this point very greatly deceive themselves. For in all right and equity, that which the Church hath received and held so long for good, that which public approbation hath ratified, must carry the benefit of presumption with it to be accounted meet and convenient. They which have stood up as yesterday to challenge it of defect, must prove their challenge. If we being defendants do answer, that the ceremonies in question are godly, comely, decent, profitable for the Church; their reply is childish and unorderly, to say, that we demand the thing in question[3], and shew the poverty

---

[1] T. C. iii. p. 171. "What an "open untruth is it, that this is one "of our principles, not to be lawful "to use the same ceremonies which "the papists did; when as I have "both before declared the contrary, "and even here have expressly "added, that they are not to be used "when as good or better may be "established!"

[2] Eccles. Discip. fol. 100. [in Cartwright's Transl. 134. "Si de "colore agitur, mihi quidem magis "decorus niger color videtur; si "autem de forma, talaris vestis ho- "nestior."]

[3] T. C. lib. iii. p. 176. "As for "your often repeating that the

of our cause, the goodness whereof we are fain to beg that our adversaries would grant. For on our part this must be the answer, which orderly proceeding doth require. The burden of proving doth rest on them. In them it is frivolous to say, we ought not to use bad ceremonies of the church of Rome, and presume all such bad as it pleaseth themselves to dislike, unless we can persuade them the contrary.

[3.] Besides, they are herein opposite also to themselves. For what one thing is so common with them, as to use the custom of the church of Rome for an argument to prove, that such and such ceremonies cannot be good and profitable for us, inasmuch as that church useth them? Which usual kind of disputing sheweth, that they do not disallow only those Romish ceremonies which are unprofitable, but count all unprofitable which are Romish; that is to say, which have been devised by the church of Rome, or which are used in that church and not prescribed in the word of God. For this is the only limitation which they can use suitable unto their other positions. And therefore the cause which they yield, why they hold it lawful to retain in doctrine and in discipline some things as good, which yet are common to the church of Rome, is for that those good things are "perpetual commandments in whose place no other can "come;" but ceremonies are changeable[1]. So that their judgment in truth is, that whatsoever by the word of God is not unchangeable in the church of Rome, that church's using is a cause why reformed churches ought to change it, and not to think it good or profitable. And lest we seem to father any thing upon them more than is properly their own, let them read even their own words, where they complain, "that we "are thus constrained to be like unto the Papists in Any their "ceremonies;" yea, they urge that this cause, although it were "alone, ought to move them to whom that belongeth to do "them away, *forasmuch as they are their ceremonies;*" and that the Bishop of Salisbury doth justify this their complaint[2].

"ceremonies in question are godly, "comely, and decent; it is your old "wont of demanding the thing in "question, and an undoubted ar- "gument of your extreme poverty."
[1] T. C. iii. 174.
[2] "And that this complaint of

"ours is just in that we are thus "constrained to be like unto the "papists in any their ceremonies, "and that this cause only ought "to move them to whom that be- "longeth, to do them away, *foras- "much as they are their ceremonies;*

BOOK IV. The clause is untrue which they add concerning the Bishop
Ch. v. 1. of Salisbury[1]; but the sentence doth shew that we do them
no wrong in setting down the state of the question between
us thus: Whether we ought to abolish out of the church of
England all such orders, rites, and ceremonies as are established in the Church of Rome, and are not prescribed in the
word of God. For the affirmative whereof we are now to
answer such proofs of theirs as have been before alleged.

That our allowing the customs of our fathers to be followed is no proof that we may not allow some customs which the church of Rome hath, although we do not account of them as of our fathers.

V. Let the church of Rome be what it will, let them that
are of it be the people of God and our fathers in the Christian
faith, or let them be otherwise; hold them for catholics or
hold them for heretics; it is not a thing either one way or
other in this present question greatly material. Our conformity with them in such things as have been proposed is
not proved as yet unlawful by all this. St. Augustine[2] hath
said, yea and we have allowed his saying, "That the custom
"of the people of God and the decrees of our forefathers are

"the reader may further see in the "Bishop of Salisbury, who brings "divers proofs thereof." T. C. lib. iii. p. 177. [It may be worth observing that the Italics are Cartwright's own.]

[1] [Cartwright's margin refers to Apol. Part i. c. 2. div. 8. by mistake for div. 9. "They cry out...that we "have rashly and presumptuously "disannulled the old ceremonies "which have been well allowed by "our fathers and forefathers many "hundred years past, both by good "customs, and also in ages of more "purity." On which Harding's remark is, "Concerning ceremonies: "if ye shew us not the use of chrism "in your churches; if the sign of "the cross be not borne before you "in processions, and otherwheres "used; if holy water be abolished; "if lights at the Gospel and Com- "munion be not had; if peculiar "vestments for Deacons, Priests, "Bishops, be taken away; and "many such other the like: judge "ye, whether ye have duly kept the "old ceremonies of the Church." Jewel replies, "Verily, M. Harding, "we hate not any of all these things. "For we know they are the creatures "of God. But you have so misused

"them, or rather so defiled and be- "rayed them with your superstitions, "and so have with the same mocked "and deceived God's people, that "we can no longer continue them "without great conscience." This passage, it will be seen, refers to the ceremonies omitted, and not to those retained in the English church. Concerning the latter, although it is well known that he would not have disapproved of further conces- sions, (see his letters to Bullinger in Strype, Ann. 1. i. 262. ii. 544.) yet it is equally certain that his views were not founded on the puritan principle of absolute unlawfulness in the use of things once abused. For in the very same year (1565–6) that he last wrote to Bullinger as above, he had refused his intimate friend, Hum- phrey, institution to a benefice in the diocese of Sarum, because Hum- phrey would not pledge himself to wear the habits. Strype, Park. i. 369. and Ann. 1. ii. 133. Wordsworth, E. B. iv. 63. How far he differed with the Puritans on Church govern- ment may be seen by a paper of his in Whitg. Def. 423. and in Strype, Whitg. iii. 21. 1 App. No. x.]

[2] [See above, b. iii. c. xi. 15.]

"to be kept, touching those things whereof the Scripture "hath neither one way nor other given us any charge." What then? Doth it here therefore follow, that they being neither the people of God nor our forefathers, are for that cause in nothing to be followed? This consequent were good if so be it were granted, that only the custom of the people of God and the decrees of our forefathers are in such case to be observed. But then should no other kind of later laws in the Church be good; which were a gross absurdity to think. St. Augustine's speech therefore doth import, that where we have no divine precept, if yet we have the custom of the people of God or a decree of our forefathers, this is a law and must be kept. Notwithstanding it is not denied, but that we lawfully may observe the positive constitutions of our own churches, although the same were but yesterday made by ourselves alone. Nor is there any thing in this to prove, that the church of England might not by law receive orders, rites, or customs from the church of Rome, although they were neither the people of God nor yet our forefathers. How much less when we have received from them nothing, but that which they did themselves receive from such, as we cannot deny to have been the people of God, yea such, as either we must acknowledge for our own forefathers or else disdain the race of Christ? BOOK IV. Ch. vi. 1.

VI. The rites and orders wherein we follow the church of Rome are of no other kind than such as the church of Geneva itself doth follow them in. We follow the church of Rome in moe things; yet they in some things of the same nature about which our present controversy is: so that the difference is not in the kind, but in the number of rites only, wherein they and we do follow the church of Rome. The use of wafer-cakes, the custom of godfathers and godmothers in baptism, are things not commanded nor forbidden in Scripture, things which have been of old and are retained in the church of Rome even at this very hour. Is conformity with Rome in such things a blemish unto the church of England, and unto churches abroad an ornament? Let them, if not for the reverence they owe unto this church, in the bowels whereof they have received I trust that precious and blessed vigour, which shall quicken them to eternal life, yet at the *That the course which the wisdom of God doth teach maketh not against our conformity with the church of Rome in such things.*

leastwise for the singular affection which they do bear towards others, take heed how they strike, lest they wound whom they would not. For undoubtedly it cutteth deeper than they are aware of, when they plead that even such ceremonies of the church of Rome, as contain in them nothing which is not of itself agreeable to the word of God, ought nevertheless to be abolished; and that neither the word of God, nor reason, nor the examples of the eldest churches do permit the church of Rome to be therein followed.

[2.] Heretics they are, and they are our neighbours. By us and amongst us they lead their lives. But what then? therefore no ceremony of theirs lawful for us to use? We must yield and will that none are lawful, if God himself be a precedent against the use of any. But how appeareth it that God is so? Hereby they say it doth appear, in that[1] "God severed his people from the heathens, but especially from the Egyptians, and such nations as were nearest neighbours unto them[2], by forbidding them to do those things which were in themselves very lawful to be done, yea, very profitable some, and incommodious to be forborne; such things it pleased God to forbid them, only because those heathens did them, with whom conformity in the same things might have bred infection. Thus in shaving, cutting[3], apparel-wearing[4], yea in sundry kinds of meats also, swine's flesh, conies, and such like[5], they were forbidden to do so and so, because the Gentiles did so. And the end why God forbade them such things was to sever them for fear of infection by a great and an high wall from other nations, as St. Paul teacheth[6]." The cause of more careful separation from the nearest nations was the greatness of danger to be especially by them infected. Now papists are to us as those nations were unto Israel. Therefore if the wisdom of God be our guide, we cannot allow conformity with them, no not in any such indifferent ceremony.

[3.] Our direct answer hereunto is, that for any thing here alleged we may still doubt, whether the Lord in such indifferent ceremonies, as those whereof we dispute, did frame his

---

[1] T. C. lib. i. p. 89, 131. [See also p. 67.]
[2] Lev. xviii. 3.
[3] Lev. xix. 27.
[4] Levit. xix. 19; Deut. xxii. 11.
[5] Deut. xiv. 7; Lev. xi.
[6] Ephes. ii. 14.

people of set purpose unto any utter dissimilitude, either with Egyptians or with any other nation else. And if God did not forbid them all such indifferent ceremonies, then our conformity with the church of Rome in some such is not hitherto as yet disproved, although papists were unto us as those heathens were unto Israel. "After the doings of the land of " Egypt, wherein you dwelt, ye shall not do, saith the Lord ; " and after the manner of the land of Canaan, whither I will " bring you, shall ye not do, neither walk in their ordinances : " do after my judgments, and keep my ordinances to walk " therein : I am the Lord your God [1]." The speech is indefinite, "ye shall not be like them :" it is not general, "ye " shall not be like them in any thing, or like to them in any " thing indifferent, or like unto them in any indifferent " ceremony of theirs." Seeing therefore it is not set down how far the bounds of his speech concerning dissimilitude should reach, how can any man assure us, that it extendeth farther than to those things only, wherein the nations there mentioned were idolatrous, or did against that which the law of God commandeth? Nay, doth it not seem a thing very probable, that God doth purposely add, " Do after my judg- " ments," as giving thereby to understand that his meaning in the former sentence was but to bar similitude in such things, as were repugnant unto the ordinances, laws, and statutes which he had given? Egyptians and Canaanites are for example's sake named unto them, because the customs of the one they had been, and of the other they should be best acquainted with. But that wherein they might not be like unto either of them, was such peradventure as had been no whit less unlawful, although those nations had never been. So that there is no necessity to think, that God for fear of infection by reason of nearness forbade them to be like unto the Canaanites or the Egyptians, in those things which otherwise had been lawful enough.

BOOK IV. Ch. vi. 3.

For I would know what one thing was in those nations, and is here forbidden, being indifferent in itself, yet forbidden only because they used it. In the laws of Israel we find it written, " Ye shall not cut round the corners of your heads, " neither shalt thou tear the tufts of thy beard [2]." These

[1] Levit. xviii. 3.   [2] Levit. xix. 27.

BOOK IV.
Ch. vi. 3.

things were usual amongst those nations, and in themselves they are indifferent. But are they indifferent being used as signs of immoderate and hopeless lamentation for the dead? In this sense it is that the law forbiddeth them. For which cause the very next words following are, "Ye shall not cut "your flesh for the dead, nor make any print of a mark upon "you: I am the Lord[1]." The like in Leviticus, where speech is of mourning for the dead; "They shall not make "bald parts upon their head, nor shave off the locks of their "beard, nor make any cutting in their flesh[2]." Again in Deuteronomy, "Ye are the children of the Lord your God; "ye shall not cut yourselves, nor make you baldness between "your eyes for the dead[3]." What is this but in effect the same which the Apostle doth more plainly express, saying, "Sorrow not as they do who have no hope[4]?" The very light of nature itself was able to see herein a fault; that which those nations did use, having been also in use with others, the ancient Roman laws do forbid[5]. That shaving therefore and cutting which the law doth mention was not a matter in itself indifferent, and forbidden only because it was in use amongst such idolaters as were neighbours to the people of God; but to use it had been a crime, though no other people or nation under heaven should have done it saving only themselves.

As for those laws concerning attire: "There shall no gar- "ment of linen and woollen come upon thee[6];" as also those touching food and diet, wherein swine's flesh together with sundry other meats are forbidden[7]; the use of these things had been indeed of itself harmless and indifferent: so that hereby it doth appear, how the law of God forbade in some special consideration such things as were lawful enough in themselves. But yet even here they likewise fail of that they intend. For it doth not appear that the consideration in regard whereof the law forbiddeth these things was because those nations did use them. Likely enough it is that the

---

[1] Levit. xix. 28.
[2] Levit. xxi. 5.   [3] Deut. xiv. 1.
[4] 1 Thess. iv. 13.
[5] [Cic. Tusc. Quæst. ii. 23. "In- "gemiscere nonnunquam viro con- "cessum est, idque raro: ejulatus "ne mulieri quidem: et hic nimi- "rum est lessus, quem duodecim "tabulæ in funeribus adhiberi vetu- "erunt."]
[6] Levit. xix. 19; Deut. xxii. 11.
[7] Deut. xiv. 7; Levit. xi.

Canaanites used to feed as well on sheep's as on swine's flesh; and therefore if the forbidding of the later had no other reason than dissimilitude with that people, they which of their own heads allege this for reason can shew I think some reason more than we are able to find why the former was not also forbidden. Might there not be some other mystery in this prohibition than they think of? Yes, some other mystery there was in it by all likelihood. For what reason is there which should but induce, and therefore much less enforce us to think, that care of dissimilitude between the people of God and the heathen nations about them, was any more the cause of forbidding them to put on garments of sundry stuff, than of charging them withal not to sow their fields with meslin[1]; or that this was any more the cause of forbidding them to eat swine's flesh, than of charging them withal not to eat the flesh of eagles, hawks, and the like[2]?

Wherefore, although the church of Rome were to us, as to Israel the Egyptians and Canaanites were of old; yet doth it not follow, that the wisdom of God without respect doth teach us to erect between us and them a partition-wall of difference[3], in such things indifferent as have been hitherto disputed of.

VII. Neither is the example of the eldest churches a whit more available to this purpose. Notwithstanding some fault undoubtedly there is in the very resemblance of idolaters[4]. Were it not some kind of blemish to be like unto infidels and heathens, it would not so usually be objected; men would not think it any advantage in the causes of religion to be able therewith justly to charge their adversaries as they do. Wherefore to the end that it may a little more plainly appear, what force this hath and how far the same extendeth, we are to note how all men are naturally desirous that they may seem neither to judge nor to do amiss; because every error and offence is a stain to the beauty of nature, for which cause

BOOK IV.
Ch. vii. 1.

That the example of the eldest churches is not herein against us.

---

[1] Levit. xix. 19. ["*Meslin*: mixt "corn, as wheat and rye." Johnson, quoting Tusser:
"If work for the Thresher ye mind for
  "to have,
"Of wheat and of meslin unthreshed go
  "save."]
[2] Deut. xiv; Levit. xi.
[3] Ephes. ii. 14.

[4] "The councils, although they "did not observe themselves "always in making of decrees this "rule, yet have kept this consider-"ation continually in making of "their laws, that they would have "Christians differ from others in "their ceremonies." T. C. lib. i. p. 132.

it blusheth thereat, but glorieth in the contrary. From thence it riseth, that they which disgrace or depress the credit of others do it either in both or in one of these. To have been in either directed by a weak and unperfect rule argueth imbecility and imperfection. Men being either led by reason or by imitation of other men's example, if their persons be odious whose example we choose to follow, as namely if we frame our opinions to that which condemned heretics think, or direct our actions according to that which is practised and done by them; it lieth as an heavy prejudice against us, unless somewhat mightier than their bare example did move us, to think or do the same things with them. Christian men therefore having besides the common light of all men so great help of heavenly direction from above, together with the lamps of so bright examples as the Church of God doth yield, it cannot but worthily seem reproachful for us to leave both the one and the other, to become disciples unto the most hateful sort that live, to do as they do, only because we see their example before us and have a delight to follow it. Thus we may therefore safely conclude, that it is not evil simply to concur with the heathens either in opinion or in action; and that conformity with them is only then a disgrace, when either we follow them in that they think and do amiss, or follow them generally in that they do without other reason than only the liking we have to the pattern of their example; which liking doth intimate a more universal approbation of them than is allowable.

[2.] Faustus the Manichee therefore objecting against the Jews, that they forsook the idols of the Gentiles, but their temples and oblations and altars and priesthoods and all kinds of ministry of holy things they exercised even as the Gentiles did, yea, more superstitiously a great deal; against the Catholic Christians likewise, that between them and the heathens there was in many things little difference; "From them," saith Faustus, "ye have learned to hold that one only God is the "author of all; their sacrifices ye have turned into feasts of "charity, their idols into martyrs whom ye honour with the "like religious offices unto theirs; the ghosts of the dead ye "appease with wine and delicates; the festival days of the "nations ye celebrate together with them; and of their kind "of life ye have verily changed nothing[1] :" St. Augustine's defence in behalf of both is, that touching matters of action, Jews and Catholic Christians were free from the Gentiles' faultiness, even in those things which were objected as tokens of their agreement with Gentiles[2] : and concerning their consent in opinion, they did not hold the same with Gentiles because Gentiles had so taught, but because heaven and earth had so witnessed the same to be truth, that neither the one sort could err in being fully persuaded thereof, nor the other but err in case they should not consent with them[3].

[3.] In things of their own nature indifferent, if either councils or particular men have at any time with sound judgment misliked conformity between the Church of God and infidels, the cause thereof hath been somewhat else than only affectation of dissimilitude. They saw it necessary so to do in respect of some special accident, which the Church being not always subject unto hath not still cause to do the like. For example, in the dangerous days of trial, wherein there was no way for the truth of Jesus Christ to triumph over infidelity but through the constancy of his saints, whom yet a natural desire to save themselves from the flame might peradventure cause to join with Pagans in external customs, too far using the same as a cloak to conceal themselves in, and a mist to darken the eyes of infidels withal: for remedy hereof those laws it might be were provided, which forbad that Christians should deck their houses with boughs as the Pagans did use to do[4], or rest those festival days whereon

---

[1] August. cont. Faust. Manich. lib. xx. cap. 4. [t. viii. 334. "Schisma aut nihil immutare debet ab eo unde factum est, aut non multum: ut puta vos, qui desciscentes a gentibus, monarchiæ opinionem primo vobiscum divulsistis, id est, ut omnia credatis ex Deo: sacrificia vero eorum vertistis in agapes, idola in martyres, quos votis similibus colitis: defunctorum umbras vino placatis et dapibus: solennes gentium dies cum ipsis celebratis, ut kalendas, et solstitia: de vita certe eorum mutastis nihil."]

[2] [Ibid. § 23. "Si usus quarundam rerum similis videtur nobis esse cum gentibus, sicut cibi et potus, tectorum, vestimentorum, &c. . . . . longe taliter aliter his rebus utitur, qui ad alium finem usum earum refert; et aliter qui ex his Deo gratias agit, de quo prava et falsa non credit."]

[3] [Ibid. § 19. "Discat ergo Faustus, . . . monarchiæ opinionem non ex gentibus nos habere; sed gentes non usque adeo ad falsos Deos esse delapsos, ut opinionem amitterent unius veri Dei, ex quo est omnis qualiscunque natura."]

[4] "Also it was decreed in another council that they should not deck their houses with bay-leaves

the Pagans rested, or celebrate such feasts as were, though not heathenish, yet such as the simpler sort of heathens might be beguiled in so thinking them.

[4.] As for Tertullian's judgment concerning the rites and orders of the Church, no man having judgment can be ignorant how just exceptions may be taken against it[1]. His opinion touching the Catholic Church was as unindifferent as touching our church the opinion of them that favour this pretended reformation is. He judged all them who did not Montanize to be but carnally minded, he judged them still over-abjectly to fawn upon the heathens, and to curry favour with infidels. Which as the catholic church did well provide that they might not do indeed, so Tertullian over-often through discontentment carpeth injuriously at them as though they did it, even when they were free from such meaning.

[5.] But if it were so, that either the judgment of these councils before alleged, or of Tertullian himself against the Christians, are in no such consideration to be understood as we have mentioned; if it were so that men are condemned as well of the one as of the other, only for using the ceremonies of a religion *contrary* unto their own, and that *this cause* is such as ought to prevail no less with us than with them: shall it not follow that seeing there is still between our religion and Paganism the selfsame *contrariety*, therefore we are still no less rebukeable, if we now deck our houses with boughs, or send new-year's gifts unto our friends, or feast on those days which the Gentiles then did, or sit after prayer as they were accustomed? For so they infer upon the premises, that as great difference as commodiously may be, there should be in all outward ceremonies between the people of God and them which are not his people. Again they teach as hath been declared, that there is not as great a difference

"and green boughs, because the "Pagans did use so; and that they "should not rest from their labour "those days that the Pagans did, "that they should not keep the "first day of every month as they "did." T. C. l. i. p. 132. [103.]

[1] "Tertullian saith, O, saith he, "better is the religion of the "heathen; for they use no solem- "nity of the Christians, neither the "Lord's day, neither, &c. but we are "not afraid to be called heathen." T. C. l. i. p. 132. [103.] "But "having shewed this in general to "be the policy of God first, and of "his people afterward, to put as "much difference as can be com- "modiously between the people of "God and others which are not, I "shall not, &c." T. C. l. i. p. 133.

as may be between them, except the one do avoid whatsoever rites and ceremonies uncommanded of God the other doth embrace. So that generally they teach that the very difference of spiritual condition itself between the servants of Christ and others requireth such difference in ceremonies between them, although the one be never so far disjoined in time or place from the other.

[6.] But in case the people of God and Belial do chance to be neighbours, then as the danger of infection is greater, so the same difference they say is thereby made more necessary[1]. In this respect as the Jews were severed from the heathen, so most especially from the heathen nearest them. And in the same respect we, which ought to differ howsoever from the church of Rome, are now they say by reason of our nearness more bound to differ from them in ceremonies than from Turks. A strange kind of speech unto Christian ears, and such as I hope they themselves do acknowledge unadvisedly uttered. "We are not so much to fear infection from Turks "as from papists." What of that? we must remember that by conforming rather ourselves in that respect to Turks, we should be spreaders of a worse infection into others than any we are likely to draw from papists by our conformity with them in ceremonies. If they did hate, as Turks do, the Christians; or as Canaanites did of old the Jewish religion even in gross; the circumstance of local nearness in them unto us might haply enforce in us a duty of greater separation from them than from those other mentioned. But forasmuch as papists are so much in Christ nearer unto us than Turks, is there any reasonable man, trow you, but will judge it meeter that our ceremonies of Christian religion should be popish than Turkish or heathenish? Especially considering that we were not brought to dwell amongst them, (as Israel in Canaan,) having not been of them. For even a very part of them we were. And when God did by his good Spirit put it into our hearts, first to reform ourselves, (whence grew our separation,) and then by all good means to seek also their reformation; had we not only cut off their corruptions but also estranged ourselves from them in things indifferent, who seeth not how greatly prejudicial this might have been to

[1] [Decl. of Discipl. 134.]

BOOK IV.
Ch. viii. 1.

so good a cause, and what occasion it had given them to think (to their greater obduration in evil) that through a froward or wanton desire of innovation we did unconstrainedly those things for which conscience was pretended? Howsoever the case doth stand, as Juda had been rather to choose conformity in things indifferent with Israel when they were nearest opposites, than with the farthest removed Pagans; so we in the like case much rather with papists than with Turks. I might add further for more full and complete answer, so much concerning the large odds between the case of the eldest churches in regard of those heathens and ours in respect of the church of Rome, that very cavillation itself should be satisfied, and have no shift to fly unto.

That it is not our best policy for the establishment of sound religion, to have in these things no agreement with the church of Rome being unsound.

VIII. But that no one thing may detain us over long, I return to their reasons against our conformity with that church. That extreme dissimilitude which they urge upon us, is now commended as our best and safest policy for establishment of sound religion. The ground of which politic position is that "evils must be cured by their contraries;" and therefore the cure of the Church infected with the poison of Antichristianity must be done by that which is thereunto as contrary as may be[1]. "A medled estate of the orders of "the Gospel and the ceremonies of popery is not the best "way to banish popery[2]."

We are contrariwise of opinion, that he which will perfectly recover a sick and restore a diseased body unto health, must not endeavour so much to bring it to a state of simple contrariety, as of fit proportion in contrariety unto those evils which are to be cured. He that will take away extreme heat by setting the body in extremity of cold, shall undoubtedly remove the disease, but together with it the diseased too. The first thing therefore in skilful cures is the knowledge of the part affected; the next is of the evil which doth affect it; the last is not only of the kind but also of the measure of contrary things whereby to remove it.

---

[1] "Common reason also doth "teach that contraries are cured "by their contraries. Now Christ-"ianity and Antichristianity, the "Gospel and Popery, be contra-"ries; and therefore Antichristianity "must be cured, not by itself, but "by that which is (as much as may "be) contrary unto it." T. C. l. i. p. 134. [103.]

[2] [T. C. i. 103.]

[2.] They which measure religion by dislike of the church of Rome think every man so much the more sound, by how much he can make the corruptions thereof to seem more large. And therefore some there are, namely the Arians in reformed churches of Poland, which imagine the canker to have eaten so far into the very bones and marrow of the church of Rome, as if it had not so much as a sound belief, no not concerning God himself, but that the very belief of the Trinity were a part of antichristian corruption[1]; and that the wonderful providence of God did bring to pass that the bishop of the see of Rome should be famous for his triple crown; a sensible mark whereby the world might know him to be that mystical beast spoken of in the Revelation, to be that great and notorious Antichrist in no one respect so much as in this, that he maintaineth the doctrine of the Trinity. Wisdom therefore and skill is requisite to know, what parts are sound in that church, and what corrupted.

Neither is it to all men apparent which complain of unsound parts, with what kind of unsoundness every such part is possessed. They can say, that in doctrine, in discipline, in prayers, in sacraments, the church of Rome hath (as it hath indeed) very foul and gross corruptions; the nature whereof notwithstanding because they have not for the most part exact skill and knowledge to discern, they think that amiss many times which is not; and the salve of reformation they mightily call for, but where and what the sores are which need it, as they wot full little, so they think it not greatly material to search. Such men's contentment must be wrought by stratagem; the usual method of art is not for them.

[3.] But with those that profess more than ordinary and common knowledge of good from evil, with them that are able to put a difference between things naught and things indifferent in the church of Rome, we are yet at controversy about the manner of removing that which is naught; whether it may not be perfectly helped, unless that also which is indifferent be cut off with it, so far till no rite or ceremony remain which the church of Rome hath, being not found in the word of God. If we think this too extreme, they reply, that to draw men from great excess, it is not amiss though we

---

[1] [See book V. c. xlii. 16.]

BOOK IV.
Ch. viii. 4.

use them unto somewhat less than is competent[1]; and that a crooked stick is not straightened unless it be bent as far on the clean contrary side, that so it may settle itself at the length in a middle estate of evenness between both. But how can these comparisons stand them in any stead? When they urge us to extreme opposition against the church of Rome, do they mean we should be drawn unto it only for a time, and afterwards return to a mediocrity? or was it the purpose of those reformed churches, which utterly abolished all popish ceremonies, to come in the end back again to the middle point of evenness and moderation? Then have we conceived amiss of their meaning. For we have always thought their opinion to be, that utter inconformity with the church of Rome was not an extremity whereunto we should be drawn for a time, but the very mediocrity itself wherein they meant we should ever continue. Now by these comparisons it seemeth clean contrary, that howsoever they have bent themselves at first to an extreme contrariety against the Romish church, yet therein they will continue no longer than only till such time as some more moderate course for establishment of the Church may be concluded.

[4.] Yea, albeit this were not at the first their intent, yet surely now there is great cause to lead them unto it. They have seen that experience of the former policy, which may cause the authors of it to hang down their heads. When Germany had stricken off that which appeared corrupt in the doctrine of the church of Rome, but seemed nevertheless in discipline still to retain therewith very great conformity; France by that rule of policy which hath been before mentioned, took away the popish orders which Germany did retain. But process of time hath brought more light into the world; whereby men perceiving that they of the religion in France have also retained some orders which were before

---

[1] "If a man would bring a drunken man to sobriety, the best and nearest way is to carry him as far from his excess in drink as may be; and if a man could not keep a mean, it were better to fault in prescribing less than he should drink, than to fault in giving him more than he ought. As we see, to bring a stick which is crooked to be straight, we do not only bow it so far until it come to be straight, but we bend it so far until we make it so crooked of the other side as it was before of the first side; to this end, that at the last it may stand straight, and as it were in the midway between both the crooks." T. C. lib. i. p. 132. [103.]

Our Rites no Stain to our Church's Independence.

in the church of Rome, and are not commanded in the word of God, there hath arisen a sect[1] in England, which following still the very selfsame rule of policy, seeketh to reform even the French reformation, and purge out from thence also dregs of popery. These have not taken as yet such root that they are able to establish any thing. But if they had, what would spring out of their stock, and how far the unquiet wit of man might be carried with rules of such policy, God doth know. The trial which we have lived to see, may somewhat teach us what posterity is to fear. But our Lord of his infinite mercy avert whatsoever evil our swervings on the one hand or on the other may threaten unto the state of his Church!

IX. That the church of Rome doth hereby take occasion to blaspheme, and to say, our religion is not able to stand of itself unless it lean upon the staff of their ceremonies[2], is not a matter of so great moment, that it did need to be objected, or doth deserve to receive an answer. The name of blasphemy in this place, is like the shoe of Hercules on a child's foot[3]. If the church of Rome do use any such kind of silly exprobration, it is no such ugly thing to the ear, that we should think the honour and credit of our religion to receive thereby any great wound. They which hereof make so perilous a matter do seem to imagine, that we have erected of late a frame of some new religion, the furniture whereof we should not have borrowed from our enemies, lest they relieving us might afterwards laugh and gibe at our poverty; whereas in truth the ceremonies which we have taken from such as were before us, are not things that belong to this or that sect, but they are the ancient rites and customs of the Church of Christ, whereof ourselves being a part, we have the selfsame interest in them which our fathers before us had, from whom the same are descended unto us. Again, in case we had been so much beholding privately unto them, doth the reputation to one church stand by saying unto another,

That we are not to abolish our ceremonies, either because papists upbraid us as having taken from them, or for that they are said hereby to conceive I know not what great hopes.

---

[1] [The Brownists, or Barrowists.]
[2] "By using of these ceremonies, "the Papists take occasion to blas-"pheme, saying, that our religion "cannot stand by itself, unless it "lean upon the staff of their cere-"monies." T. C. lib. iii. p. 178. [and i. 52.]
[3] ["Herculis cothurnos aptare "infanti." See Quintilian VI. 1. 3. and Erasm. Adag. Chil. iii. Cent. vi. Prov. 67.]

"I need thee not?" If some should be so vain and impotent as to mar a benefit with reproachful upbraiding, where at the least they suppose themselves to have bestowed some good turn; yet surely a wise body's part it were not, to put out his fire, because his fond and foolish neighbour, from whom he borrowed peradventure wherewith to kindle it, might haply cast him therewith in the teeth, saying, "Were it not for me "thou wouldest freeze, and not be able to heat thyself."

[2.] As for that other argument derived from the secret affection of papists, with whom our conformity in certain ceremonies is said to put them in great hope, that their whole religion in time will have re-entrance, and therefore none are so clamorous amongst us for the observation of these ceremonies, as papists and such as papists suborn to speak for them, whereby it clearly appeareth how much they rejoice, how much they triumph in these things[1]; our answer hereunto is still the same, that the benefit we have by such ceremonies overweigheth even this also. No man which is not exceeding partial can well deny, but that there is most just cause wherefore we should be offended greatly at the church of Rome. Notwithstanding at such times as we are to deliberate for ourselves, the freer our minds are from all distempered affections, the sounder and better is our judgment. When we are in a fretting mood at the church of Rome, and with that angry disposition enter into any cogitation of the orders and rites of our church; taking particular survey of them, we are sure to have always one eye fixed upon the countenance of our enemies, and according to the blithe or heavy aspect thereof, our other eye sheweth some other suitable token either of dislike or approbation towards our own orders. For the rule of our judgment in such case being only that of Homer, "This is the thing which our enemies "would have[2];" what they seem contented with, even for that very cause we reject: and there is nothing but it pleaseth us much the better if we espy that it galleth them. Miserable were the state and condition of that church, the

---

[1] "To prove the papists' triumph "and joy in these things, I alleged "further that there are none which "make such clamours for these "ceremonies, as the papists and "those whom they suborn." T. C. lib. iii. p. 179.

[2] Ἦ κεν γηθήσαι Πρίαμος. Il. A. [v. 255.]

weighty affairs whereof should be ordered by those deliberations wherein such a humour as this were predominant. We have most heartily to thank God therefore, that they amongst us to whom the first consultations of causes of this kind fell, were men which aiming at another mark, namely the glory of God and the good of this his church, took that which they judged thereunto necessary, not rejecting any good or convenient thing only because the church of Rome might perhaps like it. If we have that which is meet and right, although they be glad, we are not to envy them this their solace; we do not think it a duty of ours to be in every such thing their tormentors.

[3.] And whereas it is said that popery for want of this utter extirpation hath in some places taken root and flourished again[1], but hath not been able to re-establish itself in any place after provision made against it by utter evacuation of all Romish ceremonies: and therefore, as long as we hold any thing like unto them, we put them in some more hope than if all were taken away: as we deny not but this may be true, so being of two evils to choose the less, we hold it better that the friends and favourers of the church of Rome should be in some kind of hope to have a corrupt religion restored, than both we and they conceive just fear, lest under colour of rooting out popery, the most effectual means to bear up the state of religion be removed, and so a way made either for Paganism or for extreme barbarity to enter. If desire of weakening the hope of others should turn us away from the course we have taken; how much more the care of preventing our own fear withhold us from that we are urged unto! Especially seeing that our own fear we know, but we are not so certain what hope the rites and orders of our church have bred in the hearts of others.

For it is no sufficient argument thereof to say, that in

[1] "Thus they conceiving hope "of having the rest of their popery "in the end, it causeth them to be "more frozen in their wickedness, "&c. For not the cause but the "occasion also ought to be taken "away, &c. Although let the reader "judge, whether they have cause "given to hope, that the tail of "popery yet remaining, they shall "the easilier hale in the whole body "after: considering also that Master "Bucer noteth, that where these "things have been left, there popery "hath returned; but on the other "part, in places which have been "cleansed of these dregs, it hath "not been seen that it hath had any "entrance." T. C. lib. iii. p. 179. [and i. 52.]

maintaining and urging these ceremonies none are so clamorous as papists and they whom papists suborn[1]; this speech being more hard to justify than the former, and so their proof more doubtful than the thing itself which they prove. He that were certain that this is true, must have marked who they be that speak for ceremonies; he must have noted who amongst them doth speak oftenest, or is most earnest; he must have been both acquainted throughly with the religion of such, and also privy what conferences or compacts are passed in secret between them and others; which kinds of notice are not wont to be vulgar and common. Yet they which allege this would have it taken as a thing that needeth no proof, a thing which all men know and see.

And if so be it were granted them as true, what gain they by it? Sundry of them that be popish are eager in maintenance of ceremonies. Is it so strange a matter to find a good thing furthered by ill men of a sinister intent and purpose, whose forwardness is not therefore a bridle to such as favour the same cause with a better and sincerer meaning? They that seek, as they say, the removing of all popish orders out of the Church, and reckon the state of Bishops in the number of those orders, do (I doubt not) presume that the cause which they prosecute is holy. Notwithstanding it is their own ingenuous acknowledgment, that even this very cause, which they term so often by an excellency, "The Lord's cause," is "*gratissima*, most acceptable, "unto some which hope for prey and spoil by it, and that "our age hath store of such, and that such are the very "sectaries of Dionysius the famous atheist[2]." Now if hereupon we should upbraid them with irreligious, as they do us with superstitious favourers; if we should follow them in their own kind of pleading, and say, that the most clamorous for this pretended reformation are either atheists, or else proctors suborned by atheists; the answer which herein they

---

[1] [T. C. i. 53. iii. 180.]
[2] Eccles. Disc. f. 94. [p. 127. as translated by T. C. "Hæc.... "oratio de episcoporum pompa et "affluentia minuenda...gratissima "nonnullis est, qui suam causam "agi putant, et jampridem hære- "ditatem istam spe devorarint.... "Habet enim ætas nostra multos "ejusmodi milites, multos Diony- "sios, qui Deo togam auream neque "ad æstatem neque ad hyemem "commodam, sibi autem ad omnia "utilissimam et commodissimam "fore arbitrantur." Vide Cic. de Nat. Deor. iii. 34.]

would make unto us, let them apply unto themselves, and there an end. For they must not forbid us to presume our cause in defence of our church orders to be as good as theirs against them, till the contrary be made manifest to the world.

X. In the meanwhile sorry we are that any good and godly mind should be grieved[1] with that which is done. But to remedy their grief lieth not so much in us as in themselves. They do not wish to be made glad with the hurt of the Church: and to remove all out of the Church whereat they shew themselves to be sorrowful, would be, as we are persuaded, hurtful if not pernicious thereunto. Till they be able to persuade the contrary, they must and will I doubt not find out some other good means to cheer up themselves. Amongst which means the example of Geneva may serve for one. Have not they the old popish custom of using godfathers and godmothers in Baptism? the old popish custom of administering the blessed sacrament of the holy Eucharist with wafer-cakes? These things the godly there can digest. Wherefore should not the godly here learn to do the like both in them and in the rest of the like nature? Some further mean peradventure it might be to assuage their grief, if so be they did consider the revenge they take on them which have been, as they interpret it, the workers of their continuance in so great grief so long. For if the maintenance of ceremonies be a corrosive to such as oppugn them, undoubtedly to such as maintain them it can be no great pleasure, when they behold how that which they reverence is oppugned. And therefore they that judge themselves martyrs when they are grieved, should think withal what they are whom[2] they grieve[3]. For we are still to put them in mind that the cause

BOOK IV.
Ch. x. 1.

The grief which they say godly brethren conceive in regard of such ceremonies as we have common with the church of Rome.

[1] T. C. l. iii. p. 180. [and i. 53.] "There be numbers which have "Antichristianity in such detesta- "tion, that they cannot without "grief of mind behold them." And afterwards, "such godly brethren "are not easily to be grieved, which "they seem to be when they are thus "martyred in their minds, for cere- "monies which (to speak the best "of them) are unprofitable."

[2] ["when," edd. 1594, 1604, 1617.] 1886.

[3] [See a letter of Archdeacon Barfoot to Archbishop Whitgift in Strype, Ann. iii. 1. 350. (1584.) "Truly, my lord, the conformable "ministry is very much grieved "thereat. And divers said plainly, "that if they had thought this would "have been the end, they would "have joined with the other in "their recusancy, rather than have "offered themselves to such re- "proachful speeches, as were given "out of them by some of that faction.

doth make no difference; for that it must be presumed as good at the least on our part as on theirs, till it be in the end decided who have stood for truth and who for error. So that till then the most effectual medicine and withal the most sound to ease their grief, must not be (in our opinion) the taking away of those things whereat they are grieved, but the altering of that persuasion which they have concerning the same.

[2.] For this we therefore both pray and labour; the more because we are also persuaded, that it is but conceit in them to think, that those Romish ceremonies whereof we have hitherto spoken, are like leprous clothes, infectious unto the Church, or like soft and gentle poisons[1], the venom whereof being insensibly pernicious, worketh death, and yet is never felt working. Thus they say: but because they say it only, and the world hath not as yet had so great experience of their art in curing the diseases of the Church, that the bare authority of their word should persuade in a cause so weighty, they may not think much if it be required at their hands to shew, first, by what means so deadly infection can grow from similitude between us and the church of Rome in these things indifferent: secondly, for that it were infinite if the Church should provide against every such evil as may come to pass, it is not sufficient that they shew possibility of dangerous event, unless there appear some likelihood also of the same to follow in us, except we prevent it. Nor is this enough, unless it be moreover made plain, that there is no good and sufficient way of prevention, but by evacuating clean, and by emptying the Church of every such rite and ceremony, as is presently

---

"For they told him, that there was "a letter there in the country sent "from Mr. Field of London, [a great "Puritan,] to the ministers in those "parts, recusants, exhorting them "to stand stoutly to the cause; "affirming the same not to be theirs, "but the Lord's; boldly assuring, "that such as had subscribed had "made a *breach*, as he was informed "Field termed it. And therefore "rashly judging of them, that they "never would do good hereafter, "and slanderously terming them by "the name of *branded menne*. He "assured his grace, there was "great grief conceived hereat." In a schedule of complaints from Suffolk Archdeaconry, 1586. "The "communion was received by many "sitting, and those that conform-"ed to the Church called Time-"servers." Whitg. i. 497.]

[1] "Although the corruptions in "them strike not straight to the "heart, yet as gentle poisons they "consume by little and little." T. C. lib. iii. p. 171.]

called in question. Till this be done, their good affection towards the safety of the Church is acceptable, but the way they prescribe us to preserve it by must rest in suspense.

[3.] And lest hereat they take occasion to turn upon us the speech of the prophet Jeremy used against Babylon, "Behold "we have done our endeavour to cure the diseases of Babylon, "but she through her wilfulness doth rest uncured[1];" let them consider into what straits the Church might drive itself in being guided by this their counsel. Their axiom is, that the sound believing Church of Jesus Christ may not be like heretical churches in any of those indifferent things, which men make choice of, and do not take by prescript appointment of the word of God. In the word of God the use of bread is prescribed, as a thing without which the Eucharist may not be celebrated; but as for the kind of bread it is not denied to be a thing indifferent. Being indifferent of itself, we are by this axiom of theirs to avoid the use of unleavened bread in that sacrament, because such bread the church of Rome being heretical useth. But doth not the selfsame axiom bar us even from leavened bread also, which the church of the Grecians useth; the opinions whereof are in a number of things the same for which we condemn the church of Rome, and in some things erroneous where the church of Rome is acknowledged to be sound; as namely, in the article about proceeding of the Holy Ghost? And lest here they should say that because the Greek church is farther off, and the church of Rome nearer, we are in that respect rather to use that which the church of Rome useth not: let them imagine a reformed church in the city of Venice, where a Greek church and a popish both are. And when both these are equally near let them consider what the third shall do. Without either leavened or unleavened bread, it can have no sacrament; the word of God doth tie it to neither; and their axiom doth exclude it from both. If this constrain them, as it must, to grant that their axiom is not to take any place save in those things only where the Church hath larger scope; it resteth that they search out some stronger reason than they have as yet alleged; otherwise they constrain not us to think that the Church is tied unto any such rule or axiom, no not then when

[1] Jer. li. 9.

BOOK IV.
Ch. xi. 1, 2.

Their exception against such ceremonies as we have received from the church of Rome, that church having taken them from the Jews.

she hath the widest field to walk in, and the greatest store of choice.

XI. Against such ceremonies generally as are the same in the church of England and of Rome, we see what hath been hitherto alleged. Albeit therefore we do not find the one church's having of such things to be sufficient cause why the other should not have them: nevertheless, in case it may be proved, that amongst the number of rites and orders common unto both, there are particulars, the use whereof is utterly unlawful in regard of some special bad and noisome quality; there is no doubt but we ought to relinquish such rites and orders, what freedom soever we have to retain the other still. As therefore we have heard their general exception against all those things, which being not commanded in the word of God, were first received in the church of Rome, and from thence have been derived into ours; so it followeth that now we proceed unto certain kinds of them, as being excepted against not only for that they are in the church of Rome, but are besides either Jewish, or abused unto idolatry, and so grown scandalous.

[2.] The church of Rome, they say, being ashamed of the simplicity of the gospel, did almost out of all religions take whatsoever had any fair and gorgeous show[1], borrowing in that respect from the Jews sundry of their abolished ceremonies. Thus by foolish and ridiculous imitation, all their massing furniture almost they took from the Law, lest having an altar and a priest, they should want vestments for their stage[2]; so that whatsoever we have in common with the church of Rome, if the same be of this kind we ought to remove it. "Constantine the emperor speaking of the keep-"ing of the feast of Easter, saith, 'That it is an unworthy "thing to have any thing common with that most spiteful "company of the Jews[3].' And a little after he saith, 'That "it is most absurd and against reason, that the Jews should

---

[1] Eccles. Disc. fol. 98. [in T. C.'s transl. p. 131, 2.] and T. C. lib. iii. p. 181. "Many of these popish "ceremonies faulty by reason of the "pomp in them; where they should "be agreeable to the simplicity of "the gospel of Christ crucified."

[2] [Eccl. Disc. ibid.]

[3] T. C. lib. i. p. 132. [103.] Euseb. de Vit. Const. lib. iii. c. 18. [Μηδὲν τοίνυν ἔστω ἡμῖν κοινὸν μετὰ τοῦ ἐχθίστου τῶν Ἰουδαίων ὄχλου ... ἔστι γὰρ ὡς ἀληθῶς ἀτοπώτατον, ἐκείνους αὐχεῖν ὡς ἄρα παρεκτὸς τῆς αὐτῶν διδασκαλίας ταῦτα φυλάττειν οὐκ εἴημεν ἱκανοί.]

"vaunt and glory that the Christians could not keep those
"things without their doctrine.' And in another place it is
"said after this sort; 'It is convenient so to order the matter,
"that we have nothing common with that nation¹.' The
"council of Laodicea, which was afterwards confirmed by the
"sixth general council², decreed 'that the Christians should
"not take unleavened bread of the Jews, or communicate with
"their impiety³.'"

[3.] For the easier manifestation of truth in this point, two things there are which must be considered: namely, the causes wherefore the Church should decline from Jewish ceremonies; and how far it ought so to do. One cause is that the Jews were the deadliest and spitefullest enemies of Christianity that were in the world, and in this respect their orders so far forth to be shunned, as we have already set down in handling the matter of heathenish ceremonies. For no enemies being so venomous against Christ as Jews, they were of all other most odious, and by that mean least to be used as fit church-patterns for imitation. Another cause is the solemn abrogation of the Jews' ordinances; which ordinances for us to resume, were to check our Lord himself which hath disannulled them. But how far this second cause doth extend, it is not on all sides fully agreed upon. And touching those things whereunto it reacheth not, although there be small cause wherefore the Church should frame itself to the Jews' example in respect of their persons which are most hateful; yet God himself having been the author of their laws, herein they are (notwithstanding the former consideration) still worthy to be honoured, and to be followed above others, as much as the state of things will bear.

[4.] Jewish ordinances had some things natural, and of the perpetuity of those things no man doubteth. That which was positive we likewise know to have been by the coming of Christ partly necessary not to be kept, and partly indifferent to be kept or not. Of the former kind circumcision and

---

¹ Socrat. lib. i. c. 9. [Τοῦτο οὕτως ἐπανορθοῦσθαι προσῆκεν, ὡς μηδὲν μετὰ τοῦ τῶν πατροκτόνων τε καὶ κυριοκτόνων ἐκείνων ἔθνους εἶναι κοινόν.]

² [Or rather by the council called Quinisextum. vid. Labb. Conc. vi. 1124, 1146.]

³ Tom. i. Concil. Laod. Can. 38. [i. 1503. οὐ δεῖ παρὰ τῶν Ἰουδαίων ἄζυμα λαμβάνειν, ἢ κοινωνεῖν ταῖς ἀσεβείαις αὐτῶν.]

BOOK IV.
Ch. xi. 4.

sacrifice were. For this point Stephen was accused, and the evidence which his accusers brought against him in judgment was, "This man ceaseth not to speak blasphemous words "against this holy place and the Law, for we have heard him "say that this Jesus of Nazareth shall destroy this place, and "shall change the ordinances that Moses gave us [1]." True it is that this doctrine was then taught, which unbelievers condemning for blasphemy did therein commit that which they did condemn. The Apostles notwithstanding from whom Stephen had received it, did not so teach the abrogation, no not of those things which were necessarily to cease, but that even the Jews being Christian, might for a time continue in them. And therefore in Jerusalem the first Christian bishop not circumcised was Mark; and he not bishop till the days of Adrian the emperor, after the overthrow of Jerusalem: there having been fifteen bishops before him which were all of the circumcision [2].

The Christian Jews did think at the first not only themselves but the Christian Gentiles also bound, and that necessarily, to observe the whole Law. There went forth certain of the sect of Pharisees which did believe, and they coming unto Antioch, taught that it was necessary for the Gentiles to be circumcised, and to keep the Law of Moses [3]. Whereupon there grew dissension, Paul and Barnabas disputing against them. The determination of the council held at Jerusalem concerning this matter was finally this; "Touching the Gen- "tiles which believe, we have written and determined that "they observe no such thing [4]." Their protestation by letters is, "Forasmuch as we have heard that certain which "departed from us have troubled you with words, and cum- "bered your minds, saying, Ye must be circumcised and keep "the Law; know that we gave them no such commandment [5]." Paul therefore continued still teaching the Gentiles, not only that they were not bound to observe the laws of Moses, but

---

[1] Acts vi. 13, 14.
[2] Vide Niceph. lib. iii. cap. 25. ['Επὶ δὲ τούτοις Ἰούδας πεντεκαιδέκατος· οὓς ἐξ ἐθνῶν μετὰ τὴν ἅλωσιν διαδέχεται Μάρκος· τοσοῦτοι μὲν ἀπὸ τῶν Ἀποστόλων ἐς τὸν εἰρημένον Ἰούδαν ἐπίσκοποι ἐκ περιτομῆς ἐν Ἱεροσολύμοις γεγόνασιν.] et Sulpit. Sever. p. 149. in edit. Plant. ["Tum "Hierosolymæ non nisi ex circum- "cisione habebat Ecclesia Sacer- "dotem," p. 364. ed. Horn. 1665.]
[3] Acts xv.
[4] Acts xxi. 25.   [5] Acts xv. 24.

that the observation of those laws which were necessarily to be abrogated, was in them altogether unlawful. In which point his doctrine was misreported, as though he had every where preached this, not only concerning the Gentiles, but also touching the Jews. Wherefore coming unto James and the rest of the clergy at Jerusalem, they told him plainly of it, saying, "Thou seest, brother, how many thousand Jews there "are which believe, and they are all zealous of the Law. Now "they are informed of thee, that thou teachest all the Jews "which are amongst the Gentiles to forsake Moses, and sayest "that they ought not to circumcise their children, neither to "live after the customs[1]." And hereupon they give him counsel to make it apparent in the eyes of all men, that those flying reports were untrue, and that himself being a Jew kept the Law even as they did.

In some things therefore we see the Apostles did teach, that there ought not to be conformity between the Christian Jews and Gentiles. How many things this law of inconformity did comprehend, there is no need we should stand to examine. This general is true, that the Gentiles were not made conformable unto the Jews, in that which was necessarily to cease at the coming of Christ.

[5.] Touching things positive, which might either cease or continue as occasion should require, the Apostles tendering the zeal of the Jews, thought it necessary to bind even the Gentiles for a time to abstain as the Jews did, "from things "offered unto idols, from blood, from strangled[2]." These decrees were every where delivered unto the Gentiles to be straitly observed and kept[3]. In the other matters, where the Gentiles were free, and the Jews in their own opinion still tied, the Apostles' doctrine unto the Jew was, "condemn not "the Gentile;" unto the Gentile, "despise not the Jew[4]." The one sort they warned to take heed, that scrupulosity did not make them rigorous, in giving unadvised sentence against their brethren which were free; the other, that they did not become scandalous, by abusing their liberty and freedom to the offence of their weak brethren which were scrupulous. From hence therefore two conclusions there are which may evidently be drawn; the first, that whatsoever conformity of

---

[1] Acts xxi. 20.   [2] Acts xv. 28, 29.   [3] Acts xvi. 4.   [4] Rom. xiv. 10.

positive laws the Apostles did bring in between the churches of Jews and Gentiles, it was in those things only which might either cease or continue a shorter or a longer time, as occasion did most require; the second, that they did not impose upon the churches of the Gentiles any part of the Jews' ordinances with bond of necessary and perpetual observation, (as we all both by doctrine and practice acknowledge,) but only in respect of the conveniency and fitness for the present state of the Church as then it stood. The words of the council's decree concerning the Gentiles are, "It seemed good to the "Holy Ghost and to us, to lay upon you no more burden "saving only those things of necessity, abstinence from idol-"offerings, from strangled and blood, and from fornication[1]." So that in other things positive, which the coming of Christ did not necessarily extinguish, the Gentiles were left altogether free.

[6.] Neither ought it to seem unreasonable that the Gentiles should necessarily be bound and tied to Jewish ordinances, so far forth as that decree importeth. For to the Jew, who knew that their difference from other nations which were aliens and strangers from God, did especially consist in this, that God's people had positive ordinances given to them of God himself, it seemed marvellous hard, that the Christian Gentiles should be incorporated into the same commonwealth with God's own chosen people, and be subject to no part of his statutes, more than only the law of nature, which heathens count themselves bound unto. It was an opinion constantly received amongst the Jews, that God did deliver unto the sons of Noah seven precepts: namely, first, to live in some form of regiment under public laws; secondly, to serve and call upon the name of God; thirdly, to shun idolatry; fourthly, not to suffer effusion of blood; fifthly, to abhor all unclean knowledge in the flesh; sixthly, to commit no rapine; seventhly, and finally, not to eat of any living creature whereof the blood was not first let out[2].

---

[1] [Acts xv. 28.]
[2] Lib. qui Seder Olam inscribitur. [Or "The World's Order," being a summary of events and dates from the creation to the War of Bar Cochab, supposed to have been written about A.D. 130. Wolf. Bibl. Hebr. i. 491. ed. 1715. The passage cited is cap. 5, p. 16. ed. Meyer. Amstelæd. 1699. "From the Red "sea they journied unto Marah... "There were given unto Israel ten "precepts; [Exod. xv. 23, 25.] "seven of them, concerning which "commandment had been given "to the sons of Noah.] 1. עין

If therefore the Gentiles would be exempt from the law of
Moses, yet it might seem hard they should also cast off even
those things positive which were observed before Moses, and
which were not of the same kind with laws that were necessarily to cease. And peradventure hereupon the council saw
it expedient to determine, that the Gentiles should, according
unto the third, the seventh, and the fifth, of those precepts,
abstain from things sacrificed unto idols, from strangled and
blood, and from fornication. The rest the Gentiles did of
their own accord observe, nature leading them thereto.

[7.] And did not nature also teach them to abstain from
fornication? No doubt it did. Neither can we with reason
think, that as the former two are positive, so likewise this,
being meant as the Apostle doth otherwise usually understand
it[1]. But very marriage within a number of degrees being not
only by the law of Moses, but also by the law of the sons of
Noah (for so they took it) an unlawful discovery of nakedness; this discovery of nakedness by unlawful marriages such
as Moses in the law reckoneth up[2], I think it for mine own
part more probable to have been meant in the words of that
canon, than fornication according unto the sense of the law of
nature. Words must be taken according to the matter whereof they are uttered. The Apostles command to abstain from
blood. Construe this meaning according to the law of nature,
and it will seem that homicide only is forbidden. But construe it in reference to the law of the Jews about which the
question was, and it shall easily appear to have a clean other
sense, and in any man's judgment a truer, when we expound
it of eating and not of shedding blood. So if we speak of fornication, he that knoweth no law but only the law of nature
must needs make thereof a narrower construction, than he
which measureth the same by a law, wherein sundry kinds

"[the judgments]: 2. ברכת השם
"[the malediction of the name (of
"God)]: 3. ע״א [עבודת אלילים]," (more
usually עבודה זרה "strange wor-
"ship,") "the worship of idols]:
"4. שפיכות דמים [the shedding of
"blood]: 5. גילוי עריות [the dis-
"covery of nakedness]: 6. הגזל [ra-
"pine]: 7. אבר מן החי [partaking
"of any member of a living creature.]
"Israel added unto these at that

"time the Sabbath, and (דינין) judg-
"ments," (on the difference between
this and the first precept see Selden, de Jure Nat. et Gent. ap.
Heb. vii. 5. p. 809.) "and the hon-
"ouring of parents." The whole
passage is quoted and illustrated by
Selden, lib. i. c. 10. p. 123.)

[1] Heb. xiii. 4; 1 Cor. v. 11; Gal.
v. 19.
[2] Lev. xviii.

even of conjugal copulation are prohibited as impure, unclean, unhonest. St. Paul himself doth term incestuous marriage fornication[1]. If any do rather think that the Christian Gentiles themselves, through the loose and corrupt custom of those times, took simple fornication for no sin, and were in that respect offensive unto believing Jews, which by the Law had been better taught; our proposing of another conjecture is unto theirs no prejudice[2].

[8.] Some things therefore we see there were, wherein the Gentiles were forbidden to be like unto the Jews; some things wherein they were commanded not to be unlike. Again, some things also there were, wherein no law of God did let but that they might be either like or unlike, as occasion should require. And unto this purpose Leo saith[3], "Apostolical ordinance (beloved,) knowing that our Lord "Jesus Christ came not into this world to undo the law, hath "in such sort distinguished the mysteries of the Old Testa-"ment, that certain of them it hath chosen out to benefit evan-"gelical knowledge withal, and for that purpose appointed "that those things which before were Jewish might now be "Christian customs." The cause why the Apostles did thus conform the Christians as much as might be according to the pattern of the Jews, was to rein them in by this mean the more, and to make them cleave the better.

[9.] The Church of Christ hath had in no one thing so many and so contrary occasions of dealing as about Judaism: some having thought the whole Jewish Law wicked and damnable in itself; some not condemning it as the former sort absolutely, have notwithstanding judged it either sooner necessary to be abrogated, or further unlawful to be observed than truth can bear: some of scrupulous simplicity urging perpetual and universal observation of the law of Moses necessary,

---

[1] 1 Cor. v. 1.
[2] [Selden in the work above cited (which is throughout an elaborate commentary on the seven Noachical precepts) approves this construction of the word πορνεία: though he does not think that the council of Jerusalem was referring to those precepts: lib. vii. c. 12, p. 845.]
[3] Leo in Jejun. Mens. Sept. Ser. 9. [vii. c. 1. "Apostolica institutio, "dilectissimi, quæ Dom. Jesum "Christum ad hoc venisse in hunc "mundum noverat, ut legem non "solveret sed impleret, ita Veteris "Testamenti decreta distinxit, ut "quædam ex eis, sicut erant condita, "evangelicæ eruditioni profutura "decerperet, et quæ dudum fuerant "consuetudinis Judaicæ fierent ob-"servantiæ Christianæ."]

Errors about the Law: Contempt of the Lessons.

as the Christian Jews at the first in the Apostles' times; some as heretics, holding the same no less even after the contrary determination set down by consent of the Church at Jerusalem; finally some being herein resolute through mere infidelity, and with open professed enmity against Christ, as unbelieving Jews.

To control slanderers of the Law and Prophets, such as Marcionites and Manichees were, the Church in her liturgies hath intermingled with readings out of the New Testament lessons taken out of the Law and Prophets; whereunto Tertullian alluding, saith of the Church of Christ[1], "It inter-"mingleth with evangelical and apostolical writings the Law "and the Prophets; and from thence it drinketh in that "faith, which with water it sealeth, clotheth with the Spirit, "nourisheth with the Eucharist, with martyrdom setteth "forward." They would have wondered in those times to hear, that any man being not a favourer of heresy should term this by way of dísdain, "mangling of the Gospels and "Epistles[2]."

[10.] They which honour the Law as an image of the wisdom of God himself, are notwithstanding to know that the same had an end in Christ. But what? Was the Law so abolished with Christ, that after his ascension the office of Priests became immediately wicked, and the very name hateful, as importing the exercise of an ungodly function[3]? No, as long as the glory of the Temple continued, and till the time of that final desolation was accomplished, the very Christian Jews did continue with their sacrifices and other parts of legal service. That very Law therefore which our Saviour was to abolish, did not *so soon* become unlawful to be

---

[1] Tertull. de Præscript. advers. Hæret. [c. 36. "Unum Deum "novit Creatorem universitatis, et "Christum Jesum ex Virgine Maria "Filium Dei Creatoris, et carnis "resurrectionem: legem et pro-"phetas cum evangelicis et aposto-"licis literis miscet, et inde potat "fidem: eam aqua signat, Sancto "Spiritu vestit, eucharistia pascit, "martyrio exhortatur."]

[2] T. C. lib. iii. p. 171. "What "an abusing also is it to affirm the "mangling of the Gospels and "Epistles to have been brought "into the Church by godly and "learned men!"

[3] T. C. lib. i. p. 216. "Seeing "that the office and function of "priests was after our Saviour "Christ's ascension naught and "ungodly; the name whereby they "were called, which did exercise "that ungodly function, cannot be "otherwise taken than in the evil "part."

observed as some imagine; nor was it afterwards unlawful *so far*, that the very name of Altar, of Priest, of Sacrifice itself, should be banished out of the world. For though God do now hate sacrifice, whether it be heathenish or Jewish, so that we cannot have the same things which they had but with impiety; yet unless there be some greater let than the only evacuation of the Law of Moses, the names themselves may (I hope) be retained without sin, in respect of that proportion which things established by our Saviour have unto them which by him are abrogated. And so throughout all the writings of the ancient Fathers we see that the words which were do continue; the only difference is, that whereas before they had a literal, they now have a metaphorical use, and are as so many notes of remembrance unto us, that what they did signify in the letter is accomplished in the truth. And as no man can deprive the Church of this liberty, to use names whereunto the Law was accustomed, so neither are we generally forbidden the use of things which the Law hath; though it neither command us any particular rite, as it did the Jews a number, and the weightiest which it did command them are unto us in the Gospel prohibited.

[11.] Touching such as through simplicity of error did urge universal and perpetual observation of the Law of Moses at the first, we have spoken already. Against Jewish heretics and false apostles teaching afterwards the selfsame, St. Paul in every epistle commonly either disputeth or giveth warning. Jews that were zealous for the Law, but withal infidels in respect of Christianity, and to the name of Jesus Christ most spiteful enemies, did while they flourished no less persecute the Church than heathens. After their estate was overthrown, they were not that way so much to be feared. Howbeit, because they had their synagogues in every famous city almost throughout the world, and by that means great opportunity to withdraw from the Christian faith, which to do they spared no labour; this gave the church occasion to make sundry laws against them. As in the council of Laodicea[1]

---

[1] Conc. Laod. Can. 37, 38. ["Non "oportet a Judæis vel hæreticis "feriatica quæ mittuntur accipere, "nec cum eis dies agere festos. "Non oportet a Judæis azyma ac-"cipere, aut communicare impieta-"tibus eorum." Conc. Reg. II. 116.] T. C. lib. i. p. 132. [103.]

"The festival presents which Jews or heretics use to send "must not be received, nor Holidays solemnized in their "company." Again, "from the Jews men ought not to re-"ceive their unleavened, nor to communicate with their "impieties." Which council was afterwards indeed confirmed by the sixth general council. But what was the true sense or meaning both of the one and the other? Were Christians here forbidden to communicate in unleavened bread because the Jews did so being enemies of the Church[1]? He which attentively shall weigh the words will suspect, that they rather forbid communion with Jews, than imitation of them : much more, if with these two decrees be compared a third in the Council of Constantinople, "Let no man either "of the clergy or laity eat the unleavened of the Jews, nor "enter into any familiarity with them, nor send for them "in sickness, nor take physic at their hands, nor as much "as go into the bath with them. If any do otherwise being a "clergyman, let him be deposed ; if being a lay person, let "excommunication be his punishment[2]."

[12.] If these canons were any argument, that they which made them did utterly condemn similitude between the Christians and Jews in things indifferent appertaining unto religion, either because the Jews were enemies unto the Church, or else for that their ceremonies were abrogated ; these reasons had been as strong and effectual against their keeping the feast of Easter on the same day the Jews kept theirs, and not according to the custom of the West church. For so they did from the first beginning till Constantine's time. For in these two things the East and West churches did interchangeably both confront the Jews and concur with them : the West church using unleavened bread, as the Jews in their passover did, but differing from them in the day whereon they kept the feast of Easter; contrariwise the East church celebrating the feast of Easter on the same day

---

[1] T. C. lib. iii. p. 176. ["What "can be in itself more indifferent "than these two, forbidden the "Christians for that they were "used of the enemies of the "Church!"]

[2] Conc. Constantinop. vi. cap. 11. [Μηδεὶς τῶν ἐν ἱερατικῷ τάγματι ἢ λαϊκὸς τὰ παρὰ τῶν Ἰουδαίων ἄζυμα ἐσθιέτω, ἢ τοιούτοις προσοικειούσθω, καὶ ἰατρείας παρ' αὐτῶν λαμβανέτω, ἢ ἐν βαλανείῳ παντελῶς τούτοις συλλουέσθω. Εἰ δέ τις τοῦτο πρᾶξαι ἐπιχειροίη, εἰ μὲν κληρικὸς εἴη, καθαιρείσθω· εἰ δὲ λαϊκὸς, ἀφοριζέσθω. xvi. 618.]

BOOK IV. with the Jews, but not using the same kind of bread which
Ch. xi. 12. they did. Now if so be the East church in using leavened
bread had done ill[1], either for that the Jews were enemies
to the Church, or because Jewish ceremonies were abrogated;
how should we think but that Victor the bishop of Rome
(whom all judicious men do in that behalf disallow) did
well to be so vehement and fierce in drawing them to the
like dissimilitude for the feast of Easter[2]? Again, if the
West churches had in either of those two respects affected
dissimilitude with the Jews in the feast of Easter, what
reason had they to draw the Eastern church herein unto them,
which reason did not enforce them to frame themselves unto
it in the ceremony of leavened bread? Difference in rites
should breed no controversy between one church and another;
but if controversy be once bred, it must be ended. The
feast of Easter being therefore litigious in the days of Constantine, who honoured of all other churches most the church
of Rome, which church was the mother from whose breasts
he had drawn that food, which gave him nourishment to
eternal life; sith agreement was necessary, and yet impossible
unless the one part were yielded unto; his desire was that of
the two the Eastern church should rather yield. And to this
end he useth sundry persuasive speeches.

When Stephen the Bishop of Rome going about to shew
what the Catholic Church should do, had alleged what the
heretics themselves did, namely, that they received such as
came unto them, and offered not to baptize them anew;
St. Cyprian being of a contrary mind to him about the matter
at that time in question, which was, "Whether heretics con-
"verted ought to be rebaptized, yea or no?" answered the
allegation of Pope Stephen with exceeding great stomach,
saying, "To this degree of wretchedness the church of God
"and Spouse of Christ is now come, that her ways she frameth
"to the example of heretics; that to celebrate the Sacraments

---

[1] [So it stands in the original edition, p. 194. But it is most likely an oversight, the sense requiring "not done ill," or "done well:" which reading has been followed by all the editors except Mr. Hanbury. The correction appears to have been Spenser's: at least it occurs in the reprint of his edition, 1622.]*

[2] [Euseb. v. 24.]

[* The correction "had done well," is Spenser's, tacitly made in his edition of 1604; followed in the 4th edition, 1617.] 1886.

"which heavenly instruction hath delivered, light itself doth "borrow from darkness, and Christians do that which Anti- "christs do ¹."

Now albeit Constantine have done that to further a better cause, which Cyprian did to countenance a worse, namely the rebaptization of heretics, and have taken advantage at the odiousness of the Jews, as Cyprian of heretics, because the Eastern church kept their feast of Easter always the fourteenth day of the month, as the Jews did, what day of the week soever it fell; or howsoever Constantine did take occasion in the handling of that cause to say, "It is unworthy to have any thing "common with that spiteful nation of the Jews ²:" shall every motive argument used in such kind of conferences be made a rule for others still to conclude the like by, concerning all things of like nature, when as probable inducements may lead them to the contrary? Let both this and other allegations suitable unto it cease to bark any longer idly against that truth, the course and passage whereof it is not in them to hinder.

XII. But the weightiest exception, and of all the most worthy to be respected, is against such kind of ceremonies, as have been so grossly and shamefully abused in the church of Rome, that where they remain they are scandalous, yea,

Their exception against such ceremonies as have been

BOOK IV.
Ch. xii. 1.

---

¹ Cypr. ad Pomp. cont. Stephan. [Ep. 74. § 2. "Ad hoc enim "malorum devoluta est Ecclesia "Dei et sponsa Christi, ut hære-"ticorum exempla sectetur, ut ad "celebranda sacramenta cœlestis "disciplinæ lux de tenebris mu-"tuetur, et id faciant Christiani, "quod Antichristi faciunt."]
² Socrat. Ecclesiast. Hist. lib. v. c. 22. "Plerique in Asia minore "antiquitus 14 die mensis, nulla "ratione diei Sabbati habita, hoc "festum observarunt. Quod dum "faciebant, cum aliis, qui aliam ra-"tionem in eodem festo agendo "sequebantur, usque eo nequaquam "dissenserunt, quoad Victor epi-"scopus Romanus, supra modum "iracundia inflammatus, omnes in "Asia qui erant τεσσαρεσκαιδεκά-"τηται appellati excommunicaverit. "Ob quod factum Irenæus episcopus "Lugduni in Victorem per epi-"stolam graviter invectus est." Euseb. de Vita Constant. lib. iii.

cap. 18. "Quid præstabilius, quidve "augustius esse poterat, quam ut "hoc festum, per quod spem im-"mortalitatis nobis ostentatam ha-"bemus, uno modo et ratione apud "omnes integre sincereque obser-"varetur? Ac primum omnium "indignum plane videbatur, ut "ritum et consuetudinem imitantes "Judæorum (qui, quoniam suas "ipsorum manus immani scelere "polluerunt, merito, ut scelestos "decet, cæco animorum errore te-"nentur irretiti) istud festum sanc-"tissimum ageremus. In nostra "enim situm est potestate, ut, illo-"rum more rejecto, veriore ac magis "sincero instituto (quod quidem "usque a prima passionis die "hactenus recoluimus) hujus festi "celebrationem ad posterorum se-"culorum memoriam propagemus. "Nihil igitur sit nobis cum Judæ-"orum turba, omnium odiosa max-"ime."

BOOK IV.
Ch. xii. 2.

abused by the church of Rome, and are said in that respect to be scandalous.

they cannot choose but be stumblingblocks and grievous causes of offence. Concerning this point therefore we are first to note, what properly it is to be scandalous or offensive; secondly, what kind of ceremonies are such; and thirdly, when they are necessarily for remedy thereof to be taken away, and when not.

[2.] The common conceit of the vulgar sort is, whensoever they see any thing which they mislike and are angry at, to think that every such thing is scandalous, and that themselves in this case are the men concerning whom our Saviour spake in so fearful manner, saying, "whosoever shall scandalize or "offend any one of these little ones which believe in me"[1] (that is, as they construe it, whosoever shall anger the meanest and simplest artisan which carrieth a good mind, by not removing out of the Church such rites and ceremonies as displease him), "better he were drowned in the bottom of the "sea." But hard were the case of the Church of Christ, if this were to scandalize. Men are scandalized when they are moved, led, and provoked unto sin. At good things evil men may take occasion to do evil; and so Christ himself was a rock of offence in Israel[2], they taking occasion at his poor estate and at the ignominy of his cross, to think him unworthy the name of that great and glorious Messias, whom the Prophets describe in such ample and stately terms. But that which we therefore term offensive because it inviteth men to offend, and by a dumb kind of provocation encourageth, moveth, or any way leadeth unto sin, must of necessity be acknowledged actively scandalous.

Now some things are so even by their very essence and nature, so that wheresoever they are found they are not neither can be without this force of provocation unto evil; of which kind all examples of sin and wickedness are. Thus David was scandalous in that bloody act whereby he caused the enemies of God to be blasphemous[3]: thus the whole state of Israel scandalous, when their public disorders caused the name of God to be ill-spoken of amongst the nations[4]. It is of this

---

[1] Matt. xviii. 6.
[2] 1 Pet. ii. 8.
[3] 2 Sam. xii. 14.
[4] Rom. ii. 24; Ezek. xxxvi. 20; Tertull. lib. de Virgin. Veland. [c. iii.

"Scandalum, nisi fallor, non bonæ "rei sed malæ exemplum est, ædi- "ficans ad delictum. Bonæ res "neminem scandalizant, nisi malam "mentem."]

Subdivision of Things incidentally scandalous.

kind that Tertullian meaneth: "Offence or scandal, if I be not "deceived (saith he), is, when the example not of a good but "of an evil thing doth set men forward unto sin. Good things "can scandalize none save only evil minds:" good things have no scandalizing nature in them.

BOOK IV.
Ch. xii. 3.

[3.] Yet that which is of its own nature either good or at least not evil, may by some accident become scandalous at certain times and in certain places and to certain men; the open use thereof nevertheless being otherwise without danger. The very nature of some rites and ceremonies therefore is scandalous, as it was in a number of those which the Manichees did use, and is in all such as the law of God doth forbid. Some are offensive only through the agreement of men to use them unto evil, and not else; as the most of those things indifferent which the heathens did to the service of their false gods, which another, in heart condemning their idolatry, could not do with them in show and token of approbation without being guilty of scandal given. Ceremonies of this kind are either devised at the first unto evil, as the Eunomian heretics in dishonour of the blessed Trinity brought in the laying on of water but once[1], to cross the custom of the church which in baptism did it thrice; or else having had a profitable use they are afterwards interpreted and wrested to the contrary, as those heretics which held the Trinity to be three distinct not persons but natures, abused the ceremony of three times laying on water in baptism unto the strengthening of their heresy[2]. The element of water is in baptism necessary; once to lay it on or twice is indifferent. For which cause Gregory making mention thereof saith[3], "To dive an infant

---

[1] [Sozom. vi. 26. φασὶ δέ τινες, πρῶτον τοῦτον Εὐνόμιον τολμῆσαι εἰσηγήσασθαι, ἐν μιᾷ καταδύσει χρῆναι ἐπιτελεῖν τὴν θείαν βάπτισιν, καὶ παραχαράξαι τὴν ἀπὸ τῶν Ἀποστόλων εἰσέτι νῦν ἐν πᾶσι φυλαττομένην παράδοσιν.]

[2] [Concil. Tolet. iv. Can. 6, t. v. p. 1706. "Propter vitandum schis-"matis scandalum, vel hæretici dog-"matis usum, simplam teneamus "baptismi mersionem; ne videantur "apud nos, qui tertio mergunt, hæ-"reticorum approbare assertionem "dum sequuntur et morem."]

[3] Epist. ad Leandrum Hisp. [lib.

i. ep. 43. "De trina vero mersione "baptismatis nil respondere verius "potest quam ipsi sensistis: quia "in una fide nihil officit ecclesiæ "consuetudo diversa. Nos autem "quod tertio mergimus, triduanæ "sepulturæ sacramenta signamus, "ut dum tertio infans ab aquis educitur, resurrectio triduani temporis exprimatur. Quod si quis forte "etiam pro summæ Trinitatis veneratione æstimet fieri, neque ad "hoc aliquid obsistit, baptizandum "semel in aquis mergere: quia "dum in tribus subsistentiis una

"either thrice or but once in baptism, can be no way a thing "reprovable; seeing that both in three times washing the "Trinity of persons, and in one the Unity of Godhead may "be signified." So that of these two ceremonies neither being hurtful in itself, both may serve unto good purpose; yet one was devised, and the other converted, unto evil.

[4.] Now whereas in the church of Rome certain ceremonies are said to have been shamefully abused unto evil, as the ceremony of crossing at baptism, of kneeling at the eucharist, of using wafer-cakes, and such like; the question is, whether for remedy of that evil wherein such ceremonies have been scandalous, and perhaps may be still unto some even amongst ourselves, whom the presence and sight of them may confirm in that former error whereto they served in times past, they are of necessity to be removed. Are these, or any other ceremonies we have common with the church of Rome, scandalous and wicked in their very nature? This no man objecteth. Are any such as have been polluted from their very birth, and instituted even at the first unto that thing which is evil? That which hath been ordained impiously at the first, may wear out that impiety in tract of time; and then what doth let but that the use thereof may stand without offence? The names of our months and of our days we are not ignorant from whence they came, and with what dishonour unto God they are said to have been devised at the first[1]. What could be spoken against any thing more effectual to stir hatred, than that which sometime the ancient Fathers in this case speak? Yet those very names are at this day in use

"substantia est, reprehensibile esse "nullatenus potest, infantem in bap-"tismate vel ter vel semel mergere : "quando et in tribus mersionibus "personarum Trinitas, et in una po-"test divinitatis singularitas desig-"nari." II. 532.]

[1] [Euseb. Emis.] Hom. xi. de Pasch. [p. 566. par. i. t. v. Biblioth. Patr. Colon.] "Idololatriæ consue-"tudo in tantum homines occæca-"verat, ut Solis, Lunæ, Martis "atque Mercurii, Jovis, Veneris, "Saturni, et diversis elementorum "ac dæmonum appellationibus dies "vocitarent, et luci tenebrarum no-"men imponerent." Beda de Ration. Temp. cap. 4. [6.] "Octavus "dies idem primus est, ad quem "reditur, indeque [*l.* eoque] rursus "hebdomada inchoatur [*l.* semper "orditur.] His nomina a planetis "Gentilitas indidit, habere se cre-"dens a Sole spiritum, a Luna cor-"pus, a Marte sanguinem, a Mercu-"rio ingenium et linguam, a Jove "temperantiam, a Venere volupta-"tem, a Saturno tarditatem." Isid. Hist. lib. v. Etymol. cap. 30. [p. 938, ed. Gothofred.] "Dies dicti a "diis, quorum nomina Romani qui-"busdam sideribus sacraverunt."

throughout Christendom without hurt or scandal to any. Clear and manifest it is, that things devised by heretics, yea, devised of a very heretical purpose even against religion, and at their first devising worthy to have been withstood, may in time grow meet to be kept; as that custom, the inventors whereof were the Eunomian heretics. So that customs once established and confirmed by long use, being presently without harm, are not in regard of their corrupt original to be held scandalous.

[5.] But concerning those our ceremonies which they reckon for most popish, they are not able to avouch, that any of them was otherwise instituted than unto good, yea, so used at the first. It followeth then that they all are such, as having served to good purpose, were afterwards converted unto the contrary. And sith it is not so much as objected against us, that we retain together with them the evil wherewith they have been infected in the church of Rome, I would demand who they are whom we scandalize, by using harmless things unto that good end for which they were first instituted. Amongst ourselves that agree in the approbation of this kind of good use, no man will say that one of us is offensive and scandalous unto another. As for the favourers of the church of Rome, they know how far we herein differ and dissent from them; which thing neither we conceal, and they by their public writings also profess daily how much it grieveth them; so that of them there will not many rise up against us, as witnesses unto the indictment of scandal, whereby we might be condemned and cast, as having strengthened them in that evil wherewith they pollute themselves in the use of the same ceremonies. And concerning such as withstand the church of England herein, and hate it because it doth not sufficiently seem to hate Rome; they (I hope) are far enough from being by this mean drawn to any kind of popish error. The multitude therefore of them, unto whom we are scandalous through the use of abused ceremonies, is not so apparent, that it can justly be said in general of any one sort of men or other, we cause them to offend. If it be so, that now or then some few are espied, who, having been accustomed heretofore to the rites and ceremonies of the church of Rome, are not so scoured of their former rust as to forsake their ancient persuasion which they have had, howsoever they frame themselves to

BOOK IV.
Ch. xii. 6.

outward obedience of laws and orders: because such may misconstrue the meaning of our ceremonies, and so take them as though they were in every sort the same they have been, shall this be thought a reason sufficient whereon to conclude that some law must necessarily be made to abolish all such ceremonies?

[6.] They answer, that there is no law of God which doth bind us to retain them. And St. Paul's rule is, that in those things from which without hurt we may lawfully abstain, we should frame the usage of our liberty with regard to the weakness and imbecility of our brethren. Wherefore unto them which stood upon their own defence saying, "All things "are lawful unto me;" he replieth, "but all things are not "expedient [1]" in regard of others. "All things are clean, all "meats are lawful; but evil unto that man that eateth "offensively. If for thy meat's sake thy brother be grieved, "thou walkest no longer according to charity. Destroy not "him with thy meat for whom Christ died. Dissolve not for "food's sake the work of God [2]. We that are strong must "bear the imbecilities of the impotent, and not please our-"selves [3]." It was a weakness in the Christian Jews, and a maim of judgment in them, that they thought the Gentiles polluted by the eating of those meats which themselves were afraid to touch for fear of transgressing the law of Moses; yea, hereat their hearts did so much rise, that the Apostle had just cause to fear, lest they would rather forsake Christianity than endure any fellowship with such as made no conscience of that which was unto them abominable. And for this cause mention is made of destroying the weak by meats, and of dissolving the work of God [4], which was his Church, a part of the living stones whereof were believing Jews. Now those weak brethren before-mentioned are said to be as the Jews were, and our ceremonies which have been abused in the church of Rome to be as the scandalous meats, from which the Gentiles are exhorted to abstain in the presence of Jews, for fear of averting them from Christian faith. Therefore, as charity did bind them to refrain from that for their brethren's sake, which otherwise was lawful enough for them; so it

[1] 1 Cor. vi. 12.
[2] [Rom. xiv. 20, 15, 20.]
[3] [Rom. xv. 1.]
[4] Rom. xiv; xv. 1.

bindeth us for our brethren's sake likewise to abolish such ceremonies, although we might lawfully else retain them.

[7.] But between these two cases there are great odds. For neither are our weak brethren as the Jews, nor the ceremonies which we use as the meats which the Gentiles used. The Jews were known to be generally weak in that respect; whereas contrariwise the imbecility of ours is not common unto so many, that we can take any such certain notice of them. It is a chance if here and there some one be found; and therefore seeing we may presume men commonly otherwise, there is no necessity that our practice should frame itself by that which the Apostle doth prescribe to the Gentiles.

Again, their use of meats was not like unto our of ceremonies, that being a matter of private action in common life, where every man was free to order that which himself did; but this a public constitution for the ordering of the Church: and we are not to look that the Church should change her public laws and ordinances, made according to that which is judged ordinarily and commonly fittest for the whole, although it chance that for some particular men the same be found inconvenient[1]; especially when there may be other remedy also against the sores of particular inconveniences. In this case therefore where any private harm doth grow, we are not to reject instruction, as being an unmeet plaister to apply unto it; neither can we say, that he which appointeth teachers for physicians in this kind of evil, is "As if a man would set "one to watch a child all day long lest he should hurt himself with a knife; whereas by taking away the knife from "him, the danger is avoided, and the service of the man "better employed[2]." For a knife may be taken away from a child, without depriving them of the benefit thereof which have years and discretion to use it. But the ceremonies which children do abuse if we remove quite and clean, as it is by some required that we should, then are they not taken from children only, but from others also; which is as though because children may perhaps hurt themselves with knives,

---

[1] Vide Harmenop. [Harmenopuli Promptuarium Juris.] (Greek jurist and canonist, 1320-1383. His Πρόχειρον νόμων was first printed 1540, and by Gothofr. 1587.) lib. i. tit. 1. sect. 28. [παραβαίνουσι γὰρ οἱ νομοθέται τὸ ἅπαξ ἢ τὸ δὶς γενόμενον. p. 20. ed. Gothofr.]

[2] T. C. lib. iii. p. 178. [156.]

we should conclude, that therefore the use of knives is to be taken quite and clean even from men also.

[8.] Those particular ceremonies, which they pretend to be so scandalous, we shall in the next Book have occasion more throughly to sift, where other things also traduced in the public duties of the Church whereunto each of these appertaineth, are together with these to be touched, and such reasons to be examined as have at any time been brought either against the one or the other. In the meanwhile against the conveniency of curing such evils by instruction, strange it is that they should object the multitude of other necessary matters, wherein preachers may better bestow their time, than in giving men warning not to abuse ceremonies[1]: a wonder it is, that they should object this, which have so many years together troubled the Church with quarrels concerning these things, and are even to this very hour so earnest in them, that if they write or speak publicly but five words, one of them is lightly about the dangerous estate of the church of England in respect of abused ceremonies. How much happier had it been for this whole Church, if they which have raised contention therein about the abuse of rites and ceremonies, had considered in due time that there is indeed store of matters fitter and better a great deal for teachers to spend time and labour in! It is through their importunate and vehement asseverations, more than through any such experience which we have had of our own, that we are forced to think it possible for one or other now and then, at leastwise in the prime of the reformation of our church, to have stumbled at some kind of ceremony: wherein forasmuch as we are contented to take this upon their credit, and to think it may be; sith also they further pretend the same to be so dangerous a snare to their souls that are at any time

[1] T. C. lib. iii. p. 177. "It is "not so convenient that the minis-"ter, having so many necessary "points to bestow his time in, "should be driven to spend it in "giving warning of not abusing "them, of which (although they "were used to the best) there is "no profit." [See also i. 56, ap. Whitg. Defence, 277. The words are, "A counsell not so convenient, "that the ministers and pastors, "which have so many necessary "points to bestow their time on, "and to inform the people of, should "be driven to cut off their time "appointed thereto, to teach them "not to abuse these things, which "if they use never so well, they can "gain nothing."]

Whether we should defer to Foreign Churches. 471

taken therein; they must give our teachers leave for the saving of those souls (be they never so few) to intermingle sometime with other more necessary things admonition concerning these not unnecessary. Wherein they should in reason more easily yield this leave, considering that hereunto we shall not need to use the hundredth part of that time, which themselves think very needful to bestow in making most bitter invectives against the ceremonies of the Church.

BOOK IV.
Ch. xiii. 1.

XIII. But to come to the last point of all; the church of England is grievously charged with forgetfulness of her duty, which duty had been to frame herself unto the pattern of their example that went before her in the work of reformation. [1] For "as the churches of Christ ought to be " most unlike the synagogue of Antichrist in their indifferent " ceremonies; so they ought to be most like one unto another, " and for preservation of unity to have as much as possible " may be all the same ceremonies. And therefore St. Paul, " to establish this order in the church of Corinth, that they " should make their gatherings for the poor upon the first " day of the Sabbath[2], (which is our Sunday,) allegeth this " for a reason [3], That he had so ordained in other churches." Again, " As children of one father and servants of one family, " so all churches should not only have one diet in that they " have one word, but also wear as it were one livery in using " the same ceremonies." Thirdly, " This rule did the great " council of Nice follow[4], when it ordained, that where " certain at the feast of Pentecost did pray kneeling, they " should pray standing: the reason whereof is added, which " is, that one custom ought to be kept throughout all " churches. It is true that the diversity of ceremonies ought " not to cause the churches to dissent one with another; but " yet it maketh most to the avoiding of dissension, that there " be amongst them an unity not only in doctrine, but also in " ceremonies. And therefore our form of service is to be " amended, not only for that it cometh too near that of the

Our ceremonies excepted against, for that some churches reformed before ours have cast out those things, which we notwithstanding their example to the contrary do retain still.

[1] T. C. lib. i. p. 133. [104.]
[2] [" Saboth," A. B.; " Sabbath," 1617. V. note p. 372.] 1886.
[3] 1 Cor. xvi. 1.
[4] Can. 20. The canon of that council which is here cited doth provide against kneeling at prayer on Sundays, or for fifty days after Easter on any day, and not at the feast of Pentecost only. [ii. 202, 226; iv. 450.]

BOOK IV. "Papists, but also because it is so different from that of the
Ch. xiii. 2, 3. "reformed churches[1]." Being asked[2] to what churches ours
should conform itself, and why other reformed churches should
not as well frame themselves to ours; their answer is, "that
"if there be any ceremonies which we have better than others,
"they ought to frame themselves to us; if they have better
"than we, then we ought to frame ourselves to them; if the
"ceremonies be alike commodious, the later churches should
"conform themselves to the first, as the younger daughter to
"the elder. For as St. Paul in the members, where all other
"things are equal, noteth it for a mark of honour above the
"rest, that one is called before another to the Gospel[3]; so is
"it for the same cause amongst the churches. And in this
"respect he pincheth the Corinths[4], that not being the first
"which received the Gospel, yet they would have their several
"manners from other churches. Moreover, where the cere-
"monies are alike commodious, the fewer ought to conform
"themselves unto the moe. Forasmuch therefore as all the
"churches" (so far as they know which plead after this
manner) "of our confession in doctrine agree in the abroga-
"tion of divers things which we retain, our church ought
"either to shew that they have done evil, or else she is found
"to be in fault that doth not conform herself in that, which
"she cannot deny to be well abrogated[5]."

[2.] In this axiom, that preservation of peace and unity
amongst Christian churches should be by all good means
procured, we join most willingly and gladly with them.
Neither deny we but that to the avoiding of dissension it
availeth much that there be amongst them an unity as well
in ceremonies as in doctrine. The only doubt is about the
manner of their unity; how far churches are bound to be
uniform in their ceremonies, and what way they ought to
take for that purpose.

[3.] Touching the one, the rule which they have set down
is, that in ceremonies indifferent, all churches ought to be
one of them unto another as like as *possibly*[6] they may be.
Which *possibly* we cannot otherwise construe, than that it

---

[1] T. C. lib. i. p. 182, 183.
[2] [By Whitgift, Def. 481.]
[3] Rom. xvi. 5, 7.
[4] 1 Cor. xiv. 36.
[5] [T. C. iii. 183.]
[6] [T. C. i. 104.]

Augustine and Calvin on Uniformity in Rites. 473

doth require them to be even as like as they may be without breaking any positive ordinance of God. For the ceremonies whereof we speak, being matter of positive law, they are indifferent, if God have neither himself commanded nor forbidden them, but left them unto the Church's discretion. So that if as great uniformity be required as is possible in these things; seeing that the law of God forbiddeth not any one of them, it followeth that from the greatest unto the least they must be in every Christian church the same, except mere impossibility of so having it be the hinderance. To us this opinion seemeth over extreme and violent: we rather incline to think it a just and reasonable cause for any church, the state whereof is free and independent, if in these things it differ from other churches, only for that it doth not judge it so fit and expedient to be framed therein by the pattern of their example, as to be otherwise framed than they. That of Gregory unto Leander is a charitable speech and a peaceable[1]; "In una fide nil "officit ecclesiæ sanctæ consuetudo diversa:" "Where the "faith of the holy Church is one, a difference in customs of "the Church doth no harm[2]." That of St. Augustine to Casulanus is somewhat more particular, and toucheth what kind of ceremonies they are, wherein one church may vary from the example of another without hurt: "Let the faith "of the whole Church, how wide soever it have spread itself, "be always one, although the unity of belief be famous for "variety of certain ordinances, whereby that which is rightly "believed suffereth no kind of let or impediment[3]." Calvin goeth further, "As concerning rites in particular, let the sen-"tence of Augustine take place[4], which leaveth it free unto "all churches to receive each their own custom. Yea some-"time it profiteth and is expedient that there be difference, "lest men should think that religion is tied to outward cere-"monies. Always provided that there be not any emulation, "nor that churches delighted with novelty affect to have that "which others have not[5]."

BOOK IV.
Ch. xiii. 3.

---

[1] Epist. lib. i. p. 41.
[2] Ep. 86. al. 36, c. 9.
[3] ["Sit ergo una fides universæ, "quæ ubique dilatatur, Ecclesiæ... "etiamsi ipsa fidei unitas quibus- "dam diversis observationibus cele- "bratur, quibus nullo modo quod in "fide verum est impeditur." t. ii. 77.]
[4] [Ed. 54. t. ii. 124.]
[5] Respon. ad Med. ["Responsio

[4.] They which grant it true that the diversity of ceremonies in this kind ought not to cause dissension in churches, must either acknowledge that they grant in effect nothing by these words; or if any thing be granted, there must as much be yielded unto, as we affirm against their former strict assertion. For if churches be urged by way of duty to take such ceremonies as they like not of, how can dissension be avoided? Will they say that there ought to be no dissension, because such as be urged ought to like of that whereunto they are urged? If they say this, they say just nothing. For how should any church like to be urged of duty, by such as have no authority or power over it, unto those things which being indifferent it is not of duty bound unto them? Is it their meaning, that there ought to be no dissension, because, that which churches are not bound unto, no man ought by way of duty to urge upon them; and if any man do, he standeth in the sight of both God and men most justly blameable, as a needless disturber of the peace of God's Church, and an author of dissension? In saying this, they both condemn their own practice, when they press the church of England with so strict a bond of duty in these things; and they overthrow the ground of their practice, which is, that there ought to be in all kind of ceremonies uniformity, unless impossibility hinder it.

[5.] For proof whereof it is not enough to allege what St. Paul did about the matter of collections, or what noblemen do in the liveries of their servants, or what the council of Nice did for standing in time of prayer on certain days: because though St. Paul did will them of the church of Corinth [1] every man to lay up somewhat by him upon the Sunday, and to

"ad versipellem quendam media-
"torem, qui pacificandi specie rec-
"tum Evangelii cursum in Gallia ab-
"rumpere conatus est." "Quantum
"ad ritus particulares, vigeat sane
"Augustini sententia; ut singulis
"ecclesiis liberum sit morem suum
"tenere; immo interdum utile est,
"ne externis cærimoniis alligetur
"religio, aliquid esse varietatis;
"modo absit æmulatio, nec alii ab
"aliis novitate illecti diversum ali-
"quid habere affectent." Tract.
Theol. p. 414, Genev. 1597. The "versipellis mediator" was Cassander, who in 1561 published a tract "De officio pii ac publicæ tranquil"litatis vere amantis viri in hoc reli"gionis dissidio."]

[1] T. C. lib. i. p. 133. [104.] "And therefore St. Paul, to esta"blish this order in the church of "Corinth, that they should make "their gatherings for the poor upon "the first day of the Sabbath, "(which is our Sunday,) allegeth "this for a reason, That he had so "ordained in other churches."

Allegations from St. Paul to the contrary inconclusive. 475

reserve it in store, till himself did come thither to send it unto the church of Jerusalem for relief of the poor there; signifying withal, that he had taken the like order with the churches of Galatia; yet the reason which he yieldeth of this order taken both in the one place and the other, sheweth the least part of his meaning to have been that whereunto his words are writhed. "Concerning collection for the saints, (he mean-
"eth them of Jerusalem,) as I have given order to the church
"of Galatia, so likewise do ye," saith the Apostle; "that is,
"in every first of the week let each of you lay aside by him-
"self, and reserve according to that which God hath blessed
"him with, that when I come collections be not then to
"make; and that when I am come, whom you shall choose,
"them I may forthwith send away by letters to carry your
"beneficence unto Jerusalem[1]." Out of which words to conclude the duty of uniformity throughout all churches in all manner of indifferent ceremonies will be very hard, and therefore best to give it over.

[6.] But perhaps they are by so much the more loth to forsake this argument, for that it hath, though nothing else, yet the name of Scripture, to give it some kind of countenance more than the next of livery coats afforded them[2]. For neither is it any man's duty to clothe all his children or all his servants with one weed, nor theirs to clothe themselves so, if it were left to their own judgments, as these ceremonies are left of God to the judgment of the Church. And seeing churches are rather in this case like divers families than like divers servants of one family; because every church, the state whereof is independent upon any other, hath authority to appoint orders for itself in things indifferent: therefore of the two we may rather infer, that as one family is not abridged of liberty to be clothed in friar's-grey for that another doth wear clay-colour, so neither are all churches bound to the selfsame indifferent ceremonies which it liketh sundry to use.

[7.] As for that canon in the council of Nice, let them but

---

[1] 1 Cor. xvi. 1.
[2] T. C. lib. i. p. 133. [104.] "So that as children of one father, "and servants of one master, he "will have all the churches not only "have one diet in that they have "one word, but also wear as it were "one livery in using the same cere-"monies."

BOOK IV.
Ch. xiii. 7.

read it and weigh it well. The ancient use of the Church throughout all Christendom was for fifty days after Easter, (which fifty days were called Pentecost, though most commonly the last day of them which is Whitsunday be so called,) in like sort on all the Sundays throughout the whole year their manner was, to stand at prayer; whereupon their meetings unto that purpose on those days had the name of Stations given them[1]. Of which custom Tertullian speaketh in this wise; "It is not with us thought fit either to fast on the "Lord's day, or to pray kneeling. The same immunity from "fasting and kneeling we keep all the time which is between "the feasts of Easter and Pentecost[2]." This being therefore an order generally received in the Church; when some began to be singular and different from all others, and that in a ceremony which was then judged very convenient for the whole church even by the whole, those few excepted which brake out of the common pale: the council of Nice thought good to enclose them again with the rest, by a law made in this sort: "Because there are certain which will "needs kneel at the time of prayer on the Lord's-day, and "in the fifty days after Easter; the holy synod judging it "meet that a convenient custom be observed throughout all "churches, hath decreed that standing we make our prayers "to the Lord[3]." Whereby it plainly appeareth that in things indifferent, what the whole Church doth think convenient for the whole, the same if any part do wilfully violate, it may be reformed and inrailed again by that general authority whereunto each particular is subject; and that the spirit of singularity in a few ought to give place unto public judgment: this doth clearly enough appear, but not that all Christian churches are bound in every indifferent ceremony to be uniform; because where the whole hath not tied the parts unto one and the same thing, they being therein left

---

[1] De Cor. Milit. c. 3. ["Die "Dominico jejunium nefas dici- "mus, vel de geniculis adorare. "Eadem immunitate a die paschæ "in Pentecosten usque gaude- "mus."]

[2] T. C. lib. i. p. 133. [104.] "This rule did the great council of "Nice follow, &c. Die Dominico et "per omnem Pentecosten, nec de "geniculis adorare, et jejunium "solvere, &c. De Coro. Militis."

[3] [Ἐπειδή τινές εἰσιν ἐν τῇ κυ- ριακῇ γόνυ κλίνοντες, καὶ ἐν ταῖς τῆς Πεντηκοστῆς ἡμέραις· ὑπὲρ τοῦ πάντα ἐν πάσῃ παροικίᾳ ὁμοίως παραφυλάτ- τεσθαι, ἑστῶτας ἔδοξε τῇ ἁγίᾳ συνόδῳ τὰς εὐχὰς ἀποδιδόναι τῷ Θεῷ. Can. 20. ap. Routh, Scrip. Eccles. Opusc. 367.]

each to their own choice, may either do as other do or else otherwise, without any breach of duty at all.

[8.] Concerning those indifferent things, wherein it hath been heretofore thought good that all Christian churches should be uniform, the way which they now conceive to bring this to pass was then never thought on. For till now it hath been judged, that seeing the Law of God doth not prescribe all particular ceremonies which the Church of Christ may use; and in so great variety of them as may be found out, it is not possible that the law of nature and reason should direct all churches unto the same things, each deliberating by itself what is most convenient; the way to establish the same things indifferent throughout them all must needs be the judgment of some judicial authority drawn into one only sentence, which may be a rule for every particular to follow. And because such authority over all churches is too much to be granted unto any one mortal man, there yet remaineth that which hath been always followed as the best, the safest, the most sincere and reasonable way; namely, the verdict of the whole Church orderly taken, and set down in the assembly of some general council. But to maintain that all Christian churches ought for unity's sake to be uniform in all ceremonies, and then to teach that the way of bringing this to pass must be by mutual imitation, so that where we have better ceremonies than others they shall be bound to follow us, and we them where theirs are better; how should we think it agreeable and consonant unto reason? For sith in things of this nature there is such variety of particular inducements, whereby one church may be led to think that better which another church led by other inducements judgeth to be worse: (for example, the East church did think it better to keep Easter-day after the manner of the Jews, the West church better to do otherwise; the Greek church judgeth it worse to use unleavened bread in the Eucharist, the Latin church leavened; one church esteemeth it not so good to receive the Eucharist sitting as standing, another church not so good standing as sitting; there being on the one side probable motives as well as on the other:) unless they add somewhat else to define more certainly what ceremonies shall stand for best, in such sort that all churches in the world shall know them to be the best, and so know them that there may not remain any question about this point, we are not a whit the nearer for that they have hitherto said.

[9.] They themselves, although resolved in their own judgments what ceremonies are best, yet foreseeing that such as they are addicted unto be not all so clearly and so incomparably best, but others there are or may be at leastwise, when all things are well considered, as good, knew not which way smoothly to rid their hands of this matter, without providing some more certain rule to be followed for establishment of uniformity in ceremonies, when there are divers kinds of equal goodness; and therefore in this case they say, that the later churches and the fewer should conform themselves unto the elder and the moe[1]. Hereupon they conclude, that forasmuch as all the reformed churches (so far as they know), which are of our confession in doctrine, have agreed already in the abrogation of divers things which we retain; our church ought either to shew that they have done evil, or else she is found to be in fault for not conforming herself to those churches, in that which she cannot deny to be in them well abrogated. For the authority of the first churches, (and those they account to be the first in this cause which were first reformed,) they bring the comparison of younger daughters conforming themselves in attire to the example of their elder sisters; wherein there is just as much strength of reason as in the livery-coats beforementioned. St. Paul, they say, noteth it for a mark of special honour, that Epænetus was the first man in all Achaia which did embrace the Christian faith[2]; after the same sort he toucheth it also as a special preeminence of Junias[3] and Andronicus, that in Christianity they were his ancients[4]; the Corinthians he pinched with this demand, "Hath the word of God gone "out from you, or hath it lighted on you alone[5]?"

But what of all this? If any man should think that alacrity

[1] T. C. lib. iii. p. 183. "If the "ceremonies be alike commodious, "the latter churches should conform "themselves to the first," &c. And again, "The fewer ought to conform "themselves unto the moe."
[2] Rom. xvi. 5.
[3] ["Junias," so A. B. 1617, as if like "Amplias," &c. by mistaken analogy. He takes the gender to be determined by the following qualification: "τοὺς συγγενεῖς μου.. οἵτινες:" "*Cognatos et concaptivos meos qui..;*" but comp. v. 3.] 1886.
[4] Rom. xvi. 7.
[5] 1 Cor. xiv. 36.

and forwardness in good things doth add nothing unto men's commendation, the two former speeches of St. Paul might lead him to reform his judgment. In like sort, to take down the stomach of proud conceited men, that glory as though they were able to set all others to school, there can be nothing more fit than some such words as the Apostle's third sentence doth contain; wherein he teacheth the church of Corinth to know, that there was no such great odds between them and the rest of their brethren, that they should think themselves to be gold and the rest to be but copper. He therefore useth speech unto them to this effect: "Men instructed in the "knowledge of Jesus Christ there both were before you, and "are besides you in the world; ye neither are the fountain "from which first, nor yet the river into which alone the "word hath flowed." But although as Epænetus was the first man in all Achaia, so Corinth had been the first church in the whole world, that received Christ; the Apostle doth not shew that in any kind of things indifferent whatsoever this should have made their example a law unto all others. Indeed the example of sundry churches for approbation of one thing doth sway much; but yet still as having the force of an example only, and not of a law. They are effectual to move any church, unless some greater thing do hinder; but they bind none, no not though they be many; saving only when they are the major part of a general assembly, and then their voices being moe in number must oversway their judgments who are fewer, because in such cases the greater half is the whole. But as they stand out single each of them by itself, their number can purchase them no such authority, that the rest of the churches being fewer should be therefore bound to follow them, and to relinquish as good ceremonies as theirs for theirs.

[10.] Whereas therefore it is concluded out of these so weak premises, that the retaining of divers things in the church of England, which other reformed churches have cast out, must needs argue that we do not well, unless we can shew that they have done ill[1]; what needed this wrest to

---

[1] T. C. lib. iii. p. 183. "Our "church ought either to shew that "they have done evil, or else she is "found to be in fault that doth not "conform herself in that which she "cannot deny to be well abrogated."

BOOK IV. draw out from us an accusation of foreign churches? It is
Ch. xiv. 1. not proved as yet that if they have done well our duty is to
follow them, and to forsake our own course because it differeth
from theirs, although indeed it be as well for us every way
as theirs for them. And if the proofs alleged for confirmation hereof had been sound, yet seeing they lead no further
than only to shew, that where we can have no better ceremonies theirs must be taken; as they cannot with modesty
think themselves to have found out absolutely the best which
the wit of men may devise, so liking their own somewhat
better than other men's, even because they are their own,
they must in equity allow us to be like unto them in this
affection; which if they do, they ease us of that uncourteous
burden, whereby we are charged either to condemn them or
else to follow them. They grant we need not follow them, if
our own ways already be better: and if our own be but equal,
the law of common indulgence alloweth us to think them at
the least half a thought the better because they are our own;
which we may very well do, and never draw any indictment
at all against theirs, but think commendably even of them
also.

A declara-tion of the proceed-ings of the Church of England for estab-lishment of things as they are.
XIV. To leave reformed churches therefore and their ac-
tions for Him to judge of, in whose sight they are as they are;
and our desire is that they may even in his sight be found
such as we ought to endeavour by all means that our own may
likewise be; somewhat we are enforced to speak by way of
simple declaration concerning the proceedings of the church
of England in these affairs, to the end that men whose minds
are free from those partial constructions, whereby the only
name of difference from some other churches is thought cause
sufficient to condemn ours, may the better discern whether
that we have done be reasonable, yea or no. The church of
England being to alter her received laws concerning such
orders, rites, and ceremonies, as had been in former times an
hinderance unto piety and religious service of God, was to
enter into consideration first, that the change of laws, especially concerning matter of religion, must be warily proceeded
in. Laws, as all other things human, are many times full of
imperfection; and that which is supposed behoveful unto men,
proveth oftentimes most pernicious. The wisdom which is

learned by tract of time, findeth the laws that have been in former ages established, needful in later to be abrogated. Besides, that which sometime is expedient doth not always so continue: and the number of needless laws unabolished doth weaken the force of them that are necessary. But true withal it is, that alteration though it be from worse to better hath in it inconveniences, and those weighty; unless it be in such laws as have been made upon special occasions, which occasions ceasing, laws of that kind do abrogate themselves. But when we abrogate a law as being ill made, the whole cause for which it was made still remaining, do we not herein revoke our very own deed, and upbraid ourselves with folly, yea, all that were makers of it with oversight and with error? Further, if it be a law which the custom and continual practice of many ages or years hath confirmed in the minds of men, to alter it must needs be troublesome and scandalous. It amazeth them, it causeth them to stand in doubt whether any thing be in itself by nature either good or evil, and not all things rather such as men at this or that time agree to account of them, when they behold even those things disproved, disannulled, rejected, which use had made in a manner natural. What have we to induce men unto the willing obedience and observation of laws, but the weight of so many men's judgment as have with deliberate advice assented thereunto; the weight of that long experience, which the world hath had thereof with consent and good liking? So that to change any such law must needs with the common sort impair and weaken the force of those grounds, whereby all laws are made effectual.

[2.] Notwithstanding we do not deny alteration of laws to be sometimes a thing necessary; as when they are unnatural, or impious, or otherwise hurtful unto the public community of men, and against that good for which human societies were instituted. When the Apostles of our Lord and Saviour were ordained to alter the laws of heathenish religion received throughout the whole world, chosen I grant they were (Paul excepted) the rest ignorant, poor, simple, unschooled altogether and unlettered men; howbeit extraordinarily endued with ghostly wisdom from above before they ever undertook this enterprise; yea their authority confirmed by miracle, to the end it might plainly appear that they were the Lord's ambassadors, unto whose sovereign power for all flesh to stoop, for all the kingdoms of the earth to yield themselves willingly conformable in whatsoever should be required, it was their duty. In this case therefore their oppositions in maintenance of public superstition against apostolic endeavours, as that they might not condemn the ways of their ancient predecessors, that they must keep *religiones traditas*, the rites which from age to age had descended, that the ceremonies of religion had been ever accounted by so much holier as elder[1]; these and the like allegations in this case were vain and frivolous.

Not to stay longer therefore in speech concerning this point, we will conclude, that as the change of such laws as have been specified is necessary, so the evidence that they are such must be great. If we have neither voice from heaven that so pronounceth of them, neither sentence of men grounded upon such manifest and clear proof, that they in whose hands it is to alter them may likewise infallibly even in heart and conscience judge them so: upon necessity to urge alteration is to trouble and disturb without necessity. As for arbitrary alterations, when laws in themselves not simply bad or unmeet are changed for better and more expedient; if the benefit of that which is newly better devised be but small, sith the custom of easiness to alter and change is so evil, no doubt but to bear a tolerable sore is better than to venture on a dangerous remedy.

[3.] Which being generally thought upon as a matter that touched nearly their whole enterprise, whereas change was notwithstanding concluded necessary, in regard of the great hurt which the Church did receive by a number of things then in use, whereupon a great deal of that which had been was now to be taken away and removed out of the Church; yet sith there are divers ways of abrogating things established, they saw it best to cut off presently such things as might in that sort be extinguished without danger, leaving the rest to be abolished by disusage through tract of time. And as this was done for the manner of abrogation: so touching the stint

---

[1] [Min. Felix. c. 5. p. 50. ed. Gronov. "Venerabilius et melius, "antistitem veritatis majorum ex- "cipere disciplinam: religiones "traditas colere; deos, quos a pa- "rentibus ante imbutus es timere "quam nosse familiarius, adorare; "nec de numinibus ferre senten- "tiam, sed prioribus credere." And see before, p. 159, note 1.]

How respectfully it dealt with old Customs.

or measure thereof, rites and ceremonies and other external things of like nature being hurtful unto the Church, either in respect of their quality or in regard of their number; in the former there could be no doubt or difficulty what should be done, their deliberation in the later was more hard. And therefore inasmuch as they did resolve to remove only such things of that kind as the Church might best spare, retaining the residue; their whole counsel is in this point utterly condemned, as having either proceeded from the blindness of those times, or from negligence, or from desire of honour and glory, or from an erroneous opinion that such things might be tolerated for a while; or if it did proceed (as they which would seem most favourable are content to think it possible) from a purpose, "[1] partly the easilier to draw papists unto "the Gospel" (by keeping so many orders still the same with theirs), "and partly to redeem peace thereby, the breach "whereof they might fear would ensue upon more thorough "alteration;" or howsoever it came to pass, the thing they did is judged evil. But such is the lot of all that deal in public affairs whether of church or commonwealth; that which men list to surmise of their doings, be it good or ill, they must beforehand patiently arm their minds to endure. Wherefore to let go private surmises, whereby the thing in itself is not made either better or worse; if just and allowable reasons might lead them to do as they did, then are these censures all frustrate.

[4.] Touching ceremonies harmless therefore in themselves, and hurtful only in respect of number: was it amiss to decree, that those things which were least needful and newliest come should be the first that were taken away, as in the abrogating of a number of saints' days, and of other the like customs, it appeareth they did; till afterwards the Form of Common Prayer being perfected, Articles of sound Religion and Discipline agreed upon, Catechisms framed for the needful instruction of youth, churches purged of things that indeed were burdensome to the people or to the simple offensive and scandalous, all was brought at the length unto that wherein now we stand? Or was it amiss, that having this way eased

BOOK IV.
Ch. xiv. 4.

---

[1] T. C. lib. ii. p. 29. "It may "well be, their purpose was by that "temper of popish ceremonies with "the Gospel, partly the easilier to "draw the papists to the Gospel, &c. "partly to redeem peace thereby."

the Church as they thought of superfluity, they went not on till they had plucked up even those things also, which had taken a great deal stronger and deeper root; those things which to abrogate without constraint of manifest harm thereby arising, had been to alter unnecessarily (in their judgments) the ancient received custom of the whole Church, the universal practice of the people of God, and those very decrees of our fathers, which were not only set down by agreement of general councils, but had accordingly been put in ure and so continued in use till that very time present?

[5.] True it is, that neither councils nor customs, be they never so ancient and so general, can let the Church from taking away that thing which is hurtful to be retained. Where things have been instituted, which being convenient and good at the first, do afterwards in process of time wax otherwise; we make no doubt but they may be altered, yea, though councils or customs general have received them. And therefore it is but a needless kind of opposition which they make who thus dispute, "If in those things which are "not expressed in the Scripture, that is to be observed of the "Church, which is the custom of the people of God and "decree of our forefathers; then how can these things at "any time be varied, which heretofore have been once or-"dained in such sort[1]?" Whereto we say, that things so ordained are to be kept, howbeit not necessarily any longer, than till there grow some urgent cause to ordain the contrary. For there is not any positive law of men, whether it be general or particular; received by formal express consent, as in councils, or by secret approbation, as in customs it cometh to pass; but the same may be taken away if occasion serve. Even as we all know, that many things generally kept heretofore are now in like sort generally unkept and abolished every where.

[6.] Notwithstanding till such things be abolished, what exception can there be taken against the judgment of St. Augustine, who saith, "That of things harmless, whatsoever "there is which the whole Church doth observe throughout "the world, to argue for any man's immunity from observing "the same, it were a point of most insolent madness[2]?"

---

[1] T. C. lib. iii. p. 30.   [2] Aug. Epist. 118. [al. 54. c. 5. t. ii. 126.]

And surely odious it must needs have been for one Christian church to abolish that which all had received and held for the space of many ages, and that without any detriment unto religion so manifest and so great, as might in the eyes of unpartial men appear sufficient to clear them from all blame of rash and inconsiderate proceeding, if in fervour of zeal they had removed such things. Whereas contrariwise, so reasonable moderation herein used hath freed us from being deservedly subject unto that bitter kind of obloquy, whereby as the church of Rome doth under the colour of love towards those things which be harmless, maintain extremely most hurtful corruptions; so we peradventure might be upbraided, that under colour of hatred towards those things that are corrupt, we are on the other side as extreme even against most harmless ordinances. And as they are obstinate to retain that, which no man of any conscience is able well to defend; so we might be reckoned fierce and violent to tear away that, which if our own mouths did condemn, our consciences would storm and repine thereat. The Romans having banished Tarquinius the Proud, and taken a solemn oath that they never would permit any man more to reign, could not herewith content themselves, or think that tyranny was thoroughly extinguished, till they had driven one of their Consuls to depart the city, against whom they found not in the world what to object, saving only that his name was Tarquin, and that the commonwealth could not seem to have recovered perfect freedom, as long as a man of so dangerous a name was left remaining [1]. For the church of England to have done the like in casting out of papal tyranny and superstition; to have shewed greater willingness of accepting the very ceremonies of the Turk [2], Christ's professed enemy, than of the most indifferent things which the church of Rome approveth; to have left not so much as the names which the church of Rome doth give unto things innocent; to have ejected whatsoever that Church doth make account of, be it never so harmless in itself, and of never so ancient continuance, without any other crime to charge it with, than only that it hath been the hap thereof to be used

---

[1] [Liv. ii. 2.]
[2] T. C. lib. i. p. 131. "For indeed "it were more safe for us to conform "our indifferent ceremonies to the "Turks which are far off, than to "the papists which are so near."

by the church of Rome, and not to be commanded in the word of God: this kind of proceeding might haply have pleased some few men, who having begun such a course themselves must needs be glad to see their example followed by us[1]. But the Almighty which giveth wisdom and inspireth with right understanding whomsoever it pleaseth him, he foreseeing that which man's wit had never been able to reach unto, namely, what tragedies the attempt of so extreme alteration would raise in some parts of the Christian world[2], did for the endless good of his Church (as we cannot choose but interpret it) use the bridle of his provident restraining hand, to stay those eager affections in some, and to settle their resolution upon a course more calm and moderate: lest as in other most ample and heretofore most flourishing dominions it hath since fallen out, so likewise if in ours it had come to pass, that the adverse part being enraged, and betaking itself to such practices as men are commonly wont to embrace, when they behold things brought to desperate extremities, and no hope left to see any other end, than only the utter oppression and clean extinguishment of one side; by this mean Christendom flaming in all parts of greatest importance at once, they all had wanted that comfort of mutual relief, whereby they are now for the time sustained (and not the least by this our church which they so much impeach) till mutual combustions[3], bloodsheds, and wastes, (because no other inducement will serve,) may enforce them through very faintness, after the experience of so endless miseries, to enter on all sides at the length into some such consultation, as may tend to the best reestablishment of the whole Church of Jesus Christ. To the singular good whereof it cannot but serve as a profitable direction to teach men what is most likely to prove available, when they shall quietly consider the trial that hath been thus long had of both kinds of reformation; as

---

[1] [Sarav. de divers. Ministr. Evang. Grad. in Prolog. "Ejectis "Tarquiniis Roma, Regis nomen "postea non tulere Romani, quasi "cum nomine ejecta esset quam "oderant tyrannis: quitamen postea "plures tyrannidis formas perpessi "sunt, quam si Regis nomen et "authoritatem retinuissent. Non "enim in regia potestate aut regis "nomine ulla inerat tyrannis, sed "in Tarquinio. Sic dico tyranni- "dem, quæ Ecclesias Christi vas- "tavit, non fuisse in primatu Episco- "porum et Archiepiscoporum, sed "in iis qui primatu abusi sunt."]

[2] [France, Westphalia, Flanders, Scotland.]

[3] ["Combustious," A. B.; "combustions," 1617.] 1886.

well this moderate kind which the church of England hath taken, as that other more extreme and rigorous which certain churches elsewhere have better liked. In the meanwhile it may be, that suspense of judgment and exercise of charity were safer and seemlier for Christian men, than the hot pursuit of these controversies, wherein they that are most fervent to dispute be not always the most able to determine. But who are on his side, and who against him, our Lord in his good time shall reveal.

[7.] And sith thus far we have proceeded in opening the things that have been done, let not the principal doers themselves be forgotten. When the ruins of the house of God (that house which consisting of religious souls is most immediately the precious temple of the Holy Ghost) were become, not in his sight alone, but in the eyes of the whole world so exceeding great, that very superstition began even to feel itself too far grown: the first that with us made way to repair the decays thereof by beheading superstition, was King Henry the Eighth. The son and successor of which famous king as we know was Edward the Saint: in whom (for so by the event we may gather) it pleased God righteous and just to let England see what a blessing sin and iniquity would not suffer it to enjoy. Howbeit that which the wise man hath said concerning Enoch (whose days were though many in respect of ours, yet scarce as three to nine in comparison of theirs with whom he lived) the same to that admirable child most worthily may be applied, "Though he departed this world soon, yet "fulfilled he much time[1]." But what ensued? That work which the one in such sort had begun, and the other so far proceeded in, was in short space so overthrown, as if almost it had never been: till such time as that God, whose property is to shew his mercies then greatest when they are nearest to be utterly despaired of, caused in the depth of discomfort and darkness a most glorious star[2] to arise, and on her head settled the crown, whom himself had kept as a lamb from the slaughter of those bloody times; that the experience of his goodness in her own deliverance might cause her merciful disposition to take so much the more delight in saving others, whom the like necessity should press. What in this behalf

[1] Sap. iv. 13.
[2] ["That bright Occidental Star, "Queen Elizabeth of most happy "memory." Dedication to King James by the Translators of the Bible.]

BOOK IV.
Ch. xiv. 7.

hath been done towards nations abroad, the parts of Christendom most afflicted can best testify. That which especially concerneth ourselves, in the present matter we treat of, is the state of reformed religion, a thing at her coming to the crown even raised as it were by miracle from the dead; a thing which we so little hoped to see, that even they which beheld it done, scarcely believed their own senses at the first beholding. Yet being then brought to pass, thus many years it hath continued, standing by no other worldly mean but that one only hand which erected it; that hand which as no kind of imminent danger could cause at the first to withhold itself, so neither have the practices so many so bloody following since been ever able to make weary. Nor can we say in this case so justly, that Aaron and Hur, the ecclesiastical and civil states, have sustained the hand which did lift itself to heaven for them [1], as that heaven itself hath by this hand sustained them, no aid or help having thereunto been ministered for performance of the work of reformation, other than such kind of help or aid as the Angel in the Prophet Zachary speaketh of, saying, "Neither by an army nor strength, but by my Spirit, "saith the Lord of Hosts [2]." Which grace and favour of divine assistance having not in one thing or two shewed itself, nor for some few days or years appeared, but in such sort so long continued, our manifold sins and transgressions striving to the contrary; what can we less thereupon conclude, than that God would at leastwise by tract of time teach the world, that the thing which he blesseth, defendeth, keepeth so strangely, cannot choose but be of him? Wherefore, if any refuse to believe us disputing for the verity of religion established, let them believe God himself thus miraculously working for it, and wish life even for ever and ever unto that glorious and sacred instrument whereby he worketh.

[1] [Exod. xvii. 12.]   [2] Zach. iv. 6.

END OF VOL. I.

www.ingramcontent.com/pod-product-compliance
Lightning Source LLC
Chambersburg PA
CBHW052109010526
44111CB00036B/1576